The Making of

MODERN
LONDON

The Making of

MODERN LONDON

GAVIN WEIGHTMAN
AND
STEVE HUMPHRIES

CONTRIBUTING AUTHORS
Joanna Mack and John Taylor

EBURY
PRESS

1 3 5 7 9 10 8 6 4 2

Published in 2007 by Ebury Press, an imprint of Ebury Publishing
Previously published as four volumes by Sidgwick & Jackson in
1983, 1984, 1985, 1986

A Random House Group Company

The Random House Group Limited Reg. No. 954009

Addresses for companies within the Random House Group can be found at
www.randomhouse.co.uk

A CIP catalogue record for this book is available from the British Library

Mixed Sources
Product group from well-managed
forests and other controlled sources
www.fsc.org Cert no. TT-COC-2139
© 1996 Forest Stewardship Council
FSC

The Random House Group Limited supports The Forest Stewardship
Council (FSC), the leading international forest certification organisation. All our
titles that are printed on Greenpeace approved FSC certified paper carry the FSC logo.
Our paper procurement policy can be found at
www.rbooks.co.uk/environment

To buy books by your favourite authors and register for offers visit
www.rbooks.co.uk

Typeset by SX Composing DTP, Rayleigh, Essex
Printed and bound in Great Britain by Clays

ISBN 9780091920043

CONTENTS

ACKNOWLEGEMENTS

A VERY LARGE NUMBER of people contributed to the London Weekend Television series *The Making of Modern London* and the four books which accompanied them between 1983 and 1986. We would like to thank them all, once again: colleagues at LWT, academics, museums, libraries and the many interviewees whose memories make this a genuine 'people's history'. For help with the up-dating of the last six chapters we would like to thank Professor Sir Peter Hall, whose knowledge of urban history and current urban issues is unrivalled. Professor Tony Travers, Director of the Greater London Group at the London School of Economics, was consulted on the radical changes in London politics over the past twenty years. Professor Ken Young of Kings College, London provided some very useful material through his research interests have now moved away from urban politics. On fashion, Sonia Ashmore of the London College of Fashion and Alistair O'Neill provided a valuable commentary on what had happened since the Sixties and we would like to thank Professor Caroline Evans of the University of the Arts, London for permission to quote from her chapter in *The London Look: fashion from the street to the catwalk*.

We owe a special thanks to Kevin Morgan, Head of Publishing at Granada Ventures for clearing rights in the original books. At Ebury Publishing we thank Publishing Director Carey Smith for commissioning this edition, and Vicky Orchard and Laura Higginson for their assistance with its production. In the design of the plate sections, we thank Ed Pickford for his patience with innumerable changes and for creating such a striking presentation. Finally we would like to thank Charles Walker and Lydia Lewis at Peters, Fraser and Dunlop for their diligence in drawing up all the agreements necessary for this collective enterprise. Any errors of fact or interpretation are, naturally, the sole responsibility of the authors.

Gavin Weightman, Steven Humphries, Joanna Mack and John Taylor
London, 2007

INTRODUCTION

THE ORIGINAL FOUR volumes of *The Making of Modern London*, now gathered here in one edition, were the product of a unique project. It began as a proposal for a series of historical documentary programmes to be made by London Weekend Television for its regional audience. At the time oral history had become fashionable and the search for a specialist to work on the programmes led to Steve Humphries, then a lecturer at Essex University. With the producer, Gavin Weightman a format was devised for the series whereby thoroughly researched themes were to be enriched with living memory gathered over the period of a year. This approach was then applied to three more series, each of which had an accompanying book.

Victory at Waterloo in 1815 was chosen as the starting point for the first series. With Europe torn apart by Napoleon's armies, London prospered and grew at a tremendous pace, its population rising from around 900,000 at the time of the first census in 1801 to 6 million before the Great War. That was the period covered in the first documentary series and book and, because the research was carried out in 1982–3, it was still possible to find elderly people whose memories of London went back to the Edwardian era. To spread the net as wide as possible, letters were written to every local newspaper in the London area as well as to magazines whose readers might just have the kind of memories that would bring the past to life.

The themes for the programmes and chapters had been outlined so that the search for stories was narrowed to some extent: Do you remember the London Season? Did you work in the docks? Can you remember riding in a horse-drawn hansom cab? Did you ever work in a sweatshop in the East End of London? The stories that were unearthed, many of them reproduced here in this new edition, were truly astonishing. Ted Harrison of Hoxton recalled riding on horse trams around 1904 and the conflicts the drivers had with the horse bus men. Lady Charlotte Bonham-Carter remembered vividly the terrible mess that horse-drawn traffic made in

London and how her new white boots were ruined as she hurried to attend a lunch at St James's Palace (with no crossing sweeper to clear her path she had to wade through rain-soaked manure).

With their recollections from two quite opposite ends of the social spectrum, Ted and Lady Charlotte were the stars of the first series and also provided wonderful stories for the second series which covered the period from 1914 to 1939. The mailshot to newspapers and magazines for the second series generated an enormous response and a wealth of stories. The letters were opened with mounting excitement. One came from a woman who recalled the day in 1917 when, as her mother sat ready to set her watch by the whistle of a train into London, the front of their house was blown off (the whistle had been the sound of a bomb falling from a huge airship, a German Zeppelin, on one of the few raids they made on London in the Great War). Then there was Lady Marguerite Strickland, one of the great beauties of her day whose handsome face advertised cigarettes and gin, though she herself never drank or smoked. Living the life of a wealthy 'young thing' in London she would stay in nightclubs until late then be whisked off to Boulter's Lock on the Thames to swim naked (except for her heavy jewellery).

When the third series was made and the accompanying book written covering the years of the Second World War, Joanna Mack joined Steve Humphries while Gavin Weightman took the opportunity to make a series about wildlife in the capital. Again there was a huge response to the mailshot and some very vivid memories of the hardships of the war were recorded. The six chapters of the original book, which run in this edition from page 255 to page 336 provide a uniquely intimate account of the way in which Londoners came to cope with the terrible destruction of the Blitz, the separation of families and the final terror of the 'doodlebugs' and V-2 rockets. In 1939, the population of Greater London had been more than 8 million. At the end of the war it was down to 7 million and falling. The politicians and planners thought that was no bad thing and encouraged Londoners to move away from the bomb-damaged inner city.

The last chapters of this edition, adapted from the last volume of *The Making of Modern London* which covered the period from 1945 to 1985, capture the mood of the 1950s when there was plenty of work and money about but not much to spend it on besides football and the cinema. For this series Steve Humphries teamed up with John Taylor, a reporter and presenter on *The London Programme*. A spectacular event in this period was the Coronation in 1953 at which Britain's colonial subjects paraded in all their glory. In retrospect, however, it was not the dawn of a new Elizabethan age so much as the sunset on an Imperial nation. As one colonial nation after another won independence, London industries hitherto tied into empire trade, began to close. The lives of many working-class Londoners had been closely linked with their work for major employers like Tate & Lyle the sugar refiners. They had social clubs and sports grounds and employees enjoyed a paternalistic form of management. But, as the Empire shrank and the old trades began to die, so did major London firms. AEC which had once made the London buses was one of the biggest to go and the capital, once the largest industrial area in the country, rapidly lost nearly all its manufacturing jobs.

The poignancy of this period is captured in interviews with those whose entire lives had been dedicated to the success and reputation of a company unable to survive in the face of world competition. But at the same time as old industries were dying, new ones were being created and London began to develop a reputation for streetwise art and fashion that it has never really lost. The final episodes in this people's history capture the excitement of the sixties when London, according to American journalists, was 'swinging'. It is surprising how quaint that all seems now – the Mods and rockers and skinheads. But it is very much part of the capital's history and is brought back to life here with the memories of those who were a part of it.

The Making of Modern London was a four-year project. Only a small number of interviewees could be filmed for the television programmes, although far more went into the books. And to ensure that all of the material gathered was not lost, a large archive was deposited with the Museum of London where it is available to researchers who first seek permission to view it. The material collected here and in the archive is exceptional in two respects. Firstly, there is a collection of memories of a generation of Londoners who were close to the end of their lives in the 1980s. Secondly, it is unlikely such an extensive exercise in the gathering of oral history in the capital will ever be undertaken again. The whole project was funded by London Weekend Television's factual programmes department at a time when the stricture that commercial companies produce worthwhile and educational programmes regardless of ratings had to be taken seriously; if LWT or any other independent television company failed to fulfil its public service responsibilities it risked losing its franchise and, in the celebrated quip of Lord Thompson, its 'licence to print money'.

The books were written on the back of that commitment to fund good, well-researched programmes. As it happens, the series did very well on television, despite an inauspicious start when the very first programme was scheduled against a showing of *The Godfather*!

The last book and series were completed in 1986 and this omnibus edition would have looked oddly anachronistic without some essential updating. The series had left London with a falling population, a frightening loss of jobs, the abolition of the Greater London Council and an ongoing bombing campaign by the IRA and its factions. In the twenty years since then a great deal has changed: from 1998 the population began to rise, quite unexpectedly; the IRA bombings eventually ceased; jobs in London began to multiply; and in place of the old Greater London Council London in 2000 the city got an elected Mayor who is now in his second four-year term of office.

Today London is a relatively young city, certainly younger than it was in the sixties. There is a constant flow of people in and out of the capital (about 350,000 each way) from other parts of the country in recent years. As might be expected it is the young who are looking for excitement and the best jobs who move in, and the older people who tend to move out. The capital's population would be more or less stable if it were not for two new factors. Firstly, there has been a significant number of migrants from abroad, many from Eastern Europe and a growing number from some African countries. Nobody really has any idea what the scale of this migration is for it is not at all carefully monitored. Secondly, with its young age profile, which includes some groups of immigrants, London now has more births a year than recorded deaths, so there is 'natural' increase in its population.

What this will mean for the future, nobody knows. And what this history of the capital shows, among other things, is that it has never been possible to predict how London would evolve. It is a great and vibrant city driven by many forces and remains in the minds of billions around the world, including some Londoners themselves, a truly global city more cosmopolitan and wealthier than it was in the heyday of Empire.

PART ONE

The Heart of the Empire 1815–1914

CHAPTER ONE

The Influence of the City

EVERYONE IN LONDON knows about the City, conjuring up, as it did, images of bowler hats and business deals. But very few people could tell you exactly what went on there, or where the City began and ended. Nor would they be quite sure why its civic ceremonies seem to be far more lavish and pompous than those of any other part of London, even rivalling those of royalty. But images of the City are contradictory. On the one hand it symbolizes money, and a peculiarly well-dressed and tidy way of acquiring very large quantities of it. On the other, its guilds and livery companies seem to be a resplendent repository of surviving ancient ritual.

In fact, the City likes to promote both images of itself. It is the dynamic centre of international finance earning for Britain and London a vital income. Yet it is the oldest and quaintest part of the capital, the history of which is kept alive in its ceremony, even if most of the physical fabric of the past has been buried several times over in stone and concrete. The City cannot escape the fact of its overriding, and still not-quite-acceptable commercialism, but it can hide behind its anachronistic ritual. These opposing images of the City are a reflection of its past, for it is the original site of London, a former merchant stronghold which has evolved into a crucial part of the economy of a much greater metropolis of 7 million people. It has done so, not by hanging on to its past, but through a series of dramatic adjustments which have ensured that it retained the lion's share of the nation's fortune during an era of revolutionary changes in international trade and commerce.

The City's ancient past and its dynamic present are graphically illustrated whenever a new building goes up in the old Square Mile. Archaeologists dig frantically for Roman remains in the foundations of a demolished edifice before the historic treasure is once again sealed over by a new office block. But here we are concerned with neither the City's ancient glorious past nor its modern form, but with a period in between.

In the early years of the nineteenth century, the City of London began a transformation from a bustling centre of tradesmen, small industries, shopkeepers and wealthy merchants, with a sizeable resident population, into a square mile of financial institutions and offices. For the first half of the century its total population remained more or less stable at about 130,000, but this overall figure concealed a fundamental change. Merchants, tradesmen and shopkeepers were moving out, their old premises taken over by banks, insurance offices, and financiers of various kinds. Although not a great deal is known about those who remained in the City, they were almost certainly people who were too poor to move of their own accord and who remained in increasingly crowded conditions until demolitions for new offices, roads and railways drove them out.

From 1850 onwards, the population of the City plummeted, and by 1900 had fallen to just 27,000. By the early 1980s there were barely 5,000 residents in the old square mile and the only reminder now that this was once a densely inhabited area is the surviving steeples of the City's fine seventeenth-century churches. The change began at the same time as London's growth outwards in great waves of suburban development which, by the 1870s, was to make it the largest and wealthiest city the world had ever seen. This was no mere coincidence: the two factors were governed by many of the same forces. The City was a financial power-house which was not only essential to the expansion of the metropolis but indirectly provided much of its character as well.

One of the most remarkable aspects of London as it grew in the eighteenth and nineteenth centuries was that it sprawled outwards, unconfined by any city walls. Furthermore, it grew not from one centre, but from two. The older and more important of these centres was the City of London, tracing its history back to the Romans and possibly before. The other centre, which developed from the eleventh century onwards, was Westminster, where the kings and queens of England and Parliament became established. These were originally two quite separate places, the former representing commercial power, the latter political power.

Two hundred years ago, maps still marked the two places as distinct, although by that time they had been joined physically by building to the north of the Strand and east of Westminster. But politically the two retained their old distance: a relationship in which they recognized their mutual dependence but always distrusted each other. The division of power between the City and Westminster was a crucial factor not only in London's development but in the way the British Empire took shape. By the end of the nineteenth century the capital was the centre of an imperial power governing a quarter of the world's population and controlling a quarter of its land mass. For most of its history this Empire had been essentially a commercial operation, built up by adventurers and merchants with government backing.

The City and Westminster, though they were often in disagreement, had worked together to carve out new markets overseas. Merchant adventurers would get government backing for their expeditions, usually through some contact at Court, and if they were successful in finding a fruitful trade overseas they would be granted a monopoly in a particular part of the world. From the sixteenth century onwards a number of powerful chartered companies were established in this way, each with the sole right to deal in a market. The first was the Muscovy Company established when a merchant found his way to the court of Ivan the Terrible in Russia. The Hudson Bay Company, which dealt in furs and still survives today in the City, the Levant Company, and the largest of all, the East India Company, were all founded in this way.

At home, too, the City's prosperity was guarded in the seventeenth and eighteenth centuries by protective laws giving it legal monopolies over many markets and trades. This was partly because it was believed that in order to remain economically sound a company *needed* to have a monopoly, but the City's position was made especially powerful because the Crown and Parliament frequently relied on it for funds and for men in times of war. Its charters were the reward. Thus the City controlled the main food markets – Smithfield for meat and Billingsgate for fish – and its craftsmen, such as the silk weavers of Spitalfields, were protected from foreign competition by a ban on imports. And throughout its modern history the City has managed to exact from successive governments the right to run its own affairs in its own way. When the Metropolitan Police was formed in 1829, the City got its own force; when the London County Council was established in 1889, the City remained independent.

In a sense there is no more telling a monument to the City's uniquely independent position than the Tower of London which stands just outside the old wall to the east, dwarfed now like a toy fortress by the great glass and concrete creations of modern financial power. William the Conqueror began the building of the Tower as a show of strength to the people of London, of whom he was understandably wary. But around Guildhall today they still like to say that the Norman King never conquered *them*.

THE BUILDING OF THE DOCKS

The very privileged position of the City was nowhere more evident by the end of the eighteenth century than in the Pool of London. Here, in a ludicrously crowded stretch of the Thames, below London Bridge and at the 'legal' quays, all ships bringing goods into London had to unload their cargo. Customs duties were among the City's most valuable sources of income and, despite the problems created by the maintenance of this monopoly, it was reluctant to give them up. It was only when the scale of pilfering from ships forced to wait several weeks to be unloaded seriously threatened the commercial profits of the port that the big merchant companies campaigned for the building of new and bigger docks.

Around the turn of the nineteenth century, the City was finally forced to concede that existing arrangements were unworkable. The quantity of goods arriving on the Thames was increasing all the time, and sooner or later the Pool would be totally unable to cope. The City authorities produced their own proposals for the building of a new dock out in what was then a no-man's land on the northern tip of the Isle of Dogs, well away from the East End of London. When the new West India Dock system opened in 1802, followed quickly by the London Docks on the north bank of the Thames nearer the City and the East India Docks, the old monopoly of the City of London had been broken. Throughout most of the century the dock and wharf facilities on the Thames continued to grow in a series of cut-throat booms and the old Pool of London lost its former significance as the scale of trade grew to an unprecedented size. The building of the new dock system in fact signalled the rapid dismantling of the ancient privileges of the City of London. Although some of the great trading companies survived, their heyday was over, and a new, much more competitive economic order swept away the monopolistic system of the previous centuries.

The City of London did not, of course, change overnight. In the first half of the nineteenth century its older leading institutions, such as the great merchant companies, were in decline, while the elements of the square mile's commercial activities that had been less significant in the eighteenth century now emerged as a new and powerful force. It's a process that still goes on, as the merchant banks – City leaders in the nineteenth century – find themselves in turn overtaken in sheer wealth and investment power by insurance companies or pension funds.

What happened in the early 1800s, and continued throughout the century, was that those elements of City life that dealt in pure money, rather than goods, became immensely powerful. At the same time, the nature of the City itself changed dramatically, particularly after 1850, as its teeming urban life of shops, slaughterhouses and industries either moved out or was expelled to other parts of the metropolis. The City itself made a spectacularly successful adjustment to the pressures and needs of a new economic order in its transformation into the leading financial centre of the world. And in so doing, it provided the wealth on which much of the growth of nineteenth-century London was founded.

The strands of City life and monetary dealings are all interwoven and it is futile to search for crucial dates relating to this: what really occurred was first a steady, then a rapid evolution in its affairs. Take, for example, dealing in stocks. In the eighteenth century, and in fact earlier, there was in the City a band of dubious characters called stock-jobbers, as well as more reputable men known as brokers. Their history and character are rather obscure, but it is possible to say roughly what they were up to. For there to be any stock-jobbers there have to be stocks. These are the creation essentially of a system in which a company is formed by a number of people putting money into it, entrusting its direction to some form of management, and hoping it will prosper so that their investment will produce a decent rate of interest and will increase in value. The stock-holder has a stake in the enterprise without running it.

The first of these enterprises was the sixteenth-century Muscovy Company, funded by a group of merchants who put up the money to equip ships that went in search of riches in Russia. The Bank of England, founded in 1694, operated on much the same lines. In order to raise funds for the government, this private institution attracted investments from a very large number of people – 'fund-holders' – who left the management of the Bank to its governors, again hoping for a decent return on their lending. It was a way of raising very large amounts of money from a large number of people. By the eighteenth century, there were a number of such joint-stock companies. All the merchant companies, such as the East India, the Hudson Bay, or the New River Company – which provided much of London's water supply – but, above all, the Bank of England offered a place for those who wanted to invest their money. And the stocks and funds supplied a livelihood to those who would gamble on the value of them rising or falling.

At that time the stock-jobbers were men who dealt only in stocks, buying and selling them in the hope of making a profit. Brokers might also deal in stocks, but they dealt in just about everything else as well, including gold, fish and clothing. There is a long and involved history of the evolution of these two branches of what became Stock Exchange activity, but the essential point here is that in the eighteenth century neither jobbers nor brokers had a great deal of choice in what they dealt in. Most companies were private: that is, they did not raise money – and could not unless granted special permission by Act of Parliament – by issuing shares in the enterprise; they could not have more than six members; and could not ask the general public to invest in their enterprise.

The laws restricting joint-stock companies had followed a catastrophic episode in 1720 known as the South Sea Bubble, when uncontrolled investment resulted in the collapse of the South Sea Company. In any case, the scale of eighteenth-century economic activity did not generally require massive funding. For example, all banks other than the Bank of England were private. There were plenty of them both in the City and the West End, as well as in country districts, but they were small. There were also plenty of commercial, industrial and manufacturing firms, but they, too, funded themselves privately. Similarly, there were restrictions on dealing in insurance of ships at sea – the main branch of the business in the century – and only two companies were allowed to involve themselves in it, though individuals, if they wanted, could gamble their savings on private insurance. And that is precisely what a large number of monied people chose to do.

COFFEE-HOUSE COMMERCE

One of the most colourful aspects of eighteenth-century London was its coffee houses. The first of these had been opened in 1652 in Cornhill in the City by a Turk named Pasqua Rosee. Rather like the fashionable Parisian café of the 1920s, the coffee house became a cultural institution and, as their numbers spread, each began to acquire a reputation with a particular clique of people, some literary, some political, some commercial. In the City of London itself there were, by the early 1700s, no fewer than twenty-six coffee houses as well as thirty taverns where financiers of various kinds met, mostly situated around 'Change Alley at the back of the Royal Exchange, between Cornhill and Threadneedle Street.

For the stock-jobber, later in the eighteenth century, Jonathan's and Garroways had become the most popular. Those who wanted to chip in on the insurance of a ship – which they could do as private individuals – would go to Lloyds coffee house. It was in these boisterous surroundings that the modern institutions of the Stock Exchange and Lloyds of London Insurance became established. Both took on greatly increased importance, and dealt in far greater funds in the nineteenth century, as the number of joint-stock banks multiplied.

This was an age of extraordinary industrial expansion. It required massive capital investment and saw the gradual dismantling of the restrictive eighteenth-century legislation on joint-stock companies. With the coming of the railways, when for the first time very large numbers of people with small amounts of money to invest were excited by the prospect – often disastrously – the Stock Exchange came into its own. However, the City gained chiefly not by raising funds for British industry but by 'exporting' the surplus wealth of Britain in overseas investments.

At the same time, the scale of British shipping, and hence insurance, expanded enormously. The Lloyds coffee-house men were in an odd position. In order to get round the eighteenth-century rule forbidding companies to insure ships at sea, they had got together as *individuals* to put up the cash to insure merchant vessels, the deal being organized by an underwriter. When, in the 1820s, the law was changed so that any company could go into the business, the Lloyds system was badly rattled. It survived, and still survives, because it had developed an information system on shipping with agents around the world. This gave it an advance on others in terms of intelligence on insurance risks – and it always paid up. By the mid-century, it was insuring not only ships but property and all kinds of other risks worldwide.

The banking system was also transformed in the first half of the nineteenth century. In 1824, the Bank of England lost its monopoly on joint-stock banking. The private banks were rapidly undermined as bigger operations took away their business and, in a series of amalgamations, a whole new breed of joint-stock banks like Barclays, Lloyds and the Midland rose in the City, capturing the national market. With the decline of the great merchant companies came the emergence in London of the merchant bankers. It has never been possible to distinguish absolutely between an *ordinary* bank and a merchant bank, and their activities have often overlapped. But the merchant banks, which became the wealthiest and most powerful institutions in the nineteenth century, specialized in raising money for the government and overseas investments. In the previous century, though many merchants would also act from time to time as bankers, there had been only one merchant bank as such in the City – Baring Brothers. But between 1804 and 1839 another eleven were founded, several by Jewish financier dynasties from Europe, such as Rothschilds (the leaders), Hill Samuel, Hambros, Schroder, Brandt, Kleinwort Benson, Arbuthnot, Brown Shipley and Gibbs.

The Napoleonic Wars had created havoc and uncertainty. Rival international financial centres, in particular Antwerp, were undermined, and the City of London – while raising almost £1,000 million to fund Britain's successful challenge to Napoleon – became a haven for the international banker. And the century of peace for Western Europe which followed Wellington's victory at Waterloo provided the social and political climate in which London could operate effectively as the world's bank. It took up this opportunity with phenomenal success, investing thousands of millions of pounds in the industrialization of overseas countries, financing, for example, many labour works, mines and railways. In fact, merchant banks invested far more overseas than they did in Britain – around £4,000 million by the end of the century, financing railways and other enterprises in the Empire. It was they who exported the capital created by the success of British industry. If this explosion of financial activity in the old square mile is added to the rise of life insurance companies – still very few in the eighteenth century – and house insurance, the scale of monetary dealings in the City of London by 1850 was quite extraordinary. And this transformation in the foundations of wealth within the City not only changed its own internal social structure, but gave to the Greater London which grew around it a very particular kind of character still noticeable today.

Between 1800 and 1850, the physical appearance of the City of London itself does not appear to have changed all that dramatically. It was still largely as it had been since the rebuilding after the Great Fire of 1666, when new fire prevention regulations demanded much more use of brick and stone than had existed in medieval London. Grand planning of London along European lines, which a number of architects, including Christopher Wren, had advocated after the Fire had been rejected, so much of the old street pattern was retained, and is still discernible in the City today. The finest buildings were its churches, including, of course, St Paul's Cathedral.

The City was still a busy shopping area, on the eastern end of what had become two long avenues of stores running from the West End through the Strand to the City in the south, and along Oxford Street through to Holborn in the north. In Jane Austen's time, in the early 1800s, the City was still a place to buy all kinds of goods from drapers and others, who would live above the premises. Wealthier merchants, who were usually distinguished from tradesmen by the fact that they dealt in foreign goods, still had their courtyard houses in the City, rather like those buildings that can still be glimpsed through doorways in European cities such as Rome or Paris. Horse-drawn traffic would daily jam the streets with terrible snarl-ups: the bottom of Ludgate Hill was a blackspot for jams. On market days cattle and sheep were driven in from the countryside to Smithfield, where they were sold and slaughtered in a veritable Armageddon of small butcheries. Right up until 1855, when that part of the market's activities moved out to Copenhagen Fields in Islington, livestock on the hoof were regular visitors to the old square mile.

The emerging financial institutions of the City were for the first half century mostly housed in its old buildings. When, after the building of Regent Street in the West End, the City declined as a shopping district, their premises would be taken over as offices for insurance companies or some other new business. In an earlier period, the Royal Exchange itself, which had been a kind of bazaar where all kinds of goods could be bought, had been given over to dealing in commodities and stocks, until the stock-jobbers moved out – or possibly were thrown out, nobody is quite sure – into coffee houses. The first stock exchange as such was a modest affair: Jonathan's coffee house, where brokers (the relatively respectable side of the broking business) met, was burned down and a new one built, called New Jonathan's. Then, in 1773, according to the *Gentleman's Magazine* of 15 July: 'Yesterday, the brokers and others at New Jonathan's came to a resolution that instead of its being called New Jonathan's it should be called The Stock Exchange, which is to be wrote over the door'.

By and large, the new institutions wove themselves into the old fabric of the City, with perhaps abandoned merchants' houses becoming tenements for clerks or offices or warehouses. Although the City's population remained at 130,000 (more or less) from 1800 to 1850 there was quite a sudden change in its social composition. Greater London was growing very rapidly: from just under 1 million in 1800 to around 2.5 million by 1850. New districts of London that had hitherto been villages or open tracts of countryside and market gardens were springing up. In the eighteenth century, on the main roads leading in to the City, lines of Georgian houses had been built by speculators catering for the City merchant's taste in a new kind of suburban living. They can still be seen in Camberwell, Kennington, Hammersmith, Islington, Mile End and Hackney: elegant, flat-fronted, three- or four-storied terraces, their Georgian façades now often obscured by shop fronts.

THE PIONEER COMMUTERS

Although there had been some movement out of the City of London after the Great Fire, when merchants took houses in the new West End squares, such as Inigo Jones's piazza in Covent Garden, the real exodus on a large scale of the wealthy from the old square mile got under way around the early 1800s. Nobody is quite sure which kind of City person favoured which of the new suburban developments made available by landowners and speculative builders. But it is possible to provide a rough guide to the nature of this suburban exodus. The largest group that could afford to move out of the City – in the sense that they could pay the rent on a new house and their hours of work allowed them time to commute – would undoubtedly have been the clerks. Their number increased greatly as the City's financial institutions expanded, creating more and more paperwork. (Before the invention of the typewriter the clerk would painstakingly produce bills and letters in handwritten script.)

Not all clerks were equally well off, however. Generally speaking, and this was true throughout the nineteenth century, those who worked for small businesses – the commercial clerks – were among the poorest, whereas those who worked in the Bank of England would be relatively comfortable. A very large number would be able to afford at least one servant, perhaps a maid-of-all-work. The presence of a servant in the household did not mean the clerk was very high up the social scale as there was an enormous number of domestic servants in London: about 250,000 by late Victorian times. And a clerk would not be able to afford a carriage in the way that today, an equivalent on the social scale would almost certainly own a car; only the very wealthy had their own means of transport. When the suburbs around the City began to grow there was no form of public transport besides stagecoaches and these, for the most part, were not designed for commuter travel and were anyway quite expensive.

So the clerkish population's suburbs grew up within walking distance of the City, principally to the north in places like Islington and Hackney and to the south in Camberwell. There are very few records of what a clerk's life was actually like in the early nineteenth century, though there are innumerable references in the books of Charles Dickens to clerks who would walk all the way home to their semi-detached villa or terraced house in Holloway or Islington. Quite often, although they occupied with their family a whole house the size of which today seems very large, clerks would take in lodgers – frequently a young clerk just arrived in London – in order to make ends meet. By the end of the century, the clerk's attempt to sustain a genteel lifestyle on a similar income or less than that of an artisan was the subject of much condescending humour.

George and Weedon Grossmith's *Diary of a Nobody*, published in 1892, chronicles the daily life of a City clerk, Charles Pooter. He lived with his wife Carrie and one servant in a semi-detached villa called 'The Laurels' in Brickfield Terrace, Holloway. The joke about Pooter – and a very snobbish one it is in its way – is that he attempts to keep up appearances in really rather shabby surroundings, and tries to lead a genteel life though tradesmen are always duping him. His social round is very dreary and he has to keep The Laurels in order by his own amateurish efforts. On the first page of his diary, Pooter proclaims:

> We have a nice little back garden which runs down to the railway. We were rather afraid of the noise of the trains at first, but the landlord said we should not notice them after a bit, and took £2 off the rent.

Pooter was very much a product of the City in the sense that his social aspirations were formed there in a working atmosphere requiring punctuality, formal dress, and mixing – by working in the same institution – with the wealthy. The suburbs that were built to cater for Pooterish tastes reflect in their detail of miniature grandeur a kind of scaled-down version of the lifestyle of the wealthy. Much of the character of nineteenth-century London is derived from the fact that it was built to cater for this sort of taste. Other towns in England have very similar buildings, but on nothing like the scale to be found in the inner suburbs of London.

Of course, by the time Pooter arrived on the scene in the late nineteenth century, new forms of public transport, first the horse bus, then the train and the horse tram, had carried the clerkly commuter as far afield as Ilford in Essex, so the Pooter-style suburb spread out far and wide across London. It could be found everywhere to the north, south, and west – out in Hammersmith, Acton and Ealing, Camberwell, Peckham, Hackney and Islington. In the middle of the century, however, the greatest population of clerks was still confined to those places within three or four miles of the City – considered to be a reasonable walking distance. In fact, in some places there are streets which in the 1850s housed nothing *but* clerks: the 1851 census shows Ripplevale Grove (formerly two streets, Albion Road and Albion Grove) in Barnsbury, consisting of pretty villas, now very fashionable and 'gentrified', to have clerks, many of them City commuters, in almost every house.

But the City spawned many other – wealthier – suburbanites. They might take a house on one of the main roads into London (the terraces referred to earlier) or the semi-detached villas built in the 1820s and 1840s as far away as Herne Hill or Denmark Hill in Brixton. It was this sort of City person which incensed the journalist and social reformer, William Cobbett, when he observed on his way to Croydon from Southwark: 'two entire miles of stock-jobbers' houses'. Clearly Cobbett used the term 'stock-jobber' to mean City people in general, for he would have no clear idea who lived in the spreading suburbia that housed what he saw as a parasitic class.

Certainly City merchants would take up such houses and a glance at the earliest available census data – for 1841 – on, say, Brixton Hill, once lined with villas, or Denmark Hill, reveals a range of inhabitants including merchants, doctors and others. John Ruskin's father, a City wine merchant, moved out to Herne Hill in the early 1800s, for example. The census returns also show a number of people describing themselves as 'Independent' or 'Fundholder', from the very large group in London who lived off the interest from government loans. In the early part of the century there were around 250,000 people living off 'the Funds', that is the National Debt, or borrowing by the government for the financing of state enterprises, principally war. These people would have their own carriages to take them to and from the City, though Cobbett records people whom he calls 'stock-jobbers' travelling from Brighton to 'Change Alley in the City in the 1820s by stagecoach.

In fact, before the horse bus arrived in 1829 (see Chapter Four), a network of 'short stage' coach lines had developed around London to provide a kind of commuter service. Later, areas like Paddington or Belsize Park were to develop horse-drawn commuter links with the City. The hours people worked must have been fairly short as the travelling time would not allow long periods in town. John Ruskin says that his father arrived home from the City every day at 4.30pm for his evening meal. Merchants, fundholders, stock-jobbers and brokers provided a growing custom for the new 'villa' suburbs. Tradesmen, too, who had formerly lived over their shops in the City, moved out to similar areas. It was pointed out in the 1850s that the people who dominated local politics in the City no longer lived there.

The very wealthiest City people could, of course, live the life of the English landed aristocracy, with a country mansion and a house – or several houses – in town. The merchant bankers, who specialized in lending to governments, were by far and away the wealthiest people to emerge from the City of London in the early 1800s. A great many of them were European Jewish dynastic families like the Rothschilds: in fact, more than half the millionaires in nineteenth-century London were Jewish. The Rothschilds were the wealthiest and most flamboyant of the City financiers. The British branch of the family had originally established themselves as cotton merchants in Manchester, dealing with luxury goods. The merchant bank was established in the City, basing its fortune on the financing of rival armies in the Napoleonic Wars. The Rothschilds bought Gunnersbury Park in Acton in 1835 as a suburban residence, while they owned half a dozen mansions and 30,000 acres of land around Tring and the Vale of Aylesbury, their country headquarters. In London, by the second half of the nineteenth century, they had several opulent houses in Piccadilly: Lionel Rothschild lived at 148; Ferdinand at 143; his sister at 142; and Mayer at 107. The family also had houses in Grosvenor Place, Seymour Place and Hamilton Place.

Essentially the big merchant bankers could live like the aristocracy in the West End of London, though many City people were not considered to be socially acceptable. Right up to the end of the nineteenth century new wealth based on industry and commerce was thought vulgar compared to old wealth based on land ownership. Wealth derived from City finance was somewhere in between, and much more acceptable to the aristocracy: later in the century there was to be quite a close relationship between the City and landed wealth. The City was also responsible to a considerable extent for the very large number of professional people in London who grew greatly in number in the nineteenth century. Districts such as Hampstead, which were not essentially aristocratic like the West End but were a cut above the middle-class suburbs, housed many lawyers, doctors and artists whose livelihood depended at least in part on City wealth.

Altogether, the emergence after 1815 of the City of London as the financial centre of the world provided the single most significant source of wealth for the growth of London. But however 'middle class' London's style as a city, the mass of the population were working class and poor. The capital's population expanded partly through 'natural increase', that is the excess of births over deaths, but it was continuous immigration from the countryside that enabled it to grow at such a rapid pace. Some of these immigrants would get no further than the new suburbs, where there was a living to be made providing services as grooms, servants or building workers. However, the poorest newcomers ended up in the centre in the most miserable housing available.

Until the mid-century the poor could not move out of the City of London itself as new housing was much too expensive. Nothing was built for them in the suburbs and, in any case, they generally had to be on hand early in the morning to go to market or to provide many of the essential services for the commuters who arrived later in the day. The wealthier workers had moved out, from the clerk and better-off artisan upwards, and new recruits to the City workforce at this level would settle in the suburbs when they arrived from the countryside. The poor remained trapped in the centre, in housing conditions which became more and more overcrowded.

However, from 1850 onwards the poor were, in effect, evicted from the City by the redevelopment of the old centre, the driving through of new roads, the building of railways and railway stations and the construction of fine Italianate office blocks for the new financial institutions of the City. The number of City residents plummeted, and by 1900 was down to 27,000. So the transformation of the City of London itself in the nine-teenth century began a pattern of suburban development and depopulation of the inner areas and this would continue in great waves well into the twentieth century. It also had a great influence on London's *style* as a metropolis insofar as it provided a particular kind of clientele for the speculative builder who was concerned to attract, for the most part, middle-class tenants. And none of the great expansion around the City, with the exception of the relatively careful estate management by big landowners in the West End, was really planned in any way.

London was essentially a commercial city, run on commercial principles, with no single authority to oversee its expansion. The City of

London itself wanted nothing to do with the administration of the suburbs to which it had given rise and it continually thwarted half-hearted attempts made in Westminster from time to time to do something about governing the unchecked growth of the metropolis. Of course, not *all* of London's expansion can be explained in terms of the commercial transformation of the City itself. London was, after all, the single largest manufacturing city in the country right through the nineteenth century, although it developed little of the characteristic factory industry of the Industrial Revolution. Essentially it made things for Londoners themselves, importing far more goods through the docks than it ever exported. Many of those employed in London, including the colourful costers, flower-sellers and prostitutes described by the brilliant mid-century journalist, Henry Mayhew, got their living from a metropolitan economy which existed largely to satisfy the needs of the well-to-do. And the very building of London, funded to a large extent through the accumulation of money in the City, provided an enormous amount of employment, which would not have been there had there been no demand for middle-class suburbia. But there was one other great source of wealth for London in the nineteenth century.

Though the 'new money' of the City created an expanding class of wealthy people, the landed aristocracy and gentry retained until the 1870s an overall supremacy not only in the running of the country but in terms of riches. Their wealth was derived from their estates, many of which had increased greatly in value with the Industrial Revolution and the demand for coal and minerals. The fact that London was their cultural and political centre and that they came into town for a few months every year on spending sprees formed the basis of a different kind of London economy in the West End. It is to that part of London that we go in the next chapter.

CHAPTER TWO

The West End – from Season to Shopping Centre

I F THE CITY has for long been a place where tidy sums of money are made in an inscrutable way, the West End is a part of town where people spend money openly, conspicuously, and in large quantities. Most Londoners would describe the West End as a shopping and entertainment centre, the most fashionable part of town where the wealthiest tourists and businessmen can be found in tower block hotels along Mayfair. But where is the West End? Is it Oxford Street, Savile Row, Bond Street or Kensington High Street? Nobody is quite sure: all they know is that it conjures up images of opulence.

While it may not be easy to define where the West End begins or ends today, it has an unmistakable quality quite distinct from most of the other parts of London. Its nineteenth-century buildings are on a larger scale, and the Victorian terraces and villas are built in a stuccoed 'wedding cake' style, all the way from Bayswater and Belgravia to Notting Hill and Holland Park. Towards the centre of town the surviving old housing has been converted into smart offices with porticoed entrances, and in the smartest shopping streets, like Savile Row, the old tailors seem to be set in something of a social aspic which delights the wealthiest tourists. A kind of West End influence spreads away westwards until it begins to crumble in the cracked stucco of North Kensington squares; these sank in social esteem after they were built, or never really made it as a salubrious addition to fashionable London.

Although the character of the West End has changed quite radically in the last century, its extraordinary past can be sensed from the scale and style of its older buildings. In Victorian times, everybody who was anybody absolutely had to have a place in Mayfair or Belgravia, principally so that they could take part in what was known as the London Season. Every spring and summer the aristocracy, gentry and the wealthier merchants gathered in this part of London and in just four months spent millions of pounds on food, fashion and extravagant entertainments. A great army of labour, from footmen to fashion designers, were recruited to service them, so that by the Edwardian era almost a million people made a living, whether directly or indirectly, out of this West End economy. As the seasonal round drew in a wider section of society in the course of the nineteenth century, the frontiers of the West End spread westwards, and so did its influence, shaping the social and economic character of a large slice of the metropolis.

As a result of industrial and imperial expansion both the aristocracy and the new middle classes had much more money to spend than at any time before. The aristocracy had profited from their enormous landholdings by selling material rights, by collecting rents from the housing and railway building booms and by investing their surplus thousands of pounds at high rates of interest in all corners of the Empire. And the rise of government borrowing – the National Debt – created about 250,000 'fundholders' who could live a genteel life on their investments, and thereby help to support thousands of doctors, lawyers and others.

THE LONDON SEASON

To understand why so much of this spending power and wealth became concentrated in and around the West End, we must go back to London's pre-industrial past. A London 'Society' revolving around the Court, together with its accompanying calendar of events known as 'the Season', had existed since the time of Charles I. As Parliament increased in power and importance so the Season came to coincide to a large extent with parliamentary sessions, when upper-class MPs brought their households up to London with them. By the end of the eighteenth century the Court and Parliament were the two main forces attracting the propertied and the powerful into Westminster.

The London Season lasted for only a few months. The aristocracy and the landed gentry spent the rest of the year in their country seats, so that their London town houses, however grand the surviving examples in Mayfair or Belgravia may appear to us today, do not really reflect the full scale of their wealth. With the exception of such palatial mansions as the Duke of Westminster's Grosvenor House on Park Lane (demolished in the 1920s) the West End town house of the Georgian period was generally a typical London residence on a larger scale than could be found in the same period in Camberwell New Road or Upper Street Islington. There are several examples in Brook Street, Hill Street and Bedford Square in Bloomsbury. Moreover, the process of building development in the West End was very much the same as it was elsewhere in London.

The landowner would grant leases to a speculative builder, who would put up the squares, streets and terraces in the hope of letting the completed houses at a profit. Considerable control over what the builder built, and who might ultimately be allowed to rent or buy (in a few cases) the houses could be exerted by the way in which the building lease was drawn up by the landowner, and its conditions enforced by his estate staff. But in the West End the opportunity for planned and well-controlled estate developments was much greater than in most other parts of London. This was because so much of the land was held by single owners who were concerned that what was built there should remain valuable when the leases expired and full ownership of the property reverted to them. A walk around the Duke of Bedford's estate in Bloomsbury, or the Grosvenor estate in Mayfair, takes you into a well-ordered world of squares and streets set out on a grid pattern quite unlike the higgledy-piggledy medieval street pattern found in many other parts of the capital.

The very earliest examples of this kind of aristocratic suburban development were not in what we now think of as the West End proper. Covent Garden, for example, was laid out by the great architect Inigo Jones for the Duke of Bedford in the seventeenth century. The estate's church, St Paul's, which still survives with some original features, and the two arcaded terraces set at right angles, comprised a fashionable residential area. This was subsequently to go downhill as the piazza was taken over by market stalls and the wealthy residents moved to newer developments to the north and the west. Bedford Square, the best-preserved of all eighteenth-century estate developments in London, was extremely fashionable when it was first completed in the 1770s. But the best-documented account of any West End estate covers the land owned by the Duke of Westminster in Mayfair, the Grosvenor estate, which includes such famous thoroughfares as Park Lane, Brook Street, Duke Street, and, of course, Grosvenor Square itself. This has been the subject of an exceptionally detailed study by the Greater London Council's *Survey of London*.

An intriguing glimpse of life in old Mayfair in the eighteenth century is provided by a few surviving estate documents. Most of the buildings date from the 1720s onwards, and by the later part of the century it was *the* address to have in London. At that time, the parliamentary session was usually begun in November, December or January. The magazine *The World* reported in January 1790:

> London is now almost at the fullest – every avenue yesterday was crowded with carriages coming into town.

Though the calendar of seasonal events varied considerably in different historical periods, the West End of London was always at its quietest and emptiest in the mid-summer months. In the eighteenth and early nineteenth centuries Grosvenor Square would be almost entirely inhabited during the Season by titled families with a large retinue of servants – more than twenty in many cases. In the mid-eighteenth century, Baron Conway (later the Marquess of Hertford) kept twenty-two servants at 16 Grosvenor Street, and spent £3,000 while in London, mostly on tradesmen's bills rather than on his staff.

A remarkable survey of 1790 gives a complete social breakdown of the residents and tradesmen on the Grosvenor Mayfair estate, though it does not include the poorest classes who inhabited a slum area that had grown up just to the south of Oxford Street. In Grosvenor Square itself no fewer than thirty-one of the forty-seven householders were titled; and on the estate as a whole there were thirty-seven peers, eighteen baronets, fifteen 'Honourables' and thirty-nine 'Ladies'. But this was only a small proportion – less than 10 per cent – of the inhabitants. Among the other residents were one or two foreign diplomats, and a number of professional people including civil servants – such as Timothy Caswell of Davies Street, a commissioner of the Salt Tax – or Court officials, such as the King's organist. There were also army officers, doctors, architects and lawyers. But by far the largest group of residents were the tradesmen, who had shops in the area over which they lived. In fact, shops at the time were generally not purpose-built, but were established in private houses. The main shopping streets were Davies Street, Duke Street, Mount Street, North and South Audley Street, Oxford Street and Park Street.

All of this area – or nearly all of it – was redeveloped by the Duke of Westminster at the end of the nineteenth century in a costly late Victorian style, and the 'feel' of the place has undoubtedly changed enormously. For example, the 1790 survey lists among the tradesmen fifty-five butchers who at that time would still drive livestock, bought at market, to their shops in Mayfair, where they would be slaughtered. There was a market where thirty-five butchers had their stalls, and these brought a complaint from a lady living in Brook Street. In 1801 she protested that the stable yard behind her house was so crowded on market days that she couldn't get her carriage 'aired' without running the risk of being 'gored by bullocks'. As well as the butchers, there were many other tradesmen providing food and wine, dairymen (including a cow-keeper), carpenters, bricklayers, masons, plumbers, upholsterers, cabinet-makers, dressmakers, tailors, milliners and so on.

In a sense, then, the West End Season provided a self-enclosed and self-perpetuating economy. Thousands of building workers were needed to put up the fine squares in which the rich lived. Houses were elegantly furnished by the cabinet-makers and master manufacturers who were concentrated around Tottenham Court Road. The family coaches would be built in Long Acre, in Covent Garden. Little luxuries, like beautifully designed barometers and clocks, kept thousands of precision metal workers in Clerkenwell busy throughout the year. Fine meals reached the tables of the rich thanks to a complex chain of human labour made up of dealers and traders, gangs of porters in the docks and markets, poorly paid Irish men and women who humped heavy baskets of vegetables on their heads from markets to shops, carters, shopkeepers, delivery boys, and, finally, domestic servants.

A clothing industry also arose, dependent to a significant degree upon the luxury market of affluent West End London and the Season. Every member of a rich family would have a wardrobe of expensive, tailor- or hand-made clothes for every type of social occasion, changed and supplemented every 'Season' according to the dictates of fashion. The most famous members of this industry were the bespoke tailors, who catered for their rich clients' whims in gentlemanly garb, and who populated the streets either side of Regent Street and on the Burlington estate. Later they congregated in Savile Row. In the nineteenth century, this kind of economy was to expand enormously, culminating in the development of great department stores to cater for the newcomers who invaded the West End from all over London, Britain and, indeed, the world.

Not all eighteenth-century West End estates were run in quite the same way as the Grosvenor estate, and not all would have the same social composition, but they probably had more in common with each other than with the new fashionable areas which began to develop in late Georgian times and which spread out across the countryside and market gardens to the west of London in the Victorian period. The scale of the West End increased vastly and became more akin to a classic Victorian suburb built on a relatively grand scale. The single most important development marking out the West End from the rest of London in the nineteenth century was the building of Regent Street and the laying out of Regent's Park. This was a scheme devised by John Nash (the architect favoured by the Prince Regent) carved out of Crown land though built, like everything else, as a speculation. It is about the only example to be found in London of grand planning on a scale common in European cities, and typically it was never completed and was altered not long after what had been built was finished.

Nash's plan was to create on open fields in Marylebone, just north of the New Road (now Euston Road/Marylebone Road) – then virtually the northern boundary of built-up London – a kind of aristocratic garden city, with individual villas set in landscaped parkland. From here, there would be a broad street running down to Carlton House, providing an exclusive thoroughfare between the Park and the Prince Regent's residence.

To avoid the impression that the new Regent Street simply crossed the New Road and Oxford Street, circuses were to be built, providing elegant junctions to continue the style of the dominant thoroughfare. Regent Street, moreover, was to turn its back on London to the east – less salubrious areas such as Soho, where common mechanics lived – and to look to the west. Few roads were allowed in from the east, and the whole project was deliberately designed as a social barrier marking off the West End.

Not all of the scheme was finished: the fine terraces around Regent's Park certainly did become very fashionable residences, as they are today, but the circus on the New Road was only half-completed, and Marylebone Park never did get off the ground as an aristocratic suburb. But Regent Street itself, after a faltering start, became one of *the* most fashionable haunts of London Society. As Nash had intended, it was to rival the attractions of Bond Street, with shops all the way along, and exclusive lodgings above for bachelors, beaux, and visitors to town. Butchers, greengrocers and the like were not to be allowed to trade there. Regent Street was not, in the way it is now, a main road in London: rather, it was a genuine shopping centre in which the rich could park their carriages and parade up and down, the ladies popping into shops between the fashionable hours of two and four in the afternoon, while their footmen waited outside. 'Only here,' wrote Francis Wey, a visitor in the first half of the nineteenth century, 'could you find the fashionable world so perfectly at home in the middle of the street.' And in 1866, the *Illustrated London News* contrasted the bustle of Regent Street during the Season with its sad emptiness when the carriage class were out of town:

> In the former case, all is bustle and gaiety; in the latter, gloom and desolation. The brilliant ever-shifting scene presented daily in Regent Street during the season is dizzying in its confusion. On days of court ceremonial strings of carriages filled with beauty, rank and fashion, creep at a snail's pace towards St James's or Buckingham Palace. At other times, the fireflies of fashion glance rapidly hither and thither, and the West End streets are thronged with a promiscuous jungle of carriages, horsemen and horsewomen, cabs, omnibuses, and wagons; the pavements being crowded with fashionable loungers. With what dignified ease the gorgeously bedizened footmen attend to their mistresses or lounge about in attitudes of studied grace.

BELGRAVIA AND THE NEW WEST END

By the 1860s the extent of the West End itself, in the sense of the development of fashionable estates for the titled and wealthy, had expanded way beyond the old boundary of Hyde Park. In the 1820s in Belgravia, formerly a rather swampy piece of land, builders had begun the development of an entirely new fashionable quarter. Thomas Cubitt, one of the greatest of London's nineteenth-century builders, was a major figure. It was an inspirational bit of speculation, as he had recognized that the area would become attractive because of its proximity to Buckingham Palace, into which George IV moved in the 1820s. It was also close to Westminster, and was therefore likely to attract both titled and untitled parliamentarians.

The cutting of the Grosvenor Canal in 1823 proved also of great importance as it made feasible the transportation of building materials on a large scale, as well as the movement of a massive amount of earth required to make the site workable. Much of this infill probably came from excavations that had been made in the cutting out of the St Katharine Docks to the east of the City in the 1820s: thus a fashionable area of the West End had as its foundations the excavations of one of the developments that were to turn the East End of London into the least fashionable part of town.

At more or less the same time as Cubitt and others were developing Belgravia, the Bishop of London's land in Paddington, a district then known as Tyburnia, was being turned into a newly fashionable suburb in a similar way. And by the 1840s, new West-End-style estates were being established square by square and street by street in Bayswater.

Meanwhile, some of the older West End estates to the east of Regent Street were by this time becoming less fashionable. This was true of Bloomsbury, where in 1840 Christopher Hawdy, the Bedford estate agent, noted the pull towards Belgravia and Paddington. He wrote to the Duke of Bedford:

> The great struggle not infrequently is between men in business and their wives and daughters. Their convenience would keep them here within easy reach of their places of business, but their wives and daughters would give the preference to a more fashionable address at the west or north-west end of this town.

This suggests that City men moving westwards were to a considerable extent responsible for the demand for new housing in places like Paddington and Belgravia. From about the mid-century onwards the beginnings of a mixing of landed wealth and commercial wealth can be detected in that part of London. In fact, the shape of the capital, just like the social composition of Britain as a whole, was changing quite rapidly in this period. For one thing, the first railways in the north of London carved great canyons into first Euston, then King's Cross and, by the late 1860s, St Pancras, creating another social divide between east and west. Islington, which could attract the carriage trade to its shops in the 1850s, quickly went out of fashion as these three trunk lines created a twilight zone of marshalling yards and smelly steam sheds to the north of the Euston Road.

At the same time, the railways – built to cater for long-distance rather than suburban traffic in the first instance – made the West End more accessible as a shopping area to people from the provinces. Previously they had relied on their own carriage or the stagecoach and had been restricted to fairly short distances for shopping expeditions.

By 1850, too, the horse omnibus had become quite a feature of the West End, and the hansom cab, introduced in 1834, provided a taxi service around town for those without a carriage always at their disposal. This 'new' West End, far more extensive than in 1800, and accessible to a greater range of people, was given a tremendous boost with the staging of the Great Exhibition in Hyde Park in 1851. The number of horse buses increased to cater for the crowds and they became an accepted part of London life although they were still too expensive for the poorer sections of the population.

The Great Exhibition, in effect, took the West End further west, giving rise to new fashionable developments in the old Court suburb of Kensington which was built up from the 1860s onwards. As the demand for grand housing on this side of London increased, estate owners and speculative builders went to work in Notting Hill, on the Ladbroke and Norland estates behind the older 'ribbon' development of villas and terraces which had existed since the 1820s along Holland Park Avenue. There were other districts, too, which were not quite West End, but emerged as salubrious suburbs for professionals and tradesmen who might take part in some of the fringe activities of the Season, though they were not really members of Society proper. Belsize Park and Chalk Farm were developed piecemeal from the 1840s and 1860s, forming a kind of wedge of respectability all the way from Hampstead through St John's Wood to the truly fashionable West End squares.

By this period the Season itself had grown, in the sense that more and more people seemed to be taking part in its activities. It still brought a flood of people into town, the peak in the mid-century normally being in May, June and July. Society proper continued to hold the central parts of the West End as a kind of semi-private area, with the exclusive squares often protected by gates controlled by gatemen who prevented driven cattle, buses and other 'low' traffic from passing through. The gardens in the squares were also private, as many of them are today. One reason why more people were taking part in the Season in the last quarter of the nineteenth century was that it provided a social introduction between the new commercial and industrial wealth of England and the old landed wealth. Families flocked to the West End and spent thousands of pounds participating in the Season's events, principally because in so doing they gained entry into an exclusive upper-class marriage market in which the stakes were often as high as in the money market in the City.

The rush of new blood given to the Season came from upper-middle-class families of bankers, businessmen and merchants, eager for the opportunity to mix with and marry into other eligible families, preferably those with some sort of aristocratic pedigree. The comic drama of the ambitious bourgeois family aping the aristocracy, but failing miserably to 'make it' into High Society, was not lost on contemporaries: in 1841, for example, *Punch* ran a monthly series of sketches called 'Side Scenes of Society' chronicling the social adventures and disasters of a vulgar 'nouveau riche' family, the Spangle Lacquers. And there were the Veneerings in Charles Dickens's novel, *Our Mutual Friend*. A large part of the round of balls that were held when people were in town was to provide a social milieu in which eligible young ladies could find eligible young men. Lady Charlotte Bonham Carter, whose first Season was before the First World War, vividly remembered these occasions:

> In the Season, *The Times* had an enormous list of dances each night, and I'd be invited to one more or less every night. Parents were very particular about the young men their daughters knew, and in your first year in Society you were chaperoned all the time. The mothers sat in elegant gold chairs all round the ballroom floor, whilst the daughters danced with their young men friends. Parents were very careful because they hoped that their daughter might meet a suitable marriage partner at one of these events. We would meet lots of eligible young men, a few were in the army and navy – they were always awfully nice – some from the diplomatic world, landowners, and City businessmen, young men from the City, there were masses of them, they were almost the only people one saw.

Among the round of seasonal events bringing people into town was the opening of Parliament. This might occur at different times but would generally be in late January and the arrival of the Court in town would be at around the same time. The opera season began in mid-March, followed by state balls, the Royal Academy Exhibition and the big race meetings, Ascot and the Derby, which were generally visited from the London house. This social round, which ended in the late summer when grouse shooting or yachting at Cowes took the fashionable people away from London, became less private as the century went on. But it survived well into the twentieth century as an observable set of occasions when Society was in town and might be seen parading in Rotten Row in Hyde Park or queuing up in carriages in the Mall on days when debutantes were to be presented at Court, as Lady Charlotte Bonham Carter again remembered:

> Everyone was frightfully excited about being presented. One would arrive in the Mall, and line up and wait in one's carriage. Then one queued up, went into the beautiful throne room, and waited in line. I wore a simple white satin dress with a motif of white satin lilies, and then, of course, I had a train. A Gentleman in Waiting called out our names and first mother, then I curtsied to King George, then Queen Mary.
>
> Every year I went to Ascot. There one went into the Royal Enclosure, but one had to send in an application first. People who had been presented at Court would automatically be allowed in when they applied. One had a special dress for that, a very smart garden party dress. There were only two cricket matches that were part of the Season, the Oxford and Cambridge, and the Eton and Harrow. My brother was at Eton, so we went to the Eton and Harrow, and my mother and I used to give a very jolly lunch party. One took a long table in one of the large halls in Lords, and some other friend took another table and one treated it as a kind of lunch garden party.
>
> In the daytime the young ladies would go to Hyde Park, and there would be lots of people riding up and down Rotten Row, or walking up and down the paths talking to the riders, exchanging pleasantries and discussing events; it was most delightful.
>
> All the women rode side saddle, no female rode astride at all in those days. It was so inconvenient, in fact, the inconvenience in life, especially for women, was quite extraordinary. Then, in the evenings, people in lovely horse drawn carriages drove up and down between Hyde Park Corner and Marble Arch, and crowds of people would be walking along waving to them.

THE RISE OF THE DEPARTMENT STORES

From the middle of the nineteenth century, around this Society proper in the West End, a quite new, brasher, middle-class way of life was developing. It is interesting that William Whiteley, who founded one of the most successful of the new department stores that developed in the last quarter of the century, looked at both Westbourne Grove and Upper Street, Islington, when deciding the location for his new store. At the time (1863), Upper Street was established, but Westbourne Grove, on the fringes of the West End, was hardly developed at all. However, the first Underground, the Metropolitan Line, had just opened from Paddington to Farringdon, and fashion was certainly heading in that direction. Whiteley chose Westbourne Grove, and he chose well, for by the end of the century the carriage trade had gone from Upper Street. In fact, nearly all the new department stores were established in the West End, for this was now almost exclusively London's fashionable shopping district.

Whereas at the start of the century, the shopping streets had run to the City in parallel lines along Oxford Street in the north, and the Strand in the south, this pattern was now well and truly broken. The City was given over more and more to commercial offices and wholesalers' warehouses. It is interesting, too, that the new style of department store – Harrods in Knightsbridge, Whiteley's in Westbourne Grove, John Barker's in Kensington, and Tom Ponting's in Bayswater – developed in what might be called the 'new' West End. One of the principles on which they were all founded was that goods should be paid for in cash, rather than on credit, as was the custom in the old-established shops patronized by the upper classes. So not only did the department store represent retailing on quite a new scale, with a single retailer selling just about every imaginable kind of item, it also broke with the conventional habits of shopping in the West End.

Most of the department stores developed from small shops, like Peter Robinsons in Oxford Street or Harrods, expanding gradually and then undergoing a major redevelopment. The new stores aimed to provide a complete day out for their customers, more and more of whom were visitors to the West End rather than local residents. Restaurants were provided, as well as 'retiring rooms' – that is, lavatories – for ladies, who could spend the day not only buying things, but reading magazines, drinking and chatting, just as men had been able to do in their West End clubs in Pall Mall and St James's since the 1820s. Had the department stores not provided a kind of clubroom, ladies would have been greatly inconvenienced in town: though the Ladies' Lavatory Company did open its first facilities in Oxford Street in 1884, they were apparently something of an embarrassment to those who dared to use them. By the 1880s, a day trip to the West End from the provinces was quite acceptable. As one genteel lady put it:

29

Now that the train service is so perfect between London and Bath, it is quite possible to spend a day in town and return to Bath the same evening. This is no small advantage when you have a day's shopping to get through, or winter gowns and mantles to be tried on at your favourite London modistes.

With the arrival of yet more department stores, such as Selfridges, Liberty's, Swan & Edgar, and Debenhams, the seasonal trade of the nobility was eclipsed in the West End economy by the more continuous trade of the new middle classes. This was to include, in the fiction of *Diary of a Nobody*, the hapless Mr and Mrs Pooter from Holloway. As Alison Adburgham writes in *Shopping in Style*, 'Even they preferred to go to the West End for special purchases. It was at Shoolbred's in Tottenham Court Road that Carrie bought her 3/6d white fan; and it was Liberty silk that made the bows she arranged at the corners of their enlarged and tinted photographs. When Mr Pooter was promoted at the office he told her, "At last you shall have that little costume that you saw at Peter Robinson's so cheap."'

But the entire edifice of the West End, all the way from Mayfair to the fringes of Notting Hill, was – like a large part of the London economy – underpinned by money made elsewhere and spent in town. This really did not change dramatically as the West End grew bigger. The lifestyle of stockbrokers, landed gentry, or ex-colonials living in Bayswater did, however, require a much bigger army of poorer people; from the crossing-sweeper, clearing the streets of the pollution of horse-drawn traffic, to the shop assistant; from the seamstress in the West End sweatshop, working into the night to finish a fashionable dress, to the footman in an elegant household.

The big new department stores drew many new workers into the West End, where they lived mostly on the premises or in nearby hostels, run in an authoritarian manner. William Whiteley, for example, was a hard master, keeping his men assistants in one set of lodgings and his women in another. Girls slept two or three to a bedroom, and they were allowed no chairs, though this was the only living space provided. Staff had to obey no fewer than 176 rules and could be dismissed at a moment's notice. On Sundays their lodgings were closed to them during the day, whatever the weather. Whiteley did, however, provide various clubs and societies, as well as a library (paid for by regular deductions from the assistants' salaries), and this was more than most department store staff were offered.

SERVANTS AND SEAMSTRESSES

By the standards of the time, shop assistants were not badly off: there were many other West End workers whose lives must have been miserable to an extent almost unimaginable today, and they in fact comprised the bulk of the population in many areas. Even in Mayfair today, behind the main streets which were redeveloped to a large extent in the late nineteenth century, you can find many blocks of 'industrial dwellings' – the prototype Victorian council housing, put up by philanthropists or profit-making builders of dwellings for the working classes – which replaced the old slum districts. On Chesham Buildings, just off Duke Street in Mayfair, a plaque put up as an obituary to the Duke of Westminster in 1899 reads:

> Lessor to the Improved Industrial Dwellings Company Ltd, of this and other buildings on his London Estate, accommodating hereby 4,000 persons of the working class. The friend and benefactor of his poorer brethren.

One of the largest single sources of employment was domestic service. Moderately wealthy families might employ up to eleven women (including a housekeeper, lady's maid, nurse, two housemaids, laundry maid, kitchen maid and scullion) and thirteen men (including a butler, valet, house steward, coachman, three grooms, two footmen, gardeners and possibly a labourer).

Male servants, especially footmen, were a particular status symbol in the West End, but were rarely found in other parts of London. This was principally because footmen played such an important role in the Season's rituals of socializing and social climbing. They would accompany the wife and daughters on many social occasions that determined the family's social standing in Society. For example, they would escort the lady of the house on her afternoon 'calling', a ritual in which ladies called on families to follow up friendships and potentially profitable alliances, after having been introduced at social events. Footmen would also chaperone daughters at countless balls, concerts and garden parties, thus minimizing any possible mistakes that might be made on the marriage market. Families particularly valued tall, imposing footmen, and social investigator Charles Booth discovered in the 1890s that their wages varied according to their stature. A five-foot six-inch (1.67-metre) tall footman could secure only £20 to £22 per annum, while one over 6 feet (1.82 m) might command between £32 and £40. But footmen were as vulnerable as any other West End workers to the harsh laws of supply and demand underpinning its economy.

This West End luxury economy sucked in labour from the provinces or from other parts of London, primarily for the Season, then spewed them out when it had exhausted their labour power or when they were surplus to requirements. The experience of young domestic servants provides a graphic illustration of this process. Most domestics in West London were recruited from the countryside as they were considered to be more honest and diligent than city girls. These country girls, often innocent of the ways of the world, were particularly vulnerable to the threat of seduction by predatory city men, frequently their social superiors. Detection of pregnancy led to dismissal without a character reference and many turned to prostitution as an alternative to destitution. Other servants turned to prostitution simply because of the seasonal nature of much domestic employment in the West End. As a result, former servants made up between a third and a half of the thousands of prostitutes in the metropolis, many of them plying their trade in the back streets east and south of the City. In fact, the prostitutes who crowded the Haymarket and other West End resorts were simply the most visible and exotic element in the peculiar economy of this part of town.

The seasonal West End economy in women's dressmaking, which employed around twenty thousand in fashion houses, many of them concentrated around Oxford Circus, Bond Street and Conduit Street, also took its toll on the workforce. During the Season dressmakers and needlewomen commonly worked twelve- to fourteen-hour days, or even seventeen hours when there were urgent Court orders. Consequently they aged very quickly and by the time they reached their thirties their fingers were no longer supple. As a result they could not work as quickly or as intricately as younger girls, and they would be dismissed, drifting eastwards to work in the 'slop trade' of sewing and sweated labour.

However, for the many girls who willingly toiled for long hours to keep their heads above the poverty line, overwork was infinitely preferable to lack of work. As May Pawsey, who was employed by a fashionable West End dressmaking house in the early part of the century, recalled, the end of the Season, signalled by the call of the lavender girls in the streets at the end of July, was a time of sorrow for it meant less work and less food in the winter months ahead:

We didn't like to hear the girls singing in the streets. They used to sing, 'Who'll buy my blooming lavender, sixteen branches for a penny'. We hated it because we knew that it was the end of the Season and that we would get short time. If you earned twenty-five shillings a week and they put you on three-quarter time, there wasn't much left to live on. The races, the Derby and Ascot, were very important, then it faded out because London became empty in August and they didn't want us, so they sacked the work crew.

It wasn't just individuals but entire communities that could be plunged into poverty when the Season ended. Slum settlements sprang up as economic satellites of affluent West London suburbs in the course of the nineteenth century, four of the most squalid being the shanty-town communities known as the Potteries, Notting Dale, Jennings Buildings and Kensal New Town in Kensington. Many of the inhabitants – predominantly Irish – settled here after being evicted from their slum dwellings which were then razed to make way for new roads, railways and shopping arteries. A lot of poor families in Kensington teetered on the verge of destitution in the winter months because the main male occupations of brickmaking, building work, street selling, market gardening and casual labouring were dependent upon the increase in demand generated by the influx of rich families for the Season in the spring and summer. For many of these families backbreaking laundry work made the difference between survival and starvation. So great was the demand for laundresses in West London that there were around sixty thousand in London towards the end of the nineteenth century. In Kensal New Town, laundries were such a dominant feature of the landscape that it became locally known as 'Soap Suds Island'.

Because rich suburbs needed to be serviced, many were soon surrounded by colonies of workers, like those that sprang up in Kensington, housing the labouring poor, from lamplighters to laundresses and from shop assistants to sweeps. Pockets of poverty like this quickly lowered the 'social tone' of a residential area and tarnished its reputation among the well-to-do. Grandiose housing developments built for the rich and requiring extensive servicing encouraged the growth of substantial working-class communities and were particularly vulnerable to a rapid crash from aristocratic opulence to suburban seediness.

This happened in Pimlico and parts of North Kensington, Bayswater and Paddington during the final quarter of the century. Pimlico, fashionable and aristocratic shortly after it had been built in the 1840s, had thirty years later been almost deserted by the really rich, becoming a byword for shabby gentility in London. Paddington was listed in mid-century London directories as one of the most elegant parts of town, principally occupied by aristocrats, wealthy merchants and statesmen. But from this time onwards a steady stream of workers and their families came into the area and soon there were slums and select residential districts side by side. Its poorest community, made up largely of building labourers, gas workers and navvies, grew up around the canal basin at the heart of the mid-Victorian suburb. As a result, Paddington was definitely passé by the 1880s, though it still retained its aristocratic quarters with their carriages and footmen.

At its core – in Belgravia and Mayfair, the better parts of South Kensington and around Bayswater – the West End residential areas managed to retain their upper-class character until the end of the century and beyond. But the fringes, North Kensington for example, were far more vulnerable to the kind of social change affecting suburbs all around London. In fact, the wealthiest families responded to the ever-present threat of social decay either by moving further into town, or by moving much further out to the areas to the north-west and south, served by the railways.

This outward push, the dispersal of fashionable 'Society people' away from the central areas, was further accelerated by the development of a new office economy in and around the West End. For, as well as being the hub of the Season's social round, areas like Belgravia and Mayfair were now becoming places where people worked in offices. Many companies established themselves in the West End because of its convenient central position and because of the high prestige enjoyed by the area. In a sense this development was simply an extension of the whole, large-scale commercialization of the area from the mid-century onwards.

But the West End was never as completely transformed as the City, retaining something of the air of an opulent suburb. And its style still distinguishes it from other well-heeled places in London. Socially, it has always been in a different league from Hampstead, for example, and the aristocratic wealth it brought to London provided employment for all the professional people – lawyers, doctors and artists – who lived in the suburbs one social rung down.

CHAPTER THREE

The Rise and Fall of the East End

THERE USED TO be a great deal of sentimentality about the East End, and about the Cockney – that archetypal Londoner found behind a market stall or at the wheel of a taxi, always at the ready with a bit of wit and wisdom on any subject. There was always plenty of Cockney pride too, with many older East Enders claiming they were true Cockneys because they were 'born within the sound of Bow Bells'. This has caused some confusion, especially among those who went in search of that Cockney shrine, Bow Church. Quite understandably they expect to find it out along the Mile End Road, beyond Stepney and Mile End in the district of Bow. This used to be typically East End, a vast expanse of small-scale industry, sad dereliction, growling lorries and new council blocks. In fact, you won't hear the famous Bow Bells ringing in Bow: they are right in the centre of the City of London, in the bell tower of St Mary-le-Bow, Cheapside, whose history goes back to the eleventh century.

So the true Cockney is not somebody born in the East End at all: to be 'born within the sound of Bow Bells' is a definition of the true Londoner dating back to the early seventeenth century. Although there is no convincing derivation of the term 'Cockney', it probably referred to the working classes of the City itself, to the colourful crowd of cab drivers, watermen, porters and others who made their living on the relatively rich pickings of the old square mile. The former rector of St Mary-le-Bow, Canon Hudson, maintained that the origin of the 'Bow Bells' Cockney pedigree was the old curfew rung in the City, which ended a night on the town for the young apprentices. The idea of the Cockney as the archetypical East Ender derived from the late eighteenth and nineteenth centuries, and this change in definition closely followed the change in character of the area from semi-rural to solidly working class, and the eastward drift of poor people from the central areas.

As the City turned into a depopulated and highly successful financial centre, serviced by the new suburbanites of Camberwell or Islington, so the East End became the site of massive dock building, of industry – particularly the most noxious manufactures, as they were expelled from the City – and of 'sweated' trades in which shoe and furniture makers and clothing workers were kept on the poverty line. Thus, the East End progressively lost all fashionableness as London expanded, and though it was never entirely abandoned by the middle classes, by the 1880s it had become the byword for poverty and suffering.

The East End was not always like this, and the district of Bow, out by the River Lea, was a village in 1800. Charles Dickens, as a chronicler of the seamy side of London life, rarely wrote about any person or place east of Aldgate Pump. His most desperate characters invariably emerged from the slums and rookeries of central London, such as St Giles in the Field. When Dickens was writing in the mid-nineteenth century the East End wasn't the potent symbol of urban poverty that it was to become. In the first half of the nineteenth century places south of the Thames, like Southwark and Bermondsey, home of the leather trades and hat making, had far more of the character of manufacturing districts than did Bethnal Green or Stepney. Wandsworth, too, with its bleaching and calico industries along the River Wandle – said to be the hardest-worked river of its size in the world at that time – presented more of an industrial scene than the East End.

It was the old Port of London, and shipbuilding and cottage industries that gave the East End its character. On the north bank of the Thames there was a string of hamlets from the Tower to Limehouse. These housed stevedores and lumpers who loaded and unloaded cargoes, rat catchers, ship repairers, ship's bakers, marine store dealers and watermen. The servicing of sailors in turn provided much work for the women of Wapping and Shadwell, who would launder their washing. In Limehouse there were shipbuilding yards – as distinct from cargo docks – and these, along with a thriving shipbuilding industry in Deptford, south of the Thames, supported communities of skilled sailmakers and other craftsmen. The villages of Poplar and Blackwall were built around the East India Company's main shipyards, and the Company shaped the life of the whole community: time was told by the Company's shipyard bell; most local people worked in the yards making and repairing East Indiamen; they worshipped at the Company chapel, their children went to the Company school; and they often ended their days at the Company almshouses.

However, the really distinctive quality of the East End at this time, which is entirely absent today, was its seafaring tradition stretching back many centuries. This smacked of immorality and illegality and the authorities spent most of the nineteenth century trying to stamp them out. There were, for example, many disreputable lodging houses, public houses and brothels, especially along the Ratcliffe Highway in Shadwell – a sort of sailors' Regent Street aiming to make a profit out of their shore-leave indulgences. Until the mid-century, young beaux and bloods from the West End, accompanied by their minders, would 'slum it' down the Ratcliffe Highway, watching the continuous procession of sailors and ogling at the fighting, swearing and soliciting of the prostitutes for which this street was so famous.

In fact, an old seafaring tradition – the bribing of crews and the pilfering of cargoes by waterside workers – provided an important impetus for the building of the heavily fortified dock system that would change the face of the East End. For by the end of the eighteenth century pilfering in the old Port of London had reached such scandalous proportions that more than half a million pounds' worth of goods were stolen each year, especially from West Indiamen (laden with rum, sugar and tobacco), while they were moored four or five abreast in midstream, waiting for their cargoes to be rowed ashore in 'lighters', huge barges so-called because they 'lightened' ships.

The Thames was a pilferer's paradise. This was because of the City's ancient restriction on imports, which specified that all cargoes should be loaded and unloaded on the quayside north of the river between London Bridge and the Tower – the stretch of the river known as the Pool of London. With the phenomenal increase in trade in the previous two centuries, this had created a bottleneck and a long tailback of ships frequently delayed for days or even weeks. The volume of trade passing through London had become so great that by the late eighteenth century it was accounting for around three-quarters of all British imports and exports. Eventually the City gave in to pressure from merchants and lifted their old restriction on where goods could be landed and allowed new docks to be built downriver. Much of this enormous trade was controlled by the merchant companies, the most important of which was the East India Company. This had been one of the first companies to trade with India, China and Japan and the East Indies, and had made a fortune out of importing tea, coffee, silks, spices and sugar (all of which spawned local industries handling and processing the goods). In addition, the Muscovy Company was busy importing timber from Russia and Scandinavia, the Levant Company was importing silk and cotton from the Middle East, and the Royal African Company was heavily involved in the slave triangle.

With the lifting of the Pool of London monopoly, the London merchants involved in this overseas trade formed separate companies to build a series of docks, gigantic in both scale and cost. For they didn't just want protection against pilfering: they believed in building on a grand scale because they were confident that the Port of London was destined to achieve even greater wealth and prosperity in the new era of industrialism and international trade. In 1802 the magnificent buildings of the West India Dock rose on the Isle of Dogs between Limehouse and Blackwall. This massive, fortress-like dock, half a mile in length and big enough to accommodate six hundred ships, was surrounded by twenty-foot (six-metre) walls and patrolled by armed guards to prevent pilfering. Shortly after, the London Dock Company built the London Docks at Wapping, and the East India Company built the East India Dock at Blackwall. By the time the St Katharine Docks had been added hard by the Tower in 1828, London possessed by far the largest dock system in the world. The vast warehouses, enclosing the docks and housing exotic goods from all over the Empire, rose from the riverside as a splendid monument to Britain's seafaring power. For the only time in its history, the East End and its docks were a sight that every visitor to London wanted to see.

This spate of dock building changed the whole character of the East End as the riverside area became a vast dormitory for tens of thousands of dockers and waterside workers. As they moved in, so the few middle-class people living in the area, such as merchants and retired sea captains, moved out to escape from the dirt and disease. They were followed by company clerks, dock foremen and senior dock officials. Cottages and courts were flattened to make way for the land-hungry dock system, for the Commercial Road and the East India Dock Road built to link the docks with the City, and for street after street of jerry-built houses for dockers, labourers and their families. The whole area became set in a solidly working-class mould, with identical two-up and two-down rows of pocket-sized Georgian-type terraces, with continuous parapet lines to hide the chimneys and roofs.

DOCKLAND DECLINE

To begin with, the docks prospered. Trade steadily increased, merchant ships were discharged within a couple of days instead of a month, and pilfering was practically eliminated. Just as the City was emerging as the centre of world finance and the West End was establishing a worldwide reputation as the hub of High Society, so the East End appeared to be moving towards an unrivalled position as the foremost centre of world trade, which might bring prosperity to the people of Poplar, Wapping and West Ham.

But already by the 1830s it was becoming clear to more perceptive observers that the East End expansion was built on shaky foundations and that it would not necessarily benefit from free trade as did the City. Indeed, the reverse was the case: free trade and the competition from rival manufacturers at home and abroad that it brought in its wake threatened to topple long-established East End industries and the domination of the Port of London itself.

Silk weaving was one of the first to be struck by free trade, and its rapid decline was a portent of the economic malaise that would later cripple the East End. The story of the silk weavers graphically illustrates how deep-rooted East End communities with quite distinctive cultures were ground down into the 'casual poor' by economic change and unemployment. Silk weaving had been carried on in London since the seventeenth century, when Huguenot refugees escaping from religious persecution in Catholic France had settled in England. Later, when it was concentrated in Spital-fields and Bethnal Green, the industry was protected by a ban on the importation of foreign finished silk fabrics and cotton goods. The weavers turned raw silk, which arrived from the Far East on East Indiamen, into beautiful brocades, damasks and velvets, many of which were sold in exclusive West End shops. Trade prospered so much that by the early nineteenth century they were fifty thousand strong. Many of the original weavers had a passion for music, and they would enliven their long hours by singing cantatas and madrigals or by listening to the singing birds they were renowned for training. The community also supported a thriving Mathematical Society, formed in 1717, which possessed microscopes, telescopes and many other scientific instruments, and which was only abandoned when the silk industry fell into serious decline.

This decline began in the early nineteenth century when the lifting of customs duties on finished silks left the industry totally uncompetitive. By the 1830s, thirty thousand Spitalfields silk weavers were unemployed and on the verge of destitution; by the end of the century the industry was dead and their culture had died along with it.

Silk weaving was the first in a long line of casualties, including sugar refining and the associated sack-making industry – both was crushed as soon as their life blood of monopoly and privilege was drained away.

One of the keys to the rather mystifying rise and fall of many East End industries in the era of free trade lies in the monopolies, which until this time were enjoyed by London's merchant companies. In previous centuries City-based merchant companies such as the East India Company had used their connections at Court and in Parliament to gain monopolies to trade in particular products and with particular countries or continents. They had attained their power and wealth in the seventeenth and eighteenth centuries by combining a number of imperial roles: exploring new territories, forming treaties with natives, establishing plantations and mines and developing administrative and military bases to ensure that contracts and treaties were honoured. The East India Company, for example, had a standing army of fifty thousand in India in the nineteenth century.

But the movement towards free trade gradually undermined all of this. The royal monopolies granted to the merchant companies in tea, coffee, sugar and so on were withdrawn one by one, leading to their demise by the 1850s. The wealth created by these companies was transferred more and more into banking and insurance, thereby boosting financial institutions in the City at the expense of commercial operations in the Port of London.

The great merchant companies were still a powerful force in the early 1800s, as were the companies they spawned to build docks and warehouses, but they were past their heyday and the cut-throat competition in dock building soon began to undermine them all.

The first, the West India and East India Dock Companies, had monopolies on handling goods from their part of the world for twenty-one years. But when those monopolies were lifted in the 1820s, it was a free-for-all from which none benefited. The profits of the dock companies were undermined to a considerable extent by a legal victory of London's lightermen who unloaded the cargoes of ships into their huge 'dumb barges' which travelled up and down the river on the tides: they had no motors and were too heavy to row. The lightermen argued that they had an ancient right giving them 'freedom of the river' and as some of the water of the enclosed docks was from the Thames they had the right to enter them and take goods out to warehouses along the river. Dock companies had banked on being able to get the fees for storing goods, but the lightermen's victory took much of their profit away.

The substitution of steam for sail in the course of the century further undermined the early docks. The use of steam meant building larger ships which the older docks, seemingly built for all time and into which so much capital was sunk, were too shallow and narrow to accommodate. The desire to overcome this deficiency sparked off a further period of ruinous competition between the major dock companies who constructed the Royal Albert Dock, the West India South Dock and the Tilbury Docks in the second half of the century.

This constant dock building, together with the steady increase in the total volume of goods handled by the London docks resulting from the increase in international trade in the nineteenth century, makes it difficult to conceive that their relative national importance and their profitability were in serious decline. But, by the end of the century, most companies, like the East and West India Dock Companies, were forced to merge to make ends meet.

Despite these setbacks the development of the docks created an enormous demand in the East End for labour. Some was skilled: the docks required coopers, ropemakers and other suppliers of equipment. Some, like the stevedores who worked on the holds of the ships, managed to carve out relatively regular work, but they were a minority and about two-thirds of dock labour was casual. There was no guarantee of work from one week to the next and the vast majority of labourers were hired or fired on a day-to-day basis. The precarious nature of the work was a consequence of seasonal slumps in trade: China tea came in July and November; wool arrived in February and July; sugar and grain in September and April, and so on. Also, unpredictable winds and tides could delay or hasten the arrival of sailing ships by days or weeks, thus presenting the dockers with too little or too much work. In one week in 1861, 42 ships berthed in the London docks, in the next 131, in the next 209 and in the next only 29.

Even though dock work was both hard and precarious it was beginning to attract people to the East End from all corners of the world. In particular it lured a flood of Irish immigrants, especially in the 1840s and 1850s when they were escaping from famine in their homeland. As a result London's Irish population increased to over a hundred thousand by 1860. Many who made for the East End settled in St George's-in-the-East, Stepney and

Whitechapel. For the most part, poverty forced them to live in slums amid disease, drunkenness and violence. A section of the Irish population controlled key positions in the docks as middlemen who hired and fired the casual labour and made deals with shipowners on the unloading of cargo. But many Irish simply joined the queue of displaced workers who made for the docks as a last resort.

Henry Mayhew, the mid-century social investigator, reported:

> . . . we find men of every calling labouring at the docks. There are
> decayed and bankrupt master builders, master butchers, publicans,
> grocers, old soldiers, old sailors, Polish refugees, broken down
> gentlemen, discharged lawyer's clerks, suspended government clerks,
> almsmen, pensioners, servants, thieves – indeed everyone who wants a
> loaf and is willing to work for it.

By the mid-century, then, the image of the East End was beginning to change rapidly from a seafaring centre to a seedy home of misfits, ne'er-do-wells and outcasts from all over the world. But it still had a long way to go before it became the poverty trap that gripped the late Victorian popular imagination and that, according to social reformers, was inhabited by the desperate, the destitute and the degenerate. More than anything else, it was the peculiar effect of industrialism on the East End that accelerated the growth of a backward economy too weak to support the massive workforce it attracted.

The initial impact of industrialization was further to undermine the position of the London docks. The Industrial Revolution had created major manufacturing areas in the North of England which conducted their own import and export trade through more convenient and cheaper ports, like Liverpool and Hull. By the mid-nineteenth century Liverpool, for example, came to dominate the cotton trade. And while the railway, the child of the Industrial Revolution, helped to make the City and the West End rich, boosting the Stock Exchange and the Season, it sometimes had the opposite effect on the East End, and in particular the docks. For the railway took away some of the 'coasting trade' that linked the Thames warehouses with the south and east coast ports. For a while it looked as if the most significant trade in coal from the North East of England would be lost to the railways, but the building of power stations on the river revived the business, which survived well into the twentieth century.

However, the decline of the traditional port trade in domestic coal reduced the demand for the 'coal whippers' who earned relatively high wages to compensate for the backbreaking work and appalling conditions they endured. Coal whipping involved lifting huge sacks of coal from the hold, then at a precise moment, whipping it from ship to shore: one slight error and the whipper finished up in the water or in the hold with broken bones. The job was made even more dangerous by the thick coal dust which filled the ship's hold, contact with which led to a blackened body, choking fits and sometimes an early death. These dangers, however, were considered infinitely preferable to the prospect of being reduced to a casual dock hand, which was the fate most of London's two thousand coal whippers were faced with from the mid-century onwards when railways and machinery for unloading coal deprived them of their jobs.

LONDON'S SWEATED LABOUR

The Industrial Revolution had another fundamental and fairly unusual effect on life and labour in the East End. Artisans and small masters weren't simply swept away, as in many other parts of the country, by factories producing cheaper goods by mass-production methods. Because London was many miles away from crucial supplies of iron and coal, necessary to power steam-driven machinery, industrial innovation was costly and risky. Instead small masters, many of whom were Jews working in the cheap clothing and furniture trades in areas like Bethnal Green and Shoreditch, took advantage of their proximity to the large metropolitan market and the pool of unemployed labour in the capital to pioneer their own revolution in production. This revolution, which could be easily accomplished by many East End employers with little or no capital, used not steam, but human sweat and toil, to power simple hand-driven machinery.

The origins of sweated labour are obscure but it probably began during the Napoleonic Wars when the demand for military uniforms led the government to put contracts out to tender with middlemen. The fundamental first principle of 'sweating' was to keep costs down to an absolute minimum. It took a similar form in many industries, such as clothing, furniture making and shoe making, which catered for the mass consumer and retail market in the capital, from West End department stores to cheap suburban shops. The sweating system was controlled by small employers and wholesalers who sold to the shops. They subdivided the production process into its unskilled component parts so that whereas previously a tailor invariably made a complete garment, now a different pair of hands cut, sewed by machine, sewed buttonholes, ironed and packed it. Artisans who could not compete with the cheapness of goods produced in this way joined the labour pool of unemployed men, women and children, who had no option but to work for sub-subsistence wages.

This system began in the early 1800s but it was made more efficient and widespread by the invention in the middle of the century of simple, inexpensive hand-driven machinery like the sewing machine and the bandsaw. The work was done at home or in small, overcrowded workshops, thus keeping rent costs, which were very high in London, to a minimum. And the production itself was small-scale. The vast majority of East End employers hired only a handful of workers. Only about a pound was needed, for example, to set up as a master tailor, and many did this by saving up their wife's earnings from domestic and laundry work. Also, many second-hand dealers became small employers. In fact, the cheap clothing trade catering for the working classes grew out of the Jewish-dominated second-hand clothes or 'slop trade' it replaced.

The sweating system, concentrated in Whitechapel, Bethnal Green and Stepney, was based upon gruelling sixteen-hour working days, desperate overcrowding, insanitary conditions and sub-subsistence wages. Together with work in the docks, it gave the East End much of its nineteenth-century character. However, the East End could still boast in mid-century that it possessed the most prosperous and prestigious engineering and shipbuilding industries in the land. There were four Royal Dockyards and 160 private yards in London, most of them on the section of river between London Bridge and the Woolwich Ferry. This stretch of river had, since the sixteenth century, equipped England with most of the battleships, merchant ships, fishing boats and barges that she needed. The yards at Blackwall, Limehouse, Millwall and Rotherhithe were famous for the quality of their work, while most of the men who worked in the London shipyards were highly skilled, eminently respectable and superior members of the working class. They often segregated themselves from other workers, living, for example, in the more exclusive New Town and Hatcham areas of Deptford, in the Maze Hill and Greenwich Park areas of Greenwich, and in the Plumstead New Town and Burrage Town areas of Woolwich.

The shipbuilding industry in London successfully adapted to the change from wood to iron and from sail to steam, for it was served by a highly inventive engineering industry, concentrated along the south bank of the Thames in Southwark and Lambeth, in which the Brunels and Robert Stephenson were leading figures. Like the docks, the shipbuilding industry imagined it had a splendid and secure future, servicing Britain's seapower in the new age of industrialism and international trade. However, the fate of Isambard Kingdom Brunel's iron ship, the *Great Eastern*, launched at Millwall in 1857 and at the time the largest ship in the world, symbolizes the grandiose plans of the docks and their sister industries which were doomed to end in financial disaster. Thousands of tickets were sold for the launch, but the noise of the crowd prevented the many men involved in this delicate operation from hearing their commands. As a result the ship remained high and dry, and 'The Leviathan', as she was called, became the subject of many contemporary satirical cartoons. In her brief life of thirty years she was a financial failure, and when she entered the breaker's yards in 1888 the London shipbuilding industry was also practically dead.

It was knocked down, like the docks, by the double blow of industrialization and free trade. London was a long way from centres of iron and coal production, and the increasing use of high-quality iron to replace wood in shipbuilding made the cost of raw materials very high. With the breakdown of merchant company monopolies and privileges previously enjoyed by the City of London, employers cut their costs in a mass exodus to Tyneside and Clydeside. This collapse brought the East End aristocracy of labour, especially mechanics, ship-builders and sailmakers, to their knees. By 1867 there were 30,000 destitute in Poplar alone as a result of the industry's collapse, and unemployment forced them to take any casual work that was going in the docks in order to survive.

At the same time as opportunities for skilled work in reputable industries were shrinking in East London, so unskilled work in disreputable industries was expanding at a rapid pace, especially during the second half of the nineteenth century. For a very important force, contributing to the prodigious increase in people and poverty concentrated in the East End, was the entry of industries and inhabitants pushed out from central London. This exodus was a consequence of the rapid growth in the power and wealth of the City and the West End, who wished to flush out 'noxious' industries and people into other areas.

From the 1850s onwards there was a steady march of 'offensive' trades, for whose products there was a growing consumer demand in the metropolis, into the East End heartland of Stepney and Whitechapel, and across the River Lea into areas like Bow, Old Ford and Hackney Wick. These 'stink industries', manufacturing glue from boiled blood and bones, manure, matches, rubber, soap, tar, and various other chemicals and products, were pushed out by high rents, by lack of space for expansion and by tighter public health regulations in the City. They found a niche in the East End because there was no body powerful enough to resist their entry and because they at least promised new jobs in a chronically under-employed community.

These sprawling industries not only scarred the local landscape but, more seriously, their chimneys spewed out a thick, obnoxious fog which discoloured houses, killed plants, contaminated the water and induced nausea among some of the locals. The worst polluters were the companies who manufactured manure from blood by boiling it in open cauldrons. Another serious offender was the Rothschild family who established a mint a comfortable distance from their New Court offices, but uncomfortably close to Whitechapel. The emission of sulphuric acid gas from its gold refinery was a constant cause of complaint, leading to sore throats and smarting eyes.

Those who suffered most, though, were the workers in these industries. In the white lead factories which were the last resort of the starving, men were taken on by the day and not allowed to work more than three days consecutively as the lead had such a damaging effect on their health and strength. In the Bryant & May match factory in Bow, the young women workers, who in 1888 staged the celebrated 'match girls' strike', were subjected to appalling conditions resulting in premature baldness and 'phossy jaw' – rotting of the jawbone caused by phosphorous poisoning.

The expulsion of poor people from the central areas, many of whom gravitated to the East End either to find work or to remain fairly close to their original workplace in and around the central markets, was even more important in shaping the East End's economy of poverty. The growth of the City as a commercial and financial centre induced landlords to demolish houses and evict tenants to make way for more profitable office building. The development of the City and the West End was partly dependent upon railway links into central London, and this also led to a great loss of cheap working-class housing. Routes were chosen to pass through these areas, since they were the cheapest to purchase and demolish. In addition to this, the building and extension of docks in riverside areas and the construction of new roads feeding into the City and the West End also led to the widespread demolition of old slums. Indeed, it was a deliberate policy for new roads to cut through rookeries and slums – for example in the West End, St Giles was sliced in half by Oxford Street – in order to disperse the poor to other areas.

As a result, the poor families who were turfed out of places like Mint Street and Old Nichol Street in the city, turned more and more of the streets in Bethnal Green, Hackney Wick and Poplar into overcrowded slums. This huge demand for accommodation in the East End was exploited by rack-renting landlords who subdivided tenement 'doss-houses' and terraced houses so much that by the 1880s large families were often forced to live in one or two rooms, to pack four or more into each bed and to share their toilet and washing facilities with the rest of the street. For this they would be charged an extortionate rent, which normally comprised around a quarter to a half of their weekly wage.

Despite this endemic poverty in the East End, its population continued to increase in leaps and bounds. For example, between 1841 and 1901 the numbers living in Bethnal Green rose from 74,000 to 130,000, Poplar's population increased from 31,000 to 169,000, and Stepney grew from 204,000 to 299,000. This is because the nature of the East End economy acted like a magnet, drawing in the destitute and the displaced not only from other parts of the metropolis but, more important, from all over Britain and the world. Many of those who arrived were poorer than those who already lived there. By the First World War there were 140,000 London Jews – most of whom had arrived from Europe having fled persecution in the 1880s – and 140,000 London Irish.

Most of the Jewish immigrants became involved in the sweated trades, dramatically increasing the numbers working in tailoring, furniture making and boot and shoe manufacture. Many set up their own workshops employing other Jews. Although some were successful, like Montague Burton who landed in 1901 and whose name later became synonymous with the working man's 'Sunday Best', most worked fourteen-hour-plus days for a meagre wage and lived in varying degrees of poverty. The appalling working conditions endured in the East End sweated trades are graphically recalled in the recollections of Rachael Silver, who was born in Stepney in 1890:

When I first started work, I worked in houses, part of which would be used as a workshop, and we used to go around Stepney looking in house windows to see if there were any hands wanted. My first job was on trousers, doing the buttoning and the fly, that was in a house with bare walls, bare floorboards and no fire. It was freezing cold, and in the winter you'd work with all your clothes on and a scarf over your head to keep warm. Went in there at eight in the morning and you'd work right up till eight at night, doing piece work, then take home work and keep going for an hour or an hour and a half to make up your money. Sometimes the conditions were so bad you'd end up crying. Then after a few weeks or a few months you'd get the sack, there was no more work, and you'd go around looking for another job.

The presence of so many Jews adding to the severe competition for a limited pool of jobs and housing aroused anti-Semitic feeling in the East End. This was expressed in minor riots against the Jews in times of panic: for example, when there were serious trade slumps; at the time of the Jack the Ripper murders in 1888 (he was popularly assumed to be a Jew); and in restrictive legislation curbing immigration in the 1900s. Competition for jobs was made even more severe because much of the East End economy was dominated by the casual labour. The real pinch came in the harsh winter months, especially in January and February, when fog, rain and snow frequently brought the building industry and the docks to a complete standstill.

In exceptionally severe winters, like those of 1879, 1887 and 1891, seasonal unemployment aggravated by lack of food, clothing and heating provoked bread riots in the East End. Some occupations were hit more severely than others: the sweated trades, for example, maintained a more constant flow of work than the docks which was one of the most insecure industries in the East End. The casual labour system in the docks revolved around a degrading scene, the 'call on' in 'the cage', enacted every morning on the quayside and encapsulating the desperate insecurity and poverty experienced in the East End. The scramble for work tickets or tallies that it involved continued in a diluted form into the age of containerization, and was only outlawed in the 1960s. The system was remembered by Jack Banfield, who worked on the docks in the early part of the twentieth century:

We'd have to be at the dock gates at quarter to eight in the morning for the call. This meant leaving home sometimes at six o'clock, because you had to get there early to hear the whispers, because you would need to know whereabouts on the docks the work was. So the obvious place was the tea shop or the urinal. Now you never knew whether it was going to be a half a day, one day, or a week's work. So you can imagine you have been out of work for a fortnight, how humiliating it was to present yourself like cattle for half a day's work. Medland Wharf used to have a system where they had some little brass tallies, and if they gave you a brass tally, you was employed. The thing was, when you got that brass tally in your hand, you had to grab it quick, because if you didn't what used to happen was that someone would knock it out, away would go your brass tally, and whoever picked that brass tally up got the day's work.

Of course, the fewer the ships there were to unload the more brutal the fight for the few available tickets would be: 'Coats, flesh, even ears were torn off. Men were often crushed to death in the struggle.'

Some of those who literally fought for jobs were on the verge of starvation: but most breadwinners and their families managed to survive the unemployment and seasonal slumps thanks to massive charity handouts and also because there were different seasonal cycles in different trades. For, even though there was a maximum convergence of depressed trades and hence distress in the winter months, a number of trades in fact prospered at this time. For example, the heating needs of private consumers brought much work to gas workers, sweeps and woodchoppers in the winter and, conversely, when these trades declined in the summer, gas workers and sweeps would work on building sites or in the docks.

To make ends meet – and to enjoy some fresh air – East Enders developed their own version of the seasonal migration of London Society. At the end of the summer, as many as thirty thousand casual workers and their families left town to pick fruit in the orchards or to go 'hopping', harvesting hops in Kent, as Ted Harrison remembered:

We used to go down to Kent every autumn, hop picking. There was mother, my granny, my sister and brother and some friends from school. It was hard work in the fields, but we kids looked upon it as a holiday. When we used to go down hopping, they used to give us the worst bleedin' carriages; they were cattle trucks, really. We'd go about twelve at night, freezing cold, get there about three o'clock in the morning, then the gypsies would often take us to the hop houses in their carts. We'd have a box with our valuables, knife and fork, spoons, cups, oil lamps, candles, hopping pots – that was just a round pot with a wire handle, and you used to put it on the fire that you made down there, and put potatoes in there with the bacon. We used to take all our oldest clothes, then throw them all away or burn them afterwards.

For many, seasonal unemployment did bring appalling hardship. Those who experienced it would often revert to street trading to earn a few pence a day, and in the late nineteenth century there were as many as fifty thousand scratching a living from the city streets during the winter months. At this time bricklayers' labourers took to hawking hot potatoes and chestnuts, while Irish dockers joined their wives and children selling oranges and nuts. They would push their barrows many miles searching for customers, often gravitating to fashionable suburbs like Belgravia and Paddington, where their street cries, which began at seven in the morning and continued throughout the day, provoked petitions from angry rate-payers who wanted to ban them for disturbing the peace.

The most desperate characters on the streets were those who chopped up old boxes and sold them door to door as firewood, those who were reduced to scavenging in gutters, rubbish tips and sewers and those who chose to survive by begging rather than enter the workhouse. A few families actually starved to death, while many others were saved from destitution by mothers and children who worked long hours in sweated trades or, as a last resort, by turning to crime or casual prostitution.

Ernest Burr was brought up in Canning Town in the early part of the twentieth century. Because his father was often away at sea and his mother turned to drink as an escape, he was left with the responsibility of providing for his younger brothers and sisters much of the time, even though he was only twelve years old:

We were hungry and I've gone upstairs, I've looked around, nothing you could sell, because we had nothing to sell. At the finish I'd get them to go up Rathbone Street, that was the market, and fetch some orange boxes back to me, and I used to chop them up in the scullery and I used to send them out selling the wood to get some grub for us.

I was walking about with no boots and stockings on and my feet was in a terrible condition. I used to knock them on the kerbs and take no notice, and they used to have tar on the pavement and my feet would be full of tar. I used to go and get a little bit of margarine and get the tar off with it.

This sort of degradation and misery shocked late Victorian and Edwardian social investigators into promoting a picture of the East End as a kind of human dustbin overflowing with the dregs of society. There was a new awareness from the 1880s onwards that London had become a class-divided capital. The middle and upper classes in the metropolis had in the course of the nineteenth century succeeded in harnessing the forces of industrialization and imperialism to enhance their power and wealth. But in so doing, they were often ruthlessly exploitative and distanced themselves from most of the duties and obligations that they might previously have felt towards the poor by turning their backs on them to live in class-segregated suburbs.

There was still, of course, much poverty in the West End but one reason why this was often overlooked and why the East End came to symbolize urban disintegration, and even the end of civilization in the eyes of some middle-class commentators, was because mob demonstrations and strikes by the unskilled in the last decades of the nineteenth century were concentrated in the East End. The nightmare of the powerful and the propertied was that this reserve army of the unemployed in the East End was beginning to turn traitor and to stage a riot or revolution, and to pillage the West End. This was the threat of what was called 'outcast London'. It was a threat that was never realized, despite frequent riots throughout the century. Nevertheless it would shape many developments in provision for London's working-class population, and we shall be looking at these in Chapter Six.

CHAPTER FOUR

The Horse and the Railway

V ERY FEW RELICS remain of the chief means of transport used in the suburban development of London in the first half of the nineteenth century: there is a horse water trough here or there; a street in the West End and a theatre are still called the Haymarket; a few stables survive, one converted into a flea market in Camden Town; and, of course, many a mews in the West End has been converted into bijou flats and houses. But the horse as a means of everyday transport has been almost forgotten. Interviewed in the early 1980s, however, Lady Charlotte Bonham Carter could clearly recollect calling a cab when they were all horse-drawn and the awful pollution that horse-drawn traffic produced, giving that Dickensian figure, the crossing-sweeper, a very important social function:

> We often travelled in four-wheelers or hansom cabs – these were really only for people who could afford them. The four-wheelers, which would be going around the West End streets waiting to be called, would be summoned by one whistle. Then there were two whistles for the hansom, which took only one or two people. They were adorable, with the spanking horse trotting along in front, and they always had a bell.
>
> But with all the horse traffic, there was an awful amount of dirt on the streets, some of them were in a dreadful state. There were crossing sweepers, rather oldish men, and if one gave them a coin they would be very pleased to sweep a path across the street in front of one. I remember once I was going to lunch with an officer from the brigade of Guards, and I had to cross at the bottom of St James's Street into St James's Palace where the King's Guard was, and there wasn't a crossing sweeper. It began to pour with rain, so I rushed across the street, arriving in St James's Palace looking simply frightful; my lovely white suede shoes were utterly ruined for the time being.

Nowadays, a horse in London is a rare sight: it is likely to be one ridden by a police officer or it may be a shaggy-hoofed Shire in an Easter parade in Regent's Park. And the sight of a horse-drawn vehicle seems more reminiscent of a pre-industrial era than of the Victorian 'steam age'. But that is a mistake, encouraged by an oddly blinkered view of horse power held by conventional accounts of Victorian industrialism. The nineteenth century, we are always told, was the age of the train – a revolutionary form of transport which covered long distances much faster than any vehicle the world had seen. And the assumption is made that when the railways arrived, the horse was doomed, which in one specific sense was true: the railways did quickly bring the end of the old long-distance stagecoach, of the coaching inns and the romance of the old roads. But off the main roads, in the countryside and in the towns, not only did the horse survive the coming of the railways, it became more important than before.

This was as true of London as everywhere else. During a century in which the population of the metropolis rose from nine hundred thousand to around 6 million, the Victorian suburbs were built, and London grew to cover an area eighteen miles across, hay and oats represented as important a source of fuel as did coal. And in the centre of London, where there were no railways before the first Underground opened in 1863, transport remained almost entirely horse-drawn until the arrival of the motorbus and the car in the early twentieth century. The historical importance of the horse needs to be re-emphasized. This is not because it was wonderfully efficient – it was not – nor is it out of any perverse preference for animals over machines, but because, before petrol engines and electric power, the horse was vital to London's existence.

The railways certainly did have a dramatic effect on London. But until the 1860s, and arguably until the end of the century, their least important impact was in providing transport within London itself. And the railways were not the chief reason for London's growth: no transport system could have been solely responsible for that. For suburban traffic to develop, there must be jobs in the centre of town for people to go to and houses built further out for them to live in. Both of these require sources of wealth and in London these were provided by the rich economies of the City and the West End. The railways did help to concentrate more and more wealth in London, and they provided many thousands of jobs, swelling London's population. But they did not create the first London suburbs.

A good deal of what was regarded in the Victorian era as suburban development pre-dates the widespread availability of even horse-drawn transport. Thousands of commuters walked from their houses in Islington or Camberwell all the way to the City. Those arriving from south of the Thames had to pay a toll on privately owned and run bridges. Southwark Bridge made a charge on its foot passengers until the City bought and 'freed' it in 1856, greatly increasing this 'traffic'. In his early *Sketches by Boz*, Charles Dickens recorded: '. . . the early clerk population of Somers and Camden Towns, Islington and Pentonville, are fast pouring into the city . . . middle-aged men, whose salaries have by no means increased in the same proportion as their families, plod steadily along, apparently with no object in view but the counting-house . . .'

The establishment of these 'walking suburbs' was obviously quite feasible when the distance between the edge of built-up London and the centre was two miles or less, and people were prepared to walk. Even when buses and trains had arrived, there was often a good deal of walking to be done at the start and end of a commuter journey. In south-east London in particular, regular pedestrian short cuts were established over fields and ditches between the main roads. They were known as 'half-penny' hatches, as the owners of the land would set up a barrier and charge a toll. In fact, when London's first railway line, running along a four-mile viaduct from Deptford to Spa Road in Bermondsey, was opened, a gravel path for pedestrians was built alongside and a toll of one penny charged. In 1839, it is estimated that 120,000 people used it. Similarly, when the Rotherhithe Tunnel under the Thames was opened in 1845, it attracted 17,000 pedestrians a week: nothing like the numbers crossing the toll-free bridges and not sufficient to make it pay, but another indication that the walking commuter was commonplace.

At the same time as the walking suburbs were being established, there were commuters who lived much further out. These were people who were wealthy enough to afford their own carriage, or the long-distance coach fares, and whose working hours were fairly flexible. A few stockbrokers lived as far away as Brighton, but more commonly the carriage folk might take up the lease on a villa in Brixton, Paddington, Clapham or St John's Wood. So, early on, transport established a very important influence on the way in which suburbs grew, with the better-off people living a rural or semi-rural life further out, and the less wealthy confined to the districts closer to central London.

Throughout the period from 1800 to the First World War, the cost and availability of transport affected the character of the London suburbs, and helped to shape social divisions. The walking commuter, with a terraced house in the suburbs, was very well-off compared with the thousands of workers trapped near the centre by their long working hours and the fact that they could never afford the rent on a new suburban home.

Another form of transport had, in a restricted way, an early influence on suburban development. The Thames was not only the highway to the Port of London but for centuries had provided passenger transport services through the centre of the city. Before most of the Thames bridges were built in the eighteenth and nineteenth centuries the river was also a barrier, which could only be crossed at the behest of the watermen. In one of the earliest battles between rival forms of transport in London, the watermen had fiercely opposed the building of bridges and survived the spanning of the Thames by road only to be faced by competition from steam-ships in the early nineteenth century.

In fact, steam-powered transport first made its appearance in London not with the railways, or the unsuccessful attempts to launch steam buses, but with the steam packets which began regular services in 1815. In the following decades they were carrying passengers as far downstream as Margate and Ramsgate. The *Observer* reported in 1837:

> The public are now able to avail themselves of the River Thames as a
> highway, and a healthful, safe, quick and economical conveyance
> between Westminster Bridge, Hungerford Market and London
> Bridge, by means of commodious steamboats.

By the 1840s steamboats were carrying several million passengers a year. Much of this custom was from pleasure trippers going downriver to Greenwich Fair, for example, but there does appear to have been considerable – and, inevitably, wealthy – commuter traffic as well. As early as 1831, an MP was claiming that Gravesend, Margate and Ramsgate had been built to cater for London commuters, though the trip to Margate took six hours by steamboat. The river, however, was strictly limited in its potential: it provided only one route; transport suffered badly in rough weather; and steamboats were not always 'healthful and safe'. Between May 1835 and November 1838, forty-three people were drowned by steamers upsetting other craft, a dozen boats were badly damaged in collisions, and seventy-two people had to be rescued. In 1845, the *New Cricket* steamboat exploded, killing seventeen people and injuring sixty. Thus, the real revolution in London transport lay not with coal and steam, but with hay and oats, on dry land.

A new, more extensive and more complex pattern of commuting arose with the introduction to London of a Parisian invention, the horse omnibus. As a carriage pulled by horses, it wasn't, of course, radically different from a stagecoach, particularly the 'short stage' operating in and around London. What was new, however, was its ability to carry more – twelve to fifteen – passengers over short distances, its aim to provide a stopping service within town, and its cheaper fares. It was also slower than the short stagecoach, with which it competed for some years. George Shillibeer, who brought the omnibus to London, opened the first route between Paddington – then a wealthy suburb without a railway station – and the Bank of England. He had to operate in very difficult conditions. The route along the New Road (now Marylebone/Euston Road) – London's first bypass, built in the mid-eighteenth century – was fine, but the old hackney cab drivers in the City still had a monopoly of public transport in the old Square Mile. Shillibeer's buses couldn't pick up or set down passengers between the City boundary and the Bank. His omnibuses were, anyway, too bulky for the narrow City streets.

But the idea caught on quickly and other bus companies managed to succeed where Shillibeer failed. The City's hackney cab monopoly was lifted (like so many ancient City privileges) in the 1830s, during a period when there was a 'bus mania' comparable to the railway mania which had gripped the whole country. It was a while before buses ran at regular intervals, at times suitable for the commuter. And in south London, the system of turnpike roads, on which a toll had to be paid, slowed the development of regular services for some time. In fact, the turnpike trusts set up new barriers and tried to ensure all traffic was channelled along toll roads when the railways took away their long-distance traffic and their main source of revenue. By the 1850s, the turnpike trusts were desperately trying to recoup their losses by getting every penny they could from road traffic in the suburbs. A letter to *The Times* in 1850 complained that new tolls in Peckham had put a penny on the bus fare into town.

Nevertheless, fierce competition between new bus companies – many of them formed, no doubt, by job-masters and coachmen whose long-distance trade had been killed off by the railways – brought fares down, and London's first public transport system was established. By 1850 horse buses were carrying commuters and day-trippers from suburbs in north and west London into the City and, to a lesser extent, the West End. Each company had its own 'livery', with buses identified by their decoration rather than a number. As with nearly all Victorian private enterprise ventures, the system somehow managed to keep going, despite constant bankruptcies among those who ran the services. And, typically, fierce competition between services led to amalgamations as the weak or unlucky operators went to the wall.

In 1855, the London General Omnibus Company was formed: or, rather, *La Compagnie Générale des Omnibus de Londres*, for it was founded and owned by a group of Parisian businessmen who tried to copy in London the omnibus monopoly that existed in Paris. They failed and were never free from competition from rival bus companies. At this time, although there was a large enough network of routes in London to constitute a public transport system, only a small section of the population could afford to hail a bus regularly or use it as a means of getting to work. Fares were high because buses were still quite expensive, and the price of their fuel remained dependent to a large extent on the English climate: a bad harvest, and hay and oats were at a premium.

THE ARRIVAL OF THE RAILWAYS

But during this period, yet another new form of public transport arrived in London. From the beginning the railways were faster than buses, but the routes they could take were much less flexible, and they could not, of course, use the existing network of roads. They had to carve out entirely new channels into the growing metropolis and presented their builders and promoters with an entirely new set of engineering, financial and political problems. Railways excited the imagination of the age – particularly the imagination of the middle classes who could afford to use them – and, in retrospect, often appear to have been built for their own sake rather than for any clearly defined purpose. Like all other developments at the time, they were established and run by individual commercial companies and their activities were for the most part only haphazardly controlled by Parliament. It was only gradually that their impact on London was under- stood, and then it was never quite what had been anticipated in the flurry of activity that created them. They were certainly never planned, as were motorways in the 1960s.

It is, therefore, not all that surprising that the first railway to start operations in the metropolis was opened not between London and some other important centre of trade and commerce, but between Deptford and Spa Road, Bermondsey. That was in February 1836 and by the following December the line had reached London Bridge. It was designed to compete with the steamboat and the stagecoach from Greenwich to central London, and its financial backers had worked out that the journey could be completed in a quarter of the time. For most of the route, this first railway line was supported on brick arches, raising it above adjacent property. This was a device that became common to avoid the expense of closing off existing roads or demolishing buildings. The spaces beneath the arches were let off – as some still are today – for warehouses, and even a pub. Some private houses were built in the arches, although the railway company would not allow tenants to have coal fires in case the smoke from the chimneys obscured the drivers' view. This experiment did not prove successful. The company running the railway was never able to pay the dividend it promised, an optimistic 20 per cent: most railways struggled to make a profit. The company anticipated a demand for cheap travel by introducing third-class fares for passengers willing to go without a seat. Much of its custom came from pleasure trippers rather than commuters: like many steamboats on the River Thames, the railway would be busier on a holiday weekend than at any other time.

Not a great deal of demolition was required as most of the line ran through what had been market gardens. However, the very modest London Bridge Station – not much more than a shed – did involve the removal of some slum property. But the devastation, pollution and blight railways could bring to a large city were not anticipated in the construction of this line. The London & Greenwich was set up to compete for suburban traffic while the majority of other railways that were opened in the great boom period up to 1855 were not interested in carrying commuters. The Greenwich line, by pushing its terminus to London Bridge, managed to get closer to the centre of London and the City than any lines built in the north and the west. It was easier for the railways to get close to the centre from the south, where the land was not so heavily built up, and where there were fewer of the wealthier classes to resist the invasion. The southern lines did not manage to cross the Thames until the second railway boom in the

1860s but London Bridge remained a useful site for a terminus and was used by several companies. The only other station to be opened in this early period and to penetrate the centre was Fenchurch Street on the London & Blackwall line. All the other main-line stations were kept at a distance from the West End and the City.

Landed interests in the wealthier West End of London were able to resist the infiltration of the railways. A Royal Commission of Metropolitan Termini, set up to monitor new projects during the mania of the 1840s, recommended that termini be kept outside the line of the New Road, London's old northern bypass built in the mid-eighteenth century. The cost of acquiring sites in town was anyway far greater than any railway company anticipated; the further in, the more costly they were. So Euston (1837), King's Cross (1852) and Paddington (1854) began to form the familiar ring of main-line stations around north London. The North London line (then the East and West India Docks & Birmingham Junction Railway) approached the City in a great loop through Hackney, Bow and Stepney, before arriving at Fenchurch Street.

The first major effects of the arrival of this railway network in London, as it put out feelers and shoots this way and that, were to drive canyons between one area and another; to destroy and blight a good deal of poor housing; and to cause serious traffic jams. It carried an increasing load of suburban traffic, beginning a process that allowed a larger number of better-off Londoners to live further out of town. But the main lines in from the north and west were not originally interested in commuters: the first station out of town on the London & Birmingham line in 1837 was at Harrow; the Great Northern's was at Hornsey; and the Great Western's was at Ealing. It wasn't until the 1860s that a large number of stations opened along the main-line routes, serving areas which were often already built up or well on the way to development.

HORSE-DRAWN LONDON

The railways offered some competition to the horse omnibus, but in central London and inner areas not served by the railway, the omnibus remained the only form of public transport other than the hackney cab. Moreover, the new railways greatly increased the demand for horses: all the goods and people they brought into London had to be distributed by road. As

Professor F. M. L. Thompson has eloquently put it in his monograph *Victorian England: the horse drawn society* (Bedford College, 1970):

> Without carriages and carts the railways would have been like stranded whales, giants unable to use their strength, for these were the only means of getting people and goods right to the doors, of houses, warehouses, markets and factories . . .

In 1873, a House of Commons Select Committee set up to examine whether the country could supply sufficient horses for the demand was told by a stable-keeper: '. . . for every new railway you want fresh horses; fresh cab horses to begin with; I know one cab proprietor, for instance, who used to keep sixty horses and who now has one hundred and twenty.'

By the 1840s, there were 2,500 hackney cabs in London, a thousand more than ten years previously, while the number of buses had increased from 620 in 1839 to 1,300 in 1850. The railway companies themselves kept thousands of horses to haul their goods vehicles from depots to shops and warehouses and there were many thousands more goods vehicles in private hands. In the same period, the number of privately owned carriages belonging to the multiplying middle classes increased rapidly.

Even before the railways arrived there had been congestion on London's streets, and a number of schemes had been hatched to cut new thoroughfares through the old fabric of the capital. In the West End there was, of course, Regent Street. In the City a start had been made on Farringdon Street, and King William Street had been cut through from the north to London Bridge in 1835. But the increase in traffic brought about by the railways, along with the need to serve a rising and increasingly wealthy population, caused severe traffic congestion. New Oxford Street was built in 1847; Victoria Street in 1851. The building of both displayed Victorian concern to combine social and traffic engineering.

The extension eastwards of Oxford Street also demolished a rookery, thus removing a 'noisome neighbourhood' and replacing it with a 'spacious open street'. In the same way the line of Victoria Street was chosen as much for reasons of slum clearance as for traffic improvement. John Nash's pupil, James Pennethorn, whose scheme for the road was successful, told the Royal Commission on Metropolitan Improvements in 1845 that he had chosen the route for 'sanitary' reasons, which included 'opening communications through the most crowded parts'.

This was the conventional approach to Victorian 'improvements': the poorest housing was demolished to make way for new roads and railways. It was often the assumption, the pious wish, or occasionally the far-sighted proposal of those who thought about the matter that the homeless would be able to move out to a new suburb, and travel to work on the new forms of mass transport that were being made available. But, of course, the poor were unable to do so and the chief effect was to increase the housing density in those poor districts that remained standing.

Apart from swelling the traffic in London, leading to new swathes being cut through the grimmest parts of the centre of town, the building of railway lines and termini itself inflicted a direct hit on the poorer parts of town. The estimates of the numbers of people thus displaced have undoubtedly been exaggerated by those who had the laudable aim of putting an end to this kind of 'improvement': some said 100,000 people had lost their homes. But even a very cautious, recent estimate of the destruction puts the numbers made homeless between 1857 and 1869 at 37,000.

A new spate of railway building took place in the 1860s, by which time the companies had come to understand the commercial value of the commuter and had opened many more stations closer to the centre of town. To overcome the congestion on London Bridge, Cannon Street was opened on the north bank of the Thames. This was followed shortly by a station at Holborn Viaduct – by then a road bridge across the Fleet Valley, again built to alleviate appalling traffic congestion as horse-drawn traffic had great difficulty negotiating the steep slopes in and out of Farringdon Road.

In the north, the great monument to Victorian railway architecture in London, St Pancras Station, with its hotel, rose up between Euston and King's Cross, while Broad Street Station took the North London line right into the City. In 1863, the first underground railway in the world began to run between Paddington and Farringdon Street, and then on to Moorgate in 1865. Road traffic could no longer cope with commuter or long-distance passengers arriving at the main termini. The Metropolitan Railway was the answer, and it proved to be very successful on this first, northern spur, though, as it was later extended to form the Circle Line, it ran into financial difficulties.

During this second great phase of railway building in London, it appears that the trains began to carry more passengers than did horse-drawn vehicles, and had become the most important public transport network in the metropolis. Railways had by this period certainly allowed those who were better off to live much further out than any horse-drawn service would allow. Quite large numbers of City workers, for example, could travel in from as far away as Ealing or Harrow. Had London's transport system ceased to evolve at this point, it is difficult to know what shape the metropolis would have taken. It's possible that much larger numbers of the middle and lower middle classes would have remained in their semi-detached villas and terraces, while the working-class population remained trapped in the centre. But two new developments in the 1870s provided some escape routes for the poorer people in London, and took them out into Pooter Land.

First, the horse made an extraordinary comeback. An American invention, the horse-drawn tram, began operating in London in 1870: it ran on rails, could carry more passengers than the omnibus, and was therefore cheaper. In addition, all horse-drawn transport was given a boost by the import of cheaper grain from abroad. As the costs of road transport fell, so both buses and trams began to overtake trains in the number of passengers they carried within the built-up area of London. Whereas in 1875 buses and trams were providing 115 million passenger journeys a year and the trains between 150 and 170 million, by 1896 the position had changed. Horse-drawn transport was pulling 600 million passenger journeys, compared with the railways' 400 million. Not only did the horse overtake the train – a new pattern of transport was established.

The first experimental horse-drawn tram was brought to London by an American called George Train. He obviously did not understand the social geography of London because in 1861 he laid out his trial tram rails on the Bayswater Road between Marble Arch and Porchester Terrace. He had chosen the most fashionable part of town, thus raising a howl of protest from the carriage-owning classes. They could not tolerate these new vehicles hogging a fixed section of the road, on rails sticking up above the road surface and proving an obstacle to carriages. Train's tram was scrapped.

When successful tramways were established along a whole series of new routes in the early 1870s, they could not penetrate the West End or the City or get further than the railways into the intervening central area. And, although trams were more comfortable than buses, they became a working-class form of transport as they were cheaper, and had room for carrying the tools and baggage of working people.

In just four years, an entirely new and largely successful transport network of 'street railways' – the American term – had been opened in London. They ran from the Archway Tavern through Kentish Town to

Euston and King's Cross; from Newington Green in Islington to Finsbury Square; from Stratford and Poplar to Aldgate; from Brixton to Westminster Bridge; from Camberwell Green through the Elephant and Castle to Southwark Bridge. The tramways were particularly strong in the inner suburbs, north, south and east of the centre. In the centre itself, buses retained their supremacy as trams were excluded. Horse trams were much slower than trains, as vividly illustrated by Ted Harrison's recollection:

> The old trams used to be drawn by two horses. To get up steep hills like Stamford Hill, they would stop, and there would be a chain horse waiting at the bottom, and they'd attach it to the front to give them extra power. Then the chain horse would be led back down to the bottom of the hill to wait for the next tram. As the tram was going along, the driver would ring a big bell to clear the street and to warn carts in front to get out of the way. But sometimes they wouldn't and the tram would have to go very slowly, and of course there would be a real slanging match between the drivers.
>
> When we were kids we couldn't afford the fare very often, even though it was a halfpenny or a penny, so when the conductor was upstairs or right inside, we'd jump on the back where they fastened the horses, and get a free ride. When the conductor came downstairs, we'd jump off again and run along with it until he went upstairs again: you could usually keep up – they only went at six or seven miles an hour most of the time.

But, despite this lack of speed, the horse trams had great advantages over the railways: they were cheaper, they ran frequently, and at times that suited a large section of the working-class population. Unlike the buses, trams had to provide 'cheap' workers' fares. So, in the inner suburbs they were able to compete with the trains, and allowed people who could not previously afford it to become commuters. In 1884, the chairman of London Tramways was able to boast:

> We have relieved London of an immense number of poor people by carrying them out to the suburbs . . . building has been going on very largely on our line of roads in South London.

THE FLIGHT TO THE SUBURBS

This was probably one of the main reasons for the flight of the more genteel classes to suburbs further out: the working classes were moving in, splitting up the old terraced houses into multi-occupied tenements. And speculators were providing new and cheaper housing in the remaining spaces in the inner suburbs. London's suburban expansion had always tended to proceed in that way: the pioneers established themselves along main roads, so that building took place in 'fingers' spreading out from the centre; gradually the gaps between the fingers were filling in. By allowing a larger section of the population to become commuters, the tramways almost certainly played a part in changing the social composition of the inner suburbs, and although many lower-middle-class clerks and other low-paid workers used them, their image remained essentially working class.

Secondly, at more or less the same time another development, this time on the railways, was making it easier for the poorer classes to travel in to work. There had always been two or three classes of travel on the trains, though the companies themselves were keener to carry better-off than poor passengers. But they were encouraged to cater for the working classes by people who felt it was wrong that the trains should benefit only the relatively well-off. It was well recognized that even with a third-class fare, the extra costs of suburban living were preventing a large section of poorer people from moving out. Lord Shaftesbury made the point that the wives of poorer families needed to remain in the centre of town for the charring and laundering jobs that provided extra income. Men with casual employment had to be in the queue early for the chance of getting a job. The extra cost of commuting, and the extra inconvenience, discouraged any movement away from the centre.

Yet the railway companies, believing that they could profit most by serving the middle and upper classes, would resist pressures to introduce cheap travel as long as they could. The *Economist* was critical of this attitude as early as 1844, urging the railways to cash in on the new 'mass markets' that were emerging in consumer goods and to seek profits in quantity rather than quality. Most railway companies thought this economic nonsense. However, they were gradually forced to change their policy by legislation giving them the responsibility of doing something for the people they made homeless by the building of new stations. The North London had to agree to provide special workmen's trains with low fares in order to get parliamentary approval for the demolitions involved in building Broad Street Station in 1865. The Great Eastern had to do the same to get into Liverpool Street a few years later. And in 1883, a Cheap Trains Act gave railway companies in general the responsibility of providing special trains for workmen.

At first, those travelling on these trains had to 'prove' they were working class by giving their employer's name and address and details of their job. But the system eventually settled down to one in which anyone travelling before a certain time in the morning could get a cheap ticket. Workmen's fares began to succeed where third-class tickets had failed: thousands of poorer Londoners began to use them. The value they got for their fare varied, however, from one railway company to another. In 1905, the Royal Commission on Traffic in London estimated that for a two-penny workman's fare a passenger could travel less than three miles on the London & North Western, the Midland, the London & South Western, and the London Brighton & South Coast. But the same money could buy a journey of over seven miles on the South Eastern & Chatham, and nearly eleven miles on the Great Eastern. To what extent this affected the distribution of working-class commuters around London is not certain, but to the north and east, new 'working-class' suburbs began to emerge and the movement in these directions was more noticeable than in the north-west. Moreover, the workmen's fares were, according to contemporary observers, having the same sort of effect on middle-class suburbs as the horse tram. The manager of the Great Eastern said in the 1880s:

> Wherever you locate the workmen in large numbers, you utterly destroy that neighbourhood for ordinary passenger traffic. Take, for instance, the neighbourhood of Stamford Hill, Tottenham and Edmonton. That used to be a very nice neighbourhood . . . but very soon after this obligation was put upon the Great Eastern Company . . . of issuing workmen's tickets . . . the district is given up entirely, I may say now, to the working man.

By the turn of the century, the availability of workmen's fares was also affecting south London to a considerable extent. About a quarter of the total number of suburban fares were workmen's tickets. In the inner area, six to eight miles from the centre, the proportion, at 40 per cent, was much higher. The arrival of the working classes again hastened the flight of the middle classes who could afford the time and the money to live further out. The growth of London's transport system, from the steam-boats and horse omnibuses to the railways and horse trams, with their workmen's fares, obviously had a powerful influence on the way in which districts rose and declined. But these effects were not simply confined to the ways in which the system prevented or enabled people to move out of the city centre.

Throughout the second half of the nineteenth century, London's population was growing at an astonishing pace: the number of people in a suburb could increase tenfold in fifteen or twenty years. Quite a large part of this increase resulted from people moving *into* London from the surrounding towns and villages, so that the social composition of any suburb was not dependent on the sort of people who had moved out of the centre of town. It was really a matter of what sort of person could be attracted from both inside and outside London and, once a suburb was established, it quickly took on a life of its own, providing more employment for people locally than was available in town for those who commuted. Generally speaking, it was the wealthier suburbs which required the largest workforce of domestics, tradesmen of all kinds, grooms and other stable-workers, delivery men and so on. The commuter, in a sense, brought back the wealth from the centre and spent it in the suburb, creating a satellite economy. All Victorian suburbs, from the grandest in the West End to the most threadbare lower-middle-class enclave, reflected this. They carried within them a working-class population which was always liable to lower the tone of the district and send those higher up the scale scuttling off elsewhere.

By 1900, not all middle-class families had fled to the farthest ends of the commuter railway line. Many quite fashionable areas remained as islands of gentility in the general sea of decline: for example, parts of Hackney, Hampstead, Dulwich or Brixton. Before the arrival of the motor car, it was common for the well-to-do to live along the main roads, and the maps that the social investigator Charles Booth produced in the 1890s show this clearly. Booth had his own colour-coded class classification which he used to shade in the social and 'moral' character of the whole of the inner part of the metropolis. All over London, the main roads are lined with the brown that indicated his category of people second in the social scale, namely shopkeepers living above their premises, or middle-class families in semi-detached villas.

The West End did contain pockets of severe poverty, but the central part of it was never subject to the waves of social change affecting more modest suburbs. In the second half of the nineteenth century a distinction was becoming established between commuter traffic and the traffic problems of the central area – which was given over more and more to commerce, offices, government buildings, shopping and entertainment. As new forms of transport developed in the nineteenth century, a pattern had been established whereby the West End was protected from invasion by the railway and the horse tram. Most commuter routes were to the City, while the horse bus and the hansom cab provided transport in the West End – the railways were regarded as too destructive to be tolerated, and the horse tram was socially unacceptable.

The cutting of the first underground railway, the Metropolitan, and its extension around London's core with the building of the Circle Line, did not radically alter the situation. A passenger could travel from Euston to Victoria on the Circle, but it was a long and sooty way round. Remarkably, this age of steam on the London Underground can still be recalled. Interviewed in 1983, George Spiller remembered working on the footplate around 1900:

> We worked ten-hour days, eight times round the Circle. Then we
> used to run out into the open, perhaps do three Wimbledons a day, or
> three Ealings, or Upminster – that was the longest one – took nearly
> half a day to get there from the other side. It was all right when we got
> out into the open, but there were a lot of tunnels we had to go
> through first. In the summer you could hardly breathe going through
> the tunnels, it was so hot. It was enough to boil you on the footplate.
> You took your jacket off and stripped down to your shirt. There was a
> terrific wind and smoke going through the tunnels, then sometimes we
> had rotten coal and we used to get smoked out on the footplate, but
> that didn't happen very often. I'd shovel about two hundredweight in a
> day's work: it was a dirty, hot, sweaty job, but we had to put up with
> it. And there was no cover outside. So we had to put up with the rain
> and the wind and the snow.

But this type of travel – and the impenetrability of the central areas – was transformed by the development of deep tunnelling methods in the late nineteenth century. In 1890, the first Underground using this method burrowed all the way from King William Street in the City to Stockwell. It was now possible to criss-cross London without destroying buildings or upsetting the carriages and sensibilities of the upper crust. The Central Line, connecting the West End and the City, was opened in 1900, and the whole of the Underground system in central London – with the exception of the Victoria and Jubilee lines – was established in the few years of the Edwardian era. The successful electrification of railway lines was essential for the deep new Underground system, while above ground electric power replaced horse power on the trams in the first years of the twentieth century.

With the development of the Underground, the old pattern of transport in London came to an end: trains ran right through the centre, opening up the West End for office building in the 1920s and gradually undermining its exclusivity. On the buses, the petrol engine quickly replaced horse power, though horses continued to pull carts and goods wagons for another half century. For the most exclusive, the motor car replaced the carriage, again marking a new era in London's transport. Between the two world wars, London's built-up area was to continue to expand at a phenomenal rate. A new kind of semi-detached suburbia – 'Metroland' – was built along the tube lines. It was the growth of this Metroland that finally marked the end of the era of horse-drawn traffic.

CHAPTER FIVE

The Making of the Suburbs

IT TAKES QUITE a leap of the imagination now to picture places like Paddington, Kensington, Islington, Camden Town, Camberwell or Acton as newly built suburbs on the edge of town, their streets leading off into fields and market gardens. We know that they must once have been like that, and that London was not dropped in one large block on the landscape; still there is an odd fascination in examining old photographs showing meadows and trees that became another suburban road in, say, Hornsey or Muswell Hill. An imaginative reconstruction of the way in which the countryside around London became built up does help to explain why places which are now part of the 'inner city' – a term which is a by-word for urban desolation – were once thought of as suburbs. Whatever else 'suburban' means, it has always been a term to describe the residential border areas between town and country.

But to imagine that Victorian suburbs were simply an older version of the places which go by that name today is misleading. The suburban 'ideal' of a house away from the noise and bustle of the centre of town may not have been very different, but the physical reality of Victorian suburbia was in many ways another world. Even the most salubrious new developments in Kensington or Paddington contained in stinking enclaves terrible slums. Until late in the nineteenth century, most suburbs had defective sewage systems, the roads were liberally spread with the manure of horse-drawn vehicles, and for all their comparative grandness they could never have achieved the scrubbed primness of later, semi-detached suburbia.

In fact, the more the word 'suburbia' is examined, the more puzzling it becomes. Over the centuries it has been used to describe just about every condition of town life imaginable. In Elizabethan times it referred to the miserable settlements of outcasts and poor immigrants who couldn't find a place in town. It has been applied to the habit of wealthier merchants and financiers from the City setting themselves up in country villas way beyond the urban frontier in the late eighteenth and early nineteenth centuries.

And much later in the nineteenth century, when artisans and poorer clerks could afford to live in places like Tottenham and Walthamstow, we hear of 'working-class' suburbs. What part of London is left that was never 'suburban' at one time or another? The truth is that London is a metropolis of suburbs and really has been so since the seventeenth century. Whereas most European cities, such as Paris, developed within a clearly defined boundary marked by defensive walls, London began to spread out from the Square Mile of the City very early on. And from the very earliest developments a distinctive pattern of building was established which remained characteristic of London and the English until suburbia became a common form of townscape throughout the world in the twentieth century.

It has always amused foreigners that Londoners liked to live in separate houses rather than flats. A Frenchman remarked in 1817:

These narrow houses, three or four storeys high . . . one for eating, one for sleeping, a third for company, a fourth underground for the kitchen, a fifth perhaps at the top for the servants . . . and the agility, the ease, the quickness with which the individuals of the family run up and down, and perch on the different storeys, give the idea of the cage with its sticks and its birds.

On the other hand, the more pompous English Victorians thought the French upper crust very peculiar because they did not mind living in the same block as their social inferiors. An article in the magazine *Architecture* commented in the 1870s:

It would be difficult to quote any custom of the French which English people might less readily fall in with than that which assigns the tenancy of the half dozen successive storeys of the same house to just as many utterly dissociated and indeed discordant people, ranging from a jaunty viscount of the *premier étage*, not merely to a very small rentier on the *troisième*, but to a little nest of the humblest work people on the *cinquième*, all meeting on the common stair . . .

Why well-to-do Londoners should have developed a taste for individual houses rather than apartments is not at all clear, but it had important consequences for the way in which suburbia developed. The desire to live away from the workplace and the centre of town was never simply the result of a taste for a semi-rural kind of existence, as has often been suggested. It always seems to have had more to do with establishing one's superior social status and other practical and quite unromantic considerations. For example, was a banker who set himself up in a 'country' villa in Dulwich in the early 1800s seeking rural tranquillity or a lifestyle to mimic that of the landed gentry? Was the clerk who settled in a house in Islington or Camberwell really trying to experience a semi-rural existence, or was he simply fulfilling his ideal of living in a house of his own, and these were the only places sufficiently near work in which he could afford to rent?

It is really impossible to answer such questions, but a good deal of writing on suburbia seems to assume that it was the rustic idyll that provided the essential appeal, and that the back garden is the suburbanite's imaginary field and hedgerow. Whatever truth there is in the idea, it should not obscure the much more serious business of suburbia, which involved establishing one's class position and finding a house in which one could afford to live. One illustration of this aspiration towards social superiority was the common and characteristically lower-middle-class habit of christening a small terraced house or villa with a grandiose and pretentious name. William Head, for example, brought up in Stafford Road, Hounslow, in the 1900s, remembered:

> We lived in a villa with a lovely bay window which my father bought for £250. The house was designated Longleat Villa, I suppose to be a spot above the rest of the neighbours and to keep up our connection with Wiltshire where Father came from.

Moreover, the idyllic portraits of Victorian suburbia which sometimes appear in contemporary advertisements and nostalgic middle-class memoirs should not mask the fact that what made most comfortable suburban homes tick was the regimented and unremitting toil of low-paid domestics. Ronald Chamberlain, whose father worked as a post office clerk in the City, was brought up in Canonbury in the early part of the twentieth century. He remembered how the young domestics employed by the family would occasionally desert their duties when it all became too much for them.

> In our home we always had a little maid-of-all-work of about fourteen or fifteen, who had to work hard all day. The little girl would bring in her alarm clock to be wound and my father would set it for half past

six, when she would be expected to get up sharp. She'd have her meals by herself in the kitchen and would go to bed about half past nine. On more than one occasion these little girls would run away and go home, they couldn't stand it any more.

SPECULATING ON SUBURBIA

Although suburbia was based on the ideal of an individual home of one's own, the great mass of detached and semi-detached villas and terraces that were put up in the eighteenth and nineteenth centuries were not custom-built for particular clients. Few people had the luxury of ordering a particular style of house and popular taste was established in the market place by estate owners and speculative builders. Land around London was plentiful and cheap and most of it was suitable for building, or could be made so once the art of drainage had been developed. It was therefore sensible to put up relatively simple, individual structures with a low density of population. And, as the demand for housing grew with the great increase in population, it was inevitable that London would simply spread outwards. Those who were supplying the houses may therefore have been as influential as those renting them in shaping the suburban character of the capital.

House building and the creation of suburbia constituted a major London industry. They required capital from the City, and in fact drew in funds from all over the country. For the landowner it was a way of raising ground rents way above those provided by market gardeners or farmers. It gave work to professional surveyors and solicitors who not only handled the legal work but who were also commonly responsible for raising money for speculative builders. The speculative builders themselves – from the giants like Thomas Cubitt to the mass of smaller 'master builders' or craftsmen – could make a fortune, although more frequently they went bankrupt. And the building industry employed tens of thousands of labourers, as well as all those involved in supplying essential materials such as bricks.

On the ground, the ideal of suburbia was a very serious business. For the most part, the owners of the large country estates surrounding London in the eighteenth century – many of which still exist as valuable town properties today – were anxious that when their land became ripe for development it should become as fashionable a part of town as possible. On the other hand, they were not usually prepared to take the risk involved in putting up houses themselves. What they preferred to do was to grant a building lease to a speculative builder, and though they might lend him some money towards the cost of putting up houses, he took the gamble on whether or not they would be let. In the short term, the estate received increased ground rents from the property; in the long term, the entire development would come back into its ownership when the lease expired, and the wealthier the tenants were the more valuable the estate would be in the future. Good estate management, therefore, involved ensuring that the 'right' sorts of houses were built to attract the 'right' sort of people.

The owners of land north of Westminster and west of the City had a head start in the eighteenth century. Proximity to the royal palaces and Parliament was obviously a good selling point if you wanted to attract the aristocracy and gentry. The fact that the Grosvenor estate, for example, owned large unbroken tracts of land made planned development relatively easy on a large scale. The Duke of Bedford's estate, north of the Strand, was similarly well placed to provide new housing for both the titled Londoners who had a country estate and the wealthy merchants of the City who, since the Great Fire, sought a home outside the old square mile.

But building was always a gamble: if, for some reason, the housing you put up did not attract the clientele you were aiming for, the estate could quickly go downhill. It was not enough simply to build large, elegant houses – the supply of these was constantly being renewed by developers elsewhere, seeking the same kind of tenant. You had to do what you could to keep out the sort of people who might make the estate unattractive. In the 1850s, the leases on the Bedford estate prohibited an astonishing array of tradesmen from occupying its buildings: 'Brewer, slaughterer, distiller, dyer, goldbeater, tanner, bone boilers, soapboilers, working hatter . . .' These and many others were banned.

In addition, the Bedford estate and many other Georgian developments put up gates to keep undesirables out of the squares and streets occupied by the wealthiest tenants and to keep down the noise – an early example of what modern local-authority planning has tried to do (in a more democratic way) in 'environmental areas' by cutting out through traffic from residential streets. On the Bedford estate the gatekeepers were instructed to allow in only gentlemen on horseback and carriages, as well as pedestrians. Droves of cattle, omnibuses, carts and other 'low vehicles' were kept out. And the gates were closed at night. In 1879, people protesting about the inconvenience to normal traffic caused by such gates estimated that there were about one hundred and fifty in London.

The types of people and traffic that the estate tried to exclude give an indication of the enormous range of essential activities that took place in nineteenth-century London but which were always being pushed into some corner and hidden away. Where did the cow-keepers, chimney sweeps, tripe-sellers, poulterers, die-sinkers, and dealers in old iron go? Or live? Most of them had to stay near their work which was closely linked to the fashionable places from which they were excluded. So they ended up in appalling slums, jam-packed into tiny back alleys, disused stables and buildings that, for one reason or another, had fallen into disrepair. On the Bedford estate, some shoddily built housing in Abbey Place became a slum, and there were no grand housing developments anywhere that did not develop their hideous slum quarters.

Away from the estates, on the fringes of the built-up area, Victorian shanty towns developed. Not far from Bedford Square, just to the north on the other side of the New Road, was Agar Town. In a technical and legal sense, this had been built in the same way as Bedford Square: the Church Commissioners leased the land to a developer, a lawyer called William Agar. But Agar did not insist on a high standard of building or strict leasing arrangements when he brought in cheap labour – bricklayers and carpenters working in their spare time – to put up the streets of houses. Agar Town became an instant slum, described by Charles Dickens in 1851 in the magazine, *Household Words*:

> Along the canal side the huts of the settlers, of many shapes and sizes, were closely ranged, every tenant having his own lease of the ground. There the dog-kennel, the cow shed, the shanty, and the elongated match-box style of architecture . . . Through an opening was to be seen another layer of dwellings at the back: one looking like a dismantled windmill, and another perched upon a wall . . . Every garden had its nuisance . . . In the one was a dung-heap, in the next a cinder-heap, in a third, which belonged to the cottage of a costermonger, was a pile of whelk and periwinkle shells, some rotten cabbages, and a donkey.

The contrast between the heavily fortified elegance of Bedford Square and the squalor of Agar Town is a classic example of the extreme range of wealth and social conditions to be found in Victorian London. There was always tremendous social tension in suburb building, and though estate management undoubtedly became much less rigorous as the nineteenth century wore on, the same battle to create a fashionable area – whether it was to appeal to the upper classes or the lower middle classes – was played out in Hampstead, Islington, Acton, Ealing, Camberwell, Hackney, Peckham and just about everywhere except the lost tracts of the East End of London. It is arguable that the Georgian estates, like the Bedford development, were not true suburbs in the sense that they were really extensions of London's centre, and built in an urban rather than suburban fashion. It could also be said that places like Agar Town, shoddily built on land blighted by the new railway yards carved out of the fringes of London, were not truly suburbs because they had such a low social character. The suburb proper was middle class and essentially tied in with the habit of commuting into town to work, by foot, horse bus or train.

It all depends, of course, on what you classify as suburban. Do you include the scatter of detached and semi-detached villas that were built in the countryside around London in the early nineteenth century, as well as the isolated terrace rows that sprang up in places like Camberwell, Stockwell, Canonbury, Stoke Newington and Hackney? They were suburban in the sense that they provided semi-rural homes for those linked socially and economically to the centre of town. There were other forms of suburban development, too, which do not quite fit the classic image of suburbia. Squares and streets of terraced houses were built to form small-scale urban centres on the outskirts of the City and the West End. They were often called 'towns' and bits of them remain as a kind of nucleus around which much more extensive suburbia took place: Camden Town, Kentish Town, Kensington New Town, or De Beauvoir Town. There were some built to the east of the City – Tredegar Square or Bromley New Town, for example – before the East End took on its later nineteenth-century character.

The villas with their parkland (now built over, or turned into municipal parks, such as Marble Hill in Twickenham or Clissold Park in Hackney) and the new towns obviously embodied a kind of suburban ideal, but at the time they were built they really remained distant from the social forces that were shaping the greater London which grew out to engulf them. For the most part their *distance* from the centre would ensure their relative exclusivity at least for a time, whereas the inner-London estates had to create an artificial remoteness. On the whole, however, nineteenth-century suburbia had neither gates nor distance to protect it from the ever-present threat of social decline.

SUBURBAN SNOBBERIES

No two suburbs developed in quite the same way, because the intricacies of the land dealings and speculations, together with the foibles of builders, ensured an odd mixture of individuality within the general conformity. And though we tend to imagine suburbs as clearly defined places, their boundaries were never very clear, just as the districts of London today – Clapham, Highbury, Chelsea, Kensington or Hampstead – really have no identifiable borders. The names of areas and streets reflected a host of influences: the titles of landowners, the original names of villages, builders' names, and often some obscure references to members of their families.

You can find, for example, in Brixton, a Minet Road. It's named after the Minet family, French Huguenots who came to England in the early eighteenth century to escape religious persecution. They became bankers in the City and in Dover, and bought land in the Brixton area which remained almost entirely rural until the early 1800s. As London pushed outwards, the Minet estate, along with others in the Camberwell and Brixton areas, became ripe for development. Typically, the first housing built on Brixton Hill and Denmark Hill was in the form of detached villas or terraces that followed the main roads. In 1826, for example, the Minets were granting building leases for a terrace called 'Surrey Villas' on Camberwell New Road.

Brixton and Camberwell were then very salubrious areas, and remained fashionable with City people until the early 1900s. But the Minet estate was only extensively built up after the 1860s, with the opening of Loughborough Junction Station and, after 1870, with the arrival of the horse tram. This brought in a new population of clerks and some artisans, and Brixton itself developed as a local shopping area, where the Bon Marché, one of the first – though not very successful – department stores, was built in 1877. In the 1880s a guidebook, *The Suburban Homes of London*, declared the Brixton Road 'as good a specimen of a modern suburban thoroughfare as can well be met with'. And in 1889, the social class maps produced by Charles Booth show little poverty in this area. The Minet estate was in fact a classic Victorian suburb, quintessentially 'genteel' according to the guidebook.

One of the best descriptions of the way in which a nineteenth-century suburb developed is given in Professor F. M. L. Thompson's history of Hampstead. The whole district derived its character from a mixture of local peculiarities, geography, its position in relation to central London and forces that made the metropolis grow. The small town of Hampstead had been, briefly, a spa attracting artists, and doctors among other professionals. In the period before the great explosion of housing that joined it to central London, villas and terraces such as Church Row were built, making Hampstead an out-of-town suburb with a professional rather than an aristocratic character. By the 1860s it had more domestic servants per household than any other district of London. What Hampstead lacked – and the West End districts of the gentry had in plenty – were footmen and other male servants associated with the very top, carriage-owning class.

Between the small town of Hampstead and Regent's Park lay a large estate owned by Eton College. This tract of land covered what is now known as Chalk Farm, as well as parts of districts called, uncertainly, Belsize Park, Swiss Cottage and Primrose Hill. In the early nineteenth century the lessee had sublet the land to a farmer who used it as grazing land for livestock and dairy cattle. As Regent's Park took shape and St John's Wood developed into the prototype upper-middle-class suburb of villadom, it became clear that Eton College's land would be very valuable for building development. As far as estate development was concerned, the College does not appear to have been too dynamic: it received a good rent from farming and could increase the rate when leases expired. But in 1826 it did take the first step that all landowners required if they were to grant building leases: an Act of Parliament was obtained to abolish existing manorial rights on the land. (Hampstead Heath remained open country because the landowner, Sir Thomas Maryon Wilson, uniquely among would-be developers, for complex legal reasons could not get his Act through Parliament.)

In 1829, the Eton College surveyor offered fifteen acres of the estate for development with the recommendation:

This very desirable property, which is too well known to render
necessary any description of its eligibility in all respects for Villas and
respectable residences, combining the advantages of Town and
Country.

But this was not a boom period in London building and, although 300 yards (275 m) of Adelaide Road were laid out, nothing much happened in the way of house building. For in 1831 the railway chugged on to the scene.

The London & Birmingham wanted to push its line to Camden Town and Euston right through the Eton College estate. The farmer protested, the College equivocated, and a compromise was reached. The railway would have to cross the estate in a tunnel built deep enough and strong enough for houses to be safely constructed above it. In 1838 the tunnel – the first in London – was opened. As the trains emerged from the elaborately detailed entrance so they attracted sightseers. But the building speculators stayed away. There was some talk at the time of the railway 'opening up' the area for development, but this was rather absurd. The London & Birmingham was a long-distance line with no local stations until Kilburn was opened in 1852 and South Hampstead in 1879. By that time, the Eton College estate had already been developed.

With the railway – which elsewhere, in Kentish Town and Camden Town, caused almost instant blight – safely tucked in its tunnel and deep cutting, the building speculators eventually began to turn up. One grand scheme, proposed by a developer, was to put up villas like those that John Nash had built not long before in Regent's Park. But the College rejected it. In the meantime, the prime site of Primrose Hill was preserved when Eton College agreed to give it to the Crown, in return for a chunk of Crown lands near Eton.

Typically, the area then took shape over a long period as builders turned up, took parcels of land, and put up the sort of housing – such as the semi-detached villas along Adelaide Road – they thought would attract an upper-middle-class, St John's Wood type of clientele. As new roads were cut, and new houses built, it was recognized that there were no community facilities on the estate. This worried the local builders whose sentiments were passed on to the College by the surveyor, John Shaw:

> I find there is a general need for a Chapel on the estate . . . Mr
> Wynn, the builder of many houses, and other persons, have led me to
> believe that it would be profitable even as a speculation to establish
> one . . . Undoubtedly the existence of such a building on the estate
> would most materially lead to the formation of a neighbourhood
> around it.

Developers commonly regarded a church as the essential feature of a middle-class suburb and a selling point. The other community facility was the public house – and this very often arrived sooner than the church. The Eton College estate was provided with the Adelaide Hotel in 1842 and the Eton Hotel in 1846 (both pubs), but had to wait until 1856 before St Saviour's Church was completed. By the 1870s, the estate had two churches and two pubs, making it a classically respectable middle-class area in Victorian London.

The estate's 'success' in these terms was something of a fluke because the development had never been really well planned, and the most important decision of the estate turned out to be the sinking of the railway under ground. Had the rival landowner, Sir Thomas Maryon Wilson, been able to develop all his estate in the area, Eton College might well have suffered from the competition. There was no provision made for industry, which not only polluted areas but brought in a working-class population, and the people who moved in were not generally carriage-owning folk, so not many stables were built: when a mews was not used for horses, it was, of course, commonly turned into a slum.

The experience of a district not far away from Chalk Farm, and still close to Hampstead Heath, was very different, and gives a good idea why some suburban building didn't quite take off in the way intended. Land owned by the Dean and Chapter of Westminster on the Belsize estate was let out on long leases effectively preventing the estate owners from overseeing building themselves. One of the leaseholders was William Lund, who had forty-five acres off Haverstock Hill. He decided to go in for a kind of 'St John's Wood' development, and called his estate St John's Park. It was close to the newly opened Hampstead Road Station on the North London Line, and Lund hoped that he might attract City people.

Lund lived in Haverstock Lodge, with eight acres of grounds, and set about developing the estate himself by building around his home. He surrendered his existing lease and took out a ninety-nine-year building lease only loosely drawn up by the Dean and Chapter of Westminster. Everything went well at first, and within ten years he had built sixty semi-detached villas. But uncontrollable elements soon set the estate on a downhill path. First, St John's Park sloped away down to the River Fleet, which had become an open sewer by the 1850s; it was not put into underground pipes until the following decade. The sewer blighted one corner of the estate. Next, a branch of the Midland Railway into St Pancras was tunnelled under the estate, creating uncertainty among builders about its desirability. Finally, in 1869, the Metropolitan Asylums Board took over an area of unused paddocks next to the estate and put up wooden fever wards to cope with smallpox epidemics, one of which duly broke out in 1870. This obviously did nothing to increase the area's popularity and Lund was left with unlet houses and an exodus of residents from established parts of the estate.

In 1865, a distraught resident of Upper Park Road had written to the Dean and Chapter of Westminster about the blight on the area and the deterioration of the Fleet Road end of St John's Park:

> The older houses are already greatly deteriorated in value and will be
> still more so if these shops are opened as being in Upper Park Road,
> and after expending a large sum of money in purchasing, furnishing,
> and fitting up this house it will be very annoying to be driven away.

Most of the Belsize estate did not deteriorate in this way and, in fact, the area to the east of Fleet Road did not become a slum: more the home of artisans and respectable working people. Also, significantly, while the horse trams were kept out of Hampstead as a whole, as they were from other middle-class areas, they arrived in Fleet Road and South End Green in the 1870s to put the final lower-middle-class and working-class stamp on this fringe part of Hampstead.

As the building of suburbia continued throughout the Victorian and Edwardian eras, so the same kinds of influences shaped the social character of districts everywhere. Railways linking a far-flung village with London, helping it to become a salubrious suburb, blighted districts along the route. Unattractive elements – such as a mental institution, a cemetery or an established industry – branded the future development of large areas.

In west London, for example, Turnham Green and Ealing developed as middle-class suburbs, while Hanwell, Acton and Brentford never provided the necessary attraction. Although short stagecoaches and horse buses linked Turnham Green and Ealing with the City in the 1830s, there was not a great deal of house building at this period. It was not until the 1850s that a continuous line of housing took shape along the principal roads leading from Notting Hill, Hammersmith and Turnham Green to Brentford. Gunnersbury Park, once a royal residence, and bought by the Rothschilds in 1835, was one of a number of earlier, remote and semi-rural out-of-town developments.

The fate of Hanwell was sealed early on when a large lunatic asylum was built to the west. In 1854, moreover, Kensington and St George's, Westminster, decided to bury their dead in the same area, creating large cemeteries. Around the same time, a Central London District school for a thousand Poor Law pupils was established in the area. Such was the stigma attached to these developments that attempts were made to get Hanwell's name changed, but without success.

In Acton, where a large estate was developed by the British Land Company, the housing does not seem to have attracted a sufficient body of middle-class people to protect the area from poorer tradespeople. In 1872, there were sixty laundries – an essential Victorian service provided by women with a reputation for heavy drinking which shocked respectable middle-class opinion – on the Land Company's South Acton estate, as well as slaughter-houses, and factories for the manufacture of manure from bone crushing.

Brentford, an urban area rather than a demure residential village when the great suburban expansion took off after 1860, was similarly marked out as less salubrious than Ealing or Turnham Green. It was a centre of the brewing industry and had a soap factory and gas works. Another reason that some estates did not 'make it' in the fierce competition to attract wealthy, or at least respectable, people was a failure of the development at some stage before it was finished, leaving houses without roofs or windows. This would prove useless to the rich but very attractive to the poor who were being pushed out of central London by clearances for new roads, railways and office building. North Kensington developed in this way when ambitious builders went bankrupt.

It seems also to have been at least one of the reasons why one of the worst slums in London was created in Campbell Road, Finsbury Park, built in the 1860s. Freeholders on the Seven Sisters estate decided to cash in on the North Islington housing boom of the 1850s by selling off individual plots for house building on a new street running north from Seven Sisters Road. This policy of selling off to builders plot by plot – rather than any attempt to orchestrate a continuous development – left gaps between houses and unfinished shells. The houses themselves appear not to have been any worse than the average, three-storey, flat-fronted buildings that were put up in their thousands all over London. Moreover, they did attract the lower middle classes – this wasn't, after all, far from Charles Pooter's fictitious home, 'The Laurels', Brickfield Terrace (see Chapter One). In 1871 there were some residents with servants: an accountant, a barrister's clerk and a law stationer. But the incomplete state of the road, described later by a local vicar as 'unfinished, unpaved, unmade and unlighted . . . little better than an open sewer', made it less desirable, led to reduced rents and allowed in coal porters, charwomen, shoe-blacks and chimney sweeps.

Very soon, the houses intended for single occupation were being turned into lodging houses and tenements. In 1888 three of the houses were sold to one of the thousands of London landlords who made a good living by packing families into single rooms and getting a return on their property by creating overcrowding. By 1900 Campbell Road was one of the most notorious slums in London. But for the most part these great tracts of Victorian suburbia did not go into instant decline. The very poorest people were crammed into pockets of appalling housing, while the majority of working-class and lower-middle-class Londoners found, by the standards of the time, a reasonable house somewhere. It should be remembered that inside toilets and bathrooms were very rare features, even in better households, until quite late in the nineteenth century.

Hackney, perhaps, provides as good an example as any of the standard London suburb of the period. No more than a village at the start of the nineteenth century, it began to form part of London in the 1850s. It had its typical outrider development of De Beauvoir Town – laid out in the 1830s and 1840s in a grid pattern in a modest version of a grander estate in town. In 1851, the *Illustrated London News* reported that W. G. D. Thyssen, the descendant of a Flemish merchant, had begun to lay out his land for building development. The railway had just arrived – again the North London Line – always a spur to building, though the horse omnibus had linked Hackney with central London from the 1840s.

Typically, small-scale building speculators put up the semi-detached villas and terraces designed to cater for the tastes of City people. Often a builder would be responsible for only one house in the street, and few operated on a large enough scale to build more than half a dozen houses. Thus the variations on the theme of villa and terrace – with architectural style and detail gleaned from the many handbooks available – took shape.

In Hackney, housing was graded to some extent and, where a middle-class family might not be attracted, smaller, lower-grade terraces were provided for the working classes. Dalston Lane in the 1860s housed a number of clerks, as well as master craftsmen, printers and commercial travellers, in three- and four-bedroom terraced properties with steps up to the front door. Leading off this main road were poorer streets, where labourers, boot-makers and plasterers lived.

Parts of Hackney would never make it as a 'clerk's paradise'. Homerton, for example, had a smallpox hospital and two workhouses, all established before suburban development began; Hackney Wick, meanwhile, was too near the industries of the Lea Valley. But, by and large, Hackney became well established as a desirable middle- and lower-middle-class suburb, and remained so until the end of the century. In the long run, however, Hackney was in the wrong part of London to retain its social pretensions. As the East End developed, so it began to encroach on, and to surround, a suburb that had been built close to open country and away from industry. Cheap workmen's fares introduced on the Great Eastern Railway allowed a new section of the trapped central population of London to move out to places north and east of Hackney, where speculators put up a meaner form of housing to cater for a new clientele. And industry, pushed out of the City and kept away from the fashionable West End, moved towards Hackney, until it was almost incorporated into the East End.

A myriad legal, economic, geographical, political and other influences shaped the districts of inner London. It's the story of the creation of a kind of suburban ideal by market forces which never amounted to planning in the modern sense; which often went wrong from the developer's point of view; and which created, at the height of the Empire, a capital city of terraces and villas quite distinct from anything to be found in Europe.

CHAPTER SIX

Riots and Reform

FROM TIME TO time an outbreak of violent crime or public disorder in London, whether real or lent credibility by the popular press, gives rise to a fear that the social problems of the vast inner city will destroy its normal, workaday calm. In the 1980s the riots in Brixton (which in a few days of arson and looting destroyed a sizeable amount of property in a run-down London borough) and in Tottenham (where a police officer was hacked to death) aroused widespread fear of the collapse of law and order in the capital. The IRA bombing campaigns from the 1970s until the 1990s led to death and destruction and in this new century the horror of suicide bombers on the Underground has inevitably filled Londoners with anxiety (see Chapter Twenty-three). As in most comparisons between the present and past, there is a tendency to believe that things are getting worse; that a great city which once hummed along harmoniously is disintegrating under new social and economic pressures.

There have been periods of relative calm in London's history, but the Victorian era was certainly no less violent than recent times. There were occasions in the nineteenth century when the capital's wealthier citizens feared that the great mass of the poor, whose lives and sufferings might surface from time to time, were about to rise up and destroy the city in revolution. Many parliamentary committees enquired into the social conditions of working-class Londoners; countless descriptions of the appalling conditions in which the poor lived were given by medical officers of health; and, bit by bit, social reform took effect. It was gradually recognized that a vast metropolis could not cope with its administration by leaving it to a bundle of charities and antiquated authorities able to do little more than tackle its problems piecemeal. Yet for most of the nineteenth century, there was no general awareness among the propertied and the powerful of the fact that the growth of the metropolis had given rise to an urban desolation on a scale never before known.

But in 1886, the complacency of the fashionable West End appeared for a few days to be directly threatened by what was referred to as 'the mob'.

Regent Street in 1866 at the height of the London Season. The few months of the year when the upper crust were in town underpinned an entire 'West End' economy of trades people.

Overcrowding on the London to Brighton stagecoach in 1822. Some of those enduring the rough and tumble on the road are quite likely stockjobbers from the City whose families lived as far away as Brighton.

A slum just south of Kensington High Street in 1869. There were enclaves of terrible poverty even in the most fashionable parts of London. A year after this photograph was taken of Kensington Market Court it was demolished.

Local photographer Alfred Braddock had workmen and locals pose in Clapton Passage, Hackney in 1882. This archetypal London Victorian suburban street was just nearing completion.

A young costermonger with his donkey and cart selling strawberries to a suburban maid in 1885.

A wonderful illustration of the way in which Victorian London suburbs were built with millions of bricks baked from London clay. This huge stack was photographed in 1880 in Wood Street, Walthamstow. There appears to be a child sitting high up on the stack.

A silk weaver at work in his loft in Spitalfields in the East End in 1895. By that time very few of these once prosperous weavers, many of whom were descended from French Huguenot refugees, survived.

Customs officials in the London Docks go about the very sober business of sampling casks of wine. This photograph was taken in 1893 when London had the largest acreage of enclosed dockland in the world.

Towards the end of the nineteenth century horse drawn trams running on street rails provided the cheapest form of transport in London and enabled modestly paid workers to live in the new suburbs. This is the North Metropolitan Horse Tram outside West Ham Union Workhouse around 1890.

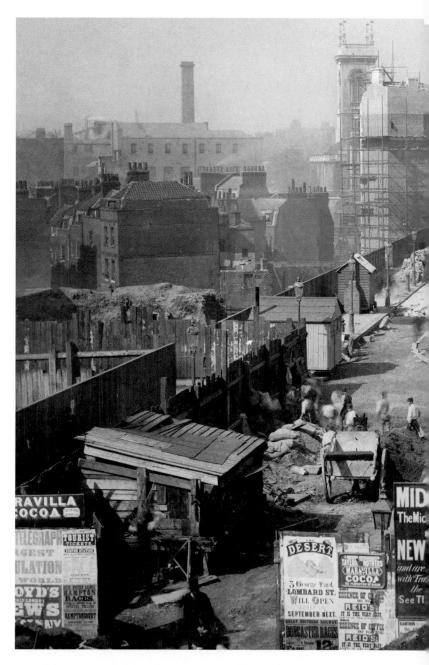

One of the most ambitious schemes to ease traffic congestion in Victorian London: the building of Holborn Viaduct in 1869. Horse-drawn vehicles had struggled to negotiate the slopes of Farringdon Street which runs in the valley of the Fleet. Bridging it involved the eviction of about 2,000 people.

A scene of traffic chaos in London around 1900, just before the arrival of the motor car and motor buses eased congestion. This photograph was taken at the Mansion House junction in the City.

Charles Tyson Yerkes, the American financier who came to London to make a killing modernizing its transport system. He raised money to electrify the District line and to buy up existing underground line schemes which formed the first sections of the Bakerloo, Northern and Piccadilly lines.

Yerkes (picture bottom left) believed that new underground lines would give rise to new suburbs around London. This 1908 poster gives an idealised image of Hampstead Garden suburbs that grew up after the opening of Golders Green station.

Lady Charlotte Bonham Carter who had vivid memories of the London Season before the First World War. She is pictured here in the dress in which she was presented at Court during the Season of 1913.

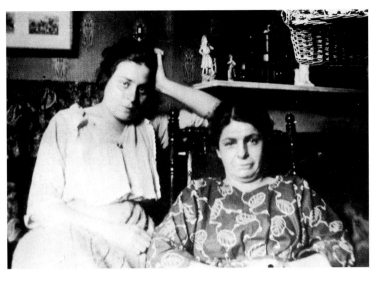

May Pawsey at home in Chelsea with her mother at the end of the West End Season. As a seamstress for a West End dressmaker she only had work when the aristocracy and upper crust were in town for the annual round of balls and events such as Ascot.

In the heart of carriage owning London, Park Lane photographed in 1895. Horse trams were barred from the more exclusive districts of London.

Elevator girls in uniform stand to attention by the lifts in the store that brought American style department store shopping to London. Gordon H. Selfridge opened his store in Oxford Street in 1909 and embraced the Art Deco designs of the 1920s and 1930s.

Commuter chaos in 1919 when a rail strike left Londoners dependent on buses and trams. This desperate scramble was for an electric tram near Embankment station.

The expanding West End economy of London in the late nineteenth and early twentieth century employed thousands of shop workers many of whom lived in dormitories. These young women are making dresses for the Army & Navy Stores in Victoria Street around 1900.

On Monday, 8 February, during a bitterly cold winter, which had put many Londoners in the building trades and the docks out of work, a demonstration was organized in Trafalgar Square. A crowd of about twenty thousand, many of them reportedly dockers and building workers from the suburbs, turned up. *The Times* reported that: 'Their numbers were increased by a very great many of the idle class – of that large body in London who are spoken of by workers themselves as the class who want no work to do.'

The demonstrators demanded employment and were addressed with revolutionary rhetoric by Ben Tillett, the dockers' leader, and John Burns from the Social Democratic Federation (a militant socialist group). An attempt was made to wind up the demonstration in an orderly fashion, but a breakaway group headed for Pall Mall. Stones were thrown at the Carlton Club windows, and several were broken. Nobody is quite sure what happened. But one witness, the Socialist Henry Hyndman, later acquitted at the Old Bailey for his part in the riot, said that the Reform Club staff had thrown nailbrushes and shoes at the demonstrators. In retaliation, the windows of a number of clubs were broken with cobblestones picked up from St James's Street, which was being repaired.

The angry crowd continued to Hyde Park, smashing windows of fashionable shops, and turning over carriages, in one case stripping a coachman of his livery and taking his place on the box. Big West End stores like Marshall & Snelgrove and Peter Robinson also suffered broken windows. The demonstrators marched home with their pickings from the West End singing 'Rule Britannia', but the fear of the mob did not lift for several days.

W. H. Smith, founder of the bookshop chain and then a Member of Parliament, told the Commons that it was 'almost incredible that, for at least an hour, the most frequented streets in the West End of London should be entirely at the mercy of the mob'. His sentiments were shared by many others. A dense fog descended on London and, frightened of a repetition of the disorder, shopkeepers and some householders shuttered their windows. Wild rumours spread of a vast army coming out of the East to attack the West. Then the fog lifted, and with it the fear that London would be overturned by the downtrodden mass of its labouring classes. The crowd had never held any real threat of revolution, but the complacency of the West End had been shaken.

In fact, it now seems astonishing how those in power were willing to risk a mass revolt of the capital's working class rather than make concessions. For all the conditions were there for revolt: dreadful poverty, once highly skilled artisans reduced to 'sweated', lowly paid labourers and radical movements led by disenchanted workers whose interests were utterly opposed to those in power. But the revolutionary threat was for the most part restricted to the plots of a small group of radicals and the recurrent nightmare shared by Parliament and London's wealthiest citizens of 'the mob' sacking the West End never became reality. When, painfully slowly, the government of the capital was re-formed, the threat of revolution was only one of an extraordinary mixture of Victorian impulses that brought about change.

One of the most important reasons why London lagged behind many other cities in tackling problems of poverty, disease and slum dwellings in the early part of the century was because the City of London jealously guarded its power and independence. While it did not want to take on responsibility for the metropolis that had grown around it, at the same time it put up fierce resistance to any proposals in Parliament to make the new and greater London self-governing. The City of London itself had had for a long time a highly developed, though not necessarily very efficient, system of local government. But by 1800 only a tenth of the people of what might be called greater London lived in the old square mile. Every other district of the capital had to make do with essentially rural parish vestries, quite unsuitable for the urban areas they now controlled.

Services now regarded as essential to a major city, such as the supply of fresh water, were provided by private companies with little or no regulation in the first half of the century. By 1800, well water was scarce or polluted by the spread of housing to the places where it had been sourced. The New River Company, established in the seventeenth century, did bring in supplies of good water from villages to the north of London and distributed this through hollowed-out elm logs from a reservoir at Rosebery Avenue in Islington. But many more companies used steam engines to pump out raw Thames water that was increasingly polluted with sewage sent straight into the river from the newly popular flush toilets of the 1820s.

There were eight Commissioners of Sewers covering London outside the City, but by all accounts they were hopelessly inefficient. They neither insisted on proper sewerage being provided in new building developments, nor did they build efficient sewage systems themselves. In fact, much of London's sewage, even in the most salubrious areas, accumulated in cesspits under the houses, their contents removed by scavengers or 'night soil' workers who would trundle the refuse out in the dark hours to hideous middens or market gardens. But often the cesspits filled up and became cesslakes, impregnating the cellars of houses with filth. If such a large house were abandoned it might become inhabited by the most desperate of all London dwellers, who spent their lives in low, unlit basements with sewage seeping through the walls.

POLICE

As the sanitary condition of London became steadily worse and the Thames filthier, another social problem – crime and disorder – posed a more immediate threat to the capital. In the early 1800s there were highwaymen on the main roads into London, operating in the countryside that was later to become suburbia. For example on Hounslow Heath the carriages of the rich were held up as they travelled along the Great West Road to Bath. In the City itself a notorious gang would hang around on the eastern outskirts and drive a bullock along the streets in front of them until it was so maddened that it would smash open the boarded shop fronts so that they could be looted. Nimble-fingered young pickpockets frequented markets and crowded thoroughfares: their favourite ploy was 'shoot flying' – gold watch-chain snatching from rich gentlemen. Countless footpads as well as garrotters (who would throw a cord around their victim's neck and rob him) – the muggers of the early nineteenth century – lurked in the streets after dark.

The upright citizens of London had only a rather ragged band of unpaid, and extremely reluctant, local constables and parish watchmen to protect them and they were on duty only at night. There were, too, the famous Bow Street Runners, created in the eighteenth century by Henry Fielding (the novelist, magistrate and reformer) and his brother. But they quickly acquired a wide reputation for tracking down criminals and stalked the country way beyond the edge of London on celebrated cases, often in the pay of wealthy gentlemen who wanted some score settled. In effect, London was very poorly policed.

When there was an outbreak of civil disorder, the troops had to be called in, worsening tension and creating fear of outright conflict between people and authority. In the Port of London itself, as we have already seen, the scale of pilfering from ships anchored and waiting to be unloaded became serious enough to threaten even the complacency of City merchants. It was on the Thames that the first proper police force was organized in 1798, signalling a major psychological change in an age when the very idea of professional policing was considered an infringement of personal liberty.

When, in the 1820s, the first proposals for a London-wide, professional force was foward, the City of London greatly objected: it would be a 'violation of all the Chartered Rights of the City'. But in this one respect, law and order, Parliament and a shrewd Home Secretary, Sir Robert Peel, were prepared to challenge the authority of the City – up to a point. A second attempt was made to establish a police force, this time allowing the City of London to have its own officers, and this was pushed through despite widespread suspicion from all classes of society.

The creation of the Metropolitan Police in 1829 was, in a sense, the first time that Parliament recognized London to be a single, indivisible metropolis. However, the police managed to create an essentially London service without setting up a local administrative body which rivalled the power of Westminster or the City. There was always a fear that if the largest city in the country were granted any kind of political autonomy, it would threaten the traditional authorities in the City and Westminster. So that the new police force did not *look* like a military force, they were dressed up in blue uniforms with reinforced top hats and they carried truncheons rather than swords or guns. This did not make them instantly popular, and it took some time before they managed to establish any public respect.

However, by the middle of the century the Metropolitan Police had become a model force deployed around the country to quell disturbances. During the 1840s they played a very important role in controlling the Chartist movement in the capital, arresting activists and breaking up public meetings. London had become one of the Chartist centres in the country, providing the movement with leaders like William Lovett and Ernest Jones, who published the most widely read Chartist newspaper, *The Northern Star*. Among the Chartist demands was the vote for the working class. They often spoke in revolutionary rhetoric, believing that if poorer people had the vote they would oust the parasitic aristocracy who lived in luxury by levying taxes on the productive classes and profiteering employers who exploited their labour.

The Chartists were not, however, for the most part revolutionary. And what threat they did pose was relatively easily contained by the Metropolitan Police. But the wave of revolutions in European capitals in

February and March of 1848 suddenly made revolution in London seem a real possibility to those who feared it, and they took extraordinary steps to secure the capital against insurrection. The Chartist leaders announced that on Monday, 10 April there would be a mass rally on Kennington Common, followed by a march to Westminster to present the Charter containing the signatures of 5 million working men and women from all over Britain, demanding universal suffrage.

This declaration created a panic in Parliament. It was decided that the defence of the capital could not just be left to the Metropolitan Police – although four thousand of them were to be stationed along the Thames bridges to prevent the protesters marching back to Westminster to present their petition, which the authorities feared might be the flashpoint leading to a revolution. Just about every major public building was to be guarded by 'special constables', sworn in for the occasion and armed. There is great disagreement about the number of 'specials' on duty that day and about what the motives of the majority of those who joined up were. Much newspaper comment claimed that the working classes were prepared to defend the capital by being sworn in as 'specials', but it is quite clear that a great many did so under threat of losing their jobs if they refused. A carefully balanced estimate of special constables on duty on 10 April puts their number at eighty-five thousand.

At the same time, the Duke of Wellington, who masterminded the operation, brought in more than seven thousand soldiers who were billeted in the West End and the City. They were kept out of sight but were there in case of emergency. As an absolute safeguard for the monarchy, Queen Victoria left London on 8 April for Osborne House on the Isle of Wight. The most heavily fortified building was the Bank of England: sandbags were stacked along its parapet walls with loopholes for muskets and small guns and musket batteries were set up at each corner of the building. Even the British Museum was armed with fifty muskets. One hundred cutlasses and other weapons were issued for the defence of the capital's prisons.

Quite early in the day it was recognized that all this had been quite unnecessary: the demonstration was largely peaceful and broke up without any rioting. London began to say that it had not been frightened after all and, though there were further protests and outbreaks of violence in that turbulent year, the threat of Chartism quickly faded. It is now generally believed that the one major administrative reform in London in the first half of the nineteenth century, the creation of the police force for the whole metropolis, was an important factor in the prevention of insurrection, giving Parliament the confidence to reject out of hand Chartist demands for reform.

Whether or not the political reforms that the Chartists sought would have led to a different development in London's government is a matter for conjecture. What is indisputable is that, from the middle of the century onwards, political control of the metropolis was fragmented, shared between outmoded local vestries, the City of London which was always resistant to change, and ad hoc interference from central government. It is worth noting that the *order* in which the great social problems of the metropolis were tackled does seem to reflect the preoccupations of those in power: the problem of crime and the threat of disturbances were tackled first with the creation of the Metropolitan Police in 1829; the problem of sewage was met with the setting up of the Metropolitan Board of Works in 1855; but the housing problems were left to private and philanthropic endeavour until the 1890s, although Parliament did introduce a series of more or less unsuccessful laws to encourage a solution to overcrowding and the elimination of slums.

LONDON LEFT BEHIND

In 1835, extensive reform of local government in England and Wales set up recognizably modern local authorities, elected by ratepayers, to tackle a host of social problems. But this Municipal Corporations Act excluded London. So too did the Town Improvements Act of 1847, which allowed local authorities outside London to involve themselves (with parliamentary approval) in drainage, water supply, street paving and so on. Parliament was simply not prepared to tread on the toes of the City of London or to challenge the vested interests of the largely incompetent parish authorities who controlled greater London by reforming the system of local government in the capital.

By the 1850s, by which time London's population had reached 2.5 million, the social conditions in which many lived are barely believable today. Here, for example, is a description of the water supply available to the poverty-stricken inhabitants of the notorious Jacob's Island in Bermondsey:

In Jacob's Island may be seen at any time of the day women dipping
water, with pails attached by ropes to the backs of the houses, from a
foul and foetid ditch, its banks coated with a compound of mud and
filth, and with offal and carrion – the water to be used for every
purpose, culinary ones not excepted.

The private, profit-making water companies had a virtual monopoly of
particular areas, and often did not bother to lay on a regular supply.
Invariably they found the cheapest source of water, often the hideously
polluted Thames. In other cases, water came from wells that were shallow,
filling from soil impregnated with filth. In Clerkenwell it was said that the
water of the parish 'received the drainage water of Highgate cemetery, of
numerous burial grounds, and of the innumerable cesspools in the district'.

A number of government investigations of the state of public health in
London were instigated, some of them as a result of outbreaks of Asiatic
cholera which claimed its first victims in England in 1832, and recurred
sporadically in the capital. Cholera was by no means the biggest killer among
the diseases which continually swept through the slum districts of London:
'the fever' and smallpox were to prove more deadly. But cholera had a terrible
symbolic significance, though not quite terrible or threatening enough to get
Parliament to act effectively. In 1847 a Royal Commission on the Health of
the Metropolis led to a reform of the administration of the sewers, with new
sets of commissioners under a central body, and in the previous year a
General Board of Health was established, but it had few powers.

It was not until the Metropolitan Board of Works was set up in 1855
that any really fundamental change was brought about in the city's sanitary
condition. The Board provided London with its first recognizable system
of local government: thirty-eight new local authorities, or district boards,
were established and they, along with the City of London – which
remained, of course, independent and untouched – elected the Board
members. Although this marked the beginning of the end of the hopeless
fragmentation of local administration in London it took a few more years –
and a hot summer in which the stink of the Thames became too much for
members of the House of Commons – for the Board to be given the go-
ahead to solve the problem.

For two years the government and the new Board argued over the best
way to create a new drainage system in London. The Board was required
by law to obtain government approval for any schemes costing over £50,000

and the go-ahead from Parliament for anything over £100,000. In June 1858 rival projects and costs were still being argued over when members of the Commons Committee, including Benjamin Disraeli, were seen making a dash from their deliberations holding handkerchiefs over their noses. The Thames, which had become more and more heavily used as a sewer, finally made its point by stinking out the Commons Committee. From then on, the Board was given a free hand to solve the problem.

A SOLUTION FOR LONDON'S SEWAGE

In fewer than ten years, under their chief engineer, Sir Joseph Bazalgette, the Board completed a new main drainage system consisting of eighty-two miles of sewers, which carried a large proportion of London's effluent under the new embankment far downstream along the Thames. Gradually, the other rivers of London, such as the Fleet in Hampstead, or the Effra River in Brixton, were enclosed in pipes: in under half a century they had been transformed from country streams into tributaries of the main drainage system. London's water supply remained in private hands, however, until 1904.

The Metropolitan Board of Works not only laid out a new drainage system: it was also heavily involved in road widening and slum clearance. But it soon became clear that one of the consequences of its improvements was the destruction of yet more working-class housing of the cheapest sort, with no provision for its replacement. This further round of 'improvements', added to all the other road building schemes, railway and dock construction and depopulation of the City to make way for warehouses and offices, aggravated terribly the problem of housing the poorest classes in London. In the first half of the nineteenth century the evidence of government inquiries and the investigations of social reformers had demonstrated that in central London housing conditions were getting worse rather than better. The worsening sanitary condition of the capital also concentrated the poorest in foul tenements and lodging houses without a decent water supply or sewage system.

But it was not at all clear to the early Victorians who was to blame for this, and the dominant view seems to have been that the poor brought degradation on themselves. Much of the impulse for reform was based on the belief that what needed changing was the moral and spiritual welfare of slum-dwellers, though there were plenty of people who believed it was unreasonable to expect improvement if they lived in pigsties. The terrible spread of gin drinking, crime and the threat of social unrest were all being connected with housing conditions before mid-century. Charles Dickens wrote in *Sketches by Boz*:

> Gin drinking is a great vice in England, but wretchedness and dirt are greater and until you improve the homes of the poor, or persuade a half-famished wretch not to seek relief in the temporary oblivion of his own misery, with the pittance, which, divided among his family would furnish a morsel of bread for each, gin-shops will increase in number and splendour.

Lord Shaftesbury in 1851 made the connection between slum life and crime: 'Who would wonder that in these receptacles, nine-tenths of the great crimes, the burglaries, and murders and violence that desolated society were conceived and hatched?' And he, like Dickens and other reformers, warned that, whereas slums might breed revolution, better housing could be of real importance to national security. 'The strength of the people rests upon the purity and firmness of the domestic system,' Lord Shaftesbury was quoted as saying in the 1860s. 'If the working man has his own house, I have no fear of revolution.'

But these arguments that social and political stability could be achieved through improved housing were, in a sense, ahead of their time, and neither Parliament nor the City of London was prepared to look at the problem in an efficient way. There were attempts from the mid-century onwards to force landlords to comply with new health regulations, but these neither tackled the roots of the problem, nor were they generally enforced. Housing and the relief of poverty were left to charity. This led to a range of responses, from the patronizing moral and educational approach of such people as Octavia Hill, who in the 1860s attempted to teach household management to her tenants, to the frankly commercial philanthropy of the Metropolitan Association for Improving the Dwellings of the Industrious Classes.

At its first meeting in 1841, presided over by the Rector of Spitalfields, Henry Taylor, the Metropolitan Association included in its founding resolution: 'That an association be formed for the purpose of providing the labouring man with an increase of the comforts and conveniences of life, with full compensation to the capitalist.' In other words, the housing problem should be solved at a profit. This became the most popular solution, and was responsible in London – as elsewhere in the country – for the erection of large numbers of barrack-like tenement buildings, stark and cold to this day, but undoubtedly an immense improvement on the rookeries they replaced.

PHILANTHROPY AT FIVE PER CENT

There were many other such commercially minded charitable organizations, including the Society for Improving the Condition of the Labouring Classes, founded in 1844, which managed to win the admiration of Prince Albert so that their model dwellings were exhibited at the Great Exhibition in 1851. The whole movement became known as 'philanthropy at five per cent' though, compared with other investments, working-class housing was never a good bet and had difficulty attracting funds. In a sense, the most successful of all philanthropic housing associations was that set up by the American millionaire George Peabody, who came to England in 1837 and established himself as a merchant and banker. He donated £500,000 for a trust to be used solely to improve the conditions of the poor of London, regardless of religious or political sectarianism. The money went into building housing for the working classes, a huge project that began with a formidable and rather ornate block in the Commercial Road in 1864. Peabody estates are still standing all over central London from the Wild Street estate in Covent Garden, to the massive development in Blackfriars.

Although the Peabody Trust was certainly charitable in its aims and some commercial companies accused the trustees of undercharging on rents and undercutting prices, the poorest of Londoners remained excluded: despite the sparseness of the interiors of Peabody Buildings – the first blocks had no running water in the flats and no plaster on the walls – the rents were still too high for a large section of the population. In effect, Peabody was operating just like the 'philanthropy at five per cent' housing associations, and until the 1880s it remained unthinkable that the homes of the poorest class of Londoners might in any way be provided for or subsidized by a public body not interested ultimately in profit.

An anonymous poem published in 1862 in the *City Press* expressed, apparently without irony, the mood of these endeavours:

Men of Money! shrewd and skill'd
In putting capital to nurse,
Ready to pull down streets, or build
If either helps to fill the purse, –
Now let me tell your wit a plan
How to reap a royal rent
Out of doing good to man –
Charity at cent per cent

But philanthropic housing did not make much of a profit. As the cost of central sites rose, so landowners such as the Duke of Bedford would sell off their slums to such companies and could ask a good price. It was very difficult to build to decent standards and at sufficient density to accommodate the same number of tenants – though not *the* same tenants – on the site of old housing that had been demolished. The people who moved in were very often lower middle class: clerks, policemen and 'respectable' artisans. The poorest classes were excluded on any significant scale, partly because they couldn't afford the rent, but also because they could not, or would not, conform to the rigid rules imposed by these associations, designed to make the poor respectable and to inculcate values of cleanliness, orderliness and thrift. Rules which specified no animals or 'home work' on the premises led to the exclusion of the underworld of Londoners who survived on messy and unsightly trades, like the coster-mongers who sold vegetables from barrows. These strict rules continued into the twentieth century and were clearly remembered by Ellen Hill, who lived in the Peabody Dwellings in Stamford Street, Blackfriars, before the First World War:

The stairs and the landing had to be polished until they were shining every week. All us children had to be vaccinated and you weren't allowed to play in the square outside after seven in the winter or after eight in the summer. And if you broke the rules or you didn't pay the rent each week, you were given a couple of hours to do it, to put your house in order, or you were out. Our superintendent was a real sergeant major type, a stickler for the rules, and we were a bit frightened of him, so most people did as they were told.

Charity, pure and simple, had by the 1880s become the principal means by which the wealthy in London tried to do something about the poverty created by the great expansion of the metropolis. It existed on a fantastic scale but was entirely disorganized, and so it was the central aim of a new organization, the Charity Organization Society (COS), founded in 1869, to bring some order to this chaotic and inefficient form of social service. It believed that haphazard payments to the poor encouraged a 'scrounger' mentality so it introduced a kind of moral means test for applicants for charity, making relief dependent upon respectable behaviour.

The COS and the Poor Law authorities were the forerunners of modern council-run social services. But in the 1880s the COS was chiefly concerned with ensuring that charity handouts were not squandered on poor people who did not repay philanthropy with cleanliness or godliness. It was at this time that a really influential pamphlet was published which began a shift in national attitudes towards the problems of metropolitan poverty. In 1883, *The Bitter Cry of Outcast London* – published anonymously, but generally attributed to the Rev. Andrew Mearns – once again laid bare the horrors of working-class housing. According to *Reynolds's Newspaper*, 'The revelations concerning "Outcast London" caused a tremendous sensation and thrill of horror throughout the land.'

The first impulse of those affected by this, and by a whole spate of newspaper reports, was to step up charitable activity. It became common for fashionable ladies to go 'slumming' in the East End, held up as the region suffering the worst poverty, although many other districts of London were in as miserable a condition. After the 1886 riots, described at the beginning of this chapter, the flow of charity turned into a torrent. A fund had been launched for the unemployed by the Lord Mayor of London and on 8 February – the day of the riot – stood at £3,300. By 23 February it had reached £60,000 and finally totalled £78,000.

The Charity Organization Society, which detested any kind of un-thought-out, emotional giving, was severely critical of the fund. Finally Parliament too began to realize that dependence on this kind of spontaneous and disorganized solution to the immense problems of housing and poverty was unsatisfactory. London did need some form of local government that would begin to relieve the misery of a large and increasingly threatening section of the population. The old *laissez-faire* doctrine that private enterprise could best find a solution was beginning to crumble, and the connection between housing and poverty became not just the theory of social reformers but the received wisdom.

A COUNCIL FOR LONDON AT LAST

Although the argument that London's government should be re-formed for once and for all was gradually accepted, there was a protracted argument about whether it would be best served by a single authority or by a number of new local authorities which took into account the new districts Victorian expansion had created. The powerful West End vestries opposed 'centralism' while the East End vestries supported it. In the end the 'centralists' won and in 1888 the London County Council (LCC) was founded. Throughout the 1880s, when radical liberal groups were pressing for a single London authority, they wanted control of the police. But the Home Office fiercely opposed this and won.

The first elections were held in 1889, and the LCC took over the area and functions of the Metropolitan Board of Works. It was an authority split between radical and liberal groups, and in the first few years lacked any effective powers. But London had almost, for the first time, been recognized for what it was: a single metropolis, the largest the world had ever seen. The first and most pressing task of the new authority was to tackle the housing problem which, by the end of the century, it was beginning to do in a much more extensive way than had ever been possible before. After the Housing of the Working Classes Act of 1890, enabling public authorities to build housing themselves, the LCC began its building programme with the Boundary Street estate in Bethnal Green, which replaced a notorious slum, the Jago.

But the fear of a powerful London authority able to challenge the power of Westminster and the City had not entirely receded. Ten years after the creation of the LCC, the first London boroughs were set up, partly with the intention of undermining the new metropolitan county's position.

London went into the twentieth century with a brand-new administrative structure finally recognizing its massive existence, although the LCC boundaries were already well inside the *de facto* frontiers of the metropolis, which was still expanding at a considerable rate. The City, by now with a population of only twenty-seven thousand out of a total of well over 5 million Londoners, remained proudly aloof, as it does today.

London did not change overnight with all these new developments, but it had entered a new phase in its history. In the fields of social policy and local government, the foundations had been laid for the enormous expansion of the built-up area of London in the 1920s and '30s, when the LCC engaged on a massive housing programme, building new suburbs along the electric tube and tram lines, while the centre of town became rapidly depopulated. But, with the outbreak of war, before this new London began to take shape there would be a four-year hiatus in its long development.

PART TWO

Boomtown London
1914–1939

CHAPTER SEVEN

The Invasion of London

WHEN WAR WAS declared on Germany in 1914, the great edifice of Victorian and Edwardian London ceased to expand after more than a century of phenomenal growth. The nation's wealth and energy were rapidly consumed by the war effort; the capital's physical fabric froze like a modern Pompeii, while its social life underwent a revolution. Liveried footmen, who not long before had served cakes to young ladies in the grand houses of the West End, were in the trenches. Women domestics exchanged their frilly aprons for overalls and were fitting detonators into the nozzles of shells. Wealthy young men who had paraded in Hyde Park during the London Season were recuperating there now in Bath chairs or hobbling around on crutches. Their lady friends ran canteens for munitions workers, nursed wounded soldiers, took office jobs in the City and the Ministry of Munitions, ate out alone at night unchaperoned, and smoked cigarettes in public. Bankers, solicitors and accountants, too old to fight, doffed their daytime dress and donned blue uniforms to man the search-lights for London's air defences, and were amused to find they were mistaken in this unfamiliar attire for porters on the Underground.

It was as if the old London had been re-inhabited by a quite different people. And when the war was over, and London's great economic machine began to work again, it seemed to many contemporary observers that a race had disappeared: Victorian attitudes and values had died in the trenches and in the great domestic upheaval of the war years. Nearly all of London's physical fabric was still there, intact: the great houses of Park Lane, Mayfair and Belgravia; the solemn edifices of the City of London's great counting houses; the canyon-like dockland and miserable workshops of the East End; and all those miles of nineteenth-century terraces and semi-detached 'villas' built to house London's vast, servant-employing middle class in modest, antiquated comfort.

But the world that had built that immense metropolis had come to an end, and when, very soon, London began to expand again beyond its pre-war frontiers it took on a quite unfamiliar appearance. No more Kensingtons, Claphams or Islingtons, with their serried ranks of terraced houses, ornate churches and railway stations, were created. Instead, there were gnomish rows of semi-detached houses with their miniature shopping parades, and jazzy new factories built along expanses of 'arterial' road. By 1939, when war once again put an end to the outward growth of the capital, this new, semi-detached London completely surrounded the old capital like the encampment of a foreign power. It was as if London had been invaded by an alien culture, and the same forces which had given rise to semi-detached London had swept through the old Heart of the Empire and given it a zest and glitter which was quite un-Victorian and not quite English.

There seemed to have been a loosening of the old social order and a more egalitarian mood was somehow reflected in the clean, 'modernistic' lines of new office buildings along the Embankment, eschewing the ornate paternalism of the Victorians. Everything was brighter, neater, smarter, electric-lit: at night an illuminated façade proudly displaying the stylish modernity of a new building. Piccadilly Circus, flashing giddily above the subterranean splendour of its Art Deco Underground station, was the ultimate showpiece of this new, nocturnal, neon London.

In the 1920s, when the fabric of the capital began to be renewed, it was generally believed that the cataclysmic experience of the Great War had somehow brought about the transformation of London's Victorian heartland. The entire social order had been shaken up and when it settled again people were different. In their new mood they had set about restructuring the capital, and without the war London might have continued to grow and evolve and there would have been no sudden break with the past. Historians continue to argue about the significance of the Great War in the social and economic evolution of Britain: did it change everything or merely interrupt a constellation of powerful forces which would have transformed it anyway? Though it's an impossible question to answer, it is worth pursuing as the attempt reveals a great deal about London and its history. There is no doubt that between 1914 and 1939 the capital was radically changed. But was it by a threat of invasion from the Kaiser's Germany, or a much more successful invasion of another kind, which began well before 1914 and which was led by the nation which was emerging as the leader of a new world economic order, America?

When war broke out in 1914, Britain was for the first time in centuries threatened by direct assault from an enemy. It appears quite bizarre now that the first attack on the Island Fortress was the shelling in December 1914 by German battle cruisers of Hartlepool, Scarborough, and Whitby, leaving 230 people dead and 500 injured. London at that time still seemed to be relatively safe from bombardment, but it was the prize the German army wanted most and they had developed an extraordinary new weapon which, they believed, would smash the capital into submission and bring about a swift victory. This was the Zeppelin, an enormous gas-filled airship named after Count von Zeppelin, who had supposedly got the idea while fighting in the American Civil War, in which hot-air balloons had been used for reconnaissance. Before 1914, a peaceful Zeppelin passenger service had been started in Europe.

These airships were extremely cumbersome contraptions which floated along at 10–15,000 feet (3,000–4,500 m) at a speed of about fifty to sixty miles an hour, their crew suspended in a small carriage below an enormous cigar-shaped gas bag. High winds and bad weather were a great problem for the Zeppelin commanders and they were always being blown off course, snooping around the sky trying to work out where they were. It was some time before the first of them made the long journey from Germany, across eastern England to London.

For Londoners, the threat of an air attack by these otherworldly craft was uniquely terrifying. The capital had no air defences to speak of – a few pom-pom guns left over from the Boer War which were useless, and aircraft which could not at first climb fast or high enough to attack the Zeppelins. There were no air-raid shelters or air-raid warnings to begin with and the anticipation of bomb attacks was like a futuristic nightmare. When a primitive blackout was organized, Londoners stumbled about peevishly in the gloom, there was a spate of road accidents, and Summer Time was brought in to make better use of the daylight hours.

THE ZEPPELIN RAIDS

The first raid on London came at near midnight on 31 May 1915 when a Zeppelin slipped unchallenged and, in fact, unnoticed over east London, and dropped a string of incendiary and explosive bombs and one hand grenade in a line from Stoke Newington down to Hackney, peppering Stepney, West Ham and Leytonstone en route back to Germany. Six people were killed and thirty-five injured. From then on, on star-lit nights there was constant vigilance, and though there were few Zeppelin raids on London, the sight of a silver-grey airship, lit up by a searchlight, became one of the most haunting images of the Great War in London. A fairly primitive warning system was developed involving maroon rockets being fired when a Zeppelin was detected on its way to London and policemen cycling or motoring around with signs saying 'Take Cover'. Boy scouts with bugles sounded the all-clear.

People sheltered under kitchen tables, ran into open country, made a dive for the basement if they had one, but more often than not, it seems, could not resist the temptation to stand at the window or in the street to watch the aerial display of a Zeppelin lit up in a searchlight beam, shells exploding around it from a barrage of guns. The airships' engines became a familiar sound to Londoners, 'like a train in the sky'. Michael MacDonagh noted in his diary *In London During the Great War* (1935) that the attitude seemed to be: 'You can hear the Zep' afar off, so that when it appears to be coming near you, you can make a bolt for shelter.'

In September 1916, an airship was shot down by a young pilot over Cuffley in Hertfordshire and several million Londoners saw the great gas bag turn into a ball of flame. Among them was G. S. Occomore who was a boy at the time:

> It was about two o'clock in the early hours of Sunday morning, September 3rd. An air raid was on and two other children were under the kitchen table with me, peeping out from underneath, looking up through the window at the searchlights criss-crossing the sky. All of a sudden they got the Zeppelin. It looked like some silver cigar . . . it turned, ducked, weaved, but still the searchlights held it. Suddenly it disappeared behind a cloud and then the searchlights picked it up again. Almost at once the flames shot up from the top of the Zep' and immediately there were shouts and cheers from the streets outside. We all rushed out. But now the Zeppelin was all alight, slowly falling like some burning firey star . . .

Con Young remembered how, as a seven-year-old child, her East End domestic routine – and that of her cat – was suddenly and dramatically disrupted by a direct hit from a Zeppelin bomb.

> We were all in bed. I was asleep in my bedroom with the cat at the foot of my bed in his usual place. My mother, so she told me later,

was in her bedroom sitting on the edge of her bed waiting to pick up and set her clock by the 10.00 through-train whistle as it passed the back of our house.

It was the London to Southend train, and it would whistle each night before it went through our station, so it was my mother's habit to check her clock by it. This night she heard the whistle, so she thought, but it was a bomb whistling down through the uncanny silence. The Zeppelins were very quiet, we never heard them, but sometimes we would catch sight of them drifting in the clouds.

I'll never forget that awful night, the bomb dropped behind us, slicing off the backs of the houses in the next road with a deafening crash, and a brilliant green crackling light. Everything moved in that room. My poor cat went past me high in the air and was drawn through the hole where the window had been. My long thick hair saved me from being cut when the broken window frame, bits of door, needles of glass, all sorts of things, flew into my corner on top of me.

By then my mother had managed to get to me and was pulling the debris off and she picked me up bedclothes and all. She walked through the broken glass with only stockings on her feet, then she dropped me in an armchair just inside where the front room had been, and it was like putting me in the front garden, as it was open to the street. I remember her saying quite calmly, 'Don't worry, it's only the Germans! I will get my shoes,' as if it was quite normal to be bombed.

Then came the police, ambulances, firemen, the gas people and people from miles around, and our road was soon packed tight. Nobody could control the crowd, they just walked over the bricks of our front room, all over the house, they were getting wedged in the passages and pushing and shouting and it was still not daylight, but we were powerless – we had to stay just where we were. People were so sorry for us they left money everywhere, and the big glove box on the hallstand was filled with so much money that we had to keep emptying it because it wouldn't close.

Three months went by and we'd searched everywhere and asked everybody about the cat. Then one day, I was picking some beans and he walked up to me in the garden and nobody believed it was him. 'Oh it isn't', they said. 'It's another cat.' But it was him. But he would never come in the house. He came for his food and would eat it in the garden, but he would never enter the house.

The Zeppelin raids on London were, however, in military terms, a failure. In all an estimated 670 people were killed and 1,962 wounded in twelve airship attacks, and nineteen aeroplane raids which came later on in the war. Germany failed to frighten London into submission, or to hit the most prized target in the City, the Bank of England, symbol of Britain's great financial might. But the dimming of lights and the fear of air attack were significant in creating an atmosphere of common peril, and a kind of camaraderie achieved by no previous war. There was, too, a deeply felt symbolism in the realization that London was vulnerable, after all those centuries, and Michael MacDonagh recalled the extraordinary occasion when MPs and peers left the Houses of Parliament to watch a Zeppelin raid from Palace Yard:

> How strikingly it appeals to the historical imagination! The thought in my mind was that England's insularity was at an end, that her Navy could no longer keep her safe from an enemy entry into her Island Fortress.

So strange was the attack from the air that quite a number of people apparently refused to believe that Zeppelins could really fly all the way from Germany, and their appearance in the sky helped to fuel the witch-hunt on Germans in London, all of whom were suspected of being spies and of sending secret signals to their compatriots. MacDonagh records a conversation his wife had with their charlady, Annie Bolster from Battersea:

> 'Isn't it an extraordinary thing, Annie,' said my wife, 'that the Zeppelins, great ships like Atlantic liners, should be able to sail through the air from Germany to London and back?'
> 'Don't you believe it, Ma'am,' Annie replied, 'Don't you believe it. We know in Battersea that these 'ere Zeppelins are hidden away in the back yards of German bakers.' And many a German shopkeeper had his windows smashed and goods looted in the East End.

The Zeppelins may have provided the most haunting image of the Great War, but they did not lead to an evacuation of the capital, or to any dispersal of the war effort, as the threat of the blitz did in the Second World War. In fact, the 1914–18 war *concentrated* activity in London, for new government departments created to deal with the national emergency grew up around Westminster, in particular the enormous Ministry of Munitions, which by 1918 was employing sixty-five thousand people, and was responsible for around 3 million workers in engineering, munitions and on the railways. The central part of town teemed with government office workers and soldiers home on leave or returning to the front.

WARTIME TRANSPORT

All this activity put a great strain on the transport services, which by then included the electric tube lines, mostly built between 1900 and 1907. Motorbuses, which had just begun to replace horse-drawn vehicles, were commandeered for service on the front. Trams were used as mobile searchlight trolleys, and the drivers and conductors were lost as men volunteered, or, after conscription in 1916, were called up. It was mostly after 1916 that women were recruited on a large scale as surrogate men and appeared on the London streets in unfamiliar guise, as Lloyd George's 'munitionettes', or as bus conductresses and ticket collectors on the Underground or as drivers of delivery vans for Joe Lyons. In the City, the banks began to train women clerks on an 'experimental basis', as they put it; by the end of the war nearly a third of Lloyds Bank staff were women.

To what extent the experience of the war altered the way in which Londoners thought about and used the centre of town is not clear, but there are some intriguing bits of evidence to suggest that it was at this time that the capital really began to develop its contemporary character. In her memoir, *How We Lived Then*, Mrs C. S. Peel dated the rise of Soho as a night-club-cum-popular-restaurant area, which anyone might venture into, from this period when girls, working as government clerks, found it a convenient place to meet off-duty soldiers. The ban on restaurateurs serving officers after 10pm with alcoholic drinks – the 'Beauty Sleep' order – gave rise to a whole colony of new nightclubs. And as early as the autumn of 1915, the *Daily Mail* had noted in the centre of town the appearance of a new breed which it called 'Dining Out Girls': 'The wartime business girl is to be seen any night dining out alone or with a friend in the moderate-price restaurants in London. Formerly she would never have had her evening meal in town unless in the company of a man friend. But now, with money and without men, she is more and more beginning to dine out.'

War work took many women out of domestic service, still by far the most important source of employment for them in London in 1914. Just under half the first recruits joining the London General Omnibus Company in 1916 gave domestic service as their previous employment, and though nobody has calculated what the effect was on middle- and upper-class life, it is quite clear that much of the West End and the wealthier parts of London abandoned their formerly flamboyant existence. Their staff were depleted but, perhaps more important than anything else in this total war, displays of wealth were not acceptable. In the 1920s the Season and the household with a substantial number of servants returned, but not on the scale of the Edwardian era.

The Great War affected every aspect of London life, and it is quite understandable that the generation who lived through it felt that the changes they saw in the capital in the 1920s were a direct result of those four years of upheaval. In the twenties, morals and manners seemed to become free and easy, personified by the flapper dressed boyishly, smoking a cigarette and dancing to a jazz band at the Savoy. There were those who thought there might be a return to the old ways when the lightheadedness of the post-war days wore off, but by the 1930s it was clear that London was being transformed. And now the overriding impression was that everything was in one way or another becoming American. In *London in My Time*, written in 1934, Thomas Burke said:

> The bulk of our entertainment is American in quality and largely in personnel. All our latest hotels derive from American models. Our snack-bars and all-night supper-stands are pirated from America. Our electric night-signs are an American idea. Our street songs are American . . . The American yeast, working constantly these last twenty years, has done so much good that we now regard the zest and pungency of London life, which the States gave us, as our own growth.

It would be quite reasonable to assume that the trauma of the First World War and the disruption of the British economy had allowed in the American invader in the wake of the Zeppelins. But the position of Britain, and London, in the world had been threatened well before 1914 and the foundations for most of the changes that became so evident in the inter-war years had really been laid at the turn of the century. The period from 1890 to 1914 had been one of great international economic, political and imperial rivalry, and though London was still the undisputed leader among great cities of the industrialized world, a change in its position was becoming evident.

THE AMERICANS ARRIVE

It was the West End in particular which began to undergo a series of changes that would undermine its former character as primarily an aristocratic quarter, built up around the royal Court and Parliament. The rise of large department stores, such as William Whiteley's of Westbourne Grove and Harrods of Knightsbridge, had signalled the opening up and expansion of this part of town from the 1870s onwards. But in the early years of the twentieth century the erosion of the West End's exclusivity began to accelerate and American interlopers played a considerable part in helping it on its way.

The most conspicuous example of the American invasion was the arrival at the western end of Oxford Street of a brand-new store, built by Gordon H. Selfridge. It was the creation of an American who had made his fortune in Chicago, having risen from a store boy working in the basement of Marshall Fields to a brilliant manager. Selfridge was in his fifties, and was looking around for a new challenge when he decided to come to London and build a superstore that would shake the dust out of the old capital. Like so many American businessmen in this period, to him London represented a vast untapped market, served as it was by rather old-fashioned tradesmen and antiquated industry. Even the immense new edifice of Harrods, being rebuilt when Selfridge arrived in London, appeared to represent no more than a worthy rival that might soon be overtaken.

It was the received wisdom that the site Selfridge chose for his store, at the run-down western end of Oxford Street, was disastrous. But it was not his intention to build his store in an already established district, such as Knightsbridge or South Kensington: he would create his own fantastic world inside a brand-new building as a kind of late Edwardian Disneyland. The opening of the store in 1909 was preceded by an extravagant promotion, with full-page newspaper advertisements – still relatively novel in Britain – and an invitation to everyone in London to visit without any obligation to buy.

The windows along Oxford Street – which were to be added to as Selfridges grew – caused quite a stir as the like of their exotic displays had not been seen in London before, and the fantastic interior included an American soda-water fountain and barber's shop. It was Selfridge's policy that customers should not be harassed by floor walkers, and the free and easy atmosphere of the place was probably the most unfamiliar part about it. At the top of the store was an exotic pergola roof garden, which at various times incorporated a practice range for golfers, a setting for ragtime orchestras and an ice-rink. When the roof was extended in the 1920s, Selfridges could claim to have the largest roof garden in the world.

Though other stores, such as Harrods and Swan & Edgar, did not seem to take the threat of this interloper too seriously, they did stage fashion shows and concerts of their own as a counter-attraction to the extraordinary opening day. However, it was not long before the American influence was evident throughout the West End, and it really came to prominence after the First World War when many of the established London stores were rebuilt. Large, ground-floor window displays became the rule, as did the open interior shopping areas – a number designed by Americans brought in especially for their expertise.

Today, the Quadrant of Regent Street, which sweeps from Oxford Circus to Piccadilly Circus, does not look to us to be particularly 'modern' or even characteristically 1920s. However, nearly the whole of it was rebuilt after the Great War. By the early 1900s, the stuccoed buildings designed by John Nash in the Regency period were in poor repair, and the Crown, whose property this was, began to consider plans for redevelopment. There were great arguments about the Quadrant's design and how the work should be carried out, but only a small part – notably the Piccadilly Hotel – was rebuilt, in grand metropolitan style, before the outbreak of war had put an end to the project and it was not until the 1920s that most of the rebuilding took place.

When it was rebuilt Harrods had incorporated luxury apartments above the showrooms, but these had to be rapidly re-absorbed as the store expanded. Similarly in Regent Street, plans for flats above the shops were abandoned. It was clear evidence that the West End was continuing to lose its residential character and becoming more and more a national and international shopping centre. The official reopening of Regent Street in 1927 was marked by a passing visit by King George V and Queen Mary, and the *Daily News* thought that it did 'in a sense typify the spirit of the age – in its vitality and brilliance and audacity. It is more suited to the flashing bus and the rapid streams of polished motor-cars than to the old-fashioned coach-and-four.'

In Kensington, too, the 1920s saw the rise to prominence of Barkers' store. This had been an important shopping area before the 1914–18 war, and by 1920 the Barker Brothers had already bought up their rivals, Pontings and Derry & Toms, though the three stores continued to function as separate businesses. The electrification of the District Line from 1905, and the redesign of High Street Kensington Station, enabling shoppers to walk straight from the octagonal booking hall into Pontings on one side and Derry & Toms on the other, had given the area a tremendous boost. Rebuilding of Barkers' began in 1923, and though it was not completed until 1958, the great ocean-liner style more nearly reflected 'the spirit of the age' than anything in Regent Street. Here, too, the management looked to American department stores for the interior design, and brought in architects for some of the work. And here, too, the expansion of the store, in particular the demolition of houses next to Kensington Square to make space for staff quarters, and the crowding of the street with shoppers from all over London, began to change the predominantly residential character of the area. In the late 1930s, a roof garden was added to the attractions of Derry & Toms – clearly inspired by Selfridges.

The growth of the new superstores in the West End represented not an entirely new departure, but more a continuation of the evolution of this wealthy part of London from the preserve of the upper classes during the annual round of balls and dinners in the Season into the playground for the whole of London. It was a creeping kind of development that had been going on since the late nineteenth century, marked by the appearance of new kinds of buildings and new forms of shopping and entertainment. The style and tone of much of this were American, because it was in the United States that the mass consumer society had developed first: London, in a way, was catching up.

Hollywood completely dominated the cinema in the interwar years. Not only were London audiences in the West End entertained by American movies, but much of the exotic picture palace architecture was influenced by American design, though the buildings were actually created by English architects. The black granite Odeon in Leicester Square, which replaced the Alhambra Theatre in 1937, is a good example of such an un-English incursion in the West End. However, the picture palaces in the heart of London's entertainment centre had much less of an impact than those built in the suburbs, where their interior splendour completely overshadowed their surroundings (see Chapter Eleven).

The significant social influence of the cinema was, first, that it was much cheaper than the theatre, and, second, that it promoted an American culture that was much more accessible to the mass of London's population than previous forms of entertainment. Thus the cinema was to play its part in opening up the West End to many more people. So, too, did the arrival of new chain stores, such as Woolworths – another American import – which got its first foothold in Britain in Liverpool in 1909 and arrived in London with a store in Oxford Street in 1924. And if you look above the jumble of shop fronts in Oxford Street today, you can see in the interwar design of many of the buildings the relics of thirties' mass consumerism brought in by the likes of Marks & Spencer.

So, from the late nineteenth century onwards, the influence of private wealth was slowly giving way to the more vigorous forces of a new kind of commercial wealth in the West End. And it was in the 1920s and 1930s that the culture and style of the old and new societies were fused in a fascinating and often comical way in this part of London. The landed aristocracy were still rich, but the basis of their wealth was being slowly eroded by taxes, death duties and a fall in the value of the basis of much of their income as agriculture slumped, and coal – out of which many had made fortunes – fell in value. At the same time, the rise of mass consumerism had produced an increasingly powerful new clientele in the West End.

Here, too, the Americans – attracted to London by its size, its traditions and its culture – played an important role in the transformation of the capital's high society. Americans had been arriving in London and seeking an entrée into aristocratic society well before the 1920s, and in fact the old established East Coast families had first been accepted back in the 1870s. In the years just before the Great War, American music had captivated London with the ragtime craze, which disturbed a few old colonials like Rudyard Kipling, who remarked that 'one doesn't feel very national when one is hummed at nasally by an alien'. In 1912 *The Times* had called ragtime 'the music of the hustler and the feverishly active speculator'.

But it was in the interwar years that the American invasion reached its climax with wealthy Americans trying to break into London Society and the ailing aristocracy gradually giving way as well-heeled millionaires pursued their daughters and transatlantic heiresses found themselves titled husbands. The whole of the Season – that great gathering of the upper crust in the West End – was jazzed up and social life was played out less and less in grand houses and more and more in the big new hotels, where the music was provided by an American band or by an English favourite, such as Ambrose, who echoed the transatlantic syncopated beat.

The American 'invasion' also had an important effect on the changing architecture of the West End in the interwar years. The most conspicuous transformation that took place was the rebuilding of much of Park Lane, where two of the grandest aristocratic mansions, Grosvenor House (home of the Dukes of Westminster) and Dorchester House, were demolished in the 1920s to make way for hotels and flats. There had been attempts to let Grosvenor House privately in 1919 when the Duke of Westminster decided not to live there any longer. However – and this is absolutely characteristic of the era – an aristocratic tenant was less valuable than the building of the kind of block of hotels and flats that was the latest thing in New York and which might attract American visitors. In fact, the speculator who first put up the rebuilding scheme said that the new Grosvenor House was designed specifically to cater for the American market, and though the building may not look very transatlantic to us today, it was the first hotel in London to have a separate entrance lobby to each bedroom, and a separate bathroom with running iced water: a peculiarly American taste. It was the interiors of English buildings in the 1920s and '30s, rather than their façades, that came under American influence.

Two years after Grosvenor House Hotel was completed in 1929 the Dorchester was built on the site of Dorchester House, and it was said that Park Lane was beginning to resemble Fifth Avenue in New York, though perhaps the most obvious connection between the two was the booking office that the Grosvenor House opened in Fifth Avenue to attract American tourists. No skyscrapers were built in London in this period, perhaps only because of a regulation laid down in 1894 that no buildings in the capital should rise higher than 80 feet (24 m) – a ruling which, incidentally, prevented Gordon Selfridge from carrying out his plan to build a St Paul's-type dome on top of his new store.

However, there were still in the 1920s, and even in the 1930s, quite splendid old-style residences surviving, such as Londonderry House at the Hyde Park Corner end of Park Lane. Lord Jessel recalled going to dances there, where one might be attended by five footmen and the total staff might amount to twenty. But the American hostesses provided rival attractions, and their lavish parties were attended by the aristocracy, who had great fun at the expense of their vibrant but 'uncultured' hosts. There were many stories, perhaps mostly fabricated, but telling none the less, about the misunderstandings of American hostesses. Lord Jessel remembered an American hostess who was told that Lord So-and-so had married the hat-check girl from a certain nightclub. 'Oh, I don't know the Hatchecks, are they a good family?' the lady enquired. Lady Charlotte Bonham Carter remembered how Society eagerly embraced the American 'invaders', principally because they injected new life – and money – into an ailing London Season:

> The rich Americans, I think, were interested in our nobility and they
> were fascinated by Society. We were interested in them because they
> were so well off. They brought a liveliness to the West End – before
> they came it had all been rather serious and formal – their approach
> was to call each other by their Christian names from the word go.
> They were terribly amusing and they brought the new fashions with
> them. Cocktail parties, they were all the rage, they were so convenient,
> you could drop in and didn't have to dress up. Then there was jazz
> and wonderful reviews with comedy and music.
>
> Life became much more vibrant, and what was particularly
> noticeable was the change in the way women behaved and the way
> men behaved towards us. The female became a person in her own
> right, she was utterly different. Before, a lady of the British leisured
> classes did not make up, all foreign ladies did and they often looked
> utterly artificial with a completely painted face, but it was thought to
> be very bad style if one made up. That changed completely after the
> war, we all made up, it was a continental thing we adopted. Until then
> it was the Americans, the French, or Italians who did it. There was so
> much more freedom for women than before.

THE NOUVEAUX RICHES

It was not, of course, simply the influence of Americans that was changing the aristocratic heart of London. British society was evolving quite rapidly and the exclusiveness of the aristocratic way of life, set in grand houses around the royal Court, had begun to break down in the late nineteenth century, as wealthy capitalists were able to buy their way into fashionable addresses. Even before 1914, it was remarked that Park Lane was becoming rather *nouveau riche*, with businessmen like Barney Barnato living there.

The landed aristocracy were losing their grip, and struggling a little to maintain their old way of life.

On the Duke of Westminster's estate in Mayfair, it was becoming difficult to let large houses in the early 1900s, and hardly any new mansions for single-family occupation were built. Living in flats or apartments was the exception rather than the rule for the wealthy and the poor alike until the end of the nineteenth century. But from the 1880s, luxury flats became fashionable not only in Kensington, but right in the heart of Mayfair. When the area around Mount Street, just at the back of Park Lane, was rebuilt in the 1890s by the Grosvenor estate, flats were constructed above shop premises. It was already clear that this kind of arrangement would prove much more profitable for a landlord as apartments were easier to let than large houses, and by the 1920s and 1930s the apartment was more or less the only kind of new housing development in the West End. The massive Grosvenor House development on Park Lane included, as well as a hotel, apartments built in the style of New York blocks with a staff of communal servants. This was the system adopted, too, in Grosvenor Square when it was rebuilt from the late 1920s onwards.

Life for the aristocracy became much more streamlined, more attuned to the modern world. Motor cars rapidly replaced horse-drawn carriages in the early 1900s, and the first recorded case of an old stable being converted into a bijou mews house in Mayfair dates from 1908. Cars required fewer servants than carriages, and were in the long run not only faster but cheaper and more efficient. Likewise, the cocktail party was not only very new and fashionable, it was also, according to *Harpers Bazaar*, the *cheapest* way to entertain. Less and less of the aristocratic social round involved the enormous expense of horses, teams of servants, and massive houses. More and more of it moved to hotels and to nightclubs, with the guests whisked from one to another in chauffeur-driven cars. It was still very lavish and very glamorous for those who enjoyed it, but quite different from the old way of life. Lady Marguerite Strickland was one of the great beauties of her day:

> I went to a lot of nightclubs every night. The Florida – that was the first nightclub – was popular with the debs, and that was great fun. The men wore black cloaks and there were telephones on all the tables, so that you could be rung up by a man across the room, it was very romantic. The Florida was semi-dark, but the most popular club was the Four Hundred; everyone loved it because it was completely

dark. Then there were The Monsignor, The Embassy, The Nest, The Kit Kat, there were lots and lots of them, and often you didn't know where you were, you'd go from one to another when a party dragged on and it was all dark.

And the idea of the darkness was that you'd be dancing with someone else's husband and your husband was across the room with the man's wife. The dancing was so important, the new band music was so marvellous, I used to know all the tunes and the band leaders who used to play in the clubs were all friends of ours. It was all so exciting.

The old and new ways of life in the West End overlapped. It was generally the dashing younger set who most readily adopted the cocktail, the dance-band, and the Art Deco apartment. A domestic servant might be required to move from one world to another, as Stanley Agers discovered when he began work 'below stairs' in Belgrave Square in 1921. On one occasion he might be a footman with powdered hair; on another he was learning to mix a cocktail for the new breed of aristocrat with American friends:

We had about eighteen staff and my job as steward room boy was really to look after the upper crust of the servants, including the butler, the housekeeper, the lady's maid, the valet, the under-butler, the groom of chambers and the chef. The people who were struggling to keep going with this way of life were old people like Lord and Lady Coventry, who were really Victorian.

My livery in the daytime would probably be fawn, with a chocolate collar and a striped waistcoat. At nighttime it would be dark blue with a black velvet collar. Any evening, from about eight o'clock onwards there might be two or three dinners going on around the square, and as guests arrived, the red carpet would be out. It lived at the front door and was rolled across the pavement, with a footman stationed outside to stop people walking on it. A big carriage umbrella was also always kept by the front door in case of any rain or pigeons.

By the time the Americans were flooding in, I was second footman in Cadogan Square and my employer was quite, shall we say, one of the Bright Young Things. He had an American publisher and American friends. This was when the cocktails came into the big houses, before that it was all straight drinks. We didn't know anything about mixing cocktails and I was sent round to the Savoy to see one of the barmen. He showed me how to make a proper Martini, and a real winner was a White Lady, which was always made with fresh passion fruit juice, which you could only buy at Fortnum & Masons.

With the Americans it was very difficult for us. They really didn't know how to handle us at all, they were either too friendly or the other way around. They always wanted iced water, and we had no refrigerators, just the old-fashioned ice box. We used to buy our ice by the hundredweight. The only way to keep these people happy was to chip off some of this ice and cool their water that way.

It is extremely difficult to gauge accurately the extent of the shift in the social life of the upper crust in the interwar years. The Season was still very much alive, and the royal Court remained the centre for great occasions, such as the presentation of debutantes. But new occasions were invented which had little or nothing to do with the established social round; the best-known being Queen Charlotte's Ball for debs. Much less exclusive than presentation at Court, this began in 1922, and though its origin is a little obscure, it was and remained a fundraising event for Queen Charlotte's Maternity Hospital and had absolutely nothing to do with any social tradition.

From the time that the Grosvenor House Hotel was completed in 1929, the Ball was always held there, along with the cardboard cake and the girls all dressed alike, as if they were out of a Hollywood pageant. At the same time, the position of royalty within British society was changing, with consequences for London's West End. Though most people imagine that the British have always been masters of royal pageantry, this expertise in fact dates only from the late nineteenth century. Before that, pomp and ceremony often lapsed into the ludicrous and it was the staging of Queen Victoria's Golden Jubilee in 1887 that established the great tradition of British royal ceremonies – at a time when the monarch was losing the last vestiges of real political power and was becoming much more of a national figurehead. Splendid occasions followed: the Diamond Jubilee of 1897, Queen Victoria's funeral in 1901, the coronations of Edward VII and George V in 1902 and 1911, and an area was rebuilt to provide an appropriate setting for the processions. Between 1906 and 1913, from money provided by the Queen Victoria Memorial Fund, Buckingham Palace was refaced and the Mall widened, with Queen Victoria's Memorial at the palace end, and Admiralty Arch by Trafalgar Square. So the stage was set for the fashioning of the monarchy into a kind of theatrical company, which would go on to perform regularly for the world's television cameras and for millions of snap-happy tourists who have become so important to London's economy.

THE LONDON OFFICE BOOM

In the nineteenth century, it was the Square Mile of the City itself which had been transformed into London's great commuter centre, as the old shops and housing gave way to Victorian office blocks built to accommodate armies of clerks and financiers. By the early 1900s, the financial institutions of the City had begun to colonize the area surrounding the old Square Mile. But the City had by this time reached a historical plateau, and though it made a remarkable recovery from the destruction of its overseas investments in the Great War, and much of it was rebuilt in the interwar years, it was not at this period a major force in the expansion of central London employment. Economic vigour came from quite a new direction and, as with so much else in the twentieth century, it was triggered by a threat from overseas.

In international economics, there were two great rivals to Britain in the years before 1914: Germany, which had developed systematically state support and a highly trained, scientifically based industrial structure powerful in the manufacture of chemicals and new technology; and America, the birthplace of the new consumer society, where mass-production techniques, backed by aggressive advertising methods, supplied a mass market of relatively well-paid workers. By the early 1900s these two rival economies began to look to Britain, and London in particular, as a great potential market for their goods and their investment. Britain's industry was, in contrast, for the most part relatively antiquated, fragmented and badly organized.

The first great shock to British pride came in 1901 when the giant American Tobacco Company attempted to buy up the British industry. A flamboyant 'Yankee' – a popular term of abuse at the time – called James Buchanan ('Buck') Duke arrived in Liverpool, went straight to the firm of Ogdens and bought it. A fierce battle ensued in which the British industry banded together to beat off the American invader and for weeks the newspapers were full of pages of invective from both sides attempting to win public support. A piece of British doggerel ran:

Don't be gulled by Yankee bluff
Support John Bull with every puff!

In the end, the British manufacturers formed themselves into a giant consortium, the Imperial Tobacco Company, carved out the home market and came to an agreement with the Americans on which of them had control of what part of the world. A new company, British American Tobacco, was formed and built itself a brand new headquarters at Westminster House on Millbank in 1915.

In the interwar years a challenge from America, or sometimes Germany, was often the catalyst that pushed British industry into the formation of giant companies to compete on the world market. The whole process was greatly helped by the experience of the Great War, when the need to manufacture armaments killed off the old liberal philosophy of 'free competition' and a belief in the benefits of having a small number of rival firms. The gigantic Ministry of Munitions brought together for the first time civil servants and businessmen, and former commercial competitors had to work alongside each other. This experience, which brought home the benefits of large-scale organization as well as the challenge from abroad, made 'rationalization' all the rage in the 1920s and '30s, and the result was the emergence in London of enormous office blocks, employing a new type of commuter working in management and corporate clerical departments.

On the north side of the Thames Embankment is the enormous structure of what was once Imperial Chemical House, almost rivalling its neighbour, the House of Commons, in stature, and built as the headquarters of ICI, formed in response to the challenge of the German chemical industry. Going east, Shell-Mex House and Unilever House were further great symbols of interwar rationalization, built in the latest architectural style with touches of Art Deco as headquarters for the new corporations. Such totems to the new corporate age arose all over central London, and might be said to include Broadcasting House in Portland Place, home of the British Broadcasting Corporation. The BBC was created by government intervention as a quasi-public body to prevent the free-for-all that characterized early American commercial radio.

In 1940, with its overseas department expanding rapidly, the BBC took over part of Bush House, another wonderful monument of the era. It was the brainchild in 1919 of an American, Irving T. Bush, who designed it as a trade centre, and was finished in 1935. The enterprise proved a failure, but the building was quickly colonized by institutions that would become essential to the new economy of central London.

The combined effects of the growth of the corporate economy and the apparatus of the new consumer economy were greatly to swell the amount of office work available in central London. The capital's economy benefited enormously from the foreign invasion, while the areas of Britain still dependent on the now antiquated economy of coal and heavy engineering went into decline. Whereas before the First World War, only about a fifth of the largest companies in Britain had headquarters in London, about half of them did by 1935.

So London's middle-class population – swelled in the previous century by the growth of the City and of all the professions that served the old square mile, the government and the West End – was sustained in the interwar years by the growth of the corporate economy. The much greater state intervention in public affairs also increased the number of civil servants, while the growing importance of local government – symbolized by the rise of County Hall on the South Bank opposite the Houses of Parliament – further added to the demand for white-collar workers.

One of the clearest indications of the way in which the West End of London was opening up to new kinds of office workers and to a wider range of shoppers was the growth of modestly priced restaurants, the most famous being the Joe Lyons chain of tea shops and Corner Houses. These became a kind of lower-middle-class institution, a genteel oasis for the typist or clerk at lunchtime, and for the cinema-goer at night. Like so much else in the story of interwar London, the origins of mass catering go right back to the mid-Victorian period. In the 1870s, the capital was badly served with cafés, particularly for the day visitor not wealthy enough to belong to a gentlemen's club and not wishing to partake in the unsavoury fare offered in pubs and chop-houses. The situation was especially difficult for women, who had to brave a rough-house atmosphere if they wanted any refreshment.

The first efforts to improve catering in London came from the Temperance Movement, which wanted to provide an alternative to the public house. They opened coffee houses, of which there were a hundred in London by 1879, but most of them seem to have been badly run and lasted only a short time. More successful were the purely commercial caterers who applied the techniques of mass production in food to the problem of eating out. The Aerated Bread Company and the Express

Dairy opened hundreds of milk and bun shops in the late nineteenth century. At the same time, more expensive restaurants were being established to offer the novelty of a place where a man might take his wife out to supper.

It was in this social context that Joe Lyons first emerged. The firm was founded by Salmon and Gluckstein. They were tobacconists who wanted to branch out into a new line of business and their first venture was to provide the catering at the Newcastle Exhibition of 1887. It took the name Joe Lyons when it was formed as a public company in 1894; the name comes from a relatively minor figure in the venture, Joseph Lyons, who, through his family connection with the Glucksteins, was invited to join the company.

The first tea shop in London was established at 213 Piccadilly in 1894, and the first of the more plush, though still inexpensive, Corner Houses was opened in 1909 at the corner of Coventry Street and Rupert Street.

Before 1914, the tea shop business expanded rapidly and Lyons's competitors in the field of mass catering were left behind. By the 1920s, Lyons had 250 tea shops nationally, and its three London Corner Houses could each seat up to three thousand people. It was in this era that Lyons really became established as a national institution, and its waitresses – who were given the nickname 'Nippies' in 1925 – were regarded as the perfect 'public' servants. In the Corner Houses, Londoners on quite modest incomes could enjoy an evening out with live music, cheap but wholesome food, and a degree of luxury in décor that seemed spectacular at the time.

But Lyons did not confine themselves to tea shops and Corner Houses: as early as 1896 they had opened the Trocadero, a high-class restaurant in Piccadilly Circus; they built the Strand Palace Hotel, on the Strand, in 1909; the Regent Palace, at the back of Regent Street, in 1915; and the Cumberland Hotel, at the junction of Oxford Street and Park Lane, in 1933. And, more profitably, they became the leaders in the mass production and packaging of food – particularly of tea, ice cream and cakes and buns. Their production centre was at Cadby Hall near Olympia, and in 1931 they were boasting that 500,000 rolls were daily dispatched from the bakery there while 160 million meals were served in their restaurants, Corner Houses and tea shops during that year.

By the 1930s, Joe Lyons's catering was already on the wane, as the shorter working day took away the breakfasts and teas that they had once served to office workers and more firms provided meals in canteens. It was the food manufacturing side of the business that thrived. However, Lyons was synonymous by then with a new way of life in London's neon-lit West End, and as the Nippy whisked around the Corner House, she might be chatted up by a group of ordinary lads on a night out, or by a more elevated customer, as Dora Dyer remembered:

> When you were a Nippy, you always got somebody that took a little
> bit of a fancy to you, and once I used to have a very elite gentleman
> sat at my table. One day, when he went out, he left his card, and
> much to my amazement he was the Consul General for Brazil.
> Anyway, the next time he came in he asked if I would go to dinner
> with him. He was an older man, but I did go and he took me to the
> Savoy and I had a wonderful time; I felt like a queen.
>   And I met the man who was to become my husband when I was
> working at Lyons as well. There was a group of men came in, they'd
> been playing cricket, and I could tell from their conversation they took
> it in turns to ask girls they met out. Well it wasn't my husband's turn,
> but he said 'I don't care even if I fall out with you, I'm going to take
> this one home', and that was the start of our romance.

Mass consumerism was to have its effect on every level of London society. The upper classes retained their glamour, and a Society wedding might still draw crowds of sightseers anxious to get a glimpse of the latest fashions, but the allure of the aristocracy was rapidly being eclipsed by that of Hollywood film stars – they were now setting the pace and, increasingly, influencing fashion. In the thirties a beautiful debutante, dashing about in sports cars, spending every night at the Kit Kat Club or The Embassy, was almost like a film star, fêted in the popular newspapers. As a result she would be sought after by advertisers – particularly those from America – to promote a cosmetic, a cigarette or a drink for the mass market. The advertising agency, J. Walter Thompson – which set up office in the 1920s in Bush House – recruited flocks of young aristocratic Ladies to promote Ponds Cream. Among them was Lady Strickland, who remembered:

> When I was eighteen I had a letter from Ponds offering fifty pounds
> to do an endorsement. That was a fortune to me because, due to a
> very bitter divorce, I wasn't living with my father and had no money.
> So I did it and my picture went in the paper more or less straight

away. My father must have seen it, because I had a telegram from him saying it was disgusting and to send the money back, which of course I refused to do. Then later on I did more advertisements; one of them was for Gordon's Gin, although I told them at the time that I never drank alcohol because I disapproved of it. I only drank milk at nightclubs.

No image captures the face of London's heartland in the thirties better than Lady Strickland's memory of her own photograph ablaze at night in Piccadilly Circus, advertising Horlicks:

There was a picture of me up in Piccadilly Circus, about thirty feet high, with a spotlight on it. And it had written across it. 'Do You Suffer From Night Starvation?' One evening Jimmy Horlick and my father were going past in a taxi and Jimmy Horlick, not knowing who the picture was of, because my name wasn't on it, asked, 'Have you seen my advertisement up there?' My father replied, 'Yes, that's my daughter.'

It was up very high and we used to drink its health in milk at four in the morning, after we'd been nightclubbing. Then we'd go off into the country.

CHAPTER EIGHT

Empire and Electricity

WHEN THE TWIN towers of Wembley Stadium were demolished in February 2003 to make way for a new arena, there was a bout of nostalgia for the loss of what was surely the most familiar monument to interwar London. It had been the home of the world's most celebrated football matches, the FA Cup Final, since it was built in 1923 and in the public mind was always associated with soccer. But, set in a sea of north London's semi-detached houses, this stadium was in reality a relic of the most lavish and exotic display of the cultural and economic riches of the British Empire ever staged in the capital.

The 1924 British Empire Exhibition, for which the stadium was built, put Wembley well and truly on the map of London. But the exhibition is of more than parochial interest: the story of how it came to be there, what it was meant to achieve, and what eventually happened provides a colourful illustration of the way in which London remained a thriving metropolis between the wars, while the rest of Britain floundered economically as the foundations of its nineteenth-century industrial wealth began to crumble.

London was still, in the interwar years, the capital city of an enormous Empire which continued to grow in size until 1937, its territory extended by the conquests of the First World War and piecemeal additions after it. But what proved ultimately much more important for London's continuing prosperity was the fact that it became the most powerful magnet in Britain for new industries, many of them first developed in America. The imperial capital itself was, in a sense, the happy victim of a kind of economic colonization which brought it a new kind of wealth.

The idea for an Empire Exhibition of some kind seems to have been suggested first in the early 1900s, at the time when American and German businessmen and industrialists were making forays into the British market. Even at that early date there was a sense that the riches of the Empire, which had historically reflected British economic superiority, might now be harnessed to preserve the nation's position in the face of fierce foreign competition, though there does not seem to have been any great awareness in Britain about what was really going on. American and German manufacturers had been making inroads into the markets of the Empire since the late nineteenth century; Britain was already living on borrowed time. The idea for an Empire Exhibition was put forward again in 1914, but the outbreak of war soon put an end to the plans.

When in 1920 an Empire Exhibition was proposed yet again, the world had changed. At a meeting in the Mansion House on 7 June the assembled dignitaries gathered to endorse the enterprise (first put forward by two private companies which became the British Empire Exhibition Incorporated) saw it at once as a victory celebration and a chance to promote Empire trade. Sir Robert Thorne, President of the Board of Trade, captured the mood well when he said that the manifestation of the power of the Empire in the war had perhaps been the most remarkable fact in all human history; but he would not talk about that – 'I wish to speak on the business side of the project.' The post-war economic boom would soon be over, he warned, and the time might come when 'trade will sag, and when we may come very near the point of depression'. If that happened, the Empire – and Britain – could do with all the trade it could generate.

There was an understandable and, as it turned out, quite justified concern behind the exhibition. It was not, as Viscount Milner, Secretary of State for the Colonies, emphasized, mere 'vainglorious display'. It was hoped that by bringing together the immense natural resources of its Empire Britain might survive in a much tougher world.

In many ways, the design and mood of the British Empire Exhibition reflected perfectly Britain's ambiguous position between the wars when new technology was undermining its dominant world position, while it remained a great imperial nation. The exhibition's siting in Wembley, on the fringes of the built-up area of north-west London, located it in what was to become one of the great boom districts during the worst years of the Depression.

Wembley Stadium was the first exhibition building to go up, and became a showpiece of interwar modernity. About two thousand men were employed to put up the reinforced concrete structure, and some of them were marched around the newly completed terraces – along with a platoon of soldiers – to test its strength. The stadium was able to cope with the vast crowds attending the Cup Final held there in 1923 when the admission system went wrong and thousands of football fans spilled onto the pitch, holding up the start of the game in which Bolton Wanderers beat West Ham 2–0. The following year the exhibition proper opened, the whole 216-acre site amounting to a kind of imperial Disneyland.

To illustrate the theme of the Empire's resources there were re-creations of African villages, a replica of the Taj Mahal, and a scale model of a West Indian waterfall. Central to the Canadian contribution were life-sized, refrigerated sculptures of the Prince of Wales in butter. There were also vast Palaces of Engineering and of Industry. As with all exhibitions, it attracted a great deal representing the height of modernity, such as the 'all-electric house' – still a rarity. The section which prophetically, however, seems to have caught the imagination of the vast number of visitors – 17 million in the first year – was the amusement park. Here, America – the bit of the Empire Britain had lost long before – introduced the first dodgem cars, and a roller-coaster. And when the exhibition was held again in 1925, among the displays was Henry Ford's assembly line for mass-producing cars.

Wembley, in the end, might easily have been a celebration not of Empire, but of the new consumerism invading Britain. For the Empire Exhibition did little or nothing for Britain's economy: its lasting effect was to help lay the foundations for a part of London's extraordinary manufacturing success between the wars. After its second year, the exhibition closed down and a large number of its buildings were handed back to the nations that owned them or were sold for scrap. They were designed as temporary accommodation and quite a number were dismantled for use elsewhere. The Palestine Pavilion became a Glasgow laundry, East Africa's a furniture factory, Sierra Leone's a restaurant in Ireland and New Zealand's a dance hall.

This asset-stripping was carried out by a man who had arrived at the exhibition to run a small cigarette kiosk, and managed to get the demolition contract when it was over. Eventually Arthur Elvin scraped the money together to buy Wembley Stadium but it remained like a ship stranded in a sea of dereliction, making a profit not from football but from greyhound racing. There were one or two grand plans for the use of the site, such as the proposed British Hollywood, but none of them came about. Instead, the area was colonized bit by bit, as manufacturers searching for suitable factory sites close to London moved in. The remaining shed-like exhibition buildings, the open aspect of the area, the new roads that had been created to handle the traffic into Wembley, the railway, and the relatively low rents combined to make the exhibition site almost perfect for industrial growth in the 1930s. For Wembley, no more than a small piece of Metroland – the middle-class housing development promoted in north-west London by the electrified Metropolitan Line Railway Company – was perfectly situated on the fringes of a metropolis enjoying an extraordinary prosperity in a historical period remembered chiefly for unemployment and industrial decline.

ALL ROADS LEAD TO LONDON

London was a boom town within declining Britain. While the old, coal-based heavy industries of Wales and the North East of England, which had been the basis of nineteenth-century industrial wealth, were seriously threatened by foreign competition, the new consumer industries, mostly electrically powered and comparatively small-scale, grew enormously. Even during the worst years of the slump, from 1929 to 1931, a host of relatively cheap, mass-produced goods made their first appearance, some of which still have a familiar ring today. Gillette razor blades, Smiths crisps, Marconi radios, Hoover vacuum cleaners, 'silk' stockings made of rayon (manu-factured from wood pulp), canned foods, gramophone records were all being churned out for the mass market, promoted by new forms of advertising in popular daily newspapers, in the cinema and on radio.

London was the single greatest consumer market in Britain, and one of the most valuable in the world, because of its immense size, with a popu-lation approaching 8 million in the mid-1930s (a figure not yet matched since). Throughout the previous century London had been, in fact, the largest manufacturing region in the country, and its industries concentrated on satisfying the needs of the metropolis. But in the consumer boom of the interwar years it moved even further ahead of the field. Between 1923 and 1939, something like *two-thirds* of the new jobs in Great Britain were created in Greater London. And nine hundred new firms, employing twenty-five or more people, were set up in the London area between 1932 and 1938, about half the national total during that period. London tightened its historic grip on the national wealth, and by the end of the interwar period government committees were inquiring into the causes of this great regional imbalance.

Droves of jobless descended on the capital in search of work: immigration from the rest of Britain added 600,000 to London's population between the wars. Many were single men who travelled long distances hoping to get a job on spec'. Having little or no money, the newcomers developed their own community networks in the capital, enabling friends and relatives to get jobs, and if necessary helping them to dodge the train fare to London which many could not afford, as Billy Rounce from Jarrow remembered:

> When I finished my time after six and a half years as an apprentice shipwright, I had five days' work and then six and a half years on the dole. From the age of twenty-two to twenty-eight, I was out of work. And there were thousands of us on the dole and we wanted a job more than anybody can understand. The best prospects were in London at that time but it was getting there was the problem; the lads couldn't afford to go to London.
>
> So, the only way there was to dodge the fare and the dodge was done by the platform ticket trick. You got the platform ticket at this end, the Newcastle end, and you got on the station, you got on the train and you had a mate meet you with a London platform ticket at King's Cross. Or on a more official basis, one of the lads who did the trip regularly would supply you with a King's Cross platform ticket for a couple of bob. I went down to London doing this and I worked with some of our lads who got me a job on a block of flats in Mornington Crescent.
>
> All the people from Jarrow lived in different parts of London, but if you fell sick or if you felt you could do with a handout, you always knew where to go – the path leading to Speaker's Corner on Hyde Park, and the seventh lamp on the left if you were going away from Speaker's Corner.

One of the most poignant stories of the period is that of the Jarrow march from Tyneside to London in 1936 aimed at drawing government attention to their desperate condition. The marchers met their sweethearts and relatives in Trafalgar Square, the women having moved down to work as domestics, factory hands or clerks. Indeed many of the marchers themselves were not seeing London for the first time, having made the journey by train in previous years, seeking out whatever work was going in the boom town of the Depression years, as John McNulty recalled:

It wasn't the first time we'd been to London – the majority of the lads had been before; you'd come down on spec' to look for work. I'd worked on the Great West Road for six weeks, putting the drains in. There was a lot of Geordies, and Irish and Welsh working as navvies, hardly any Londoners though. But when we got into London, I remember, it was pouring with rain, and my mother and my two sisters were at Marble Arch waiting for us to come past – they'd been down in London for some time, working. I made a dash across to them and hugged them. Then we marched on to Hyde Park, there were crowds of people there, and a well-wisher gave me an old wireless. Of course, I brought that back on the train with us. We never had a wireless before, we were one of the only ones in our street with one – everyone was coming in to listen to it after that.

In contrast with the rest of the country, which, with the exception of the Midlands, was in decline, the prosperity of London and the South East was visibly quite striking in the 1930s. It made a sharp impression on the novelist and broadcaster, J. B. Priestley, whose book *English Journey* is a vivid account of a tour he made in the mid-1930s. Priestley contrasted nineteenth-century England, which had been built on coal, iron, steel, cotton, wool and railways and now provided a landscape of 'Sham Gothic churches, Town Halls, mills and foundries . . . cindery waste ground, mill chimneys . . . and sooty dismal little towns', with modern England. Whereas the old 'is not being added to and has no new life poured into it', the new was growing fast, and as he crawled back into London in a chauffeur-driven car, fog-bound on the Great North Road, he could conjure up in his mind's eye this odd, futuristic world obscured by the mist:

If the fog had lifted, I knew that I should have seen this England all round me at the northern entrance to London, where the smooth wide road passes between miles of semi-detached bungalows, all with their little garages, their wireless sets, their periodicals about film stars, their swimming costumes and tennis rackets and dancing shows . . . You need money in this England, but you do not need much money. It is a large-scale, mass-production job, with cut prices. You could almost accept Woolworth's as its symbol.

Like many other observers, Priestley found it hard to define this post-First World War England, and resorted to a kind of catalogue of consumerism in order to capture its spirit: 'Cocktail bars, motor-coaches, wireless, hiking, factory girls looking like actresses, greyhound racing and dirt tracks, swimming pools, and everything given away for cigarette coupons.' He thought it all 'belonged more to the age itself than to this particular island' and imagined its birthplace must be America. This new world, which was so characteristic of the London created between the wars, was, in fact, the product of a host of technological changes which had begun to take shape in the late nineteenth century and which came to fruition in the 1930s. They amounted to a second industrial revolution, particularly favourable to London.

THE ELECTRIC REVOLUTION

The development of electricity was, indirectly, one of the most important of these technological changes. Though the nature of electricity was understood several centuries ago, its practical application goes back to the mid-nineteenth century when the electric telegraph first came into use. It was as early as 1848 that its use for lighting was first demonstrated in London when battery-powered arc lamps lit up a part of Trafalgar Square. In the later part of the century electricity was mainly employed for lighting, generated by small and usually inefficient stations on site. The Savoy Hotel was electrically lit in the 1890s, as were some expensive blocks of flats such as Kensington Court. The first large-scale generating stations were developed by local authorities for street lighting and by the tramway and railway companies to replace horse or steam power. Before the First World War, Lots Road power station on the Chelsea Embankment was built to run the new electric tubes, and Greenwich power station for the London County Council's newly electrified tramways.

A good deal of electrical inventiveness went on in Britain during the pioneer days, the work of brilliant individuals such as Michael Faraday, Sebastian de Ferranti and Charles Merz. But in the crucial decades just before the Great War, electricity's practical application was hampered. For one thing, the political ideal of *laissez-faire* – or free competition – led the early law-makers to ensure that electricity supply was fragmented, with each licensee allotted only a small area of operations. As the supply of electricity is a classic industry in which large-scale production brings considerable advantages, this proved a setback. Britain also had ample supplies of coal and there was little incentive to experiment with new forms of power in industry, while the new electricity undertakings had to wage a fierce battle with the gas industry, which competed for the claim to be the truly 'modern' fuel, both in the home and in the factory.

As a result, the development of electrical equipment and its use was not as rapid or dynamic in Britain as it was in the United States or Germany, where neither the law nor traditional reliance on coal presented the same obstacles. British firms wanting to use electric machinery often had to import the equipment from abroad, but even then they were in trouble if they did not have their own power stations, for there was a mass of suppliers. In Greater London in 1917 there were seventy companies and local authorities supplying electricity to the public, with seventy generating stations, fifty different types of systems and twenty different voltages. It is understandable, then, that a factory inspector should lament in 1901 that: 'in the age of steam this country led the way, whereas in the age of electricity we seem to follow America and other countries'. The foothold the Americans gained early on in the electric revolution coloured much of its future development in London and elsewhere, and was yet another strand in the 'Americanization' of life between the wars.

The experience of the Great War, however, helped to shake Britain out of its archaic approach to the use of electricity. The great value of electrically driven machinery was recognized in the manufacture of munitions and, during the four years of the war, the output of the industry was doubled. Electricity was essential for new munitions works set up away from coal supplies, often on the north-east and north-west fringes of London. In fact, about 90 per cent of the First World War munitions factories were electrically run, proving the value of this new form of power where new plants had to be set up rapidly.

The war experience was a catalyst, but there is no doubt that electricity would anyway have been rapidly adopted by industry as the major source of power because of its tremendous flexibility in driving machinery. It was the legal and political tangle in which the emergent electrical industry had got itself embroiled that held things up, and ensured that it was not until after the war that the revolution in industrial power took place. The generation and supply of electricity were divided so that there were power companies producing the current and a mass of small firms and municipal authorities selling it. A committee investigated the ludicrous state of the industry and, in the Weir Report, came up with the obvious answer: get rid of the inefficient stations, standardize the system nationally, and connect new and larger power stations through a 'national gridiron' (this quickly became known as the National Grid). The Electricity Supply Act of 1926 did not, in fact, get rid of the fragmented system but it did set up the Central Electricity Board (CEB) whose job it was to impose some kind of order on the existing muddle. It set about establishing the National Grid and standardizing the whole system so that the first stage of the grid was in operation by 1933.

It was not the CEB's job to generate electricity: it bought it from power supply companies and there was no nationalization of the industry until 1948. In the interwar years the grid was not effective in creating a truly national system from which power stations in rural or coastal areas might have supplied the big cities. Inevitably, therefore, as the demand for electricity both industrially and domestically grew enormously from the twenties onwards, London required massive new power stations. The siting of these was critical as water was needed for cooling the generators, and along the Thames – once the main highway for coal barges bringing London's fuel – new cathedrals of the electric age were built.

Battersea Power Station, which became a giant symbol of what might be called the 'early modern' industrial age, was planned by the London Power Company in 1927. It was designed by the celebrated architect, Sir Giles Gilbert Scott, and opened in 1931, its giant chimneys fitted with sulphur extractors to reduce pollution in the surrounding area. Battersea Power Station was regarded as the most advanced generator in Europe in the 1930s and represents that period in the rationalization of industry when the benefits of large-scale production were recognized. It continued in operation into the 1970s but was gradually closed down and the power finally turned off in 1983. Since then the huge carcass of the building has remained a mournful shell while plans for its redevelopment have floundered. It is currently on English Heritage's list of buildings at risk.

The fact that industry was rapidly becoming electrically powered, and that London could now supply its own current, greatly encouraged the colonization of the outskirts of the capital by new firms. London's big strength as a manufacturing region had always been that it provided the richest market in Britain, and one of the wealthiest in the world, for consumer products. A large part of its industry was small-scale, tucked away in back streets and alleys. In the 1920s, and to a greater extent in the 1930s, much of this cramped industry was searching for new sites not far from London, but with room to expand. At the same time, new mass-production techniques and the growth of electrical products created a great many new firms in search of convenient and economic sites close to London. These two developments laid the foundations for the capital's spectacular interwar industrial expansion which spread right around London but which was particularly strong in the north west, around Wembley and the area known as Park Royal.

Most of this region was ideal for firms moving out of the centre or for those setting up for the first time because it was largely open country with some of the services required by industry already available. Park Royal provides the classic example. It takes its name from a Royal Agricultural Society showground established on the site before 1914: outside the enormous Guinness factory built there in the late 1930s stand two oak trees planted in 1903 by Edward VII and by the Prince of Wales. As a showground it was apparently a failure and during the First World War parts of it were used as munitions factories and as a horse compound for the Royal Army Service Corps.

COLONIZING THE RUINS
OF THE EMPIRE EXHIBITION

Park Royal was served by the Great Western Railway (which owned a good deal of the land) and the Grand Union Canal. After the Great War, former munitions factories which had been built around the fringes of London were quickly colonized by firms moving out of the centre. At Park Royal, the story of one firm – Allnatt's – provides an example of the way in which the process worked. Major Allnatt was a caterer from Reading, who took over some disused munitions sheds at the time of the Empire Exhibition to provide food and accommodation for children visiting Wembley in 1924 and 1925. When the exhibition finished, he realized there was a demand for factory space, and decided to build a small unit for lease. The first road he laid out was named after his foreman, Mr Gorst, and retains that name today. As demand picked up he built more and more small factory units and was completing one every two weeks by the 1930s. By Gorst Road is Standard Road, named after Standard Motor Cars (the first firm to arrive there), as well as Sunbeam Road and Minerva Road, both named after motor car manufacturers who were the first leaseholders. Allnatt went on to build factories on the Great West Road, making a fortune out of the inter-war industrial boom.

Park Royal lies just to the south of Wembley Stadium, the abandoned site of which was colonized by firms mostly supplying the London market. Wembley was especially favoured because new roads had been laid to cope with the visitors to the Empire Exhibition, and very soon the whole of the area was to benefit from an extraordinary programme of road building linking the new industrial areas with the centre at the very moment of great expansion for motorized transport. Although canals and railways remained important for bringing in bulk raw materials, new roads were revolutionizing goods transport in Britain. In and around London, roads were generally in bad shape before the Great War. The long-distance highways linking the capital with other main cities had gradually fallen into disrepair during the second half of the nineteenth century as the railways creamed off the goods and passenger traffic of the stagecoaches. The turnpike trusts, which maintained the roads by tolls, had all gone bankrupt through lack of traffic. The road system, if it could be called that, was administered by a hopeless confusion of authorities, with no incentive to spend money to aid through traffic. At the same time, in central London, traffic had increased enormously and congestion was a serious enough problem to be made the subject of a Royal Commission of Inquiry in 1905. However, the Commission's proposals for reorganizing the administration of roads and the building of new central thoroughfares were largely ignored. And it reported, as fate would have it, just at the time when a new form of transport, the motor vehicle, was beginning to make its impact on the capital and the country.

The Royal Commission of 1905 did, however, lead to the formation of the London Traffic Branch of the Board of Trade, which had few powers but was at least able to formulate some kind of policy for future road building. In 1907, this small outfit commissioned a survey of the traffic problem from one Colonel Hellard, and the basis of future road policy started to take shape. It was evident then that motor traffic was beginning to overtake horse-drawn traffic in central London. A survey in Westminster, comparing the flow of vehicles in 1903 and 1908 at selected points, revealed that the number of private horse carriages and cabs going by had fallen from 43,790 to 29,967, while the flow of private motor cars had risen from 1,064 to 6,961 and that of motor taxis from zero to 19,718. Because motor vehicles were nippier and smaller than horse-drawn vehicles it was duly noted that the 'change from horse to motor cabs is distinctly beneficial to traffic'.

At the same time, there was a noticeable increase in vehicles in outer London, 'almost entirely attributable to the growth of mechanical traffic'. In other words, the Traffic Branch appears to have come to the conclusion that the real problem to be solved was in outer London, where the approach routes to the capital through the narrow main streets of outlying suburbs, such as Brentford, were very congested. Schemes for cutting new avenues through central London were pushed into the background, perhaps because it was thought that the motor vehicle was beginning to solve the problem by its superiority over horse-drawn vehicles.

In 1909, the Development and Road Improvement Act provided an important step towards the solution of the tricky problem of how new roads were to be financed, and who was to plan them. In his budget speech, the Chancellor of the Exchequer, Lloyd George, brought in motor vehicle and petrol taxation, which was to be used to finance new road building – the Road Fund – and with the act a Road Board was created to administer the fund. There followed a series of Greater London Arterial Roads Conferences and in a patchy and very muddled way a kind of plan emerged to build a network of new, wide roads on the fringes of London to ease traffic congestion on the approaches to the capital. It was during the war years that the Road Board came up with schemes for the Great West Road, a new North Circular Road and Western Avenue.

It was never made clear what the new roads were really for, particularly in the case of Western Avenue, which was to run from the built-up area out into open country. Such roads could bypass congested routes into London, but would also lead into areas that would become ripe for development. As they were to be built mostly through open country, they could be properly planned and made wide enough for modern traffic conditions. Of Western Avenue the eminent planner Colin Buchanan remarked: 'There was, in fact, complete confusion as to the road's function, whether it was to be a traffic artery or a development road, and such confusion was to bedevil road planning for the next twenty years.'

When the road building actually began after the First World War, encouraged in the 1920s by extra finance provided by schemes to reduce unemployment, it provided around the western, northern and eastern fringes of London a web-like structure of new avenues which became the focus of rapid, unplanned development. And in west Middlesex the opening of Western Avenue, the Great West Road and the linking North Circular Road was an added impetus to the development of what was to become the single greatest concentration of industry in the country, running from Wembley through Park Royal south and west to Twickenham. By the mid-1930s, the new roads were bustling with motorized transport, carrying goods from showpiece factories into London and to other parts of the country. The most spectacular of the new avenues was undoubtedly the Great West Road, which had been officially opened by King George V in 1925. It had begun as a bypass for Brentford, where traffic congestion in the narrow high street had been regarded as a problem since the middle of the nineteenth century. The coming of the electric tram in 1901, hogging the middle of the road, had been the final straw, and the act to build the new road had actually been passed in 1914, but was delayed by the war.

The official programme of the opening suggested that the new road was the most spectacular highway achievement since Roman times: it was laid out in a clean curve running from the fringes of Brentford into open country, with space alongside the carriageway for the laying of mains gas, electricity and water pipes. One of the first firms to find a site here was Smiths Crisps, which moved out from Cricklewood in 1927. There followed a succession of new factories, such as Isleworth Winery, Macleans Ltd (makers of toothpaste and stomach powders), Trico-Folbert (a British subsidiary of the American car windscreen manufacturers), Firestone tyres, Curry's cycles and radios, and Gillette UK Ltd (the American safety razor manufacturers).

In time, this stretch of the Great West Road close to the London exit became known as 'the Golden Mile' and even today, with its somewhat forlorn air, it is still just possible to imagine how strangely gleaming and futuristic it must have looked to the motorist of the 1930s. It became a kind of roadside gallery of modern architecture as each firm used the aspect of its site to project a brand-new image to the world. American firms, in particular, favoured this stretch of road, and it was estimated that about 60 per cent of those set up in Britain between the wars came here. Infected by the style of the area, British firms liked to trumpet the splendour. In 1936, Curry's journal proclaimed:

It is a worthy home for our great national concern. Its publicity power must be incalculable. Well might Mr Albert Curry suggest that perhaps the advertising department should contribute £1000 per annum for such astounding publicity value!

It is indeed true that nowhere in the whole of the British Isles is there a road which will advertise Curry's to the world as the Great West Road . . .

Have you seen this building by night? It's worth motoring many miles to see. Curry's on the front: Curry's on the tower; Cycles and Radio on the tower, all ablaze with vivid Neon lighting; and the whole front flood-lit with glorious intensity – a really marvellous spectacle.

It was in daylight, at the start of his travels for *English Journey* in 1934, that J. B. Priestley took in the spectacle from one of the new motor-coaches which were now competing with railways on long-distance routes, and he could hardly believe his eyes:

After the familiar muddle of West London, the Great West Road looked very odd. Being new, it did not look English. We might suddenly have rolled into California. Or, for that matter, into one of the main avenues of the old exhibitions like the Franco-British Exhibition [at the White City] of my boyhood. These decorative little buildings, all glass and concrete and chromium plate, seem to my barbaric mind to be merely playing at being factories.

The new factories were certainly quite unlike those of Priestley's Victorian Northern England, but in the context of London manufacturing they were, in fact, a natural extension of an old tradition of the capital making things chiefly for its own consumer market. What was new, however, was the style, the use of new technology, and the concentration on the products of rising mass consumerism. On the Wembley Exhibition site in the 1930s you would find, for example, Claude-General Neon Lights Ltd in the shell of the South Africa Pavilion, Modern Kitchen Equipments Ltd in the old India Pavilion, and the Expanded Rubber Company Ltd in what had been the Palace of Arts. Here, and in the area around, were gathered a host of mostly small-scale manufacturing concerns, many of which had been established, previously in inner London and have chosen to move out, while others were brand new.

The same thing had occurred all the way around the North Circular Road and in Park Royal; printers, coach builders, radio works, cosmetic manufacturers, metal goods factories had established themselves. It is doubtful whether much of this expansion could have taken place without the development of electricity; this freed old industries from dependence on steam and mechanical power and gave them much greater flexibility in their sites. Nor would the distribution of the goods have been nearly so convenient without motor lorries and new roads. And the whole edifice of this new consumer society required new breeds of men and women to run it, and to sell its goods.

On the roads, the lorry driver began to replace the cabman with his horse-drawn vehicle. In 1921, there were 49,000 cabmen – twice as many as there were lorry drivers. But by 1931, the number of goods vehicle drivers overall had increased from 73,000 to 86,000 and the motor men represented a clear majority – 49,000. The foundation of the motor road haulage business was laid when the government sold off army surplus lorries cheaply after the Great War. Many of the ex-servicemen who had learned to drive them in the forces became lorry drivers. Firms with fleets of horse-drawn vehicles had to retrain the cabmen who were used to a slow and pungent routine of reins and harness, straw and oats. According to *The New Survey of London Life and Labour* it usually took a cabman six weeks of fairly constant teaching before he could drive a motor with any confidence. It was quite a different routine!

> A horse shares the cabman's knowledge of routes frequently traversed, and often leads the way, moving at a steady speed of about seven miles an hour. On the other hand, motors need constant control and move three or four times as fast as the horse. The cabman turned motor driver at first forgot that he had to steer all the time, and was a bad judge of short distances in manoeuvring his vehicle.

Primitive motor vehicles, long journeys and overnight stops in the truck or in the new cafés and lodging houses springing up along the trunk roads made lorry driving in the early days demanding, exciting and somewhat disreputable. Bill Taylor, who drove long distance in the 1920s and '30s, needed more than a little resourcefulness to get by:

> I couldn't read or write, so when a firm gave me a delivery note, they used to give the orders of a night-time for the following morning. So I'd take the notes home and try and work out a route which I was

going to do, using a map. I'd look on the map for names of places that were the same as those on my delivery notes. I'd make a line right the way across the map, say, from Holloway right up to Barnet and up on the North Road to Darlington or, say, York, and each big town I was going through I'd mark on the map. So, when I pulled up at that town I'd get the map out and ask people which was the best way to the next town I'd marked. This was how I got on.

As long as I was behind the wheel driving, I was happy. And when I used to go away on journey work, I'd perhaps be away a week at a time and we used to have to sleep rough in the lorry because often the guv'nor had no money. I've come home lousy, white lice running in my jersey, that's how bad it was in those days. You slept under canvas to keep you warm in the back of the lorry. And there used to be these lorry girls in the cafés, and they'd clean your lorry for a few bob, and you'd take them from one town to another. Sometimes they'd stop with you a whole week, sleep with you and keep you company. This is the way they lived. Sometimes you'd give them a lunch or kept them in grub and cigarettes. When the wives found out about these lorry girls, that used to break their marriages up.

In the new factories themselves, a very large number of single women were employed on routine, sometimes soul-destroying work under an extremely strict regime. Lateness, talking on the job and untidiness could easily lead to dismissal. Some of these women, like Edie Bedding, left the old West End cottage industries which had in the past serviced the aristocratic Season but which were now shrinking, to look for better and regular money on the factory floor:

I was at a private little firm, doing dressmaking in the West End. There was only four of us, and we made hand-made things for well-to-do people – a lot of outfits for weddings, like lady's suitings. I liked the work very much but it was seasonal, you were working from September to January, then they put you off until May.

I went to a dance and I met some girls who were working for Heinz, and they said what a good firm it was and they said, 'Oh, you could come to our place, the money's good and the girls are ever so friendly, you'll like it there'. I told my parents about it, but they didn't like it. They'd seen the girls from the Fullers chocolate factory in

Hammersmith Broadway and they looked messy. They had chocolate all over them when they came out, and they used to go down the local pub at lunchtime.

Well, I kept on and I got my own way in the end. But to start with I didn't like it at all. When I went to Heinz my job was sorting beans. When these beans came along on the conveyor belt, they were coming along ever so thick, you just had to turn them ever so lightly with your hand, just to make sure there were no black ones in there, and there was a small container where you dropped the black beans. But you didn't have many to put in there because the beans were so perfect anyway. And I was doing this for eight hours a day, sitting by the belt watching these beans go past, and it used to almost send me to sleep staring at them, because we weren't allowed to talk at all, we had to get on with our work.

At the really sharp end of the new consumerism was the door-to-door salesman, a much less respected figure than the commercial traveller who dealt with tradesmen and was better paid. Many of them sold vacuum cleaners. But the vacuum cleaner – the electrically powered symbol of suburban, labour-saving housewifery – was not taken up as enthusiastically as one might have expected in the interwar years. Electricity was expensive and it took time for people to get used to the idea that this new gadget could actually be worth the expense. It was therefore quite a task for vacuum cleaner manufacturers like the American firm Hoover to convert London householders to their machines. But Hoover brought with them from America the aggressive sales pitch of the new industry. They built themselves a showpiece factory on Western Avenue in 1932, and the company drilled the door-to-door salesman, who carried the vacuum cleaner to the customer, in high-pressure sales techniques and unquestioning loyalty to the product. By all accounts he had a thankless if sometimes amusing job, as Sam Tobin, whose patch was Arnos Grove, Enfield and Palmers Green in the late 1930s, remembered:

You knocked on the door. 'Good morning Madam, I represent the North Metropolitan Electric Power Supply Company' – that was the authority in the area prior to nationalization. 'I have been sent along because you are entitled to have one of your carpets and some of your furniture cleaned with the latest Hoover vacuum machine.' Very often it would be, 'Not today thank you', but if you got inside you would follow a script almost down to the last letter that they taught you in a training course. I laid out the Kapok, I laid out the sand in strips, and I laid out the saltpetre, plugged in the Hoover and cleaned them up, trying to charm and persuade the housewife all the while. And whatever objection they had, you were taught an answer to it. They might say, 'Oh my husband wouldn't like me to get involved in buying one of these,' and I would say, 'Now I see you've got a very nice lawn. No doubt your husband has one of these cylinder machines that he cuts the grass with. Not using the old shears method is he?'

It could be pretty soul-destroying though, because you could go for weeks without a sale and if it was bad weather, or if Electrolux or newspaper subscription salesmen had done your territory, it was very difficult to get a demonstration anywhere. You had to survive on the £2 a week retainer they gave you, and even when you made a sale, your commission, say £3 for a Hoover Senior, was taken off your retainer, so you only ended up being £1 better off. So to encourage the salesmen, and to put the spirit of the firm in their hearts, sort of thing, the company would have these singsongs and some salesmen used to sing them in the storerooms before they went out on the road on Monday mornings. They would be standard popular tunes of the day, with Hoover words. [This verse was sung to the tune of the American military ditty, 'The Caissons go rolling along'.]

All the dirt, all the grit,
Hoover gets it every bit,
For it beats as it sweeps as it cleans.
It deserves all its fame, for it backs up every claim,
For it beats as it sweeps as it cleans.

Oh it's hi-hi-hee, the kinds of dirt are three,
We tell the world just what it means,
Bing bing bing, Spring or Fall,
The Hoover gets 'em all,
For it beats as it sweeps as it cleans.

By the late 1930s, something like 40 per cent of households owned a Hoover, and though the consumer revolution in Britain was not in full swing until after the Second World War, it was during this decade that much of the groundwork was laid. American-style advertising was then established and the Victorian industry shaken up by newcomers from across the Atlantic. After Hoover abandoned its Art Deco building in the 1980s it was left empty but was saved from demolition when it was listed Grade II for its architectural value. In 1989 it was bought by the Tesco supermarket chain, which restored much of the complex of buildings and kept the façade of one as the store entrance.

PIRATE RADIO AND OTHER ENTERPRISES

In one field in particular, namely in radio, the American advertising agencies, such as J. Walter Thompson, who arrived in London in 1919, stole the march on their established British counterparts. In America, commercial radio was accepted early on, and the sponsored programme had become a feature of life from the 1920s. Britain was typically much more cautious, first resisting the spread of radio and then allowing five major radio manufacturers to form the British Broadcasting Company in 1922. Visits by Lord Reith and others to America led swiftly to a political decision not to allow in commercial radio. National newspapers, fearful for their advertising revenue, were also hostile. The British Broadcasting Corporation, surviving on Post Office licences rather than advertising, was established in 1927.

A couple of sponsored broadcasts had been transmitted before 1927. Harrods tried it as early as 1923, and Selfridges – always in the forefront of new ideas – organized a fashion talk from the Eiffel Tower in 1925. The formation of the BBC two years later was supposed to put an end to commercial radio in Britain, but the pressure for a new advertising medium was such that a way was found to foil the government's monopolistic system.

A few enterprising individuals, notably Captain L. F. Plugge, set up stations on the continent and began to broadcast sponsored programmes to England. Plugge founded Radio Normandy in 1930 and, over the next few years, Athlone, Hilversum, Madrid and Toulouse (evocative names from the dials of thirties radios) all had a go at beaming advertising into Britain. However, the most successful and best-known station was Luxembourg. The British press behaved as if Radio Luxembourg and the other stations did not exist, never mentioning them or publishing programme information, and putting pressure on established British advertising agencies to ignore them. But American concerns, like J. Walter Thompson, persuaded their clients to give radio a try, and before long the commercial radio stations were carrying advertisements for Lifebuoy toilet soap, Rinso, Palmolive, the Ford Motor Company, Colgate dental cream and so on.

J. Walter Thompson, who moved into Bush House in 1922, converted the swimming pool in the basement into a sound studio, and recorded up to forty-four different sponsored programmes every week for Radio Luxembourg. Londoners tuned in, and surveys suggest that there was a very large listening public in the 1930s, some of whom could be heard humming jingles like the 'We are the Ovaltineys' song as they went about their daily work. At the same time another powerful American influence had invaded the capital: the cinema.

There were already about ninety cinemas in London before the First World War, and an embryo British industry had been established which competed with the American imports. But the war wiped out British cinema and in the 1920s Hollywood completely dominated the market. This became the subject of great national concern, not least because it was felt that the diet of American movies was advertising American products and undermining British industry. The Cinematographic Films Act of 1927 put a block on the showing of imported films and required cinemas to show a quota of British films.

Though many of the British films subsequently produced were regarded as second-rate 'quota quickies', the act did allow a considerable industry to grow up before the Second World War. Inevitably it became established around London, characteristically on the fringes of the new industrial zone, but also in the more run-down of the Victorian suburbs which were becoming increasingly industrialized in this period. Film studios were set up in Elstree, Croydon, Denham, Surbiton, Pinewood, Cricklewood, Ealing, Fulham and many other places within Greater London. They all worked on electric power, of course, and provide perhaps the most vivid illustration of the fact that this new form of energy enabled industry to set up more or less wherever it liked, and most of it liked London.

Sir Alexander Korda's Denham Studios in Buckinghamshire, built in 1936, had their own power plant, but most used public supplies, by then much better organized. London's great attraction for the film industry was that it remained the cultural centre of Britain and West End actors found it convenient to dash from the studio to the theatre as they enjoyed the employment of both the old and new industries.

A great deal of the new industrial development around London was related to its traditional manufacture: coach builders of the horse-drawn era moving to Park Royal to make the bodies of motor vehicles, which would then be displayed in gleaming showrooms in Regent Street, Piccadilly and Mayfair. The consumer society greatly expanded the scale of production and the size of the market, but industry still clung to London. In fact, the extraordinary story of the rise of the western industrial belt was extended via the North Circular Road and new arterial roads, such as Eastern Avenue, right around the north of London to the Lea Valley in the east. Some of this, so evocative of the 1930s, still survives in buildings of brick with metal-framed windows, a kind of miniature grandeur which to us today looks so tatty and uninspiring.

For the most part, the East End, London's principal industrial zone of the second half of the nineteenth century, did not share this new prosperity. But there is one gigantic and, in many ways, anomalous exception: the Ford Motor factory at Dagenham in Essex. Ford was operating in Britain before 1914, and had built his original factory in Old Trafford, Manchester. But in the 1920s, Henry Ford wanted to establish a European base and, after a good deal of argument, decided on a site near London, against the advice of his leading English representative who had marked out a part of Southampton's dockland. Exactly why Ford went to Dagenham to build his monster production works is not clear, but the lure of London for Americans was clearly very influential.

The great complex was built on marshy land by the Thames and supported on enormous concrete piles. It had its own foundry and during the 1930s the furnace was fuelled partly by LCC rubbish that had formerly been dumped on the site. Nearby was a mass of unskilled labour, which had also been recently 'exported' from inner London to live on the vast Becontree 'cottage' estate (see Chapter Ten). However, Ford's move southwards was an unusual episode in the story of London's prosperity in the interwar years. Most of the industry which grew up in the new industrial belt was either entirely new, and related to electrically powered manufacture, or had moved out from the centre in order to find space. Very few industries arrived from the North: it was the people, not the factories, who made the great migration to the capital.

CHAPTER NINE

The Heyday of London Transport

OR MORE THAN half a century, from the 1930s to the 1980s, London's tubes and buses were run by a public authority. It seemed to most Londoners only right and proper that the transport system of their great metropolis should be administered in the public interest rather than as a profit-making enterprise. The brilliantly designed Underground maps certainly give the impression that sometime in the past the whole of the tube system was designed and thought out by a single authority, even if transport in London is today handed over to highly subsidized private companies.

It might come as a surprise, therefore, to the gloomy commuter waiting for the lift to ascend to ground level on, say, the Northern Line at Belsize Park Station to learn that this was the creation in 1907 of a private company headed by an extraordinary American financier called Charles Tyson Yerkes. And how many hurrying travellers have noticed that at Oxford Circus two stations have been welded into one? From the street, the original stop on the Central Line, opened in 1900, can still be seen alongside the Yerkes station, with its familiar 'ox-liver' tiling of 1906. Both of these were built by private enterprise, which is responsible indirectly for the fact that passengers on the old tube lines are sometimes flung about as the train negotiates a tight corner into a station. The cheapest routes lay under roads because no 'easement' had to be paid to the owners of buildings above, so that Underground companies burrowed round corners to follow a bend; your electric Underground carriage is probably following a route established long before the Great War by horse-drawn traffic!

The truth of the matter is that what survives of London Transport today was largely the creation of private enterprise before 1933, the year in which the capital's tubes, trams and buses were first put in the charge of a public authority. And the shape and extent of the system were dictated by the pursuit of profit, often with very disappointing results for investors. The

Underground map is, in fact, a very clever distortion of the *actual* route the capital tubes take and seeks to make some logical sense out of a network of tunnels and tracks which were never planned as a system but which came about by the piecemeal efforts of a number of railway promoters.

Although the commercial nature of London Transport before 1933 produced a rather haphazard system, it was also in many ways a very vigorous operation and by use of new sources of power – electricity and petrol – which became available around 1900, laid the foundations for what might be called the heyday of public transport in the capital in the late 1930s. For between 1914 and 1939 Londoners used buses, tubes, trams and trolley buses much more than they had ever done before. Only in recent years have the number of journeys overtopped those of interwar London. Though motor cars were already contributing to serious traffic jams in the 1930s, few Londoners in this period owned a car and they therefore spent much more of their money travelling for work or pleasure.

A survey of the rides per head of population in London shows the extraordinary increase in travel. For tubes, buses and trams the average Londoner took 210 rides a year in 1911 and 388 in 1938–9; if railways are included, the increase is from 250 to 443. The absolute highpoint was 1949 when the private car gradually began to take passengers away from public transport. Private transport operators, particularly the Underground Group, made great efforts to improve transport, but it is a mistake to imagine that the commuter of the 1920s or '30s had a much easier time of it than his or her successor today. For one of the reasons for the increase in travel was that from the 1890s right through to the interwar period a host of social and economic changes fundamentally altered the pattern of journeys between home and work in London.

Before the Great War, London already had a huge army of commuters who travelled to work by train, tube, tram and bus. Cheap workmen's fares, introduced from the 1860s to compensate the poor for the destruction of housing involved in much railway building, had allowed hundreds of thousands of the lower-paid clerks and artisans to live in modest, terraced suburbs, particularly in the north east of London as the railway company operating there had the lowest fare policy. The war itself had a profound effect on the nature of travel in London, however. In answer to the demands of munitions workers the government froze rents, and this discouraged movement from one home to another as people remained where they were to benefit from rent control. At the same time, the rise of armament factories, many of them set up on the fringes of London, altered the distribution of jobs. As a result, the amount of travel increased enormously between 1914 and 1918.

After the war, the trends of industrial development continued to pull homes and workplace apart: the LCC was building enormous 'cottage' council estates in places like Becontree in the east, while much of the new employment was growing in the west. Despite the continuation of workmen's fares on the railways and trams (they were never available on buses) the cost and inconvenience of travel were considerable and the cause of a great deal of concern. The physical and mental distress of commuting was a lively issue. So, even though many people gained through an interwar reduction in working hours – the eight-hour day became more and more common – they had to spend much more time travelling to and from work. Moreover, the traveller could only get a cheap workman's ticket up to 8 am – if he or she missed that train, they paid more. So often, in order to save on fares, people would arrive in London far earlier than they needed to, having been jam-packed into the early morning cheap train. George Matthews was one of those who experienced the commuter crushes of the 1930s as he tried to board the train from Eltham:

> When you got to the station it was like a football match, absolutely solid packed with people. To get a workman's ticket, you see, you had to arrive in central London by eight o'clock, so you had to catch the 7.36 train. Everyone wanted to catch it. Because a lot of us on those new estates didn't have any money to spare (we were all paying for our houses) you'd even find people who didn't start work till nine or ten o'clock, clerical-type people, they would all catch that last workman's train as well to get the cheap fare.
>
> And even when it arrived, it was practically full up with people travelling in from Dartford, so we'd be waiting on the platform four or five lines deep, and so people opened the doors to get in, you'd have two or three blokes nearly falling out. It was really unpleasant, everybody would be shoving, pushing, there would be shouting, elbowing, near fighting sometimes; oh, it was absolutely murder. Sometimes you couldn't get on, but even when you did, you'd stand all the way, about twenty of you in a compartment meant for eight.

George was one of the many people who eventually turned to pedal power as the cheapest, most efficient and most enjoyable way of getting to and from work. Though cycling was never a statistically substantial part of commuting, it was a popular option for many poorer-paid workers and there would be great armadas of bicycles along roads bordered by factories at clocking-in and -out times. It's estimated there were 2 million cyclists in the London area in 1936. Some of the cyclists, like Les White, travelled quite extraordinary distances every day, and they developed ways and means of making the journey as painless as possible:

> I used to live in Bow, and I worked at Hoover's in Perivale, which is some seventeen miles away, and this journey I used to do by cycle. I'd be on my bike doing thirty-two or sometimes forty miles a day – thought nothing of it. I started work at seven o'clock in the morning, which meant I had to leave home at about a quarter past five. When I got to Aldgate I used to meet my friend from West Ham and we'd cycle together most mornings, side by side, chatting about all sorts of things, the weather, football, family – it helped pass the time.
>
> We had a few dodges as well to get to work more quickly, because if you were late at Hoover's, they locked you out. Oxford Street was full of traffic lights and we used to get to know these lights quite well travelling morning after morning, and being early morning there was little traffic about, so you could see almost the whole length of Oxford Street, all the traffic lights from one end to the other. So we worked it out that, if you caught one light, if you pedalled like mad, you'd be able to catch the next seven lights without stopping – they'd all be green. We got expert at that. Another thing we did, was to get lifts. If a market lorry or a cart was going our way we'd reach out and grab the tailboard and get a pull-along for as long as possible, it might be a couple of miles, or just fifty yards, it depended how lucky you were.

The widening distance between home and work led to a boom in restaurant catering, which in turn had the effect of increasing the number of people using public transport. Many women chose to become waitresses rather than domestic servants, which meant that they themselves now travelled to work. And quite a number of firms, anxious to keep up with the times and to cope with the problem of staff who travelled long distances, brought in canteens – an innovation encouraged by the First World War. At the same time, transport companies, notably the most powerful of them, the Underground Group, made a deliberate effort to extend the frontiers of the capital in their never-ending search for new passengers. They were able to pursue a policy of colonizing new areas of countryside because London's population, swelled by immigration from the depressed areas of Britain, continued to grow, rising by 1.5 million between the wars.

While 'inner London' lost population, the new suburbs expanded rapidly. The problem for the commercial companies running the buses and tubes was to generate enough traffic to repay the enormous capital investment involved in building new lines and modernizing old ones. They did this by encouraging suburban development and the use of the transport system outside the commuting 'rush hours'. This policy carried over into the era of public ownership of London Transport, for the same people who ran the single most influential company in London dominated the Passenger Transport Board of 1933. This transport imperialism came to an end with the beginnings of a Green Belt policy – designed to prevent more suburban building on the outskirts of the capital – and finally with the outbreak of the Second World War.

The crucial technological revolution in London's transport system took place before the First World War. In the nineteenth century, Londoners were taken to and from work and about town on steam railways and in horse-drawn vehicles. In the heart of the capital, the West End, the horse bus held sway as the horse tram – a working- and lower-middle-class form of transport – had been banned in the 1860s. Trams ran from the boundaries of the central area out to places like Camberwell, Peckham and Archway, providing a cheap service invaluable to those who lived in the new suburbs of terraced houses. London's steam-driven Underground went around the central area, linking up the mainline railway stations, which, like the tram, had been kept out of the West End.

The first break with this pattern of transport came with the building of the 'deep level' tube, using a technique for burrowing below the surface of the capital's streets perfected in the boring of tunnels under the Thames. The blue clay subsoil proved ideal for this and the first underground railway proper of this type was the line from Stockwell to King William Street in the City in 1890. All previous Underground lines had been built using the 'cut and cover' method, which involved demolishing property, digging a large trench, and filling it over again. Steam trains were, anyway, quite unsuited to deep tunnels as ventilation was a serious problem. Lines running near the surface had to have frequent open cuttings.

In fact, the initial plan for this first tube railway (the City & South London) when it was being tunnelled in the 1880s was to use cable power to pull the trains. But during the time it was being built, the technological problems presented by using electricity to power trams was solved. Railed transport had proved a significant factor in United States cities in the second half of the nineteenth century because roads there were so bad that horse-drawn, carriage-wheel vehicles had only a limited use. The wide open spaces of the New World were moreover ideal for experimentation with electric power carried in an unsightly fashion on overhead wires supported by poles: something the big city authorities in New York and London were not keen on.

American horse tramways were rapidly electrified in the late nineteenth century and the opportunity to experiment, as well as the great demand for new equipment, gave the Americans a vital lead in developing this new form of traction. The Germans, too, were quick to develop electric power and, in fact, had provided the world's first passenger electric train in Berlin in 1881. In Britain, a seafront electric train in Brighton was opened in 1883 and an electric tramway system in Blackpool in 1885. Electric power had therefore arrived just in time for the City & South London, which in fact installed equipment of a British make – a rarity in the early days of the Underground.

London's second electric tube was the Waterloo & City Line, built in 1898 and early dubbed 'The Drain'. It was, significantly, a project promoted by a mainline railway company, the London & South Eastern, which wanted a way of getting its passengers direct from Waterloo to what was then still the central goal of the commuter, the City. A spate of tube proposals came up in the 1890s at a time when London's population was rising rapidly and its old horse-drawn and steam-driven transport system was creaking under the weight of travel to and from the centre. Four main schemes emerged in these years, three of them supported by mainline railway companies: the Baker Street to Waterloo; the Great Northern & City Railway from Finsbury Park to Moorgate; and 'The Drain', which was the first to be built. There was one other proposal for a line from Hampstead to Charing Cross, with a branch off to King's Cross.

Yet another line had been authorized by Parliament in 1891, and this was to prove the most successful of the pioneers. This was the Central London Railway to run from Shepherd's Bush to the Bank. In a period when the financial success of tube lines was in some doubt – the City &

South London was not paying much of a return – this Central Line was the best bet. It traced underground the heaviest flow of horse-drawn traffic in the capital from the Bank alongside Cheapside, through Holborn and Oxford Street to the Bayswater Road and finally to Shepherd's Bush. The density of horse-drawn traffic on the roads was, at this time, a good guide to the potential profit of a tube line beneath it.

The basic technical problems of building these lines and providing electric power had been solved. The stumbling-block that remained was how to convince investors it was worth putting money into railways which required an enormous capital outlay, but often gave little back. International support was found for the Central Line from investors in Paris, Hamburg, Frankfurt, Berlin and New York, as well as from Britain; and with its equipment supplied by General Electric of America, the first section began to operate in 1900. It had a flat fare of 2d and was quickly dubbed the 'Twopenny Tube'. But the other schemes were floundering for lack of finance: part of the line from Baker Street to Waterloo had been burrowed out, but the company behind it went bust. It was at this point that that extraordinary figure appeared on the London scene: Charles Tyson Yerkes, capitalist and speculator from America.

Yerkes was in his sixties and had a very murky past as an operator in corrupt American finance in the late nineteenth century. His speciality was overvaluing some pretty shoddy assets, including tramway systems, and he is reported as describing his line of business as 'to buy up old junk, fix it up a little and unload it upon other fellows'. In America he had spent a few months in jail for his shady dealings. But, as far as American investors were concerned, he had a good track record in building the elevated railway – 'the EL' – in Chicago. Yerkes was, in retrospect, the ideal man for London's Underground railways, in the sense that he had a gift for persuading people to put their money into something that was not really profitable. He proceeded to do so by buying himself into the District Railway, which was in financial trouble, as well as the proposed Hampstead tube and other lines.

This was a period in history, as we have seen in earlier chapters, when American financiers were particularly keen to break into the London scene. Yerkes clearly thought he could make a killing in London, though he told a Commons committee: 'I have got to a time when I am not compelled to go into this business, but seeing the way things are in London, I made up my mind that this would be my last effort.' And it was, for he died in December 1905 before any of the schemes he masterminded were completed.

In the few years he was in London, Yerkes and his associates laid the foundations for the Underground system we know today. By bringing together the management of a number of tube lines, the District, Bakerloo, Piccadilly and Hampstead, a basis was formed out of which the great combine, the Underground Group, grew. And he brought to London an unmistakable American flavour and drive; this survived his death, thanks to the American managers and experts he and his successors imported. Prompted by the success of the Central Line, proposals for new tube lines were being put forward all the time in the early 1900s and Yerkes and his associates had to fight off a challenge from another group of American financiers headed by J. Pierpont Morgan.

The ins and outs of this battle are too complex and subtle to go into here, but what they amounted to was an attempt by two groups of tube railway backers to convince parliamentary committees that the lines they proposed were worthwhile, that they would do a decent job, and that they had the money to complete their schemes. The Morgan Group had teamed up with a tramway company and proposed, among other tube lines, one that would run through north-east London. Through a bit of sharp dealing, in which his company gained a controlling interest in one of the Morgan company associates, Yerkes undermined the opposition and emerged as the victor, scuppering the proposed North East London Line and allowing his undertakings a clear field for developing the Bakerloo, Piccadilly and Hampstead lines.

In America it had become the practice of tramway promoters to build out into open country, well beyond city boundaries, and to capitalize on increased land prices when housing was put up around the tramway stops. They often opened amusement parks at the end of the line to encourage traffic. If you provided the transport, housing would surely follow. For the most part, the London tube schemes had not reflected this policy. They simply attempted to provide a new form of urban transport, which would cream off traffic within the existing congested built-up area. This was the case with the original scheme for the Hampstead tube, but when Yerkes came in, he quickly proposed that the line be extended into the undeveloped fields of north London at Golders Green.

The story goes that Yerkes took a carriage to the top of Hampstead Heath with a colleague, who had earlier been sent out to scout along the route. Stepping out of the carriage, Yerkes asked: 'Where's London?' It was pointed out to him and he determined there and then to build the railway. He also wanted a station under the Heath, beneath the Bull and Bush Pub, part of which was excavated, but this was abandoned and the terminus established at Golders Green. In putting the case for the extension of the line to Golders Green, counsel for the Yerkes Group told a committee in 1901:

> It is a very pretty part of the country right away to the North, and a country which is eminently suited for building both the better class of houses and also houses for the labouring classes.

The American speculators' instinct for extending transport into the countryside was complemented in England by the 'garden city' movement. This grew up in the late nineteenth century in opposition to the Victorian lack of urban planning and sought to create a new townscape where housing was segregated from the industrial heart of the city. At Golders Green, the two impulses came together when, soon after the station was opened in 1907, work began on Hampstead Garden Suburb.

What might be called the 'Yerkes' part of the Underground system – the Bakerloo, Piccadilly and Hampstead lines, as well as the electrification of the District – was completed by 1907. Their characteristic stations, still seen in many parts of London, are faced in deep red, glazed tiles. On the technical and management side, Yerkes brought over to London a team of American engineers who introduced to London a transatlantic railway lingo, including 'OK', supposedly of Native American origin, and the terms 'northbound' and 'southbound' instead of the English 'up' and 'down' for the direction of trains. And prim commentators at the time thought the Americans had encouraged in Underground staff a foreign brashness: letters in *The Times* complained of stations' names being distorted by Cockney accents, Hampstead becoming 'Ampstid' and Highgate 'Igit'.

A TRANSPORT FREE-FOR-ALL

At the same time as the tube railways were being established, there was a revolution in the capital's surface transport provided by trams, buses and cabs. Tramways were being electrified, making them brighter, cleaner, faster and capable of much longer journeys. And the first motorized buses and cabs were being experimented with on the city streets.

The battle between the American financiers over the tube lines had caused quite a stir and there was a feeling that it was wrong that the planning of London's transport system should be left to competition between capitalists. As the Chairman of a Commons Select Committee said of Yerkes's fight with Morgan, it all seemed to be 'a game in which it was proposed to make the London roads pawns on the chequer board of Wall Street'.

One London authority could, however, reasonably claim to be in a position to take over and plan the transport system: the London County Council. Set up in 1889 the LCC was run for the first few years by 'progressive' liberals, among them Sir John Williams Benn, grandfather of Anthony Wedgwood Benn. Legislation enabled the LCC to purchase and operate the commercial horse tramways laid down in the 1870s and the progressives were keen to do so and to use this section of the transport system to further their social policies of providing cheaper travel for the working classes from city centre to suburbs. Between 1896 and 1906 the LCC bought the assets of nine tram companies north and south of the river and proceeded to electrify the lines, becoming one of the major transport operators in the capital.

The LCC pressed for a government inquiry into London's transport and hoped that it might be given some overall planning powers as had happened, for example, in New York, where the subway lines were built by the Rapid Transit Commission and run by private companies. Instead of an inquiry, a Royal Commission was set up in 1903 and deliberated for two years. It recommended the creation of a London Traffic Board, but no action was taken. London's transport was left as a most extraordinary jumble, with the LCC and private companies jostling for power and trying to make sense of their own bits of the system. Electrification of the tramway system therefore came in bit by bit.

A group called Imperial Tramways, based in Bristol, teamed up with American associates, bought out an ailing horse tram line in Hammersmith run by West Metropolitan Tramways and, on 4 April 1901, created the first permanent public electric tramway in the capital, the London United, which ran from Shepherds Bush to Acton. On the east and south-east sides of London, the local authorities outside the LCC area (which was much smaller than the built-up area of London) took over and built tramways, East Ham running its first electric service in June 1901. The LCC itself was slow to shift to electrification, partly because it lacked technical expertise, but also because it rejected the use of overhead wires for power – acceptable in outer London – and favoured the 'conduit' system, which involved digging up roads to provide the power lines for the trams. The Highways Committee of the LCC got the council started by buying an entire demonstration system of conduit trams from the American Westinghouse firm at an exhibition in the Agricultural Hall, Islington, in June 1900. They even bought the tram driver – motorman in American parlance – and installed him with the system at Camberwell. This began to operate in December 1901.

At this time electric traction appeared to be the thing of the future – the petrol engine was still in its infancy. The Royal Commission on London Traffic concluded that the motorbus was of minor importance and a tramway manager proclaimed in evidence that 'it is an anachronism and is looked upon more or less as a fit object for a museum and not for public service'. Around the world, there were futuristic schemes for light railways, which many people believed would solve the transport problems of great cities. In 1901, the LCC's tramway manager and engineer went to Boston and New York to look at the shallow subways developed there and came up with the idea for something similar in London.

A great problem with the tramway system in London was that its northern and southern sections were not connected as the lines had never been allowed across the Thames. The LCC planned to solve this by creating a subway tunnel under Kingsway, a grand new avenue that formed part of a slum clearance scheme from Aldwych to Holborn. The Kingsway tunnel would link the northern system, ending at Theobalds Road, with that on the other side of the Thames. The tunnel was completed around 1904, but remained unused until the LCC had won permission to run trams along the Embankment and across Westminster Bridge at the end of 1906 (part of Kingsway Tunnel is now an underpass for road traffic). Trams crossed Westminster Bridge and Blackfriars Bridge for the first time in 1906 and 1909, and something like an integrated system was beginning to emerge in the centre as the LCC took over the tram system in its own area. But within Greater London the whole thing was fragmented, the boroughs outside the LCC running their own services on the east side of the capital, and private operators running the trams to the west.

Electric trams were, nevertheless, a great boon to Londoners: they were cheaper than buses, started earlier and were much more comfortable and better lit than the old horse-drawn vehicles. The murky journey home redolent of the Victorian era was greatly brightened by this innovation. Their heyday came just before the First World War, when competition from their great rival on the roads, the motorbus, was just beginning to take effect. The Great War put an end temporarily to the challenge of the buses, as so many vehicles were commandeered for service at the front. At the same time, troop movements around the capital, the influx of office workers to keep the home front operating, and the travel of munitions workers increased the 'travel habit' in London, and it was in these years that many people became accustomed to tube travel. The trams, too, despite a shortage of men and equipment, were carrying more passengers at the end of the war than at the beginning.

METROLAND AND THE NEW SUBURBS

Before the war, there had been some co-operation on fare structures among the competing elements of the transport system, and the Underground Group – the biggest owner of Underground railways – had absorbed the London General Omnibus Company and three major tramway companies to become easily the most powerful element in the system. The experience of the war itself, as in so many other aspects of British life, won many people over to the idea that a co-ordinated system was economically and socially better than fierce competition. But the old *laissez-faire* transport system was still a muddle in 1918.

Its development in the 1920s and 1930s was carried out by three main groups which had to operate, to a considerable extent, in their own 'territories'. The best-known of these operators – perhaps because of its evocative advertising and the many nostalgic revivals – is the Metropolitan Railway. In extending the Metropolitan Line (London's first steam Underground railway) out into the countryside of north-west London in the nineteenth century, it had been forced to buy far more land than it needed for its tracks. It created a surplus land company which became party to a number of ventures.

One of these, involving a separate Tower Company, with Sir Edward Watkin, the Metropolitan Railway's chairman, at its head, leased land at

Wembley Park and attempted to promote an amusement park in the 1880s, with a bigger and better version of the Eiffel Tower as its centrepiece. The Tower, in fact, remained unfinished; it was abandoned for many years, dubbed 'Watkin's Folly', and was removed to make way for Wembley Stadium in the early 1920s. But the Metropolitan continued to encourage development along its lines and in 1915 adopted the term 'Metroland' for advertising purposes, the origin of the term possibly being a little ditty composed by the journalist, George R. Simms:

> Hearts are light, eyes are brighter
> In Metroland, Metroland.

Just after the war, the Metropolitan set up a new company, Metropolitan Country Estates Ltd, which acted as a housing developer in places like Pinner and Harrow.

To the south of London, the amalgamation of three railways in 1923 produced a new company, Southern Railways. Some of the lines it took over had already been electrified, but like other mainline railway companies operating in London, much of it was still steam-powered, quite antiquated and unsuitable for short suburban journeys with frequent stops. Southern was exceptional in that it got more of its money from passengers than freight, and it proceeded to carry out a swift electrification of its suburban lines which was virtually complete by the 1930s. This gave it a huge territory in Kent, Surrey, Sussex and Hampshire which was not invaded by the electric tube, with the exception – and a contentious one as far as Southern Railways were concerned – of the line to Morden which the Underground Group pushed through in 1928.

The complexity of the rest of the transport system is mind-boggling, with the LCC running the trams in the centre, local authorities such as West Ham or Croydon outside the county area running them in the east and south east, private tramways operating in the west, and a number of bus companies competing for custom in the centre and the 'country' areas around London. But one concern was more powerful than all the others and, in effect, set the tone and style of London Transport between the wars.

That anything like a co-ordinated system should have emerged from this muddled situation in the years between 1918 and 1933 is quite remarkable. But it did, and this was largely due to the efforts of two men who had joined the Underground Group before the First World War. One was Albert Stanley, later to become Lord Ashfield. He was born in England, but his family emigrated to America, where he became the dynamic manager of a New Jersey tramway company. He was brought over to London in 1908 by the Underground Group, anxious that an American should be in control. The other man was Frank Pick, who joined the Underground Group in 1906, and became their commercial manager in 1912. In terms of style, approach and philosophy, Albert Stanley and Frank Pick created London Transport in the interwar years and their influence is still evident in the Underground design today.

Between them, Stanley and Pick brought some unity to London's transport system, the one overseeing the expansion of the Underground Group's activities, and the other devising ways of making the whole thing more 'modern', attractive and dynamic.

When the London General Omnibus Company became part of the Underground Group, Frank Pick set off on a kind of walking tour to map out new routes for the buses, with the idea that road and tube services should be linked in a supporting system. It was Pick who developed the Underground posters that are collectors' items now. There was a sound commercial reason for commissioning these works of art. The Underground railways had to provide a 'peak' service for commuters but the trains were under-used outside the rush hour. Attractive posters urging Londoners to have a day in the country, or a night in town, could increase the traffic in off-peak hours. Pick brought in artists such as Graham Sutherland to design these posters and out of his efforts grew a particular genre of British design. During the Great War, he commissioned Edward Johnston to design a new typeface appropriately called 'Underground' for use on the tubes. And Pick experimented with the 'bulls-eye' design for the tube railways, which was to become the familiar London Transport symbol.

As existing tube lines were extended during the interwar period, and the old stations were modernized to cope with the increase in travel, Pick was able to develop with architects a distinctive style of station design. It is for this reason that so many Londoners imagine that the Underground was essentially a creation of the 1920s and 1930s. After the Great War there many proposed extensions to tube lines remained outstanding, having been halted by the shift to a war economy. Economic conditions were now quite different; everything was more expensive. Though the Underground Group was anxious to push out into new territory finding the money proved impossible until, during the first real depression of the interwar period in 1921, the government offered money for schemes to relieve unemployment. Lord Ashfield quickly put forward a proposal to claim government finance for the Underground Group. He secured £5 million to build an extension of the Hampstead Line out to Edgware, to modernize existing lines and to create a new junction at Euston.

The Edgware extension, with its neat little stations designed by the Underground Group's architect, S. A. Heaps, laid the foundations for that district's suburban prosperity. The new line was opened to Hendon Station in 1923 and reached Edgware in the following year. One station on this line, Burnt Oak, remained isolated among fields until the LCC began to build its 'cottage' estate of council houses at Watling in 1926. Under the same unemployment scheme (the Trade Facilities Act of 1921) the Hampstead Line was joined with a modernized City & South London tube at Euston and Camden Town, to form the two branches of the present Northern Line. The contractors, Mowlem, brought in Welsh miners to excavate the tunnels for the complex new junction.

Shortly after the Underground Group began work on the extension to Edgware, it pushed southwards into Southern Region mainline railways' territory with the line from Clapham Common to Morden. Once again this was part of an expansionist policy with lines going out into open country in the belief that new traffic would be generated by the creation of suburbs around stations. But pushing tube lines out into open country was a costly gamble, and Lord Ashfield is reported as saying on the opening of the Morden Line that 14 million passengers a year were needed to make it pay.

As it turned out, the Underground railways did not pay a respectable return on capital. One major reason for this was that they faced such fierce competition from electric trams and, particularly in the 1920s, from motor-buses. The Great War had abruptly stopped the rapid development of the motorbus and it took some time to recover; only 250 were returned to London streets by the War Office after 1918 and the railways and trams at this time carried the great majority of the capital's passengers. But the bus had always been potentially the most lucrative branch of public transport in the capital and quickly reasserted itself as new designs were developed that were more comfortable and could carry more passengers.

In fact, within the Underground Group, which owned both buses and tubes, the former paid the dividend. During the Great War Lord Ashfield had pushed through a 'Common Fund' scheme to which all the branches of

London Transport contributed according to a formula based on the ability to pay. The Fund survived the war and the bus service made the single largest contribution. To some extent this reduced competition among the various services, which Ashfield found so wasteful, but the success of the buses in the early 1920s put a strain on the whole system.

Until 1924 there were no authorized bus routes, and independent operators or 'pirates' could compete with the larger companies wherever and whenever they liked. This led to some extraordinary scenes on the busier streets of the capital, as a pirate bus attempted to get ahead of a 'General' while the 'General' buses tried to get either side of the pirate to 'nurse' it away from passengers. There were even stories of pirates doing U-turns because more passengers were waiting on the other side of the road, and of conductors jumping from their own bus to a 'General' to rob them of fares. Ted Harrison remembered how the pirates operated quite a different sort of service from the 'Generals':

> If you wanted to catch a pirate bus you had to wait at a stop where
> there was about three people, because if you waited at the stop where
> there was just one, he'd whizz past and you wouldn't catch him at all.
> They were just after the crowds of passengers, and if there was a
> General bus in front they'd want to overtake it. They were speedies,
> express buses we called them, because no sooner had they stopped than
> they were away again; you hardly had time to sit down. If you wanted
> to get anywhere quick, you'd use a pirate. They were good drivers, in
> and out of the traffic like nobody's business.

By 1924 there were about 460 pirate buses operating in London, squeezing the profit margins of the 'General' and other large companies. In that year, bus routes were regulated for the first time, but the pirates continued to compete until the 1930s, hoping to attract passengers with convenient schedules and comfort rather than reduced fares. The peak year for the pirates was 1926 when there were more than 550 of them on the road, carrying nearly 200 million passengers. From then on, the independent buses were gradually swallowed up until the coming of the Passenger Transport Board in 1933. But their activities and the relative profitability of buses in general ensured that there was little investment money for new tube lines, even though the great increase in traffic around the capital made this a growing concern.

Once again, government money came to the rescue. In 1929 the newly elected Labour administration offered funds for public utility works to help reduce the number of unemployed. The Underground Group snapped up the opportunity and put forward its proposal to extend the Piccadilly Line from Finsbury Park to Wood Green, Arnos Grove, Southgate and Cockfosters. The expansionist policy was under way again, with thirty thousand free tickets offered to local residents travelling from Arnos Grove after 10am when that station was opened in 1932. And there was a new opportunity for Frank Pick to bring in his 'modernistic' architecture, with stations designed by Charles Holden.

Dipping into the same government unemployment relief kitty, the Metropolitan Railway found the money to improve its stations and rolling stock and to build a new line from Wembley Park to Stanmore, completed in 1932. In fact, in the interwar years, the bulk of the modernization and extension of London's tube system was financed by the Treasury. The great achievement of these years was the co-ordination and modernization of a transport system which was revolutionized by electric traction and motorization before 1914, but which remained archaic in many ways. Travel on London Transport increased enormously and the stations built in the days of Charles Tyson Yerkes could not cope. Frank Pick of the Underground Group was the real genius of the modernization system, and it was his almost fanatical concern with providing London with the best transport system in the world that established the character of the buses and tubes that are now a sadly run-down relic of London Transport in its heyday.

Pick's attention to detail was legendary: he always wrote in green ink so that his missives could be instantly recognized. Though not a very public figure, he personally investigated some aspect of the Underground Group (and later the Passenger Transport Board) activities every week. New Underground stations were designed not only to look pleasing and up to date, but were carefully planned to handle a very heavy traffic flow with maximum efficiency. Escalators, for example, replaced lifts in many central stations in the 1920s and 1930s. Pick's *pièce de résistance* was Piccadilly Circus Station, which had opened in 1906 as an old red-tiled Yerkes model but was hopelessly inadequate for the traffic of the 1920s. Whereas 1.5 million passengers had used the station in 1907, the number had risen to 18 million by 1922. Pick chose the architect Charles Holden for the major rebuilding project in the centre of town: an entirely new labyrinth of tunnels was excavated below Eros in Piccadilly Circus, the statue being removed for safe-keeping for a couple of years while work proceeded. When the new station opened in 1928 it attracted world attention with its Art Deco booking hall, subdued lighting, and shopping arcade. It was the new 'Heart of the Empire' and a specially commissioned painting adorned the interior, showing Piccadilly as the very centre of the world. This was Pick's vision of the Underground system; it was not simply a commercial enterprise, it expressed a utopian vision.

The Underground Group was building itself a new headquarters at 55 Broadway, above St James's Park Station, at the same time as Piccadilly Circus was being redesigned. Again, the architect Charles Holden was brought in, and famous sculptors, including Henry Moore and Jacob Epstein, were commissioned to provide works of art as part of the building's façade. They remain there today, as monuments to Pick's remarkable influence, largely unnoticed by passers-by who are aware only of the stark grey building towering above them.

Most of the redesign of London Transport was carried out before it finally became a public corporation in 1933. Its character was already established, and Lord Ashfield and Frank Pick, the two figures largely responsible for its creation before 1933, were put in control of the London Passenger Transport Board. Since the beginning of the century, the London County Council had been arguing that it was absurd for the capital's transport system to be left in the hands of a mass of competing private operators, and a number of inquiries and committees had recommended much greater co-ordination of services. But any kind of 'nationalization' was anathema.

The creation of a Passenger Transport Board became a possibility in 1929, when the first government in which Labour had a real say was elected, and Herbert Morrison – the leading London Socialist politician of the day – became Transport Minister. He began work immediately to try to bring transport under public control. The fact that he was successful was due largely to Lord Ashfield's willingness to co-operate, for, by the early 1930s, Morrison, the Socialist politician, and Ashfield, the businessman concerned with rationalizing an industry which had never been very profitable, were of similar mind. Ashfield persuaded the Underground Group's shareholders that selling out to a public corporation was the way forward and, without his conviction that the system was best run in this way, public ownership would almost certainly have been delayed until the 1940s.

THE IMPACT OF THE MOTOR CAR

In the 1930s the public transport system was being threatened by the rapidly growing influence of the motor car. Lord Ashfield recognized this and issued warnings to the Transport Board that the motorist was beginning to take traffic away from buses and Underground trains:

> The private car has completely revolutionized passenger transport. It has set higher standards of speed, convenience and even luxury, which must have their reactions on standards to be aimed at by those who provide public forms of passenger transport. Indeed, it may be said that failure to maintain a rising standard of comfort in our services, both rail and road, must have the effect of further increasing the competition of the private car.

As early as 1933, Ashfield told Underground Group shareholders: 'The theatre traffic, which at one time was carried upon the railways and omnibuses, has now largely passed to the private car.' Furthermore, by the 1930s the motor car was beginning to worsen the traffic congestion in central London, already jammed with motorbuses, taxis and goods vehicles. Traffic lights were a rarity until the 1930s; the first set of electric signals in London, operated manually by policemen, were installed in Piccadilly Circus in 1925. White lines dividing lanes of traffic did not arrive until the 1930s and constant road works and slow-moving goods vehicles ensured that the traffic flow was generally slow in the centre of town. However, the great pleasure of those who could afford cars in this period was to bomb out of town onto the country roads, or along the new bypasses that were being built. In 1930, speed limits were lifted completely, there were no driving tests and the roads around London were used as a race track by Bright Young Things who bought cars built for speed. Lady Strickland recalled the madness of those early motoring days:

> My boyfriends, the very rich young men, they had marvellous cars, very fast cars, MGs, Bugattis, Bentleys. Of course, in those days you didn't have to pass a test, a friend took you out on the road a few times to learn the gears, then off you went. They did some terrible things. One friend of mine used to go up a very curvy road near Godalming on the wrong side for a thrill. He was killed quite quickly. Another

one used to go over humpback bridges at seventy for a thrill, risking meeting something in the middle. My uncle tried to drive his MG over a passenger bridge in a railway station and was had up.

After we'd been to three or four nightclubs in evening dress, we'd go down the Great West Road at about eighty, at three or four in the morning in the dark, to Cuckoo Weir near Windsor. I'd slip the dress off and the shoes and swim in all my heavy silver jewellery. And then it started to get light and you had to clamber out with nothing on, it was great fun. My husband used to drive badly when he'd had a bit to drink and I remember threatening to swallow the ignition keys unless he let me drive.

As the motor car replaced horse-drawn vehicles, the number of accidents on the roads rose rapidly. In 1901, just before the first cars began to replace the horse-drawn carriages of the aristocracy, there were 186 fatal road accidents in the London County Council area. By 1929, when the wealthy all had cars and the capital's roads were full of motorbuses and lorries, fatalities reached 1,362 and there were 55,000 injuries. The slaughter was such that in 1934 a new law brought in the 30 miles per hour speed limit and driving tests. But as motorists began to be more effectively controlled, so their numbers rose rapidly. By 1939 there were 2 million cars in Britain, a quarter of them registered in London and the Home Counties. As mass production stepped up, so the price of cars fell. The first £100 British car was the Morris Minor Tourer of 1931, but it was relatively primitive in engineering terms and did not sell widely. The real breakthrough came in 1935 when Ford produced the 'Popular' for £100. Many other models were offered by manufacturers for just over £100, and hire-purchase terms became easier.

London Transport had expanded rapidly between the wars and had become a powerful vehicle for the empire building of Ashfield and Pick because at precisely the time when the need and ability of Londoners to travel more frequently and over longer distances had greatly increased, *public* transport was for the majority the only available means. In America, where mass car ownership arrived much earlier, public transport – particularly the well-organized Inter-Urban rail service – was undermined much sooner. In London, however, public transport retained its dominant position until 1939, by which time London Transport could boast with some justification that it was the best-run system in the world.

CHAPTER TEN

The Battle for the Suburbs

TRAVEL OUT OF London by car or train in any direction, and after about eight to ten miles' journey from the centre you reach a border at which the scenery changes suddenly and completely. It's almost like a geological break in the structure of the rock, with one historical flow of bricks and mortar being deposited and ceasing to expand, while another, later, flow begins. You are leaving the built-up limits of Victorian and Edwardian London, and entering the vast expanse of a very different and much newer London. The skyline is lower, the doors and windows of the houses are smaller, and everything from the tube station to the shopping precinct is built on a reduced scale, so that it has an oddly toy-like quality. You are in semi-detached suburbia.

The very term 'semi-detached' is evocative of a kind of tidy, private, polished, vacuumed way of life, in which the horizon extends no further than the garden shed. It seems to be a denial of the great metropolis it surrounds like a gnome-built reef, and intellectuals and architects have generally dismissed the whole thing as a kind of cultural disaster, without vision or style. In his cuttingly comical classification of building design, *A Cartoon History of Architecture*, Osbert Lancaster dubbed much of it 'By-pass Variegated', a catch-all term for the jumble of mock-Tudor and faintly modernist influences in design. Nobody thinks of suburbia as exciting, except in the sense that it induces in those who hate it a fierce indignation.

But the story of how it was built, and how, during an era largely remembered for its Depression and disappointment, this new suburbia arose at such a rate that it doubled the size of the capital in twenty years, is every bit as intriguing as any episode in London's history. And though the new London that was created may not appear in itself to be a thrilling place, the forces which gave rise to it and the political battles involved were as ferocious as any that took place in the previous century. For the nature and appearance of semi-detached London reflect a historical revolution in social life and policy which began before the First World War, was influenced by the experience of the war itself, and took shape in the troubled years of peace, when fears of a Communist revolution were real, and the propagandist catch-phrase, 'Homes fit for Heroes', had not yet been dismissed as a politician's pipe-dream.

There was, in a sense, a battle for the new suburbs between two political ideals: the first, of public provision for the mass of the population; and the second, of allowing private builders and landowners to provide Londoners with homes. And though there was some doubt in the early 1920s as to which would be dominant, there was no question that private housing was the victor by the end of the period. Of the enormous number of new houses built around London between the wars – something like seven hundred thousand – three-quarters were put up by private builders for homeowners. Though the London County Council began in a confident mood in the twenties to create its own kind of municipal suburbia with funds provided by the government, by the 1930s it had run into a host of social and economic difficulties which forced it to pull back and to put its greatest effort into slum clearance in the centre of the capital. The battle for the suburbs was won decisively by the building society, the landowners and the homeowner.

However, in terms of style and philosophy, both council and private estate building of the period was influenced by the same reforming ideas that had arisen at the end of the nineteenth century in response to the unplanned and often squalid nature of the Victorian city. In the eighteenth century, the larger and wealthier landowners in London had attempted, often with some success, to impose a kind of planning on their estates, forbidding the entry of noxious trades into their new streets and squares and often defending their developments with gates and gatekeepers. But the pressure of London's relatively impoverished majority, as well as the loosening of estate control, combined in the nineteenth century to undermine such planning, and the ideal of *laissez-faire* discouraged any kind of state control in town planning.

The idea that on the fringes of town a pleasant, semi-rural environment could be created for Londoners, away from the smoke and noise of industry, first emerged in the late nineteenth century. An innovative development was built at Bedford Park, Chiswick, as early as 1878. Here you can see the beginnings of what would evolve into the semi-detached house. But in 1898 the concept was crystallized by Ebenezer Howard in his book *Garden Cities of Tomorrow* in which he analysed the advantages and disadvantages of town and country. The first provided excitement, entertainment and jobs; the second offered natural beauty, a healthy environment and cheaper housing. The town was polluted and overcrowded; the country did not provide jobs or entertainment. Howard's garden city would offer the best of both worlds in a planned environment which kept home and work apart, but not too far so that the misery of daily commuting would be minimized.

What Howard proposed was not suburban development but quite new towns around London. These would have a population limited to about 30,000 people of all social classes, and would be surrounded by a 'Green Belt' separating them from the built-up area of London. He would have liked government backing to carry out his dream of building such places, but before 1914 the state did not provide funds for putting up houses or towns. So Howard got private backing for his ventures at Letchworth, begun in 1903, and Welwyn Garden City, where building started in 1920.

Howard's vision was immediately appealing and, in a diluted form, influenced other pre-war developments, such as the privately built Hampstead Garden Suburb, begun as the new Hampstead Underground Line was being extended into the fields of Golders Green in 1907. It also influenced a mock-Tudor revival in the early years of the twentieth century that expressed a nostalgia for a lost world of rustic innocence and sturdy country folk.

In the public sphere, too, Howard's ideals were having some effect. For example, the London County Council in the early 1900s began a policy of building new garden suburb-style estates on the edges of London at Norbury and White Hart Lane, Tottenham. These were the prototypes of the two styles that would flourish in the interwar years and dominate London's ever-expanding suburban landscape. On the one hand there would be largely unplanned speculator suburbs for those who could afford a semi-rural retreat, fresh air and the modern conveniences of a new home. And on the other there would be 'cottage' style estates – often carefully planned and architect-designed but much more modest in their architecture and amenities – provided for the working classes to rent by the LCC and local councils.

But the First World War put an end to building altogether and this hiatus would ultimately ensure that Victorian and interwar styles of building would look so very different from each other, for London did not begin to grow again until the 1920s, when the world had changed.

SOCIAL UNREST AND THE HOUSING CRISIS

As nothing had been done during the war to improve the conditions of the poor, and hardly any housing of any kind had been constructed, there was a serious shortage of homes in 1918. During the four years of the war rent strikes by militant munitions workers had managed to win a freeze on rents in poorer housing, and at the lower end of the market had taken away any incentive landlords may have had – which was not much – to provide rented accommodation for working people. Shortly after the war, this rent freeze was extended to higher income groups, in recognition of the fact that there was a desperate shortage of private, rented accommodation for the middle classes and that without such a constraint, landlords could have charged what they liked.

Prices had risen steeply, and there was a shortage of raw materials as well as labour, which made house building costly and difficult. There was little incentive, moreover, for people to invest in housing for rent. Before 1914 it was quite common for small investors to take out a mortgage on a house which was then rented to someone else. The mortgage incurred a fixed rate of interest over an indefinite period and could be sold at any time. After the war, not only rents, but the interest paid on such mortgages, was frozen. Investing in property was no longer 'safe as houses' as the saying had been before 1914. It appeared unlikely, therefore, that private developers would be able to build the 'Homes fit for Heroes' that were promised in return for the sacrifices of the war. This presented the government with a serious problem for, unless something was done to improve housing conditions, there seemed a real prospect of serious social unrest or even a revolution. The First World War had involved the effort of the whole nation – including women who took over armaments work, helped to run the transport system and kept industry going – and people had been led to expect something in return. The situation was made even more worrying for the government because it felt it could no longer depend on the traditional loyalty of the army to quell any major disturbances. After 1916, when conscription was introduced, it was no longer a professional band, but a mass of ordinary men, still armed until they were demobilized, and therefore potentially dangerous. Fears were heightened by a wave of mutinies and soldiers' strikes in 1919, by men frustrated with the delay in their return to civilian life.

In addition, race riots against immigrant groups who settled in ports like London after the war, youth riots against the police on the capital's streets, and a police strike for better pay and conditions all seemed to point to an impending breakdown of law and order immediately after the war. And, of course, this was an era of revolutions in Europe (the most disturbing of which for the British ruling class was the Russian Revolution of 1917) and politicians like Lloyd George were frightened that shattered dreams of a better life might trigger a similar Socialist revolution at home.

It was against this background that for the first time in history a British government decided to put national funds into house building. In 1919, what became known as the Addison Act – after the Minister of Health who initiated it – was passed, giving generous grants to local authorities to put up new housing; any cost above a one penny rate was borne by the government. In effect, this was a *carte blanche* for councils to build as many houses as they wanted, and a great many took up the offer with enthusiasm. Among them was the single largest housing authority in the capital, the London County Council, which not only began to extend its existing pre-war estates on the fringes of London, but also went out to buy new land to plan new estates.

A special study commissioned in 1918 from the Liberal MP Sir Tudor Walters had recommended a very high standard of house construction, with a bathroom for each unit, and a low density of building limited to twelve houses to the acre. Armed with all the money they needed, and some of the ideals of the garden city movement, as well as instructions to produce high-quality dwellings, the LCC set to work. In 1920, an estate was begun in Roehampton in south-west London, on the site of what had been a private park owned by an American financier. In the same year, building began at Bellingham near Catford in south London and at Becontree in Essex, on open land way out to the east of London. Of these, Becontree was to become by far the largest – in fact the single biggest council development in the world.

Other London councils took advantage of the generous Addison Act, and between 1919 and 1922, something approaching 30,000 local authority houses were built in Greater London, representing 60 per cent of all housing put up in the period, as compared with only 6 per cent built by councils before 1914. The quality as well as the quantity of council house building in this period was high. As the average houses had three or four bedrooms, an inside toilet and bathroom, hot and cold running water, and front and back gardens, they must have seemed idyllic for those leaving the run-down rented accommodation of inner London. The 624 houses completed at Roehampton under the Addison Act are good examples of the standard of building achieved in this short-lived period, when the 'Homes fit for Heroes' dream appeared to be coming true after all.

But in 1921, the dream ended as abruptly as it had begun. An economic crisis led to cuts in public spending, and the generous subsidies for council housing that had alarmed the Treasury were withdrawn. Councils, which had been spending at a tremendous rate during the two-year bonanza of the Addison Act, some buying properties built by private builders for £1,000 and renting them to tenants, had to cut back. Never again in the interwar period did they provide the generous kind of accommodation of the early Roehampton houses, though subsidies were renewed, and then withdrawn, as the political climate changed in the twenties and thirties. And all the time there was a belief among Conservatives that private builders could solve the housing problem.

From 1919, subsidies were offered to builders putting up cheap semis for rent or sale, and in 1923 this aid to the homeowner was increased as grants became more generous and the government made it easier for people to get mortgages on lower-priced housing by allowing councils to offer them or to guarantee payments to building societies. In a period when private building was still in the doldrums this was important for its survival, and represented a critical shift of finance and encouragement away from council housing and towards the private homeowner.

Nevertheless the 'cottage' estates begun by the LCC on the fringes of London continued to expand under new laws varying in their generosity and effects. It took eighteen years to complete the vast Becontree Estate, with a railway line built through it to carry building materials up from the Thames, and fifty miles of roads laid out as it pushed north and eastwards into Essex. By the time it was finished, Becontree had a population of nearly 120,000 and was already bigger than many English provincial towns – Bath, for example. Though the uniformity of housing of the estate was often a cause for criticism, the ever-changing laws on subsidies ensured considerable variation in style; generally speaking, as time went on houses became smaller and less convenient: hand basins in the bathrooms, which were standard fittings in the Roehampton houses, were no longer provided.

However, throughout the 1920s, the LCC continued to pursue a policy of buying land on the outskirts of the capital, beyond its own boundaries, to establish new cottage estates. It was able to do so because the Wheatley Act, passed by the Labour government in 1924, gave relatively generous subsidies for council house building. The LCC began to build estates at Watling in north London, on the route of the tube line extension to Edgware, at White City in west London, and to the south near Morden, on an estate named St Helier after a former LCC councillor. These estates continued to expand until the early 1930s, but by that time the council building boom on the fringes of London was well and truly over. State-funded suburbia had run into many difficulties – for example, living out in the suburbs and paying higher rents and travelling costs proved prohibitively expensive for many working-class people. But, most important, council housing was unable to compete with private housing, into which the nation's small investors poured their money.

The peak year for local authority building had been 1927, but it had already been overtaken by private building, which by chance had benefited from the very same economic and political twists and turns which first put money into council housing, then took it out again. For the building of London's private, semi-detached suburbia was not simply the result of the rise of an ideal of a quasi-rural existence among the moderately well-off middle classes: it was made possible and encouraged by an economic revolution, in which a large part of the nation's investments were poured into housing.

THE RISE OF THE BUILDING SOCIETIES

Before 1914, only a very small proportion of English people owned their homes. People rented their housing, whatever their social class, and many put their savings into property for a small but steady return. After the Great War, as we have seen, that system collapsed as far as new building was concerned because of the freeze on rents and on the interest from mort-gages, and because of the high cost of building. However, since the eighteenth century a building society movement had been developing in Britain, its origins tracing back to friendly societies and freehold societies. These were relatively small groups of people who got together to acquire property and build houses for one reason or another.

The freehold societies, for instance, had originally been set up as a means to win the vote, which was only enjoyed by the owners of plots of land worth forty shillings (£2). Many of these societies were wound up after a few years, but others remained in existence after the founders had acquired their property and so called themselves *permanent* building societies. Though these societies had been established originally to encourage or enable relatively small groups of artisans and middle-class people to become property owners, they began to attract investors who wanted a safe place to salt away their money.

But the virtual disappearance of house building for rent after 1918 and the loss of all kinds of overseas investment brought about by the war greatly increased the incentive to invest in building societies. There were tax break too, allowed by a government keen to encourage home ownership. A private deal between the Inland Revenue and the building societies gave them an advantage over rival forms of investment.

Immediately after the war, the largest building societies had been located in the North of England. But a series of amalgamations, as well as the steady take-off of house building in the South, changed the situation. By the 1930s half of the biggest societies were established in the South. Throughout the 1920s, the amount of money available for private house building for sale therefore increased steadily, and the number of people to whom home ownership appealed grew with it. This was for a number of related reasons.

First, the number of white-collar workers, clerks and lower-grade professionals multiplied, creating, in effect, a middle class that was much larger but rather poorer on average than its Victorian counterpart. For this emerging social group, domestic servants were a luxury. The young girl who might have become a maid-of-all-work and cook found that there were many rival jobs in industry, catering and hotels which pushed up her wages. Whereas the wealthier families of the West End were able to hang on to a living-in staff of maids and cooks, the middle class in general rapidly gave up the employment of servants.

At the same time, the age of marriage fell steadily, so that the number of new households – that is, husband and wife wanting to set up a separate home from their parents – rose, while the number of children in the average family fell. The result was that there were more but smaller households, in search of smaller, more convenient, housing.

Buying a home and investing in a building society are two sides of the same coin and the appeal of exchanging rented accommodation for a 'home of one's own' was heightened by the feeling of financial uncertainty that many middle-class people experienced in the interwar years. So by the mid-1920s, the supply of money for home ownership, as well as the demand, were created by much the same social and economic forces. The first slump, in 1921, followed by the Depression of 1929–31, greatly increased the attractions of investment in building societies, as the future of manufacturing industry seemed to be so uncertain.

So the idea of home ownership caught on, and the building of private suburban houses grew steadily after 1922, rapidly outstripping the output of local authorities. Land was relatively cheap on the outskirts of London because agriculture was depressed, and the large landowners one by one began to sell plots to builders. And just as the building societies grew in size, so did a number of building firms, many of whom moved from the North of England to cash in on the London market. Taylor Woodrow, Costain, Laing and Wimpey were among those who expanded in the inter-war years during the house building bonanza.

THE END OF THE LCC RURAL IDYLL

From about 1926 onwards, as the new machinery for building private suburbia for home ownership was gathering momentum, the LCC's attempts to create idyllic, semi-rural 'home and hearth' settlements on the fringes of London were running into trouble. The LCC planners and architects were proud of their achievements, and in their way had taken considerable care in house design, within the constraints imposed by the ups and downs of government financial support. But the planners' vision had not been matched on the ground, for the people who went to live in the new estates were confronted with many difficulties, even though the houses they lived in were far superior to anything they had known before.

In fact, it was not the poorest of Londoners who were allowed to move to the 'out-county' estates in the first place. A whole constellation of factors combined to prevent the poor from escaping from the inner-city slums. Those applying for new accommodation were required to provide a regular and punctual record of rent payments and the visiting LCC inspector would check the rent book to determine this. He would also note whether or not the family was of clean and respectable appearance – this was widely accepted as the litmus test of good character, which in turn was likely to influence whether or not a family would be good tenants on the cottage estates. The LCC understandably wanted to recruit respectable tenants who could be relied on to give the lie to the middle-class fear that their suburbs were being invaded by hordes of roughs. But poor families, almost by definition, frequently got into rent arrears during seasonal slumps and hard times and it was a constant and sometimes unsuccessful struggle to keep large families and overcrowded rooms looking respectable on a shoe-string budget. Many poor families, then, fell at the first hurdle.

But many more families were to be excluded by the ruling – rigorously imposed in the early 1920s – that their income had to be five times greater than the amount they had to spend each week on rent, rates and fares to work. The rents themselves were quite high – on average 11–15s a week in the 1920s. So were transport costs, which could frequently mount up to 10s a week since most estates were essentially 'out-county' dormitories, situated several miles away from where most breadwinners actually worked. This was particularly marked in Becontree where there was only one station, located in the first part of the estate to be built, leaving the rest for years without adequate transport into London, where nearly everyone worked. As the majority of unskilled and semi-skilled workers in central London earned only about £3 a week at this time, large numbers had simply no chance of qualifying for a council cottage.

Also, in the first years, there were few or no schools on the new estates, partly because of the opposition of local education authorities to LCC cottage estate schemes (they were not keen to spend money educating exported Londoners and were often sluggish in their provision). So hundreds of children spent months or years roaming the streets when they should have been at school. Thus the suburban council tenant was stranded in a vast and often inhospitable environment without the economic means to do anything about it. And there was no single authority within the Greater London area to co-ordinate transport, education, health and housing in such a way that the 'garden city' ideal was even approached. As a result there was a massive turnover of tenants on the early estates, sometimes as high as 20 per cent a year.

At the same time, opposition to LCC 'out-county' estates was often fierce. Local authorities outside the county area did not want poor people billeted on them, as this lowered the tone of their area, threatened to increase the rate burden and might discourage better-off people from moving in. In 1924, for example, the LCC tried to buy some land in Edgware and, despite the fact that it was not the poorest of Londoners who would ever be offered homes in such a district, the *Golders Green Gazette* was quick to respond: '. . . this will lead to a big slum development;

impairing the good work already in hand in the north of the Chandos estate, and completely "knocking out" any chance of private residential development at Burnt Oak.'

Often local authorities in these outlying districts were prepared to house what they thought of as their 'own' working classes in their council houses, but they did not want the LCC's poor. Thus when the LCC began to expand the Downham Estate, near Bromley, local residents objected at an inquiry saying: 'Such a scheme will reduce the respectability of the . . . streets by inundating the neighbourhood with working classes.'

In fact, in 1926 the sensitive residents of a private estate abutting the southern edge of Downham took the law into their own hands and actually built a brick wall across a road that led straight from the private part of the street to the council houses. Bromley Council refused to co-operate with LCC demands for its demolition and it was not pulled down until the early years of the Second World War when it impeded emergency services. The inconvenience and bad feeling caused by this 'Berlin Wall' were recalled by Betty Trigg:

> It was about seven feet high and it had broken glass on the top. Well, when I was a child I lived in the council houses and we used to climb over the wall because we used to scrump apples and throw things up at the conker trees to get the conkers down – there were trees over on the Bromley side, you see. And of course they didn't like us doing that; we got shouted at. As I grew older I realized how inconvenient the wall was for the mothers, because to catch the bus to Bromley they had to do a detour with the wall being there.
>
> I used to live in the house next to the wall on the council side. One day a young girl decided it wasn't right to have a wall up there when there was a war imminent and she decided she'd start knocking a lump off it. I suppose there were about a dozen teenagers around her, encouraging her, but the police came and stopped her.

The story of the Downham Wall is a small but graphic illustration of the kind of opposition the LCC and its tenants faced in territory regarded not only by private residents and local authorities, but by many Conservative politicians as well, as the preserve of the middle classes. In fact the LCC, dominated politically by the Conservative Municipal Reform Party until 1934, had incorporated this notion in its original plans for cottage estates: one of the four basic principles it adopted was to take into account the possible detrimental effects on middle-class areas of large-scale working-class developments.

Partly as a result of these sorts of difficulties, by the late 1920s the LCC planners seemed to have a change of heart and they began to think again in terms of rehousing the poor in the centre of town, not in 'cottages' but in grand blocks of flats. This in many ways provided the fashionable architect of the day with a more interesting challenge. But here the LCC still experienced problems in finding the sites on which to build: land assembly in the centre of town was not easy. So when in 1929 a Labour government came to power at Westminster, launched a slum-clearance drive, and put money back into the system, the LCC valuers set out again on a land hunt on the suburban fringes of the capital. But they were far too late. The slump of 1929–31 gave building societies a tremendous boost, as they became the easiest, safest and most profitable place for investors to put their money.

HOW THE BUILDING SOCIETIES GREW

The story of the Abbey Road Building Society provides a colourful example of the building society boom. Formed in 1874, it took its name from its first address, Abbey Road, NW6. The founders were members of the Free Church and met in a schoolroom attached to the chapel. By the outbreak of war in 1914 the Society had assets of £750,000. By 1925, assets had increased to £3.5 million, and it was developing rapidly into a modern-style building society, drawing funds from a wide range of investors and advertising itself extensively to both investors and borrowers. It had grown to such a size by 1927 that it moved out of Abbey Road and built a new headquarters in Upper Baker Street. Between 1929 and 1935 its assets rose dramatically from £19.1 million to £46.1 million and, outgrowing its headquarters yet again, it moved in 1932 to another head office in the street, the clock tower of which was its familiar landmark until a new head office was built. It amalgamated with the National, to become Abbey National, in 1944 and since the war has had many incarnations, floating on the stock exchange in 1989 and finally being bought by a Spanish bank in 2004.

The Woolwich founded earlier, in 1847, was a substantial local society by the turn of the century, its strength founded on the contributions of working men from Woolwich Arsenal. It too took off after the First World War, its assets rising from £1.6 million to £27.1 million by 1934. It began to open branches all over London, in the City, in Ilford and Romford in Essex, in Finsbury Park, Ealing and many other expanding semi-detached suburbs. A system of builders' 'pools' was agreed whereby the developer of an estate would underwrite the initial cost of acquiring houses so that the first-time buyer – as most people were – had to put down only 5 per cent, instead of 20 per cent, of the cost. At the same time, building society propaganda stressed the stupidity of paying rent. One builder, Laing, estimated that the pooling system tripled the rate of house sales, and by the 1930s the whole private housing system was thriving.

Whenever a new electric railway station opened, as on the Edgware or Morden Lines in the 1920s, semi-detached suburbia would develop at an astonishing rate. In south London, it was not uncommon for a developing builder to put up the money to make a contribution to the building of a railway station that would open up land for building. Houses were built along the new arterial roads in north, west and east London, along bypasses – anywhere that promised some access to the centre of town and to the local shopping precincts that sprang up at some focal point in the unplanned developments. For example, soon after the opening of the Kingston Bypass in 1927, it became lined with rows of spec'-built houses, as well as shops, pubs and factories. This came to be known as the problem of 'ribbon development', which was a public nuisance for many reasons, not least because it blocked through-roads with local traffic and pedestrians. Eventually – but too late to prevent most of London's arterial roads from being sandwiched in by spec'-built housing – this nightmare of unplanned development was controlled by special legislation, the Ribbon Development Act of 1935, which gave local councils the power to restrict frontage developments along main roads.

A further boost to this building boom was given by the fall in the price of raw materials during and after the slump, and by a lowering of the wages of building workers who – despite all this activity – were in constant supply as industry outside London declined. This pool of unemployed or under-employed labourers enabled employers to demand a long working week of forty-seven hours, and to keep wage rates down to a meagre 1s 8d an hour. When a job came to an end, or when depression hit the building industry in the winter months due to bad weather, some of these men who helped to build the new London suburbs – navvies, brickies, painters and plasterers

– found themselves on the bread line. John Neary was one of the many Irish labourers who worked on London's building sites in the days when you could be hired and fired on a daily or weekly basis. He recalled:

> You'd tramp from one building site to another, and when you got there you'd sleep rough out in the fields sometimes – that would impress the foreman that you were tough and he'd be more likely to give you work. I used to dig manholes and trenches, and it was tough digging manholes. It would be six foot square and each man was given a manhole to dig and very often the last man to dig his manhole was fired. And when you were digging a trench, if you were working alongside one of the navvies, great big hefty men that could down twenty pints a day, they might try and 'dig you out', dig much more than you, and if they did that and showed you up, you might have to go as well.
>
> It was a very hard life, in the mornings, about one minute to eight, the foreman would come out and let out a big shout, particularly the Irish foremen – they were demons. He'd shout, 'Jump to it, you so and so's', and people never answered back, and very often he would go along the trench and look down and he'd shout, 'If I don't see steam rising off your bloody backs I'll know you're not working'. And we'd always be stripped to the waist, whatever time of year it was, because they said it was a bad sign if a man worked with his jacket on, he wasn't sweating.

All sorts of people moved into the building business, and estate agents' clerks frequently set up on their own in an effort to make a fortune in the boom. Scouts scoured the countryside in search of new sites. And house prices actually fell as a result of fierce competition between builders and an eventual over-supply, with average prices of £500 and some as low as £395. Builders began a massive campaign to sell estates, and houses came to be marketed in almost the same way as other mass-produced consumer goods that were coming on the market. New developments were advertised with firework displays, concerts, visits from politicians and in one case, in Surbiton, a free car in the garage for the purchaser of a diminutive detached house. Film and radio stars were brought in to give a glamorous launch to very ordinary estates and a whole range of newspaper advertising in the mass circulation dailies was used to lure the middle classes into the suburbs.

Among the free gifts on offer to purchasers were railway season tickets, fridges and furniture. Modern Homes Ltd actually tried to entice buyers to its relatively expensive estate at Joel Park in Pinner, where houses were on sale from £850 to £1500, with an electric refrigerator, washing machine, cooker and seven fires free in each home.

This building bonanza spawned a great variety of private estates. The 'up-market' ones, comprising substantial semi-detached and detached residences, were concentrated for the most part in London's northern and north-western suburbs; for example in Edgware, Southgate and Northwood. Characteristically these would be cottage-style houses made up of a mixture of period decorative features, the most popular of which were mock Tudor. Timbered gables, elaborate porches with red-tiled roofs, lattice and coloured glass windows, oak doors with Gothic panels, plus the inevitable bay windows, were all highly fashionable and helped to evoke a rural-romantic image. The period styling continued indoors with oak-panelled halls and dining rooms.

The keynote of the private interwar estates was individuality, and spec' builders with a keen eye for the middle-class market made architectural variety a major selling point, ensuring that every home could boast some unique decorative detail, however insignificant. Many homes would be given their own names, such as 'Dunroamin', 'Coze-cot', 'The Gables', and so on, for this was the land of the 1930s-style successful Mr Pooter, whose house was not only the sentimental centrepiece of his life, but also a supreme statement of his family's social status. The whole enterprise has been much criticized – both at the time and since – for its banality, pretentiousness and ugliness, but there is little doubt that the builders gave homeowners what they wanted, namely an 'olde worlde'-style retreat, and definitely not the clean lines and concrete and glass of the modern movement.

There was also a large potential demand for more 'down-market' properties. With firms such as New Ideal Homesteads making available houses in places like Sidcup for a £5 deposit and as little as 8s 1d a week repayment, home ownership became a real possibility for many lower-middle-class families and also for a substantial minority of working-class people. The proportion of working-class homeowners rose from around 5 per cent in 1929 to 14 per cent in 1939. They would live in much smaller semis or in short terraced rows, with appropriately scaled-down architectural details and sometimes just one reception room and two bedrooms. Even clerks, whose salaries and security nose-dived with the financial crashes of the period, could just about scrape together enough for the deposit and mortgage repayment on a cheap home in the new suburbs – as Dora Dyer recalled:

> My husband was chief teller in a private American bank, and when the Wall Street Crash happened he lost his job. From then on he was a tally clerk in the docks and we had very little money coming in. Anyway, I couldn't stand it, living in our rooms any more, it was driving me mad, we lived just off the Old Kent Road and it was rough around there. I knew they were building a lot of houses down Sidcup way, so I went down one day. I saw a house I liked – it was £250 but it was yours for £5 down – then I came back that evening and told my husband we were moving. He said, 'All right, you can move but you'll move on your own, you know we've got no prospects at the moment.' Anyway, he eventually agreed, and I had a friend with an open-top lorry. We tied what little furniture we had on with ropes, and when we pulled up outside our new home you should have seen the look on our neighbours' faces, they were horrified, thought we were rough. I only had one room downstairs and one bedroom furnished, all the rest was floorboards, but we managed.

THE ROMANCE OF THE PLOTLANDERS

But even the very low mortgage repayments on the cheapest of houses were often too much for those earning the average wage of £3 10s a week. Fares, rates and other expenses, in addition to the mortgage repayment, might amount to nearly half of that sum. Even at rock-bottom prices, the suburbs remained therefore the home of better-off Londoners – with one romantic, and little-known, exception. There were, after the Great War, some Londoners who had neither the means to buy a suburban house, nor the qualification or inclination to become council tenants. Yet they had been gripped by the suburban impulse which swept the capital, and longed, like so many after the war, for a 'home and hearth' in some peaceful rural setting.

These were the 'plotlanders', suburban frontiersmen and women who set out to build their dream home in the country with their own hands. They might live in London during the week, in miserable privately rented accommodation, but at weekends they could set out for the countryside, usually beyond even the most far-flung of the railway suburbs and council estates, to a plot of their own. Farmers in Essex, in particular, were only too keen to sell off poor parts of their farms during the agricultural depression and these patches of pasture could be bought for a few pounds. To begin with, that was all that was there, until the plotlander pitched a tent and, bit by bit, began to build.

To places in Essex like Pitsea, Peacehaven, Laindon and Canvey Island they carted out bits of timber, often carrying building materials on bicycles. They created shanty towns which caused much greater shocks to the idealistic planners of the day than the sprouting suburbs proper. Anything with a roof might serve as a holiday and weekend home: disused railway carriages, garden sheds, ex-army huts and bus bodies. In time, a more elegant edifice might take shape and the family might settle there. Some of these shanty towns became quite large, attracting a rather unusual social mix of bohemians, back-to-the-landers, and working-class families with the homeowner's pride but without the resources for a 'proper home'. These shanty towns were fondly remembered by many Londoners, like Lydia Bonnett:

> I remember the first I heard of a place called Dunton. We were living in Hackney in 1924, and Dad came home from work one day and said Mr Sawyer, his foreman, had shown him an advert in the *Hackney and Kingsland Gazette* advertising plots of land there for five pounds a plot. They both went out there at the weekend, and Mr Sawyer bought some but Dad couldn't afford it. Anyway, the next weekend Dad took Mum to Dunton and she fell in love with the place. Secretly she got a part-time job in a jam factory and saved up the money, then without Dad's knowledge she bought some plots next to the foreman's. The next time they went to Dunton, Dad was looking at these plots and Mum said:
> 'You would like some of those wouldn't you Bill?'
> 'Yes.'
> So Mum said, 'Don't just stand there, get cracking, you want some posts and barbed wire, it's yours, I've just bought them.'
> After this the whole family, we'd go to Dunton at weekends whatever the weather. We used to travel to Laindon railway station then walk. Dad bought a bell tent, and we used that in the summer. But when it was very cold a permanent resident there, a Mrs Taylor in First Avenue, used to let us sleep on the floor in her small bungalow. I

loved sleeping in the tent and being out there – the fresh air, the dawn chorus and the fields everywhere, that all made up for the lack of amenities. Mum would cook the meals on an oil stove.

Then as time went by, Mum and Dad saved up a bit more money and brought out some building materials, and they started to build their little bungalow hoping when it was finished they would retire there. I've seen my mother with a pair of Dad's old trousers on, climb up a ladder to the roof and sit astride while Dad handed up the ridge tiles for her to fix and cement along the roof; those ridge tiles were very heavy. She was more at home with a trowel than a rolling pin! We all mucked in to help build it and we had many happy times there going out on Friday night and coming back late Sunday.

In the end the post-1945 planners cleared most plotlands away: Basildon New Town in Essex was built on the site of one of the largest of the settlements. Most of the plotlands were, however, established well away from London's central suburban battleground, which still hugged the areas served by transport to the centre. It was in these non-central areas that the LCC, with new money from the Labour government of 1929, set out once again to look for land to build more cottage estates. In its first phase of 'out-county' building in the 1920s, the LCC had effectively been excluded from Hertfordshire, Kent and Surrey; the Becontree estate in Essex on London's eastern fringes, which were traditionally working class, had absorbed the single greatest concentration of the Council's building. Now, in the 1930s, despite the injection of funds from the government, the LCC seemed doomed to be thwarted in their plans. Land prices had risen too sharply and the large landowners were now unwilling to sell to the LCC. In Stanmore, Middlesex, for example, any LCC bid for land was followed rapidly by a counter-bid from private interests. After a number of failed attempts the LCC abandoned the suburbs to private enterprise and looked into rehousing slum dwellers in the centre of London.

THE RISE OF THE INNER-CITY COUNCIL BLOCK

'Up with the houses and down with the slums' was the Labour Party slogan in 1934, when for the first time the Party, led by Herbert Morrison, gained control of the LCC. But the houses they built were blocks of flats, giant developments described by a contemporary critic as 'worthy of Socialist Vienna'. Morrison said he still believed in the garden city, or satellite town ideal, but it was not practicable now. Even when it turned its attention to inner London, the LCC was not able to build where housing was most needed. Many of the more radical boroughs like Bermondsey, Finsbury, Fulham and Woolwich had their own extensive housing programmes and built blocks of flats themselves: they felt they did not need the LCC. Other boroughs were dominated by the Conservative Municipal Reform Party and would not allow the LCC in, or allowed only small-scale slum clearance, whether they were tackling the problem themselves or not. Whereas Bermondsey, a Labour-controlled council, built 2,700 dwellings between 1929 and 1938, the Conservative boroughs of Kensington, Paddington, Holborn and St Marylebone built only several hundred between them.

The LCC was able to operate extensively in only a few places, where there was no rival Labour programme and opposition to their presence was weak. Almost half of the LCC's new tenement blocks were put up in only four boroughs: Southwark, Lewisham, Wandsworth and Lambeth, where land was available at reasonable prices and there was sympathy from the local Labour parties. So in the 1930s, the great bulk of the LCC's programme – as well as local authority housing as a whole – was in the form of flats, not houses. And it was nearly all within the LCC's own administrative boundaries. At the same time, far from seeking to build on the remaining open land of London's outer suburbia, Herbert Morrison resurrected the concept of the 'Green Belt'. This had originally been conceived as part of an entirely new structure for the capital whereby it would be ringed by satellite towns, separated from the central core by countryside.

Morrison's Green Belt was rather different – simply the preservation of the countryside which for one reason or another had survived the suburban building boom. The LCC offered county councils in these areas up to half the cost of acquiring land on the condition that it would remain open, and made available £2 million for this purpose. This proposition was taken up much more enthusiastically than previous attempts to rehouse London's poor in such areas and by 1939 about 13,000 acres had been acquired.

By this time, however, much more dramatic political events were bringing the expansion of London to an end. With the declaration of war in 1939 the rate of building slowed down, grinding to a complete standstill a year later. Before this the threat of war and the concern about the vulnerability to air attack of such a vast capital had, in fact, provided useful propaganda for selling suburban houses. Builders advertised houses in so-called 'safety zones' with concrete shelters provided in back gardens. One enterprising builder in Southall supplied windows with seventeen hinges that could be tightened to form a seal in the event of a gas attack.

But it was the last gasp of the private building boom that had won the interwar battle of the suburbs and had covered the countryside around London with wave after wave of bricks and mortar. There was a growing realization that the spec'-built suburban dream had serious drawbacks – its haphazard growth was responsible for appalling land wastage, the destruction of valuable open spaces and traffic chaos. When, after the war was over, the Town and Country Planning Act was passed in 1947, the spec' builder was to be controlled to a much greater extent by local and central government.

CHAPTER ELEVEN

Ideal Homes

THE FACT THAT semi-detached London built between the wars looks and feels so very different from the capital's Victorian and Edwardian fabric is a reflection not simply of developments in building styles influenced for instance by the garden city movement. This London could not have grown so rapidly had it not enshrined an evolution in lifestyle which the speculative builder attempted to cater for in his efforts to sell houses, and the London County Council sought to encourage in the planning of its semi-rural cottage estates. For the way of life that emerged in the new London built in the 1920s and 1930s represented a clear break with the past for both middle- and working-class people.

The home, and in particular a new concept of the ideal home, was at the heart of this change in lifestyles. The Victorian middle classes did, of course, idealize the home and family life. But electricity, the radio, the reduction in the size of families and, as far as middle-class households were concerned, the disappearance of resident servants and the maid-of-all-work gave the home a quite different atmosphere during the interwar years. For the better-off Londoner, buying a home for the first time, the semi-detached house in the suburbs meant an essentially servant-free house, wired for electricity, scaled down and rearranged so that it could be run by the housewife on her own or with a minimum of outside help. One or two builders, falling behind the times, did design kitchens to be operated by servants, with no windows looking onto the garden (to ensure the privacy of the owners), only to find that this detail was quickly modified and a hole knocked in the wall to give the housewife a view while washing up. For some of the housewives who spent their lives in these suburban homes it was a dream come true, but others – as we shall see later – found it terribly lonely and depressing.

For poorer London families, moving from rented rooms to council house suburbia in Becontree or Downham meant a more comfortable home life with greater living space, inside toilet and washing facilities and a garden. But – at least to begin with – the move also meant a weakening of community bonds between relatives and neighbours. The sense of community in the new working-class suburbs was often not as intense as it had been in the old inner-city areas, the new pub of the suburbs (whether a mock-Tudor roadhouse or a giant council estate tavern) was a less-frequented and more family-centred sort of place, while the cinema and the radio set trends which transcended locality and class. Llewellyn Smith, editor of the *New Survey of London Life and Labour* compiled in 1929–30, was quite sure that because of the influence of the cinema local working-class accents were becoming less pronounced. And J. B. Priestley thought the same was true of personal appearance, with 'factory girls looking like actresses' – that is, film stars. The old parochialism and the distinctive working-class image of poorer parts of London were breaking down.

In the forefront of the new lifestyle and the consumer revolution of this period – despite the fact that they represented a minority of the population – were the more prosperous middle classes living in the new suburbs. By the mid-1930s they were buying electric cookers, vacuum cleaners, washing machines, electric fires and motor cars, while the majority of the population had to wait until the affluence of the 1950s before they could begin to acquire these amenities. And it was those same middle classes who aspired to home ownership in the greatest numbers and who set the pattern for a more private suburban family life, revolving around the housewife.

In every period in London's history, old ways of life have existed alongside the new. But the contrast between emerging and disappearing lifestyles was particularly sharp in the interwar years, partly because the pace of change was unusually rapid for one section of the community – the middle classes. Upper-class families, though perhaps living in slightly reduced circumstances, could still afford a much grander lifestyle in which domestic servants rather than machines did the work for them. For the many poorer working-class families living in the run-down villas deserted by the middle classes – in places like Finsbury, Hackney and Islington – home life was worlds apart from that in the new suburbs. It often meant sharing a house with one, two or several other families; terrible overcrowding, with all the beds jam-packed into the same room; humping water up the stairs from a standpipe in the back yard for all cooking or washing; and sharing an outside toilet with several other families. Here it was not so much a question of aspiring towards an ideal home but of struggling to keep any sort of home together at all.

The foundations of the new ideal home suburbia were laid before the First World War and its pioneers came from an essentially new class of salaried person: there were the professionals whose ranks doubled nationally from 744,000 to 1,500,000 between 1911 and 1921; there was the rising number of civil servants brought about by the creation of new government departments such as the Ministry of Health and the Ministry of Pensions; and there were more clerical and managerial workers associated with the emergence of big business. London, as always, provided more work than anywhere else in Britain for this new class, and therefore supplied the new suburbanite in greater numbers.

In effect, as a group, the middle class had become much more numerous since the Victorian era, but individually they were relatively less well off than their forebears. The great increase in taxation during the Great War, which remained in force in the 1920s, was one reason. But, more fundamentally, their sheer numbers ensured that they could not sustain the lifestyle of the Victorian person of private means. At the same time, the social aspirations of this middle-income group were moulded in an era when a technological revolution brought about by the development of electricity and the advances of its great competitor, gas, affected the home as much as it did transport and industry.

LABOUR-SAVING DEVICES

Home ownership in itself encouraged a new attitude towards domesticity, while the slogan 'Let electricity be your servant' shifted the emphasis in social status from the employment of maids to the ownership of 'labour-saving' devices, such as cookers, electric irons and vacuum cleaners. Central to this series of social changes was the position of women, for it was the new housewife in command of the servant-free house who was the key figure. And the decline of domestic service – which had been carried out almost exclusively by women – was intimately bound up with the new Ideal Home.

The story of the decline of domestic servants from the turn of the century is rather confused, because the official information on how many there were, and the kind of work they did, is difficult to interpret. Their numbers seem to have reached a peak around 1901, when there were nearly a quarter of a million women in service in the County of London – and certainly more if the whole built-up area is included. Their numbers then began to decline, and the 'servant problem' – always a subject for debate in Victorian times – surfaced as a major social problem, becoming the subject of special government investigation. What confuses the issue here is the fact that 'living-in' servants were to some extent being replaced by part-time daily maids who lived in their own homes and became, statistically speaking, 'invisible'.

The reason for the decline in female servants is not properly understood, but almost certainly the drudgery of the work ensured that if women could find alternative employment, they would. The young maids-of-all-work had a particularly hard time, as the tragi-comedy of Lil Truphet's recollections of her tasks in New Cross before 1914 illustrated:

> I was up at six in the morning and I didn't run in till ten at night, all for five bob a week. I was a slave to the missus. And the job I hated most, two or three morning a week I used to have to vacuum certain rooms. But it wasn't a vacuum like we have today; it was like a bellows. I used to have to push the handle back and forwards with one hand, and with the other hand I used to have to put the nozzle round the carpet to pick up the dirt.
>
> And when each room was done I used to have to take the vacuum down, empty the dirt out of the paper bag and the missus would weigh it and look at it, and if I hadn't got enough dirt she used to make me go back and do it again. So I used to save bags of dirt in the pothouse. If I got a lot of dirt one day, I'd put some in there. So in the pothouse I had all different bags with different colours of dirt in them, taken from different carpets, and if I was a bit short, I'd get the right bag out and top up the dirt before I took it to show her. So I'd get the right quantity of dirt and that used to satisfy her.

Like a great many women of her generation, Lil Truphet was only too thankful when, in 1915, the trades unions and the government reluctantly agreed that they should be employed in munitions work and other formerly all-male occupations:

> Then when the jobs came up in the munitions, I couldn't get out quick enough. It was much more comfortable, it was more money – I was on two or three pounds a week – and with all the girls together we'd have singsongs and make friends, and it was more or less like a jolly party.

The experience of the freedom and camaraderie of the factory provided only a brief liberation, however, for the hundreds of thousands of women who ran the buses, became bank clerks, drove delivery vans and kept the home front going during the Great War. When men returned from the trenches, and the munitions industry closed down, many had to return to their old jobs or seek new ones in industries where male opposition was not strong enough to keep them out. The number of women domestic servants did decline in London, but not as sharply as many imagine. In the LCC area there were still 157,000 in 1921, and in the wealthier boroughs there was no dramatic disappearance of the cook and the 'tweeny' – or maid-of-all-work.

Working conditions had always been much better in richer households with a large staff than in the modest middle-class home, so perhaps this was the main cause. Wages for domestic service were also higher and could compete with factory work. In 1921 a comparison was made by the *New Survey of London Life and Labour* of domestic service in wealthy and middle-class boroughs. In the former, there were still 40 women servants per 100 families, a decline of 25 per cent since 1901, while in the latter there were only 13 per 100 families, representing a dramatic fall of 60 per cent in the same period. This was despite the fact that in the 1920s all kinds of pressures were put on working-class women to stay in domestic service. Former women servants could not get dole money from Labour Exchanges, and were excluded from unemployment insurance schemes, while training schemes for women were concentrated on domestic service.

The survey did not cover the new suburbs, but it was evident that by 1920 a large section of London's middle-class population had no servants at all. And perhaps the main reason for this was that while the middle classes had *increased* in numbers, domestic servants were slowly disappearing. Therefore a new middle-class household set up on marriage would have no expectation of employing a resident maid.

THE HOUSEWIFE AS SERVANT

In this respect, the position of women after the war was crucial. In 1918 the suffragette battle for the vote was partly won – in the sense that women over the age of thirty could now vote for the first time. But this new power was not matched by a liberation of women from a conventional view of their essential role in life. They had shown they could make bombs, repair aeroplanes and accomplish just about any task the average man was asked to do. But that was not the point: all this was unwomanly, as Lil Truphet discovered even before her war work was over. She remembered:

> I was working on the bullets, then I was sent to the danger zone, and you had to wear a trouser suit, it was all khaki colour, and a bonnet cap. Well, all the girls got together and we had our photographs taken in our trouser suits, and my father was proud of it and he showed it to his friends. But my husband-to-be, he showed off, he didn't like me wearing trousers, he thought that was a disgrace. The war was pretty well over by then and they were laying the women off. He came in and saw the overseer lady and said he didn't approve of me working there, it wasn't women's work. And he saw to it that I was dismissed, so I left about a fortnight after.

Although a Sex Disqualification (Removal) Act had been passed in 1919 to provide some protection for women in work, the general ethos was that they should know their place. Whereas working-class women were encouraged to return to domestic service (so as to solve the problems of the middle-class housewife), middle-class women were encouraged to stay at home. For example, in the 21 January issue of *The Times* in 1921 the continued employment of over two thousand women by the War Office was described as a 'monstrous injustice' – they should make way for men. However, single women did manage to consolidate some gains that they had made during the war. This was particularly so in the new light engineering industries, and in clerical work.

The number of women working in the Civil Service had risen to 102,000 from 33,000 during the war. But *married* women were expected to leave their jobs on or before their wedding day. Exactly how and why this bar on married women working came about is not clear. In some instances it was legalized: in the case of the Civil Service in 1921, for example, where single women actually supported the ban as it effectively reduced competition for their jobs. Similarly, in 1924, the London County Council determined that for women employees – which meant clerks, doctors, teachers, and so on – 'the contract shall end on marriage'. Justification for the ban was usually couched in terms of the need for women to raise a family and keep the home happy. And among middle-class and 'respectable' working-class men it became a matter of pride and status that their wife did not go out to work. It was also, of course, a way of ensuring that your dinner was ready when you got home. In the 1930s, Ivy Willis gave up her job as a bookbinder, even though she earned more than her husband and they needed the money. She reflected:

> My husband, just before we were married, said he felt I shouldn't go out to work. He felt he should be able to come home from work and find me there – not the little slave, because we both agreed on this – but I should be home ready to look after him and keep the home tidy. My boss was very angry when I said I would have to leave. He came down to see my husband and begged him to let me stay until somebody was trained to take my place, but my husband said 'No', he wouldn't allow me to go to work.
>
> Every day I'd do my chores – cooking, cleaning and washing – and I used to watch for my husband coming home. Where I lived we could see the tram coming up the hill, and I used to watch for the tram coming at the usual time, and I'd run along the passage and open the door for him. He was what I call a steak and kidney pudding man, so I'd always make sure there was an enormous pie or pudding, and an apple pie or something like that for afterwards, on the table. I'd do everything myself; he didn't even wash up. He used to say he didn't keep a dog and bark himself, so he disagreed with doing anything, unless I was ill. Then he'd be very kind and do the work.

And Lil Rodgers, who worked as a Lyons 'Nippy' in the 1930s, was also pressurized into giving up her job. She remembered:

> I'd been courting for a little while and my husband and I decided to get married. Well, the hours I was working, sometimes it could be ten till six in the evening. If Hubby got home a bit early he didn't appreciate that, he'd be sitting there, because men didn't think much of doing their own meals in those days, and he used to say, 'This is a fine time to come home'. And he kept getting annoyed, he used to say, 'You give that bloomin job up', 'I'm going round my mum's for me Sunday dinners, I'm seeing nothing of you hardly' and 'I don't like the hours you're coming in of a nighttime'.
>
> We quarrelled because I wanted to carry on working, we needed the money and I didn't have any children at that time. But after about

three months he said to me, 'Either give the job up or give me up', which seemed a terrible thing to do in those days, and we discussed it and discussed it, and in the end I gave my job up. He said he found it beneath his dignity to have a wife working, and of course he wanted his meal on the table.

It was such social mores, rather than any legal disqualification, which appear to have been chiefly responsible for the fact that the great majority of married women did not work in the interwar years, whether or not they had children. On the other hand, women were having fewer children; the birth rate in Britain went down steadily from the late nineteenth century, spreading to all but the poorest working-class families by the 1930s. Why the birth rate should have declined in this way, so that the average family size was reduced, from more than five children at the turn of the century to only two by the thirties, is not clear.

As early as the 1870s the better-off middle classes in Britain began to have fewer children, and one of the explanations given for this is that they were trying to maintain a kind of genteel lifestyle with carriages and servants on a barely sufficient income. Children also became more 'expensive' in that they were being educated to a higher level at greater cost. So from the start, the fall in family size was linked to an attempt to maintain a particular lifestyle. Similarly, in the twentieth century, it was the new middle class who had smaller and smaller families, and their decision to do so was probably connected with their desire to have a house of their own and to maintain the new suburban lifestyle, with mortgage repayments and consumer goods.

Large families – except among the very wealthiest – were associated with poverty, and it was the poor who had most children in the 1930s. Though it is difficult to disentangle cause and effect, the creation of the Ideal Home, with an ideal 2.2 children, did go hand in hand with and was part of the desire to enjoy a modest, well-ordered way of living on a small income. And this small family size was achieved by a large number of people by the 1930s, despite the fact that modern contraceptives were not widely used and despite official campaigns encouraging bigger families, for there were fears that the population of Britain was going into decline.

This greatly reduced the burden of motherhood for most women, so that by the 1920s a new being – the lone housewife in her semi-detached home – was being created. A rash of new magazines sprang up, replacing those that had earlier catered for the Victorian lady administering a household staff. The leader in the field in 1922 was *Good Housekeeping*, sold for a shilling. It had been developed in America, where there had always been a shortage of servants, and the concept of the 'housewife' had been created earlier. Among many other monthly magazines that followed there was *Woman and Home* in 1926, *Wife and Home* and *Harper's Bazaar* in 1929. And in the 1930s came the weekly magazines with higher circulations: *Woman's Own* in 1932, *Woman's Illustrated* in 1936, and *Woman* in 1937. The tone and picture of life presented in these publications encouraged what *Woman's Life* in 1920 referred to as 'the return of the feminine type': 'The tide of progress which leaves woman with the vote in her hand and scarcely any clothes upon her back is ebbing, and the sex is returning to the deep, very deep sea of femininity from which her newly-acquired power can be more effectively wielded.'

THE GAS AND ELECTRIC HOME

In the home, this reincarnation of the feminine woman was to have a new source of power, which in time she was expected to wield almost like a specialist domestic technician. It came from electricity and from gas – two industries which fought each other bitterly in the interwar years to capture the attention and admiration of the woman in the servant-free household. By the 1880s, private homes were being lit by electricity, though the equipment was cumbersome and expensive and, as there was no centralized supply system, small generators had to be set up to provide the current. One such was installed in the 1880s in the Grosvenor Art Gallery in Bond Street by Sir Coutts Lindsay; he called in the young Sebastian de Ferranti to develop a private distribution system which carried the excess power by overhead wires to more than three hundred customers, as far away as Regent's Park and the Law Courts.

There were other early electricity power schemes for domestic consumers, such as the small station built for the expensive block of flats, Kensington Court, in the 1880s, but before 1914 most electric power went into transport undertakings. Even in 1918, only about 6 per cent of homes were wired for electricity used almost exclusively for lighting. But in the next few years a very rapid expansion of the industry, both in the manufacture of equipment such as light bulbs, which became cheaper and more efficient, and in the development of wiring systems, brought about a rapid rise in the use of electric power.

Prices and availability varied widely around the country, as the whole supply industry was run by private enterprise or by local authorities, covering only a small patch of territory. However, the creation in 1926 of the Central Electricity Board with powers to pool the industry's resources brought some order to the chaos, and the systematic wiring of new houses was undertaken. Nearly all the semi-detached suburbs of London had electricity laid on, as well as many of the council cottage estates. But, as electricity was more expensive than coal or gas a great many poorer people could simply not afford to use it or have it installed, which was also costly.

The middle-class housewife was the chief target for promotional organizations such as the Electrical Development Association, which in the 1920s and 1930s made a number of films extolling the wonders of the new electric home. *Edward and Edna*, a silent film made by the Association, showed a young couple deciding to get married because the wife-to-be offered to run the all-electric home without a servant. There was, too, the Electrical Association for Women, founded in 1924 which was still offering courses in electricity for £5 a day sixty years later. This organization was set up by Caroline Haslett, who had received an engineering training during the First World War and wanted to consolidate the gains made by women workers. In fact, perhaps inadvertently, it helped to promote not the new woman engineer, but the housewife competent in the use of electricity to run the home. For it was the electricity industry, and its efforts to persuade women to use more and more electrical appliances in the home to make housework easier, that was largely instrumental in creating a view of the housewife as a home-bound 'professional'. *Good Housekeeping* called house-wives the 'craft workers of today'.

An American book, *Scientific Management in the Home* by Christine Frederick, published in Britain in 1920, actually applied the 'time and motion' studies of production-line industry to the kitchen, with diagrams setting out the best layout of equipment. Research was carried out on the number of hours the housewife spent on each task and suggestions were made as to how the workload could be reduced. Cleaning proved one of the most onerous tasks, and the substitution of the coal fires and the coal range in the kitchen with gas and electric appliances greatly reduced the amount of dust in the house. Electric irons cut down the time heating up the old models; vacuum cleaners saved brushing time; electric light meant that dust could be more easily seen and that it could be cleared up later in the day.

In the creation of the Ideal Home, the gas industry fought electricity fiercely. Gas lighting in the nineteenth century had been by naked flame, and the gas mantle, which provided a brighter, more even light, was actually developed to compete with electric light bulbs. Electricity won the battle over lighting and ironing, but cheaper gas was favoured for cooking: by 1939 there were probably about eight or nine gas cookers for every electric one. Heating was still largely by coal fires. By that time, of those houses – about two-thirds nationally – with an electricity supply, nearly all would have electric lighting, 77 per cent an iron, 40 per cent a vacuum cleaner, 27 per cent electric fires, 16 per cent a kettle, 14 per cent a cooker, and fewer than 5 per cent a water heater. Generally speaking, electric appliances remained too expensive for the majority of people, despite the fact that both private companies and local authority suppliers – such as West Ham – had 'assisted' wiring schemes, and hired out equipment from their glossy showrooms.

Not surprisingly, therefore, many modern electric appliances were restricted to middle-class homes. But the suburban housewife's new 'professional' role involved not only taking over some or all of the tasks previously performed by a servant, but also raising standards of comfort and luxury in the home itself. Women's magazines encouraged a concern with style extending from buying 'tasteful' carpets, curtains and furniture, to experimenting with new foods. The overall desired effect – the good taste of the interwar years – was a fusion of modern and historical styles. In the kitchen, new labour-saving equipment like an electric cooker would be set among cottage-style furniture, such as a scaled-down dresser. Similarly, in the living room modern elements like a three-piece suite with an Art Deco couch would be balanced by a Jacobean-style table and chairs with 'twist' legs. And fireplaces, with their characteristic oak or mahogany surround and tiled centrepiece, would combine shapes with historical overtones, perhaps of Aztec altars or Devon cottages, with Art Deco motifs; for instance, the ubiquitous fretwork sunblaze: strips of wood radiating from a disc to represent rays of sunlight.

But the jewel in the crown of the suburban middle-class home was a luxurious or at least a comfortable bathroom. During the 1920s and 1930s the old-style bathroom with its cold white walls and mahogany furniture was transformed into the recognizably modern bathroom suite, with a coloured and enclosed bath, a heated towel rail and tiles replacing the old carpets and wallpaper. It has been argued that this great concern with the bathroom represented a reassertion of an old status symbol of the better-off. In the past the working classes could not afford plumbed-in baths and were always thought to smell, but in the interwar years those who lived on cottage estates were provided with rather primitive, bare-walled bathrooms – thus the stress on luxurious bathrooms could be seen as a new attempt by the better-off to once again differentiate themselves from those beneath them on the social scale. Many, however, who lived in the run-down inner areas still had to make do with a zinc bath in front of the fire.

THE IDEAL HOME AND THE REALITY FOR THE POOR

So, an extraordinary range of lifestyles existed in London in the interwar years. In the upper-middle-class household of the West End, Sunday lunch might still be served up by a maid and prepared by a cook, while in her semi-detached, scientifically designed kitchen the suburban housewife probably produced the roast from her new enamel (therefore easier to clean) gas or electric cooker. And in the inner-city slum areas of London, the working-class housewife might still be obliged to light a coal fire to cook, or the family might take the meal out to be cooked in the local baker's oven, a ritual Lal Brown recalled from Hoxton in the 1920s:

> We used to go down Essex Road Market on a Saturday night, half
> past nine, ten o'clock, and they'd be selling off meat cheap. They
> didn't have no ice blocks or fridges, they had to get rid of it cheap. So
> we'd buy a shoulder of lamb, for perhaps one and sixpence; they used
> to auction it off and you'd try and knock them down.
> And then Sunday, you would prepare it, put your potatoes and your
> meat in a big dish, put your lump of fat on, cover it over, and take it
> down the street to the baker. He'd cook it for tuppence. We did that
> in the summer – not so much the winter, because in the winter you
> had a coal fire going anyway, so you could stick your dinner in the
> oven which was at the side of the fire, and it didn't cost you anything
> extra. But in the summer it was cheaper to take it to the bakers. And
> you'd have to wait a couple of hours before you went to collect, then
> there would be lots of women walking up and down the street with

these big steaming dishes, and you'd lay the table with last week's *News of the World* – you mustn't read the *News of the World* because you weren't old enough – and then you'd get stuck in. That would be your best meal of the week.

While the middle classes went out to fashionable department stores to furnish their ideal homes, the poor would often kit themselves out on the cheap from the local street market. In fact, the centuries-old street markets actually grew in number in the interwar years, so that by the late 1930s there were nearly a hundred of them in inner London – practically all to the east, in poor working-class districts like Brick Lane and Mile End Road and Portobello Road to the west. Over thirty thousand costermongers succeeded in scratching a living out of these colourful places. The markets promoted a great deal of recycling of furniture, carpets, curtains, ornaments, and so on. The contrast between these age-old market scenes with their bustle, bartering and repartee, and the affluent technological society of the 1920s and '30s could not have been greater. It was around this time that it became fashionable – because it was so 'different' – for better-off people to go rummaging around these places looking for bargains.

This more sociable and boisterous way of life, which survived in the run-down rented districts of inner London, was the very opposite of the new, ordered, and much more home-centred world emerging in the middle-class suburbs, which working-class people were urged to adopt on council cottage estates. There was often a mixed reaction among the first generation of cottage estate housewives to the sudden change from a communal life in the overcrowded streets and slums to a more comfortable and private life in the new working-class suburbs of Becontree, Downham and Watling. On the one hand, they welcomed modern conveniences like an inside toilet and bathroom, more rooms, and a kitchen with running water as a godsend, releasing them from much of the drudgery of slum life. The greater privacy also reduced the danger of flare-ups over such matters as noise and dirt, an ever-present peril when families lived virtually on top of each other, sharing basic cooking and toilet facilities.

At the same time, many experienced a psychological shock when they were exported to the suburbs and quickly discovered that their new, more private family life could have practical drawbacks as well. For tenement living in places like Bermondsey and Poplar fostered, over the years, all sorts of communal bonds – looking after neighbours' children, borrowing sugar, running errands and, perhaps, going on an annual charabanc outing to Southend. And in the old inner-city areas whole families – mothers, grans, uncles, cousins, and so on – often lived within walking distance and would see each other almost every day. All this added up to a mutual support system of and for the poor. This was disrupted, at least temporarily, in the suburbs, where everybody – to begin with – was a stranger in a more isolated environment. For those who moved away, like Doris Scott, who spent two years on the Dagenham Estate between 1937 and 1939, the Ideal Home they had dreamed of in the country proved a bitter disappointment, making the advantages of city life doubly attractive, as she recalled:

> I hated it; living out there altered your whole way of life, really. The streets were very long and you had to trek half a mile or a mile to the nearest shops. Well, I didn't approve of that – that was too far for my liking. Especially after I'd been used to living quite close to a market in Canning Town, that was much cheaper and more convenient. And it was terribly lonely and boring, it seemed so dead. I was used to being with people all the time, and I used to know most of the people in our street. But out on the estate the lights seemed to go out at eight o'clock everywhere and there was nothing to do. Another thing was you spent so much time travelling and it took your husband so long to get home, that by then it was too late to do much, like in the way of going out for a drink. In any case the pubs out there were very few and far between.
>
> And where I'd lived before, Mother was on hand to babysit. I remember I spent so much time going back on the bus to see mother and my old friends that she said, 'You might as well live here'. So that's what we did. We went back to rooms in Canning Town. I wasn't the only one that did; lots couldn't settle, droves of us went back. We were glad to get back to civilization.

To what extent the Ideal Home of the middle-class housewife was a lonely place leading to a sort of suburban neurosis in the living rooms of Croydon, Ruislip and Wembley is a matter of some conjecture. There was a social life of sorts for women in the better-off suburbs, usually centring on coffee mornings, tennis clubs, amateur dramatic societies and residents' associations. But for the young mother in her 'semi', whose husband left on the 8.05 and arrived back on the 6.25, the Ideal Home could turn into a prison. For practically everything revolved around her home, her garden and her family, which meant that few friendships were usually made beyond immediate neighbours and relatives.

STAYING AT HOME

The increasing home-centredness of life in the 1920s and 1930s was encouraged by a number of changes in leisure activities and entertainments in the interwar years. One of the most conspicuous changes was the decline in drinking after the First World War. This was partly due to higher prices of beer and new opening- and closing-time restrictions. In addition, improvements in housing conditions were making the home a more attractive place to spend an evening in; prior to this many working-class people had been regulars at the local pub partly because it was warmer, more comfortable and more spacious than their overcrowded homes. But this change was also partly engineered by authorities like the LCC and licensing magistrates who, in an attempt to defeat the problems of crime and violence associated with heavy drinking, hardly built any pubs at all on the new council estates.

Whereas in central London there was an average of one pub for every 500 people, on the Becontree estate just six pubs were provided to cater for 120,000 – a ratio of one pub per 20,000 people. Though the Downham estate was the largest of its kind in Britain with a population of 35,000, it was allowed just one pub. And the pubs themselves tried to encourage drinking habits that differed from the raucous, rough-and-ready pub scenes of inner London. They encouraged the sale of soft drinks and a family atmosphere with most of the space devoted to areas where families could eat, drink and be entertained together. Indeed, they weren't actually called pubs at all, but refreshment houses, and they were huge, relatively impersonal places lacking the cosy intimacy of the old smoky bars. The Downham Tavern had no stand-up bars when it was first built – an LCC member had said he was against 'perpendicular drinking' – and offered a waiter service, with a staff of thirty-two in 1932. Many working-class Londoners found it all a bit of a nuisance, especially when they had to tip the waiter to make sure he would answer their call for drinks during the evening, as Bill Peek recalled:

You couldn't go to the bar yourself, you had to call the waiter. And they were all in monkey suits, bow-tie and so forth. And there were liveried men outside to open the door, 'Good evening Sir. Good evening, Madam', trying to make working men things they were not. I thought it was an imposition, you couldn't go and get your own pint, you had to wait for the waiter and if you couldn't give him a half penny or a penny tip, you had to wait until he served all his regulars from whom he got the tips.

All this, plus the fact that to get a pint you could easily find yourself walking one or two miles each way to the nearest pub, must have provided a powerful incentive to stay at home. For many, home-centred activities like gardening began to take over from drinking and socializing in the pub as the main leisure pursuit.

The cinema, of course, did not directly encourage a home-centred way of life. But the entertainment it provided, with its celebration of romantic love and the American Dream, helped to reinforce the new aspiration towards family activities and consumer comforts. It was the sort of place courting couples, husbands and wives, or entire families might go for a night out. Even the poor were greeted by uniformed doormen and shown by usherettes to their seats in palaces decked out in as exotic a style as any opera house.

Whereas many of the old theatres and music halls had been concentrated in the central areas, the enormous new picture palaces, built in the 1920s and '30s, rose up all over London. In Brixton, Tooting, Kilburn and Hackney, for instance, cinemas looking like modern cathedrals dwarfed the suburban buildings around them. These cinema chains of Astorias, Granadas, Gaumonts, Odeons and Roxys, showing films made in Hollywood, provided entertainment on a much cheaper and grander scale than ever before. They quickly outstripped the theatre and the music hall. Some of the new cinemas had vast seating capacities of up to 4,000 and by 1929 there were 266 of them in the LCC area alone with accommodation for 268,000 people. In six typical working-class boroughs – Stepney, Shoreditch, Bethnal Green, Poplar, Southwark and Bermondsey – with a combined population of 1 million, there were in 1929 only five theatres and music halls but fifty-nine cinemas.

This new form of entertainment, which could be enjoyed for up to four hours at a stretch without a trip to the West End, was the cheapest available – 'truly the poor man's theatre' as the *New Survey* put it. The price of cinema seats, at around sixpence, matched the cheapest music hall of the day, and was a third or less of the price of the theatre. For sixpence people of all classes could experience an extraordinary fantasy world: they could admire the grandiose and opulent designs of the cinema interiors and enjoy the glamour of the Hollywood stars. One of the most lavish interiors was found in the Tooting Granada – now a bingo hall – with its gigantic foyer designed like a medieval baronial hall, a marbled columned hall of mirrors, and a 3,500-seater auditorium in a Venetian Gothic style complete with chandeliers and rows of cloistered arches lining the walls. It was classified as a Grade I listed building in October 2000.

There were, from time to time, panics about the morally dangerous effects of the cinema. It was blamed for encouraging people to buy American rather than British products, for provoking unbridled sexual desire and reckless violence and it was even suggested that darkness in cinemas might produce moral dangers – particularly in the back row. Most of these fears were almost certainly unfounded but the cinema, by bringing Hollywood stars to a vast audience, helped to create an image of womanhood that was taken up by women's magazines of the period. Together the magazines and the movies brought the feminine fantasy all the way back home to the housewife, who was now not only expected to be a 'craft worker', but one modelled in the fashion of film stars.

One of the few entirely new influences on people's lives in the 1920s – the radio – also encouraged a new home-centredness and provided an alternative to the boisterous life of the public house and the streets. When the British Broadcasting Company (BBC), a consortium of five manufacturers, began to broadcast in 1922, there were 36,000 licence holders, pioneers from the early days of amateur enthusiasts. The first commercial sets were primitive and mostly battery-operated, but the technology improved very rapidly. By 1931 4.3 million people had radio licences, and by 1939 the figure had more than doubled to 9 million. Just about everyone in Britain listened to the radio.

It is interesting that as an entirely new product, the radio – or the wireless as it was known at the time – had to be designed without any reference to an older appliance. This raw piece of technology brought an alien element into cottage-style homes. To overcome this, some manufacturers tried to blend it into the scenery by disguising it as a drinks cabinet or hiding it in a chest. Other manufacturers brought in a modernist Art

Deco style, employing well-known designers, some of whom decorated the speaker surrounds with sun motifs. Radio sets therefore brought design into some people's homes for the first time. But much more than that, radio provided a form of home entertainment that was more continuous and absorbing than anything available before.

The BBC – which became the Corporation in 1927 – attempted under Lord Reith to instil a 'high' culture and a pious Christian morality through the new medium. On Sunday classical church music was broadcast. It was the commercial stations, broadcasting from Europe – Radio Luxembourg, Radio Normandy, and many others – who could capture an audience longing for some livelier entertainment. The commercial stations survived on advertising and sponsored programmes, which meant that they were promoting products – and what better medium for reaching the housewife than the radio in her own home?

Advertisements for Johnson's wax polish, Palmolive soap, Heinz beans and the like helped to reinforce the 'housewifely' way of life. Children were catered for too, with the very first recorded programme broadcast by Radio Luxembourg: 'The Ovaltiney Concert Party' sponsored by Wonderfoods, the makers of Ovaltine. It first went out in 1934, and from it grew the League of Ovaltineys, a nationwide band of five- to fourteen-year-olds, who were sworn to do the things their parents told them, to study hard at school, to eat the things their mother wanted them to eat and to drink Ovaltine every day. There were over 1 million Ovaltineys by 1938, huddled round their radio sets and taking down coded messages which, when deciphered, told them to help their mothers and suchlike. The main target area was the new, middle-class suburbia, where good little children might be raised – and who might encourage their mothers to buy Ovaltine.

In its own way the BBC also helped to build up the sense of homeliness with programmes about things to do about the house, and with gardening talks given by Mr Middleton. He enjoyed a personal following of millions, and gardening – both in the middle-class suburbs and in the new cottage estates, which gave many working-class people a piece of land to tend for the first time in their lives – became one of the most popular pastimes of the interwar years. The gardens enjoyed by homeowners in the semi-detached suburbs were, however, often substantially bigger than those provided for council tenants. And although the council-house garden was sometimes just a scaled-down version of its private counterpart, there were important differences.

What characterized the middle-class suburban garden most of all was a concern with the privacy of the family. At the front the barrier to outsiders was merely symbolic. Most commonly it comprised a privet hedge nestling behind a low brick wall topped with iron chains – which was suggestive perhaps of the drawbridge and the castle wall. But at the back seclusion was considered even more important, especially in the area close to the house, and the customary 5-foot-high (1.5 m) fences erected by builders would often be raised by the householder to a height of 8 feet (2.4 m) or more, using openwork trellis trained with roses. The back garden would usually be divided into two zones, the lower end being devoted to vegetables – fresh food for the family – while the half closest to the home would have a lawn, flower beds and borders, and perhaps a rockery. Suburban couples cultivated in this part of the garden a sort of tidy, miniaturized version of natural beauty, but they also ensured there was space for the children to play, for the dog or the cat to mark out its territory, for Mum and Dad to sunbathe and for the family washing to be hung up. And the finishing touches which gave the garden that 'olde worlde', natural feel – perhaps a symbolic escape from the ever-changing interwar world of big business and scientific advance – were crazy paving, a bird table, a sundial and a cluster of red-hatted gnomes wielding axes or fishing rods.

In the working-class garden this sort of privacy was often not possible or even aspired to. The gardens were smaller, so that a conversation could be held with somebody two houses away and high fences were considered an unnecessary expense as most of the money was needed for more essential items like food and the rent. In the council garden there would commonly be a small lawn, flower bed and vegetable patch, but it was all scaled down with few of the frills which graced the miniature 'estates' of semi-detached and detached homes.

A Mass Observation survey into housing, part of which asked 'gardenless' working-class people in north London what they would do with a garden if they had one, gives a good indication of the uses gardens were put to on council estates in the interwar years. Their answers, listed in order of preference, were growing vegetables, growing flowers, growing 'things', keeping chickens, relaxation, space for children to play in, nothing, drying washing, having a dog kennel, keeping rabbits and keeping pigs. Their preferences show how the keeping of livestock – which provided a cheap supply of fresh food, particularly useful in hard times – was probably more important than it is today. The LCC, in fact, had rules preventing the keeping of livestock, but these only seem to have been imposed when animals became a nuisance. Rather than a manicured suburban garden, many working-class people favoured a 'take us as you find us' farmyard style. Doris Hanslow, whose father was a taxi driver, and who moved with her family from Bermondsey to the Downham estate in the mid-twenties, recalled:

> When we first moved out to Downham, we used to invite all our old friends from Bermondsey down for the weekend to stay. Sometimes there would be twenty-five of us in the one house, and it would be treated like a mini-holiday. It was a big attraction then, our friends were thrilled to bits with our lovely new house, and so were we. We'd give them a guided tour, first they wanted to go upstairs and look at the bathroom and toilet, because no one had got one you see, and they couldn't get over how lovely it was.
>
> Then they'd see all the rooms – there was so much room to move in them – and the garden, that was my father's pride and joy. And they'd all have to see the animals we were caring for.
>
> There was the goat we had. My dad always went up and brought the goat in to introduce it, and of course there used to be screams of delight and 'get away from me'. Then we had a pigeon that had broken its leg, and Dad had put a little splint on it; there was Gertie the duck, she just used to follow us in and out all the time; and the most horrible cockerel that used to go for you if you tried to feed it. It was like being out in the country, because there were fields at the back of us in those days, and we'd often go for walks and come back and have a sing-song in the evening around the piano.

So the new suburban London growing up between the wars did, in a great many ways, represent a new lifestyle. Not everyone could enjoy it, and not everyone wanted it, but it marked a sharp break with the past. This was most true for the middle-class owner-occupier family and, in particular, the housewife in her servant-free home. The municipal suburbia drew in people with less money to participate in the new consumer lifestyle and less inclination to hide away in Arcadia. As they became more firmly rooted in the suburbs the community bonds severed in the slums were to some extent restored. Relatives moved out to be close to each other, neighbours built up community networks, and children – unlike many of their middle-class counterparts – played on the streets. Nevertheless, their lifestyle was more home-based than it had ever been before.

CHAPTER TWELVE

A Brave New World

AN AWARENESS AMONG working-class people of the important part they had played in the Great War, the promises of politicians to create a better world and the extension of the franchise giving many men and women in London the right to vote for the first time in 1918, all combined to create a strong demand for social reform in London between the wars. Much faith was invested in the Labour Party – by the early 1920s an important political force in the capital, especially at a local level. Socialist candidates were particularly successful in working-class areas and the Labour Party gained control for the first time in places like Poplar, Bethnal Green, Bermondsey and Hackney, with dustmen, postmen, general labourers and the like, who had little or no formal education, being elected as councillors and mayors.

In each borough the Labour Party set about creating what they believed might become a municipal Utopia. After the war there was little conception that a Socialist majority in Parliament could be achieved in the foreseeable future, so with urgent social problems to deal with, it made sense to these town hall visionaries to aim for a local revolution in health and housing, using what powers they had. Public parks were created or given a facelift with landscaped gardens, swimming pools and lidos; some of the worst slums were knocked down with garden village estates and later modern blocks of flats taking their place; and local health services were improved.

A characteristic campaign of the early twenties was Labour's mission to 'Beautify Bermondsey'. It was initiated by the council, who provided free bulbs and seeds for local residents and was so successful that after six years of Labour rule there were hundreds of window boxes blossoming with colour, and trees could be seen in almost every street and alley. For a time the council even attached pots of hanging flowers to lamp posts.

Building the 'New Jerusalem', however, cost a lot of hard cash and Labour councils ran into trouble with the LCC (which until 1934 was controlled by the essentially conservative Municipal Reform Party) and with the government itself over their spending on local services. In the early twenties some of them were prepared to defy the law if necessary and their zeal to form what was then seen as a revolutionary local state led them to be dubbed 'Little Moscows' in the press. The most dramatic revolt occurred when Poplar took the lead in transforming the whole basis of the Poor Law and the workhouse system in London. To understand what this rebellion was all about, we must first briefly look at how the Poor Law worked and the terrible suffering it could cause to those forced to resort to it for relief.

In London, as elsewhere, welfare handouts and help for the aged, the poor, the sick and the unemployed were largely administered by the Poor Law Boards of Guardians, of which there were twenty-seven elected in the LCC area. The poor relief they provided varied enormously from one area to another, but generally in London immediately after the Great War they offered a spartan and subsistence form of welfare, invariably administered in a punitive way. The poorest widows, unmarried mothers, orphans, the chronically sick, and the disabled were incarcerated in workhouses where they were often subjected to a harsh regime which had changed little since Charles Dickens attacked the system in his novel, *Oliver Twist*.

Able-bodied men were given 'outdoor relief', whereby they could continue living with their families only if they completed a 'labour test' which usually involved eight hours of stone-breaking in the labour yard in return for a small payment or food tickets. The Poor Law authorities had for almost a hundred years been deliberately cultivating a mean image for the workhouse in order to deter what they saw as society's 'lame ducks', who, it was thought, would take advantage of a cosy berth rather than do an honest day's work. This severity was reinforced by the self-supporting principle whereby relief was financed out of the local rates – here was a powerful inducement to keep costs as low as possible.

The system was in most parts of London antiquated and inadequate at the best of times, but when a new wave of unemployment hit the capital in the early 1920s, it was overwhelmed. There was, in fact, a government insurance scheme, but payments were small and could only be claimed for short periods. In any case, the vast majority of the unemployed were ineligible for the benefits. So, thousands of respectable families who had never before contemplated the idea of going to the Poor Law Guardians suddenly found themselves at the mercy of the Poor Law during the slump of the twenties.

One group who were hit particularly hard by the severity of the Poor Law was single-parent families and their children. Boards of Guardians had for many decades adopted a policy of breaking up such families and dispatching the children to orphanages, so that they would not be such a burden on the rates. In the post-war years there was a big increase in single-parent families due to the death of a parent, most often as a result of the war or the killer 'flu epidemic of 1918–19. Most of the Guardians, with little money to play with, reacted in a traditionally harsh way, showing little of the concern for children and family welfare that would emerge in 1930s London.

This threat of the orphanage often sparked off remarkable struggles to hold families together, particularly in the immediate post-war years. Doris Scott recalled how after her father was drowned one foggy night in the Thames, she, as the eldest daughter, had to make almost as many sacrifices as her mother to save their Canning Town family from being dispersed:

> Our Mum, with myself trailing behind, called on the Board of Guardians to try to get outdoor relief. Well, when we went in, it was a kind of board, and Mother had to stand on the carpet in front of them while I was left holding our dear new-born baby in my arms – we'd left the other four at home – and we waited for the verdict. 'Madam,' announced a bloody bloke like Scrooge, 'we will give you food tickets but not enough to keep your six children. You may keep the new baby in your own care as it's breast fed, but your eldest child – that was me – must leave school straightaway to earn some money. The four other children will be sent to an orphanage.'
>
> Mother said 'Orphanage? I couldn't think of parting with any of my children. I don't care if I have to scrub floors and work all hours, I won't part with my children.' So off we went. From then on Mother scrubbed floors and did sweatshop tailoring, anything to keep us kids all together. My sentence was to leave my lovely school almost at once, which really upset me. I'd won a scholarship to a Central School and I used to cry myself to sleep at the thought of leaving. A lady who lived in our street said, 'I'll speak for her, get her a job in the jam factory.' The factory was just across the road from us and the advantage was I'd have no fares to pay. So, I started work in the jam factory, no less, I got nine shillings and ninepence a week.

Anne Hitchins, then a young mother in Limehouse, recalled being forced to resort to more desperate means to keep her children:

I did apply for assistance, and when someone came to interview me, they told me I'd have to put the children away in a home before they'd give me any money. But I didn't want to lose my children; my children were my treasures. I had a baby that would have been about six months and a boy of two, and I was in such a quandary, I didn't know what to do, you see. I told the person to get out, so he said, 'What are you going to do, start stealing?' I said 'No'.

Then I thought, which way can I turn? I knew that my children were hungry and I swore that my children would never go hungry again, and no one was going to take them away from me. So, after I'd put them to bed I went out and sold myself for just a few shillings. I went to an all-night café, I bought a tin of Nestlé's milk for my baby and a sponge cake and some ham sandwiches for my boy, and I woke them up. And I gave my little boy a ham sandwich and when he got half way through he said, 'Mummy, I don't want any more,' and this picture is engraved in my memory.

Then I started doing it as a regular thing. I used to go up to the café just up the street, and there would be sailors, a lot of them were Chinese sailors, or American tourists, or businessmen. They'd come up and speak to the children, I'd get into conversation, and that's how I used to meet them. Some would be regulars, boyfriends, and they'd be kind to me. I'd take them back to my place, or arrange to meet them there. I'd always do it in the other room when the children were asleep. Some would be a pound or two pounds. See, the more money I got the less I'd do it. They'd always have to pay first, because beforehand they'd promise you the world, then when they'd had what they wanted it was bye, bye. I was caught like that.

THE POPLAR REBELS

The idealistic Labour councillors who swept to power after the war were not prepared to accept harsh treatment of the poor, and the misery and desperation which followed from it. In some areas like Poplar they were winning control of the Board of Guardians as well as the council – sometimes the same people were elected on both bodies – and they took immediate action. In Poplar they fixed relief scales above those offered by most other Guardians, and they refused to impose a maximum family rate

– standard practice in most other areas – which meant that the 'handout' was often inadequate to support a large family. Because of this rule a large single-parent family in Poplar could survive fairly comfortably on the Poor Law. Elsewhere, the family might well have broken up, the children going to an orphanage. But all this benefit had to be paid for out of the local rates and by 1921, with increasing unemployment forcing more than one in five of Poplar's breadwinners to claim relief, this was becoming a crippling burden to the local people. For Poplar, a dock area overshadowed by railway goods yards and gasworks, and cut through by canals bordered with wharves and warehouses, was the poorest borough in the capital.

The councillors, led by George Lansbury, future Labour Party leader, refused to put pressure on the Guardians – who were overspending – to reduce their relief rates. Instead they made a stand to reform the whole rating system. They decided not to levy rates due to the LCC, the Metropolitan Police or the Metropolitan Asylums Board, until rate equalization was brought in whereby richer boroughs like Westminster and Kensington paid their fair share towards the social costs of poverty and unemployment. These were a new breed of politician, invariably working-class men and women, born and bred in the areas they served, whose life and political work were deeply rooted in their local community. They commanded much respect in Poplar, and they quickly became local heroes when, after a long legal battle, thirty of them, including the Mayor, were sentenced to be imprisoned. Their arrests were announced in advance in the press and were used by the Labour Party to whip up local popular feeling by organizing peaceful demonstrations whenever and wherever the arrests took place. When Poplar's five women councillors were arrested at the town hall, they were driven at walking pace down the East India Dock Road to Holloway, escorted by a procession of ten thousand local sympathizers.

The revolt became front-page news in national newspapers throughout the autumn of 1921, and was referred to sneeringly as 'Poplarism'. *The Times* denounced it as a 'revolutionary movement for the equalization of wealth'. Yet, remarkably, in the face of hostility to their actions the Poplar councillors triumphed, the Conservative central government and the LCC dropped all charges against them and they were released from prison after six weeks amid great victory celebrations. The people of Poplar's support was probably the key factor in the victory, for the government's trump card, the appointment of officers to collect the outstanding rates from local residents, would have been met by a rent strike organized by the Tenants'

Reform League in which thousands had quickly enrolled. Also, the government was well aware that other Labour councils, like Bethnal Green and Shoreditch, were considering direct action on rate equalization and to penalize them would have further disrupted local government, possibly triggering violent resistance. The end result was that the richer London boroughs were forced to contribute far more substantial sums to help pay for unemployment and deprivation in poor areas like Poplar.

Similar battles to improve welfare services and living standards were fought by rebellious London Labour parties in the early 1920s. The Poplar Guardians paid relief rates over and above a new maximum fixed by the Ministry of Health and, after an official investigation, continued to defy government orders, spending £2,000 a week above their limit. After twelve months the Guardians faced a surcharge of £110,000, but no attempt was made to retrieve the money. The Poplar Guardians also openly made illegal unemployment benefit payments to local men involved in the unofficial London dock strikes of the summer of 1923. Likewise, the Labour councils in Bermondsey, Battersea, Bethnal Green, Poplar and Woolwich resisted strong government pressure to reduce the wages they paid to council workers, which they generously fixed at about £4 5s for skilled workers and £4 for the unskilled; this compared very favourably with wage rates in the private sector. Dustmen in run-down inner London were in the early 1920s among the best-paid in the country. In 1925, though, after five years of what the government saw as 'overpayments', the councils were forced by the Law Lords to lower their wage rates. Eventually, from 1929, central government began to take away Poor Law Boards' powers, and created a new system of public assistance committees.

The kind of direct action in which the Poplar councillors engaged, challenging the authority of central government, was quite common in the twenties. In a rather different guise, it came to a head in 1926 with the General Strike. For nine days in May, a substantial section of London's working class came out as part of a national strike to give industrial muscle to a long-standing dispute in which miners were resisting a wage cut. On the surface the strike was all about solidarity and sympathy with the miners. But underneath it was a battle between the classes, in which the well-to-do were holding off the demands of a Socialist-led working class for a more equal society in which they had a bigger slice of the economic cake. Many people thought, at the time and since, that this was a potentially revolutionary situation. At the very least it was a very important test case, for if the government and employers had caved in, many more workers would have joined the queue for wage increases and better conditions.

The London dockers came out en masse and huge gatherings of strikers, supported by Port of London Authority clerical and supervisory staffs, immobilized the docks for several days until the government moved in troops and forced the unloading of ships with machine-guns trained on pickets. London's railwaymen, including their clerical staff, also solidly backed the strike. Practically all London's bus and tram drivers answered the strike call, though some Underground staff accepted an offer of bonus payments and operated a skeleton service. Middle-class students, some ferried in especially from Oxbridge to 'do their bit' for the government, tried to maintain bus services, though many had to be fenced into their cabs with barbed wire to give them protection from pickets trying to stop them. Still, a number of buses were ambushed by angry crowds who overturned them and set them on fire.

The BBC transmitted anti-strike radio news broadcasts and speeches by Conservative Prime Minister Stanley Baldwin and other notables, urging the strikers to return to work. The unions were given no access to this new medium. Tens of thousands of middle-class car owners drove their vehicles to work, offering office workers lifts on the way. In fact, the government had long prepared for this battle with the unions and the motor car commuter service was part of a whole volunteer system devised to maintain 'business as usual' and keep essential supplies and services going.

After only nine days, trades union leaders, fearful of provoking a revolution, conceded defeat. This came as a crushing blow to the Labour movement as a whole, but in London it was only a temporary setback. The capital's industrial prosperity helped to sustain strong trade unions and Labour politics, and the Co-operative Movement, which had previously been largely concentrated in the North, continued to flourish in mini-Socialist republics in the London boroughs. Before the First World War this sort of radical activity had been so rare in London that it had almost come to be seen as part of an alien northern culture which could never take root in the South.

Nevertheless, the defeat of the General Strike did dampen the spirit of direct action that was flowering in the poorer parts of London. It was the last major act of popular protest in the capital until the massive anti-Fascist demonstrations of 1936 and the long-running busmen's strike a year later. Legislation was passed to prevent disruptive industrial and political action in the future, and in 1927 all sympathy strikes calculated to coerce the government were banned. Two years later the Local Government Act, passed by the Conservative government, eliminated any threat of a new wave of Poplarism by disbanding Poor Law Unions and Boards of Guardians. Central government was eager to close any local loopholes through which 'Little Moscows' might emerge.

THE LONDON POOR

It was in this era of concern about poverty and the reactions it provoked that Charles Madge and Tom Harrisson launched the project called Mass Observation, the reports of which have already been quoted. Both men had studied anthropology and had what was then the new idea of using an anthropological approach closer to home to capture the minute detail of people's everyday lives. They organized a body of observers, many of them volunteers, to go out into pubs, markets, Labour Exchanges – in fact everywhere – and record what they saw, whom they met and what they said. People were recruited to enter in detail in a diary everything they did on the twelfth day of each month.

Thus Madge and Harrisson gathered together an astonishing array of facts. Some of these were published, covering everything from juvenile delinquency, to doing the football pools, popular jokes and how many men wore bowler hats in pubs. The observers sometimes went to absurd lengths, verging on voyeurism, in their pursuit of the facts, as seen in the following edited report of a man undressing in the East End in February 1939:

Description of male 25, Cockney (Irish) undressing for bed

Time 11.40 to 11.48.40 p.m. Male came into bedroom dressed in blue shirt, dark suit only. He undid the front of his braces and slung them over his shoulder, sat down on bed, immediately got up and lit a cigarette, stood facing bed smoking his cigarette, 20 secs. Talking and motioning with his arms to someone already in bed, 10 secs. Holds his head in his hands, 25 secs. Rolls up his shirt sleeves, picks his nose with his left hand, and rubs it on his shirt. Throws cigarette into fireplace. Motions to person in bed and shows the motions of a boxer, an exhibition lasting 15 secs, pulls off his trousers. Rubs his legs from ankles to knees. Climbs on bed, throws back clothes and slides slowly into bed and pulls clothes over him. Time taken 8 mins 40 secs.

James 'Buck' Duke, head of the American Tobacco Company, with straw hat and cigar, arriving at Liverpool in 1901. When he began to buy up British companies a deal was done with Imperial Tobacco and British American Tobacco was formed to carve up the world market. Its HQ was in London.

A sea of summer hats and bowlers as some of the 5,000 West End staff employed by the Army and Navy Stores arrive for work. In this period, around 1900, men outnumbered women among department store and shop workers.

London was first attacked from the air in May 1915 when a Zeppelin dropped a trail of bombs across north London. There were few raids in World War 1 but some private houses advertised their cellars as bomb shelters. This photograph dates from 1917.

The 1914-18 war gave women the chance to take over men's jobs. This cheerful group are painting stations on the London Underground in 1916.

il Truphet when she was a lowly
domestic servant in 1913, a job
he hated: the woman who
employed her would weigh the
dust swept from each room to
check for thoroughness.

il Truphet (front row, second
from right) in a job she loved,
working in a munitions factory.
Near the end of the war her
husband-to-be objected to her
wearing the trouser outfit and
made her leave the factory.

A volunteer social worker from a 'Care Committee' making
her calls in Hoxton in 1938, then a poverty stricken enclave
in east London.

Lidos, open air swimming pools, were opened all
over London between the wars as part of the fresh
air and sunshine cult. Named after the Poplar rebel
councillor and Labour leader this is the George
Lansbury Lido in Hyde Park in 1937.

A protest march in Poplar in 1921 in support of the local councillors who went to jail for refusing to levy rates for the London County Council. They won their battle to have rich boroughs subsidize poor councils.

The Joe Lyons catering company with its Corner Houses all over London typified the opening up of the West End as an entertainment centre for all Londoners. Here a van is loading up from the Cadby Hall bakery in Olympia which made half a million bread rolls a day.

These children are being treated in Bermondsey Health Centre with a sun ray lamp thought to be a cure for tuberculosis and rickets (caused by a lack of Vitamin D). The dangers of such treatment, especially the risk of skin cancer, were not known in the 1930s.

Many debutantes were recruited in the 1930s to model for advertisements. Lighting up here is Lady Marguerite Tangye, a non-smoker and teetotaller who also advertised gin. A great beauty, her picture also advertised Horlicks in Piccadilly Circus.

An independent or 'pirate' bus of the 1920s which would compete with the General Omnibus Company on popular routes. Note the crudely chalked names on the destination board.

While housewives in the semi-detached suburbs were planning modern kitchens for the servant-less home, in poor districts women were still taking their Sunday lunches to be cooked in the baker's oven. This happy threesome were pictured in Limehouse in 1933.

Begun as a bypass for Brentford in west London the Great West Road attracted modern industry after its opening in 1925, much of it American, and housed in Art Deco buildings.

An electricity company showroom in the 1930s. Many local councils as well as private companies supplied electricity and fought fierce advertising battles with the gas companies.

The building of London's interwar suburbia doubled the built up area of the capital and provided new housing for a few pounds down and weekly instalments of a few shillings. After a slow start, private house building outstripped local authority housing programmes.

The quintessential image of London's West End in the
1930s, Piccadilly Circus in its brash neon night-time,
captured here by the brilliant Picture Post photographer
Kurt Hutton.

American industries were attracted to the new arterial roads running out of West London, one of the most famous of which was the Hoover Factory in Perivale on Western Avenue. Here London Hoover salesmen set off on a selling spree around 1930.

Hudson Motors on the Great West Road in the 1930s. In the Park Royal area there were many motor manufacturers competing for a growing market. This car, with its dummy occupants, was illuminated at night.

A page from a brochure for new Wates built semi-detached suburban houses in which the modern bathroom was considered a great luxury.

. . .luxury

Hot water without restriction — gleaming tiled walls and chromium fittings — a deep hand-basin of fine quality — a comfortable Bath that tempts you to linger. . . . These are advantages you can enjoy as soon as you take occupation!

Smiths Crisps proudly display on their trade card the brand new modernist factory building they opened on the Great West Road in 1927 soon after it was completed.

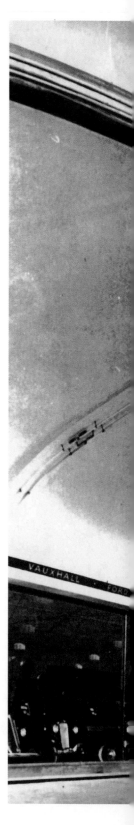

The leading motor agent of the late 1930s, Henlys opened this showroom and garage on the Great West Road in 1937, yet another Art Deco building on what had became known as the Golden Mile of Brentford. The writer J.B. Priestley thought driving along it was like 'rolling into California'.

Holborn Station at rush hour in 1937. London Transport, by then a semi-public company, prided itself on a flair for design with subdued lighting and clean lines. The travelling public are smartly dressed and nearly everyone is wearing a hat.

One of the most thorough investigations into poverty in London in fact predated Mass Observation and was completed in 1930 by Llewellyn Smith and his team of researchers from the London School of Economics. They aimed to review the condition of London's poor, forty years after Charles Booth's original poverty survey. Although the report, published in 1934, did record significant improvements in life and labour in London, it documented how half a million people, about one person in eight of the working class, was living below the poverty line. And this wasn't just a definition of poverty appropriate to interwar consumer London. Llewellyn Smith was using the minimal subsistence definition of poverty that had formed the basis of Charles Booth's 1889 survey of the capital.

The investigation discovered that poverty was concentrated among old people, half of whom lived in need because of the meagre pensions of ten shillings a week they were expected to survive on. Single-parent families, families with several children, and the unemployed were also among those most likely to be living on the breadline. What poverty meant in London in the 1930s was a 'bread and marge' diet with only occasional meals that included meat; it meant hand-me-down clothes and shoes; and it often meant living in an overcrowded tenement, sharing basic washing, cooking and toilet facilities with other families. Naturally, it inevitably involved an exclusion from most of the modern consumer comforts like an electric iron, a vacuum cleaner and a motor car, that were enjoyed by many middle-class families in London.

Llewellyn Smith's poverty survey was pieced together from a mass of census returns, questionnaires, door-to-door interviews and information obtained from School Attendance Officers, Employment Exchanges and Boards of Guardians. But the nitty-gritty of people's actual experiences of poverty is usually drowned in a sea of statistical tables and numerical summaries. Rare glimpses of the scenes his investigators saw appear in a few accounts of interviews with old people, such as Mr N., who eked out an existence on a ten-shillings-a-week old-age pension, plus six shillings outdoor relief.

Mr N. lives alone in a two-roomed house which is in a very dilapidated condition; most of the paper has come off the walls and the rest is peeling off. The kitchen was very barely furnished and only had a table, a chair and a couch in it, all very dilapidated and almost falling to bits. The room was altogether very miserable and cold, as Mr

N. never has a fire until teatime. His clothes were very shabby and
needed mending badly. He never got a hot dinner excepting on
Sundays; all the rest of the week he has cold meat and bread and
cheese. Quite cheerful, he manages to jog along happily and has
nothing to worry him and is very contented living alone with his cats.
Mr N. goes for a long walk in the park each morning, provided it is
not raining and only gets home just in time for dinner. After dinner
he cleans up his house and lays the fire and then goes for another
walk, coming in just in time for tea. He says that he walks five or six
miles every day and feels very fit on it. After tea he sits in front of the
fire and reads and smokes. He said that he had great difficulty in
getting the Relieving Officer to give him his relief in money; he used
to get it in kind as a meat ticket for 3s. 6d. and he said that was of no
use to him as he did not want 3s. 6d. worth of meat in a week. He has
now got his money and says that he can now save a little in the
summer when he has no coals to buy, and with this money he can get
things like extra clothes that otherwise he could not get.

Poverty, it was discovered, was widely dispersed around many different
parts of inner working-class London. The five poorest areas were Poplar,
Bethnal Green, Bermondsey, Stepney and North Kensington, which
housed some of the worst in London.

In a few slum streets there was a concentration of poverty, which
marked them off as quite beyond the pale of respectable society. These
enclaves were marked black on Llewellyn Smith's social map of London.
One such street was Campbell Road in North Islington, often described as
'the worst street in North London'. Its tenements were peopled by council
labourers, street sellers, the incapacitated – the deaf, the blind, the
physically and mentally handicapped – former tramps, the long-term
unemployed, prostitutes and small-time crooks. There was appalling
overcrowding with an average of five people living in each room, meaning
that two thousand people were jam-packed into this small street. A number
of houses had no front, back or lavatory doors as these had been chopped
up for firewood in hard times.

The old sweatshop economy, in which small masters survived the
onslaught of factory competition by demanding long hours of labour in
return for subsistence wages, trundled on through the 1930s. Blighted by
seasonal unemployment, it continued to play an important part in the

clothing, boot and shoe, and furniture industries in inner London, especially in the East End. There were still thousands of tiny workshops – usually run by Jewish masters in converted tenements, employing a predominantly Jewish labour force – in the streets of Whitechapel, Bethnal Green and Stepney. London was the last major outpost of this workshop economy in Britain.

There were some glimpses of the twentieth century. A few factories sprang up in the East End, one or two of them supplying the cloth cap craze, which became part of the working-class indentikit in the 1920s and '30s, while others produced cigarettes, catering for the modern fashion of smoking. But many factories migrated to the fringes of London, clustering around the new arterial roads like the Great West Road, the North Circular Road and to a lesser extent Eastern Avenue, where the land was cheaper, and where mass production geared to the needs of the new chain stores like Marks & Spencer and Woolworths was possible. Thus for the most part industry in inner London bore little or no comparison to the modern, Art Deco-style, prosperous factories that were sprouting up in and around the new suburbs.

Where nineteenth-century industry survived in London, it was as a rule associated with the same kind of poverty found in the depressed areas of Britain. London's dockland, for example, had collapsed completely as a commercial venture and had been taken over by the Port of London Authority in 1909. The Authority was formed to try to avert the crippling losses made by many of the old dock companies and to solve the terrible casual labour problem which dragged many dockers and their families down below the poverty line. The building of one of the few major dock extensions of the interwar years, the King George V Dock at North Woolwich, opened in 1921, was thoroughly in keeping with this image – it was constructed with government funds for the relief of unemployment.

The PLA did help dockers a little through its system of recruiting only from a limited pool of registered dockers, and through its unemployment benefit scheme which assisted those who experienced irregular employment. But still the low wages and the insecurity of unemployment remained. On many occasions, particularly in the slack summer months, there were many more registered men than there was work, with the result that the daily 'call on' at the dock gates sometimes turned into a desperate scramble to be taken on by the foreman. The way the new breed of dockers in the 1930s coped with this system – still dominated by the old hook used to grab bags and boxes – was a vivid memory for Alex Gander, who recalled:

The hook was important in the life of us dockers. Like the carpenter would have his tools, we'd have our hooks, and when we went to look for work we'd have an S hook in our belt and a bag hook in our pockets. And we'd go on the stones, that was the dockside, or in the 'cage' at the West India Dock, for the call on, to get a day's work. We were like animals in the struggle to get close to the foreman and catch his eye, men would get hooked up to each other. That would lead to aggro, sometimes fights. And you'd get trouble sometimes in the London dock area because a lot of the foremen were Irish and they'd favour their own, so to get around that you'd put a green scarf on so they'd think you were one of them, an R. C.

But the work was irregular and when there wasn't anything doing on the morning call, we'd go to the local coffee shop for a cup of tea and 'two out of the pan', [bread and] dripping dipped in the pan. Then it was on to the local police courts to see the drunks and the prostitutes and petty thieves, then on to the library to read.

We'd look at Lloyds to see when and where the boats were coming in, and if there were some due in at Tilbury, we'd go down there on spec' to look for work. Usually, though, we'd stay around for the afternoon call, and if there wasn't any work then we'd go to the billiard hall or go home. If you had three consecutive days in a week without any work you got some dole money. So if we'd had two days off we weren't very keen to work on the third because you ended up losing money. And if we worked three days and the other three were on the dole, we had a saying, we'd call it 'three on the hook and three on the book' or 'the bomper'.

LONDON'S OWN WELFARE STATE

The rediscovery of this sort of hardship and poverty in the interwar years went hand in hand with a renewed attempt to do something about it. Charitable and voluntary work, initiated through a complex web of care committees, housing trusts, settlement missions, and so on, was given a new sense of urgency. One pioneering voluntary project in London at this time was the launching of the Peckham Health Centre. Two radical doctors – George Scott Williamson and Innes Pearse – first established an experimental centre in a small house in London's declining mid-Victorian suburb in 1926. Their aim was to monitor and devise ways of maintaining health and preventing illness in the local community – preventative medicine was then quite a novel idea. The centre was later closed down for a few years while a massive effort was made to raise enough money to construct a new purpose-built home. It opened again in 1935 in a modern, open-plan building boasting a swimming pool, a gymnasium and a cafeteria. The centre sought to create an attractive meeting place where all the family could be together – only whole families were allowed to join – and which would integrate exercise, sport, health care and check-ups into the everyday life of the local community.

But the most successful attempt to build a 'New Jerusalem' in a run-down part of London was in Bermondsey. Here a radical Socialist and philanthropist, Dr Alfred Salter, joined forces with working-class Labour councillors to create a miniature welfare state, incorporating the latest medical equipment. In 1926 the Labour Council opened a 'Sun Cure Institute', the first municipal solarium in Britain. Sun treatment helped to cure and keep at bay tuberculosis, which flourished in Bermondsey's environment of malnutrition, overcrowding and bad air. A year later one of the most magnificent baths in the country was opened, which included two swimming pools, 126 private baths, and Turkish and Russian vapour baths. This was a badly needed amenity because only one home in a hundred had a bath in Bermondsey. But the pinnacle of the Labour Council's achievements came with the creation of a purpose-built, modern health centre in 1936 – they saw it as the Harley Street of Bermondsey – which re-housed the solarium and boasted among its many departments a foot clinic, a clinic for ear, nose, throat and eye ailments, an antenatal clinic, and a dental surgery. As a result of their efforts, both the death rate and the infant mortality rate fell dramatically in Bermondsey between the wars.

This kind of social reform was given much wider currency and was heavily promoted when the London Labour Party under Herbert Morrison gained control of the LCC in 1934. Labour got into power on a rising tide of concern – particularly among the middle classes – that local authorities should take a more active role in tackling the social problems of the capital. Morrison's vision of municipal socialism was different from that of George Lansbury and the rebellious Poplar councillors in the early twenties. The latter had used the language of class war and favoured direct action: if necessary, they did not hesitate to break the law. What Morrison offered was a more moderate programme of change, planning by professionals, and improvements in housing and public services to be voted in through the ballot box. It was a package designed to attract not just working-class voters, but also middle-class voters with a social conscience.

He recruited sympathetic advertising men and women to streamline his party's image and give it a vigorous and progressive look. They came up with slogans like 'Let Labour Build the New London', 'Labour Gets Things Done', 'A Healthy London', 'A Decent Treatment for the Poor', and 'For the Children's Sake'. This formula won Labour control of the LCC from 1934 to 1940, and during these years new directives from County Hall further changed the face of the capital. This was the era of a Morrison-style 'brave new world' for Londoners: the heyday, in a way, of the LCC, which had much wider responsibilities in those pre-welfare state days.

The party quickly drew up three-year programmes for housing, health, education, town planning and parks. Most effort was put into housing, and hundreds of blocks of modern council flats rose out of the rubble of the worst slums, which the LCC bought through compulsory purchase orders in places like Camberwell, Lambeth and Poplar. The LCC also began to refashion the workhouse hospitals it took over from the Boards of Guardians in 1929. Under the new Morrison regime hospitals were modernized and re-equipped, sun balconies were built, more staff were recruited, diets were improved, and wirelesses were installed for patients. In the field of education, what were termed the 'Tory Shylockisms' – the economy cuts – were abolished, staffing levels were increased, free milk supplied, and health inspections provided. School prizes were restored, more scholarships to secondary schools introduced and children in residential schools were given a camp holiday every summer.

Morrison's municipal socialism was channelled into improving and increasing the number of parks, playing fields and open spaces: a change very much inspired by the thirties' enthusiasm for fresh air, healthy exercise, sunbathing and sport. Many parks, like Victoria Park in Hackney, were provided with more facilities such as paddling pools, modern lidos with purified water, sun-bathing terraces, cafés, bowling greens, and tennis courts. Morrison was particularly proud of the amenities for open-air entertainment that were provided during school holidays when comedians, conjurors and story-tellers attracted big crowds of children in the parks. By 1938 the LCC provided 347 cricket pitches, 436 football pitches (of which 140 were on Hackney Marshes) and 713 tennis courts.

Morrison's most controversial act was the rebuilding of Waterloo Bridge. The old bridge, dating from 1817 and opened on the anniversary of the Battle of Waterloo, had been in poor condition since the 1920s, but Parliament was reluctant to demolish it, or to contribute to the cost of a new bridge. There was great conservation pressure to save the old bridge, which was regarded as an architectural masterpiece. However, when he came to power, Morrison set in motion a rebuilding programme: he wanted a functional bridge to carry LCC trams. The new Waterloo Bridge should have been completed by 1940: in fact it had to wait until 1945 as the war delayed construction. But the rebuilding was regarded as a great symbolic triumph of the LCC over central government and of socialist pragmatism over reactionary conservation.

By the time Morrison came to power, the continuing expansion of London was beginning to become a political issue and it was he who began a scheme for limiting its growth. This was the beginning of a 'Green Belt' policy, to ring the capital with fields and parkland protected from further suburban development (see Chapter Ten). It was an expression of the ideal of city life which, in a sense, epitomized the belief in planning for a new, cleaner, healthier world.

There is no doubt that municipal reform in the interwar years achieved a great deal: it was a kind of prototype welfare state run at a local, rather than a national level. But there were inevitably limits to what it could accomplish, and then, as today, central government was wary of the power local authorities could wield. The actions of the Poplar councillors in flouting the conventional administration of the old Poor Law, for example, and similar subsequent protests elsewhere, were taken as reasons for the gradual dismantling of this Victorian system of welfare from 1929 onwards. Power was progressively removed from local Guardians, and from the Public Assistance Boards that replaced them, as a more standardized, nationally controlled system replaced the variable local administration. Though Poor Law Guardians were rarely generous, the Assistance Board inspectors enforced a 'social security' administration quite heartless by later standards.

Despite the fact that London was very prosperous compared with the rest of Britain in the 1930s, some districts, such as Poplar and Stepney, suffered severe unemployment, rising to 15 or even 20 per cent. Poverty-stricken families in such areas had now to pass the 'means test' if they were to get public assistance – the income of the whole family, including children and their possessions, was scrutinized and totted up before they were eligible for help. Inspectors could go into any claimant's home, demand that anything deemed a 'luxury' – such as the radio or gramophone – be sold, and the proceeds would be docked from benefit payments.

There was nothing the idealistic municipal Socialists could do about this, and while they might provide solariums and parks for poorer Londoners, more fundamental economic need persisted. In this climate, the unemployed remained a potentially aggressive and perhaps revolutionary force whose sympathies could be sought by the Communist Party, or by the Communist-controlled National Unemployed Workers Movement, which staged many of the hunger marches on the capital, as well as one or two sensational publicity stunts in London itself. In the nineteenth century, there had been riots in the West End: in the 1930s, groups of penniless, unemployed workers invaded the Ritz and asked to be fed, as Chris Cansick, a revolutionary diner of the period, recalled:

There was about fourteen of us, and we'd decided, 'We're gonna have dinner at the Ritz'. So we went in smartly, walked to the table, sat down, we had our working clothes on, the only clothes we had, you know. The waiter come up, 'Gentlemen what do you want, what are you here for?'

'We would like a dinner please'.

'Dinner! Dinner!'

He said it so many times, so we said 'Yes'.

'I'll get the manager'.

So he got the manager. Now they didn't want trouble, the Ritz, because the unemployed were there and the unemployed could wreck the place, that's what they thought. So the manager got onto the police and they were waiting outside, but we still said, 'We're not going, we're going to stop here till we have something to eat'.

I was really afraid, I said to myself, 'this is it'. Anyway, they didn't call the police in, they didn't want it in the papers, 'the unemployed at the Ritz', bad publicity, the big nobs go to the Ritz. So some dinners came up, always remember it, meat and potatoes we had, and sweet afterwards, and tea. We thoroughly enjoyed it.

So we got up after the meal, we was on pins and needles, we were saying, 'That's our lot, "Pentonville now".'

'No, sod Pentonville,' old Sid said. 'We'll do it on our knees'.

Anyway, we marched out, and the police didn't touch us, and there was a van drawn up outside, full of our mates, and they gave us all these bills and banners they'd just made, and we marched all around Piccadilly, saying it was the finest meal we'd ever had. That was a great day for the unemployed.

A much more serious threat to the peaceful, gradualist mainstream of social reform in the capital was the emergence in the 1930s of pockets of strong support for the Communist Party on the one hand, and for the British Union of Fascists on the other. Both represented essentially European, radical approaches to solving the problems of poverty and inequality. The key ideological battleground at the time was in Spain where, during the Civil War, the entire nation was divided by these competing political philosophies.

When the Fascists organized a march through a Jewish quarter of the East End, the Labour Party advised opponents to stay at home. The Communist Party, however, adopted a policy of direct opposition on the streets and organized a counter-demonstration of about a hundred thousand supporters, a great many of them Jewish. Barricades were thrown across the streets by the Communist opposition, and many fights broke out, including a flare-up in Cable Street in Bethnal Green, before the march was finally abandoned. In broad political terms, the Cable Street incident was not of lasting significance, but it did provide ammunition for reformers such as Morrison to argue the case for social change to remove the underlying causes of discontent. And it was quickly overshadowed by the threat of war in Europe – a threat, which by 1938, was being taken seriously. The reformist movement, which had attempted to improve the lives of the poor through a healthier environment, was now complemented by a national concern for the health of a people who would need strength to fight a war with Germany. Schemes like the National Fitness Campaign, launched in 1938, encouraged the provision of more recreational facilities.

A SWANSONG FOR THE OLD LONDON

London was now regarded in quite a new light. Until the Green Belt policy of 1935, almost nothing had been done to prevent its continued growth and the social problems thereby created. In 1938 the Committee on Imperial Defence estimated that in the first twenty-four hours of war, 175,000

Londoners would be killed, and the toll would rise to 1,800,000 after two months. There were plans for mass war graves, as someone had calculated that 20 million square feet (1.8 million sq m) of timber would be needed if the dead were all buried in coffins. Winston Churchill commented that London was 'the greatest target in the world, a kind of tremendous, fat, valuable cow, fed up to attract beasts of prey'. So London's great strength in economic terms during the interwar period had by 1938 become a liability.

An era in London's history was coming to an end in 1938 – a period in which its Victorian culture and structure had been replaced by a brave new world of council housing, mock-Tudor suburbia, sun-bathing by the Serpentine, American jazz, electricity and the motor car. This sense was expressed in an extraordinary outburst of nostalgia in a song-and-dance routine, 'The Lambeth Walk', performed by Lupino Lane in the West End show *Me and My Girl*. The lyrics conjured up a sentimental image of Victorian London's back-street community spirit, while the dance routine involved much marching up and down, head waving, and the shouting of 'Oi' as the hand, thumb cocked, was swung in an over-the-shoulder gesture.

It was such a success, both nationally and internationally – Mussolini is said to have ordered a pretty girl to teach it to him in Italy – that Mass Observation made a study of it. They could not really explain the phenomenon, except in terms of a harking back to the old days – a kind of wild rejection of the new – and marvelled at the scenes it brought to London, where dancing had been a great interwar craze. One Mass Observation report stated:

At Highbury Fields, Islington, on August 11 [1938] the crowds totalled some 20,000 and the official arrangements broke down under the strain. The inner ring of asphalt meant for the dancers became lined on both sides with onlookers as well, leaving only a narrow lane for dancing. One had to fight to get in or out of this ring. Announcements and speeches were drowned by the voice of the crowd in spite of powerful loudspeakers. The Lambeth Walk was the chief excitement, though the dancers in the end just tramped and bombed around in a solid mass, speeding into a blind scrum.

PART THREE

Surviving the Blitz
1939–1945

CHAPTER THIRTEEN

In the Front Line

IN SOME WAYS Sunday, 3 September 1939 was just like any other Sunday. Throughout London housewives prepared the family lunch, husbands read their newspapers, young men and women put on their Sunday best. But beneath the familiar routine there was an unusually tense atmosphere. In every home the wireless was switched on. At 11.15am the voice of Prime Minister Neville Chamberlain came on the air:

> I am speaking to you from the Cabinet Room at 10 Downing Street. This morning the British Ambassador in Berlin handed the German government a final note, stating that unless we heard from them by eleven o'clock that they were prepared at once to withdraw their troops from Poland, a state of war would exist between us. I have to tell you now that no such undertaking has been received, and that consequently this country is at war with Germany.

People wondered what would happen, what a truly modern war was like, with its new technology of death. Just seven minutes after the declaration of war it seemed as if they were about to find out. The eerie wail of the air-raid sirens sounded over London. Policemen on bicycles pedalled furiously up and down the streets wearing 'Take Cover' placards. There was a stampede to the shelters. People began to run frantically, children screamed and terrified mothers pushing prams were caught up in the race for safety. Odette Lesley remembered how she, her mother Marjorie and her sister Jean sat in their suburban home in Hendon, awaiting Armageddon:

> I remember when the first siren went, how we struggled with our gas masks, because they were the most awkward things possible to put on. I remember my mother's landed up round the back of her head, I think my sister's landed up on her left ear and, if I remember rightly, it seemed to me somehow that mine landed up on my chest.

But it was a very terrifying time. We had this awful fear of the air attack on London because, obviously, it was the age of the plane. I used to imagine swarms of planes, always black, with evil-looking pilots in them coming over, raining down death from the sky and I could see buildings all round me collapsing, I could hear screams, terrible noise, terrible panic. Everything was destruction, it was terrible to imagine, and now it became very real in my mind. We thought we were going to get gas raining down. We thought, this is it, we are just going to die.

Everyone knew that the main thrust of the German attack would be upon London because of its enormous strategic and symbolic importance as the centre of government, communications, trade and industry. Also London, by virtue of its sprawling size, was a sitting target for air attack. If Germany wished to disrupt the machinery of government, cripple production and break civilian morale, its bombs would achieve maximum impact if dropped on the capital. Londoners realized that they themselves were in the front line.

Some experts predicted that hundreds of thousands might die or be injured if the German airforce – the Luftwaffe – mounted serious bombing raids on the capital. This danger had prompted the government to make early preparations to protect London against such an attack. For months Air Raid Precautions volunteers had been trained to provide backup – as firemen, nurses, wardens, and ambulance drivers – should war be declared. A quarter of a million Londoners, most of them part-time volunteers, were now enrolled in the ARP services. Air-raid shelters, usually made out of brick, concrete or corrugated iron, had been hastily built in streets, back gardens, parks and basements of buildings, and sirens installed to warn of approaching enemy aircraft.

Coupled with the nightmare of air bombardment was the fear of gas attack. Many Londoners remembered the damage done by poisonous gases in the trench warfare of 1914 to 1918 and it was assumed that gas would be used in any future war. The government had issued a handbook describing in lurid detail how phosgene produced gangrene and how mustard gas resulted in blindness and decomposition of the flesh. Many pillar box tops in the capital had been painted yellow with a gas-detector liquid which changed colour when there was poison in the air, alerting people to the danger. And everyone, even babies, had been issued with a pig-snouted rubber gas mask to protect them from the evil effects of this sort of warfare. Many Londoners had their gas-mask boxes slung over their shoulders as they sat in their shelters waiting for the word from wardens to put them on.

Although on the first day of the war Londoners had a taste of what an air attack might be like, it wasn't the real thing. The 'all clear' soon sounded. A civilian plane had set off a false alarm and an hour later the shelters were empty. The incident, nevertheless, highlighted the new role Londoners were to play in the age of 'total war' that would bring London into the front line of the war. As Londoners rushed about on that first day frantically making last-minute preparations against air attack, the government set about establishing an unprecedented network of official observers to monitor what the 'ordinary' Londoner was doing and thinking.

High morale was seen to be of paramount importance and the government immediately set up a new Ministry of Information. Based in the Senate House at the University of London, its staff of a thousand had to know what people were thinking. A new unit called Home Intelligence co-ordinated observers who provided information from all over Britain with special emphasis on monitoring morale in the capital.

Officials of the London Passenger Transport Board, branch managers of W. H. Smith and Sons, supervisors of cinema chains, workers in Citizens' Advice Bureaux, trade unionists, local council officials, social workers, had all to report regularly on Londoners' feelings about the war. This information was co-ordinated by regional information officers who also employed full-time observers through the independent survey organization Mass Observation. These observers gathered their information through interviews, observation, and eavesdropping on conversations of unsuspecting people. Nina Hibbin was a full-time observer in the East End during the early part of the war. She recalled:

> We tried to get beneath the ordinary sort of 'yes' or 'no' or 'don't know' kind of statement, underneath to what people were feeling. For example, we would not only ask direct questions but we would also ask indirect questions, slipping them into conversations. So I'd perhaps go into a shop and say, 'Five Woodbines, please. Looks like rain. What do you think of the news?' Or we would note down overheards from people's conversations. We had all kinds of rather ingenious ways of assessing morale like, for example, counting how many people had gas masks or how many people we saw in pubs and things like that.

Because, if they weren't carrying gas masks they were likely to be feeling happy. If they were feeling rather bad, they'd be carrying the gas masks. From all these sources I'd put together reports on what Londoners were thinking about the war. And the Ministry of Information commissioned various studies, like how people reacted to their 'hush' posters, 'Careless Talk Costs Lives', and things like that, and we did surveys for them on evacuation, and on shelters, and so on.

There were also other secret sources of information – police duty room reports and postal censorship. The monthly intelligence reports on morale from Postal and Telegraph Censorship were based on the scrutiny of around two hundred thousand letters opened to check on the unintentional leaking of military information. From all these sources the regional information officers produced detailed reports on what people in their area were doing and thinking. These Home Intelligence reports were top secret and the material was considered so sensitive that it was not released to the public for thirty years. Much of the material in this account of Londoners was gleaned from those documents.

From the start, there was a huge discrepancy between government records of what was really happening and the accounts given at the time by the Ministry of Information and taken up by the press, radio and newsreels. Evacuation is the first major event to highlight this distinction between the official 'myth' and the official 'reality'. The government's mass evacuation plan – finalized in the months preceding September 1939 – was seen as a military counter-move to the enemy's expected strategy of demoralizing the civilian population through air attack, and was presented as a great success for military-style organization.

In the first days of war 750,000 Londoners were ferried away in official parties to avoid the expected bombardment. Most of these official evacuees were schoolchildren. Mothers, given only a few hours' notice before the final departure, packed suitcases and sandwiches for their children, tied identity labels around their necks and marched them off to join school groups supervised by teachers. The newsreel and press pictures all showed the mothers happily waving goodbye to their departing children. But the reality was very different. The mothers, often tearful, found the parting painful. They did not know where their sons and daughters were going or when, even if, they would meet again. The children frequently faced horrendously long train journeys into the unknown. Mollie Matthews, then thirteen, recalled how she and her sister Joan said goodbye to their mother on Canning Town Station:

> Quite a number of us set off this particular morning, all the mums waving off their children, mine included. Then eventually came the really sad part where we had to get into the carriages and leave our parents behind. The journey seemed to take for ever and the awful thing was, as far as we were concerned, that the longer the train was going, the further away from home we were going. It wasn't a very nice feeling. Ultimately the train did pull in at the station, and there we were at our destination. Miles and miles from home, we wondered whether or not we'd ever see our mums and dads again.

When the evacuees arrived, they were gathered together in reception centres. In some places, the children waited days to find a home. In others 'receiving' families would seize upon boys and girls who were tidily dressed and old enough to help with farm work or domestic chores, but ignore the raggedly dressed, the weak and the innumerable bands of inseparable brothers and sisters. Doreen Holloway and her brother, William, who had never left Battersea before, recalled how they found themselves being looked up and down in Binfield Village Hall in the heart of Berkshire:

> We all stood in a circle with our cases and packages. Some of the villagers came here to select the children they wanted. It got so that my brother and I were left almost till the last and I began to feel most unwanted and rejected because we seemed to be overlooked all the time. Nobody wanted a boy and a girl. At one point a man wanted to take me from my brother and I got very frightened. He wanted to take my clothes out of my case but I stopped him. But we were eventually taken to a home in the village.

THE PHONEY WAR

Back in London, people were becoming swiftly disillusioned. Now that the war had begun, Londoners expected some military action by the Allies. Troop trains chugged out of Waterloo and Victoria Stations taking soldiers on the first stage of their journey to the battlefront. Crowds of Londoners gathered around maps of Poland in shop windows to work out where the British army might be heading. There had been an air of excitement. But when, on 27 September, Warsaw fell and there was no attempt by Britain and her ally France to provide military support to aid the resistance against Germany, people began to wonder what the war was all about.

On the declaration of war, many Londoners had seen it as an epic struggle between good and evil. Since the mid-1930s refugees fleeing the violence and anti-Semitism of Nazism had been arriving in London, and by the end of 1937 almost twenty thousand German Jews had entered Britain, the majority settling in London. Popular feeling against Hitler increased as he extended his empire by annexing Austria in 1938 and then by taking control of Czechoslovakia in March 1939. These conquests resulted in an even greater flood of refugees. In the eighteen months prior to the war almost fifty thousand more refugees – among them Austrian and Czech Jews – had arrived in London. Art historian Klaus Hinrichsen escaped from Lübeck in Germany. He remembered:

> I had had encounters with the Gestapo. I could not work in any of my
> intellectual fields. I was at constant risk of denunciation under the
> Nuremberg racial laws. We were second-class citizens and when I
> came to London I had a feeling of relief that I could say what I
> wanted, that I could behave as I wanted and that, although I was in a
> foreign country, nevertheless I was accepted as a human being. This
> friendship extended even to accepting my accent. All the
> organizations, the Church of England, the Quakers and so on, with
> whom we had registered, understood the situation and were extremely
> helpful, extremely sympathetic, and introduced us to English life and
> institutions. There were lectures put on by the British Council and we
> got invited to British homes and things like that. I was so happy that
> now I could join the British in the war against fascism.

But in London the war had not yet begun. The German bombers failed to arrive. Hitler did not seem to want to engage the Allies – at this stage Britain, her Empire and France – in a fully-fledged war. This period of inaction was to become known as the 'Phoney War'. Because of this feeling of unreality people became less concerned about the dangers they faced and more and more angry at the restrictions imposed upon them by the war.

By December wishful thinking had taken over from fear. Many felt that now the capital had had time to protect itself with an array of barrage balloons in the sky and anti-aircraft guns on the ground it was relatively safe; Hitler would probably never dare or be able to attack it. Odette Lesley recalled this change in attitude from commitment to complacency:

My mother enrolled us in the ATS and I thought oh, this was marvellous, I was going to be part of the war effort, I was going to do something for my country, I was going to be a soldier. I was absolutely thrilled. And I was only fifteen years old at the time, but of course they didn't think to ask for a birth certificate, and I hoped they never would. And just one month after the war broke out, there we were into uniform, mobilised, and sent away to be soldiers. At least that's what I thought they were going to do, because I saw myself doing drills, learning about guns and holding rifles, and potting away at the enemy. But of course it wasn't like that. I was an officer's orderly, making cups of tea and generally being a lackey. And in the evenings I'd go out with all the fellahs. It was a wonderful time socially but we forgot the war altogether, it was just a giggle, nobody took it seriously. After a bit we got fed up with the inconvenience and pointlessness of it all and I declared my real age – I was dismissed and the ATS had to get along without me.

From the start evacuation had been painful, but after three months of Phoney War, it had become a major source of discontent among Londoners, a fact that was largely covered up at the time. The main problem was that the parts of London from which many children were evacuated housed most of the poorest families. These children found themselves billeted with provincial or rural families who were often better off and more 'respectable'. The result was often a tragi-comic confrontation in which the big-city children disrupted many a quiet, rustic routine in country villages.

The receiving families were frequently shocked and disgusted at the poverty of appearance and manners of the London children billeted on them. Late nights, head lice, rough street games, smoking, swearing, chips with everything, bedwetting, some or all of which were common to children from the poorest areas in London, provoked a storm of outrage within the receiving communities. And though most families tried to be welcoming, many of the evacuees found their middle-class ways terribly formal and their attitudes snobbish. Sometimes richer households, used to servants, could treat evacuees as second-class citizens. Doreen Holloway, for example, remembered feeling totally rejected by the lady who eventually picked out her brother and herself from the Binfield Village Hall:

> The house that we were evacuated to was enormous, at least by our standards. We rarely saw the lady of the house and were put in the care of two servants who obviously resented us. You know, we felt the resentment from the beginning. We had to sleep on sacks filled with straw outside the kitchen, although at the time there were spare beds upstairs in the house. The back garden was rather large but we were not allowed out there, it was out of bounds. My parents were never asked inside when they came to visit us, they had to wait outside the fence in the street. And during one of the meals there the cook actually told me that we were lucky to have the food we were given, as we were eating the same sort of food the lady of the house had. And she made me feel very unworthy and that everything that was going wrong was all my fault. We were not happy at all; we felt really out of place. We felt most unwanted and wanted to get back straight away to London with Mum and Dad again.

Within a few weeks a trickle of evacuees began to go home – they preferred to face the possibility of attack by the Luftwaffe than to live lives of deprivation in the country. So desperate were some of the children that they ran away from their 'reception' homes, intrepidly making their own journey of tens, even hundreds, of miles back to London.

By December 1939, the aerial bombardment predicted by the government had still not materialized. In addition, the government had by then made parents pay towards the costs of billeting, though people had originally assumed it would be free. Poorer families could ill afford the money. The trickle of returning evacuees turned into a flood. Parents, many of whom were themselves bored and lonely without their children, responded to the unhappy letters which sons and daughters wrote to them and brought them back home. Molly Matthews came back to Canning Town:

I wrote to mum and dad and explained that we had really had enough by then and if they didn't come to collect us, we would walk home. So consequently we had a letter saying that they would be down that weekend. When they came, they arrived in a taxi. Now I presume it must have taken the best part of their savings, if not all of it. Coaches weren't booked in those days to go anywhere and trains were unreliable, because of all the stations being out of order, so the next best thing was a taxi. So the taxi arrived and the delight, the joy. Then we left and I came home. And I'd rather have faced at home the bombing and things than go back there.

By Christmas 1939 more than half of the seven hundred and fifty thousand people originally evacuated from the capital had returned. Though relieved at being reunited, many families were nevertheless angry and disillusioned with the way they had been treated. A new mood of despondency was in the air.

Feelings of aggravation were heightened by another air-raid precaution – the blackout. From the beginning of the war the government insisted that street and shop lights should be turned off and house windows blacked out with thick curtains, paper and blinds as essential precautions to protect the city from night attack by German bombers. The blackout was unpopular right from the start, partly because it curtailed many Londoners' leisure activities. Floodlit evening sports, like greyhound racing and speedway, were, for example, suspended straight away. Commuters could no longer read on the blacked-out buses and trains bringing them home from work. Many women became frightened of going out to the cinema, to the theatre or to see friends; fearing harassment, they often stayed at home.

Wardens, with nothing else to do, were often over-zealous in reporting those who broke the elaborate blackout regulations and magistrates, anxious to demonstrate their patriotism, were too ready to impose fines. There was also a dramatic increase in road deaths, especially of pedestrians. A Gallup Poll found that 18 per cent of the population had suffered some accident – bumping into sandbags or lamp posts, being knocked over in the dark, and so on – in the first year of the war. As the 'phoney War' continued, the blackout seemed to be cutting off Londoners from one another, increasingly undermining their cheerfulness and confidence.

By the winter the problem of rising food prices and food shortages – which particularly affected the poorer sections of London's working class – was further fuelling the chorus of discontent in the capital. Taxation on items such as beer, sugar, and tobacco – raised partly to help pay for the war – pushed families in places like Stepney and Bermondsey further into poverty. In early January butter, bacon and sugar were rationed. However, the distribution of most foods was still uncontrolled and rich ladies with cars at their disposal could get more than their fair share of non-rationed goods by buying from shops in many different areas, causing considerable resentment.

The scarcity of goods also pushed up the cost of living, again hitting those on the breadline – often the unemployed and the elderly – hardest. All Londoners, however, were affected to some degree and with the war apparently more imaginary than real, they grumbled bitterly about such deprivation, wondering just what they were being asked to make these sacrifices for.

By the beginning of 1940, a deep anxiety had developed in government circles at the rising level of public dissatisfaction and apathy towards the war. The Ministry of Information launched a campaign with the aim of 'replacing public bewilderment with a strong sense of what they were fighting for'. By February all London was festooned with posters displayed in pubs, shops, libraries, tube stations, buses and factories one of which featured Britannia exhorting: 'It's up to you'. The MOI film department began to stress in its propaganda shorts the importance of individual effort and vigilance. And to try to overcome the dangerous complacency developing towards the threat of air raids, a booklet, *How to Make Your Home Safe*, was distributed to every householder in London.

However, by the MOI's own reckoning, the campaign had little impact. This had been their first major attempt to change the public's mood and they were still learning the technique of effective propaganda. Morale remained low.

Concern now spread to the Metropolitan Police, who feared that they would be unable to maintain public order and morale after air raids on the capital. They were worried that given the mood in London, serious air raids might result in panic, looting and widespread disorder. They were already training their men in the use of firearms, partly to cope with public disorder. Frank Whipple remembered when he became a reserve policeman at the outbreak of war:

> We were trained to use arms in case of an emergency in London.
> They took us out on the Metropolitan Police Range and we were
> firing old Canadian 1914 rifles. I remember saying to the inspector,

'Who are we going to use these on, the invader?' And he said, 'You'll use them on Londoners if you have to. If they get out of control when the invasion and the bombings come you'll have to use them on them.' I remember being quite shocked at the time.

There were already several thousand troops deployed in London whose main role was not originally to defend the capital against a German attack but to 'support the police'. They could regularly be seen patrolling vulnerable points of strategic importance like the docks, arms factories, railway bridges, and aerodromes. There was always a strong presence of soldiers outside the Bank of England, Broadcasting House and the West India Docks. They were there not only to prevent sabotage by 'extremist' groups like the IRA, or by German agents and parachutists, but also to avert disorders from Londoners themselves.

BLOOD, SWEAT, TOIL AND TEARS

Then in April a new blow hit morale. Hitler unexpectedly invaded Norway. The British attempt to repel the intruder quickly turned into a fiasco, a military failure that was seen by many as evidence that the nation was not geared up for war. The Phoney War was over. Home Intelligence reported: 'Norwegian defeat staggered people . . . public morale was at a low ebb. Although there were for the first time signs of psychological healthiness: people were facing facts and were not bathed in fantasy. The earlier mood of complacency entirely disappeared.'

But even as the Norwegian debacle was sinking in, a new crisis emerged. On 10 May, Germany invaded Belgium and Holland. Home Intelligence reported an increase in fear, noting that 'anxiety was deepened because it must be remembered that the defence of the Low Countries had been continually built up in the press'. The crisis toppled Neville Chamberlain who was blamed for being a weak leader, and Winston Churchill, First Lord of the Admiralty, was that day chosen to replace him as Prime Minister. He declared in his first speech, 'I have nothing to offer but blood, sweat, toil and tears', setting a new tone of determination so that the war effort was being taken very seriously by everyone. One of the first acts of Churchill's new government was the formation of the Local Defence Volunteers, rapidly renamed the Home Guard.

On 26 May the whole war effort was given a sudden and even greater sense of urgency. Newspapers reported that the British Expeditionary Force of 325,000 men was being evacuated from Dunkirk. Just two weeks earlier, the force had advanced confidently into Belgium to join French and Belgian troops. But the German army had bypassed France's main defence system, the fortress-like Maginot Line, and were advancing at incredible speed towards the coast. The Allies had swiftly retreated. To begin with it seemed that only a few thousand would escape. With the cream of the army and most of its equipment captured, Britain would be defenceless.

Dunkirk came as a terrible shock for Londoners. Many of the injured soldiers were taken by train to London for treatment in the capital's hospitals, and for numerous Londoners the sight of these dishevelled and shaken men pouring into Waterloo Station brought home the nearness of the battle. It had been assumed that the battle would be fought on continental soil, and, though Londoners had been prepared for rationing and air raids, they were taken aback by what faced them now.

The invasion of Britain suddenly seemed likely. Military chiefs began to implement plans to resist the invasion, which it was assumed would spearhead on London. The Home Guard helped with a lot of the donkey work, eagerly dismantling signposts, railway signs and any evidence of place names, to confuse the invaders. To stop German troop-carrying gliders using London's roads as runways, vast hoops of metal were erected over dual carriageways and ring roads like the North Circular and the Kingston Bypass. Hundreds of wooden stakes were hammered in rows across open spaces like Hackney Marshes so that they could not be used as enemy landing grounds.

Children were sent away in their thousands by parents who could afford the liner fares to distant parts of the British Empire or to the United States. An official emergency scheme to ship children to safety was swiftly overwhelmed by a rush of applications despite the fact that Germany had refused to grant evacuee ships a safe passage.

But the German army, instead of attempting the immediate invasion many Londoners expected, turned south to complete its conquest of France. Everyone, from cabinet ministers to assembly line workers, realized the urgent need to take advantage of this valuable breathing space to replace all the military hardware – tanks, transport, machine-guns, rifles and artillery – that the British army had left behind at Dunkirk. For Britain – and London – to be able to resist Hitler it was crucial that she should be armed.

People came to call this new spirit of determined resistance 'the Dunkirk spirit'. J. B. Priestley coined the phrase in his talks on BBC radio, referring to the defiant and miraculous evacuation of British troops when all seemed lost. Within weeks this new catchphrase had captured Londoners' imagination as the 'never say die' fight for democracy in which everyone had an important part to play. People all over the capital were saying that this new spirit would get them out of trouble.

The 'all-out effort' of those first few weeks after Dunkirk certainly boosted the rearmament drive and helped to generate a strong spirit of resistance in London. Hard work and vigilance were to be the watchwords of the summer. But just as the war effort in London was gaining some momentum and people were resolving to do everything they could to resist the invasion, two more bitter blows had to be faced.

On 10 June, Italy, led by the Fascist dictator Mussolini, declared war on Britain and France. That night there were riots in Soho with window-smashing crowds seeking early retribution on the Italian community, now seen as another enemy. Then two weeks later, on 25 June, France, rapidly being overrun by the German army, finally surrendered. Nina Hibbin was then out on the streets of east London to record for Home Intelligence people's reaction to this latest blow:

> I have a very vivid memory of the fall of France because I had to go out and, as usual, slip the question in, 'What did you think of the news?' which you just simply couldn't do because on every street corner there were little groups of people, and they were crying. It was the only time I'd ever seen people actually crying in the street. It was not just fear of invasion, it was like, 'That's the end of our alliance, and what's going to happen now?'

ROUNDING UP THE ALIENS

Suddenly Britain stood alone – all her Allies had been defeated. Churchill stiffened the mood of resistance with speeches promising, 'we'll fight in the fields and in the streets'. The new spirit of resistance emerging out of Britain's isolation became increasingly insular and xenophobic. 'Now we know where we are! No more bloody Allies!', a tug skipper shouted across the Thames to the writer A. P. Herbert.

There was a feeling in the capital that only the British could be trusted in the coming battle. Such feelings found their most extreme form in a sort of collective anxiety about the 'fifth column', the enemy within. It was assumed, first, that fifth columnists had infiltrated London life – Churchill spoke of this 'malignancy in our midst' – and second, that those who had no claim to British citizenship were likely to be the traitors. In short, the foreigner or the 'alien' was not to be trusted. Suddenly, not only was the Home Guard on the lookout for fifth columnists – it became a preoccupation of the entire city.

The anxiety was particularly strong in London because, as the capital, it formed the political, military and administrative heart of the nation's war effort. This concentration of power seemed, moreover, to be threatened by London's cosmopolitan nature, by its mass of immigrant groups – Jewish, Italian, Irish, German – which formed more than ten per cent of its total population. This immigrant community had, of course, been 'topped up' by fifty-five thousand or so German, Austrian and Czech refugees from Nazi oppression. Originally they had been welcomed and treated sympathetically by the capital, but by the summer of 1940 popular opinion was turning dramatically not only against the Italian community but against the German and Austrian Jews too. Klaus Hinrichsen remembered how the warm welcome that the German refugees had first received evaporated:

Up to that time the population had been quite extraordinarily tolerant. But once the Germans had started overrunning the Low Countries and Belgium, rumours began to spread, particularly through the Press, that German parachutists had descended on those countries dressed as nuns and priests, and that they'd been assisted by fifth columnists. Suddenly the Press, particularly the *Daily Mail* and the *Sunday Express*, took up a vicious campaign against the refugees, suspecting that most of them were fifth column and that they were a danger to the nation. Boarding-house owners suddenly put up notices, 'No Germans, No Jews', which was particularly offensive to the Jews, who had been Hitler's first victims. And I began to be afraid to talk in Underground trains and public places because, although I spoke English, it was quite obvious I was German because of the accent. You could feel that the situation was tense and that it was a fraught situation to run around as an able-bodied young German.

Popular imagination was haunted by images of refugees transmitting information back to the Fatherland on secret radios; of Italian waiters eavesdropping on the conversations of cabinet ministers as they dined in Soho restaurants; of 'foreign' domestics rifling through the secret papers of their high-ranking employers; and of expatriate and German businessmen turned saboteurs blowing up bridges, power stations and aerodromes all over London. The press further whipped up this suspicion and hostility, demanding that the government 'intern the lot'.

Internment had in fact begun at the outset of the war when a handful of known Nazi supporters and sympathizers – some of them German – classified as Grade 'A' risks to the nation, had been transported to special camps for prisoners of war. However, the British government maintained a liberal approach and recent immigrants who did not seem to pose any real threat had been classified as Grade 'B' and Grade 'C' aliens and were allowed to retain their liberty. In June, when Italy declared war, the Italian community of chefs, waiters, restaurateurs and shopkeepers concentrated in Soho and Seven Dials – many of whom had lived in London for generations and who identified with the British cause – was also rounded up. Victor Toliani who had lived in London since he was a small child recalled:

> I was brought up in this country, I was educated here, and actually I felt like a Londoner. But when war was declared with Italy on 10 June I was arrested a few hours afterwards by Special Branch officers and the shock was enormous. I had no tribunal, no trial, and I was just taken away from my family and home, and shunted around the country to different prison camps. And the treatment was actually very bad. There was one occasion when we were marched through the streets, and on a street corner was a teacher with a group of school children, and she turned round and said, 'Look at the dirty Germans, spit on them,' which these kids promptly did. On the other corner was a little old lady standing by. She looked at us, and said, 'Well, whoever you are, God help you.'

On 24 June panic measures were taken. At Churchill's direction, the police rounded up and interned more than fifteen thousand Grade 'C' foreigners living in London. The vast majority were Jews who had escaped from Germany and Austria, who would have been sent to concentration camps by Hitler and who were eager to fight against him. Among those rounded up by the police was Klaus Hinrichsen:

At that time I lived in a small attic flat in Glenlock Road, near Haverstock Hill in Hampstead. One morning very early, came a knock at the door and there were two CID officers. They had come for details of another German refugee who was living in the house and they asked the landlady, 'Are there any other Germans in your house?' She said, 'Yes, there is someone living on the top floor.' The officers came up and told me to get dressed and pack my suitcase. I was just about to go off with the Pioneer Corps, which was a non-combatant regiment established for refugees to help the war effort. My call-up was due any day and I thought that in fact it was the postman bringing me the note. I remonstrated with them and said, 'You cannot possibly take me, I have been classified a friendly alien and I am waiting to join the British army.' They said, 'You can explain this to our superiors.' They put me in the Black Maria outside and I was driven off to Hampstead Police Station and later that night to Lingfield Race Course.

In the atmosphere of this 'collar the lot' campaign all 'aliens' were arrested, even those who, like Jewish refugee scientists, were playing an important role in the war effort. They were interned in hotels or hastily converted holiday camps, many of them on the Isle of Man or in seaside towns and, to begin with, they were subjected to a harsh and often punitive regime. Boatloads of internees were quickly deported to the colonies. Victor Toliani was one of the many Italian internees who were packed into the liner, SS *Arandora Star*, to be shipped to Canada. It was torpedoed in the Atlantic with the loss of six hundred lives. It was for him a terrible memory:

Two days out to sea, first thing in the morning, I was still fast asleep under a trestle in the main lounge when a German torpedo hit us. The ship immediately started to list. My friend and I decided to go overboard into the sea, just as the captain was shouting out, 'abandon ship'. This all took place within twenty minutes and the water was already filled with wreckage, and floating bodies. But luckily a raft came by with a person sitting in it, and he helped us into it. We spent ten to eleven hours floating around on this raft, it was like an eternity, and we were sure we were going to die. Then a Canadian destroyer came along and picked us up.

The witch-hunt was extremely divisive and even loyal British citizens were interrogated by the police and shunned by neighbours if there was the slightest suspicion that they were fifth columnists. Odette Lesley remembered this happening:

I came home one night to the flat where I lived in Hampstead and found that the police had broken in. They started to interrogate me in an awful sort of way, saying things like, 'You're an enemy agent, you're a fifth columnist, who's paying you?' And this interrogation seemed to go on for such a long, long time, until I realized what had happened. I had left a light on without drawing the blackout curtains and, of course, it was shining out like a beacon across the Heath which to them was a signal to the enemy, because it was thought that this sort of thing was being done by fifth columnists. I realized the awfulness of what I'd done. Imagine me signalling the enemy. Eventually I did convince them that I was not an enemy agent, it was a pure accident and in the end I was just fined two pounds at the local magistrates' court. But the outcome of it was that many of the neighbours around shunned us for quite some time, whispering 'Look, fifth column', which was to me so dreadful because nobody was more anti-Nazi than I was.

Anyone, whoever they were and whatever their background, became a potential object of suspicion. There was a spate of prosecutions for careless and defeatist talk as police and informers tightened their grip on comment and criticism of government action. After only a week, this had led to serious discontent in London. The Home Intelligence reports for London record 'many people feeling nervous about anti-gossip campaign and that they are afraid to open their mouths'. Londoners were saying that the policy was 'turning us into a nation of spies'.

PREPARING FOR INVASION

The main problem concerning the British government at this time, however, was one of high-level strategy involving the defence of Britain, and especially London, against invasion. Throughout the summer British Intelligence desperately tried to piece together scraps of information to predict the invasion date.

The search was given even more urgency in mid-July when Hitler announced, 'I have made a decision to prepare for and if necessary carry out an invasion of England.' His plan was to establish a bridgehead on the south-east coast between Folkestone and Worthing and to advance on London, the capture of which, he thought, would end British resistance. A Gestapo 'hit list' of thousands of London notables, featuring ministers, politicians, civil servants, industrialists and journalists, was created, plans were made to remove national treasures – including Nelson's column – to the Fatherland, and a scheme was drawn up to transport men of working age to camps in Europe.

The people of London, knowing that they were to be the main target for the coming German onslaught, prepared for a last stand. Churchill declared that we would 'fight for every inch of London, down to the last street and suburb'. Londoners comforted themselves with the thought that resistance would be strengthened by the presence of the evacuated British Expeditionary Force and by a new wave of conscription adding another five hundred thousand to the armed forces. Most of these were to be deployed in mobile forces to attack the Germans when they arrived and advanced from their coastal positions. They would have been aided by a secret plan to drop mustard gas on the invaders as they landed on the beaches. In the South they aimed to prevent the enemy crossing a 'stop line', which ran all the way from Maidstone in Kent to the Bristol Channel.

The defence of London itself lay in the hands of a number of battalions of the regular army and the Home Guard. Together they prepared three lines of defence for the capital. The first two, on the outskirts, were anti-tank lines with deep trenches, barriers, pill boxes – squat, concrete firing points – and road blocks. The outer line circled London's suburban frontiers linking together Rickmansworth, Potters Bar and Epping Forest in the north with Hounslow, Kingston-upon-Thames and Bromley in the south, bordering Uxbridge and Yiewsley in the west and Redbridge and Woolwich in the east as part of its grand sweep around the capital. The next line of defence ran several miles inside this outer barrier linking together Enfield to the north, Harrow to the west, West Norwood in the south and Wanstead in the east. The third inner line of defence was bounded to the south by the River Thames, and to the east and west by the Rivers Lea and Brent with the circle finally meeting to the north at the Dollis Sewage Works. This inner line was seen to be crucial to London's defence and was to be manned entirely by the regular army.

Finally, a last stand was planned in Whitehall and on street corners by crack troops like the Royal Marines and the Scots and Grenadier Guards. Machine-guns were placed inside or on top of strategic buildings, and on street corners all over the area. Rapidly erected pill boxes were often disguised as tea stalls. Contingency plans were made for special protection to be given to notables like the royal family, the Prime Minister and leading government officials; they were to be flown away to safety if the enemy advanced this far and if the fall of London looked inevitable.

The Home Guard was to play a key role in the defence of London's two outer anti-tank lines. It was stressed at the time that these lines should be held to the last man – no withdrawal was permitted without direct orders from headquarters. The efforts of those volunteers, who spent evenings and weekends practising techniques to sabotage tanks, shooting from uncovered positions at imaginary German planes, or laying trip wires across the roads (thereby threatening local drivers more than the Germans), have been affectionately parodied in the sitcom *Dad's Army*, filmed for television in the 1960s. It is certainly difficult to envisage this ill-equipped and ill-trained civilian army of clerks, retired bank managers and ageing colonels holding up Hitler's advance. Len Jones, a member of the 57th Surrey Home Guards Unit, recalled preparing to repulse any enemy advance across the Mitcham part of London's outer defence line:

> We were told to dig great anti-tank trenches across the sewage farm
> by Hackbridge Junction. The plan was that the tanks would fall into
> them and they would be so steep that they wouldn't be able to get out.
> We thought this was a waste of effort, so we only dug shallow trenches
> and covered them over with branches so the top brass wouldn't notice.
> Another plan we had was to creep up on the German tanks at night
> when they were still, kill the sentries and plant sticky bombs on the
> caterpillar tracks so that when they started up next morning they
> would explode and dislocate the tracks. Then, when they got out of
> the tank to repair it, we would throw sulphuric acid balls at them. Our
> favourite sabotage tactic, though, was trip wires. We practised
> stretching wires between trees. We were going to use that trick to get
> German motorcyclists as they went along the road – if they had been
> going fast, the aim was to take their heads off.

Fears of a massive air attack on London had engendered a feeling of helplessness: the vision now of Nazi divisions attempting to march upon London had, by contrast, created the feeling that there was an active role for everyone. Commuters bought guerrilla warfare booklets on station bookstalls and middle-class women in places like Hampstead formed private armies teaching themselves weapon handling. Government leaflets advised civilians to stand firm, demobilize motor cars and give no assistance to the enemy. Every Londoner had a part to play in the defence of the capital. From this mood emerged an exhilarating feeling of confidence. The Home Guard, for example, believed that they really could stop the massively well-equipped panzer divisions of the German army, as Len Jones remembered:

> Most of the men in the unit worked in engineering and we could use
> all the latest engineering equipment, so we managed to improve
> beyond recognition all the old weapons we got lumbered with in the
> Home Guard. The old Smith guns we were given were very crude, but
> we machined new barrels and fitted sights onto them to make them
> very accurate. We modified the sten guns we were given to make
> them more accurate and our stock of bayonets and knives we made
> razor sharp. And we made our own acid bombs and sticky bombs. We
> really thought we could stop the German army. In hindsight, we
> weren't aware of how difficult it would be to get anywhere near the
> German troops and tanks without being killed, but we felt that our
> dogged determination would get the better of them.

This feeling of confidence was given a tremendous boost during the summer of 1940 by the success of the RAF. The Battle of Britain, as the air war between the RAF and the Luftwaffe came to be called, was close-run. Many British pilots were killed and the Germans nearly destroyed a vital ring of seven aerodromes around London. The Luftwaffe was, however, held at bay, and this resistance was heralded as a major triumph in the propaganda of the time. The RAF seemed to most people, including Churchill, to be winning the day.

The Battle of Britain was, however, not so much being won, as changing course. In the last week of August, a few German raiders who had lost their way emptied their bombs on the capital by mistake and in direct contravention of Hitler's orders. Though small in scale, this seemed to be the sort of targeting of the London population that had been so feared and expected at the outbreak of war. On subsequent nights, the RAF bombed Berlin. The German response was to shift from military to civilian targets.

On 4 September Hitler proclaimed, 'In England they're filled with curiosity and keep asking, "Why doesn't he come?" Be calm. He's coming. He's coming. When they declare that they will increase their attacks on our cities, then we will raze their cities to the ground.' But Londoners now believed that the RAF had mastery of the air. Their fears – which had so dominated the outbreak of war – receded just as the Battle for London was about to begin.

CHAPTER FOURTEEN

The Battle for London

A T AROUND FIVE o'clock on 7 September 1940, a hot, summery afternoon, East Enders were drawn on to the streets by the approaching roar of several hundred bombers. Most of them thought the planes were British for they had come to believe that the capital was no longer vulnerable to such an air attack. Then the bombs began to fall, first on the Arsenal in Woolwich, then thousands raining down on the vast complex of docks on both sides of the Thames – especially the Victoria & Albert, the East India and the Surrey Commercial – setting them ablaze. Very quickly as they crouched in the official street shelters, or in their own living rooms, Londoners realized that they were themselves targets as the maze of narrow streets and blocks of flats from West Ham to Bow, from Bermondsey to Whitechapel and from Limehouse to Poplar were blitzed. One of those standing in King Street, Poplar, was eighteen-year-old Len Jones who recalled:

> That afternoon, around five o'clock, I went outside the house. I'd heard the aircraft, and it was very exciting, because the first formations were coming over without any bombs dropping, but very, very majestic; terrific. And I had no thought that they were actually bombers. Then from that point on I was well aware, because bombs began to fall, and shrapnel was going along King Street, dancing off the cobbles. Then the real impetus came, insofar as the suction and the compression from the high explosive blasts just pulled you and pushed you, and the whole of this atmosphere was turbulating so hard that, after an explosion of a nearby bomb, you could actually feel your eyeballs being sucked out. I was holding my eyes to try and stop them going. And the suction was so vast, it ripped my shirt away, and ripped my trousers. Then I couldn't get my breath, the smoke was like acid and everything round me was black and yellow. And these bombers just kept on and on, the whole road was moving, rising and falling.

The first wave of bombs was hitting the poorest and most overcrowded parts of London, and some slum buildings, like the jerry-built tenements of Canning Town, disintegrated into rubble, burying their occupants underneath. In the shelters men and women were shouting and screaming hysterically as each blast rocked the very structures that were protecting them.

The East End faced the full brunt of this attack. Gladys Strelitz remembered the first instinct of her and her family in East Ham was to run away from the bombs:

> We had been bombed all day long and there was a lull. My brother said, 'Come on girls, get all the children's clothes in a bag and we've got to get out of London, there is a lull.' And so we got this bus, and we went to Bow. And when we got to Bow the bombing was going so badly that the conductor pulled the bell and said that we wouldn't go any further. So the only place to go was to run under this crypt, under this big church. And there the sight that met my eyes, it overcome me. Because there was people praying, and crying and asking God to help us, because there was bombs going on and this crypt, it was actually shuddering. And, well, it was too much for me, I just passed out.

Len Jones ran into a nearby street shelter in Poplar, which he was to share with several Chinese families that lived in the area:

> The shelter was brick and concrete built, and it was lifting and moving, rolling almost as if it was a ship in a rough sea. And the suction and the blasts coming in and out of this steel door, which was smashing backwards and forwards, bashed us around against the walls. The extent of injuries at that stage was just abrasions really, the shoulders and chest getting crushed against the wall, or across the floor. The worst part was the poor little kids; they were so scared, they were screaming and crying, clutching at their parents. The heat was colossal; the steel door was so hot you couldn't touch it. And everybody was being sick and people were carrying out their normal human needs, and the smell was terrible.

The second attack came later that evening and continued into the early hours of Sunday morning. By this time four hundred and thirty East Enders had died and many corpses lay in the streets and gardens. Sixteen hundred were seriously injured, and tens of thousands were made homeless. Len Jones was shocked by what he saw when he emerged from his street shelter early that morning:

> I went out to see how our house was, and when I got there the front door was lying back, and the glass of the windows had fallen in, and I could see the top of the house had virtually disappeared. Inside, everything was blown to pieces, you could see it all by the red glow reflecting from the fires that were raging outside. Then I looked out the back and suddenly I realized that where my father's shed and workshop used to be, was just a pile of rubble, bricks. Then I saw two bodies, two heads sticking up, I recognized one head in particular; it was a Chinese man, Mr Say, he had one eye closed, and then I began to realize that he was dead.

When fire-fighters arrived at the docks, they faced a uniquely terrifying spectacle. Bill Ward, who was one of them, remembered:

> We go into Surrey Docks and the flames are all over the place. There's telegraph poles alight, the fences were alight and, when we get nearer to the canal, there's even barges alight. Everything was alight including the warehouses, and everything inside them was burning, the fumes choked you. We'd have to walk in the middle of the road because the Germans overhead were flinging down the bombs and walls and masonry were falling everywhere. I don't think any firemen had ever seen anything like it before.

During and immediately after these attacks the emergency services almost broke down. Nurses in the ill-equipped first-aid posts dotted around the East End were besieged by the walking wounded. Ambulances found it difficult to get through the bomb-cratered streets to ferry the seriously injured away to hospital. Weary rescue squads – swamped by the magnitude of the devastation – worked furiously to free as many of those trapped in the debris as they could.

The next morning some homeless families wandered aimlessly around the ruins of their shattered streets while others formed long queues outside the rest centres provided for them. Bombed-out families, desperate for food, clothing and shelter, were bewildered to discover that practically no provision had been made for them. The abiding memory of that first and awful night of bombing – known locally as Black Saturday – was one of shock, panic, helplessness, confusion and hysteria. The nightmarish experience remained with many East Enders for the rest of their lives. Gladys Strelitz recalled:

> As we got out of the crypt, we could see the Home Guard actually digging out bodies. And the smouldering flames and the stench was terrible and the sky all lit up with flames. It was a terrible sight. Shattering to relive it, to remember.

Some of the panic that night was caused by the army. It seemed possible that the mass bombing, combined with favourable moon and tide conditions, could mark the beginning of Hitler's long-awaited invasion. The code word 'Cromwell' – which meant that the invasion was imminent – was signalled around Britain. This was widely interpreted as meaning that the invasion had actually started. The Home Guard were called out and in one part of Eastern Command the army blew up strategic bridges. All this added to the confusion in the East End as fire-fighters were warned to look out for parachutists and fifth columnists.

RUNNING FOR SHELTER

On Black Saturday, and during the first few days and nights of bombing which followed, many Londoners felt defenceless. They were disturbed by the fact that there was at first little anti-aircraft fire deployed against the raiders. They did not know that the sound location equipment on which the gun crews relied to locate their target had turned out to be totally ineffective. The feeling of terrible vulnerability was heightened by the government's failure to make provision for protection against air raids. These attacks were unprecedented in their ferocity and the received wisdom was that sheltering from bombs would be hopeless. Instead, millions of cardboard coffins were ordered and preparations made for instant burials in quicklime. Teams of psychiatrists were on standby to provide therapy for mass neurosis. Another assumption was that air attacks would be by daylight and would be over fairly quickly so that shelters would be primitive, without provision for overnight stays.

Before the outbreak of war, but in anticipation of the first bombing raids, the Home Secretary John Anderson had, in 1938, asked for a cheap back garden shelter to be designed. This was done very speedily by a team of engineers who approved a standard design. Shelters were constructed from fourteen sheets of corrugated iron forming a shell which was buried in the ground to a depth of 4 feet (1.2 m) with at least 15 inches (38 cm) of earth above. These so-called 'Anderson' shelters were not roomy: they were only 4½ feet (1.4 m) wide and just over 6 feet (1.8 m) long and high.

The first Anderson shelters were distributed in the borough of Islington as early as February 1938, and before the blitz began two and a quarter million Anderson shelters had been dug into London gardens. During the Phoney War they were of no use and were damp and cold when the terror of the bombing raids drove Londoners into them. But they proved their worth: only a direct hit by a bomb put the sheltering families in danger. There was a limitation on the use of the Anderson shelters, however. To dig one in you had to have a garden and many Londoners, especially East Enders huddled in densely populated treeless streets, did not. Another kind of brick shelter was provided but these proved to be less effective than the Andersons, chiefly because they were poorly built. Emily Eary remembered the frailty of these shelters in the Aldgate district:

The warning had gone, we all ran to the shelter. There was my mum, my two sisters and my brother. We ran down the stairs, and we all sat huddled together on a form. It was very cold, damp down there, and there were crowds of people. Then the bombers came over, and in the early hours this bomb came down, it whooshed down. We didn't know where it had hit; we just sat there. It shook the shelter, we were covered in dirt and dust, it was choking everybody and we all got into a bit of panic. We couldn't move, we just sat there. Everybody was saying, 'What's happened, what's happened?'

Then we realized that the buildings had had a direct hit, collapsed onto the entrance of the shelter, and we couldn't get out. And we had to crawl out the far entrance. We were crawling over old forms that people had turned over to get out in a panic. We crawled to the end and as we got out we saw daylight, and we saw a big space where our flats had been. There were many people killed down there, but we were just relieved to get out that day, and wondered where we were going to go next night.

London's East End took the brunt of those first few days and nights of saturation bombing between 7 and 11 September. Its familiar cityscape of terraced rows, warehouses and factories was, in just four days, shattered by bomb blast and fire into what looked like a smouldering shanty town. Whole streets were reduced to rubble. The horror of it all and the feeling of defencelessness created a sense of shock and panic. The Home Intelligence report for 9 September noted that: 'In dockside areas the population is showing visible signs of its nerve cracking from constant ordeals.' And the following day it reported: 'Increased tension everywhere and when the siren goes people run madly for shelters with white faces . . . Bermondsey Citizens' Advice Bureau is inundated with mothers and young children hysterical and asking to be removed from the district . . . Exodus from East End growing rapidly. Taxi drivers report taking party after party to Euston and Paddington with belongings.'

Thousands of terrified East End families trekked out of London. They struggled through cratered streets, pushing babies in prams, the elderly in wheelchairs and their possessions loaded in hand carts. Gladys Strelitz recalled:

> The day after everybody was fleeing for their lives because it was still blazing. And we got the children and we knew we got to run for it like everybody else was running out of London. You had to escape, so we just managed to get into a baker's van that took us to the station. And we decided to go to Maidenhead and take the children there.

Refugees also fled to Epping Forest in Essex, Reading, Windsor, Oxford, and to the Kentish hopfields, where they camped out under the trees or in makeshift wooden huts. Mary Price remembered setting off with her young baby:

> There was destruction and flames and smoke everywhere and the noise was terrible. We were petrified. We didn't know where to go and what to do. The only thing we could think of was to get to Kent to the hopfields. At least we'd be safe getting out of London. Some cousins of mine came round; they'd borrowed a lorry and they said, 'Come on, we're going', and I just took two bags of clothes with the baby. I had a five-month-old baby. We made our way to Kent. It was just like a convoy of refugees going out. Everything on wheels, old cars, old

lorries, anything that moved, it was one steady stream going towards the coast. We got to the hopfields and there's this wonderful sense of peace, nothing was happening. We slept in the huts on straw that the farmer provided.

Some official attempts to bring an atmosphere of greater calm by organizing the evacuation in an orderly fashion went disastrously wrong. West Ham Council, for example, gathered several hundred people who wanted to be evacuated – mostly homeless mothers and children – into South Hallsville Road School, Canning Town, which had no air-raid shelter. The coaches to take the refugees away were directed to Camden Town instead of Canning Town, leaving the women and children waiting in the school to be evacuated the following day. That night the school suffered a direct hit and almost everyone inside was killed.

DEFYING AUTHORITY

London's growing sense of vulnerability was reinforced by a widely held belief that the authorities could not be trusted to tell the truth about what was really happening in the war – and, in particular, the cost to London of the blitz. The government took the view that the sight of death and destruction on London streets, or the knowledge of its extent, would have a demoralizing effect. Thus any film or photograph showing deaths from an air raid was banned and press reports on casualties of bombings were censored. The Ministry of Information stipulated that any film of a bombed-out street had to end with a building that was intact. It was forbidden to give the names and localities of damaged buildings for twenty-eight days. This cover-up process was completed by the body-disposal squads, whose job it was to collect quickly the shattered remains of dead bodies and transport them to mortuaries.

Censorship was a breeding ground for suspicion and during the first few days of the blitz there were plenty of demoralizing rumours that London was about to grind to a standstill. Such talk gained a widespread currency in the first few days of the blitz and to many in the battered East End the chaos was real. In particular the main provision for the homeless – rest centres – was proving to be disastrously inadequate. The principal problems were severe overcrowding and insanitary facilities. In one rest centre in Stepney – a converted elementary school – three hundred people had the use of ten pails and coal scuttles as lavatories. Though most of these families had been bombed out, the overcrowding was further aggravated by the arrival of temporary evacuees.

Hundreds of unexploded bombs littered the streets waiting to be defused, which meant that whole communities had to be evacuated and all roads closed within a 300-yard (275 m) radius of each bomb. The handful of troops trained to deal with bomb disposal had received only the most basic training. Bert Woolhouse, who was a sapper (private) with the Royal Engineers, remembered:

> When we went out on a bomb, we used to draw lots to see whose turn it was to be in the hole first. And we used to evacuate the area around for three hundred yards and we were very inexperienced, didn't know hardly anything about bombs or explosives, and we were young – only 'squaddies' – and I can assure you that we were very, very frightened when we got into a bomb hole on our own. On this particular occasion, when we were digging the bomb, we found a fuse which we knew was an anti-handling fuse and then, when we tried to get this bomb out, it exploded. I was thrown many yards, and covered with rubble and my ears were bleeding. I was crying and a chimney pot hit me on the head. All my comrades were killed, blown to pieces. The most found of anybody was a piece of leg in a Wellington boot.

While fire brigades continued to struggle bravely to contain each conflagration, and heavy rescue squads tried to dig out survivors, the bombed and evacuated buildings provided rich pickings for looters. There was often a narrow line between 'helping yourself' and criminal activity. Children would rummage through rubble looking for salvageable items, and some poor families would ensure that they had enough food by lifting it from shops with their fronts blown in. Sometimes policemen and civil defence workers would 'rescue' goods that, they argued, were about to be destroyed. Petty criminals took advantage of the dark streets and empty houses to steal goods for the black market, now growing fast as shortages began to bite. Frank Whipple, a reserve policeman, remembered patrolling the dock areas:

> There was a terrible lot of looting. You'd find bent wardens, heavy rescue men, even police doing it. People were like vultures, going into

bombed-out houses and shops, and they'd even take rings and valuables off dead bodies. We would have to accompany them to the mortuary to stop that happening.

Reports of such incidents were censored, but a lot of people knew what was going on: shopkeepers found their stocks depleted after raids and families found their prized possessions missing from their damaged houses. For many, suffering already from the strain of the raids, this seemed to be the last straw. Gladys Strelitz remembered that when she returned to her home, having evacuated her children, she was in for a shock:

> We went home to find that all around us was shattered. We had just
> had our windows blown out, but people had been in and looted my
> home and all the bed linen and everything was stolen and, well, we
> were full of despair. It was sad enough leaving the children, but to
> come home to that.

On 11 September Churchill tried to raise people's flagging spirits with a speech broadcast to the nation. Londoners, huddled around their wireless sets, heard the Prime Minister tell them that the barges for the invasion lay in wait across the Channel. He described the Luftwaffe's attempt to win air mastery as 'the crux of the whole war'. He said that the week that followed would rank in British history 'with the days when the Spanish Armada was approaching the Channel and Drake was finishing his game of bowls; or when Nelson stood between us and Napoleon's Grand Army at Boulogne'. He finished saying: '... every man and woman will therefore prepare himself to do his duty whatever it may be, with special pride and care.'

Although some Londoners greeted the speech with cheering and many were moved by it, there was still deep government concern that their morale was cracking. This concern peaked on the fifth day of the blitz – 12 September – when thousands of East Enders stormed tube stations in east and central London to use as shelters.

Officials had rejected the use of the Underground for this purpose fearing that those inside would develop a 'deep shelter mentality', leading a troglodyte existence, never daring to come to the surface until the war was over. Also they wished to keep the Underground railways clear so that movement of troops, the injured and the evacuated could be carried out under London without hindrance. But when the idea that the tubes could provide a safe refuge from the bombing took hold of the popular imagination there was a stampede to the stations and the officials could not stop it. Sheltering in the tubes began when hundreds of families bought tickets, rode the trains, then evaded station staff in a bid to stay on the platforms all night. But after a few days, crowds just brushed past the police and London Transport officials trying to keep them out. Emily Eary and her family were among them:

> When we got down there we would travel the tubes. And the porters, the station staff, used to say, 'Clear out, get out, you're not supposed to be down here', so we would travel, just pretend we were travellers, just to be down there, because we knew it was illegal. When the trains stopped running, we'd put our bits and pieces, our old blankets and our pillows on the platform and we'd lie there against the wall.
>
> But gradually, it just caught on, and people were so frightened they had to force their way down. They were determined that they weren't going to be thrown out. People would rush to the tubes, almost knock you over to get down the escalator because when bombs were coming down, people were getting panic-stricken to get out of the noise and the devastation.

People camped where they could – on the platforms, in the corridors, even on the stairs. Though the authorities disapproved, they found themselves powerless to move the swelling crowds. Within days more than a hundred and fifty thousand people were taking refuge in the safety of the tubes. The way in which the Underground system had been taken over by the people, against the wishes of the authorities, became symbolically important, signalling the beginning of an attitude of self-reliance and community initiative. This would help to build a new spirit of resistance in the next, and critical, weeks of the blitz.

This emergent mood was reinforced by the commencement of an intense barrage of anti-aircraft fire. British night fighters were withdrawn and London's anti-aircraft guns, which bristled across Hyde Park, Battersea Park and Richmond Park, had the opportunity to blaze away at the bombers. General Pile, the ack-ack (anti-aircraft guns) commander, issued orders that every possible gun should fire, however remote the chances of hitting anything. The terrible noise that the resulting barrage made kept many people awake all night. The shells, in fact, killed far more civilians –

through falling fragments – than German bombers, while unexploded shells added to the chaos already caused by unexploded bombs. However, people did not realize all this and the thunder of British guns, which at least forced enemy aircraft to fly higher, gave a boost to Londoners' morale. Also, now that the Luftwaffe's new strategy of relentless bombing of the capital had become clear, Fighter Command deployed many more aircraft to protect London.

CIVILIANS TO THE RESCUE

At last it seemed something was being done to defend the city. The panic and anarchic exodus of the first days were dramatically reduced. But the British defences could not stop the bombers. The Luftwaffe kept coming through day after day, and in greater strength night after night. While the eastern riverside boroughs – from Stepney to Canning Town and from Bermondsey to Deptford – continued to take the brunt of the attack, the more central areas of the City, the South Bank and the West End were now also being heavily hit.

In the front line in the fight to withstand the saturation bombing and to keep London ticking over stood the emergency services. The fire service played a critical role because of the widespread use of incendiary bombs. Fires, many times worse than any confronted in peacetime London, blazed every night. The burden of fire-fighting fell on the 2,000 professional firemen of the London Fire Brigade, backed up by the 23,000 full- and part-time auxiliaries called up at the beginning of the war. The volunteers came from many backgrounds: bus drivers, labourers, journalists, artists, salesmen and a number of conscientious objectors. In the long lull prior to the blitz they had been openly derided by the public as 'war dodgers, loafers and parasites'. As a result, many left the service and from June 1940 the government had to stop any more men from resigning in order to maintain the fire service's strength.

The fires now threatening to engulf whole communities and reduce built-up areas to ashes gave the firemen the opportunity to answer their critics and to end the stigma of cowardice. This they did in the most emphatic way. They battled night after night against the flames, often not sleeping or resting for days. The danger they faced from collapsing walls, falling masonry and poisonous fumes was made more horrifying by the fact that their work was often done in the thick of air raids. The Luftwaffe often preceded a major bombardment with an incendiary attack, causing widespread fires forming easily identifiable targets for their bombers. As a result, hundreds of firemen were killed or injured on duty.

Rescue squads dug out the living and the dead from bombed buildings. Many of the rescuers had been building workers – bricklayers, plumbers, carpenters – who used their knowledge of construction techniques to dig survivors from the ruins. Stretcher carriers lifted the injured away from bombed-out buildings. Doctors performed endless operations on blitz victims. Repair gangs worked round the clock attempting to restore broken electricity cables, sewage pipes, gas mains and telephone cables. All these groups had to brave the bombs that were raining down day and night, hampering their work. They all played a key role in keeping London going and making some sort of civilized routine possible. Many were professionals but, as with the firemen, there was also a large number of volunteers from all walks of life.

At the heart of the air-raid defence system was the air-raid warden. A network of thousands of air-raid wardens, nine-tenths of whom were voluntary part-timers, covered the capital. On average there were ten per square mile. Their job was to report incidents, call up the appropriate rescue services and, if they were first on the scene, to do their best to rescue the trapped and provide first aid for the injured. They also had the dangerous task of investigating unexploded bombs. In the first days of the blitz a number of wardens had shown themselves to be totally incompetent and some had even run away; but those who remained, together with new recruits, provided for the most part an invaluable service to their local communities.

Women made a crucial contribution to maintaining essential services during the blitz. Because this was very much a civilians' war and because there was such a shortage of manpower, there were many opportunities for women to become involved in all sorts of ARP and civil defence work. Many thrived on this new freedom. About one in six wardens was a woman and most were middle-aged housewives who carried out their duties on a part-time voluntary basis.

Women also volunteered in large numbers to drive fire engines and ambulances – in fact, most of London's ambulance drivers were women. This was a popular option among the more prosperous, for the ability to drive was at this time relatively rare. They faced unprecedented dangers, driving in virtual pitch darkness – only dimmed sidelights were allowed – along hazardous cratered streets strewn with glass and rubble. For June Buchanan, Society 'deb' turned ambulance driver, the contrast with life before the war could hardly have been greater. She remembered:

> There was such a remarkable difference between my life on and off duty. When I was off duty, I'd be shopping in the West End, dining at the Ritz, wearing smart dresses, going to balls, generally enjoying the social scene in London that I'd just been introduced to after I was presented to the King. Then on duty, I'd do my shifts twelve hours a day, driving the ambulance to and from incidents in my plain cotton coat and cap – it was a completely different world. We all just did what we had to do. I'd often find myself carrying the dead and injured on stretchers into the ambulance and rushing them back to hospital along the blacked-out streets. I just took it in my stride. The bombs would be falling all around, but you felt better out doing something to help rather than waiting for them to drop on you.

Many women also acted as dispatch riders while others played a key role in maintaining communications in the capital – usually by telephone, staffing emergency control centres during the blitz. This was often more dangerous than it sounds, for it meant working through air raids to ensure the co-ordination of emergency services.

But probably the most arduous and exhausting job performed by women in the front line was nursing. State-registered nurses were bolstered by thousands of auxiliary nurses who were given only a few weeks' emergency training, often with the Red Cross or the St John Ambulance Brigade. They provided care and comfort for the injured in air-raid casualty wards, at first-aid posts, and in bombed-out houses where heavy rescue teams searched for survivors. The conditions they worked in were often primitive, overcrowded and dangerous. When they were working alongside rescue teams, they were sometimes lowered down through narrow holes in the rubble to give morphine injections to those buried beneath. For all this they received just 25 shillings a week – barely enough to survive on.

The example of calm and courage set by the emergency services, and the order that began to emerge out of the chaos as a result of their efforts, helped to foster a growing stoicism among Londoners. Indeed, the government was startled that when they hastily revived their evacuation scheme for children it was not taken up en masse by London families. Many mothers preferred their children to remain at home during the bombings than to face another upsetting evacuation. When the heavy bombing began on 7 September there were around 500,000 children of school age in the London evacuation area, but by the end of September only 20,000 unaccompanied children had been evacuated despite official encouragement. Here was clear evidence that people were adjusting to the challenges of air attack.

Even those who had been bombed out and lost practically everything seemed to be coping better with the crisis. In the first days of the blitz many had simply panicked. Now people could often be seen on the day after the bombing carefully going through the wreckage of their homes trying to salvage the remains of their possessions. Commentators noted that finding small personal belongings seemed to help people through the ordeal. Some would recover enough to recreate the feeling of home in a corner of the shelter where they spent their nights. Others would gain immense relief from learning that a pet canary or parrot had survived and would then carry it around in its cage wherever they went.

Those who had not been bombed out often took treasured family items, like wedding photographs, and practical things, like brushes or a spare pair of shoes, to the shelters with them. If their homes were hit then these would become prized possessions – a link with a familiar past – giving them greater personal strength.

And when all seemed lost there was always the reassuring cup of tea. People were observed going back to their homes to find the windows blown in and splinters of glass everywhere, and proceeding calmly to put the kettle on for their morning 'cuppa'. The propaganda films of the blitz regularly played on this routine to illustrate people carrying on as normal. Tea acquired almost a magical importance in London life and the comforting cup of tea actually did seem to help cheer people up in a crisis.

THE HOMELESS CRISIS

But new crises continued to emerge. The first stemmed from the damage and destruction wrought on thousands of homes by the bombings. For those at home, the conditions that people had to put up with – especially in the worst-hit East End where only a third of the population was able to remain in their houses – were often rather primitive during these early days of the blitz. Suddenly, people who were getting used to a world of running water, electricity, and wireless sets were plunged back into Victorian conditions. Most houses suffered some sort of damage in the first few weeks of raids even if this amounted only to shattered windows and cracks in the ceilings and roof. This, together with the regular cut-offs in the electricity, gas and water supplies, made any sort of normal family life impossible.

At the same time there was a host of problems emerging from the lack of adequate shelter. One solution taken by some Londoners was to return to the habits of their early ancestors. They discovered the existence of a set of caverns at Chislehurst in Kent and, as with the London Underground, they simply broke into them. Families each took over a small section. Sometimes double beds, armchairs and tables were transported down in carts and lorries. After a week of the blitz more than eight thousand Londoners were living in these caves. Most were homeless families and older people who had no work to go to, but some commuted daily to their offices and factories in central London.

Much worse conditions were to be found in the mass shelters in the East End where there was appalling overcrowding. The largest and most notorious – the Tilbury shelter – was a massive underground goods yard beneath the Tilbury railway arches in Stepney. It housed as many as 14,000 to 16,000 people each night. Nina Hibbin, working for Mass Observation, provided regular reports on 'the Tilbury':

> The first time I went in there, I had to come out, I felt sick. You just
> couldn't see anything, you could just smell the fug, the overwhelming
> stench. It was like the Black Hole of Calcutta. There were thousands
> and thousands of people lying head to toe, all along the bays and with
> no facilities. At the beginning there were only four earth buckets
> down the far end, behind screens, for toilets. It was terribly hard on
> the old people because they were obviously terrified. They'd usually
> come down in their pyjamas and dressing gowns and they'd have to sit
> up all night huddled together. The place was a hell hole, it was an
> outrage that people had to live in these conditions.

Overcrowding also became especially bad in many of the tube stations. People had to sleep as best they could in cramped and uncomfortable conditions, on floors and against walls. Platforms were packed tight with bodies, people slept on the escalators and slung hammocks over the rails (the power was turned off after the trains had stopped running at 10.30pm). Often, there were no sanitation or washing facilities on the platforms and people walked down the tunnels to relieve themselves. The stench was dreadful and in the older Underground stations a plague of mosquitoes thrived on the heat and the unwashed bodies.

Though these deep shelters were grim and unhealthy, their main advantage was the relative insulation from the noise of bombings and the feeling of safety – not always justified – that they engendered. As a result people were able to sleep a little better in them than in the much more vulnerable surface shelters, where sleep was practically impossible. However, even in the tubes, only three or four hours' sleep would be snatched each night. This dramatic change from private home life to a much more public existence was a severe test for the resistance of East Enders.

In a few shelters committees were democratically elected to try to improve the squalid conditions. They introduced daily cleaning rotas, regularly emptied lavatory buckets and controlled the flow of people in and out by issuing tickets. One huge, stinking cellar in Stepney, which nightly housed ten thousand people in conditions of appalling discomfort and overcrowding, was improved in this way by the remarkable efforts of Mickey Davis, a hunchback only just over 3 feet (91 cm) tall. The shelter, later dubbed 'Mickey's Shelter', quickly became famous for a spirit of self-help and democracy, and Mickey himself became a local celebrity.

However, there was a limit to the changes that could be made by a committee with practically no money or political influence. Substantial improvements, such as the provision of canteens, bunks and decent toilets, were dependent on assistance from local and central government – aid for which the shelter committees began to campaign strongly.

Meanwhile, Hitler put the invasion date back from 15 to 21 September hoping to buy time in which to deliver a knockout blow to the morale of London and the RAF. After making this decision, on 15 September, he launched a massive air attack on London to prepare the way for the delayed invasion. The RAF won a famous victory destroying around fifty German planes while sustaining losses of only about half that number. Londoners, watching the Luftwaffe's humiliation in the sky above them, were given their greatest morale booster to date.

A RIFT BETWEEN RICH AND POOR

Hitler's response was an intensification of the major offensive against the capital and in this next wave of air attacks a new terror weapon was deployed. It was a huge naval mine with considerable blast effect which fell slowly and silently on to its target by parachute. The blast from a 'land mine', as it was called, could blow a man a quarter of a mile away and toss railway carriages into the air like broken toys. The redoubling of Hitler's efforts to bomb London into submission coincided with an awareness in official circles of the re-emergence of an old and potentially damaging social problem in the capital: class resentment.

During the first week of bombing the East End and dockland areas were severely hit while many well-to-do parts of London were little affected. This was becoming a cause of a great deal of potentially divisive anger and hostility. In addition, working-class people heard about or saw the high life of the hotels and clubs and restaurants thriving in the West End despite the bombings. They knew about the luxurious deep shelters underneath the hotels and exclusive department stores offering night-time accommodation to wealthy clients, but often refusing to take in the East End poor who migrated west searching for a safe refuge from the bombs. Their anger was heightened by rich youths who would amuse themselves at night by 'slumming' around the tube shelters sniggering at the awful sights and smells. Emily Eary remembered the feeling of being looked down upon:

> In the evenings you'd get ladies and gentlemen going home after the theatre and night-club people. And you felt they were staring and sneering at you, as much to say, 'Look at them'. You'd be there on the platform, putting your curlers in or whatever and you felt a bit humiliated. Really it was degrading because they gave the impression they were looking down on us. In fact, we were a bit resentful about it, what with them going back to their safe areas and their comfortable homes. They didn't have to go through what we did.

Car owners would frequently sail past long queues of workers – even civil defence workers – and refuse to take any passengers. Those involved in actively defending and saving the capital became particularly irritated by better-off citizens whose lives were carrying on as before. One typical example of the kind of behaviour that angered the civil defence workers occurred when a group of firemen, resting after a night-long battle against the flames, were shouted at and abused for laziness by a passing party of nightclub revellers. Home Intelligence reports noted an escalation of 'class feeling' based on a popular resentment that the sacrifices of the war were being borne unfairly and unequally.

The authorities were aware that this sort of class conflict could seriously undermine Londoners' will to resist. The feeling of resentment did not end even when a lone German raider attacked Buckingham Palace on 13 September. Newspapers and newsreels made much of the fact that everyone from the greatest to the lowliest was, in a sense, on an equal footing in the civilian front line. Queen Elizabeth was widely quoted as saying, 'I'm glad we've been bombed. It makes me feel I can look the East End in the face.' But a few days later MP Harold Nicolson noted in his diary that there was still much bitterness in the East End and that the King and Queen had been booed when they visited the destroyed areas. At about this time, a hundred East Enders under Communist leadership rushed the Savoy Hotel demanding that they be allowed to use the hotel's shelter. The unexpected sounding of the all-clear saved the management from an embarrassing situation.

Paradoxically, the change in German bombing strategy generated a greater sense of unity in the capital. During the next weeks of bombing, rich and upper-class areas like Belgravia and Kensington in inner west London were hit far more frequently and heavily. So were suburban areas to the south and east, like Croydon, Wandsworth, Plumstead and Ilford. Now all Londoners, wherever they lived, had to face the terror of the blitz and the sense of shared suffering helped to promote a new sense of co-operation and comradeship.

A NEW SOLIDARITY

The first sign of this new spirit was the appearance of thousands of hitchhikers – many of them city clerks and secretaries – thumbing lifts to and from work. With many rail and bus services disrupted by the bombings, hitchhiking, which had previously been frowned upon, became the proper and patriotic thing to do. Motorists, who had earlier refused to give lifts, began to ferry around hitchhikers who quickly developed thumbing into a fine art by holding up destination boards and wearing badges with slogans like 'I want to go to Pimlico' and 'Say Old Bean, I'm Golders Green', or even the slightly more risqué 'Say, boys, I'm sweet, what about a seat?'

At a local level too, a new spirit of co-operation was emerging. Neighbours in middle-class areas, previously known for their standoffishness and snobbery, now found they were dependent on one another for their survival. In places like Edgware and Carshalton the residents formed rotas for voluntary street fire-watching duties. They kitted themselves out with stirrup pumps, sandbags and pails of water to put out the incendiary bombs. Notice boards displaying street rotas sprouted in front gardens, while in back gardens housewives improvised field kitchens to cook for bombed-out families. WVS volunteers collected food and blankets for the needy, secretaries and clerks doubled as fire-watchers and families helped to clear the debris of the previous night's raid.

The new spirit of community and unified resistance mushrooming all over London often revolved around the air-raid warden, who took on the position of being the leader and adviser to the neighbourhood. Quite apart from their emergency and rescue work, wardens provided information and support, guiding the people in their unit through the new jungle of war bureaucracy that was springing up: how to claim for war-damaged property, where to go to get new ration books; what were the latest evacuation and rest-centre arrangements. The good warden – and there were hundreds – inspired confidence and was of immense value in the struggle for survival.

Yet, despite this growing sense of community solidarity throughout London, the suburban way of coping with the bombing remained more private than the working-class mode of inner London. Whereas many East Enders packed into public shelters and entered into a communal lifestyle, suburban families still preferred to keep themselves to themselves. They sheltered either in a safe part of the house – such as a basement strengthened against collapse by wooden 'pit props' – or in the family's Anderson in the back garden. Some of the better-off families even had specially built garden shelters; these, though still cramped, were more comfortable than the Anderson.

The blitz was often, as a consequence, a less traumatic experience for suburban families than for those living in places like Stepney and Bermondsey. The family's evening routine carried on much as before, though parents and children might find themselves reading books and listening to the wireless in a cramped shelter rather than in the living room. Phil Barratt remembered how each night he and his family would go to the shelter in the back garden of their house in Carshalton in Surrey:

> We had a very happy little atmosphere in our shelter. My father had it specially built just before the war and it was quite spacious. We had a little cooker, electric light, all the necessities of life. And life went on very much as usual. We had books, we had a little Pifco toaster which gave us the chance of doing a bit of toast and dripping if we felt a bit peckish in the night. There was a supply of water as well.

Suburban houses were far less vulnerable to direct hits and mass destruction than the packed streets and tenements in the central areas of the city. But whatever the differences in lifestyle, after two or three weeks people all over London were adapting themselves more easily to the blitz. In the first few days of bombing air-raid warnings had created chaos: buses drew up and unloaded their passengers into the nearest shelter; post offices and shops had shut; and some older people went into a state of near panic. But by the end of September most Londoners carried on, casually and uninterrupted, with whatever they were doing when the sirens went – something that even began to acquire a certain glamour.

The pride and sense of purpose were particularly strong in people who had experienced some sort of near miss – preferably not too near. After an initial feeling of shock, they would chatter and joke about the experience and come out of it feeling more important than before. In self-defence some people wore badges declaring 'I've got a bomb story too'. Nothing demonstrates this more clearly than the 'business as usual' attitude of shopkeepers when they suffered mild bomb damage. Remaining open became a symbol of defiance, and amusing signs like 'More open than usual' or 'Blast' were soon displayed on shop fronts to show that spirits remained high.

The fact that Londoners kept going to work was of critical importance to the war effort, for the capital housed hundreds of munitions factories as well as being at the heart of national communications. To keep the wheels of wartime industry whirring Winston Churchill brought in on 17 September 'lookout men' who scanned the skies from London rooftops to distinguish a minor raid from a major bombing offensive. The idea was to prevent disruption of factory and office work through constant air-raid warnings which sent people scurrying for shelters when only a few bombers were in the air. It was a brilliantly successful scheme, more than halving the number of working hours lost. Equally important in keeping up the work drive was the astonishing resilience of London transport workers who daily traversed the bomb-cratered routes to take people to work.

Stoppages and strikes were unheard of during the blitz, and absent-eeism was minimal, partly because people thought their workmates would worry that they were dead if they didn't turn up each morning. Also, work was part of a normal, thus comforting, routine in a time of extraordinary disruption. The fact that people had to be somewhere and do something for eight hours each day helped them to cope with the horror. Most did not have the time or the energy to reflect too much on the incessant raids. Their preoccupation with work provided a valuable defence against the psychological damage that fear of death might otherwise have imposed upon them.

Although the blackout, night attacks and the pressure of shelter life all meant that people went out less during the evening, after the initial shock and disruption of the bombings, many continued to go to their local cinemas, dance halls and pubs. The Granada chain offered night-long shelter and entertainment for their clients, and those who stayed could look forward to five feature films and community singing. Many brought their blankets to the last house.

On 12 October, Hitler – confronted with the continued success of the RAF and the interminable resistance of Londoners to his attacks – was forced to abandon his invasion plan. The blitz itself was set to continue but its purpose was no longer to pave the way for an invasion of Britain: as it heightened in intensity the grim intent was to smash British morale. Londoners had to learn to live with the nightly raids that they feared would never end.

CHAPTER FIFTEEN

Living with the Blitz

ON THE EVENING of 15 October 1940 Londoners prepared for yet another night of bombing which had been almost continuous since 7 September. The spotters on the roofs stared into the sky straining for a first sight of the planes. The wardens in their control centres waited for the word that the Luftwaffe had been seen, ready to go out into the streets and warn people to take cover. The firemen at their stations checked their damaged equipment and mentally prepared themselves to face yet another night fighting the flames. When darkness descended, the bombers arrived, as regular as clockwork. Suburban families left the comfort of their homes for the tiny, damp Anderson shelters buried in their back gardens and inner Londoners huddled together in crypts, cellars, street shelters and tube stations. However, it was soon apparent that this raid marked a new stage in the Luftwaffe's assault on the capital. The number of bombers had doubled and the destruction they would wreak was unprecedented.

At 8pm six hundred people sheltering under Balham Station in south London heard a terrific explosion directly above them. A mountain of ballast, sand and water cascaded down through a huge hole at the end of the platform. The passage to the exit had been blocked by bomb blast. The whole station was rapidly submerging under this slime. Some scrambled to safety through an emergency hatch. Others remained trapped below, watching the water level rise, while the rescue service struggled to reach them. Bert Woolridge remembered being on duty at the ARP centre in Balham when the station was struck:

> As I went into the entrance hundreds of people were racing out in real
> panic. I got to the bottom of the stairs and the entrance to the bombed
> platform was blocked. All you could hear was the sound of screaming
> and rushing water. We managed to get to the platform by wading along
> through the sludge on the track, and it was terrible. People were lying
> there, all dead, and there was a great pile of sludge on top of them. Lots

were curled up in sleeping positions on the platform. One of them – he was the porter – had had his clothes ripped off by the bomb; he lay there naked. We put the people on stretchers and carried them away through the water. I don't think we found any survivors that night.

Sixty-four Londoners died at the Balham tube disaster in what proved to be just one tragic incident among many that night. The effects of this night of bombing, the worst so far, were devastating. The bombs had rained down from East Ham to Fulham and from Tottenham to Lewisham. Shelters were hit in Kennington, Poplar, Southwark and Waterloo, killing and injuring many. Some nine hundred fires were started. The Fleet sewer on the western outskirts of the City of London burst, pouring its contents into the Farringdon Street area. The terror lasted from dusk until five o'clock the next morning. When dawn broke and the night raiders departed, four hundred Londoners had been killed and nearly nine hundred seriously injured. Many had been made homeless, some having lost everything they possessed.

It was the worst toll since the opening days of the blitz, when people had been completely unprepared. Londoners were shaken, for they had believed that they were beginning to cope better. They felt they had begun to adjust to the tremendous emotional and psychological pressures of the blitz. They had been repeatedly told, in the propaganda catchphrase of the time, that 'London can take it'. But the sheer scale of the attack made people wonder how much longer the capital could survive under this seemingly endless and ever-increasing bombardment.

More urgently, nowhere now seemed safe. Within three days, three other Underground stations – Trafalgar Square, Bounds Green and Camden Town – were also the scenes of death and injury. And serious loss of life in a number of other mass shelters, including Druid Street railway arches in Bermondsey, St Peter's crypt in Southwark and several in Stoke Newington and Stepney, bit further into people's confidence.

The secret Home Intelligence reports on London recorded 'a lowering of morale' and reported that many people felt that 'in a few months' time there will be little left of London or its people'. Growing anxiety was shared by Churchill and he instructed that a search be made for the capital's strongest buildings which could be used to house the government war machine. 'It is probable indeed,' he said, 'that the bombing of Whitehall and the centre of government will be continuous until all the old or insecure buildings have been demolished.' The cabinet could see no reason why Hitler should call off his attack.

Although the German High Command had by now abandoned their plan to invade Britain that autumn, they had not abandoned their faith in mass bombing. Even if Britain could not be conquered by invasion, it might nevertheless be possible to force her surrender through extensive devastation. The lesson the Nazi commanders drew from their failure to bring Britain to her knees was that the intensity of the bombing had been insufficient and the time-scale too short. What was needed was an intensification of the bombing campaign.

The Luftwaffe's attack on London was set to last. Moreover, there was nothing at the time that Britain could do about it. During the early days of the blitz, when the Luftwaffe had been making day as well as night raids, the RAF had been able to destroy a considerable number of enemy planes. But now that the raids took place only under the cover of darkness, Fighter Command found that it was impotent. London was reliant on the anti-aircraft guns which rarely hit a German plane, leaving the capital practically defenceless against the night raider. The military was giving top priority to developing an effective system of defence but airborne radar was not yet operational.

LONDON TESTED TO THE LIMIT

As the air attacks continued relentlessly, the problem of homelessness reached crisis proportions in bomb-ravaged London. A host of difficulties were mounting and two became critical: the provision for those growing numbers of Londoners whose homes had been damaged or destroyed by bombing, and the conditions in the mass shelters. Without action to solve these problems, London's ability to keep on 'taking it' was in doubt. Each night hundreds of houses were hit and streets all over the capital were cratered, the network of pipes and mains beneath ruptured.

Each morning, many were left homeless, often with no possessions. About 40 per cent of the houses in Stepney, one of the worst-hit boroughs, had become casualties by early November 1940. Thousands more people found that though their home was still standing the basic services – gas, electricity, water – had been cut off. On one night, the bombings left a fifth of London's households without gas.

In the first weeks of the blitz, people had resolutely put up with not being able to cook or wash but, by now, they were expecting greater support from the authorities. In the East End families faced these problems daily, yet often there was still nowhere they could go for a good cheap meal, or to wash themselves or their clothes. George Golder recalled how when he, his mother Hannah and two sisters, Emily and Alice, were bombed out from their dockside home in Silvertown, they camped out in a brick street shelter:

> We hadn't had a proper meal for days so I went back home to try and knock something up. There was no gas or water or electricity in the house, but I managed to salvage some bacon and I made a bonfire in the back garden with some broken wood. I was in the middle of cooking the bacon when the landlord came along and asked about the rent. I told him to clear off. I had my little meal but the house was in too bad a state to try and live there again.

Gladys Strelitz was slightly more successful in feeding her family, with a do-it-yourself kitchen in the back garden of her bombed-out home in East Ham. She recalled:

> We had no light you see, there was no gas, no electricity – that had been cut off – and all we could rely on was a candle. The house was a mess. Well, I found these four bricks and I put them like a diamond on the back step, and filled it up with paper, bracken and a piece of wood. I'd put the saucepan on that, and stir and make the porridge for the children. 'When will it be ready, mummy?' 'Not long now.' We would put the kettle on and have a cup of tea. We really were scouts.

Voluntary groups like the Women's Voluntary Service, the Young Men's Christian Association and the Salvation Army had struggled to provide at least some of the most basic services since the early days of the blitz. They ran mobile canteens for families unable to cook for themselves. But this army of volunteers, who were largely funded through the collection box, could not cater for people's needs en masse. They did not have enough mobile canteens and, anyway, this was only a temporary 'morning-after' solution. If your gas was cut off for days, a cup of tea and a bun served in the street was clearly inadequate. A proper public meal service was needed but that required indoor canteen facilities and the voluntary groups had neither the buildings nor the equipment to supply these. Most important, those whose homes had been destroyed needed to be rehoused – and the voluntary groups simply did not have the power to do this.

The responsibility for tackling this emerging crisis lay with London's local authorities. The inner-London area came under the authority of the London County Council (LCC), which covered twenty-nine boroughs stretching from Hammersmith to Woolwich and Islington to Lewisham. As a large and well-resourced organization, the LCC proved to be more dynamic than the individual borough councils. Working in close co-operation with voluntary groups and the Ministry of Food, it put more mobile canteens on the road. But the homeless also needed shelter, clothes, household goods and money. Emily Golder recalled:

> It was difficult to manage without being able to wash yourself or your clothes and without anywhere to go. We went to the council who bused us out to the Majestic cinema in Woodford. It was a great tall building, terribly unsafe. There were no facilities, nowhere to wash or eat. We slept in the cinema seats, you could only get a cat nap. And after a few days we were moved to St Stephen's church in Walthamstow. There was nothing there. We slept on straw on the floor. We didn't know what was going to happen next. We couldn't get to Silvertown from there and so we lost our jobs. Then we were moved again to Finchley Rest Centre. We felt like refugees.

Helping the homeless came under the Poor Law Acts and, despite reforms in the interwar years, they still maintained a rather punitive attitude towards poverty. Consequently, provision tended to be meagre and parsimonious and access to welfare handouts was governed by the old 'means test'. People who had already gone through the devastating experience of losing everything they had then faced the bureaucratic and humiliating process of 'proving' that they were penniless. The secret Home Intelligence records carried a report from one of their observers in Chelsea:

> Bombed people don't enjoy answering more than a certain number of questions and they hate being treated as criminal paupers. People know that Americans and Canadians have sent warm things for the unfortunate of Chelsea. They know that it is no easy thing to get them

from those experienced in the tough administration of Charity who dole them out after the Town Hall has satisfied itself that the applicant is sufficiently near death from exposure . . . This business is a scandal. People are talking about it and they don't like it. They are treated like rabble.

The rest centres – the converted church halls and schools temporarily housing the homeless – were totally inadequate. They desperately needed more blankets, mattresses and camp beds for sleeping, more cups and teapots, and more chairs and tables to make people feel welcome, even 'at home'. A new approach was required – one that would be both more generous and would provide help on the basis of 'need' alone without the means test.

There was considerable support in the coalition government, particularly among the Labour members, for such a change. Most significantly, Herbert Morrison, who had campaigned against the Poor Law in the pre-war years, was now, as Minister for Home Security, one of the key figures involved in the debate. And at the Ministry of Health, the other key department directly responsible, officials had become convinced of the need for change by the urgency and seriousness of the problem. However, the Treasury held out against such moves throughout October.

BOMBING REFUGEES

The crisis of homelessness was, in the meantime, steadily worsening. By mid-October, roughly two hundred and fifty thousand Londoners had been made homeless by the bombings. Given the lack of help from local councils, most went to stay with friends or relations. Such arrangements were, of course, far better for the homeless than having nowhere to live, but they generally resulted in serious overcrowding and did not offer a long-term solution to the problem. Len Jones recalled how he and his entire family descended on his sister's maisonette in Carshalton:

We all went to 32 Wrythe Lane to my sister's little maisonette. There were eighteen of us there in two rooms because we were all bombed out. My father fixed up scaffold boards along the walls and at night ten of us would sleep in one room, all in line, and eight in the other little room. Of course we didn't get much sleep. Outside my father fixed up some buckets for washing for the men and built a latrine. In the garden there was a bit of a grass patch and my brother-in-law fixed up a ridge tent, so I used to sleep in that with three or four of the other men.

Charlie Draper and his family had an even more tragi-comic time in his aunt's back garden in Peckham. He recalled:

Our family ended up all of us living in Aunty's Anderson shelter. We were bombed out, the house was in ruins, so Aunty let us stay with her. It was incredible inside, there was six of us but there was only room for one big bed so we all slept in it, and it was a case of one turns and you all turn. And I used to wear Wellington boots at the time and I had very smelly feet and often they wouldn't let me in until I'd taken them off or washed my feet, and the bombs would be raining down and I'd be saying, 'Let me in'.

During the first six weeks of the blitz, the councils in the London region had rehoused only a little over 7,000 of the 250,000 homeless in the capital. Although some progressive councils like Bermondsey and Lambeth had in the interwar years developed mini welfare states in their boroughs, many others were run by an 'old guard' of councillors and officials who were set in their ways and who jealously guarded their power.

There was a glut of empty houses in London at this time and the councils had the power to requisition these properties and then use them as billets for homeless families. Yet they were not using this power: in one local authority, left unidentified in the official records, the council's chief billeting officer was also the local estate agent, who looked after his own business interests to such an extent that not one property had been requisitioned by the end of October. Ministry of Health reports repeatedly emphasized the slowness of requisitioning in London:

In one borough which is full of empty houses only three have been requisitioned and got ready in a week, another was still relying on voluntary billeting on householders, another had on a certain day eight hundred people needing billeting and only six vacancies available. There appeared to be a universal shortage of billeting officers, the work of finding billets being left to the Women's Voluntary Service.

The most inefficient boroughs were also often the worst hit. The people of Stepney, for example, faced not only the heaviest air attacks but also a borough council which, according to government inspectors, was in 'unbelievable chaos' with no billeting or rehousing departments despite two months of bombing. The war cabinet discussed taking away responsibility for rehousing from local councils and handing it to a special commissioner for London, a sort of 'London dictator', but they decided against it.

The government's own attempts to alleviate homelessness were equally unsuccessful. The Ministry of Health, for example, organized through local councils the transfer of several thousand East Enders into empty houses in well-to-do western and north-western boroughs like Paddington, Hampstead, Finchley and Westminster. But the newcomers, many of whom were poor, complained of the extra travelling costs to work and the lack of cheap shops locally. Alice Golder, sister of George and Emily Golder, remembered how she and her family were eventually billeted in Finchley:

> When we arrived we all looked a bit dirty and dishevelled and the lady
> of the house decided that she didn't want us in and she wouldn't open
> the door. The billeting officer said 'You've got to open the door by
> law and let them in' and eventually she did. We felt awful. We were
> put in the attic; there were two rooms. Me and my sister had to share
> a bed with mum and my brothers went in the other room. There was
> nowhere to cook and the lady wouldn't let us bring food in the house.
> She didn't like us in the house in day-time and so we spent most of
> the day in the park. We'd eat some sandwiches, sit on benches or walk
> around to keep warm. We would have gone back to the East End if
> we could, but our home was totally uninhabitable.

The government also attempted to alleviate the crisis of homelessness in London by extending their evacuation scheme, which had been hastily restarted for children after the first heavy raids back in September. Mothers and their children from anywhere in London were now entitled to a place. Among them was Gladys Strelitz and her children, on the move once again. She recalled:

> We couldn't live a life like that much longer, there was still no light,
> no gas no electricity, it's been cut off, and we were living in draughts

and cold. We had to put all our blankets round the windows to keep out the draughts. And all the children were running round in the debris and I was trying to cook in the back garden. It was all so much of a worry that in the end we had to do something about it so we decided there and then that we'd go to Reading.

In October eighty-nine thousand mothers and children were evacuated under the official scheme. But, like the first evacuation, this exodus into the provinces turned sour once the London families reached their destination. The bombed-out families were usually dirty, bedraggled and surprised to be treated with contempt by some of the receiving families. As censorship meant that few people outside London realized the devastating impact of the blitz, many in the reception areas did not appreciate the appalling conditions from which the evacuees were escaping. In addition, numerous day-to-day problems arose. By the beginning of November 1940 the numbers leaving London were reduced to a trickle.

This all meant that the problem of rehousing the homeless was left primarily to the individual borough councils. But the councils were by now sinking into deeper difficulties. As well as failing to requisition empty houses, they were falling way behind with dealing with bomb-damaged property. Families, who could have returned to their own homes if fairly minor repairs had been done, instead joined the army of homeless. At the same time the stock of houses available for repairs continued to shrink. Moreover, the crisis was aggravating overcrowding in the shelters. With nowhere else to go, many of the homeless simply set up home in the shelters. More and more homeless East End families went down to the Chislehurst caves in Kent, which by the end of October were housing around fifteen thousand people.

The cave-dwellers had to make the best of the primitive conditions. The caves were cold and dim, lit only by candlelight. There were no washing or toilet facilities; the cave-dwellers had to walk a mile or more to relieve themselves outside. In the first days of the blitz, some families had tried to make it a real home by bringing beds, armchairs and sideboards with them. But as the caves became more and more over-crowded people were jam-packed together sleeping on the rough floors. And even then, on some nights there might be hundreds left in the open air outside, unable to get in. Similarly, squalor and overcrowding in the mass shelters in inner London were worsening. By now, some three hundred and fifty thousand were taking refuge in public shelters each night. Some of the worst conditions were in the tubes where scabies, impetigo and lice were increasing at an alarming rate. The Eary family were sheltering in the Underground at Moorgate. Emily recalled the awful health risks there:

> The sanitary arrangements were appalling. There were still no proper toilets on the station, only chemical latrines, and they were so inadequate they overflowed all the time. There was nowhere to wash and you might be sleeping next to sick people. My brother Ernest got enteritis. And we all went down with scabies. We had to go to a rescue unit and they slapped disinfectant all over us with a big paintbrush. It was horrible. We had the treatment three times. Then they baked all our clothes.

And, as winter set in, so too did the cold-weather ailments of flu, colds and bronchitis. There was concern that this ill-health was weakening people's resistance and making them vulnerable to the spread of more serious diseases like tuberculosis. The prospect of an epidemic loomed ever larger. As the difficulties mounted and as the shelterers became more weary, the limited improvements gained by the mutual co-operation that they had achieved earlier were under threat.

In the early days of the blitz a community spirit had flowered on the tube platforms and grimy shelter floors and had helped people to pull through. But as overcrowding and conditions worsened, competition and bitter rivalry for the 'best' places emerged. When people saw their own immediate safety and health, and even their lives, as being dependent on fighting for themselves and their family, community and collaboration took second place. Emily Eary recalled this frightening shift in attitudes:

> It was a real survival of the fittest. You'd queue for hours to get a good spot on the platform – you'd want to avoid the cold, draughty and smelly parts. People would spread newspapers on the floor or leave bundles to show it was their territory and somebody might come and kick them away and that would lead to arguments over who should be where. Sometimes you'd get people squaring up and fights. Mum was like a hen fighting for her brood.

Although war was not declared until September 1939 the Government had anticipated German bombing raids a year earlier. Here residents of Arundel Square in Barnsbury, Islington are beginning to dig themselves a communal shelter in 1938.

Gas masks began to appear in shop windows in 1938 as the prospect of war and German air raids threatened. Terrible though the Blitz and later rocket attacks were, they were not as devastating as the authorities feared they would be at the outbreak of war.

Bewildered and bemused, a group of undesirable aliens, mostly Germans and Italians who had been living in London when war broke out, are escorted onto trains at Euston Station in May 1940. They were interned on the Isle of Man.

In the summer of 1939, just before the declaration of war, illuminated road signs were masked in anticipation of the blackout to come. Later many road signs were taken down so that invading Germans would not know where they were.

Looking as if they had just returned from a trip to IKEA, a Mrs Rowe and a Mrs Treadwell puzzle over the construction of their Anderson shelter provided free to the poorer families in London in 1939. More than two million of these shelters were built in back yards and gardens.

Clutching a few of their possessions these three women joined a long line of refugees fleeing London during the first month of the Blitz which had begun on 'Black Saturday' 7 September 1940.

Children sitting on the ruins of their home which had been demolished in a raid on the East End of London in September 1940. Many evacuees had returned home during the so-called Phoney War before the Blitz began and many were to leave again when the bombs began to fall.

A London policeman moves to restrain an enthusiastic youngster from straying too near the line as children await a train to take them away from London in October 1940.

A festive and patriotic canteen set up on the platform of St John's Wood Tube station. It is Christmas 1944 and the Blitz was long over but the flying bombs or 'doodle-bugs' had once again brought terror from the air from June that year.

The extraordinary scene at Aldwych tube station in October 1940 when Londoners defied authority to turn the underground into night-time bomb shelters. In time some order was restored with bunk beds, refreshments and sometimes entertainment.

A concert by members of ENSA (Entertainments National Service Association) for Londoners sheltering in Aldwych tube station in October 1940. Conditions in the shelters generally improved after the first frantic dash for cover.

Three years after the end of the Blitz, and just as the D-Day landings got underway, Londoners faced a new terror, the V1 and V2 rockets. The first V1s, pilotless flying bombs nicknamed doodlebugs, droned overhead on 13 June 1944 dropping when their motors cut out.

While much of London got by with 'digging for victory', growing vegetables in parks and gardens, the Rev W. White of St Andrews Vicarage in Hackney, a volunteer Air Raid Warden, kept hens which laid eggs for victory.

Flying bombs came literally out of the blue causing death and destruction in the suburbs of London as well as the centre of town. This shocking image shows the body of a victim killed by a doodlebug which hit Aldwych on 13 July 1944.

A picture of Elsie Huntley with her son Derek and baby Roy just a few weeks before they were all buried in the ruins of a concrete shelter opposite their home in Mitcham by a direct hit from a doodlebug. Elsie and her baby were rescued from the rubble but nine-year-old Derek was killed instantly.

A genteel street party in Bedford Road, Walthamstow celebrating VE Day in May 1945.

This rayon Utility
dress modelled on
a Bloomsbury roof
in 1943 could be
had for seven
coupons plus
fifteen shillings.
Fashion was
rationed when the
war had ended and
it was calculated
that the wedding
dress of Princess
Elizabeth in 1947
would have cost
300 coupons and
£1,200.

The proud tenants of a 'prefab' put up on a bombed site at Portland Place, London tend their garden in 1947. Intended only as a short-term solution to the post-war housing crisis, these pre-fabricated homes with their brand new bathrooms and little plots of land were very popular.

Desperate for a place to live many Londoners, including returning servicemen, moved into empty buildings and demanded that basic services were connected. These squatters occupied Abbey Lodge in Hanover Terrace in September 1946. Though the protestors made their point, the squatters were soon evicted.

A last show of Imperial might at the Coronation of Her Majesty Queen Elizabeth ll on 2 June 1953. Colonial troops are followed by the British South African mounted police from Rhodesia (later Zimbabwe).

After war work in the Admiralty, Margaret Dent– you can spot her in the left hand row with her chair pulled back – stayed on as a clerk, the sole woman among serried ranks of men. But not for long. She was demoted to 'temporary' staff, lost her pensions rights, and soon, because she was married, her job.

SHELTER POLITICS

Finally the government made a complete U-turn in policy. Work began in the inner-London area on the construction of eight enormous purpose-built underground shelters, each of which would hold eight thousand people. Herbert Morrison, who persuaded his cabinet colleagues of the need to divert scarce building resources to this enterprise, argued that the plan was essential to counter Communist agitation on the deep-shelter issue, which was striking an increasingly popular chord.

At the same time, the government set about replacing the outdoor Anderson shelter with an indoor home shelter. The 'Morrison', named after the cabinet minister, was a steel-framed box which was constructed and kept in the home and could be used as a table between air raids if the side plates were removed. It took a while to put together with 219 different parts and 48 nuts and bolts but was distributed free and was effective. Now those without gardens could get protection and those suffering from winter cold and damp in garden dugouts could move indoors.

Those in the communal shelters such as Tilbury became more and more disillusioned with the way they were run as the blitz continued. Home Intelligence noted the shelterers' response to government instructions on keeping the shelter in good order:

> The experienced dwellers of the shelters realised that these were
> obviously the work of those with no knowledge of life underground.
> The notes were laughed at and produced a bitter criticism which is
> becoming more and more evident of late.

The authorities, on the other hand, were often extremely suspicious of the shelterers, especially those who agitated for improvements. The loudest voices demanding change were often those of the Communists, but they tended to be dismissed by the government as 'subversives' even though the reforms they advocated were practical and moderate, and often had widespread support among the shelterers. The authorities were also often distrustful of the elected committees which were also seen as the work of 'agitators'. Nina Hibbin recalled an incident at the Tilbury shelter illustrating dramatically this deep antagonism:

People had started to organize but of course there was a limit to what ordinary people could do. I mean they could club together and buy first-aid equipment, they could bring their own folding stools, they could allocate places or make sure that the older people had a decent place but they couldn't pump out the wet. There was so much wet on the floor, sometimes you were actually wading in it. They couldn't provide the latrines because obviously that's a professional job, so it was only the authorities, the ARP or the town hall authorities who could make any really substantial improvements. The people were so angry that they decided to take a deputation to the ARP. There already was a rudimentary shelter committee and the people who were on it got together and went to the ARP headquarters with certain demands like decent sanitation, bunks with proper tickets and bunk allocation – that kind of thing, very simple things. Well when they got to the ARP, there were about forty of us. I went along with them. All of a sudden we find that we're being charged by mounted police. They came pouring through the entrance wielding their batons, and I remember one of them got hold of a man with a bandage round his neck and began beating him up. And then a number of people were taken to the police station, and that was the end of our delegation.

The violence of this response was unusual, probably reflecting the officials' fears that the Tilbury, based as it was in the Communist Party stronghold of Stepney, was a hotbed of revolution. But even when the requests for improvements could not be dismissed as simply 'Communist-inspired', they met with little success. For example, the committees representing the shelterers in Swiss Cottage Underground – who were professional middle-class people – found that their requests for proper medical care were passed constantly between the Health Ministry, the local authority and London Transport. And while the authorities dallied, a child died of meningitis.

The Swiss Cottage shelterers, who saw themselves as a very moderate group, were incensed. In the *Swiss Cottager*, their own unique station newspaper that they managed to print, they complained 'against shameful apathy, indifference amounting almost to callousness, neglect, soulless contempt for elementary human decencies, against red tape, authority, and officialdom, and against practised experts in the time-honoured game of "passed-to-you-please".'

By early November, the government was facing an increasingly angry and disillusioned population in the blitzed capital. Whether in the nightly routine of shelter life or in the desperate plight of being bombed out, people felt that their lives were made harder by official inaction. The war cabinet's civil defence committee had been told that it was becoming difficult to restrain the press from criticism, despite the fact that censorship, often self-imposed, had meant that until now there had been almost total silence on all these problems. Morale, the country's leaders were warned, would be seriously undermined if action was not taken. Then, unexpectedly, the pressure on London was lifted.

A BRIEF RESPITE FOR LONDON

On the night of 14 November there was a clear sky, but for the first time since 7 September the Luftwaffe did not take the opportunity of bombing the capital. That night they blitzed Coventry, leaving behind a devastated city. For sixty-seven successive nights – with one exception in early November when bad weather had kept the Luftwaffe away – the capital had faced death and destruction. Now it shared the burden of air attacks with the other major industrial centres of Britain as Germany stepped up its bombing campaign. London was still to suffer more raids and more bombs than any other city, but in the next month it suffered only three raids.

There was now an opportunity to tackle the crises that the destruction of London had created. Repairs to houses could begin without the depressing prospect of even more ruins the next day. The old-fashioned Poor Law attitudes treating the victims of bombing damage as paupers had to be swept away. Those, like Herbert Morrison, who had argued from the early days of the blitz for an emphasis on people's needs, first and foremost, now began to win the day and at the end of November, the Treasury, which had previously resisted this change, caved in and agreed to finance all the costs of sorting out the problems of the homeless.

From now on, a new emphasis on welfare was to be the mark of the government's approach to the blitz victims. There was a new consensus that in this, the 'people's war', the people's needs had to be met, or, at least, be seen to be taken seriously.

People felt more and more that the ultimate responsibility for tackling the problems lay with the state. The war cabinet, in particular, had the power to determine how the nation's effort and resources were used. They could, for example, divert labour and equipment from industry and the armed services into assisting the blitzed capital. The state was set to become an increasingly important influence on people's everyday lives.

The government called in the army to help out with repairs in the most hard-pressed boroughs; dirty clothes could be taken to a mobile 'washing van' which would do the laundry for free; and meals could be eaten in one of the new public canteens equipped with requisitioned army stoves. In inner London in particular, the LCC was quick to take advantage of Ministry of Food funds and soon a new 'communal feeding centre' was being opened up virtually every day. Within three months, the LCC Londoners' Meals Service had opened 104 restaurants, serving 10,000 meals a day; in the East End there was eventually one about every half mile. The meals at these communal canteens – or 'British Restaurants' as they later became known – were nutritious and extremely cheap, costing about 10d to one shilling a head, and they were rapidly extended to non-bombed areas to supplement scanty rations.

At the same time, central government started to take greater control over local billeting procedures. Each council was instructed to appoint officers who had to ensure that billets were found. All the properties in the borough had to be surveyed regularly to see where there was spare capacity. Empty properties had to be requisitioned as necessary and made ready for immediate occupation. Furniture was to be provided, though the short supply meant that this was often very minimal. Once a family had been billeted or rehoused, a welfare officer would visit to check what difficulties they were encountering. The emphasis throughout was on trying to meet the particular needs of each individual family. Emily Golder recalled when she and her family were eventually rehoused in a semi-detached house in Hendon Lane, Finchley:

> To begin with it was very primitive. There was no heating and no
> furniture, and we had to sleep on the floorboards. But bit by bit,
> things got better. You got a welfare officer coming round and sorting
> things out and the council set us up with our cooker and made sure
> that we had water and bedding and everything we needed. And when
> the neighbours got to hear about us they were very nice, and they'd
> offer us furniture and things. And because we were settled we'd all
> been able to get jobs in the area and start earning again. We felt we
> were beginning to live again, we were really thankful for what was
> done for us.

In Chislehurst, the local district council and central government stepped in to improve the conditions and safety of the vast subterranean community of shelterers camped in the caves. They introduced electric lighting, improved sanitation and flattened the floors. In other shelters, in particular the Underground, basic facilities, such as first-aid posts and bunks, were now being provided. Some tube trains were converted into 'refreshment specials', moving from station to station serving tea and cocoa, sausage rolls and pies, cakes and buns. Sometimes entertainment would be organized with ENSA performers or even top-ranking artists like George Formby.

But the problems were so extensive and time so short that many shelters were left untouched throughout November. At the end of the month, a tube shelterers' conference was held – organized by the shelter committees from Swiss Cottage, King's Cross, Euston, Old Street, Moorgate, Tottenham Court Road and Hampstead – to press for a speedier rate of improvement. For these shelterers, as for those in other mass shelters, it seemed that they were waiting too long. The Home Intelligence reports monitored continuing discontent. In early December, the report on the East End noted:

> There are many shelters that are still dripping with water and lack
> proper sanitation, drainage and ventilation. The people habitually
> using these shelters have a sense of grievance . . . They have had
> official visits and seen many promises in the press of improvements –
> but improvement does not materialize. Bitterness and apathy grow.

While Londoners had benefited from the lull in the bombing of the capital, the London Fire Brigade had not. Since the first days of the blitz they had been hindered by a lack of modern equipment like turntable ladders, heat-resistant hosing and fire engines, while raids were more and more designed to inflict maximum fire damage.

FIRE BOMBS

On 8 December over three thousand incendiary bombs – eight times more than on the first day of the blitz – had been dropped. Then, on the night of 29 December the Germans bombed the City of London. The Luftwaffe dropped hundreds of incendiary canisters on the commercial heart of the capital when no one was on watch. Businessmen had gone home for the night, double-locking their property behind them. Banks, offices, churches and houses rapidly caught alight and the flames spread swiftly through the narrow streets.

As the fires raged through the City, the firemen found that the water in their hoses turned to a trickle. The mains in the area had been hit and their back-up systems from distant pipes failed. They turned to the Thames for help, and struggled across the mud to extract the river water. But that night the ebb tide was exceptionally low and the water could not be reached when it was most needed.

The fires spread into a massive conflagration, blazing uncontrollably across the heart of the capital, consuming its oldest and most historic area, the City of London itself. From the roof of St Paul's Cathedral, the fire-fighters could look down on a carpet of fire stretching into the distance – and could do nothing. Eventually, the tide in the Thames turned, water came back to the hoses and the fires were controlled. But by then the damage had been done.

The inferno had reduced great swathes of the City of London to charred rubble in what was one of the worst nights of destruction of the whole war. In the Barbican and Moorgate areas almost every building was ruined. On the South Bank – to which the fires had spread – a strip of houses and warehouses a mile long and a quarter of a mile wide was destroyed. The streets around St Paul's were now blackened shells, though the Cathedral itself had been saved, partly as a result of more vigilant fire-watching followed by swift preventive action. For many Londoners going to work the next morning, St Paul's symbolized a renewed defiance in the face of the enemy's onslaught as it stood majestically above the smouldering ruins.

The very next day, new fire-watching laws were brought in to ensure that no property was left unguarded. Men between the ages of sixteen and sixty had to register for compulsory fire-watching forty-eight hours a month. New equipment was ordered to tackle the shortage of water during raids. But many of the men fighting the fire felt that, perhaps, the most important problem – the lack of co-operation and co-ordination between local fire services – had been ignored. The government was still reluctant to take control of the fire service. Morrison, in particular, saw it as the 'brightest jewel in the local authorities' crown' and was afraid of offending the local councils by taking it away from them.

The problems of the shelters, too, continued to dog the government. On 5 January 1941, the LCC member Lord Cranley described in the *Sunday Times* a tour of the shelters in the London area. 'I was implored,' he stated, 'to do anything that was possible to alleviate their appalling conditions.' In early January, the heavy raids continued, causing much devastation and many a tragedy. The Bank tube station received a direct hit and 111 shelterers died. Morale was sinking to a new low.

Discontent came to a head on 12 January when the Communist Party organized a 'People's Convention' in central London. Over two thousand 'delegates' met to call for a 'people's peace'. Though the claim that these 'delegates' represented over a million people was no doubt exaggerated, the numbers involved were large enough to worry the government; a week later, Morrison banned the Communists' paper, the *Daily Worker*, which had been in the forefront of the campaign to improve conditions for shelterers and bombed-out families.

The government realized, however, that repression was a dangerous, and possibly counterproductive, way of dealing with the situation and that to maintain morale the remaining problems created by the blitz had to be tackled yet more urgently. The authorities were helped out by another lull in the attacks. In February, the weather was exceptionally bad and there were few raids on London for a month. There was a renewed chance for substantial improvements.

New equipment started to arrive in the fire service and there was even time for training sessions in its use. New water mains began to be laid on the surface and unlike the mains underground these did not shatter when a bomb fell in the area because of their greater flexibility. In the spring, Herbert Morrison, under pressure from the fire chiefs, finally accepted the need to 'nationalize' the fire service and form one fire-fighting body called the National Fire Service, which could come into operation during the summer.

The crisis in the shelters was also finally tackled. Basic facilities became widely available, with twenty-two thousand bunk beds, for example, being installed in the Underground. Shelterers in the tubes would now be allocated a ticket for a specific bunk that was theirs, as long as they slept there regularly. The physical improvements and the better organization ended the battles for the 'best' places and a feeling of neighbourliness began once again to develop. The Eary family noticed the difference. Rene, sister of Emily, recalled:

You got a real community going after it was organized better. Until then everyone had been shifting around and you didn't hardly know anyone. But now you had a regular spot with the same bunks every night, and the people around you became like regular neighbours. We'd play with the kids next door so to speak, and everyone would be gossiping and playing cards with each other. It was a settled community.

In the Chislehurst caves the combined efforts of the owner, Mr Gardiner, the government and the shelterers had created a remarkable community life deep underground in which bunk beds, canteens, a children's chapel and a cave hospital were some of the amenities provided. Charlie Draper remembered how when he joined his grandmother to live in the caves in spring 1941 the level of organization was quite astonishing:

When I first came down the caves, I was amazed; it was like a city under ground. I found my gran, and she saved me a bunk. They had two-tier bunks, and they were a luxury then. So I put my blanket and my pillow out, and put my tools under the bed, and I said I'm going to have a roam round. I went a few caves up and found there was a dance hall, and an old piano where people were sitting having a singsong, and there was a cinema the other side of the cave. In the tea room there were a couple of tables, where the WVS used to work, and they were selling pies and sandwiches and cakes, and you could get a cup of tea for a penny. Then further along there was the hospital where the children learnt to line up to get their cough mixture, that sort of thing. And then there was a little chapel, and on a Sunday I used to go by the chapel, and the kids would be singing away at their hymns. And there was a bit of luxury, they even put in washrooms and facilities, like men's and ladies' toilets. So it was quite nice, I enjoyed it.

When the better weather brought the return of the Luftwaffe, Home Intelligence reports noted that Londoners were 'very appreciative' of the new welfare services and that people did not take so long to recover as in the early days of the blitz. The radical measures needed to deal with the direct consequences of the blitz were now in place.

Moreover, a whole new set of ideals was emerging which went much further than the 'welfare' approach that had so far come out of the blitz. People began to see the changes forced on them by the war not just in terms of crises to be overcome but also in terms of new opportunities. In the shelters, for example, there were people regularly gathered together with nothing to do who could be encouraged to use the time to learn new skills or take up new interests.

In Bermondsey – building on its progressive policies of the pre-war years – the borough council set up a range of evening classes in the shelters. In some shelters you could go in any night of the week and find, say, a dressmaking group in one corner and a drama group in another, preparing a play which subsequently the rest of the shelterers would watch. Elsewhere, children would be painting. Once a week there would be a well-attended discussion group dealing with topics ranging from the latest military questions to rights for women.

In St Pancras travelling libraries were set up to take books out to the people in rest centres, shelters, billets or even to ARP units. Gladys Strelitz and her children were settling down in Caversham on the outskirts of Reading, and helped by council-run services, were beginning to recover from the shock of the blitz. Gladys recalled:

> At last we felt safe and happy again when we got to Caversham. The council helped us evacuees a lot – they provided us with this place called The Pantry, where we could have a good cheap meal with the children, and all the evacuees from London could have a chat, all together. The meals were really delicious to us in those days. We used to have swede, cheese and onion pie, black pudding, lots of cups of tea. It was all so delicious to us because we'd had to go without for so long. The government paid our billeting allowance and that helped considerably. It helped for little extra things that we didn't have before. And it was good to see the children with a little colour in their cheeks and not looking miserable and tired after the heavy bombing that we had in London.

From now on the government propaganda made much play of the brave new world that would come out of the war. The propaganda film *Post 23*, for example, showed a new spirit of idealism emerging among a group of wardens in Finchley. In reply to a comment from a 'working-class' warden about all the slums and tenements that had come down during the blitz, a 'middle-class' warden states: 'We've got to see the job's done decently this time. If we can work together now, why can't we work together in cleaning up the mess and helping build a better world in which these things can't possibly happen?'

The severest bombing raid on the capital of the whole blitz came on 10 May 1941. Fires were started from Hammersmith in the west nearly as far as Romford in the east. More civilians – 1,436 – were killed than in any other single raid on Britain. The House of Commons, Westminster Abbey, the Law Courts, the Royal Mint and the Tower of London were all badly hit. A third of the streets of London were impassable the next morning and 155,000 families found themselves without gas or electricity. Yet Emily Eary and her family now felt they could cope with the bombing, however awful it was:

> I remember the May 10 raid. The whole of London seemed to be on fire. We'd been down the tube all night, but when we came out in the morning, we had to run through fires which was raging both sides of the streets. And there was hot falling embers pouring down on us. But we weren't as terrified as we used to be because by then, you see, we had got bunks down the tube, and we had a place that was sort of secure for us. We knew that when we got down there we'd have everything we needed to get by, whatever happened on top, whether there was raging fires or bombs falling.

This terrible raid marked the end of the blitz. Days and then weeks passed, but the Luftwaffe did not return. For a reason that Londoners were yet to understand, Germany had abandoned its mass air attacks.

CHAPTER SIXTEEN

The Road to Victory

Londoners awoke on the morning of 22 June 1941 to hear the most dramatic and important news of the war so far: in the early hours of that morning, Germany had invaded Russia. The eerie peace of London during the last month was explained – the Luftwaffe had flown off to the east. The capital was no longer in the front line of the war, its citizens no longer the target of the relentless German attack. Though Londoners felt an immediate and deep sense of relief, these feelings were tempered by the belief that the Luftwaffe would soon be back. The incredibly rapid advance of the German army through Russia had led many to believe that the Red Army might collapse within weeks. Britain would then be standing alone again.

But during that summer the mood began to change. For, though the Germans were still making substantial advances through Russian territory, they were meeting fierce and courageous resistance. A wave of admiration for the Soviet people and for the Red Army swept across Britain; her new ally was turning out to be a powerful and aggressive fighting force.

For the first time since Dunkirk, people felt a tinge of optimism. Their thoughts began to turn to victory. Throughout the capital, walls were painted or chalked with the 'V for Victory' sign as Londoners spontaneously took up the BBC's slogan for the resistance movement in Europe.

But Britain was not yet on the road to victory. There was a crisis in war production. The whole economy urgently needed to be geared up for war. London's role in overcoming this crisis and putting Britain on the road to victory was to be as critical as it had been in staving off defeat. And the changes that this would bring to every waking hour of every Londoner's life were to be as radical as those brought by the blitz itself.

The first and greatest problem was that London had been Germany's prime target for air attack. In the early stages of the war, the government had desperately tried to avoid placing major orders in 'vulnerable' areas like the London region, preferring, wherever possible, the 'safe' areas of north-west England and Scotland. They feared that if key war industries were concentrated in the capital, the whole programme could be brought to a halt by the Luftwaffe.

As a consequence, the capital's resources were not fully utilized for the war effort. The massive Ford works at Dagenham in Essex, for example, had few orders for military equipment. However, by the late summer of 1940, the classification of 'safe' and 'vulnerable' areas was beginning to change. The Luftwaffe were now poised along the continental coastal areas in bombing range of the whole of Britain. Military chiefs became concerned that the building of new factories in supposedly 'safe' rural areas would attract the enemy's attention and make them prime targets, whereas existing factories in urban areas, it was now argued, might be less visible and vulnerable.

So the government decided to lift the restriction on the development of war industry in London in the early autumn of 1940, although by then the blitz had begun and there was little chance for a shift in the capital's industries to war production. By the summer of 1941, however, London was poised for a great expansion in its war effort.

The large-scale engineering and chemical factories were the easiest to draw into the war machine. They had the plant and equipment that enabled mass production for the military once they had been converted from civilian to war products. The Ford foundry at Dagenham was soon working flat out making a wide range of army trucks and gun carriers. In the East End, despite the effects of the blitz, factories managed to turn to war production. Ironically, they often made the most explosive of products, as this area had for almost a century housed the bulk of the capital's noxious chemical industries. Paint factories, though they had been heavily damaged during the bombings because of the inflammable nature of their products, made the switch. Bryant & May, the match makers in Bow, made demolition charges and safety fuses. Albright & Wilson, the chemical firm in Canning Town, became a major shell-filling firm.

But the greatest expansion came in the west and north-west parts of London, where industry in pre-war years had been booming and where, as a result, many of the factories were modern and well equipped. A wide range of war production sprang up; AEC in Southall, for example, turned from making buses to armoured cars carrying six-pounder guns. Easy access to the Midlands, where the air-frame industries were concentrated, led to the expansion of engineering production for the aircraft industry;

Napiers in Acton, for example, had gambled on the development of a new engine which was to be used in the mass production of the Typhoon and Tempest fighters.

Much of London's production remained, however, very small-scale in nature. In the north-east of the capital over two-thirds of the engineering firms employed fewer than fifty people. Gearing their potential output to the war effort was critically important, but co-ordinating these small and often fiercely independent firms proved much more difficult than drawing in the large engineering firms.

Nevertheless, when the state-run Royal Small Arms Factory in Enfield developed the sten gun – a cheap and easily produced sub-machine gun – it looked to hundreds of small local workshops for the production. Firms that once had made a glittering array of goods from sewing machines to windscreen wipers were welded together into one long war production line and lorries travelled between the numerous premises in a sort of metropolitan conveyor belt.

Perhaps the most remarkable transformation was in the furniture industry of north-east London. Carpenters turned from making chairs, tables, wardrobes and the like to mass-producing a wooden aeroplane. The 'Mosquito', as it was called, was made from sheets of paper-thin plywood and balsa wood, glued together and then heated to form a product as tough as metal but much lighter. The strengthened wooden sheets were then sawn and shaved into the parts of the plane, from the bulkhead to the tail-piece, from the fuel tanks to the wings. Alf Pearson worked in Wrighton's Mosquito factory in Walthamstow. He remembered:

> It was out of this world really, because kiddies used to make little models, little toys out of this balsa wood and we couldn't believe that we were using inch-thick balsa wood to make a plane that was going to fly over Germany and be armed. We were most of us skilled cabinet-makers and we used the same sort of tools that we did on furniture – planes, chisels, saws – to make the Mossies. We felt absolutely bucked about it, that we were doing something useful to help us win the war. But to begin with we never thought it would fly.

The end product was, in fact, exceptionally versatile. Used for reconnaissance work, the Mosquito could fly low into enemy territory and fast enough to evade interception. As a night-time bomber, it could carry the same weight of high explosive as a conventional bomber and fly in greater safety at 21,000 feet (6,400 m), and as a small passenger plane, the Mosquito was the fastest in the world. And if you wanted it to go even faster, all you had to do was give it a good wax with furniture polish.

ALL HANDS TO THE PUMP

At the same time as existing factories were being turned over to war production, new factories were hastily being built. Often these were on the outskirts of London where sites were easily available. The small towns of Slough, Watford, Hemel Hempstead and Welwyn Garden City expanded rapidly, often recruiting skilled workers from inner London. Empty premises throughout London were also swiftly converted into factories. Unused basements, cellars, warehouses, even an unfinished London Transport Underground tunnel, were all given a new life.

Perhaps the most extraordinary transformation took place under the Houses of Parliament. While the elected members moved to the House of Lords to carry on with business as usual, underneath the ruined debating chamber of the House of Commons a very different type of business had sprung up. What is called the Guy Fawkes cellar was converted to house a submarine factory whose workers toiled day and night. The whole operation was secret, only known to Members of Parliament and the staff of the Palace of Westminster who manned the factory in their spare time. Vera Michel-Downes was the factory's welfare officer and she remembered:

> We had a fantastic atmosphere in the factory, which was really totally classless. We had staff from all walks of life: the policeman, the postman, the fireman, the legal advisors, the secretarial staff, the staff from the House of Lords and the House of Commons, and, of course, close relatives of Members of Parliament. And they all were issued with the same white overalls. The ladies had foldover overalls that tied at the back and the gentlemen had overalls that buttoned down. And they were all working next to each other, and with class disappearing, most of them were on first-name terms and some very good friendships were made.

However, the demands from the military for more men and equipment were ever increasing. Ernest Bevin, the bull-headed pre-war leader of the Transport & General Workers Union, was in charge at the Ministry of Labour. He set about gearing up the war economy by passing the Essential Work Orders Act. The government turned to all possible sources.

Londoners who had been rounded up and interned as 'aliens' after Dunkirk now found that they were back at work making guns, tanks and essential products, and in their spare time were on duty in the Home Guard. Jewish refugee, Klaus Hinrichsen, who had been interned on the Isle of Man recalled:

> In the summer of 1941, I was released and came back to my little attic flat in Hampstead. The feeling in London had changed – refugees were now accepted and the war effort needed everyone's help, particularly people with any skills. I was directed by the Labour Exchange to a firm in Sunbury-on-Thames, making chemical products. I contacted a number of continental chemists I knew who knew all about ersatz, substitute materials, and we took over part of a small factory, and produced substitute shoe polishes, substitute detergents and substitute materials which at that time were something completely new. I felt this was in some way a contribution to the war effort, because we had to make things without the old raw materials – the ships bringing them to Britain weren't getting through. Then one day I went to the Home Guard barracks in St John's Wood, and asked whether I could sign on. They enlisted me, and very soon I found myself a sharp shooter and in possession of a rifle, guarding vital installations like the BBC and viaducts around London.

THE FIRST WOMEN CONSCRIPTS

From the start of the war, thousands of young women had gone voluntarily into the factories. The government now made it compulsory. At the beginning of December 1941, conscription for women was introduced for the first time in British history. This required that all unmarried women aged between nineteen and thirty register for war work of some kind. Some were conscripted into the forces, though the shortfall here was small because of the large number of volunteers for the women's services. Most of the conscripted women were directed to work in essential industries.

From now on, women moved from a marginal to a central position in the war production drive. Whether putting together the intricate mechanism of the sten gun in Enfield, lifting the molten metal casts from the foundry in Dagenham or assembling a Halifax bomber at London Transport's converted workshops in Chiswick, women were doing jobs previously thought beyond their capabilities. For many it was a liberating experience. Odette Lesley, who had been rejected by the ATS when she revealed her true age, remembered being directed to work in the Pullman Springs factory, Hendon, which had switched from making fittings for luxury railway carriages to the production of fuel tanks for Spitfires:

> I was terrified to begin with because I had never even picked up a spanner before and I thought I'll never learn it, what am I going to do? And you found that the men were resentful and wary of the women because they'd never worked with women before. But I had to learn it, it was war work and gradually I learnt the things properly and I almost started to enjoy it, not just because of the work but because I knew it was war work and therefore it was of use to the country. Of course, the longer we were there we got more and more proficient in the job and we became quite confident. Because the men and women were doing exactly the same job we felt just as good as the boys. And as new men came into the plant very often we were teaching them the job. They would be like I was originally, a bit terrified and also a bit embarrassed because a woman knew the job and they didn't.

In some workplaces women were so much in control that they started to adopt some of the old male traditions, like initiation ceremonies and practical jokes, and sprang them on young male recruits – as Charlie Draper, a refugee in the Chislehurst caves, discovered when he first began work at a sten gun factory in Peckham. He recalled:

> The majority of workers in the factory were women; all the men were away in the forces. And the women more or less took over everything. I used to get teased a lot by the women in there, sending you out to the shops for pregnant tarts, and sending you down to the stores for a long wait or some elbow grease. The women were even doing the initiation

ceremonies, like the men used to. Myself, I got my trousers taken down, and my private parts sprayed with lacquer, and I spent a couple of hours sitting in the toilets, with a tin of thinners, washing it off.

In the armed forces, women moved out of administrative 'welfare' jobs. Though they were never allowed or encouraged to fight on the military front, there were new opportunities to join 'active' units on the home front. Nina Hibbin resigned from Home Intelligence out of disgust with what she regarded as the government's manipulation of the information she provided. The call-up brought her to the WAAF (the Women's Auxiliary Airforce Association, pronounced 'Waf') where she became a flight mechanic at Hendon. Like many other women in the forces, she remembered how her work opened up a whole new world of learning and skill that had previously been the exclusive domain of men:

> I joined the WAAF because I really wanted to do something with my hands, to learn a trade, a mechanical trade. I chose engines and I was actually on Spitfires, and used to service the whole thing. But when I was on this mechanic's course to learn how to do it, it was like a most amazing revelation. I'd no idea how an engine worked before, I couldn't imagine how I'd got to the age of twenty, jumping on and off buses without understanding this marvellous theory about how things worked. To some extent it changed my whole approach, which up to then had been to have a good time and cheek the officers. And suddenly here was this whole new field of work and thought. Once I actually got into trouble for not being at a make-up lecture and being instead in the library swotting up mechanics. And really, that was the part of the WAAF that I enjoyed the most.

Many London girls were now hoisting the enormous barrage balloons that were floated above the capital to deter low-level dive-bombing attacks. Many more found themselves on anti-aircraft crews, servicing and loading the guns (though they were still not allowed to pull the trigger). Then, just a few days after conscription for young unmarried women had been introduced, the whole scale of the war escalated rapidly.

On Sunday, 7 December, the Japanese air force bombed the United States fleet at anchor in Pearl Harbor, Hawaii. This action brought America into the war and Britain declared war on Japan. In order both to release more men to fight and to provide munitions for the widening conflict, more and more women had to be drawn into the workforce. It was no longer thought that women were 'doing their bit' for the war effort by looking after their homes. Women, without the responsibility of children, now had by law to register for work, initially up to the age of forty, then up to forty-five and eventually to fifty. The most radical shift in attitudes, however, related to the role of women with children.

At the beginning of 1942 a 'women's parliament' at Conway Hall in London demanded more nurseries. This was followed up later in the year by nursery demonstrations: in Hampstead mothers and their children marched with placards proclaiming, 'Nurseries for kids, war work for mothers'. 'Hampstead mothers stage baby riot to demand more day nurseries', ran the headline in *Picture Post*, the popular illustrated weekly. The *Daily Mirror* reported that in Cricklewood there were scores of mothers willing to go into the local Halifax bomber factory if only nurseries were provided.

The official response was very divided. In some London boroughs – Ealing was one – the medical officers strongly opposed the growth of nurseries, believing such care to be bad for the children. The Ministry of Labour, meanwhile, was running a campaign to recruit mothers into the factories. Eventually, the needs of industry prevailed and nursery provision started to expand rapidly. Eighty per cent of London's married women were employed, although nursery provision, despite the growth, remained inadequate. Women whose children were too young to be placed in a nursery often did part-time war work at home. Emily Golder, still living in Finchley, had married and had a small baby:

> I noticed this part-time job advertised to assemble aircraft parts at home so I decided to do that. The money was a great help, and I also felt I was doing my bit towards the war. I used to load the pram up with the chrome parts from the garage where I collected them and wheel the pram home, my son would be sitting on top, and all the bits and pieces on the bottom. That kept me busy for a couple of hours each day on top of looking after the baby, but you just took it in your stride.

THE BELT TIGHTENS

At the same time that women were being brought into the workforce, attention was being focused on the industries making consumer products for the home market, both essential items like food as well as less essential items like furniture. Many workers from these industries had already moved or had been directed by the state into war production and as a consequence output was well below the pre-war levels. Before more workers could be switched, the problem of shortages had to be tackled more effectively – a problem that during the early part of 1942 had been made increasingly urgent by the escalation of the war. Japanese victories in the Far East had cut off traditional supplies of rubber, tin, tea and sugar, and a spate of German U-boat attacks following America's entry into the war had led to a sharp increase in shipping losses.

Rationing, which had been introduced early in the war for a number of items of food, notably butter, bacon and sugar, was extended and intensified. During 1942, many foods – including sweets and chocolate – were rationed. The precise rations varied each month according to shipping losses and seasonal supplies, but on average, the adult weekly ration was 2 oz (60 g) of tea, 4 oz (115 g) of butter or margarine, 2 oz (60 g) of cooking fat, 8 oz (230 g) of jam, honey or marmalade, 8 oz (230 g) of sugar, 2 oz (60 g) of cheese, 4 oz (115 g) of bacon or ham, 2½ pints (1.5 litres) of milk (when it was rationed), and 1½d worth of meat, which would buy about two small chops or half a pound of stewing steak. In addition, each month a person was entitled to 20 'points' worth of tinned goods (this would buy, for example, a tin of Spam, or five tins of baked beans) and one packet of dried eggs. Bread, vegetables, fruit, offal and fish were not rationed but, apart from bread, potatoes and a few basic vegetables, like carrots and cabbage, these goods were a rarity. The resulting diet seemed to all but the poorest London families to be dull and meagre.

The clothes ration, introduced a year earlier, was also tightened up. The basic clothes ration from the spring of 1942 only allowed a man to buy, for example, an overcoat once every seven years, a pullover every five years, a pair of trousers and a jacket every two years, a pair of pants every two years, a shirt every twenty months and a pair of shoes every eight months. The restrictions on women were equally strict.

But there was a limit to which the problems of shortages could be solved by squeezing the consumer. In March 1942, the government introduced 'Utility' goods. This scheme specified simple and practical designs for a whole range of products, from suits to settees, so that the same quantity could be produced by fewer workers. So, for example, the remaining furniture-makers in north London now had to make articles to a simple pattern, without time-wasting frills. As a result, it was possible to go some way at least to alleviating the furniture crisis which had been created by the blitz and at the same time to allow more carpenters to go off and make aircraft.

These principles applied to the manufacture of a great many things: crockery, pots and pans, boots and shoes, carpets, domestic electrical appliances – the list is almost endless. Perhaps most important for the consumer was the effect on clothing. The number of basic designs was limited to encourage long production runs, and each design would exclude trimmings such as embroidery or the wasteful use of materials through features like pleats or turn-ups.

Government departments ran a number of highly effective propaganda campaigns aimed at helping people to get by on their spartan rations. The 'make-do-and-mend' campaign, for example, gave practical advice on extending the life of old clothes. Sewing classes sprang up across London showing women how, for example, to reverse a collar or to make a child's skirt out of an old pair of trousers. In the home, improvisation became the watchword. Those setting up home, in particular, had sometimes to make do with old crates for tables or an empty dried milk tin as a measuring jug.

More and more, every hour was occupied in one way or another in supporting the war effort. If you weren't actually at work, mending worn-out clothes or transforming an old piece of metal into a curtain rail, then you should have been sorting out the rubbish for salvage for re-use in the war industries. Old bones, so the government propaganda claimed, could become the glue for a Spitfire, old newspapers could make shell cups, waste fats could be used for explosives. All sorts of gimmicks were used to sustain interest in the salvage campaign.

Bermondsey and Bethnal Green challenged each other to paper-collecting competitions. Paddington ran a 'Mile of Keys' campaign to collect a million keys. Often the keenest collectors were children and the Brownies managed to pay for an aircraft with their salvaged jam jars. Later the government started a scheme for children to become official salvage collectors – or 'cogs', with an official Cog anthem: 'There'll always be a dustbin', sung to the tune of 'There'll always be an England'.

Londoners were also urged to 'dig for victory'. Allotments sprouted up all over the capital dug from bombsites and the lawns of local parks, even from the Albert Memorial gardens in Kensington and the moat of the Tower of London. The vegetables produced were treasured, supplementing as they did the meagre rations. Keeping pigs and chickens, and sometimes rabbits and goats, became all the rage. Surface shelters, no longer in use for protection against the bombs, became hen houses. The snorting and snuffling of pigs could be heard in unlikely places like Pall Mall, where the swimming bath of the Ladies' Carlton Club was converted into a giant pig-sty. As Charlie Draper recalled, he and his family, back in Peckham after the blitz, turned their back garden into a mini farmyard:

> We used to keep a few chickens and a couple of geese, a couple of ducks and nine rabbits in the garden. We'd feed them on scraps from the kitchen, potato peelings, cabbage leaves, any old thing. They used to help supplement the rations. On special occasions we'd have chicken or rabbit for dinner, fresh from the back garden, go out there and see what took your fancy, and it tasted a bit better than the two ounces of corned beef that we got on the rations. Dad might sell a couple over the pub and get his beer money, or one or two of the neighbours used to have them.

MUSIC WHILE YOU WORK

Although Ministry of Food campaigns featuring characters like Potato Pete and Dr Carrot offered good advice on different ways of making a nutritious meal out of say, a few potatoes and a cabbage, in practice many mothers found it difficult and time-consuming to produce meals that their children were prepared to eat.

Women were becoming weary and during 1942 levels of absenteeism began to grow. Odette Lesley recalled the strain of the long hours spent at work:

> We worked terribly long hours. We had to work a sixty-hour week which was compulsory. You were dreadfully tired and your work was bound to suffer. You used to crawl out of the factory. I mean three

days a week we used to do eight in the morning till eight at night, and your breaks were very short.

Concern for the welfare of industrial workers began to mount. Managements, under pressure from the Ministry of Labour, started to improve working conditions. The buzzing and grinding of machinery on the factory floor were increasingly drowned by the sounds of popular music. 'Progressive' managements relayed new BBC radio programmes like *Workers' Playtime* and *Music While You Work* over loudspeakers several times a day. The women would often time their actions on the machines to coincide with the rhythm of the music, making the routine more enjoyable as well as helping to keep up their rate of work. Mary Hankins recalled working in a munitions factory in Acton:

We were on the assembly line which wasn't much fun itself but the music helped us to work faster and keep happy. Everyone would be singing along when 'Music While You Work' was on. Sometimes I'd start everybody going, get on my chair, and lead them into 'The Lambeth Walk' and 'My Old Man'. The spirit in the factories was fantastic.

Many factories opened canteens for their workers. These often turned out to be far more than halls just for eating: they became leisure and social centres as well. During the meal workers would sometimes put on their own entertainments, and afterwards the tables and chairs would be cleared away so that they could sing and dance through the rest of their lunch break. Mary Hankins remembered:

We formed a song-and-dance act in the factory. I was on the piano. We started off in the canteen then we began performing in all the factory canteens around Acton. They'd tap their knives and forks to the music, and it would be nothing for them to clear away a few tables and have a knees-up. Then the BBC heard that we were pretty good and we did a 'Workers' Playtime' concert at our factory. Everyone thought that was wonderful.

On their nights off from work, young women would regularly go to the dance halls: the Hammersmith Palais, the Streatham Locarno, the

Paramount in Tottenham Court Road or the Lyceum in Ilford. These were their escape routes to relaxation. The desire for a cheerful and communal escapism was reflected in a great demand for noisy and silly dances in which everyone could take part, like Boomps-a-Daisy, the Conga and the Palais Glide. Odette Lesley recalled going often to the Hammersmith Palais:

> Of course they used to play all the dances we liked: the waltzes, the quicksteps and the fox trots. But what we really used to wait for was the Palais Glide. This was the one we knew was going to get everyone together. You'd get strung out across the ballroom, great lines of boys and girls, and then they'd start to play, 'Horsey, horsey, don't you stop, just let your feet go clippety clop. Your tail goes swish and the wheels go round, giddyup, we're homeward bound.' And, of course, that sort of dance was marvellous, because it got the boys and girls mixed up together, and there was no shyness any more. Then we'd go in groups, and we'd sit around a table and have coffee and we'd talk. It was a great thing for us, it gave us an impetus to go to work the next morning.

In the summer of 1942, local councils throughout the capital organized all sorts of special attractions to encourage people to spend their holidays at home and thereby free transport for military use. The London County Council laid on an extensive programme of events to make 'Stay-at-home holidays Play-at-Home'. Every evening there would be a choice of thirteen different open-air entertainments with everything from stand-up comedians to Shakespeare. Every swimming pool had its own gala, every open space from Hackney's Victoria Park to Clapham Common had a fair or fête and on the hot summer evenings there was often dancing in the parks.

In outer London, there were similar, if less extensive, programmes of events. The borough of Barnes, for example, held displays of 'physical training', band concerts, 'comic' cricket matches, a Punch and Judy show, and an Olde Worlde Fayre.

All the changes in industry – from those that increased the recruitment of women and reduced consumer demand, to those that challenged the very heart of the old private enterprise system – were producing startling results. Production in London's war industries boomed, part of an upturn in the war economy throughout Britain. By the autumn of 1942 output of military equipment was dramatically higher than it was in the summer of 1941 when the production crisis had been so urgent. The number of tanks rolling off the assembly lines had more than doubled, as had the number of machine-guns. And in the late autumn of 1942, the benefits began to be reaped.

VICTORY ON THE BATTLEFIELD

On 2 November, the British Eighth Army, equipped with around four times as many tanks as the German forces, defeated Rommel decisively at El Alamein and thereby turned the tide of the war in North Africa. In London, church bells rang out across the city – in celebration and not, as would have been the case two years earlier, because the Nazis had invaded Britain. At last there was a light at the end of the tunnel.

But for Londoners there could be no complacency. The start of 1943 brought the first raids on London by the Luftwaffe since the blitz, in retaliation for an intensive Allied air attack on Berlin. They brought tragedy again to London. One of the bombs scored a direct hit on a primary school in Catford killing thirty-eight children.

Londoners were disturbed by the raids and a few panicked. On one evening the siren went off while people were queuing for shelter under Bethnal Green tube station and – quite unlike the calm behaviour during the later stages of the blitz itself – there was a stampede for the stairs. In the ensuing crush, 173 people died. This time, however, the scale of the German attack was minor and the British defences – which had been substantially improved with radar on the fighter planes and new anti-aircraft 'rocket projectors' in the ack-ack units – were far more successful. After only two raids in January and one in March, the Luftwaffe gave up.

The Home Intelligence reports on morale noted that most people in London desperately hoped that there would be a swift end to the war and that a 'second front' would now be opened up in France to push Germany back from the west. Indeed, a direct assault on northern Europe was favoured by the United States, but under Churchill's insistence the Allies adopted a strategy which took a much more long-term view of events: first, the North African campaign was to be pursued and won, followed only then by the battle in Europe. The war was set to last a lot longer and the government had to persuade people that it was essential to keep on working flat out.

A spate of propaganda films extolling the factory worker was produced

– films which contrasted sharply with the Chaplinesque portrayal of the working class prior to the war. Odette Lesley recalled alternating her trips to the dance halls with visits to the cinema:

> We used to go to the cinema whenever we could find time because the cinema, along with dancing, was certainly the biggest leisure pursuit that we loved. And we found that the jobs we were doing, with these awful machines, were being portrayed in the British films like 'This Happy Breed'. And we could identify with the people in them, because this was reality as opposed to the old Hollywood glamour that we used to escape into. We wanted reality now; we wanted to be recognized. We wanted everyone who saw the film to see what we were really doing. And in these films that is how it was, and we were really thrilled. We used to sit there and think, 'Look at that actress, she's working on a machine like I do.' And it really almost gave a bit of glamour to what we were doing, despite the miserable job that it was, and this was very uplifting. Maybe it was a type of propaganda but if it was it was excellent and it worked.

The greatest morale booster, however, was always success on the battlefield and by the late spring of 1943 the military rewards for people's efforts were becoming more visible. On 12 May, the Allies finally overcame the last of the German and Italian troops in North Africa. That summer Germany was in retreat, not only in the Mediterranean but also in the east where the Red Army was pushing the Nazi divisions back towards the Fatherland. With Germany's ally, Italy, in internal turmoil, the time was ripe to strike while the enemy was weak. Serious planning for an Allied invasion of northern Europe now began.

In August, the Allied commanders made the final decision to press ahead with their bold plan for a seaborne invasion of northern France. A vast array of equipment would be needed to give this campaign any chance of success for the proposed landings, and finally London was asked to play its part in supplying equipment for the war effort. At the beginning of the war, London's industrial capacity had been deliberately under-used. During the middle phase of the war, the pressure of war production had necessitated a rapid expansion in the capital's industries. Now, as the conflict reached its climax, London was to be at the heart of a great production drive to win the war.

PREPARING FOR THE SHOWDOWN

The invasion plan, code-named Operation Overlord, involved landing about a million men on the beaches of Normandy. The Allied commanders saw the key to success in flexibility. Hitler expected an Allied counter-attack and was building up defences and troop reinforcements at strategic points along the coast. The Allies had to be able to land in Normandy at a few days' notice. This military tactic posed tremendous technical problems for the engineering industries. While the troops themselves could be landed easily enough anywhere, they only formed an effective fighting force if at the same time tanks, jeeps, trucks, field guns, anti-aircraft guns, flame throwers and all the other military hardware of a modern army were swiftly ferried ashore. The final gathering-point in Britain for all this equipment was the Channel coast.

As London was by far the biggest industrial centre of the area, the capital had to play a pivotal role in the development and production of the special equipment needed for Operation Overlord. The core of the plan was to build enormous, hollow concrete units, or 'caissons', which could be towed across the Channel and then joined together and sunk so as to form breakwaters and harbour walls. A floating pier, joined to the shore by a floating roadway, would then be placed within these 'Mulberry harbours' – named after the codeword for this part of Operation Overlord.

As construction got under way, three large London docks were drained to house over half the estimated work: the East India Docks, the southern section of the Surrey Docks, and part of the Tilbury Docks were in this way transformed into a mosaic of building sites. At the same time, along the banks of the Thames, huge basins were dug out to form temporary dry docks.

But as this great production drive gained momentum in the autumn of 1943, a new threat was emerging. British Intelligence had pieced together evidence suggesting that Hitler was preparing a pre-emptive attack with a secret long-range weapon. From an early stage in the war, Germany had been developing new methods of bombing, exploiting the latest scientific and technological developments. There were three parts to this programme. First, there was a pilotless aeroplane carrying a one-ton warhead with an engine pre-set to cut out at a certain distance so that it nose-dived to the ground exploding on impact. This was the V-1 flying bomb, dubbed the 'doodlebug' by Londoners. Then there was the V-2, the first long-range ballistic missile actively to be used in combat. The V-2 could carry its one-ton warhead to a height of over fifty miles, almost to the outer limits of the earth's atmosphere. This supersonic rocket would hit its target silently and at such a speed that no defence was possible. And finally, there was the lesser-known V-3. This was a huge piece of artillery over 400 feet (122 m) long that would fire finned projectiles with 300 lb (136 kg) of high explosive to a distance of 100 miles. Two batteries, each with twenty-five guns, were being built to the south of Calais, all targeting London; they were known collectively as 'the London Gun'.

Hitler's plan was to have these new weapons ready swiftly so that the Allied invasion of northern France could be defeated before it ever set sail. For the Allies, preparing for Operation Overlord was becoming a race against time. But the invasion of France could not be rushed and the date was set for May 1944.

In the meantime, the Allies simply had to try to knock out Hitler's secret weapons. The intelligence services had long been tracking the development of the V-1 flying bomb and the V-2 rocket and felt that they had successfully disrupted both by bombing the testing site at Peenemünde in the north of Germany. In response to new information about the launching ramps in northern France, the British and American air forces mounted an intensive bombing campaign to destroy them. As for the London Gun, British Intelligence never knew anything about it. By early in 1944, the Allies consequently believed that the threat had been countered.

By now, the invasion preparations in the capital were also beginning to bear fruit. Ford at Dagenham had developed an invaluable waterproofing compound made of red putty. London Transport's Acton works had converted tanks to operate in water 10 feet (3 m) deep. A Thames-side submarine cable company had tested strong but flexible piping on the floor of the Thames for use in the Pluto project which was to supply the Allies invading France with oil. The furniture-makers in north London were busy expanding their range of military products. Alongside Mosquito planes, there were troop-carrying gliders specially adapted for landing on grassland behind the German lines on the French coast, assault dinghies and wooden pontoons for the floating roadway. In the London docks, the first batch of half-completed caissons for the Mulberry harbours were floated out and round to the remaining 'wet' docks for finishing off. Tom Feeney, who was recruited from his native Ireland to work on these, recalled:

They ended up as high as a block of flats, thousands of tons of concrete and steel. We'd never seen anything like it and we wondered if it would ever float. I remember the day they dug a canal to take the Mulberry out by tug into the Thames. And when the tide came up the canal we all watched secretly fearing it might sink, then as the water got higher and higher, it started floating and everyone started clapping and cheering.

Hitler heard reports that the Allied invasion plans were well under way. He wanted to disrupt these but his secret V weapons were not yet ready, partly because the Allied bombing missions had caused disruption and partly because of technical problems. So he returned to conventional bombing and on 21 January, he ordered every serviceable aircraft in the west to attack London. The raid was not a success – only 30 tons of the high explosive carried by the Luftwaffe hit their targets. However, the attack was renewed in February, when several raids by the Luftwaffe brought death and destruction back to the capital. The raids were christened the 'baby blitz' – as they were nowhere near as destructive as the blitz itself. Moreover, the improved defences of London were soon beginning to take their toll on the Luftwaffe. The German counter-offensive began to fade and, after a few more attacks, ended in late March.

The massive preparations for Operation Overlord in London and on the south coast were now reaching their climax. All along the Thames, the riverbanks were bristling with concrete barges and with converted Thames barges, their sterns cut off and replaced with ramps ready for the landings. As the first batch of caissons for the Mulberry harbour were completed these gigantic concrete units floating out of the docks and down the river were a puzzling sight for Londoners. Few people outside the docks knew what they were for as their construction had been kept a close secret by the project's workers. Indeed, every precaution was taken to ensure that information about the D-day landings was not leaked to German intelligence. Tom Feeney remembered the importance placed on secrecy at the time:

We all knew what we were doing was part of the invasion plan but they tried to keep it secret outside the East End. There were notices posted up everywhere saying 'DANGEROUS TALK COSTS LIVES'. We, the Irish, were banned from going home so that we wouldn't go out and boast about what we were doing, and let the secret out and get back to Germany. And all the letters home were opened and censored as well, to stop any secrets getting out; many was the letter I sent home which had 'opened by the censor' marked on it.

The caissons were then towed round to the Solent, waiting for the rest of the units, still behind schedule, to be finished. For separate military reasons, the date of the invasion – D-day – had to be put back from May to June. The harbours were frantically completed. Now, all the preparations were ready.

In the last weeks of May and early June, tension began to mount as thousands of troops passed through the capital on their way to the south coast. Many were temporarily housed in makeshift military camps erected on the bombed-out wilderness that had once been Canning Town and Silvertown or on London's football grounds, such as West Ham's Upton Park. Six divisions gathered in the London docks waiting for embarkation.

The weather conditions had to be right for Operation Overlord: a full moon to light the way for aircraft and to ensure a neap tide. After a tense period of waiting and watching the go-ahead was finally given on Tuesday, 6 June 1944. Hundreds of ships set off down the Thames and, as they rounded the coast, they joined thousands more vessels and tugs leaving from the south coast ports. The greatest amphibious assault in history was under way.

Very early that morning, the first troops had landed on the beaches of Normandy. For Londoners, the tension and pressure of the last few months, the hard work of the production drives over the past three years, the sacrifices of the war, all seemed worthwhile. The Allies were on the road to victory. Spirits in the capital had never been higher since the outbreak of war. Nobody had any suspicion of the terrible shock that was in store.

CHAPTER SEVENTEEN

The Final Terror

HE FIRST MISSILE arrived at 4.25am around sunrise on Tuesday, 13 June 1944 shattering the peace of Grove Road in the heart of Bow. A strange machine-like noise could be heard travelling through the sky above London. Those who were awake thought it sounded like an old motorbike or a huge clockwork toy. The Bow bomb was one of ten missiles hurled that summer morning from their camouflaged catapult bases in northern France. Of the ten, five crashed almost at once, one plummeted into the Channel, and three fell to earth in Kent causing little damage. But even though only one of these flying bombs landed on its target, its effects were quite devastating for it marked the beginning of a new air offensive on London.

The strike rate of these doodlebugs increased as the Germans rapidly improved the way in which they were programmed and launched so that within three days the flying bombs were reaching Greater London at a rate of seventy-three a day. The V-1s brought a new sort of devastation to London. Whereas during the blitz there was a chance to dash for shelter and much of the destruction had been caused by fire, the doodlebugs gave only a moment's warning and their warheads were incredibly powerful, damaging houses and shattering windows within a quarter-of-a-mile radius. The direct blast of the explosion hurled people against obstacles, crashed them into walls and, in the most serious cases, literally ripped them apart. Spears of flying glass lacerated people, sometimes causing serious injuries, such as blindness. Others were hurt by objects like flying rubble or pieces of wood striking them heavy blows or piercing them like arrows. Those who were inside their home, workplace or street shelter when the missile struck were likely to be buried alive if they were within 50 yards (46 m) of the explosion. Elsie Huntley recalled huddling with her nine-year-old son Derek and her baby Roy together with neighbours in the concrete street shelter opposite their home in Mitcham during one early doodlebug raid in south London:

It was the most terrible night we knew. We had a lot of bombing all night long. They were coming over all night, warnings coming and going. And then in the morning it had eased off quite a bit and I suggested I go in and make a cup of tea. Anyway, I went in the house to make the tea; I'd got the baby with me, he was nearly two. My son, who was nine, came running in and said, 'Mummy, there's one coming over.' So I said, 'You run over the shelter and get into your bed and I'll come in.' So I came in quickly and I hadn't been in there a few minutes when we heard the noise stop. Well, we knew when it stopped something was going to happen and then, bang, everything went dark. I leant over my baby and we were all screaming; I could hear my neighbours screaming, I was screaming, the baby was screaming. So I tried to ease myself away so that the baby could breathe, because everything was crushing us. All the concrete was on top of us. And then I just thought, 'Oh God, what's happened, please help me, get me out.'

It seemed ages, but I think it was only a few minutes when I heard above me movements and voices, and I'm saying, 'Please help me, please help me'. Gradually I managed to push my arm out and somebody held my hand and was saying, 'Hold on lady, hold on. And I said, 'I've got a baby, got a baby in my arms,' and then they pulled my baby out and got me out. We were all put in an ambulance and taken to hospital. I was laid on a bed in a casualty ward and then somebody brought the baby round saying, 'Whose baby is this?' And I said, 'It's my baby.' In the morning they said to me that my other son Derek had been killed outright. And all the women neighbours were killed as well.

To avoid any panic, and to prevent German intelligence from discovering what damage the V-1 was wreaking, Herbert Morrison, the Minister for Home Security, at first censored any reference to the flying bombs. Many of those who had seen or heard the first missiles believed they were German raiders shot down over London. But when the intensity of the attack increased concealment was no longer possible; the people of London needed to be told something of what was happening to them so that new precautions could be taken. On 16 June Herbert Morrison announced that London was under attack by pilotless planes, but the scale of devastation and demoralization caused by the flying bombs was hushed up at the time in order to maintain morale.

Most Londoners thought it inconceivable that the Allies, with their overwhelming strength, could not destroy a few hundred missile sites just across the Channel now that they had invaded France. Many blamed the government, and Morrison, once the hero of Londoners, found himself booed as he visited bomb-damaged areas. The great spirit of solidarity and faith in the state generated during the blitz and sustained till D-day was beginning to dissipate.

One of the principal aims of the flying bomb attack had been to boost German morale at the same time as demoralizing the British. Since 1942 one German city after another – and in particular Berlin – had been subjected to saturation bombing by the British and American air forces. Almost all the victims had been civilians. Indeed the Allies' deliberate aim – though this had not been publicly admitted at the time – was to break German morale by 'de-housing' the population of the industrial cities as well as destroying the factories where they worked. The results were far worse than anything that London had ever experienced. The bombing of Hamburg in July 1943, for example, created a mammoth firestorm that burned for several days and killed over 50,000. Now London was to take the brunt of an attack that was provoked primarily by a German desire for retribution. The Reich christened the flying bomb *Vergeltungswaffe*, meaning 'vengeance weapon'.

Early in 1944 Hitler spent many hours with Goebbels drawing squares on a map of London and working out how many people each missile might kill. British Intelligence had long suspected that Germany was about to use new secret weapons to attack the capital. However, the government mistakenly believed that the heavy Allied bombing raids during the winter of 1943–4 had all but knocked out the launching sites and disrupted the missile production programme. As a result, London's defences were scaled down; the number of guns protecting the capital was almost halved.

The new assault was almost harder to cope with than the blitz. Odette Lesley had a vivid memory of a new kind of panic that gripped the capital. She had been forced to give up her war work because of physical exhaustion and was making handbags in central London:

I can still remember my horror and disgust at seeing grown men avidly pushing women and children aside to get down into Warren Street tube station when the doodlebugs were coming over. I was actually shoved out of the way myself once or twice. People's nerves had gone, their nerves were shot to pieces.

The official fear of a 'deep-shelter mentality' developing among tube shelterers (which had proved groundless during the blitz) now seemed to be coming true. Some Londoners, especially those with young children, lived in the tubes day and night, refusing to leave until ejected by the police so that the shelters could be cleaned. People felt that the war was nearly over and did not want to be killed by one of the last bombs. Whereas in 1940 the mood had, in part, been one of self-sacrifice, now it was more exclusively self-preservation to get through to the end. Most civilians secretly felt, or even openly said, that the war should have been won by now anyway.

Within days, the flying bomb raids had created feelings of intense strain and anxiety. At the same time, the old spirit of co-operation and communality was being replaced by a new sort of individualism.

The doodlebugs, which by the end of June were hitting London at the rate of about a hundred a day, left the old air-raid warning system – which had worked quite well during the blitz – practically redundant. The flying bombs were so small and fast that they sometimes managed to avoid radar detection, the result being that either there was no air-raid warning or it was sounded too late for families to find shelter. At other times, the alert went so frequently that people found it difficult to remember if an alert was in force or not. To get any work done at all, many stayed where they were so they could continue working and instead listened for the flying bomb. This could be a nerve-wracking business.

There would be a distant hum rising to a raucous rattle. This would then either disappear into the distance or suddenly stop, and it was the interval between the engine cutting out and the explosion that was the most terrifying. If the noise seemed to stop directly above them people would dive for cover, flinging themselves on the floor, under tables or in doorways. The interval lasted only twelve seconds but seemed interminable.

The ever-present possibility of death and destruction combined with the shortness of the warning created feelings of isolation. Because the flying bombs could come at any moment, day or night, there was no specific period when people would come together to shelter, yet when destruction was near there wasn't time to draw strength from one another. Charlie Draper, who had moved to work repairing bomb-damaged buildings in south London, recalled how he found the constant danger a terrible strain:

> You never knew when one was going to get you. There were several
> occasions I had near misses. One was when I was blown off a

motorbike when a fly bomb dropped in Dulwich. On another occasion I was buried for five hours in a market in East Lane and was dug out. And another occasion, when I was at Penge, a fly bomb came over. We heard the engine stop and we all rushed into this ice box in the fishmongers, and it dropped just over the back of the shop and the door slammed so hard that when we got out of there we all had gone slightly deaf. I think at that time I was more or less knackered and that did me in. So I went in the shop next door, got a couple of pies, put them in my tool bag, collected my tools together and jumped on a bus and went off to the Chislehurst caves. I didn't actually go into the caves, I lay down in a field opposite and I just slept for about seven hours, so I must have been on the edge of collapse.

IRRATIONAL FEARS AND RATIONING

The robotic and depersonalized nature of the flying bombs fuelled many irrational fears. The most common was that the doodlebugs were pro-grammed to reach certain specific targets and had the power to seek them out and pursue them. This was, in fact, far beyond the capabilities of the V-1s but such fears seemed to be given substance by the remarkable frequency with which the bombs scored direct hits on hospitals in London. More than a hundred were hit by doodlebugs, among them St Mary Abbots in Kensington, Mile End, Lambeth and St Olave's. Some people believed that the weapons had been targeted against the sick and the helpless. The whole nature of these pilotless machines was like something out of a science-fiction story. The thought of being killed by a robot was for many much more unnerving than being bombed by a pilot, who might himself be shot down and killed in the process. Odette Lesley remembered these feelings:

> The doodlebugs were so much more terrifying than anything that had come along up till that time because they were supernatural, they were uncanny, they were almost science fiction. It was so awful to think about this destructive thing up there, full of explosive, with this awful flame coming out, and nobody in it. You accepted a plane with a man in it, you couldn't accept something that was automatic. It was this

that struck psychologically at us in such a way that it destroyed our nerves; it destroyed any sort of calm that we'd worked out through the war. We could not accept this.

Over half of the flying bombs rained down on the suburbs of south London, with Croydon, Lewisham and Wandsworth (in that order) worst hit. Even if the bombs did not actually fall, the residents had the unnerving experience of watching processions of doodlebugs pass overhead on their way to central London.

The new geography of the bombing brought into the front line the suburban housewife, whom Home Intelligence reported as being particularly disconcerted by the attacks. Many women strained to hear the bombs as they went about their daily chores, only to discover that the domestic sounds of running taps, sizzling food and buzzing vacuum cleaners could easily be confused with approaching flying bombs or, worse, could make the real thing inaudible. They did not have even the small benefit of roof observers to warn them of impending danger as did factories and department stores. Gladys Strelitz had now moved back from Caversham where she was evacuated, and was living with her children in Ilford, in Essex:

It was dreadful because we had a big room, with a big open window space, and we'd look out and see this flaming sword coming right over, and it always appeared as if it was coming for us. And we would have to fall on the floor, lie under the table, and wait for the crash that would come. We knew every minute that it might be our last. It was intolerable, it really was. And in the end it had its effect on me because I started sleep-walking, and I'd have to be helped down the stairs, and I knew I couldn't carry on much longer, that something would have to be done about it. All the tablets the doctor was giving me weren't helping me a little bit, so I ended up with nervous exhaustion.

In addition, the post-blitz lull in bombings had resulted in a gradual winding down of the whole civil defence network. The great demand for recruits in the forces and for war production had led to the transfer of tens of thousands of men and women away from civil defence work. Morrison, partly to compensate for this reduction in public provision, distributed thousands more of his indoor table shelters known as 'Morrisons', originally developed during the blitz to give Londoners greater protection in their own homes. However, these strong and well-designed shelters, which offered excellent protection against flying glass and masonry, served only to increase the isolation of the individual family and in particular the housewife, who was now likely to remain in her house when a raid was on.

Underlying this despondency was a deep physical and mental weariness with the war. The Ministry of Food, with its Kitchen Front publicity campaign, had raised public awareness of what were healthy foods but by 1944 everyone was becoming fed up with a miserable if healthy diet. They craved fresh eggs, oranges and onions, all of which had virtually disappeared. The strict rationing of basic items like meat, butter, bacon and cheese had for many people taken much of the pleasure out of eating. People were bored with carrot marmalade, dried eggs, and 'Woolton' vegetable pie, made out of a mixture of potato, swede, cauliflower and carrots, while the new foods like whale meat, catfish or pigs' brains which had found their way on to people's dinner plates were found repugnant by many. Women were exhausted by the constant scrimping and saving, the queuing for hours outside fishmongers and greengrocers, and the struggle to make a wholesome, filling meal from a few ingredients. And when the effort became too much or the queues too long, then they and their families went hungry. Gladys Strelitz kept going for the sake of her children:

There was all this lining up for food. A neighbour might say, 'Yes, they've got sausages down the road,' and you'd rush out, line up for an hour, two hours, and when you got to the counter, all they'd have was whale meat sausages. Take them home and while you were cooking them, these sausages were so revolting they actually smelt of fish. Well, we ate them in front of the children to prove that they were lovely, but they weren't really. The children would say, 'No, we don't want those, Mummy,' so then we would mix up swede with them to take the taste away, and we'd see the tears running down their cheeks. But we knew the children had to be fed and they couldn't go hungry. We couldn't put 'em to bed hungry. So, day after day we kept on like this. There was nothing else.

The rationing of household items was also demoralizing. Toilet paper had become scarce – most made do with the traditional working-class substitute of ripped-up newspapers (although even this was in short supply as the daily newspaper was now only four pages long). There was a shortage of millions of pieces of crockery and some families were forced to drink from jam jars as the poorest had done in the 1930s. Furniture was rigidly rationed and even bombed-out families were allowed only a few essential pieces to set up their new homes. As furniture became more and more threadbare, dyed flour sacks and sugar bags were commonly used for covers and cushions. Cots were in very short supply by the end of the war and pregnant women were advised to make one out of an old drawer, by padding it with newspaper and then lining it with an old nightdress.

Obtaining everyday items like saucepans, kettles, alarm clocks, bedding, toothbrushes, paint and carpets was very difficult, as was replacing cutlery, so that much was pilfered from canteens. By 1944 the number of knives, forks and spoons that were disappearing each year from the canteens run by the London Transport Passenger Board had risen astronomically to more than 60,000.

The growing disillusionment with rationing along with people's increasing desire to get more than their fair share helped to fuel a substantial increase in crime in the last years of the war. Professional criminals in London started hijacking lorries loaded with food and clothing and raiding warehouses. There was a boom in pilfering from workplaces – dockers, warehousemen and those involved in the transportation of goods often had the richest pickings – and most of this stolen property found its way on to the black market. Ordinary civilians increasingly dabbled in crime both as pilferers and purchasers of stolen goods. They bought the goods 'under the counter' without any rationing coupons exchanging hands, in shops and markets or from 'spivs' who would fix up deals in pubs.

FLEEING THE DOODLEBUGS

The doodlebugs continued to rain down on the capital. Within two weeks the flying bomb attacks had wrought nearly the same amount of damage as had the Luftwaffe in the first two weeks of the blitz. About 1,600 people had been killed, about 10,000 were injured, half of them seriously, and over 200,000 houses had been damaged. When the war cabinet met on 27 June opinion was unanimous that the capital faced a crisis. Morrison saw the new attacks as a real threat to Allied victory. He argued that:

. . . . after five years of war the civil population are not as capable of standing the strains of air attacks as they had been during the winter of 1940-41. I will do everything to hold up their courage and spirit – but there is a limit and the limit will come.

An official evacuation scheme was introduced in early July 1944 and quickly put into operation. Almost 500,000 mothers, expectant mothers and children were billeted on strangers in the country. Another 500,000 – including elderly people and homeless families – left London as 'aided evacuees': they made their own arrangements but were given free railway warrants and billeting certificates entitling them to a weekly allowance. By the end of August the population of London had dropped by more than 1 million.

In early July, the government opened eight new purpose-built deep shelters, four on the north bank of the Thames at Chancery Lane, Goodge Street, Camden Town and Belsize Park, and four on the south, at Stockwell, Clapham North, Clapham South and Clapham Common. Each of them was 100 feet (30 m) under ground and contained 8,000 bunks as well as canteen and hospital facilities. Those lucky enough to get tickets felt like the aristocrats of the shelter world. All this helped Londoners to cope with the effects of the flying bombs. But the most important task for the government was to try to prevent the bombs from actually landing on the capital. Here British Intelligence played a key role.

The Germans relied on a handful of secret agents that they had sent to Britain during the war to provide them with this information. These agents were all captured and were used to feed back phoney information. When flying bombs landed on central London, they reported that they had overshot their mark and hit the countryside to the north. They also reported that no flying bombs had landed south of the Thames, despite the fact that around three-quarters of the bombs had fallen in this area. In response to this false information the German crews readjusted the flying bombs' guidance mechanisms so that from then on the majority of bombs were set to nose-dive well to the south of London, in the countryside. Most northern, central and inner suburbs to the south were spared doodlebug raids and although areas like Croydon, Bromley, Bexley and Orpington were much worse off, as outer areas were much less densely populated each incident caused, on average, far fewer casualties.

The doodlebugs were also thwarted by four lines of defence that were rapidly assembled in late June and early July. First there were the squadrons of fighter planes – Hawker Tempests, Spitfires and others – patrolling the Channel twenty miles offshore between Dover and Beachy Head. At first, at altitudes of about 3,000 feet (914 m) the flying bombs were too fast for the British fighter planes. In time, however, they found a way of shooting some of them down and, occasionally, upsetting their balancing mechanism with a nudge on the wing so that the missile spiralled into the sea.

The next line of defence was thousands of anti-aircraft guns – including those which had once been in London – placed on the coast along a fifty-mile stretch behind the patrolling aircraft. The ack-ack units had by this stage been much improved with rocket projectors, radar guidance for the guns and 'proximity' fuses on the shells, which meant that the shells exploded not only when they hit their target but also when they were near.

Behind the guns were more fighters to deal with any missiles that got through the gun belt. Finally, along the North Downs, floated a wall of barrage balloons, which by mid-July numbered 1,750. To begin with, lack of experience in dealing with the flying bombs meant that most passed through the defence system intact. But by the end of July the anti-aircraft gunners and the RAF pilots were having considerable success in shooting them down. Between mid-June and early September a total of 3,916 bombs – just over a half of all those directed at London – were blown up. The fighters brought down 1,942, the guns 1,730 and the balloons 244. By then, however, the flying bombs had killed nearly 5,781 people and severely injured 15,530 more.

MYSTERIOUS EXPLOSIONS

On 5 September 1944 victory fever spread around London, with flag-waving celebrations in the streets as rumours spread that the bombings were all over. The prevailing euphoria even infected government ministers and on 7 September Herbert Morrison ordered an end to the evacuation of London. Later that day Duncan Sandys, the junior minister in charge of defeating the V-1s, told a press conference: 'except possibly for a few last shots the Battle of London is over'.

Many Londoners, hearing this news, considered the war to be virtually won and thousands of evacuated families flooded back into the capital. However, the celebrations proved to be tragically premature. On the evening of 8 September, a mysterious explosion was heard all over London, followed immediately by a second explosion. One was in Chiswick to the west, the other in Epping to the east of London.

The strange explosions went on and increased, so that by the end of October an average of four a day were heard in London. But all the time the return of evacuees into the capital continued, most of them oblivious to the new danger that now faced them; the government had ordered a total censorship on any reference to the true nature of these explosions.

Dore Silverman was one of a team of press censors who worked round the clock at the Ministry of Information headquarters in Senate House in Bloomsbury, combing through 'sensitive' copy from editors, taking out any reference to rocket damage. He recalled:

> We had to stop the knowledge of their arrival being circulated, first, so as not to inform the Germans that they had landed in any particular area, but more important, there was the question of morale of the civilian population, because these were devastating in their effect. One rocket could demolish a whole street in a working-class area. There was no defence against them. And there was no warning that they were on their way and you could not take any shelter of any kind, because you had not even five seconds' notice.

But soon the mysterious bangs had become so common that many people were frightened and wild rumours circulated as to what they might be. Some said they were exploding gas mains; others thought that German paratroopers were blowing up key installations. But each one was heralded by a double blast (so loud that even at ten miles away it sounded close by) followed immediately afterwards by a reddish flash and a large plume of black smoke rising into the sky. At the point of impact, it was clear that these explosions were the result of a new and yet more powerful type of bomb. There would be a crater, sometimes as much as fifty feet (15 m) wide and ten feet (3 m) deep. In the immediate vicinity a whole row of perhaps thirty terraced houses would be razed to the ground. Suburban streets suddenly took on the appearance of battlefields covered in clouds of dust and masses of rubble. The dead and injured lay everywhere, covered in blood, some of them dismembered. Many who were close to the explosions and survived were permanently blinded.

An earthquake effect reverberated, causing yet more damage: a quarter of a mile away, windows smashed, roofs caved in and washbasins cracked; a few miles away, the earth tremor was such that floorboards shuddered, window frames shook and clouds of soot were blown out of fireplaces into living rooms. Charlie Draper remembered seeing the effect in the Peckham, south London:

> It was a lot worse than what the doodlebugs did. It would take out a row of houses or a block of flats; the complete block would just disappear. And then, say, another hundred yards away the walls were caved in, party walls were gone, roofs blown off, the structure was in a terrible state. They were irreparable. They just pulled them down, dangerous structures. We patched up the ones further away.
>
> In some of the houses we went in we'd see some of the people that were there when it happened. They might have been in their shelter, then come out in the morning and found the house half gone. They were upset and cracking up and saying, 'Oh, this is the sixth time this has happened. You know, I don't think I'll ever start again. I've had enough.' When we were at the rocket sites, it was terrible. They were digging people out for days after, and finding bodies on roofs all the way around the area.

British Intelligence had known about the development of the V-2, a new type of 'rocket' bomb, since 1943 but had mistakenly believed that Allied air attacks in that year and 1944 had all but destroyed the rocket production process and the launching pads. They were unaware of the existence of a major V-2 assembly line (serviced by a slave army of prisoners from concentration camps) deep in the Hartz mountains outside Nordhausen in the heart of Nazi Germany. Launched from camouflaged mobile trailers in Holland (so it was impossible for the RAF to locate and destroy them before they were airborne), they reached an altitude of sixty miles, moving in a vast parabola at up to 3,600 miles an hour, twice the speed of sound. It took them only four minutes to reach their target. These technological marvels of the time rendered the British defence system of Spitfires, ack-ack and barrage balloons completely redundant.

The government had attempted in September 1944 to boost morale by replacing the blackout with a less rigorous 'dim-out', and by planning to disband the Home Guard in November. Now that the rockets were raining down on London these measures were thought to be premature. The Home Guard had given many thousands of Londoners a pride, a purpose and a real sense of participation in the defence of the capital.

Now they felt redundant and powerless to do anything about the new German onslaught. By early November many parts of London had been hit, from Bermondsey to Walthamstow and from Camberwell to West Ham, and a public statement was needed to contain the rising tide of anger and anxiety. On 10 November, more than two months after the explosions began, Churchill finally conceded publicly that London was under rocket attack.

THE TRUTH ABOUT THE V-2

The first serious incident to be widely publicized was the New Cross disaster on Saturday 25 November 1944, when a V-2 rocket scored a direct hit on the Woolworths department store, packed with lunchtime shoppers. Bodies were flung skywards and the building crumbled into a tangled mass of bricks and masonry. June Gaida, then thirteen years old, remembered the appalling aftermath:

> I was going shopping that morning for my mother, and suddenly
> there was a blinding flash of light, and a roaring, rushing sound. I was
> thrown into the air. There was noise all around me, a deafening
> terrible noise that beat against my eardrums and, when I fell to the
> ground, I curled myself up into a ball to protect myself, and I tried to
> scream but there wasn't any air. When the noise had faded, I picked
> myself up and I was coated with brick dust, with slivers of glass in my
> hair. Then I walked towards Woolworths. Things were still falling out
> of the sky, there were bricks, masonry, and bits of things and bits of
> people. I remember seeing a horse's head lying in the gutter. Further
> on there was a pram-hood all twisted and bent, and there was a little
> baby's hand still in its woolly sleeve. Outside the pub there was a bus
> and it had been concertinaed, with rows of people sitting inside, all
> covered in dust and dead. I looked over towards where Woolworths
> had been and there was nothing. There was just an enormous gap
> covered by a cloud of dust and I could see right through to the streets
> beyond Woolworths. No building, just piles of rubble and bricks, and
> from underneath it all I could hear people screaming.

The death toll – although this was not disclosed at the time – was 160, with a further 200 injured, many of them seriously. Although the location, the casualty figures and much of the horrific detail were censored, news of what had happened spread through London. This did not lead to the panic which some officials feared, but tension in the capital was heightened. For if the doodlebugs were seen as sinister, then the rockets brought an element of supernatural terror. It was impossible to hear them coming and the indoor Morrison shelters provided little protection from them. Mollie Matthews, working as a clerk at Tate & Lyle's sugar refinery in Silvertown, remembered being constantly distraught at the threat the rockets posed to her family while she was away at work:

> There were occasions when, if a rocket had dropped locally to where I worked, and I didn't live too far from work, I would go home to see if my mum and sister were OK. But this particular morning a rocket dropped and I didn't go home because my mum was due to come into work very soon. I received a phone call; the voice was a little incoherent, I couldn't quite understand what was going on, other than the fact that our house had been hit.
>
> I left work, ran out of the gate to catch a bus and no bus came. Every second seemed like ages. Consequently I decided to run home. It was about a three-mile trek so, running and walking and running again, I eventually reached our street. There was ruined houses everywhere; burst pipes, bodies in sacks. When I reached home I found that our house was a skeleton, a mess. I immediately got to the bricks and kept throwing them away, calling out for my mum and my sister and wondering if they were there or not.
>
> Eventually a policeman came and said that some people had been taken to a nearby school. I flew round to the school, but at the gate my legs turned to jelly, and for some reason I just could not move. A gentleman came along and asked what was wrong and I tried to explain to him. He said he would go into the school for me, and they seemed to be the magic words. I thought, 'If anyone's got to find them it's got to be me', and with that the use was back in my legs and off I went into the school. I searched through several rooms and eventually there was mum and my sister, covered in dirt and soot where the firemen had helped them out. Mum was injured, lying on a camp bed; my sister, fortunately, was OK.

The vast majority of V-2 rockets landed on London's eastern and north-eastern suburbs, or in the old East End. This was not what the German crews firing the missiles intended. Most of the rockets were fired from Holland and their trajectory took them over East Anglia into Essex and the eastern suburbs of London. They were targeted on the centre but the aiming of V-2s was not at all accurate and many had faulty mechanisms so they fell short, decimating some eastern boroughs. Ilford was the worst-hit area, suffering thirty-five rocket explosions in the last winter of the war, closely followed by West Ham, Barking, Dagenham and Walthamstow. The casualty figures in the north-east corner of the capital were 645 dead and 1,441 seriously injured. Heavily built up working-class areas like Islington, Finsbury and Stepney also suffered a high death rate from the V-2s as a number of tenement blocks were hit. In comparison, the southern suburbs and places to the west were relatively untouched.

The rocket attacks flattened thousands of houses and shattered millions of windows as they exploded on to the capital. Some districts were by now beginning to look like shanty towns. Those worst affected were London's working-class areas because their housing was often of poor quality and high density and as such most vulnerable to bomb damage. Also, the residents of those districts were less likely to have the money to command rapid private repairs. Ironically, although Charlie Draper repaired houses for a living, he and his family in Peckham were also victims of this housing crisis:

> We waited a hell of a time for repairs to be done to the house. The roof got blown off, windows caved in and we were waiting for repairs to be done. We couldn't just get the materials and do it ourselves because there was none available. So we had to wait for the council to come round and do them, which took a long time. We only had temporary repairs, a tarpaulin on the roof just to keep the water out. The water eventually did creep in down the sides, and most people moved from the top of their houses downstairs into the bottom to keep dry.

The situation was at its worst in January 1945 when V-2 rockets landed on London at the increased rate of five every day. This coincided with the coldest winter weather in living memory. Many householders – especially working-class families – were already living in primitive conditions with broken roofs, blown-out and papered-over windows, missing doors, smashed pipes and irregular gas, electricity and coal supplies. Now the Arctic winds, snow and sleet made the conditions practically intolerable. Many went down with frostbite, hypothermia, rheumatism, and there was a flu epidemic. Appalling housing conditions aggravated Charlie Draper's bad health:

> I was taken with rheumatic fever. I was paralysed for four weeks and the time I was lying in bed, there was no roof, there was just the tarpaulin, the canvas up over the windows and half the fireplace missing. I just lay there waiting for the repairs to be done. And there was a sort of damp atmosphere that didn't do the rheumatic fever any good, because there was no way we could keep the house warm in those conditions. It laid me up for six weeks altogether.

Absenteeism again became a major problem at work and tens of thousands of hours were lost in factories and offices because of illness. Londoners were weak, exhausted, and longed for the end of the war. Mollie Matthews recalled:

> I think there came a time when it must have affected everybody the same way. We were tired. The war had been on for six years, we had suffered from it and the rockets. And this last incident, with the rocket destroying our house had its effect, because eventually I began to feel quite tired. Obviously it was showing at work. One thing, I wanted to wear nothing but dark clothes because I thought they stayed cleaner longer, they wouldn't show the dirt. Eventually the firm for which I worked sent me away to a convalescent home at Tadworth in Surrey for a little while.

Whereas in the crisis period of 1940–41 there were virtually no strikes, the last year of the war produced a wave of stoppages and disputes in the capital. There were serious strikes in the docks, among London Transport workers and in the new engineering factories in the north-western industrial belt. What made this unrest all the more significant was that strikes had been declared illegal by the government since the beginning of the war and strikers could be and were fined and imprisoned. The press was extremely hostile to anyone taking such action.

Also underlying the resurgence of disputes was a new conflict between management and workers over industrial relationships in the post-war world. Both sides had made sacrifices during the great production drive to win the war but now that the war seemed to be virtually over, they both looked more and more to winning for themselves the best possible deal for the future. Management sought to end wartime concessions and privileges for workers, while the workers themselves took advantage of their strong bargaining position to try to institutionalize wartime gains. It seemed that the spirit of national unity and idealism generated by the war was fading. Charlie Draper's experience in the housing repair business reflected the change in mood:

> We'd put up with the guvnor and he'd put up with us because we had
> no choice. We had to by law, we couldn't leave and everyone was
> doing their bit. But by the end of the war there was a lot of bad
> feeling creeping in. My guvnor was keeping back all my £1 10s a week
> overtime I earned; he kept saying the cheque hadn't come through
> from the Ministry. I found out later he was doing this with everybody
> and salting it away for the future after the war. And he was fiddling
> our time and work sheets that he sent to the Ministry. He said we
> were doing more repair work than we were, and he gave us an extra
> quid a week to keep our mouths shut. I ended up leaving; the trust
> had broken down.

Although many Londoners looked forward to the post-war world with great apprehension, by early 1945 there was a desperate desire for the war to end immediately. This was not defeatism: the vast majority were determined to see it through to the bitter end no matter what sacrifices they had to make. But Londoners were tired of the deprivations of bomb-blasted housing, rationing and the ever-present threat of death. A deep frustration with the way the war was dragging on was welling up. The end result was a new mood, encouraged by the newsreels and the press – a mood that sought revenge and retribution against the German people. There was a widespread feeling that Germany should be bombed into submission whatever the consequences. Len Jones, whose military designs were one factor that made the bombing of German cities more accurate, remembered this new climate of opinion:

You hated Germany, you hated Germans, a bad thing, a horrible feeling, really. I only recognize it as sadistic now, but you must understand it was a desensitizing of moral values. Because there was this overwhelming feeling on everybody's part who was involved. It was revenge. Part of me hated the idea of German cities being damaged, because they were beautiful places – I loved German architecture – but at that stage you felt your whole character was changing and you wanted to punish them. You wondered where all this madness was going to end.

The Allied bombing of Dresden, ordered by Churchill on 13 February 1945, came as the climax of this new mood. The city was almost completely destroyed, consumed by a firestorm and an unknown number of citizens perished – perhaps as many as 100,000. The rocket attacks on London continued until the end of March when all rocket units were withdrawn from Holland into Germany, bringing to an end the era of bombing terror for the capital and for Britain as the Allies drove towards victory in Europe.

CHAPTER EIGHTEEN

A New Life

As Big Ben struck three o'clock on the afternoon of 8 May 1945, silence descended on the vast crowd gathered in Whitehall to celebrate Victory in Europe. Over loudspeakers specially erected for the occasion came the voice of the Prime Minister, Winston Churchill. His was the only voice to be heard. The crowd of thousands hung on his every word. Churchill's announcement that hostilities with Germany were over was greeted with loud cheers, followed by cries of joy and a waving of hats and flags as he declared that 'the German war is, therefore, at an end'.

It had been clear for weeks that Germany had been beaten by the Allies and ever since Hitler had committed suicide at the end of April, the final collapse of the Third Reich had been imminent. Indeed, the announcement of the Nazi Supreme Command's unconditional surrender had come the day before. Nevertheless, the official declaration of peace in Europe on VE day itself sparked off deep feelings of patriotic pride and relief as Londoners released the tensions and pressures of the past six years. Their city, having taken the brunt of the German air attack, had earned its place at the centre of the celebrations and that evening the crowds in the focal points of the capital went wild.

In Trafalgar Square, lines of young women and servicemen linked arms and swung along the road singing 'Roll Out the Barrel', 'Two Lovely Black Eyes', 'Oh, You Great Big Beautiful Doll' and many other songs. In Leicester Square, people hung together all trying to do the Conga and in Piccadilly Circus, a sailor stripped off his clothes and climbed on to the top of the Eros pedestal, wrapping a Union Jack around himself. Meanwhile, women swiftly lost count of the number of men they'd kissed. As midnight approached the excitement became more infectious and the crowds more boisterous. Among them was Charlie Draper:

> Everybody was just going mad and dancing and singing in the streets.
> Me and my mates had a few drinks and I ended up in the pool in

Trafalgar Square. I think it was one of those occasions when I thought, 'Well, they didn't get me,' and I was lucky to survive it and I thought, 'Well, that's it, I'll have a good drink and celebrate the fact that I'm still alive.' I must have ended up in St James's Park that night, sleeping there, because that's where I found myself the next morning.

In the suburbs the celebrations were more subdued, though the sense of excitement was still present. Most houses were decorated with bunting, Union Jacks or fairy lights. There were street parties, fireworks and bonfires. In some places, an effigy of Hitler had pride of place on the fire with the surrounding crowds cheering as it was consumed by flames. As the evening wore on, pianos were sometimes carried into the streets and there would be singalongs and dancing to the old Cockney favourites like 'The Lambeth Walk' or 'Knees up Mother Brown'.

However, the following day, when the immediate excitement had passed, there was a feeling of anticlimax. Evacuation had affected enormous numbers of Londoners. During the course of the war some 2 million people had been moved at least for a short time away from the capital, and probably 500,000 had stayed away for more than a year. The cumulative effect of these successive waves of evacuation was to change many Londoners' perceptions of what 'home' was like.

Although at the outset, evacuation had often been problematic, during the later stages of the war many of the difficulties had been ironed out and evacuees had begun to appreciate their new surroundings. Many were from London's poorest communities having previously known only damp and crowded tenement blocks, vermin-ridden back-to-backs and dirty streets. Now they had come to know open air, the countryside and houses that were often in substantially better physical condition than their own.

Some of the younger children had been away for so long that they had only faded memories of the homes they had come from; home for them now was a village or a small provincial town. Many mothers had been evacuated with the younger children and now had expectations of a house with more room – a separate kitchen and dining room, a bath – and a little garden for the children to play in. Gladys Strelitz recalled the profound effect of evacuation to Caversham on her own and her family's ideas about where they were going to live when the war was over:

It changed my mind decidedly because it was so beautiful there, all the different trees, especially in the springtime and the autumn. The children were so happy, and they could run and have a dip, and Mother always had the towel ready to wipe their feet. We decided that we couldn't go back and live in East Ham any longer, we'd got to get out of London, let the children see the beauty of the countryside, go where there were nice surroundings. We went first to Ilford and then we ended up in Romford. The children used to collect walnuts and there'd be apple trees there they could shake.

Although to begin with Doreen Holloway was very unhappy in her billet in the village of Binfield, Berkshire, she remembered how she came to develop a love of the countryside which later influenced her to move out from Battersea to Wimbledon:

We used to walk the lanes as far as White Waltham and Ascot. In fact, almost every day we went out on these nature walks with our teacher and I came to appreciate the lovely countryside, the trees and hedgerows, which were quite in contrast to Battersea, where I came from. I'd never seen primroses and bluebells and that sort of thing before. I hoped that when the war was over, should I ever marry, I would certainly like a garden of my own. I remembered all this lovely beauty that I had seen.

Many other Londoners also moved out of the capital during the war. Young men, instead of going into the traditional jobs their fathers had done in their local neighbourhood, found a whole new world had opened up to them. Military service, in particular, took them away from their locality to exotic locations in Italy and the Middle East, or to postings in other parts of Britain. Some met up with local girls or personnel in their station, and married. Their attachments to their own London communities waned.

Young women, too, often found that military service gave them the opportunity to get away from the limited options that their local communities held out for them. For example, young girls who would have got married and had children in the area in which they were brought up joined the Auxiliary Territorial Service (ATS), the Women's Royal Naval Service (Wrens) or the WAAF and travelled to distant parts, meeting a wide cross-section of people. In addition, many London girls opted for the Land Army with its outdoor life on the farms. Others were directed to factory work, often in the Midlands, where they stayed in hostels. These young women's expectations changed completely. Nina Hibbin remembered:

> Before the war, there was virtually no way well-brought-up young women could leave home and the prospect was simply that you got married to leave home. And now suddenly there was this possibility of joining the WAAF. People did feel very strongly about doing their bit for the war, but the WAAF or any of the services had this attraction because we knew that we would learn a trade, we would travel, and that's what people wanted to do. It was a great tragedy if anybody joined the WAAF and was posted back home. So I think because women's aspirations were so much less developed than they are now, just the mere fact of leaving home meant a lot, being free from the chores that were expected of women, for, you know, women were expected to be domesticated.

Other Londoners who never actually left the capital nevertheless moved around within it. Unmarried women who did not enter the services were directed to work in war production and this often meant moving away from home, to live in places like Acton and Slough. For even more women it meant leaving a life of domestic service in the grand houses of Belgravia, Kensington and Hampstead. These new jobs offered greater freedom and independence and many were not prepared to go back to a narrow and restricted life in service after the war. As a result, servant-keeping among wealthy London households declined as maids and cooks looked for a new life in factories and offices. It was a continuation of what had begun to happen during and after the 1914–18 war.

Those men who were exempt from military service because they worked in essential industries often found that their work also took them away to different parts of the capital. Many who were born and bred in inner areas like Bermondsey, Poplar and Islington went to the outer suburbs, in particular the industrial belts of the north-west, north-east and south of London. By the end of the war they had often settled in the areas where they now worked. Len Jones was one of the many thousands who moved out from the East End. He remembered:

A few months after coming to Carshalton we rented a little house, and then as the war went on, I was earning very good money, so in 1944 I bought the little house across the road. The work was here, so we stayed out here. This was now our home, Carshalton.

Destruction resulting from bombing raids and rocket attacks had made at least 1,500,000 Londoners homeless, some for a short period of time, others for months or even years. As with the evacuees, the homeless were most likely to come from the inner-London boroughs. During the blitz, in particular, many homeless families in the old East End and in declining inner areas like Battersea and Hackney had been unable to find accommodation in their neighbourhood and had moved in with relations or friends in distant parts of the capital. As the war progressed, they often found accommodation of their own in that area. Others had been officially billeted in more prosperous parts of London, like Edgware and Finchley. Billeting, again like evacuation, had at first caused problems, but eventually many families came to prefer the less crowded environments in which they were 'temporarily' living. Emily Golder recalled:

> After we'd stopped in Finchley for a while, I looked around and
> realized what a lovely place it was to live in. All the greenery, so
> different from the back-to-backs in the docks area, with outside toilets,
> smut, smoke and everything. This is where I decided I wanted to fetch
> children up when I eventually got married. There was no comparison
> with the East End; this was a residential area. So I had my son in
> Finchley and he went to the school down the road. It was very good;
> we were very happy. The houses had lovely gardens, so different to the
> East End with just the back yard. So we settled down in Finchley.

Something like a third to a half of London's population of 8 million had moved away from their neighbourhood for some period of the war. This enormous movement of people was particularly sharp in inner London and, moreover, permanent. For a long time numbers in London's poorest boroughs had been declining, but the impact of the war years was devastating; Stepney's population, for example, had dropped during the 1930s by about 2 per cent a year; during the six years of the war it dropped by over 40 per cent. While some yearned to move back, for many the ties had been broken.

Londoners who had stayed within their local community throughout the war often found that their expectations and aspirations too had been changed. The American GIs, in particular, offered the chance of friendship to young women, uninhibited by the conventions of class and respectability with which many Londoners had been brought up. Some of these friendships led to marriage and a permanent uprooting of women from their London homes. More often the friendships would be casual, giving rise to grave concern among the older generation about a decline in moral standards. But for the young women themselves the chance to meet people from very different backgrounds changed their outlook. Odette Lesley remembered:

> You see, coming to the Hammersmith Palais made a vast difference to us. We started to meet GIs, Canadians, boys from other countries, and we used to sit and talk to them, and listen to their stories of where they came from, exotic names like Texas, New York, Montreal, names we'd only seen and heard in films. And when we listened to their way of life, we realized that there was a very big new world out there that we knew nothing about at all. All I knew, for instance, was my little bit of north London, where I'd been brought up; the local streets, my neighbours, and the local dance hall. But I was hearing these marvellous stories and they opened up horizons to such an extent that I thought I might even see those places one day. I might go there. And I felt a strong sense of independence as a girl that I'd never felt before. It was so exciting. I felt anything was possible.

At the same time, new independence for some recently married women sometimes meant that, come the end of the war, they were far from sure that they wanted to settle back down with their husbands. Perhaps they had married hastily under the pressures of war and often their husbands had been away for years, coming home at most for a few weeks' leave. Divorce, which in the pre-war years had been rare, was now set to become much more common. Besides having a traumatic effect on the individuals directly involved, for London this was yet another disruption of the settled pre-war patterns of community life. Odette Lesley ended up living in the Channel Islands for a time after escaping from her marriage:

> Like a lot of girls, I really married in quite a hurry in wartime. The men were in the services. We knew they were going away, going

abroad, and we felt we wanted to get married. I was married when I was eighteen, and I got married on the Tuesday and Wednesday I was saying goodbye to him. I saw him very briefly after that, and then it was three years before I saw him again. And, of course, because I had changed through the war, through the experiences, meeting all sorts of people, I'd got this sense of independence, which coloured everything I thought about. Then I started to think about my husband. I had awful guilty feelings because I was sure that there was no way when he came home that I'd be able to settle down, into the rather dull, domestic routine which was what he would have expected. I thought to myself: 'I can't stay with him, because I can't do what he wants. I want more out of life now; I want to have more experiences.' In fact, when he was sent back to his unit for demob', I ran off to the Channel Islands, because I knew I couldn't cope with that sort of marriage and that was the end of it. This, of course, was the effect of war.

All these social changes meant that by 1945 many Londoners no longer wanted to live in the communities in which they had lived throughout the pre-war years. In particular, many who had lived in inner London had expectations of a life beyond the back-to-backs and tenements of their youth. At the same time, many Londoners could not return to the streets they had known, even if they wanted to, for those streets were often no longer there. Len Jones recalled:

> In some ways I would have loved to have come back to the East End at the end of the war, but where I used to live in Poplar was all blown to pieces. You see, I missed the wonderful community in the East End and the social life, going down the People's Palace every Friday and Saturday night with my friends. Carshalton was dead in comparison – there was nothing to do. It made me depressed being there, but I decided to stay because I worked in the area and there was really nowhere else to go.

BOMBSITES AND THE PLANNERS

While those Londoners whose homes had been destroyed reflected with pain and grief on their loss, planners and the middle-class reformers began to see the destruction as opening up new opportunities. Hitler had swept away more slums in a few months than radical campaigners had in years or even decades. A new London could rise like a phoenix out of the ashes. The unplanned, chaotic development of London over the centuries could be replaced by a planned London.

In October 1942 the Royal Academy, representing a traditional school, published *London Replanned*, a thirty-page outline of ambitious projects for the central area. At its heart was the reconstruction of the rubble around St Paul's Cathedral. They envisaged a monumental stairway leading from the banks of the Thames to the steps of St Paul's, with classical pavilions on either side and a new approach to the cathedral from the west consisting of an avenue of trees along a widened Ludgate Hill, opening up into a circular piazza reminiscent of St Peter's, Rome. Another wide vista was to be created between New Oxford Street and the British Museum, by sweeping away the intervening buildings. In Covent Garden, the Academy suggested – somewhat prophetically – that the fruit and vegetable market be replaced by a new music and drama centre and garden, carefully preserving the old colonnades of the market. South of the river, they proposed a new circular park, slightly bigger than Regents's Park, at St George's Circus, Southwark.

In contrasting styles, other architects also put forward a range of plans for opening up new vistas in central London. Two private architects, Kenneth Lindy and Winton Lewis, for example, proposed new focal points such as a 500-foot (152 m) tower modelled on New York's famous Wool-worths building; they also, more futuristically, proposed a giant helicopter landing pad stretching into the sky above Liverpool Street Station.

Many of these schemes were little more than the daydreams of architects and planners and had little chance of ever getting off the ground. Much more influential, however, were the two major studies – the County of London Plan and the Greater London Plan – commissioned by the London County Council and headed by Sir Patrick Abercrombie, Professor of Town Planning at London University.

There was to be a radical reconstruction of the Victorian heart of the capital. Those mean streets that had not been destroyed by the Luftwaffe would be swept away by the planners to make way for new and planned communities. Each newly defined neighbourhood, which would house about 10,000 people, would have a central area with open space and community facilities such as a school, nursery, health centre and shops.

Historic features, such as churches, would be preserved to form focal points and around them would be a mix of modern terraced houses with small gardens and high-rise flats.

This noble aim was seen to be overwhelmingly important. The war had brought out a strong belief that the 'ordinary' Londoner ought to have a better deal. The people of London were celebrated as heroes and there was a substantial shift of opinion among the middle classes in favour of greater welfare provision by the state. Vera Michel-Downes, active throughout the war in voluntary work in the capital, remembered the new moral climate:

> A wonderful spirit of caring developed during the war. People had been thrown together in rest centres and shelters and they really got to know each other and helped each other. There was a tremendous amount of voluntary social work of one sort or another going on, especially in the WVS, and it heightened people's awareness of social problems and poverty. Snobbery and class differences became far less important, people just wanted to help each other.

By 1941, the Home Intelligence reports on London were recording widespread support for 'home-grown socialism' which was 'growing like a jungle plant'. Londoners believed that everyone was entitled to decent housing, good health, equal opportunities and an adequate standard of living and, moreover, that the state had a responsibility to ensure that every citizen gained these rights. These aspirations were to some extent reflected and reinforced in government propaganda. The Ministry of Information and the Army Bureau of Current Affairs appreciated that visions of a better future were an important motivation to help people pull through the war. Though Churchill consistently opposed making promises of social reform, many radical ideas did seep through in government propaganda.

Towards the end of the war, many Londoners had begun to fear that these aspirations would turn out to be nothing but a dream. Many of the opportunities created by the war began to close up. This was particularly true for women, who often found themselves thrown out of their jobs when men returned from the services. Nina Hibbin, having established herself as a flight mechanic at Hendon, found there was no future for her in this job:

At the end of the war, what I wanted to do was to be a mechanic. I went to my Warrant Officer, who thought a lot of me as a flight mechanic, knew I could do the job, and I said, 'What are the chances of me getting on a course?' But he just laughed and said, 'Forget it, duck'. You know the way they do. I tried. I mean, I wrote to lots of firms, I went to lots of garages, but it was absolutely inconceivable at that time. After I'd tried everywhere I did what I suppose was the next best thing, I trained to become a teacher.

I went on an emergency training course and, although teaching is a very fine profession, it was second best, it was a sort of compromise as far as I was concerned. And I think that's what probably happened to a lot of women. Their horizons were opened out, and they wanted to do all kinds of things, but then even before the war was over, the pressures began to come down. Now the boys are coming back, you must go home and you must get ready to make homes and so forth. And I think that the best any of us could do was a compromise of some sort.

At the same time, some of the unity of earlier years began to disappear. People were slipping back into the habits of pre-war years. For example, in the House of Commons factory where, during the war years, every worker, whether they were a duke or a doorman, had been on equal terms, the atmosphere of classlessness rapidly evaporated. Vera Michel-Downes was the welfare officer at the factory:

When we were closed down, although we ended up with a wonderful party and everybody had a fantastic time, the moment the factory was closed all the class barriers raised their ugly heads again. Immediately we were back to surnames and deferential attitudes towards people. Although everybody was congratulating everybody on a wonderful job done, it was quite interesting to see that the barriers remained there and were reinstated the moment the war was over.

THE WAR HERO VOTED OUT

Soon after VE day, Londoners were given the chance to reassert their desire for a new and more equal post-war London. On 23 May, the coalition government, which had been in power for the past five years, came to an end at the insistence of the Labour members. Churchill tendered his resignation as Prime Minister and a general election campaign got under way. When the result was announced on 26 July, the greatest electoral upset of the century had taken place. Labour, led by the mild and studious Clem Attlee, won a landslide victory. Churchill was identified with the past, the Labour Party with the future.

The mood in London was clear. Across the capital, there was an 18 per cent swing from the Conservatives to Labour, one of the highest in the country. Labour had more votes in every district in London except the business areas of the centre. The suburbs, previously Tory strongholds, turned to Labour as the middle classes voted for change. In Lewisham, Herbert Morrison, the Minister for Home Security during the war, turned a safe Conservative majority into a Labour majority of 15,000.

In inner London, the vote for radicalism was overwhelming. In Fulham, Islington, St Pancras and Hammersmith, the left-wing Labour, Common Wealth and Communist parties polled 65 per cent of the vote compared to 34 per cent for the Tories, a sharp reversal of the position in the previous general election in 1935, when the Tories had a majority over the left of 52 per cent to 46 per cent. In the traditional Labour strongholds to the east of the City, the Tories were decimated: in the boroughs of Stoke Newington, Hackney, Shoreditch and Finsbury, the left polled over 72 per cent of the vote. The mood of radicalism in the inner eastern areas was such that in the seats in which the Communist Party stood, they succeeded in replacing the Conservatives for second place, polling 33 per cent of the vote. And London's first-ever Communist Member of Parliament was elected with the success of Phil Piratin in Mile End.

Londoners' hopes were high. Nina Hibbin remembered the atmosphere at Hendon Aerodrome as the election results came in:

> There was a hut that was used for lectures and we had a huge map of the whole of the country there, with all the constituencies marked. As the results came through on the radio, we were sticking in red pins for the Labour victories, and blue ones for the Tory victories, and there was a huge crowd outside that gathered all day. There were great cheers every time there was another Labour victory, because we really did feel that this was socialism, that things were going to change, it was going to be our country after all. There was a great 'us and them'

feeling and it was going to be 'us' at last, particularly, let's say, to do with housing. Because a lot of people thought that the blitz, however tragic it was, was doing the job that ought to have been done a long time ago, which was the removal of the slums. We'd seen the exhibitions for a new London and we imagined that there would be splendid housing estates, gardens and facilities for everyone. And so we thought, right, there's this marvellous victory, the whole country is wanting a new kind of Britain that would work for us, and not for them. And this was the vision, and as each pin went into the map great cheers went up, we really thought that was it.

Charlie Draper, who had recently joined the Labour Party League of Youth, believed a new and better London might now be built:

> Well, when I saw a Labour government being elected I thought, 'This is great.' I thought that they would make London a better place, because where I used to live it was slum conditions, people living on top of one another. I wanted to see something different, new estates, new playing fields for the children, better living conditions, better environment where there was more spaces. A nice new London.

On a rainy day in August, Londoners finally celebrated the end of the war – Victory over Japan. Their feelings that day were, as they had been on VE day just a few months earlier, primarily of relief that the suffering, the hardship, the destruction, the pain of war were at last over. But as Londoners celebrated the end of the war, they also remembered the dead. In London, 30,000 civilians had died during the war and thousands more of the capital's young men had been killed in action on the military front. In a world war in which around 40 million had been killed, this number may seem small, but for the very many Londoners who had lost members of their family or close friends, the feelings of loss were sometimes overwhelming. The memories would remain, for some people scarring deeply for the rest of their lives. Elsie Huntley recalled:

> They had a party and I did attend, but my feelings were very sad, to think that I had lost my son through it all, and my mother. Because when my mother got the news about the doodlebug hitting us, she

had a stroke and died. It took me a long time to get over it. That day is still very vivid in my mind and always will be.

Len Jones remembered:

Apart from the little injection of elation, I think the overall feeling for most of us was one of great sorrow because, for example, out of forty-seven blokes – schoolboy pals, blokes I'd worked with – forty of them were killed, or they weren't any good any more mentally. The sadness there was so intense that it offset the fact that you won a war.

At that time I thought I was all right physically and mentally, but there was a time bomb in my brain that was going to blow out eventually and it did. I saw some buildings being pulled down more than twenty years later and I started shaking uncontrollably just like I had on that first night in the blitz. It brought back the destruction of those people that I'd known, disintegration of them, the total destruction of where I lived, all around me, the church that I'd been to and the school, my old place of work, all smashed to pieces, all in one night. And that to me was the end of the world, just a red sky. Fire, explosions, burning, smell, total destruction, that's what haunts, has haunted me ever since.

Nevertheless, Londoners dreamed of a new life rising out of the ashes – one in which the best of the old would be preserved or rebuilt while the pre-war scars of poverty and squalor would be banished for ever.

PART FOUR

London Transformed
1945–2007

CHAPTER EIGHTEEN

Imperial Sunset

DESPITE THE TERRIBLE destruction and dislocations of the Second World War, London emerged in peacetime as a major world city and the capital of an Empire encompassing something like a quarter of the world's population. Wherever the Union flag flew there were nations that looked to London as the centre of their government and trade. The capital was still full of monuments to the Empire and Commonwealth with which its riches and power were associated, not least the towering warehouses which hugged the docks and riverside, forming the world's largest emporium of goods including everything from exotic shells and ivory to bulk cargoes of tea and grain. The very names of many concerns, like Imperial Chemical Industries, the Plantation House Commodity Exchange and the Empire Mill in Victoria Dock, reverberated with imperial associations.

It was not clear in the years immediately after the war what Britain's position would be in the world. War-weary Londoners had to put up with rationing which continued until 1956, with a host of social problems, especially the shortage of housing, and with a sense that the old imperial capital would not sustain its world position for long. The granting of independence to India in 1947, relinquishing what had been the 'Jewel in the Crown' of Empire, was a portent. However, there was, at least, peace and hope for the future. And London was still, for the time being, an imperial capital – a fact demonstrated with great pomp and ceremony with the Coronation in 1953 of a new young monarch, Queen Elizabeth II. Would this be the dawning of a new and prosperous 'Elizabethan age'?

On 2 June 1953 a million cheering people lined the seven-mile route of the Coronation procession from Westminster Abbey to Buckingham Palace via the West End. Many, like Londoner Dolly Hyne, then aged fifteen, remembered camping out all night to make sure of the best views:

Myself and my sister got down to Whitehall at about four o'clock in the afternoon on the day before the Coronation to make sure we got a good view. We decided we were going to sleep out and settled down on the pavement on a doormat with a rubberized bottom. But, as the night went on, the rain started to pour down and we were totally unprepared for it. We wrapped ourselves in my sister's bicycle cape, and all you could see were two little heads sticking out of the top of it. We both got soaking wet; we were freezing cold and we had nothing to eat. By the time the morning came we were tired out and needed a couple of matches to keep our eyes open.

The leaders of over forty Commonwealth and Empire countries paraded in horse-drawn coaches, some of them, like the traditionally dressed Queen of Tonga from the South Sea Islands, creating a great impression. The march past was a showcase of military and civil power with 13,000 troops, and armed police including the Canadian Mounties, the New Guinea Constabulary and – marching bare-legged –the Papuans included in the Australian contingent. The entire cavalcade took forty-five minutes to pass any given point along the route. To cap it all, on the very day the second Elizabethan age began it was announced that a Commonwealth team of climbers had, for the first time ever, scaled Mount Everest. The timing of this had been carefully stage-managed to coincide with the Coronation, just as the royal pageant, down to the last satin train, had itself been elaborately planned many months in advance.

Despite the fact that it poured with rain for most of the day this extravagant piece of theatre had the desired effect, striking a deep patriotic and imperial chord among the new Queen's subjects. The Coronation was followed by street parties all over the capital to celebrate the new reign. It was a day of great optimism when everyone looked forward to a better world. In the East End, for example, Ron and Rose Linford, who both worked at the Tate & Lyle sugar refinery, spent many weeks helping to organize their street party in Maybury Road, Plaistow. Ron Linford recalled:

At the time the Coronation was announced our street formed a committee and we held raffles to collect money for our party. Really, it was for the kids; we wanted to give them a day to remember. We bought toys and Coronation cups and mugs as presents for them. The women in the street did most of the work – they made all the flags and bunting out of crêpe paper. We put tables down the middle of the street and laid on ham sandwiches, and jelly and custard for the kids. There was lots of children's games, and races for the adults. It was a great day, you felt like you were coming out of the doldrums.

Rose Linford remembered:

You felt as if something had been lifted and you could go out and be cheerful. During the war years everything had been dreary. Then there was rationing and we'd been short of things we wanted. But after the Coronation you had a great feeling that you had something wonderful to look forward to and you'd be able to have a bit more enjoyment.

As it turned out, the Coronation heralded not so much the dawning of a new Elizabethan age, but the setting of the sun on the once mighty British Empire. Within a few years the Empire had shrunk, as one colonial nation after another gained independence, and the exotic trading ties of London and the River Thames with India, Africa and the West Indies faded away. For many years London's docklands stood derelict and forlorn, and there seemed little prospect that the area would ever survive. London's traditional manufacturing economy suffered a similar fate.

Ultimately, London would not only survive, but thrive in a post-imperial world; in the new world economy it would remain a 'global city', rivalling other glamorous capitals like New York, Paris and Tokyo. However, the seeds of renaissance were not evident at all in the London of the 1950s and while it still retained its imperial grandeur, much of it was fading.

SWANSONG FOR LONDON INDUSTRY

Immediately after the Second World War, trade with the Commonwealth had actually increased and throughout the 1950s was at its highest level ever, accounting for around half of the Port of London's imports and exports. This was largely due to the Commonwealth Preference System, established in the early 1930s, which allowed free trade within the Commonwealth and erected high tariff barriers to discourage trade with other countries. The great advantage of Commonwealth trade for London was that it provided an endless supply of very cheap food and raw materials. By the mid-1950s almost a third of the total exports of all the Commonwealth countries was arriving in London: tea from India, wool and butter from Australia, wheat and timber from Canada, copper and gold from South Africa, and sugar from the Caribbean. Appropriately, Silvertown Way in Newham, east London, was still known as the 'road to Empire'.

This post-war resurgence of Commonwealth trade meant that many docks and wharfs in the Port of London were busier than they had ever been before. Almost every year in the 1950s a new record was set for the amount of tonnage handled. In 1956 it reached a record 70 million tons of goods, transported in an average of 1,000 ships that docked every week. Because the Commonwealth countries were historically united in their use of the sterling currency, buying and selling on London's commodity markets was often more straightforward than elsewhere. Thus in the mid-1950s London's position as a leading world port and market place seemed unassailable. There were around 30,000 men employed in the Port of London as dockers, stevedores, carters, clerks, crane operators, and warehousemen. Lightermen – so-called because they 'lightened' ships – ferried goods by barge or tug from ship to shore, from ship to ship, or from the main docks to the many small riverside wharfs and warehouses. Among the 7,000 operating in the Port of London at this time was Ken Rigby. He recalled:

> In those days the river used to be so packed with ships and tugs and
> barges that you would often get the odd minor collision, especially
> with the barges under oars. When that happened you'd ship your oars,
> lie on the deck and hang on to something solid, to prevent being
> knocked over the side. We handled all sorts of cargoes from the
> Empire and Commonwealth trade. One of the most unusual I
> remember was large sacks of animal bones from North Africa. They
> were sent up to the mills at Bow on the River Lea and crushed for
> fertilizer. Bags would often burst – and you'd see camel jaws sticking
> out and they used to stink and have lots of green beetles all over them.

Processing of raw materials and manufacturing were done in the rows of flour mills, breweries, refineries, sawmills, furniture and food factories which lined the riverside. The classic food-processing industry in London was sugar-refining, dominated by Tate & Lyle, which had major factories in the East End on the riverside. They were the biggest sugar-refiners in the world. After the war they successfully defeated plans by the Labour government to nationalize them by fighting a propaganda war, using the cartoon figure of Mr Cube – an impish sugar-lump character that appeared in many newspapers, publicizing the virtues of free enterprise and the evils of state control. By the mid-1950s Tate & Lyle were reaping the rewards of their campaign to remain a private company. At this time they employed almost 8,000 Londoners and owned a fleet of ships as well.

Tate & Lyle's profits – like those of many other London food factories dependent on imports from new Commonwealth countries – were rooted in a plantation economy that was the legacy of the British Empire. The company owned plantations all over the Third World, a number of them in the West Indies. The way in which the trade was made to revolve around London was quite remarkable. The cane was chopped, cleaned and boiled in factories on each plantation to produce raw sugar which was then transported thousands of miles to Tate & Lyle's London factories, where it passed through a sophisticated refining process to produce granulated sugar. This then was shipped out again in millions of bags to countries all over the world, some of which had grown the sugar in the first place. By the mid-1950s a record 800,000 tons of sugar – half the total sugar refined – was exported, much of it to the Middle East, Africa and India; the rest was sold in Britain, some of it as Golden Syrup or sugar cubes.

However, far and away the most important type of export from London to the Commonwealth was not processed food but manufactured goods – especially those associated with the electrical and engineering industries. Traditionally, London had made and exported to the Common-wealth everything from lathes to lorries – goods that less-developed countries did not have the technology or know-how to produce. This supremacy was boosted even more in the interwar years by the boom in electrical industries in west London producing many new consumer items, like Osram lights and Belling cookers. This industrial base was streng-thened during the war years when the production of aircraft, tanks and other weapons was concentrated in the capital, so that in peacetime London would apply much of this new technology to the growth in travel by air and road.

In the early 1950s London's aircraft industry was given generous financial backing by the government, so that it could combat competition from America. British-made planes would fly the Empire and European routes operated by the airlines BOAC and BEA. London-based companies like Vickers at Weybridge and DeHavilland at Colindale and Hatfield benefited enormously from this government money for design and research. And in the early 1950s they seemed to be providing good value for money. The Vickers 'Viscount', equipped with jet turbo-prop engines, which ensured quiet and economical flights, quickly became the most successful British airliner ever made. There were large sales abroad, many of them to Commonwealth countries. And DeHavilland won the race to produce the world's first jet airliner when the Comet successfully came through its test flights in 1949 and 1950. Export orders to Commonwealth operators like Canadian Pacific Airlines and South African Airways were to be one of the prizes of new developments like this.

Although from the perspective of the twenty-first century it is difficult to believe, the motor car was the single most important export manufactured in London in the 1950s. Much of this output came – as we shall see later – from the American-owned multinational of Ford at Dagenham. But there were other companies which boomed at this time as builders of buses and trucks, the best-known of which were the Associated Equipment Company chassis works at Southall, and its trading partner, the Park Royal Body Builders. Together they formed one of the biggest bus and truck manufacturers in Britain, producing the world-famous London red double-decker buses. An export business established in the 1920s boomed in the 1950s with exports to Commonwealth countries. Cities like Johannesburg and Pretoria in South Africa, and Melbourne and Adelaide in Australia, had large fleets of London-built buses many of them similar in appearance and design to the traditional London bus. Even far-flung corners of the Empire like Kuala Lumpur in Malaya had a fleet of blue and white liveried buses manufactured by AEC and Park Royal. To workers at AEC like Jack Ailsby, London was still the workshop of the world. He remembered:

> It was a wonderful place to work in, we had a damn good team spirit;
> we were cock-a-hoop because we were the world leaders in producing
> trucks and buses. We had a fine body of craftsmen who produced
> these vehicles and they went all over the old Commonwealth and
> Empire, and the rest of the world as well. We were world renowned as
> the builders of London's buses and we felt we were worldbeaters. The

original logo of AEC was a triangle and across the bottom was the word 'Southall', which was the base of the plant; wherever an AEC vehicle was exported so the name of Southall was exported with it, and it became synonymous with AEC. There was a great pride to think that the name Southall was on buses all over the world.

FAREWELL TO FACTORY FUN

While home-grown engineering firms were prosperous, American-owned multinationals had settled in the capital during the interwar years attracted to cheap greenfield sites in west London and the capital's consumer market. In fact, more than half of the seventy major US companies in Britain in the 1950s could be found on the Great West Road, the North Circular Road and the Slough Trading Estate. It was along here that Hoover, Firestone Tyres, Gillette and other American companies built their Art Deco-style factories – monuments to the modern movement in architecture and to American enterprise in London.

In the 1950s Ford of Dagenham flourished. After the war there was a huge world demand for cars and the European motor industry had been wrecked by the war, allowing British-based companies like Ford a virtual monopoly of exports. One of the company's most successful models at this time was the Zephyr, selling at £607. With the Consul and the Zodiac, it was one of a trio of scaled-down American-style 'big cars', which became known as 'the Three Graces'. In the 1950s Ford were producing around a quarter of a million vehicles each year at Dagenham, most of which were exported. The output was phenomenal. To keep up with it they spent several millions of pounds on a brand-new foundry which started operating in 1957.

Working for a multinational like Ford was a novel experience for those familiar with work practices in smaller British companies, like AEC, which made great use of craft skills. The Americans introduced assembly-line methods in which the car frames moved slowly forward on a moving chain, known as the track. Workers stationed along it fitted engines, gearboxes, and wheels in sequence as the frames passed by. Rigid discipline was enforced by foremen in order for the system to work smoothly and there was an increasingly narrow division of labour, so that each worker performed just one kind of task which might take, say, two minutes to complete.

Practically every year the company would try to increase productivity by reducing the time taken for each job at Dagenham. This was known to the workers as the 'speed-up' and it was at the heart of many disputes between men and management, as Bernie Passingham remembered:

> Working on the line was filthy, dirty and noisy. Basically, you had to have a bath every night. The metal dust that was flying around would turn all your underclothes rusty. No matter how much you washed the sheets they would go rusty and so would the pillows. But what really caused the trouble was the speed-up. We used to have a works standards man come round, and he'd time you with his watch. Then the foreman would come and say, 'Well, you've got to produce faster'. But it just didn't work out like that, because you felt you were working and sweating hard enough as it was. You were given so many seconds to do this and so many seconds to do that, and it didn't go down well with the workers. They were constantly cracking the whip and trying to get more and more out of us. Well, that annual time study caused lots of disputes and strikes. Sometimes the men would try to cheat the time-and-motion man by taking longer than they needed for the job while he was timing them, but they usually took that into account.

Although in the 1950s work could become increasingly monotonous, this was the heyday of company paternalism, when major manufacturers provided canteens, sports grounds, entertainments and paid holidays for workers. The aim was to generate a strong sense of community and loyalty revolving around the company. After the war Tate & Lyle helped to run a social club organizing Saturday night entertainment for its workers and their families and friends. Ron Linford recalled:

> It was known as the Tate & Lyle Saturday night out. It was really great. All the family would go including the kids. First thing we used to do was to make sure we had our seats right alongside the bar, so that we didn't have too far to carry the drinks. There was cabaret, fancy dress with prizes for the children, dancing to the band, spot waltzes and comedians doing turns. Sometimes they used to let all the balloons down at once. There used to be hundreds of them, and all the kids would dive towards them.

At AEC there was a huge range of social activities for the workforce. Jack Ailsby recalled being involved in many of them:

> I was Chairman of the Sports Committee and we had clubs for everything: swimming, angling, football, rugby, cricket – the lot. I helped plan the annual gala day. I usually ended up running the coconut stall – that was a great laugh. Then we had all sorts of other things, like Christmas parties for the children and a club with cheap booze – you'd find me in there quite a lot! There was a feeling that the company was just one great big family.

A greater reward of the boom in London industry was a fat pay packet. By the end of the 1950s the real income of working Londoners was almost double what it had been before the war. Until the mid-1950s rationing and consumer controls meant that there was no outlet for this increased spending power, but as soon as these were lifted Londoners began to enjoy the fruits of a new consumer society, based on mass production. Labour-saving electric devices for the home, like washing machines, refrigerators and vacuum cleaners, had previously been too expensive for most people outside the middle classes, but by the mid-1950s many Londoners could afford these 'luxury' items for the first time, even if they had to buy them on the 'never never' (slang for hire-purchase agreements).

It was also the dawn of the television age, as recalled by Jack Ailsby:

> Everyone in the street had a television before us. I wasn't very interested because I was out all the time involved in the social club and the union. The wife got a bit lonely and she wanted a television, but I didn't. Anyway, every evening I expected a hot dinner on the table when I came home, and I got one as well! But one day the wife went off and got some TV rental forms and when she served up the dinner she slapped them down on the table for me. She said, 'Right! We have a telly or you don't have any more hot dinners!' That was how we came to get our first television set.

By the late 1950s most Londoners would have agreed with Prime Minister Harold Macmillan that some of them 'had never had it so good'. Many were enjoying a standard of living far above anything they had known before. But this industrial prosperity, at least as far as the manufacturing industry was concerned, was largely based on the shaky foundations of London's dominant position in Commonwealth trade – an economic weakness that would be cruelly exposed in the next decade. For during the 1960s the demand for independence in Britain's Empire and Commonwealth loosened or ended many of the old trading ties with Britain.

Twenty-seven colonies, in Africa, the West Indies and the Mediterranean and elsewhere became independent nations. The roll-call of colonies given independence in the 1960s included Cyprus (1960), Jamaica (1962), Kenya (1963), Malta (1964), and Aden (1967). Added to this, South Africa severed her links with the Commonwealth in 1961. These new nations could now choose their trading partners for the first time. And, overwhelmingly, they chose to turn away from the old dependency on London, developing their own industries and their own trading preferences. For Britain in the 1960s was being overshadowed by rival industrial giants – the United States, Germany, Japan and the Soviet Union. These nations offered a big export market for the primary products of Commonwealth countries and in return offered a wide range of manufactured goods that were often better and cheaper than those made in Britain.

As a result, during the 1960s London's trade with the Commonwealth was halved. The old inner docks were the first to suffer. They were geared to the Commonwealth trade, situated as they were close to the commodity exchanges and all the elaborate warehousing and marketing services they involved. They also supplied many of the riverside factories which processed imported foods and raw materials from the Commonwealth. In 1967, due to falling trade, the East India Dock was closed, quickly followed by St Katharine Docks and the London Docks in 1968. As a result, dock employment began to shrink. The number of lightermen fell dramatically. Ken Rigby recalled:

> The docks weren't doing so much business so in 1968 I thought I'd try
> something different and I moved out of lightering. A year later the
> lighterage company I worked for went out of business. My family had
> quite a few lightermen in it going back many years. My father had
> been one and he used to take me out on the boats from the age of six.
> I thought, to begin with, that one of my sons would follow me in the
> trade, but as the docks started to close there were just no
> opportunities; it was all dying out.

London's sugar industry was hit hard by independence and the break-up of the old Commonwealth trading links. New nations like India and Malaysia developed their own sugar refineries, and other governments (for example, in the West Indies) demanded greater control over their sugar crop and more money for what they produced. The consequence of all this was that Tate & Lyle's exports were halved and in 1967 they were forced to close down their refining operations at Plaistow Wharf. Ron Linford was one of the several hundred refinery workers who lost their jobs. He remembered:

When I took my severance pay and became unemployed I thought to myself, 'Well, I'll probably get a job somewhere else easy enough,' and at first I thought I'd have a few days off – it was a sort of novelty. Then I had to go and sign on. I'd never been to a Labour Exchange in my life, and it was horrible lining up there – I felt ashamed that you had to get in a queue and sign on, especially when you have worked all your life. Then I went to the Job Centre and the first words out of their mouths were 'How old are you?' 'I'm 47.' 'Sorry, you're too old, you stand no chance.' This was from a job centre! That was depressing in its own right, without having to go back and sit down and think to yourself: where can I go to look for a job? When can I go? I used to see adverts in papers, and went out after a few jobs, but when I told them my age they'd say: 'Well, sorry, we're looking for somebody younger.' Day after day it was the same. I stayed at home and got very down. I regularly did two crosswords in the morning, then got some jobs done around the house.

LONDON ON THE DOLE

Unemployment, which had been virtually unknown in London throughout the 1950s, began to creep back into the capital in the 1960s, as many refineries, flour mills and factories in the docklands were forced to make cuts. Job losses and company closures were worsened by the flood of cheap imports beginning to enter London from former Commonwealth countries. This was the real sting in the tail of the Empire. Worst affected was the capital's clothing industry. For more than a century many thousands of London's poor had toiled over sewing machines in sweatshops, most of them in the East End and inner London, making shirts, coats and jackets for the metropolitan market. Traditionally, the hours had been long and wages low. But now these sweatshops and small factories were undercut by places making clothing in India, Hong Kong and Taiwan, where the cost of labour was much cheaper than it was in London. An industry employing around 150,000 after the war was to be pruned to one-third of its original size.

London's newer industries – engineering, for example, concentrated in west London – were also beginning to shed workers. They too were undermined by the loss of the Commonwealth market and tougher world competition. For many years there had been an emphasis on producing for 'soft markets': for example, exporting to less-developed countries or producing for government departments like the Ministry of Defence, which were playing an increasingly important role in the economy. These protected markets masked a growing inefficiency and lack of invention in many companies and this was revealed when the crutch of Commonwealth-based power and wealth was removed.

The answer in the 1960s seemed to be for competing companies to merge to form big corporations that would be more competitive on the world market. A fundamental change in the structure of London's newer industries was to result from this equation of size with efficiency.

What happened in London's aircraft industry was typical of this process. During the 1950s there had been more than a dozen separate plane-makers in the capital, each with their own highly paid design and construction teams funded with government money. The seeds of their decline were sown at this time when a number of projects went expensively and disastrously wrong. The most spectacular failure was the Comet, which after its early triumphs was involved in a series of tragic crashes caused by technical failures. As a result, it was grounded and withdrawn from service for several years. The government – which provided most of the important orders for both civil and military aircraft – insisted that the industry be streamlined in order to increase efficiency. The upshot of all this was that many famous names like Vickers and DeHavilland disappeared in the early 1960s, as most of London's plane-making companies were swallowed up into two giant corporations, Hawker Siddeley Aviation and the British Aircraft Corporation.

The new wave of corporatism was also felt in London's bus industry. In 1962 AEC and Park Royal were taken over by Leyland, and they in turn became part of the gigantic British Leyland Group when Leyland took over Austin and Morris in 1968. It was an attempt to combat increasing competition, especially in world markets where German and Japanese companies were beginning to win orders once held by Britain for buses and heavy vehicles.

To begin with, the corporate power of the Lancashire-based Leyland company seemed to benefit the London end of the operation. In 1964, for example, the AEC division achieved record exports. However, in the long run, the creation of this new breed of bigger company or corporation was to have a crippling effect on London's economy. London was an expensive place to be; rents and rates were spiralling, workers expected higher wages, and traffic congestion meant that transporting goods was difficult and costly. It made sense for manufacturing concerns to move away from the capital to new towns like Stevenage in Hertfordshire and Crawley in Surrey, or to greenfield sites in the South East.

The American multinational, Ford at Dagenham, had not been hit by the decline of Commonwealth markets because they were by now geared to sales in Britain and Europe. Their great success story of the 1960s was the Cortina. Every part of the original version of this car was manufactured and assembled in the Dagenham plant, which had a workforce of 30,000 in 1969. More than 4 million Cortinas were to run off the production line, many of them for export. Amid much pomp and ceremony the millionth Cortina to be sold abroad was carried by helicopter from Dagenham to its new owner in Belgium.

Despite the underlying weakness of London's economy, wages rose steadily for industrial workers in the 1960s so that many working-class families were able to afford their first motor car. The 1960s were the decade of the so-called 'affluent worker', when it seemed inequalities of class were breaking down. Convoys of bicycles, once a common sight going through factory gates all over London, were replaced by a convoy of cars edging their way into new factory car parks. Bernie Passingham remembered being one of London's many industrial workers who bought a car for the first time in the early 1960s:

> Even though my job was making cars I never thought I'd own one –
> they were for the better off. But the wages improved a bit and the
> company had a sort of 'HP' [Hire Purchase] scheme and you could buy
> second-hand cars with it. So I saved up for a long time and bought a

Classic, and when I'd got it it was a big event. I'd built a garage years in advance but I couldn't actually drive a car. Now all I could afford was five lessons and, miraculously, I managed to pass my test after having just those five lessons. In the early days I was so proud of the car that I didn't want to get it dirty driving to work. So I used to leave it in the garage all day and go to work on the bike. We used the car at weekends and for holidays, and we had some lovely times.

The image of economic strength and vitality created by lots of donkey-jacketed workers driving expensive-looking cars around the capital was, however, an illusion. For, beneath this veneer of affluence, London's economy was undergoing some radical changes that would leave a large part of its traditional workforce stranded. The decline in manufacturing industry in the capital quickened when Britain entered the European Economic Community (EEC) in early 1973. In place of the Commonwealth Preference System came high tariffs on Commonwealth imports and a quota on the amount of goods that could come in from outside Europe. Tate & Lyle and London's sugar industry suffered seriously from EEC quotas on the import of sugar cane. As a result, Tate & Lyle's production was decimated in the 1970s, when refineries at Fulham and Hammersmith were closed and several thousand workers were made redundant.

The shift away from deep-sea Commonwealth trade to short-sea European trade, which came with Britain's entry into the EEC, greatly favoured coastal ports close to the continent at London's expense. Channel ports like Dover and Felixstowe were better placed and better equipped to deal with the growing trade with Europe than the London dock system, which was geared to the old-style trade with the Commonwealth and Empire. In the eyes of employers, these ports enjoyed the further advantage of not being tied up by trade-union agreements, which they believed had caused over-manning and strikes in the London docks. The London dockers' fight for job security and better wages was doomed and, if anything, hastened the decline in the London docklands' trade. The containerization of cargoes and the building of huge ships to carry goods encased in metal boxes favoured docks nearer the coast, and the Port of London Authority put its resources into Tilbury, far down the Thames in Essex. One by one all the old inner docks were closed down, ending with the Royals in 1981.

For every job lost in the docks, another three were lost in dock-related services and industries. Shipbuilding and transport companies went to the wall and more and more of the riverside factories either closed down or moved away from central London, as seaborne supplies of raw materials, upon which they depended for survival, became difficult or impossible to obtain.

At the same time, from the early 1970s London's manufacturing industry was shrinking: the great industrial zone, so modern and vibrant and redolent of American enterprise in the 1920s and '30s, was closing down as Hoover, Firestone and others pulled out of London. Engineering and electrical industries concentrated in outer boroughs such as Ealing and Hounslow suffered badly, with Ealing losing jobs at the rate of over 2,000 each year.

London had long been the single greatest manufacturing region in Britain and it had been a boom town between the wars. But the decline that began in the 1970s was not to be reversed. Between 1971 and 2001 London lost a staggering 766,000 jobs in manufacturing as well as 55,000 in energy and utilities, such as the water and gas companies, and 67,000 in construction. In total there were an estimated 4.7 million jobs in London in 1971, falling to 4.3 million in 1989 and 3.8 million in the recession of the early 1990s. The total then began to creep up again and was reckoned at 4.3 million in 2000. Tower Hamlets, the borough covering much of docklands, saw its workforce fall from an interwar high of 210,000 to just 87,000 in 1981. Overall in the thirty years between 1971 and 2001, inner London lost 10,000 jobs, while outer London gained 125,000.

One of the saddest casualties was the home-grown bus and heavy truck industry. Between 1979 and 1981 British Leyland closed down AEC and Park Royal, with a loss of 3,500 jobs. The closure – like other major industrial closures in London – dealt a cruel blow to the local community, dependent on the factory. AEC in Southall had once employed 4,000 men and women, making it the most important source of work in the area. Many of the employees who remained had spent all or most of their working lives with the company. One of them was Jack Ailsby and he remembered:

> When the company closed it was a devastating blow. It had been my life, twenty-four hours a day. I was always doing something there, either working or drinking in the bar or helping on the sports committee. The day it closed down a lot of people cried and some of my friends had nervous breakdowns over it. The company had been so important to the local community, and now all that just went.

Whereas a large number of British industries were moving to other parts of Britain, notably to the west of what became known as the 'sunrise belt', the big multinationals were beginning to pull out of the country altogether in search of cheaper land and a less affluent workforce. Ford of Dagenham provide the classic case study of this kind of development. Since the war Ford had been London's biggest manufacturing employer, but in the five years after 1979 they shed 10,000 out of the 30,000 jobs they provided in the capital as a result of redirecting work to other plants across the world. In 1975, for example, they established a major new factory in Valencia, Spain. By 1979 half the Fiesta cars sold in Britain would be made there. Also, as the Dagenham plant was drawn more and more into Ford's international division of labour, the work done there changed. Whereas in the old days cars like the Zephyr and the Cortina were completely made at Dagenham, now much of the work involved assembling parts imported from overseas. This trend, which meant the Dagenham factory was turning into an assembly plant employing fewer skilled workers, was given a further impetus by the closure of its foundry in 1984.

Most of Ford's job losses were accounted for by voluntary redundancies. Bernie Passingham remembered how he, like many older workers, was keen to accept a golden handshake because he felt angry and disillusioned about Dagenham's decline:

> Lots took early retirement like myself because the truth was they just
> didn't like working there, and it was a good excuse to get out. I felt sad
> because I felt we'd done a lot for the Ford Motor Company as
> workers. We worked hard, they made good profits – damned good
> profits – and they'd been used to buy and build plants abroad and not
> in the UK. That was sad because we were slowly losing out and
> becoming a screwdriver plant. To me that is morally wrong.

TOURISTS TO THE RESCUE

In the late 1990s it looked as if London was in serious danger of becoming a vast depressed region as unemployment rates rose to above the national average overall, and in a number of boroughs were worse than anywhere else in the country. However, London's traditional ability to reinvent itself, to find new ways of making a living, came to the rescue. While manufacturing spiralled into oblivion, jobs in business and services rose dramatically up by 620,000 between 1971 and 2001. Much of this was in the City, which not only survived a series of violent adjustments to its traditional working practices, but thrived (see Chapter Twenty-one). Over the thirty years from 1971 a quarter of a million jobs were created in 'financial services'.

London also retained and built on its worldwide reputation as a centre of creativity in design and fashion and music. And, as every Londoner is aware whenever they visit the historic centre of the metropolis, the tourist trade has become one of the capital's major industries, possibly second only to financial and business services.

London has always attracted visitors of course, from other parts of Britain as well as from overseas. Even in 1851, 6 million people visited the Great Exhibition in Hyde Park between May and October, and many came from Europe and across the Atlantic from America. The West End theatres have attracted audiences from out of town since the Victorian period and the building of the railways, and that part of London has been an international playground for well over a century. In 1902 it was estimated that 120,000 tourists visited London each day and there was already a good deal of accommodation in boarding houses, hotels and rented flats. Modern hotels, some like Grosvenor House in Park Lane modelled on the latest American lines with en suite bathrooms (see Chapter Seven) arose in the centre of town. The British Empire Exhibition in 1924 had attracted 17 million visitors to London who marvelled at the exotic displays of colonial life.

The war inevitably put an end to tourism, which had not recovered by the time the Festival of Britain was staged in 1951, attracting less than half the number of tourists who had been drawn to London in 1924–5. Nevertheless, by the 1950s tourism was emerging as a very significant industry in London and, with an estimated 1.5 million visitors to the capital by the end of the decade, its importance was acknowledged by the establishment in 1963 of the London Tourist Board.

To encourage tourism, government grants of up to £1,000 per bedroom were paid for new London hotels up to 1973. By 1977 London was host to nearly 20 million tourists, 8 million from abroad and 11 million from other parts of Britain. This constituted a huge industry, offering considerable compensation for the loss of jobs in manufacturing industry over the same period, although factory or dock workers could not necessarily find work in the newly expanding tourist trade.

By 2005 London's tourist industry was reckoned to bring in £15 billion annually, though the number of tourists had fallen from a peak in the Millennium year. The celebrations of 2000, which saw the rise of the great observation wheel the 'London Eye' on the South Bank, a new bridge linking St Paul's on the north side of the river with the Tate Modern gallery to the south and the erection of the giant tent of the Millennium Dome at Greenwich, attracted a record 31.6 million visitors to the capital. The Dome itself was a disappointment, with barely half the 7 million visitors that were expected.

Surveys of tourism continue to show that visitors are interested most in seeing 'historic' sights and art galleries. The revamped British Museum, with its huge covered square in Bloomsbury, is still the top attraction (4.5 million visitors in 2005), with the National Gallery a close second (4.2 million). There are no entrance fees, of course, and this helps to maintain their popularity as well as that of the brilliantly successful conversion of the old Bankside electricity generating station into the Tate Modern gallery (3.9 million visitors). The older gallery of that name (now called the Tate Britain) was named after Henry Tate of Tate & Lyle sugar cubes, who donated some of his fortune to found the art collection in 1897. And so, in a sense, the transition from manufacturing to tourism comes full circle.

The top entrance-fee attraction in the capital is now the London Eye, which provides visitors with a panoramic view of the capital as its glass cubicles inch their way up and around in skies which are these days usually clear of the mists and fogs that once attracted French impressionist painters to London. The Eye would have been useless in the 1950s before the Clean Air Acts took effect, yet it now attracts 3.25 million tourists a year.

Nothing, however, is settled for long in London's constantly shifting economy. From its peak the number of tourists each year has settled back to just under 25 million. Of these, 14.4 million come from abroad, the single largest contingent from America (17 per cent). Although the attack on the Twin Towers in New York in September 2001 inevitably cut back foreign tourism in London, it has been the numbers of British visitors to the capital that have fallen in recent years. Cheap flights to Europe offer a rival attraction to the annual trip sightseeing in London and taking in a West End show, and domestic visitors are down to 10 million annually.

One of the great attractions of London since the war, especially for foreign visitors, has been its status as a fashion capital. This has waxed and waned since the 1960s but London has maintained a high reputation for its creative industries. Clothes might be manufactured thousands of miles away, but London designers remain at the forefront of the international scene with a reputation for generating a distinctive vernacular style. The British Museum might be the single most popular tourist attraction, but London now is clearly not simply a modern Pompeii packed with Victoriana. No longer the heart of a great Empire, it remains one of the few great international or 'global' cities, recently celebrating its success as the chosen host for the 2012 Olympics. How that colossal enterprise will affect the capital's economy is a matter for fierce debate, as a swathe of once derelict East London is transformed by a huge investment. Meanwhile, foreign observers continue to redefine London's special qualities as a place to live in and to visit.

CHAPTER TWENTY

Style Capital

I N THE SPRING of 1966 the influential American magazine *Time* devoted its front cover to a pop art representation of London. Among the familiar images of Big Ben and the London bus were new and exciting ones: a mouthing pop star wearing a T-shirt with The Who and a 'British-made' symbol emblazoned across it; a spindly, long-haired girl wearing dark glasses and a short dress with strange black and white geometric patterns; and a discothèque. The headline read: 'LONDON – THE SWINGING CITY' and in the article that accompanied this unprecedented front cover, *Time*'s team, which included the London-based correspondent, wrote:

> . . . in this century every decade has its city. During the shell-shocked
> 1940s thrusting New York led the way, and in the uneasy 50s it was
> the easy Rome of 'La Dolce Vita'. Today it is London, a city steeped
> in tradition, seized by change, liberated by affluence, graced by
> daffodils and anemones, so green with parks and squares that, as the
> saying goes, you can walk across it on the grass. In a decade dominated
> by youth, London has burst into bloom. It swings, it is the scene.

By the mid-1960s London had become the major international centre for fashion, design and music. These were the boom industries of the decade. They, in turn, boosted a whole range of smaller industries, like photography, modelling, magazine publishing, advertising and so on, which also clustered in the capital. These industries not only created immense wealth and provided work – directly or indirectly – for almost a quarter of a million Londoners; they also gave London a new image and its people a new sense of identity and vitality. The old pride in London as the heart of the Empire was eclipsed by a 1960s-style patriotism – felt very strongly by the younger generation – based on the city's leading position in the popular arts.

The image of 'Swinging London' could not last, of course, and, based as it was in fashion, it was intrinsically short-lived. However, it is clear now, in the first years of the twenty-first century, that the foundations of an enduring industry based on talent, much of it provided by London's art schools such as Goldsmiths, St Martin's and the London College of Fashion, were laid down, and, though the capital lost much of its vibrant image in the 1980s, a resurgence came in the 1990s. Once again, it was an American publication that came up with an epithet for the capital: the 4 November US edition of *Newsweek* in 1996 dubbed London the 'coolest city on the planet':

> The moment may have come two weeks ago, when the grand Paris fashion houses Givenchy and Dior decided to install two brash young London designers as their top couturiers. Or perhaps it came in September when Trafalgar House unveiled its plan to build the 92-story Millennium Tower in London's financial district on a site badly damaged by an IRA bomb in 1992. Or was it, less grandly, two weekends ago at the Ministry of Sound, when one of the London club's bouncers was frisking a striking Australian girl and turned up a batch of shiny foil-wrapped condoms? The precise timing matters less than the consensus opinion: right now, London is a hip compromise between the non-stop newness of Los Angeles and the aspic-preserved beauty of Paris, sharpened to a New York edge. In short, this is the coolest city on the planet.

The *Newsweek* reporters did not think this would last. After all, London at the time did not even have a political leader as the Greater London Council had been abolished a decade earlier and not replaced. They quoted the historian Roy Porter as saying that London was 'a muddle that worked'. It was a metropolis not governed by any great power but driven by myriad individual commercial decisions. In the second half of the 1990s it was rich, a boom town, and this fuelled its fashionable buzz. A downturn in the market and London would be back in the drab 1950s. But, a decade after London was dubbed the 'coolest city on the planet' and despite huge shifts in its population and economy (outlined in later chapters), it is still vibrant – a gastronomic, musical, theatrical, design and fashion Mecca. As the French designer Christian Lacroix put it to the fashion magazine *W*: 'London projects the rhythm of today.' It was as true at the beginning of the twenty-first century as it was back in the 1960s, as London's youth broke away from the years of austerity.

A NEW KIND OF FASHION

Immediately after the Second World War there were few signs of the explosion of popular culture that was to emerge in the 'swinging 60s' and to make London the style capital of the world. London was a grey city dominated by austerity. Everything was on ration, from shoes to sweets and from meat to petrol. Clothes were bought with coupons saved over many months, or more enterprising people would make their clothes from curtain material. Things were in such short supply that there was a flourishing black market in most items. On many street corners 'spivs' could be seen selling – at a price – that most coveted of all articles, nylon stockings. Those women who were unable to afford a pair on the black market sometimes drew a simple black line up the back of each bare leg to make it look as if they were wearing seamed nylons. This was the limit of style for them.

Style was essentially the preserve of the rich, as it had always been. And London took its influences from other European cities, mainly Paris with its haute couture. Even hairdressers had to adopt the style and mannerisms of the French if they wanted to be successful. Raymond, the son of an Italian immigrant born in Soho, and later to be known as Mr Teasie-Weasie, took advantage of this fascination with all things French in his high-class salons during the early 1950s:

> Women at that time thought that good hairdressing could come only from French hairdressers. So I taught my stylists to use French expressions, such as 'Bonjour, Madame,' 'Comment allez-vous, Madame?' and all that nonsense. I also renamed them. If their name was Joe I called them Louis or Monsieur Emile. They were all given a new name, French sounding.

While the rich monopolized the world of fashion, the older generation imprinted itself on practically all the activities and entertainment available for young people. The immediate post-war years witnessed the zenith of traditional values, old pastimes and adult authority. Church attendance in the capital rose, as did membership of political parties and youth organizations like the Boy Scouts, and family life flourished. The main entertainments were watching football, going to the cinema, and rambling or cycling, and sometimes whole families would be involved in these activities. In the late 1940s attendances at football matches were greater than ever before: the terraces of top London clubs like Arsenal and Tottenham were packed, often with crowds over 50,000. Going to matches was still very much a family affair, with many fathers and sons going through the turnstiles together.

Deprived of these simple and familiar pastimes during the war, Londoners now returned to them with enthusiasm. They had money in their pockets but very little to spend it on in the way of consumer goods, as factories turned out all they could for export to earn foreign currency. And the war had encouraged everyone to take part in communal activities.

The younger generation did not necessarily, however, share the values of their parents or older brothers and sisters. They were unhappy when a relatively easygoing wartime regime was overturned by returning fathers and brothers who insisted on the kind of discipline they had experienced growing up and in the forces. This discipline was reinforced in the classroom by schoolteachers and in the street by policemen who were now back to full strength.

The sexual permissiveness and relaxation of moral standards that had characterized the war years also ended abruptly when family life resumed. Many London dance halls had rules controlling the dress and behaviour of their customers and the more adventurous dances like the American 'jitterbug' were banned in some places. John Kerridge, who grew up in Wood Green, north London, in the early 1950s, remembered the tedium of the weekly routine of visits to the cinema and to relatives:

> The pictures used to be packed every night, night after night, because there was practically nothing else to do. People used to wait out in the cold for ages . . . to get inside. All the time, you did as you were told. And you did a lot of visiting to relations. You'd go round to tea on a Sunday afternoon and have a family get-together. But you didn't have a choice. 'Sunday afternoon, you're coming with us to see Gran,' and that was it.

Young men at this time were also confronted by the daunting prospect of National Service. Under the terms of the National Service Act of 1948 they were called up at the age of eighteen to undergo two years' military training. This was the first time that compulsory service in the armed forces had been imposed in Britain in peacetime. Most found the experience boring and oppressive.

THE RISE OF YOUTH CULTURE

It was in the early 1950s that young people began to rebel against the stranglehold that the older generation and the well-to-do exercised over style and entertainment. Bohemian subcultures, celebrating an unconventional kind of individualism, spontaneity and style, began to emerge in London. Soho, later the heart of Swinging London, was the first and the most important centre of the capital's post-war underground culture. It had established itself as an artistic Bohemia in the late 1930s, attracting literary figures like the poet, Dylan Thomas. After the war the bars and restaurants in Soho continued to attract bohemians. But there was a shift in emphasis from literature to music.

Jazz became the driving force for this alternative culture, and by the early 1950s there was a honeycomb of jazz clubs in the basements of Soho. One of the first was the Club 11, which opened in 1948 on the corner of Windmill Street and Archer Street, and was run by jazz musicians Ronnie Scott and John Dankworth. Marijuana smoking was very popular among jazz musicians at the time and the club was raided by the police and later closed down as a result. Shortly afterwards the premises became Cy Laurie's Jazz Club, one of the major jazz venues in the country, and it was here, in 1951, that a young singer called George Melly helped to organize one of London's first all-night jazz sessions – a very daring and exciting idea at the time.

While jazz clubs were becoming established in Soho, another meeting place for young people took off in the area – the coffee bar. Serving Italian-style espresso coffee and providing a juke box and regular live music, including jazz or skiffle groups with their acoustic guitars and kazoos, these coffee bars, many of which stayed open virtually all night, acquired a powerful mystique as oases of alternative culture in London. The first to open in 1953 was the Mika in Frith Street, but it was soon surpassed by Heaven and Hell in Old Compton Street and the Home of Sam Widges (a rather indigestible pun) on the corner of Berwick Street. By the mid-1950s these new-style trends were attracting national and even international interest; their coffee bar patrons were dubbed by the press 'bums', 'beats', and 'beatniks'.

Young people, eager to distinguish themselves from 'squares' (conventional people), rejoiced in the insults thrown at them and were happy to be called beatniks. Most were young and middle class, often aspiring actors, artists or students at college or looking for their first jobs in the capital. Their emerging lifestyle valued spontaneity and creativity above all else, and this, in turn, promoted a love for jazz improvisation, poetry and anything alternative.

There was also a sharp political edge to this subculture and it provided strong support for the first 'Ban the Bomb' Aldermaston marches and Trafalgar Square demonstrations of the early CND. Young bohemians expressed their group identity and their rebellion in the way they dressed. They chose casual and informal clothes, which to outsiders appeared very scruffy. Peter Powell, an aspiring actor in London during the early 1950s, remembered:

> In the '50s everybody was very stereotyped and the clothes they wore were sports jackets, flannels and a collar and tie, and possibly suede shoes if you were really daring. I guess for the kind of people we were, who were beat, we wanted to look different. Big baggy sweaters were *de rigueur*. Probably the holier the better. Then you would have corduroy trousers, often tied with string or enormous belts, and cravats or scarves tied round your neck.

Although beatniks dressed informally most of the time, they also loved to wear outrageous unconventional gear, especially for jazz dancing. Among the devotees of this new bohemian culture were many young people who were later to rise to fame in the London fashion world of the 1960s. For example, two former art students of Goldsmith's College, Mary Quant and her then boyfriend, Alexander Plunket Green, were regulars at Humphrey Lyttelton's jazz club in Oxford Street. They were noted for their unique style of dress. Alexander Plunket Green recalled:

> My mother had been ill for a long time and I had no money, and I actually wore all her clothes all the time. I didn't wear frocks exactly, but I put on pyjamas and trousers which had zips up the side and that

sort of thing. But when I got a bit bigger and couldn't get into her blouses any more I used to paint buttons on my chest and just wear a tie with it, and pretend I had a shirt on.

Mary Quant remembered:

I hated the clothes the way they were so I used to make circular skirts out of marvellous great prints and find black tights from theatrical costumiers and black ballet shoes and black leotard tops, and these skirts were really great to dance in.

After Mary Quant left art college she worked in a high-class milliner's. Her real ambition, however, lay in designing alternative styles of dress from those she saw all around her in the London of the mid-1950s:

What I loathed was the unsexiness, the lack of gaiety, the formal stuffiness of the look that was said to be fashion. I wanted clothes that were much more for life – much more for real people, much more for being young and alive in.

After long discussions in the coffee bars and jazz clubs she decided to set up her own business and in 1955 opened Bazaar, London's first boutique. Located in the King's Road, Chelsea, its distinctive feature was its free and easy atmosphere, which allowed customers to browse around and try clothes on unattended, contrasting sharply with the formal ways of the old clothes shops. All the designs sold in Bazaar were by Quant. A further break with tradition came when Alexander Plunket Green opened a restaurant in the basement. Both enterprises were extremely successful.

The King's Road began to take off as another centre of alternative culture, alongside Soho. By the mid-1950s coffee bars, soup kitchens, small clothes shops and jazz clubs were sprouting all over Chelsea. These were the prototype bistros, boutiques and nightclubs that would become all the rage in Swinging London several years later, and they were overwhelmingly populated by the young middle classes, the more stylish of whom were dubbed the 'Chelsea Set' by the press. Few young Londoners from a working-class background felt at ease in them, and they became the preserve of people who had been to grammar school or had enjoyed higher education.

London's working-class youth, in the meantime, developed its own sub-cultural style – that of the Teddy Boy. In the early 1950s the gentlemen's Savile Row tailors relaunched the 'look' of the Edwardian (hence 'Ted') dandy for their young aristocratic customers, and with characteristic London wit, working-class boys mimicked the drape jackets and velvet collars and combined them with the drainpipe trousers or jeans and bootlace ties they had seen in American cowboy films. A Ted's most treasured possessions were his 'brothel creeper' shoes and his comb, with which he constantly groomed his Brylcreemed hair. Traditional 'bob-a-knob' barbers, whose repertoire was limited to the 'short back and sides' cut, had to adapt quickly to the changing fashions. Brian Fleiss, an early Teddy Boy in Burnt Oak, north London, remembered, 'You used to go in and ask for a Tony Curtis, and get the barber to put a quiff on the front. I'd tell him I wanted plenty on the front.' Teddy Boys had a reputation for violence and were rendered fearsome by the popular press, their chosen weaponry (and how quaint this seems now) being bicycle chains and flick-knives. The easiest way to rouse a Ted was to insult his 'style', as one unfortunate did in 1953 at Clapham Common. In retaliation for calling a Teddy Boy a 'flash cunt' he was murdered in the first of a number of violent incidents in the Ted era.

There were Teddy girls as well as boys and they too evolved their own fashions, as Jackie Fleiss remembered:

> We wore jeans a lot. They weren't tailored then – they were pretty baggy and never tight enough so we used to start off by getting in a bath full of water with the jeans on and shrink them to fit you. But it was very uncomfortable letting jeans dry on you and your parents didn't like that at all. And we used to have full skirts with thick petticoats underneath made of a material called Vilene. And you'd have maybe three or four of these things, which we used to starch. After you'd washed them and taken them off the line they were so stiff they'd stand up on their own. But they were terrific for jiving. And we always had black stockings and suspenders. You didn't have tights in those days, only nylons.

The driving force behind this new subculture was music: while the beat-niks raved about jazz, the Teddy Boys were devoted followers of the rock 'n' roll music that was arriving from America. It featured the electric guitar and was loud, brash and aggressive. To the older generation this new music seemed discordant, disturbing and even threatening, but the explosive sounds of Bill Haley and Elvis Presley captured the mood of the younger generation and their yearning for greater freedom, as Brian Fleiss recalled:

> I remember hearing Bill Haley and the Comets' 'Rock Around the Clock' in 1956, and I thought to myself, I haven't heard anything like this before – this is really wild stuff. It was just something that I had to be involved in. There was nothing before that; you were in the family environment. But through this teenagers began to break out on their own; you could identify with it.

Whereas the beatniks were in the cafés drinking frothy coffee and doing their best to look like tramps, London's Teddy Boys put on their drapes and bootlace ties, groomed their quiffs and their carefully combed 'duck's arse' sidelocks and headed out to a local dance hall for the Saturday night 'hop'. The music was loud and to win your spurs you had to be able to jive, throwing your partner around in a routine practised in living rooms and bedrooms over many weeks. John Kerridge remembered:

> If you didn't have a partner you'd go up to the bedroom with the Dansette, put the records on and use the door handle. And there you'd be shaking and turning around and using the door handle as though it were your partner.

Teddy Boy culture never really penetrated the more bohemian central areas like Soho and Chelsea and became very much a phenomenon of working-class districts like Clapham and Stepney. However, one Soho coffee bar did become popular with Teds and developed into a famous breeding-ground for British rock 'n' roll performers. This was the 2 i's in Old Compton Street where Tommy Hicks, Harry Webb and Terry Nelhams began their careers. They later changed their names to Tommy Steele, Cliff Richard and Adam Faith.

THE COMING OF THE MODS

In their different ways both Teddy Boys and beatniks were pioneers, breaking new ground and flouting the old conventions. They created exciting dress and music fashions for young people in a grey, conformist world. However, by the late 1950s a new working-class style emerged that became known as the 'Mod' fashion and characterized the era that *Time* magazine dubbed 'Swinging London'. Mods – from 'modern' – thought of themselves as smarter and more sophisticated in their dress than Teddy Boys. Beatniks, of course, were deliberately scruffy and the Mods were in some ways consciously distancing themselves from that social group.

The Mod cult began in 1958 when a small group of young men, some of them sons of tailors living in Stepney and Stamford Hill, adopted a new look combining Italian and French styles. Impeccably cut Italian suits with very narrow lapels were tailor-made for them and worn with shirts with pointed collars. Their shoes were hand-made 'winkle pickers' (so called because of their very narrow pointed toes). The image was completed by a short, neat Italian or French hairstyle, copied from foreign film stars of the day like Alain Delon and very different from the greasy, Brylcreemed look of the Teddy Boy. Willy Deacey, an apprentice printer from Islington in north London, was a pioneer of the Mod look:

> Most of us had terrific hair, French style, and you spent a lot of time on it. You had to use sugar water. What you would do was wash your hair, then get a bowl of hot water, put sugar in it, then let it cool and keep stirring it up and then plaster that on your head to get it into shape. You used to leave it on all night – the longer you left it on the better it was. If you had straight hair you left it on twenty-four hours. It was horrible stuff. But if you had crinkly hair you might have to leave it on for four days. I knew one guy, a friend of mine called Gypo, he had to keep it on four days and he just put a sort of balaclava thing over his head, but it still didn't work. But with straight hair it came out just the business.
>
> We used to go to a lot of extremes. Once I didn't go out because I put on my suit, and my shoes were a little bit dirty so I got the polish out and – disaster – I looked in the mirror and I'd splattered my shirt. So I got the hump and I didn't go out that evening; I stayed in because my shirt wasn't perfect. And I knew guys who'd get on a bus with a sheet of brown paper so they could put it on the seat so they didn't get any dirt on their suit. And they'd sit bolt upright so they were not touching the seat. I used to go to the Tottenham Royal and I knew this guy who would turn up from a building site in his wellies

and a pickaxe, and with a suitcase, and he went into a cloakroom and cleaned up and came out in a suit, tie, shirt, shoes, socks that he had in the case. Because he was working so far away he couldn't get home and he thought he'd do it there. We took it very seriously and you had to be immaculate, very dandyish.

Mods adopted their name not so much for their clothes, however, but for their taste in what used to be known as Modern Jazz in the days of Charlie Mingus and Dave Brubeck. But they had a fetish about anything that they took to be modern. They might dream of owning an E-type Jaguar, but more realistically these smart working-class boys who worked in London's factories and offices were pleased enough with stylish motor scooters, especially Italian Lambrettas and Vespas. These were smart and clean unlike the big greasy machines of their style rivals the bikers and rockers. To keep their clothes neat and clean while they zipped around on their scooters, the Mods took to wearing army surplus all-weather cape-shaped coats known as parkas. A haunt of the pioneer Mods was Le Kilt in Soho where they might rub shoulders with cool young French women.

Up to 1960 the Mods were not very prominent in London, just a smattering of enthusiasts in various parts of the capital. But that soon changed. In the sixties young men could earn good wages and they had exceptionally high 'disposable incomes', living at home with few outgoings. Most working-class families were now so much better off than they had been before the war that the tradition in which teenage sons and daughters handed over most of their wages to their parents to help pay the family bills was rapidly abandoned. It was estimated in the early 1960s that the average weekly wage of teenagers was around £10, of which about £7 was left to spend as they liked after they had paid for their 'keep' at home. Enjoying exceptionally high wages, teenagers in London had more money to spend than young people anywhere else in Britain: a lucrative youth market was rapidly developing.

Not only did young people have more money than ever before; they also had more free time. From the 1950s onwards the number of hours spent at work was gradually reduced; at the same time holidays with pay increased. Labour-saving innovations in the home, like washing machines, vacuum cleaners and convenience foods, also created more free time, especially for girls, who were no longer obliged to spend so much time at home helping their mothers as they had in the past. And in 1960 National Service, which had deprived most teenage boys of two years of freedom, was abolished.

THE YOUTH MARKET

A new market catering for the needs and wants of young people was being opened up. The young were ripe for commercial exploitation and yet the large companies and corporations dominating the worlds of fashion, design and music were staid and conservative in their approach. In the early 1960s the BBC, for example, was very reluctant to give any air time to pop music, either on radio or on television. Many bosses were fearful that pandering to the whims of youth would unleash a dangerous, antisocial culture. This attitude was not unconnected to the fact that the teenage market was overwhelmingly working class in character and taste – many young people from middle-class backgrounds spent most of their teenage years in the education system and had comparatively less money to spend.

The youth market created a new opportunity for entrepreneurs who were working class like their customers and similar in age and background, so knew what they wanted. At the same time, the 1944 Education Act had brought about an improvement in the quality of schooling for working-class children and the opportunities open to them were greater than they had ever been before. More young people from humble backgrounds moved on to further and higher education, and the newly founded colleges and universities gave working-class students a chance to develop as artists, designers, musicians and entrepreneurs catering for the teenage market.

In particular, the art colleges were transformed. Before the war they had been little more than finishing schools for well-to-do young ladies who wished to learn genteel refinements like drawing and painting between leaving school and getting married. By the early 1960s they had become much more dynamic places, encouraging students to question the status quo and teaching a whole range of commercial skills in graphics, design and fashion. And the new college life gave many more young people more time to think, develop and create their own personal style.

There was a great concentration of art schools and colleges in the London area – Chelsea, St Martin's, Central, Camberwell, Kingston, Hornsey, Harrow, Wimbledon, Croydon, Sidcup and so on – and they were a magnet for young creative talent from across a wide area. Many leading figures in 1960s London – musicians like Pete Townshend of The Who, Ray Davies of the Kinks and Keith Richard of the Rolling Stones – were educated at art colleges in the capital. Teenage disposable income in the 1960s created a very valuable youth market, while the expansion of education, and particularly the art colleges, provided people with the inspiration and drive to exploit and profit from it. London drew in many talented and ambitious young people keen to make their mark and, with luck, their fortunes in the style capital.

In the early 1960s, the Mod look was taken up by the new fashion designers. Boutique clothing shops, like Mary Quant's pioneering Bazaar, mushroomed all over the capital, offering an easygoing and relatively inexpensive way for young people to indulge their interest in the new fashions. There were about 1,500 boutiques by the mid-1960s, many of them setting the tone by playing the latest pop records while their customers browsed inside. Interpretations of the Mod style flourished in these new clothing stores, which were inspired by the shops in Carnaby Street, Soho and the King's Road in Chelsea.

By the early 1960s half a dozen Carnaby Street boutiques were owned by one man – John Stephen, a Glaswegian grocer's son who came to London in 1956 when he was nineteen. He noticed what Mods were wearing and what they wanted, and the moment a new style appeared on the streets he began stocking it in his shops. Stephen revolutionized men's clothing and his first boutique, called His Clothes, was a Mecca for top Mods, known in Mod circles as 'faces'. These fashion leaders would spend what were then astonishing sums of money on clothes. Some of the trendiest shirts would be sold for £4 or more, representing a large chunk of their weekly wages.

The 'faces' were attracted by the huge displays of well-cut suits, jackets and trousers and the many different styles and fabrics available in Stephen's boutiques. He anticipated and catered for all the latest Mod trends – at one time mohair suits, at another white suits – and also sold coloured hipster trousers, which only homosexuals had dared to wear previously because their colours were supposedly effeminate.

By popularizing and commercializing Mod styles for men, Stephen was the first really to exploit the new youth clothing market in London, then in Britain and then right around the world. The rapid expansion of his chain of boutiques was quite remarkable. Within a few years he was the millionaire owner of twenty-five boutiques in London, twenty-four in the United States and twenty-one in various European cities.

In contrast to Stephen's boutiques, those that opened in and around the King's Road in Chelsea catered chiefly for teenage girls and young women. They were run by a band of pioneer entrepreneurs, many of them young art school graduates who made and marketed their own designs. The Mod look that they sold was often a refined version of what they had seen Mod girls wearing on the streets and in the clubs of London. Mod girls were always a minority in this male-dominated sub-culture, but they too were obsessively concerned with their appearance and dress. In fact, the miniskirt was a Mod fashion which became a London icon in the sixties.

The most successful of the new clothing boutiques, some of which came and went very quickly, was Mary Quant's Bazaar. Her simple bright designs always stayed one step ahead of her competitors' and she became the most fashionable purveyor of the Mod look. By the early 1960s she and Alexander Plunket Green – her husband and business partner – realized that the appeal of their clothes was no longer limited to their friends in Chelsea. Plunket Green recalled:

> At first we thought it was just the art studenty type that wanted to look like us and buy our clothes. But what we didn't realize at the time and didn't discover for some time was the fact that we were interpreting the mood of the whole generation, not just smart art students. The whole thing caught on in a much bigger way than we'd expected. We thought we were just working for people who lived in Chelsea, but the whole thing was actually what people wanted from all over.

The Mod look for young women spread from London to other parts of Britain and, by the mid-1960s, to the United States. As Mary Quant's confidence grew so did her attacks on the fashion establishment. She changed the whole concept of the fashion show, for example, which until then had been very staid and demure. The women who modelled *her* clothes were instructed to run, jump and dance down the catwalk, often to the music of a group playing live. The publicity such daring innovations attracted gained the Quant image recognition around the world and there was soon an insatiable demand for her designs, which were licensed in many countries. In 1966 she received an OBE for her services to exports.

The promotion of the work of leading designers like Quant was made possible by a burgeoning of fashion journalism in newspapers and new glossy magazines like *Nova* and *Queen*. The first *Sunday Times* colour supplement came out in 1962 and was an important showcase for new styles. A young generation of fashion journalists eagerly embraced the Mod look, now illustrated with colour photographs. Fashion modelling and fashion photography promised those who were successful highly paid and glamorous careers. Fashion photography, as much as anything else, won London its American title as the Swinging City.

By the mid-1960s dozens of new photographic and modelling agencies had been established in central London. Young people from humble backgrounds did very well out of both professions, partly because the Mod cult was originally a working-class phenomenon and fashion editors felt that using them was a sure way of creating an 'authentic' look. Three of the most celebrated young photographers discovered during this period were David Bailey, Terence Donovan and Brian Duffy, all of whom were East End born and bred. One of the most famous models of the era was Lesley Hornby, better known as Twiggy. She was launched into stardom as 'the face of 1966' a few weeks before sitting her O levels at Neasden High School for Girls in north London. In 2005, at the age of fifty-five, Twiggy was still influencing fashion when she became 'the face' of Marks & Spencer.

A new kind of hairstylist emerged in the slipstream of the great fashion boom. Vidal Sassoon was an East End boy who had served his apprenticeship under leading stylist 'Teasie-Weasie' Raymond. Sassoon rejected the elaborate styles popular in the 1950s and, together with Raymond, he developed a much more natural look which they called the 'geometric cut'. Sassoon set up his own salon in Bond Street in the West End and by the early 1960s had become very successful, with aristocratic ladies queuing to have their hair bobbed by him in the style made popular by Mary Quant. Sassoon's 'geometric styles' complemented the unfussy clothes that Quant was designing and his cuts quickly became a great favourite with Mod girls. By 1966 he was exporting his styles and salons to the United States, where he eventually moved. Hairdressing salons for young men also appeared all over London in the 1960s, many of them run by Italians offering a full range of Mod styles. Gone were the days when pioneer 'Modernists' like Willy Deacey used home-made concoctions to get their hair looking right. Hairdressing for both men and women was now commercialized and was very responsive to the styles that young people wanted.

And just as the styles of dress and appearance of the early London Mods formed the basis of internationally famous fashions, so their musical interests provided a launch pad for dozens of rhythm-and-blues groups to go on to international fame.

THE POP REVOLUTION

The Mods' early interest in jazz had, by 1960, broadened to include black American country blues, amplified rhythm and blues and soul music. Records by American artists like Muddy Waters, Chuck Berry and Howling Wolf quickly became collectors' items, and the musical tastes and interests of Mods provided a convenient starting point for dozens of London-based rhythm-and-blues groups to gain international recognition. The most internationally famous London band of the era was the Rolling Stones. Their first residency was at the Craw-Daddy club in Richmond in 1963 where they played American R&B to packed audiences. Once the fame of the Stones spread and they became pop stars, their Mod following faded away. Their appearance was too untidy and their commercialized versions of favourite blues classics were seen as 'sellouts'. Much more in favour with Mods were other home-grown bands like the Yardbirds – featuring lead guitarist Eric Clapton – the Kinks, the Pretty Things and Georgie Fame and the Blue Flames.

At first these new groups were heard only in clubs, but in 1963 a pop music programme called *Ready Steady Go* was given a prime-time early evening slot on ITV. Broadcast from a studio in Kingsway, Holborn, it was an instant success and featured bands on the London club circuit virtually unknown outside the capital at that time. A year later Radio Caroline, Britain's first post-war 'pirate' radio station, began transmitting from an old ship moored off the Suffolk coast. It was promoted by Ronan O'Rahilly, manager of one of London's top Mod clubs, the Scene, and it plugged the Mod music that was being played in the capital. O'Rahilly's interest was blatantly exploitative, as he explained: 'Youth was bursting out all over, there was a lot of money to be made.' Radio Caroline was quickly followed by Radio London, another pirate station geared to the capital's music scene. As London's bands began to reach wider audiences they produced a succession of hit records. The Who and the Small Faces were the most popular Mod bands and soon had hits in the charts. Inspired by Pete Townshend, then a student at Ealing art college, The Who were originally called the Detours, then in 1964 Townshend's friend Richard Barnes suggested a new name:

> There was this MC at the Oldfield Hotel dance hall in Greenford, where they played regularly, and he loved to have a little joke when

introducing the group. He would say stuff like: 'And now I'd like to introduce the Detours – the Who? Never 'eard of 'em,' and other assorted witticisms. I thought we could spike his guns for him. Townshend, incidentally, wanted to call the band the Hair. The next day he even suggested a combined name, the Hair and the Who, which sounded to me more like a pub than a group.

Having chosen their name, The Who became the resident band at the Railway Hotel in Harrow. Here Townshend began smashing guitars – a form of wilful destruction and an affectation intended to express the band's adolescent nihilism. Their manager insisted that the band dress in the latest Mod styles and introduced them to top Mods in the London clubs. Their first single was entitled 'I'm the Face' but it was their third release, 'My Generation', which really launched them as a national phenomenon.

The most popular East End Mod band was the Small Faces. By 1965 they were in the top twenty, and their manager gave the band members an account at every boutique in Carnaby Street and £20 a week each to spend on clothes. They quickly developed a reputation for being Britain's best-dressed band and this, in an era of narcissism, greatly contributed to their success.

Young musicians eager to hit the big time all headed for the capital in the sixties. Everything from the recording studios to the factories manufacturing the new plastic discs was in the London area. The Beatles, established first on Merseyside, moved from Liverpool to London in 1964, recording most of their music at the EMI studios in Abbey Road, St John's Wood. Their early music, however, was too melodic and their image too respectable for most Mods. Much more popular were Zoot Money's Big Roll Band, who came up from Bournemouth, and the Animals who came south from Newcastle. Chas Chandler, former bass guitarist with the Animals, remembered coming to London in 1963:

London was a huge magnet. The recording studios were in London – the only studio we had in Newcastle, if you put a drum kit in it, you couldn't get the drummer in. It was that small. You had to come to London. All the record companies were there, the music papers were there, they didn't review you if you hadn't played in London. Everybody got a nosebleed if they went north of Watford. We came down for ten days and stayed twenty-two years.

A number of club venues for the new rhythm-and-blues music were outside central London. The most popular were the Eel Pie Island Hotel in Twickenham, the Craw-Daddy in Richmond and Klook's Kleek in Hampstead. And as the R&B clubs spread all over London so, too, did a new type of Mod haunt – the discothèque. A French import, the first London disco, La Discothèque, was opened in Soho and was the first London club to replace live bands with gramophone records. All-night dancing sessions at La Discothèque were quite common and mattresses would be positioned around the sides of the dance floor for exhausted Mods to recover. By the mid-1960s the fashion for discothèques, complete with disc jockeys, had spread not only throughout London but all across Britain. Many of the Mods who went to the London clubs and discothèques had a hectic social life. Most attended clubs two or three times a week, and top Mods like Willy Deacey would often be out every night. He was able to afford this even though he only earned £6 a week as an apprentice printer. He remembered a typical week's social diary around 1964:

> Monday was Tottenham Royal, Tuesday the Lyceum, Wednesday the Scene, or maybe stay in and wash your hair, Thursday Tottenham Royal again (because it was our little hangout), then Friday night was 'Ready Steady Go'. It got difficult to get in on that so me and a friend used to get hold of an empty film can apiece and ride up and down the lift in the studios until it was time to go in, then we would just join the crowd. Then after 'Ready Steady Go' you'd go on to the Scene later. Saturday and Sunday was either a party or the Tottenham Royal, then the next week you'd start again.

To sustain this hectic lifestyle some Mods took amphetamines (called Purple Hearts, French Blues or Black Bombers). They could be bought for a few pence in the clubs. Willy Deacey recalled:

> We used to take Purple Hearts. They were legal then – in fact, my mum used to get them on prescription. They used to keep you going most of the night, but the only dodgy night was Sunday night because you were really tired then, so we'd take a handful and we'd be OK. There wasn't any dope around then so we used to take speed.

By 1965 the young working-class men who had pioneered the Mod cult were beginning to lose interest in it as it became mainstream fashion. They had at first benefited from the commercialization of their style: Mod musicians and entrepreneurs were able to get rich quick and the records, clothes and hairstyles that the Mods wanted were much more widely available than before. But the Mod style had become a mass phenomenon and by 1965 and '66 – the years of Swinging London – a third of Britain's youth considered themselves Mods and the style had a sizeable international following too. Every weekend Carnaby Street was filled with young people from the provinces and foreign tourists in search of the latest fashions.

From late 1963 onwards new London clubs opened where heirs and heiresses could meet the new aristocrats of the pop world. The most popular among the young gentry were the Ad Lib off Leicester Square, the Scotch of St James near St James's Square, and the Cromwellian near the Cromwell Road in South Kensington. Here the new rich pop stars (Mick Jagger of the Rolling Stones and Roger Daltrey, lead singer of The Who), designers (Mary Quant and Ossie Clark), top model Jean Shrimpton, and fashionable photographers (Terence Donovan and David Bailey) rubbed shoulders with the upper crust, forming a London jet set whose private lives filled the gossip columns of every newspaper.

This image of young men and women from working-class backgrounds who had made it to the top, mixing with the 'toffs', encouraged the naive view that Swinging London had somehow become classless, while in reality, the great majority of once fashionable London Mods were by then back working in ordinary jobs, a little rueful that their 'scene' had been hijacked by high fashion. In fact a fragmentation of Mod culture occurred around 1965, giving rise to the skinhead style of big 'bovver' boots and trousers held up with braces – an outfit that mimicked old-fashioned London working-class clothing. Skinheads became associated with violence, particularly at football matches, and though their first taste in music had been West Indian and they adopted Jamaican 'rude boy' styles, they ultimately appeared to be racist and fascistic, especially when the style was adopted by disaffected youth across Europe. Skinheads were distinct from the so-called 'peacock' Mods who continued to embrace smart fashion. Fragmented and overtaken by new fashion, the hugely influential Mod scene was fading by the early 1970s.

The first generation to experience the new freedoms of youth culture were anyway growing older and were starting families. However, they did not abandon their new tastes altogether. As they began to set up home they naturally looked for furnishings to suit their lifestyles, and in so doing created another new market. Terence Conran was the most successful of the pioneer creators of a new kind of home furnishing. A graduate of the Central School of Art and Design in 1950, he spent fourteen years persevering with his furniture designs in tiny attics and workshops in various parts of London. To make ends meet he had opened in the West End cheap restaurants he called 'soup kitchens'. In 1964 he decided to open up a shop in Fulham called Habitat, selling modern, well-designed furniture and household goods at prices that most people could afford. To begin with, Habitat wasn't very successful; the first shop took only £64,000 in its first year. But by the late 1960s Habitat was booming, and on the way to becoming a nationwide chain store. Terence Conran recalled:

> I'd always believed that well-designed things should be available to the whole population, that it shouldn't be an elitist thing. And I think this coincided with a lot of people who'd had further education coming through who were discontented with the way things were. The fashion revolution was just beginning – certainly, music was well on its way – and we wanted to provide home furnishings in the widest sense of the word to this type of person. There was beginning to be a little bit of demand for it – not a great deal – but you could feel the atmosphere of discontent. Most of the other stores weren't sensitive to change in society and they thought it was only a flash in the pan.

FROM POP TO PUNK: THE 'LONDON LOOK'

The Swinging London scene faded after 1966 and for a while the centre of gravity moved to the United States, especially to California, when, in the late 1960s it became a Mecca for young musicians and designers hooked on rock music, drugs, mysticism, communal living and political dissent. However, London's extraordinary ability to reinvent and resurrect itself was soon apparent. The art colleges were still producing creative students and it was only a matter of time before a new 'London look' appeared on the streets and in the shops.

A decade after the final flourishes of the Mods came the fashion which revelled in outlandish clothing, vigorously unmelodic music and a kind of adornment with tattoos and nose- and ear-rings which had previously been the preserve of highland tribes in New Guinea. Self-consciously icono-clastic and grotesque, Punk musicians and fans nevertheless changed fashion, and though they could be found in all major cities in Britain, London was naturally the capital. Once again with Punk, fashion and music evolved together.

The Punk shrine was a shop opened in 1974 and called, simply, SEX at 430 King's Road, Chelsea; the three letters were spelt out in pink rubber. The shop, selling fetish and bondage outfits, was owned by Malcolm McLaren and his partner Vivienne Westwood. McLaren had got the idea of Punk clothing after a trip to New York in which he had tried unsuc-cessfully to manage some pop bands, while Westwood had, since 1971, made and sold Teddy Boy clothes from the same premises.

McLaren went on to manage the most notorious of all Punk groups, the Sex Pistols, who in turn had a huge following in London. Among them was a girl from Kent, one of a group of Sex Pistols fans who called themselves the Bromley Contingent. Born in 1957 as Susan Janet Ballion, she adopted the Punk name Siouxsie Sioux and found instant fame after an impromptu first appearance at the 100 Club on Oxford Street during a 'Punk Rock Festival' organized by McLaren in September 1976. According to a journalist who witnessed her unannounced appearance on the stage, Siouxsie simply emerged from the audience, and took off her raincoat to reveal a plunging V-neck dress with black net over her breasts. She wore a home-made swastika held with a safety pin on her armband, fishnet tights and black vinyl leggings, black strap stilettos on her feet and, in her short black hair, flecks of red like flames.

Siouxsie Sioux appeared with the Sex Pistols in December 1976 on the television programme *Today* presented by Bill Grundy for London's Thames Television. There was banter between Siouxsie and Grundy, who later admitted to being the worse for drink as the show went on air. Grundy playfully suggested he and Siouxsie might meet after the show, at which point the band began to insult him. Grundy egged them on and Steve Jones, the Sex Pistols' guitarist, called him a 'fucking rotter'. This made the headlines and brought Punk rock into the mainstream, vilification in the newsapapers, and on radio and television serving only to raise the movement's commercial value. McLaren was quoted as saying that fashion seemed to be 'the place where music and art came together' and, together with Vivienne Westwood, he continued to produce Punk costumes which were, in time, adopted by the top designers, safety pins and all. Some of the original T-shirts and fragments of Punk clothing are now lovingly preserved in the Museum of London collections, a reminder that the capital's 'street culture' has been an important part of its recent history.

By the 1970s, Carnaby Street had lost its fashionable edge and was rapidly eclipsed by another district, north London. Camden Town, the character of which was fixed by the arrival of the steam railway in the 1830s, was until the 1970s solidly working class with a lively vegetable market in Inverness Street and a high street of greengrocers, fishmongers, butchers and many second-hand clothes stores. The Regent's Canal runs through the centre of Camden Town and it was lined with warehouses from the days when many goods were delivered by narrow-boat. Where a road bridge crosses the canal there is a lock and a basin for the mooring of barges. A huge, multi-storey building there, used for stabling for hundreds of horses until the war, was abandoned.

Just after the war, in 1946, a merchant called T. E. Dingwall took over some of the warehousing and imported timber with which he made wooden containers. There were then, as in other parts of London, many local employers in Camden, including Gilbey's Gin and, housed in a splendid Egyptian-style block, Carreras Tobacco, which made a celebrated brand of cigarette. However, one by one all these businesses closed down and Dingwall's warehouses were left empty. Canal trade was more or less finished and Camden suffered years of 'planning blight', as discussion of how it ought to be revived produced a stalemate.

In 1971 a company called Northside Developments, which had already revived an area in south London on Clapham North Side (hence their name), bought the seven years remaining on Dingwall's lease. The cost was minimal – £10,000 – and an inexpensive conversion of the buildings created a new market and rock venue appropriately called Dingwalls. A local Member of Parliament, Jack Stollard, opened the new Dingwalls market in 1973 and it was soon flourishing. A scheme to demolish everything and build a new complex was beaten off by public protest.

As Camden Market became established it took on the same kind of creative role as Carnaby Street in the 1960s, with young designers such as David Holah and Stevie Stewart, creators of Body Map, taking up stalls giving them a shop window on the wider fashion world. Another Camden pioneer was designer Wayne Hemingway, a northerner from Morecambe, who came to London to study at University College. As a sixth former he had been disappointed by a visit to Vivienne Westwood's store Seditionaries, finding it far too expensive and sophisticated for his taste. In 1981 he set up his own stalls at Camden Lock, creating the Red or Dead label; in time he sold Dr Martens boots and became a fashion guru.

Inevitably, Camden Lock has changed as it has expanded, but it is still going strong and what was once a typical run-down former industrial district of London is now one of the most popular tourist destinations in the capital, and a Mecca for journalists and designers on the lookout for the latest trends. It is characteristic of London itself, a city not governed by any ruling elite but by myriad commercial and creative forces which may be dormant for periods but seem always to resurface, often in the most unlikely places.

Writing in 2004 in *The London Look: Fashion from Street to Catwalk* (published by the Museum of London), Professor Caroline Evans defined the capital's special qualities:

> The liveliness of London fashion emerges from its history of quirky little shops rather than big designer labels; a cultural mix that has moved during the centuries from imperial transaction to present-day immigration; the crossover between fashion, art, architecture and music; and a strong sense of a past ever-ripe for playful reworking and reconfiguring. The London Look might be best summed up as an edgy, of-the-moment 'have a go' mentality not seen in other fashion capitals . . .

Though no doubt partly mythical, the idea of the Swinging Sixties turned out to have a kernel of truth in it, for London has sustained that idiosyncratic streetwise reputation and it is a large part of its attraction for foreign visitors. Fashion and music have become a significant part of the modern economy of the metropolis, a colourful counterpart to its other great resource, business and the City.

CHAPTER TWENTY-ONE

The New Office World

IN THE 1980s it was noticeable that London's office workers were shedding the more formal dress and habits of their older colleagues who were approaching retirement. For example, the bowler hat, for so long a symbol of the City worker, had become a rarity and young financiers might be seen wearing coloured shirts. A decade later, and the same age group who had ushered in a revolution in the sartorial habits of office life could be found huddled in street-level doorways – they were the smokers, social outcasts forced to indulge their cravings in no-man's land. Alert photo-journalists were quick to spot this, snapping sequences of the guilty groups exiled by a new puritanism which followed hard on the heels of the liberation from old-fashioned rules about the correct form of dress. Whereas the new puritans were concerned about pollution the old guard had been much more exercised about appearance.

Just after the war there were around 1 million office workers in London, nearly all of them smartly dressed and conforming to codes of behaviour imposed by their bosses. In the City the standard outfit of bowler hat, rolled umbrella and pinstriped suit was still compulsory. Dundas Hamilton, who became a partner in a City stockbroking firm in the 1940s, remembered:

> The City was a very formal place; I mean, I came to work in a short black jacket and striped trousers and we all wore white shirts and stiff white collars. Everybody had bowler hats and rolled umbrellas because it was part of the uniform. In fact, it was so much a part of the uniform that when one of our young partners joined us my senior partner carpeted him because he wouldn't wear his bowler hat and he was thought to be improperly dressed. We also had a ban on the soft shirt or the coloured shirt, and if I'd worn a striped shirt and a soft collar people in my office would have said to me, 'Why haven't you got out of your pyjamas yet?'

The City offices in those days were much smaller than they are today, because businesses were smaller. Very few had central heating; most had gas fires. There was a Victorian atmosphere which came from tall desks with sloping tops where you could stand up and write if you wanted to. Or, if you wanted to sit down, you sat on a high stool. Virtually all the clerks were male. It was very much still the era of the pen-pushing clerk and the hand-written ledger.

During the war, hundreds of London's central offices had been damaged by fire and bomb blast, some of them razed to the ground. Worst hit were the Barbican, Moorgate and the streets around St Paul's Cathedral, where almost every building was ruined. From the 1950s onwards London's office world would be transformed, becoming the capital's fastest area of growth.

Although there was an urgent need for more office space, new building was tightly controlled by the Labour government that came to power after the war. London's office economy was given a low priority in the government's reconstruction plans, preference being given to public housing schemes and factory rebuilding.

Developers had to get an official licence to put up offices, and these were hard to come by. There was a restriction, anyway, on the height of any new office block: the London Building Act of 1894 had put an upper limit of 80 feet (24 m) on all buildings. Many could not reach even that as there were rules about the maximum height of buildings in relation to their immediate surroundings.

While renewal of offices was difficult, many were patched up and were little different in style or comfort from those built before the war. Office workers were still mostly men, and, in the City, they held a near monopoly of top jobs in the worlds of banking, insurance and finance. The idea of senior women executives in such companies was almost unthinkable. If clients needed to be entertained for lunch then they would often be taken to that traditional and exclusive male preserve, the gentlemen's club, which continued to thrive for many years after the war. Dundas Hamilton recalled:

When I became a partner in my firm I became a member of the City of London Club. I lunched there virtually every day, sometimes taking business clients out. The food was very much the public school type, like roast beef and two veg'. A particular delicacy was sausage and mash. This was the smallest and cheapest dish on the menu and, if you looked around the lunch room, you would see all the millionaires eating sausage and mash and thoroughly enjoying themselves. In the old days, of course, there were no women allowed inside the club, even as guests into the private luncheon rooms – partly, I think, because it was very much a male preserve and partly because the whole City was a male preserve. It was one of the rules of the club that people had to be principals in their firms, ex-directors or partners, in order to be eligible for membership and there weren't many women who were in this position.

The City continued to be male-dominated, but in offices in other parts of London half of all office workers were women by the late 1940s. Most were young and single, working chiefly as typists, telephonists, filing clerks and secretaries. There were rules making it extremely difficult for women to move up the office ladder, the most significant of which was the 'marriage bar': as soon as they married, women working in many banks and insurance companies and for public institutions like the Civil Service and the London County Council were forced to resign from their jobs. During the war this rule had been relaxed to allow married women to continue working. As soon as the war was over, however, the old discrimination returned. Margaret Dent worked for the Admiralty in Whitehall during and just after the war. She remembered:

> It was wartime when I got married and I had to stay on because they were short of staff, but it was very humiliating for I was immediately made a temporary member of staff and lost my pension rights. The whole attitude to women at that time in the Admiralty was that you were really only fit for making the tea and that you should be at home. You weren't taken seriously at all. I think if the attitude had been different I would have taken my career more seriously. But as it was I was glad to leave to get away from it all after the war, because the attitude to women there was terrible.

However, there were forces at work that would produce a boom in office building and begin to transform the staid office world.

THE HEYDAY OF THE SPECULATOR

In the late 1950s, London began to reassert itself as the Mecca of international money markets and the City led the way. At the outbreak of war in 1939, there had been only eight American banks with branches in the City and all the German banks had gone, never to return. But the relaxing of exchange controls in 1958 and the City's traditional financial expertise, exercised with fewer legal and tax restrictions on buying and selling than in other financial capitals, made it a magnet for banks and insurance companies. They prospered greatly after the war, fuelled by the increasing amounts of international money attracted into the City.

By 1959 there were 76 foreign banks in the City, rising to 580 at the end of the century – far and away the highest number in any financial capital. In fact, London in the late 1990s had more American banks than New York and more Japanese banks than Tokyo. Between the mid-sixties and the early eighties employment in financial services in the City more than doubled, to 575,000.

London's army of office workers was growing also with the continuing demand of large companies for a head office in the capital; this had also been a feature of the interwar years. Companies like ICI and Shell whose factories and refineries were scattered around the world wanted their corporate headquarters to be close to Parliament and the City. At the same time government departments were growing in size as the bureaucracy of the welfare state created by the post-war Labour government was established. With entirely new departments such as the Ministry of Housing, the Civil Service had to find much more office space than before the war. And the newly nationalized industries, the Coal Board and the Central Electricity Generating Board, were in search of suitable head-quarters in London. The pent-up demand for offices was huge by 1951 and yet the Labour government refused to lift its bar on new building.

Then, in 1951, the Conservatives returned to power, committed to growth in the office economy, and within three years this government had dismantled practically all the controls on office development: building licences were abolished as was the heavy tax on new office buildings and, suddenly, the bombsites that spread across central London became ripe for purchase and redevelopment in anticipation of an office boom.

Waiting in the wings to make a killing out of the boom were speculators who had quietly acquired land in central London, well aware of the controlled demand for office space there. As soon as restrictions were lifted, these speculators emerged and were soon denounced for their influence on the development of London and the huge profits they made from rapidly built office blocks. The property speculator needed no special knowledge of architecture or building techniques: his talent was for acquiring run-down properties cheaply and assembling sites which, with planning permission, could rise in value hundreds of times over.

The property development system was at this time very simple and straightforward. A developer would obtain planning permission to build on a bombsite, arrange a bank loan to purchase it, then employ an architect and a builder to erect the office block on it. There was a small risk element in trying to find a company for the offices when they were completed. However, such was the demand for office space that some companies were prepared to take up and pay for the lease even before the office was completed. Huge amounts of money changed hands in this way and developers like Joe Levy and Jack Rose became fabulously wealthy almost overnight. Jack Rose remembered how in those days a money-spinning deal could be clinched with just a few telephone calls:

> The demand for office space was insatiable and everyone was
> encouraging us to build more offices. When you saw a site for sale, you'd
> buy it sometimes on the same day and would be almost certain that
> you'd get planning permission and make a good profit on it. Once a site
> was on offer we'd ring up an architect (usually the same one) and he in
> turn would make a phone call to the planning authority. He would be
> told over the phone that he could apply for planning permission and told
> how many square feet of office space we'd be allowed on the site. Then
> we'd make a quick back-of-an-envelope calculation as to how much we
> could afford to pay for the site, and ring up and make an offer. What
> takes years today took days back in the '50s. And there were big profits
> to be made out of it. I left the army in 1945 with a gratuity of £18 and
> nothing else to my name. By the early '60s our company was worth £4
> million. We weren't as big as many others – one of the greatest names
> was Lord Samuel whose company Land Securities was estimated to be
> worth, even in those days, £1,000 million.

The idea was to pack as much office space as possible into a site. As it was a speculative venture, the building was completed as quickly and cheaply as possible in order to reduce the risks. Consequently, most offices had little ornamentation or individuality. The LCC gave planning permission for these new developments because modern offices were fashionable – the buildings of the future – and there was no conservation lobby to stop their onward march. At first the speculators' buildings might be quite conventional, like the eight-storey Woolworth House in Marylebone Road, developed by Jack Rose with architect Richard Seifert and completed in 1955. Three years later Castrol House, also in Marylebone Road, became the first of a new style of concrete and glass office blocks. All of these buildings changed the character of the capital and Jack Rose later believed that many of them should not have been built. He said:

> For the most part, they're nothing better than shoe boxes with glass windows in them! They should have been controlled by the planning authority who should have had a great deal better taste than they obviously had at the time. Wherever you see the boxes of that era they're being disguised – refaced and refurbished with what is now regarded as better taste. I don't believe in the preservation of a great deal of old property. Nevertheless, allowing a proper vista of St Paul's and other lovely and important buildings in London to go because of new offices was philistine. Undoubtedly, the developers of that time didn't care. They weren't interested in what the buildings looked like – just how much profit they could make out of their building. When I look at the streets of London and at the buildings that were put up in that era, I'd say we made a muck of it.

But while the 1950s had laid the foundations of a fundamental change in the fabric of London's offices, it was only in the sixties that it all really came to fruition. Offices often took several years to complete and, as time went by, they were built higher and higher, so that by about 1962 Londoners were becoming aware of the extent of the transformation of their city's skyline. In that year, for example, giant offices like the Shell Centre on the South Bank and the Vickers Tower on Millbank – both almost 400 feet (122 m) high – were completed.

Also at this time, there was another upsurge in the need for offices in London. Multinationals, especially booming oil companies, were expanding their operations in the capital and banks were prospering as a result of the development of currencies like the Eurodollar, attracting even more international money into the City. But the stock of bombsites and derelict buildings cleared and built on in the 1950s was now almost exhausted. So property developers began buying up Victorian offices, warehouses, churches and terraced houses, some of them in reasonable condition, and demolishing them to make way for new offices.

During this mania for modernizing, almost every celebrated building in London came under threat from one scheme or another. For example, there were plans to demolish the Houses of Parliament, St Pancras Station and the whole of the southern half of Whitehall including the Foreign Office.

The early 1960s, then, were the era of 'monster schemes' in which many old buildings would be bulldozed to make space for huge office developments. Developers were able to plan ambitious schemes like these because they were now rich men with massive reserves of capital to draw on. Joe Levy, for example, was a millionaire as a result of property deals, and this wealth gave him enormous power. His Euston Centre was typical of the new type of development: he bought up properties and parcels of land in the Euston Square area in about four hundred separate deals in the 1950s and early '60s, keeping the whole operation secret. If he had made his plans public, the price of the remaining property he wanted to buy would have spiralled, although Levy was prepared to pay way over the odds for the last few properties he needed to complete the jigsaw of land required. He recalled:

> I'd spent more than ten years buying up all the land I needed. I had several millions pounds tied up in it, and it came to the point where there was one more house I needed to complete it. I think it was a Cypriot who owned it. It was a run-down old place worth next to nothing, but he was holding out for as much as he could get. The agent that was working for me made him some offers and the price went up and up, but still he didn't want to know. So, one cold morning, I went down to see him myself. He refused to do a deal to start with but I said, 'There's no point in refusing, because the council will buy it compulsorily and then you'll get next to nothing.' We came to an agreement: I would give him £50,000. He wanted cash and all the documentation done immediately. I said yes and when it was done I asked, 'Have I made you a happy man?' He said, 'Yes, I'm happy now.' He was delighted with the deal, so I said, 'Now I'm going to tell

you something that will make you very unhappy. If you hadn't sold to me now I needed your house so badly I might have paid you a quarter of a million pounds for it.'

By 1963 Levy had bought up the complete proposed site and the bull-dozers moved in. The residential area of Euston Square was transformed into the Euston Centre, a mixed development containing mostly offices and shops, the centrepiece of which was a high-rise office block. Home to London's Capital Radio, this was to become the single most profitable office development in the world.

The LCC did little or nothing to control these new office dev-elopments. Deals were done with developers who in return would give the LCC small plots of land for road-widening schemes, which the office boom and the subsequent increase in commuter traffic were making very urgent. In any case, the LCC was still broadly sympathetic to the idea of clean-sweep planning and often helped large developers by making compulsory purchase orders, or by letting the property bought by developers remain unoccupied and rehousing some of the displaced residents. The Euston Centre is a fairly typical example of this kind of deal. Joe Levy was allowed to build his offices in the way that he wanted to on condition that he handed over £1 million-worth of the land he had assembled that ran through the site. The LCC used this free land to build the Euston underpass; it also gave property tycoon Harry Hyams permission to build the Centrepoint office tower on a tiny traffic island off Tottenham Court Road, on condition that he donated an adjacent plot of land it needed for a new road scheme.

TYPING POOLS, DOLLY BIRDS AND MINISKIRTS

The office world was not only transformed on the outside. What went on inside the new buildings was also changing. A new style of mechanical office was emerging, making greater use of labour-saving machinery. Some pioneering offices bought giant prototype computers. However, although these early computers were bought to save time and money on clerical work, they were prone to disastrous breakdowns. In the early 1950s Joe Lyons of London became the first company in the world to use a computer for business purposes. Norman Beasley, who was one of the operators, recalled:

Lyons decided that they would set about designing and building a computer themselves. They did, and they called it Leo. 'Leo' stood for Lyons Electronic Office. It was one of the first computers for commercial use, so nobody who was working with it really knew what to expect because no one had any previous experience of working with them. So, in a sense, it was very strange and sometimes things went wrong. We did work for other companies who of course didn't have their own computers then. One such was the Ford Motor Company. We did their payroll for them weekly and, of course, in those days it was cash in the packet on a Friday.

One week it went wrong. The first we heard of it was when they told us that a clerk in the Treasury, who was responsible for putting money in the pay packets of the Ford workers, went to her supervisor and asked for a larger envelope. When the supervisor said, 'What d'you want a larger envelope for?' she replied: 'Well, I can't get this £478 in this one.' That was the first we knew that something had gone wrong.

The use of computers for writing letters, doing accounts or sending messages was a long way off. Typewriters had been around since late Victorian times but the increasing volume of office work meant that the clatter of the keys now resonated everywhere, the 1950s and early '60s being the heyday of the typing pool. Anything from ten to a hundred women would sit together arched over their typewriter keys all day. Anne Henderson remembered working in the ABC Cinema typing pool in Holborn in the late 1950s:

It was a bit like being at school; there'd be about twelve girls in the pool, all sitting in rows with their typewriter on a desk in front of them. And the supervisor would be sitting in front of you like a schoolteacher would. It was very strict. You couldn't talk to the girl sitting next to you; you couldn't smoke and you couldn't eat. You would go up and collect your work in a folder, take it back to your desk, type it, take it back to the supervisor and then she would check it. If it was no good you'd have to collect it and do your mistakes. If that happened we'd all sort of moan and groan and pull faces. It was very boring work.

As always, new machinery created work but also took work away from established craftsmen and women. The ledger machine replaced the old ledger clerk. The dictating machine reduced the need for shorthand. The calculating machine cut down the time spent on sums and accounts, previously a source of pride for the clerk. And the first photocopying machines reduced the need for a lot of copying work. This spelt the end of the era of the pen-pushing male clerk who had occupied such an important place in the pre-war office, and closed down the big typing pools.

But office work was growing. Up to 1961, the 'typical' London worker was employed in a factory or workshop: just over 1.5 million men and women comprising just over a third of the entire workforce. By 1966 the 'typical' London employee worked in an office: again, just over 1.5 million workers and just over a third of the workforce.

Another radical change within the ranks of office workers was that whereas in the pen-pushing days of the clerk men had outnumbered women, by the early 1960s there were six women to every four men in offices in the capital. Women were preferred to men for a number of reasons. The new office work was less skilled and complex than before and this type of repetitive work – according to the prejudices of the time – was thought to suit women far more than men. Also, in the days before the Equal Pay Act, women could be employed much more cheaply than men. Women office workers were paid around two-thirds of the rate paid to men for doing the same job. Yet, despite this, more and more young women wanted to do office work. Many girls who were now enjoying a higher standard of education at London's new secondary modern and comprehensive schools saw working in offices as more comfortable and interesting than going into service or working in shops or factories.

The growing army of fashion-conscious young women recruited into offices became pioneers of a new, less formal office style. In the past, many women had had to wear sober-coloured suits or even overalls in the office. Now they began to dress more as they pleased, confident that no one would reprimand them for fear of losing their services – such was the demand for women office workers in London, as Anne Henderson recalled:

> We used to wear very flared skirts with can-can petticoats underneath, and the more petticoats you had the better it was, so you'd be walking out dressed like someone on 'Come Dancing'. If anyone had tried to stop us wearing the clothes we wanted we would have changed our jobs – just left, gone down to the agency and said we'd lost our job; there was no sort of nastiness about getting the sack or saying that

you'd walked out in those days. They'd have sent you off for a couple of other interviews the same morning; you'd be in another job by the afternoon. It was as easy as that!

The old formal office way of life was beginning to break down. The trendiest office workers spent their lunchtimes jiving and twisting to the latest sounds at places like the Lyceum ballroom in the Strand. It opened from 12 to 2 pm on weekdays and hundreds of teenagers paid a shilling a session to escape into this noisy and exciting world of pop culture. Anne Henderson was one of them:

> We really used to look forward to the lunch hours because that was the time when we used to go jiving. As soon as the lunch hour came round we would rush into the loo, get more petticoats on, backcomb the hair up another four inches, put the black lines on the eyes, fourteen-inch points on the feet and we'd be straight over the Lyceum. Jiving at the Lyceum was really the highlight of our day because the work that we were doing was so boring and this was the one thing that we really wanted to do. They would play records by Buddy Holly or Eddie Cochran or Bill Haley, and we used to dance with other girls. The girls didn't dance with the fellers because they used to stand around the side looking Teddy Boy-ish. We'd rehearse elaborate routines beforehand and then we'd do all our steps and it would have to be absolutely perfect, and then we'd sit down and wait for the next record to come up that we'd practised to. Sometimes we might be ten or fifteen minutes late getting back to the office but usually nobody said anything.

Many Victorian conventions were swept away in a wave of informality of dress and manners. The late 1960s were the era of the dolly-bird secretary with her miniskirt and heavy make-up. Companies wanting to promote a glamorous image encouraged this trend by advertising for secretaries who were 'attractive, sophisticated and vivacious', and temporary secretarial agencies like Girl Friday and Brook Street Bureau which sprang up everywhere often catered for this demand. Not all secretaries, however, were of the 'dolly-bird' breed and not all companies wanted to employ them. Banks and insurance companies in the City remained far more traditional in their attitudes than the new advertising agencies and television companies in the West End.

Nevertheless, during the sixties the image of the secretary changed from being functional to glamorous, and most men were happy to encourage this trend. The dolly-bird secretary was the latest male executive toy: an office wife to tend to business and personal needs and the greatest office status symbol that a man could possess. And the new office prosperity allowed many thousands of men in London, right down to junior management level, to employ their own secretary for the first time.

The dolly-bird secretary made the office a more erotic place than it had ever been before and one interesting consequence of this was the need for modification of office furniture to accommodate scantily dressed secretaries. Open-fronted desks and tables had become particularly fashionable in London but they now presented a new hazard for women office workers. Many complained that men were ogling their legs and looking up their miniskirts as they sat at their desks. By popular demand, a protective panel called the 'modesty board' came into vogue in the sixties. Val Hill remembered how important they were:

> I worked in an office with lots of young girls all about my age and we all wore very short skirts – it would have been rather odd not to have done – and some of them were in very bright colours. This caused embarrassment for some of the men and excitement for others. Some of them couldn't stop staring at your legs. So we had modesty boards arranged on all the desks, which covered us in nicely – not just the front but the sides – and all in all we were quite satisfied with this; everyone was happy. It became one of the perks of a job; you not only asked for a rather good salary and an electric typewriter, but also modesty boards. And if there were no modesty boards then you might renegotiate the salary.

While most male bosses welcomed – or at least accepted – miniskirts, the fashion for trousers worn by women met a quite different response. Women who wore them were reprimanded for being untidy or unfeminine. Despite this, the rules were defied and trousers became popular among women office workers because they were convenient and warm in the winter. Inspired by the new liberalism of the sixties and the beginnings of modern feminism, small rebellions were staged by women in offices in different parts of London to win their right to wear trousers. Val Hill remembered one such revolt in the Associated Television (ATV) offices at Marble Arch:

Having argued that minis were acceptable as office clothes, we went on to trousers and trouser suits. I remember once a dreadful hoo-ha about this, and memos being sent round saying that trousers would no longer be tolerated in the office worn by women. But, of course, men could always wear them. This made me very angry and everyone else very angry and so we got together and said, 'Right! We'll all come in wearing trousers and see what happens'. Jobs were plentiful then so if we were dismissed it didn't matter too much, we'd just go next door and there'd be another office ready to employ us. So we all came in trousers which I think were fairly smart; they weren't jeans. And nothing very much happened. There were a few tuttings but they seemed to be ignored. And a short while later we had another memo, individually sent to each one of us, which said it was all right for women to wear trousers in the office as long as they were not of a jean material or of a lewd nature. And we felt we'd won our case.

During the 1960s men's appearance and manners in the office were also changing quite dramatically. This was the time when more adventurous dressers wore shocking-pink shirts and suede shoes to work. The bowler hat looked ridiculous with the new longer hairstyles and the more colourful ties, shirts and suits that were becoming fashionable. Along with more informal dress came less formal manners, as Dundas Hamilton remembered:

I think in the sixties dress became less formal. I know I certainly hadn't worn my black jacket and my striped trousers for some time, and I gave up my bowler. I still carried my umbrella on wet days, but the lightweight suit that came in and the more relaxed type of dress – the soft shirt with the striped collar – all meant that the bowler never really looked quite in place any more. And when people's hair grew longer the bowler was really totally out of place. This was sad in a way because you used to be able to stand at the end of London Bridge and see what was like a colony of seals coming towards you, bobbing along in the morning – all identical black heads. That disappeared. I think also there was a greater relaxation in one's attitude and one's relations with staff. Previously one would call both one's equals and one's employees by their surname; if a person was on a par with you you called him Smith or Jones, or you might call one of your lowest servants Smith or Jones. In the sixties that changed. The Christian name term, which had only been used for closest friends before, became much more widespread. You started to call most people by their Christian names and – surprise – your staff began to call you by your Christian name, so the old disciplinarian rigidity faded out.

The established office lunchtime watering holes such as Lyons Corner Houses with their sit-down meals and waitress service were now unable to accommodate the rise in the number of workers. Their rather formal atmosphere was anyway becoming unfashionable. What the new office workers wanted was food they could buy cheaply with a minimum of waiting around. To cater for this, sandwich bars began to open up all over central London in the sixties, many of them started by Italians who were keen to run their own small catering businesses.

A perk for office workers had been the introduction in 1954 of the luncheon voucher, issued to employees as a kind of bonus by companies that did not have their own canteens. A private venture, the luncheon voucher scheme was given government backing as firms buying them and issuing them to their workers were given tax breaks and exemptions from National Insurance payments. In 1956 nine of the largest catering companies, including Joe Lyons, bought out the scheme.

THE ARRIVAL OF THE TRAFFIC WARDEN

The booming office economy that drew millions of commuters into London inevitably created some problems, notably traffic congestion. The more affluent employees who owned cars drove to work, jamming the roads and creating parking problems. The 'company car', a perk for top managers, made matters even worse than they might otherwise have been. As the company car counted as a business expense there were tax advantages in offering them to thousands of executives who would now drive to work without paying any fares or for petrol.

London's satellite towns and outer suburbs such as Croydon, Ealing and Wembley did not escape the traffic jams as many offices moved out of the central areas. Until the late 1970s, national policy was still to divest the centre of London of office employment and the Location of Offices Bureau had shifted 150,000 jobs to places like Croydon by 1978. It seemed that the whole London region might grind to a standstill as rush-hour traffic led to terrible snarl-ups every morning and evening.

There had been some parking restrictions from the 1920s but in 1958 the first parking meters were installed in London in Manchester Square, Westminster, and the first traffic wardens hit the streets in the sixties, recruited to ease pressure on the police, who were in charge of traffic control. The anger and frustration of motorists combined with the inexperience and insecurity of traffic wardens, fighting to establish a new position of authority, were an explosive mixture. Tom Cook was one of London's first traffic wardens. He recalled:

In those days we often put ourselves over as fierce NCO types. We saw it as a war – us against them, us against the motorists. We didn't smile; we didn't want to know people or listen to their excuses; the attitude was to gaze into the middle distance. We were scared of being conned. If someone broke down and they were genuine we'd think, 'He's kidding'. The reason we did this, I think, was because we were something new and I suppose we thought that we wouldn't be accepted, and that we had to take a hard line or people wouldn't take any notice of us. In those days lots of motorists didn't really accept our right to book them. If we'd had a policeman's uniform it would have been all right. But we didn't, so people were even more aggressive towards us than they'd normally be.

We took minor assault as part of the job. I patrolled Soho, which meant that I was always going to have more than my fair share of problems because it was quite a rough area in those days. I had an orange hit me on the face thrown from eight storeys up – walnuts, stones, the lot. Once I was cornered in an alleyway by a doorman about eight foot wide and thought that was the end of me, but he changed his mind after I thought he was going to do me in. Another time I *was* assaulted; I was booking someone and he threw me against a wall. As I landed on the floor a policeman came round the corner and I thought, 'Good, we'll prosecute!' But there was a traffic warden opposite and he came over and knocked the bloke out. We couldn't do anything about him then.

The spate of office building unleashed in 1951 by the Conservative government came to an abrupt end in 1964 with the return to power of

Labour. New legislation at first banned, then strictly controlled, office building in the whole of Greater London. Devised by George Brown, in charge of the new Department of Economic Affairs, the so-called 'Brown Ban' put the brakes on large-scale office developments in the capital until the end of the 1960s.

A new era of office decentralization was beginning. Companies and government departments wanting to expand had to move out of London altogether. This was government policy, and it led the way, relocating 50,000 Civil Service jobs in provincial towns such as Doncaster, Newcastle and Swansea. Private businesses, banks and insurance companies which moved away from London stayed much closer to the capital, colonizing the outer suburbs and market towns in the Home Counties around 30 miles from London.

A new kind of office began to take shape on greenfield sites in these outer areas. They were huge and in some cases came to dominate the economies of the places they settled, so that in the Home Counties there were 'one-company' towns. Typical was the Sun Alliance company's development at Horsham, Sussex, which moved there from the City in 1964. The giant 'office factory' employed up to a thousand people, most of whom were button pushers in low-grade jobs. Sun Alliance and other companies making the same kind of move generally retained a head office in central London staffed by the more senior managers and executives.

Work at the Horsham office factory was dominated by the computer. The skilled staff members were practically all men, while women were overwhelmingly used to do the routine work as computer clerks and punch-card operators. An old division of labour, in which men took the highly paid careers jobs and women did the lowly paid dead-end work, was usually replicated in these out-of-town offices. And as there were more unskilled jobs to be done, so more women were recruited to work in them. In the 1960s there was a big increase in women working in offices, largely because of mothers and housewives over thirty-five who were going back to work. They were thought by office employees to be especially suitable because they were likely to be hard workers with few career aspirations. Many suburban housewives who had been housebound found either part- or full-time work in these new offices close to where they lived. Travelling to work was easy and shopping and housework (now slightly less time-consuming thanks to new labour-saving devices) could be dovetailed into the day.

But women who had once enjoyed careers felt frustrated at the routine nature of their work even if they welcomed the chance to get away from the routines of domesticity. Margaret Dent who was formerly an executive officer in the Civil Service remembered becoming one of the first computer clerks at Sun Alliance's Horsham offices:

> After I got married I never thought I would go back to work; it wasn't the done thing then. If you did it was very humiliating for the man because it was thought that your husband couldn't support you. Attitudes had changed by the sixties and when my children were all at school I thought I'd try for a part-time job. I longed to do something to get out of the house and I liked the idea of having my own money. But I had mixed feelings about the job I got. On the one hand, it was lovely to get away from the home and to earn my own money and it was very convenient being so close. But, on the other hand, the work itself was rather boring. It took them about five minutes to train you for the job, just filling out computer cards, then they told you to get on with it. Nobody told you what the end product was, what you were doing it for. One longed to do something that one had been educated for.

HEATHROW AIRPORT

One outer London development that both created jobs on the fringe of the capital and boosted the demand for office space in the centre was the creation of Heathrow airport. The large, open site had been owned by Fairey Aviation and was used as an aerodrome for test flights before the war. In 1944 the RAF had taken it over to develop into a large military airfield. However, when the war ended this was no longer needed. At the time Croydon was the main airport for the capital, but the Heathrow site was much more suitable for expansion because there was little in the way of suburban development around it. Formally designated London Airport in 1946, Heathrow was at first makeshift, with customs, inspection, immigration and refreshments all housed in a short row of marquees and caravans. As late as 1950, a year in which 37,000 planes and over half a million passengers passed through Heathrow, there were still no permanent airport buildings.

There was a desperate shortage of aircraft at this time, which meant that many old planes formerly used in the war were commandeered for service. Airlines had always geared themselves to first-class travel, equal to that of a transatlantic liner, and the most luxurious planes boasted powder rooms, cocktail bars and promenade decks. In the austerity years, however, these standards were impossible to maintain and business flights from London Airport became incredibly primitive. Ron Bradburn remembered being a young air steward at the time:

> For the passengers at Heathrow there were just two marquee-type
> tents – one was for the customs and the other was for the passenger
> lounge and booking-in area. The primitiveness initially was such that,
> basically, all that was available was a few chairs in the passenger
> lounge, and a trestle table with a tablecloth, an urn of tea and cups and
> saucers on it. The inside of the passenger lounge was also very
> primitive in furnishings; the floors were laid down with coconut
> matting. Later on they introduced a small bar where people could sit
> and have a drink before take-off. The passengers had to walk across
> duckboards spread over muddy fields to get to the aircraft.
>
> At the end of the war there were very few planes around for
> commercial use, and so when BOAC wanted to start up very quickly
> to assist companies in London to do their business abroad once again,
> they had to use various military aircraft. The first ones that we used
> were DC3s, commonly known as Dakotas. These were totally
> unfurnished inside. There were sixteen seats, virtually bolted to the
> floor, no curtains, no carpet – nothing like that inside.
>
> As far as the flying itself was concerned there was no pressurization
> and, because of this, the aircraft had to fly below 10,000 feet – above
> that there's no oxygen. When there was bad weather the plane was
> thrown about all over the sky and naturally many people were sick. In
> fact, we had what we knew as 'puke bags' or 'honk bags' for passengers
> to be sick in. Frequently I was sick myself trying to sort out soup,
> coffee, and God knows what, at the back of the aircraft where the tail
> was swinging backwards and forwards all over the place.
>
> The facilities for the passengers were minimal. There was a toilet
> on board at the rear of the aircraft and this was a straightforward
> chemical-type toilet, with no flush. And there was also a urinal 'pee
> tube' as we called it. This was a tube linked to the outside of the

aircraft with a funnel on the end. You dangled what you had to dangle in the funnel, always being careful not to go too far because there was a suction element in the tube and, if you went too deep, the effect was like pulling a cork out of a bottle!

Despite these primitive conditions, however, air travel proved to be hugely popular. Each year the number of passengers rose astronomically: from 1.2 million in 1953 and 2.7 million in 1955 to 5.3 million in 1960, by which time Gatwick had been designated the second London airport.

The airports themselves with airline employees, ground staff and associated warehousing and hotels created a huge number of jobs: 26,000 by 1958. Now much expanded with new terminals, Heathrow employs 70,000 people, while an estimated 200,000 jobs nationally are related to its activities. With nearly 68 million passengers a year it is the busiest airport in the world for international travel.

While Heathrow was rapidly growing in importance Ted Heath's new Conservative government, elected in 1970, swept away most of the controls on office building in London brought in by the 'Brown Ban'. But this time the developers and the planners were not given the same easy ride they had enjoyed in the 1950s. A well-informed and forceful conservation movement had arisen in opposition to the destruction of so much of Victorian London in favour of drably designed office blocks. A notorious episode in those conservation battles concerned British Rail's demolition of the magnificent Euston Arch to make way for the modernization of Euston Station, incorporating new offices.

THE CONSERVATIONISTS FIGHT BACK

To begin with, the protests were voiced by a few architects or literary figures like John Betjeman, but by the early 1970s the conservation movement had become genuinely popular and radical, its aims broadening from protecting threatened buildings to saving whole communities whose future was thought to be at risk from redevelopment plans. This had happened during the 1960s in places like Euston Square where tenants, small businesses and shops were dispossessed and dispersed with little or no compensation. Now people were determined that this kind of thing should not happen again and they united to resist new developments.

Perhaps the most famous conservation battle was fought over plans to develop Covent Garden. When the long-awaited removal of the fruit and vegetable market to Nine Elms in Vauxhall was finally scheduled to go ahead in the early 1970s, the Greater London Council (GLC) came up with an ambitious development plan to replace the old buildings with new offices, shops and homes for displaced residents. Those who lived and worked in Covent Garden, as well as a group of architects who were horrified at the planned destruction of the nineteenth-century market building, formed the Covent Garden Community Association. One of its leading figures was printer John Toomey, who remembered:

> A group of local people heard of this horrific plan. We got together
> and a public meeting was called in the Kingsway Hall, and that is how
> it all started on 1 April 1971. And to our amazement six hundred people
> turned up for that meeting, so it gave you the feeling that people
> wanted to keep Covent Garden. They didn't want it turned into office
> blocks and skyscrapers and have conference centres put up in its place.
> Well, we got the people together and we marched; we held candle-lit
> processions over to County Hall; we went to Parliament; we met MPs
> – the Minister of the Environment and people like that – to fight our
> case for Covent Garden because we loved Covent Garden.

The campaign was a triumph for the conservation movement in the capital – the government bowed to local pressure by listing many of the existing buildings in Covent Garden, and the GLC scrapped its redevelopment plan. But it also proved to be a turning point in new office building in London. For a long time after this, developers were more restricted in their scope and had to show more respect for historic London than they had in the past.

A world economic recession which set in in 1973 put the brakes on major office development schemes, and a number of property development companies went bust due to the dramatic increase in interest rates. The era of the dolly-bird secretary also came more or less to an end, the recession forcing many companies to make cuts, the first of which was the personal secretary – the gift of the 1960s to junior and middle management. In central London the office space occupied by an office secretary was estimated at £8,000 a year in rental alone, so from the late 1970s onwards most managers had to share their secretary with other colleagues. New equal rights legislation putting a stop to the blatantly sexist advertisements for attractive secretaries also led to the dolly-bird secretary's disappearance.

By the mid-1980s there was a general assumption that London's office workforce, now becoming dependent on computers and electronic technology, would remain stable or possibly shrink a little. The Square Mile of the City was jam-packed, its former warehousing and retailing mostly taken over for office space. There was no question of anyone knocking down the West End of London to make way for office blocks, though some City financiers had begun to move there and to Marylebone well to the west of the old Square Mile.

DOCKLAND REVIVAL

However, to the east of the City, all along the snake of the Thames, lay the dereliction of the old docklands. There were many attempts to find a workable plan for redeveloping this vast region, but they all faltered because the local authorities and pressure groups of residents and businesses wanted to retain its working-class character with new manufacturing industry and social housing. But this could only work if industry wanted to move in and governments wanted to invest huge sums in housing schemes for which there might be no accompanying jobs. At a time when industry had been leaving London steadily, the old docklands hardly looked attractive. Transport was hopeless without good rail and road links.

There had been one relatively small-scale success story. St Katharine Docks just downriver of Tower Bridge had been closed in 1969. The Port of London Authority sold them to the Greater London Council for the bargain price of £1.25 million – a 24-acre site hard by the Tower of London. A competition for their redevelopment was won by the construction company Taylor Woodrow who built there a large hotel, boutiques and some luxury housing. They preserved dock warehouses and quaint cobbled walkways and soon St Katharine Docks were a thriving tourist attraction offering a kind of 'historic' docklands experience with trips on the river in a red-sailed barge along with very modern facilities. However, dockland councils and pressure groups were not enthusiastic: schools, theatres and local provision shops were dropped from the scheme and social housing was a long time arriving. To those wanting to preserve the former character of the docklands this was a disaster. As it turned out, it was also the future.

Though a few million pounds were spent filling in the abandoned docks, there was a stalemate on development plans until the arrival in 1979 of Margaret Thatcher as Prime Minister. Determined to reverse the apparent decline in the British economy, she took a cue or two from America: she introduced the notion of public-private partnerships and put her faith in the vigour of profit-making enterprise freed from planning controls. Whereas those activists who had opposed the comprehensive redevelopment of Covent Garden could be confident the old buildings would be quickly occupied by new businesses in that prime central London location, this was not the case in the docklands. It had to be substantially redeveloped if it was to be revived at all.

Two major measures introduced by the Thatcher government broke the docklands development deadlock. New legislation made possible the creation of a London Docklands Development Corporation (LDDC), set up in 1981 in the teeth of fierce local opposition. And on the Isle of Dogs a novel 'Enterprise Zone' was created with huge incentives for any companies moving in. The LDDC, run by leading businessmen, had charge of 5,120 acres of mostly derelict London with the power to buy land, build roads and railways and, in short, to lay the foundations that might entice new enterprises to move in without interference from other planning authorities.

At first, the LDDC tried to attract a range of businesses to the Isle of Dogs, selling off land cheaply. A drift eastwards of newspapers, including the *Daily Telegraph*, began an exodus that would take away from London's Fleet Street its long association with national journalism. In a last-ditch battle with the print unions, *The Times*, published by News International, was relocated in 1988 to the docklands behind such tight security gates that it became known as Fortress Wapping. But the first efforts of the LDDC to attract companies to the Isle of Dogs were not notably successful.

The creation in 1982 of the Enterprise Zone made the difference. Originally intended simply as a region free of rates and with generous tax breaks, in the end the Isle of Dogs scheme involved government subsidies to companies moving in. The LDDC decided to entice companies away from the City of London: some sizeable new blocks of offices and flats were put up on the old waterfront at South Quay Plaza and Heron Quays, before the defining project – the mountainous Canary Wharf development – got under way. As late as the 1950s, dockers had called the walkways of the old West India dock where the new building arose 'blood alley', as the West

Indies sugar they unloaded was so abrasive it cut their hands. However, working conditions would be much pleasanter for the 40,000 people who could be accommodated in the proposed 8.8 million square feet (820,000 sq m) of offices at Canary Wharf. The scheme was pushed through without any public scrutiny, so eager was the government to show how vigorous private enterprise could succeed where careful planning failed.

The developers were three American banks and a Texan called G. Ware Travelstead who became known as G. Whizz and was soon on his way back to his home state, leaving the project to the Canadian development company Olympia & York. A proposed light railway connecting the City with docklands was extended to Canary Wharf, as was the Jubilee Line. Finally, it seemed, docklands was taking off. However, there were the inevitable booms and busts that plague all ambitious development projects. The City, still an independent planning authority (no government ever dared meddle too much with it), saw the dockland development as a threat to its traditional monopoly of financial services. Whereas it had been conservative in its approach to new office space in the early 1980s, it now changed the rules to lure the speculators in, raising the former height limit on buildings. Between 1985 and 1989 the City added 16.5 million square feet (1,532,000 sq m) to its office space compared with the 2.6 million square feet (241,000 sq m) added in the LDDC area.

This was the era of the so-called 'Big Bang' in the City, old practices governing the sale of stocks and shares were swept away under pressure from rival financial centres in the new electronic age. In October 1986 the final stage in the transformation of the City – the deregulation of the Stock Exchange – had the champagne corks flying in the old Square Mile, though nobody really knew what the result would be.

As it happened, London as a financial centre was not only confirmed but enhanced as foreign finance houses gobbled up old firms in a feeding frenzy. London was no longer the imperial capital and had lost the largest river port of the industrial age, but it had been transformed into a powerful international centre. A study by Anthony King of the names London firms were giving themselves in 1920 compared with 1985 was very revealing. At the earlier date 149 firms had Imperial or Empire in their titles while only 118 chose International, World or Global. By 1985, however, only 102 firms still had the Imperial tag, whereas 662 were Global and another 348 European.

In the early 1990s a financial crash looked like it might undermine the new prosperity in the City and docklands. A great deal of office space stood empty, no fewer than 650 property companies went bust and the City workforce fell by 90,000. In 1992, Olympia & York, which had been the world's wealthiest property company and which was due to make a payment for the Jubilee Line extension, went into liquidation. The office vacancy rate at Canary Wharf was over 40 per cent and the LDDC got rid of 40 per cent of its staff. But then, in the first years of this twenty-first century, docklands revived. Anyone who had known it in the 1980s could not fail to be astonished by its transformation.

The Museum in Docklands housed in one of the original West India warehouses is now set in a region of bustling modernity with cafés and bars beneath the great tower of Canary Wharf. All along the riverside are blocks of flats, somehow more reminiscent of some kind of upmarket Riviera development than London and there are many who deplore the architecture. The City of London, will still not be outdone by the new dockland, for in 2004 the first really high-rise building to tower over the Square Mile appeared. Designed by the architect Norman Foster, its extraordinary shape and the greenish tinge of the windows earned it the nickname 'the Gherkin', which has stuck. It is now a true London landmark and recently put up for sale by the finance company Swiss Re.

London is now a global city and the majority of its workforce is housed in offices rather than factories or warehouses. This has been true of the City for a long time, but it represents a complete transformation for the docklands region. Redevelopment checked the steep decline in employment in the region and brought tens of thousands of jobs to boroughs like Tower Hamlets. But they are not the jobs that the traditional workforce were trained to do. Nor is most of the housing affordable for anyone earning less than a City salary. But the regeneration of the area has been a huge factor in one of the most remarkable developments in London over the past twenty years. The population of inner London, which had been in decline since the early twentieth century and which plummeted during and just after the war, began to grow again.

The chassis production line at the Associated Equipment Company (AEC) in Southall in l951 when business was booming and they, with Park Royal BodyBuilders, turned out buses and trucks that were sold around the world.

A London built double decker bus on a route in Kuala Lumpa, Malaysia, in the 1950s. The same distinctive buses were a familiar sight just after the Second World War in South Africa and in Melbourne and Adelaide in Australia.

Putting memories of wartime and the Blitz behind them Londoners enjoyed the delights of the Festival of Britain in 1951 with bright lights and firework displays. Herbert Morrison, London politician and wartime Minister said that with the festival Britain was giving itself a 'pat on the back'.

Stevenage station is re-named SILKINGRAD in a 1946 protest at the Labour Government's plan to designate it a New Town to provide homes for Londoners. Lewis Silkin was in charge of Town and Country Planning and his high-handed manner struck Stevenage locals as 'Stalinist'.

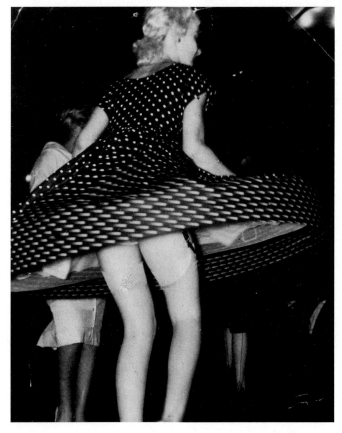

While the government encouraged Londoners to leave the capital, for young people it was the most exciting place to be, even in the 1950s. This girl is jiving in a night club: the photographer appears to be down on all fours!

Despite their spirited resistance, the people of Stevenage were forced to accept the building of a New Town which disturbed their rustic peace. For many Londoners there was the opportunity to enjoy a new life and they felt their right to be there had arrived when Her Majesty opened the new Town Centre in 1959.

A new office world arose in London in the 1950s and was to dominate the capital by the 1970s. These young women are jiving at the Lyceum Ballroom during a lunch break in 1957.

When London's industries were booming in the 1950s they provided for their staff a whole way of life. Tate & Lyle, the sugar refiners, had Saturday nights out in which there would be events for children, dancing and, pictured here, cabaret.

Terence Conran with some of his early designs at an exhibition held in Simpson's of Piccadilly in 1952. The founder of the Habitat shops, he revolutionised home furnishing and was a 'mover and shaker' from the 1960s onwards. He was knighted in 1983.

A group of Mods (short for Modernists) with their smart suits and scooters pictured in the early 1960s. In its various manifestations, Mod Culture dominated London fashion until the 1970s.

Before the Clean Air Act of 1956 took effect, London was swathed in thick fog for periods every winter and everything was covered in a sooty grime. This photograph was taken in November 1953 in a fog which claimed many lives.

Carnaby Street, the Mecca of Mod Fashion pictured here in the summer of 1967. The year before the American magazine *Time* had called London 'The Swinging City' adding: 'In a decade dominated by youth, London has burst into bloom. It swings, it is the scene.'

Smartly dressed West Indian families arriving at Victoria Station in 1956 after crossing the Atlantic on an ocean liner docking at Southampton. After the war the Labour government awarded all in the Commonwealth British citizenship though recruitment of skilled Eastern Europeans was favoured at the time to combat the labour shortages.

Mary Quant, dubbed Madame Miniskirt, on a promotional trip to Rome in 1967. She was attending the Press conference for the opening of a Pop Shop in Rome's Via Marutta. Swinging London was vigorously exported by Quant and others.

The happy pioneer 'gentrifier' Harvey Sherlock (right) who bought two run down houses in Islington back in 1952 when the area had not yet begun to come up in the world. Guests at his house-warming party were given picks and shovels to knock the two houses into one.

Families coming to England from the West Indies in the 1950s and 1960s hoped for good jobs and prosperity but many found it hard to get by and rented accommodation was often in very poor condition and very expensive.

OUT WITH AEC
IN WITH HONDA

LEYLAND

AEC

WE WERE
THE GREATEST

THE LAST ONE
1979
R. I. P.

Jack Ailsby, former AEC worker, tempering bitterness with humour when his company, bought up by British Leyland in the 1960s was closed down completely by 1981 with the loss of 3,500 jobs. London lost tens of thousands of jobs in manufacturing from the 1970s onwards.

Asian refugees arriving in London with their worldly belongings after they had been expelled from Kenya in 1968. Many Indians had migrated to Africa in the days of the British Empire to work in the colonial service.

The London Eye, revolving almost imperceptibly slowly on the South Bank of the Thames, is a fitting symbol for the modern capital as a tourist attraction rather than a manufacturer of goods. Behind it is the old County Hall once the seat of London government.

CHAPTER TWENTY-TWO

Moving Out

WHEN, ON 20 April 1959, Her Majesty the Queen opened the new centre of Stevenage, a town in Hertfordshire 30 miles from the centre of London, most of the cheering, flag-waving residents had been born and bred in places like Tottenham, Hornsey and Islington. They were among the million or so Londoners who had moved out to set up home in the Home Counties. Alf Luhman, one of Stevenage New Town's earliest residents, moved there from Tottenham in 1952 and remembered being one of those cheering Her Majesty when she unveiled a commemorative plaque in the town centre:

> I think it meant to Stevenage that at last we were recognized. The town was no longer a building site, but a real town and the Queen had come and granted us a charter so to speak, and everybody in Stevenage who had worked so hard to see the town grow felt that it was an honour. At that time we were still very much Londoners, we were visiting at least two or three times a month and we used to go up at weekends to see our family. But with the Queen coming I think we started to throw that off.

While the 1920s and '30s had seen a mass movement from the centre of London to newly built semi-detached suburbs, the post-war exodus was to places out of town altogether. This came about in response to government policies aimed at bringing London's population down to what planners regarded as a healthy size and, as it turned out, more significantly, a spontaneous diaspora from the fog-bound capital.

Just before the war in 1939 London's population had peaked at 8.5 million. The blitz and the evacuation to escape the bombing began a decline which carried on after the war and was to continue until 1988 when it had fallen to just 6.73 million. To the surprise of the planners the capital's population then began to rise again, and is expected to go on doing so in the first half of this century. Government policy and that of London's Mayor Ken Livingstone are now in favour of a growing metropolis – a complete reversal of the view of politicians and planners for long after the end of the war.

The wartime government was already planning to offer Londoners the possibility of a new life in the Home Counties while the doodlebugs were still raining down on the capital. It appointed Patrick Abercrombie (Britain's most eminent planner) who, in 1944, published the *Greater London Plan*, providing a blueprint for the post-war reconstruction of the London area. Abercrombie envisaged a million people moving out in ten years as part of a wholesale dispersal of population and industry from central and suburban London. A ring of ten new satellite towns would be built 20–30 miles away from the capital, each housing between 30,000 and 60,000 people.

The Abercrombie plan was seized upon by the Labour government elected in 1945 as it offered an immediate solution to London's housing crisis and a vision of a better future for all. Social engineering on this scale had never before been seen in Britain. Prime Minister Clement Attlee appointed Lewis Silkin as chief of the new Ministry of Town and Country Planning, with a brief to implement the new town policy as quickly as possible.

The site that was destined to be the prototype for the first generation of new towns was the small, thriving agricultural town of Stevenage. It was recommended in Abercrombie's plan and was particularly attractive to planners because it was situated on the Great North Road and on the main London to Newcastle railway line. Early in 1946 there were rumours among locals that Stevenage was to be chosen as the first new town and these were confirmed when in April of that year the postman delivered letters informing 178 residents that their property was to be compulsorily purchased by the Ministry of Town and Country Planning.

The government had assumed there would be little resistance to the new town plan, but they were quickly proved wrong. What became known as 'the battle for Stevenage' was about to begin. Angry locals, including many farmers who wanted to keep Stevenage as it was, formed a militant Residents' Protection Association.

THE BATTLE OF SILKINGRAD

Lewis Silkin first experienced the strength of local feeling when he visited Stevenage on 6 May 1946 to explain to locals why it had been chosen for what he called 'a daring exercise in town planning'. He was met by thousands of protesters and the town was festooned with posters saying, 'HANDS OFF OUR HOUSES!' and 'NO! NO! MR MINISTER!' At the meeting, he responded to barracking, saying, 'It's no good your jeering! It is going to be done!' Meanwhile, outside the Town Hall, saboteurs put sand in the petrol tank of Silkin's chauffeur-driven Wolseley and let the tyres down. The government and the Residents' Protection Association were on a collision course. If Silkin backed down then the whole new town policy would be in jeopardy. On the other hand, the homes and businesses of the Stevenage residents were at stake.

The government's strategy was to rush through a New Towns Act so that by August their policy became law and Silkin was able to issue a draft order designating Stevenage as London's first new town. The residents responded by demanding their right to a public inquiry to hear objections to the plan. As there was a unanimous local rejection of the new town and no government minister attended the inquiry to defend its action, it was assumed that the plan had been dropped. As it turned out, however, the government was so convinced its master plan was in the public interest it felt no need to justify its actions to the locals. On 11 November 1946 Stevenage New Town was officially designated and the Stevenage Development Corporation, a government-appointed body, was established to build and run it. Local protester Jack Franklin had an amusing, if futile, response:

A friend of mine coined the word 'Silkingrad', obviously after the Minister [Lewis Silkin] and we thought this was rather witty. And the three of us got together, two doctors' sons and myself, and we manufactured fake signs for the railway station and fake signposts saying 'Silkingrad'. We made these out of hardboard and cardboard and took a lot of trouble with them and then, one moonlit night in December (it was very frosty and a bit of snow was about) we put these signs up in the station. It was rather like a military operation, and we glued them on with aircraft glue and they looked quite official. I was on the top of a ladder putting a large Silkingrad sign over the booking hall when the local bobby turned up. I knew him quite well and he just wandered up, and I called down from the top of the ladder, 'Is your wife a good cook?' On being told that she was I said, 'If you look in the back of our van I think you might find a brace of pheasants.' That was the end of that. And we got these signs up and we'd tipped off the press and they came down post-haste next morning and it got in the national press in forty-eight hours. Even got in the American press!

Jack Franklin's father, a wealthy local farmer, took the government to the High Court and in February 1947 the order designating Stevenage as 'New Town' was quashed on the ground that it had overridden local objections. The celebrations of the locals were short-lived, however, for within a month the government had appealed against the decision and won. So Stevenage New Town was built after all. Over the next two years London's other new towns were designated and, although locals were often unhappy about the plans, there was no repeat of the fierce opposition put up by Stevenage: it was clear that resistance was useless. All over the Home Counties towns watched and waited to see if the planners would pick them out for development. Some breathed a sigh of relief when they learned that they were judged unsuitable. This was the case with Redbourn and Stapleford in Hertfordshire, Ongar and Margaretting in Essex, Meopham in Kent, Crowhurst and Holmwood in Surrey and White Waltham in Berkshire. The new towns to be built were, in order of designation, Crawley, Hemel Hempstead, Harlow, Hatfield, Welwyn Garden City, Basildon and Bracknell.

At Stevenage no permanent houses were built for over three years by the Stevenage Development Corporation. The only signs of activity were an information office and a team of surveyors who scurried around in Land Rovers inspecting the lie of the land. It had originally been predicted that by the beginning of 1951 Stevenage New Town would be housing over 30,000 Londoners, but when the time came the first families were still waiting to move in. There was a similar dearth of house building in the other new towns, for which Britain's heavy post-war debts and a shortage of building workers and materials were responsible.

Meanwhile, working-class Londoners were moving out to new council estates built by the London County Council (LCC) beyond the suburban fringe of the capital in places such as Oxhey and Borehamwood in Hertfordshire, and Debden and Harold Hill in Essex. They were similar in look and design to the cottage estates, such as those in Dagenham, built by the LCC between the wars. However, though the new post-war estates were a little more luxurious, with lavatories upstairs as well as down, they were 15–20 miles from the capital – too far out for many residents to commute to London and very expensive for those who did.

Abercrombie opposed the building of these new 'out-county' estates, on the grounds that they were perpetuating the interwar problems of suburban sprawl and class segregation. His vision, shared by many other planners and politicians in the post-war years, was much grander and more utopian. New towns were supposed to be not one-class suburbs but self-contained and balanced communities. Homes and jobs would be provided so that the newcomers could avoid the tiring and time-consuming business of commuting to work. A wide range of different classes would live side by side, workers next door to managers, who would share the same schools, churches and community centres.

This vision of social harmony in the new towns was embraced by post-war governments and by the staff of many development corporations. It was a curious mixture of utopian socialism and a rather backward-looking and paternalistic conservatism, well summed up by the Chairman of the Stevenage Development Corporation when he declared in 1947: 'We want to revive the social structure which existed in the old English villages, where the rich lived next door to the not-so-rich, and everyone knew everybody.' The contradictions in this philosophy would emerge in the 1950s when house building and industry in the new towns really took off.

If the new towns were to be self-contained and not just commuter dormitories they needed to attract industry and commerce that would provide jobs locally. Particularly sought after at the time were engineering and electronics, and the new towns competed to persuade companies to settle with them. If they were successful they needed to attract skilled or semi-skilled workers to take up the jobs created, which meant selecting the better trained and educated applicants from London. It was a rule in the new towns that you were not eligible for a council house unless you had a job. Inevitably therefore it was the better off who were able to take advantage of the better housing and living conditions in the new towns, while the poorest in the worst housing conditions in London were left behind. Some did manage to escape the slums, however. Alf and Anne Luhman remembered:

> Conditions were bad in London; we had no water at all and we used to share the tap with the landlady. We had to use the local baths for our own baths. There was a garden but we weren't allowed to use it.

There was no hope of bringing the children up under those conditions, they were growing up and getting bigger and as they got bigger so the conditions became worse automatically. We were desperate, so desperate in fact that because we were unable to be housed by both the council and the LCC, we decided the best thing to do was to up sticks and go to Australia. So I got myself a job and was ready to go out to Australia to ensure that the kids had a decent home. Well, at that time there was this hoo-ha with the Silkingrad business. I think it got in the news, and I said, 'Well, if they're going to build a new town in Stevenage thirty miles away I'll try it.' So, of course, I got on the train and came down here and got a job and was told that if I worked here for three or four months I'd get a house. And it was ideal; exactly what I wanted. So we sent all the papers back to Australia House and decided to come to Stevenage.

Anne Luhman:

I was thrilled with the home, it was really lovely – to think I had my own sink, my own bathroom, two toilets, one up and one down. I felt I was on holiday for months and months; the children thought it was great. There was a green dell at the side of us, and they just ran round and round. They felt free.

Londoners were generally very pleased with their new homes, though for many of them the interiors were rather *too* modern. Development Corporation architects on a mission to offer simple, functional design to ordinary families adopted an open-plan style getting rid of the Victorian 'front parlour' in favour of one large downstairs room. A study of the opinions of residents in Harlow New Town by sociologist Judy Attfield revealed that this innovation was very unpopular among families moving in, who would have preferred to keep the parlour as a kind of well-kept shrine for visitors, as it had always been. Finding themselves on show in picture-window living rooms, residents felt obliged to deck them out as tastefully as they could to make an impression on passers-by. The favourite status symbols of the 1950s were three- or even five-piece suites, television sets, bright carpets and the cocktail cabinet (which often remained empty because the proud owners could not afford to stock it). Hire purchase more often than not provided the funds for these furnishings.

The idealistic aim of integrating people from different classes in the new towns met with dogged resistance. Fundamental differences in language, culture and interests between the classes could not be wiped out by a few plans emanating from Development Corporation offices. It was originally thought that the simplest recipe for class mixing was to build larger houses for the middle classes in the same neighbourhood or even the same street as smaller houses for the working classes. However, by the mid-1950s it was clear that managers were simply not prepared to live next door to workers. Bigger houses in 'mixed' streets and neighbourhoods were very hard to let, and some remained unoccupied. In contrast, where a more exclusive one-class neighbourhood was developed, often next to a golf course or beauty spot, it quickly took off as a desirable place for professional people.

Very soon the idealism of development corporations in new towns like Stevenage and Crawley bowed to market forces and neighbourhoods became more and more custom-built for different classes. From the mid-1950s onwards choice plots of land were sold to private builders and, as home ownership among the middle classes boomed, the offer of an 'executive' home was the most effective way of attracting professional people into the new towns. Some of the better off chose to live in picturesque villages rather than in the new towns themselves, which had gained a reputation as characterless and boring places.

There was social climbing too. The more affluent and ambitious workers would, after a few years, often move into brand-new or bigger houses in newer neighbourhoods. As time went on, old neighbourhoods with lower rents (like Bedwell in Stevenage) were colonized by less well-paid workers and their families and some were regarded as 'problem estates'. By the late 1950s it was clear that the ideal of a classless new town community was no more than a utopian dream.

However, there was a flowering of community activism in the new towns, often led not by the middle classes, as might be assumed, but by working people. There was an almost complete lack of social facilities in the new towns in the early days. They had been starved of the resources they needed by the returning Conservative government elected in 1951. Although house building continued there was little money available for anything else, like schools, hospitals, shopping and community centres, roads, transport or street lighting. The first residents were shocked to find themselves marooned on gigantic building sites which, in the winter months, turned into a sea of mud, and they had to walk miles to the nearest shops, pubs and schools. A sense of loneliness and isolation, dubbed 'the New Town blues', descended on the first generation of newcomers. A few – less than one in a hundred – returned home, while the majority decided to stay and fight for better conditions.

A militant and successful Tenants' Association emerged in Stevenage to mount a series of demonstrations, marches and petitions to get things done. They fought for a school, a hospital, community centres, street lighting, better bus services, and the building of the Stevenage bypass, to prevent any more of the serious accidents resulting from the A1 running through the town. One celebrated cause was the campaign for a traffic-free town centre which, when it was completed in 1959, was the first pedestrianized shopping precinct of any size in Europe. Out of all these struggles emerged a strong community spirit. Michael Cotter, who went on to become one of the leaders of the Tenants' Association in the 1950s, recalled:

> We were determined to make it work. We had a nice home at last,
> just what we had always wanted, so we weren't going to give that up;
> we decided to fight for everything we needed. We weren't educated,
> we never spoke publicly, never had any dealings with people in
> authority; we just learnt it all as we went along. We discovered fairly
> early on it was no use being soft, they would not take any notice of us,
> so we started to take a hard line. There were no primary schools, no
> buses, no shops for miles. We didn't want it all in a few years' time; we
> wanted it now. We organized marches, mass meetings down in the
> town hall, all sorts of demonstrations. There was a great spirit that
> brought everyone together then, and the women were fantastic – they
> backed their husbands come hell or high water.

By 1959 the first generation of new towns had come of age and they had fulfilled at least some of the ambitions of the planners and politicians. They had established a strong foundation of successful industries; they offered more than enough jobs to satisfy those who lived in them; and they provided a high standard of housing, better than anything that most Londoners who moved out had ever known before. On top of this, they were by now beginning to make handsome profits from the renting of factory and office space to firms, and were proving to be one of Britain's most successful nationalized industries. More than 120,000 people were now living in London's new towns and most of them, like Alf Luhman in Stevenage, were pleased they had moved out:

It was the finest move we ever made; we had no regrets. We were able to raise our children in very good conditions. We had to struggle for things but when we got them they were brand new. We had brand-new schools and, again, we were fortunate because we were involved and helped to choose the headmasters and the teachers. And we were on the governing bodies and what have you, whereas if we'd been in London you never had that sort of opportunity. It all became a very close-knit family in those days, and everything we did was for the benefit of our kids. To us that was the most important thing.

As well as the new towns there were the so-called overspill or expanded towns that took in 30,000 Londoners. Under the 1952 Town Development Act, the LCC was able to rehouse Londoners assisted by government grants for housing and industry. This initiative was attractive to declining agricultural areas, and several East Anglian towns, like Haverhill, Thetford and Bury St Edmunds, received many families from the capital. Some Londoners went even further afield: the schemes farthest from London were in Swindon, Plymouth and Bodmin in the South West, and Grantham and Gainsborough in Lincolnshire. These expanded towns were planned like miniature new towns, and although they experienced some teething problems, most of the Londoners who moved out to them had few regrets.

When Abercrombie drew up his wartime plans he had envisaged an orderly dispersal of Londoners under government decree and controlled by the planners. What he, and those in power, had not bargained for, however, was an exodus not supervised in any way by the authorities. It was a spontaneous emigration from the capital and proved to be more significant than both the new town and overspill schemes put together. Around 200,000 Londoners just upped sticks in the 1950s and made for the Home Counties, without any invitation from a Development Corporation. In doing so they dumbfounded the planners, who imagined that they would be able to channel any mass movements to the places they had chosen for strategic reasons. The countryside immediately beyond the London suburbs was protected as a Green Belt in which private developers were prohibited from putting up housing or factories. Anyone moving beyond the Green Belt would be too far out to commute back into London. Or so it was believed. However, this assumption proved to be unfounded.

THE FLIGHT TO THE COUNTRYSIDE

For those in the best-paid office jobs, the work was in London and many were prepared to put up with long-distance commuting. Train services were improving to make this easier and there was a boom in London office work. Then the Conservatives ended restrictions on private house building and in the affluent 1950s some of the better-off families discovered they could afford to buy homes out of London. As a result new housing developments began to 'leapfrog' the Green Belt, as Londoners began to buy into villages and market towns in the Home Counties on an unprecedented scale. This invasion would transform the character of hundreds of villages in and beyond the Green Belt within commuting distance of the capital or the market towns, like Reading, where London's offices and industries were beginning to relocate. Farm mechanization and the drift from the land left many villages with dwindling populations. Middle-class families moved in from the early 1950s onwards, restoring run-down cottages or buying new detached homes built on the outskirts of villages. This colonization had begun during the interwar years, especially in Surrey, but it now advanced rapidly. The electrification of Eastern Region lines to Liverpool Street opened up many Essex villages to London commuters in the late 1950s.

Railways were important, but the single greatest impetus to the colonization of the Home Counties by affluent Londoners was the motor car. The number of private cars quadrupled in the London area between 1945 and 1960. They were faster and more reliable than ever before and there was a corresponding improvement in the road system. Many used their new car to travel direct to work in London. Frederick Keeble remembered commuting to his office in St James's Square from the picturesque Surrey village of West Horsley, where he and his family moved in 1955:

> I loved driving anyway and thirty miles each way a day wasn't too
> much for me – it only took about an hour. The only time that it was
> really tiresome was in the early days when we used to suffer from
> smog. On one occasion I was coming back and the fog was so thick at
> Raynes Park that everything was stationary for about an hour and a
> half, and passengers were wandering in front of cars with white
> handkerchiefs to lead them home. But usually it was very easy and
> when I came home in the evening the children, particularly in the

summer, were always out on the grass in the drive with their toy
tractors waiting to greet me and saying, 'How's everything gone?' and
they wanted me to take them out for a drive in the car.

Others became the first car–train commuters, driving from the village
to the railway station where they left their car for the day, then taking the
train to London and back. In one-car families it became customary for the
wife to drive the husband to the station and to pick him up in the evening.
Queues of cars with housewives at the wheel waiting for the homebound
commuter train from a London mainline station became a familiar sight in
station car parks throughout the Home Counties.

The motor car made once remote villages easily accessible, especially if
they were not too far from a railway station and a fast train to the city.
Typical was a place like Danbury in Essex, just 6 miles from Chelmsford,
in turn a thirty-minute railway journey from London's Liverpool Street
Station. Here the double garage soon became popular so that the husband
could drive himself to and from the station while the wife had her own run-
around for school and shopping trips. Practically all the new custom-built
detached homes put up in Danbury village from the late 1950s onwards had
a double garage.

Many of the post-war pioneers who settled in villages were young
middle-class couples who had been brought up in semi-detached suburbia
built between the wars. To their parents the new homes had seemed
luxurious and semi-rural. But to the children of this suburbia, semi-
detached London could appear drab, increasingly urban and choked with
traffic. There was a desire to escape further into the countryside to enjoy
the peace and tranquillity that the suburbs were rapidly losing. Village life
seemed particularly idyllic to couples with small children or those about to
start families. Valerie Keeble recalled:

> The thing that most appealed to us about village life was getting
> away from the crowds and the noise and the congestion of London.
> We liked the idea of there being fields and farmland around. And,
> most important, we wanted the children to enjoy the country life. We
> wanted them to have space to run around without coming up to a
> fence, and to throw a ball and not find it in next door's garden. The
> garden was a great excitement for the children – watching boughs of
> trees coming down and helping stack logs, and gathering fruits in

summertime, helping father pack it away for the winter. And when we got mechanized garden equipment, of course, they had a whale of a time. They were able to sit on my husband's lap and ride on a tractor and trailer when we cut the grass in the orchard, and they had great fun hay-making and watching things grow. And because they had lots and lots of space they were able to have a tent and camp out at night if they wanted to. We bought them miniature tractors and they learnt to ride bikes without having to go out on a main road, which was lovely.

Another attraction of the countryside was the architecture of the traditional English village compared to which semi-detached suburbia with its rows of identical houses was boring. More and more people were excited by the idea of restoring an authentic period home in the country, with a real history, among them Valerie Keeble:

We'd seen a lot of houses and they were mostly sort of pseudo-stockbroker-Tudor, which we didn't want. We both had a feeling that your surroundings are very important and you can be happy or unhappy in them, according to what they are, and so we'd set our hearts on a period house. We felt there was a certain sameness about a suburban street but in a village like Horsley there was a big mix with period houses, turn-of-the-century artisans' houses, and we liked the mix and the people that that necessarily brought you into contact with, and the variety and the un-alikeness of the streets and the higgledy-piggledyness of it. So we'd seen a house advertised and we had an appointment one November night. We walked up the path and, snap, we both said, 'Yes, this is it', without even seeing the inside. We made an offer there and then, and when I read the surveyor's report I was rather horrified but my husband, who'd got much better professional knowledge about building than me, said, 'No, that's fine', and so we went ahead. It was £4,500 which people wouldn't believe today. It was so right with its absolutely genuine façade (the Georgian frontage which so many people try to copy these days without studying proportions) and it somehow had an intangible atmosphere and we were just happy in it immediately. It needed some work done on it, but we knew that it was just right.

The rural idyll, however, was never quite perfect. Most villages were poorly served by main services like gas, electricity and sewers. Improvements took years and often turned out to be very costly. Many village homes, both new and old, had to make do with a smelly cesspit in the back garden. Schools were often few and far between, and some became hopelessly overcrowded as the village population boomed. The new villagers found themselves battling for facilities just as their new town counterparts had done. And middle-class people who imagined that they would be joining a friendly community of rustic villagers were to discover that the locals resented colonization by people who were much better off than they were and who wanted to bring their village into what was dubbed the 'gin-and-Jag belt'. Fond of a quiet pint of beer, villagers found their local pubs were changing character when village populations doubled or trebled in size. The closed community of the village, in which everyone knew everyone else's business, became a metropolitan outpost and a dormitory for wealthy Londoners. Dorothy Harris remembered how the village of West Horsley was transformed in the 1950s:

In the old days we had horse ploughs and there would be perhaps two men who looked after the horses, and there would be several men out working on the hedges while lots worked on the land. Well, there's still the same roads and lanes now, but much more has been put on them and lots more people live here. Up at the corner, where all the houses are, that was just one orchard belonging to the man across the road, and the kids used to go scrumping apples and pears there. Well, it changed because so many more people came to live here, and they were all such a busy kind. I mean, if they work in London they're out of the village all day so you don't really get to know them. In the old days you used to see men cycling to go up to work down the farm, but when the commuters came in they just buzzed along in a car. The car absolutely ruined it: you didn't get to know people like we used to. We would say, 'Oh, that's Mrs Johnson, that's Mrs Childs and that's Mrs Hutchins'. But that's stopped now and you don't get the old friendliness.

While the better off usually settled in and around villages, the less affluent middle classes moved into more easily accessible market towns 20–30 miles away from London, where house prices were slightly cheaper. As a result, places like Guildford, Maidenhead, Bishop's Stortford and

Woking became commuter outposts, the key attractions there for Londoners being similar to those that lured them to the villages: car ownership, faster train services, and a desire to escape from the congested capital. Although the conventional image of the London commuter is the wealthy stockbroker or the successful executive, during the 1950s even those with low incomes began to commute long distances by rail to work in the capital. This new breed of season-ticket holders included clerks, foremen and skilled workers and most of them chose to live in south Essex.

The electrification of the line from Liverpool Street to Shenfield in 1949, and then to Southend in 1956, made it convenient for people to commute from the cluster of small towns north of the Thames. Here houses were cheap and working-class people could afford to buy their own homes, put up by builders who created new estates of box-like houses all over south Essex. Towns like Billericay, Brentwood and Rayleigh soon doubled in size with between a third and a half of their working populations commuting to the capital. By the late 1950s proportionately more people commuted to London from south Essex than from anywhere else in the Home Counties.

By the early 1960s residents and councils throughout the Home Counties were up in arms about the invasion of their territory. While some areas welcomed the jobs and prosperity that the newcomers brought with them, most were unhappy about the traffic jams, the damage done to the character of historic towns and villages and the loss of treasured local countryside, which was disappearing under a tide of bricks and mortar. The middle-class Shire Counties that Londoners were moving into were overwhelmingly conservative in their outlook and politics and resented the invasion. Many of the newcomers too feared that the countryside they had moved out to enjoy would be destroyed if more housing estates were built. Confident predictions that population and industry in the South East would continue to boom in the decades to come served to increase the general anxiety in the Shires.

Clearly a new scheme was needed to replace Abercrombie's plan, which now lay in ruins. One major planning strategy, the South East Study of 1964, claimed that the population of the area would increase by over 3 million in the next twenty years. To accommodate this expansion it recommended an end to piecemeal development and the building of major new self-contained cities at Bletchley, Newbury and south Hampshire, near Southampton, and big new expansions at Aylesbury, Chelmsford, Reading and Stansted where the small airport would be developed to rival Heathrow and Gatwick. This plan never got off the drawing board but it did influence the new Labour government who were committed to grand planning, and between 1967 and 1968 they designated a second generation of London new towns at Milton Keynes, Peterborough and Northampton.

MORE NEW TOWNS

Although similar in some respects to the first new towns, there were also major differences reflecting the fundamental social changes that had occurred since the late 1940s. The second generation were built much further out than the first new towns – around 50–60 miles away from London – as there was little space for major expansion any closer to the capital. They were also much larger in size and scale than before. Milton Keynes, for example, had a projected population of 250,000. These towns were built with the motor car in mind and practically every home had a garage, whereas the earlier new towns were built with some roads too narrow for parked cars or busy traffic and with far fewer garages. Finally, these new towns placed much greater emphasis on private building and homeownership, again in contrast to the 1950s new towns, with their near monopoly of state-owned housing.

Milton Keynes was the showcase new town of the late 1960s. Conceived at a time of affluence and great optimism, it was designed like a mini Los Angeles, in the belief that those who moved there would enjoy an income and lifestyle similar to that of Southern California, one of the richest areas in the world. Public money was lavished so that it had well-designed modern homes, well-equipped schools, and every conceivable community facility. Millions of trees were planted, and open spaces were beautifully landscaped to create a semi-rural feel. The road grid system was designed so that people could drive to work at an average speed of 50 miles an hour, even during rush hours; there were no traffic jams and there were always plenty of free parking places. This was made possible by scattering industry and housing over large areas, which seemed to make good sense in the late 1960s when it was assumed that universal car-ownership was just around the corner and that there would be plenty of public money to subsidize buses.

However, it soon became clear that most people couldn't afford to run their own cars. To make matters worse, the deliberate low-density, scattered nature of houses and industry made bus services impossible to operate profitably. Those without a car had great difficulty in getting to work or to the shops and some old people and young mothers became stranded. One of the top priorities in the planning of Milton Keynes had been to achieve an efficient traffic system, yet lack of transport was to be one of its most serious social problems. Though the car-owning, California-style Milton Keynes Utopia proved to be wildly over-ambitious, for those who were able to move there life was generally better than it would have been back in London.

The building of a second generation of new towns was intended to bring the diaspora of Londoners under some kind of planning control. But private building continued in the Home Counties and in the end the county councils themselves, as local planning authorities, devised a scheme to prevent further encroachment on their countryside.

The same Town and Country Planning legislation passed after the war giving governments the right to purchase land compulsorily for new town developments gave county councils wide-ranging powers to determine who could build where. Responding to the anxieties of local residents, county councils began to extend the land designated as Green Belt. The result was that by the late 1960s each of them had doubled, trebled or quadrupled the size of their Green Belt and some were quite indiscriminate about what was included: unproductive farms, gravel pits, golf courses and wasteland were all to be protected against the developer.

In the Abercrombie plan, enshrined in post-war legislation, the Green Belt was on average only about 7 miles wide. Now it sometimes extended from between 20 and 40 miles. More or less the whole of Surrey and Hertfordshire was designated as Green Belt, and huge chunks of Berkshire and Kent followed suit. These Green Belt extensions undoubtedly did help to contain the growth of London and, in particular, the outer metropolitan sprawl that became marked during the 1950s. But the negative way in which county council powers were used to prevent development was to lead to further problems, especially for Londoners moving out.

In the metropolitan villages the immediate effect of Green Belt restrictions was to send house prices spiralling. Cottages bought in the mid- to late 1950s for a few thousand pounds in Surrey villages like West Horsley, or Buckinghamshire villages like Chalfont St Giles, were fetching prices approaching £100,000 just twenty years later. The intention might have been to preserve the rural character of these villages but the consequence was a fierce inflation of property prices. Those who had already become settled in a village found they had immensely valuable homes that were now protected from further development. But the next wave of incomers would inevitably be much wealthier, as only the rich could afford the price of a rustic Home Counties home.

CRISIS IN THE COMMUTER VILLAGE

At the same time, the consequence of the Green Belt conservation policy disadvantaged many of the old villagers by reducing their opportunities for housing, jobs and services. Sky-high property prices meant that from the 1960s onwards sons and daughters of the locals were no longer able to afford to live in the villages where they were born and bred. Many drifted to small council estates built on the outskirts of villages. However, Green Belt restrictions and class snobbery kept these council estates to a minimum despite the great shortage of housing for rent in the countryside. And most industrial developments around villages were opposed for environmental and conservation reasons. This resulted in depressed labour markets in and around metropolitan villages pushing younger people away to find work. One spin-off from this was that middle-class newcomers were able to employ older locals as cleaners and gardeners at fairly low rates of pay. Appropriately, they were often former domestic servants or agricultural labourers who had once worked for the landed gentry. Those who looked to the new metropolitan 'aristocracy' for their employment found a new brand of paternalism, often friendlier and less fierce than the old. Dorothy Harris worked as a cleaner for the Keeble family in West Horsley. She remembered:

> I'd been in service when I was a girl and I used to have to get up
> about half past five in the morning, do the fireplace and help the
> cook. But with Mrs Keeble it was different. I'd just lost my husband
> and Mrs Keeble was looking for someone to help in her home. When
> I went round there my mother saw me going off in a sunsuit. She
> said, 'You're never going round there in a sunsuit to get a job, are
> you?' I said, 'If she doesn't like it she knows what she can do.' I went

for two weeks on approval and stayed twenty years. At first her attitude was rather inclined to be, 'Well, I'm going to employ you'. But when you got to know her she was sweet. She was a perfectionist in everything she did and you had to do things properly. You didn't say, 'Oh well, I'll do that tomorrow'. But I liked it because we became great friends, we'd sweep the chimney together and do things like that, and I really loved going around there. I went there more for pleasure than for anything else.

As the composition of many villages changed, so the services geared towards the old inhabitants were replaced by others directed at the new middle-class community. Village butchers and bakers often became delicatessens or antique shops; bus services were axed because the newcomers often had two cars; and pubs and clubs were taken over by the more educated and well-to-do commuters. Thus, in the process of capturing these villages for themselves, the metropolitan middle classes inadvertently helped to destroy one of the things that had attracted them in the first place – the original village community. For, despite the new paternalism and devoted work of the newcomers restoring old cottages, the old villagers were, in a sense, dispossessed by the middle-class invasion.

The extension of the Green Belt also had a big impact on market towns and, particularly, on Londoners moving out to them. More land was released for housing and industry in these urban areas than in the countryside, but there was still a serious shortage of land for development. As a result, land prices escalated rapidly which, in turn, pushed up property prices. Homes on the new private estates built in places like Woking and Chelmsford were often attractively designed with mock-Georgian or classical exteriors and enjoyed all modern conveniences, like central heating and luxury fitted kitchens. However, because there was so little land available and because land prices were so high, these modern homes were also very small and had tiny gardens.

The average semi-detached or detached private home of the 1960s and '70s was far smaller than those built in the 1920s and '30s in suburbia, the aim of architects and builders being to pack as many houses into as small a space as possible. Whereas in the 1930s the typical suburban housing density was eight per acre, by the late 1960s this had risen to thirteen per acre. The new houses were also smaller than the council- or new town corporation-built homes of the 1950s. There were government regulations on minimum space standards but they only applied to public housing – private builders could ignore them with impunity. The box-like estates that they built, where each house stood cheek by jowl with the next, were seen everywhere, especially on the outskirts of market towns, from the late 1960s onwards.

The small size of the new houses created problems for some families moving into them. Although they were often ideal for childless couples, those with two or more children found them very cramped. There was a lack of storage space for items like prams and pushchairs, the kitchens were too tiny to prepare family meals easily and there was no room in the garden to build an extension to provide extra room. The biggest complaint was the lack of play space for children inside the house or in the back garden. Mike and Rita Brunwin and their two daughters moved out from Cheam into a three-bedroom detached home on the Goldsworth Park Estate in Woking in 1973. Rita Brunwin recalled:

> The home was smaller than what we'd been used to and that did have some advantages. It was very easy to keep warm and maintain for one thing. But one inconvenience was the small garden, what with having two children and a big dog. We never wanted our children to play outside in the road – we didn't want them to be a nuisance to the neighbours – but with there not really being the space in the garden it did happen. And because of the traffic we didn't think this was terribly good. It wasn't a safe place for children to be.

Another problem created by land shortages and by the defensive attitude of county councils towards the metropolitan expansion into market towns was the appalling traffic congestion. Councils had no long-term master plan for development and land released for housing and industry was usually made available in a piecemeal fashion. This meant that home and workplace were often separated, for there was little or no co-ordination between housing and industrial developments. The unhappy consequence was that from the late 1960s onwards a growing army of commuters travelled to work by car, creating the familiar motoring nightmare of jams, parking problems, exhaust pollution and noise in practically every market town on the outskirts of London. During the rush hours, boom towns like Reading and Woking came to a standstill and it often took half an hour to an hour to travel just a few miles. Local planners tried to keep the traffic moving by introducing bypasses, one-way systems and flyovers but they sometimes had the effect of ripping the heart out of beautiful market towns and turning them into ugly sprawls. Mike Brunwin remembered his first impression of Woking in 1973:

> The first weekend after we moved, I said to Rita, 'I'll pop down into the town and get some newspapers.' And I drove around and came back an hour later and said, 'I can't find it'. I drove round and round in circles and it was always just over there. You were stuck in this sort of great big concrete block surrounded by roads, and the result was that you couldn't actually find the town; it didn't basically exist – there was no village street or town high street. So that was, I suppose, one of the biggest shocks that we had when we first arrived, and that took a little time to get used to. But the disadvantages started to come when we found the build-up of traffic getting worse. To begin with, if you decided to drive to London and got away by about seven o'clock you could have a virtually trouble-free run into London and you could make Wimbledon in about half an hour, but after a time if you arrived on the A3 or the M3 at seven, you hit the height of the rush hour. What was happening was people were starting earlier and earlier as the build-up of traffic got worse and more and more people moved out.

Despite these disadvantages, most of those who left London to live on new estates in the market towns were, on balance, happy with the move. Factories and offices have continued to colonize the market towns, creating good employment opportunities and reducing the need for long-distance commuting to London for work. Reading, for example, became one of the fastest growth areas in the country attracting, among other companies, Metal Box's head office and Courage's Brewery from London. Constantly increasing house prices, which have partly resulted from the tension between the pressure for development and the shortage of land, have meant that homeownership in the South East has been a very profitable business. The Brunwins' home in Woking, bought for £18,000 in 1973, had increased in value four times by 1986 and today would fetch somewhere near £300,000. Property prices for private-estate homes in Woking and other Home Counties market towns are among the highest in Britain, and everyone who moved out has shared in this prosperity.

LONDON BEGINS TO GROW AGAIN

The plans laid out for London just after the war were based on the belief that the metropolis should not grow in population or built-up area. But nobody had envisaged such a rapid loss of manufacturing jobs in the sixties and seventies and the rapid decline of the inner boroughs. In reality people were leaving London in droves: in the 1970s 'net migration' – the excess of those leaving over those arriving in the capital – was 100,000 a year and it was still running at 50,000 in the 1980s. The new town and overspill programmes promoted by governments played a significant part in this, but by far the largest contingent left under their own steam for the new estates built around market towns and the edge of villages.

London's population fell precipitously for forty years after the war so that by 1988 it was back to roughly what it had been in the Edwardian era at 6.73 million. (Earlier estimates putting the low point at 1983 have been revised.) The population of the inner London area (roughly the Victorian and Edwardian suburbs such as Hackney in the north or Lewisham in the south) had peaked at 5 million as early as 1911 and fell to its lowest point of 2.55 million in 1981. Outer London's population (roughly the semi-detached suburbia of the interwar years) peaked in 1952 at 4.52 million and has not changed dramatically since; in 2004 it was close to the 1950s figure at 4.5 million.

The most remarkable development in recent years has been the growth of London's population after such a long era of decline and against the expectations of the planners. The new town and overspill projects had been effectively wound up in the 1970s with a Commission for the new towns overseeing the sale of land and other residual issues. The fears that London would grow too large if not constrained by planning controls appeared to be unfounded. Now that the population has been rising again since 1988 the view of the government and the new Greater London Authority appears to be that this is a good thing, symptomatic of a revitalized metropolis. However, not everyone is convinced of this and some believe the rise may be short-term. Certainly the astronomic rise in property prices in inner London makes it impossible for the majority of young people to buy their own home, and rents are also very high. What this means for the future is not clear, but those wanting eventually to own property will almost certainly have to move away from the capital.

An analysis of what has been going on provides a picture of a great deal of movement in and out of London. The desire to get out of the city into the Home Counties or elsewhere in Britain is still very strong. In the mid-1990s around 50,000 more people left London for other parts of the country than moved in from other areas. This trend has increased in recent years so that in 2004 the excess of leavers was 105,000. Generally speaking those leaving are older and with children around secondary school age. Of those moving in a disproportionate number are young adults seeking work and the excitement of the inner city. This to-ing and fro-ing has been a factor in changing the age structure of London, which has a younger profile now than other parts of the country.

The answer to the puzzle of London's growth when more people appear to be leaving than are arriving can be found in two influences that have more than compensated for this loss. Firstly, there has been a large increase in the number of asylum seekers and other people from abroad settling in London. The figures are not thought to be very accurate, but the International Passenger Surveys and Home Office data suggest the numbers were running at about 100,000 a year. Most of these incomers are aged between sixteen and forty-four. At the same time London has had a very high 'natural increase' in its population, which is to say each year there is an excess of babies born over people dying in the capital. Back in the 1970s, London had a relatively old age structure with fewer children than the national average. Now, a great many of those leaving the capital are around retirement age, people whose life will come to an end somewhere else in Britain or possibly abroad. So deaths in London are below average while the young population with many of the families from abroad ensures a high birth rate. In 2004 there were 114,000 births in London and just 54,000 deaths, giving a natural increase in population of 60,000. This is exceptionally high for Britain, and London contributed over 70 per cent of the natural increase for the whole country in that year.

London's population in 2007 was estimated at 7.43 million and is expected to continue rising for the foreseeable future. The shift to employment in service industries has increased the jobs available from a low in the mid-1980s, and arrivals from those countries newly welcomed into the European Community, notably Romania and Bulgaria, are expected to swell the population of the inner city. Always a cosmopolitan city, about 30 per cent of London's population is now from a black or minority ethnic group – in the 2001 census people from Cyprus, Turkey, Albania and former Yugoslavia were not counted in the 'minority ethnic group' but as 'white other'. The capital's population is now truly multicultural and would be unrecognizable to those pioneers who arrived with so much expectation from the West Indies just after the war. But it is still, in a sense, for many new arrivals the promised land.

CHAPTER TWENTY-THREE

The Promised Land

ALTHOUGH LONDON HAS been a host to immigrants from all over Europe throughout its modern history, it was never in the past as richly cosmopolitan as it has become since the end of the Second World War. In the nineteenth century there were enclaves which took much of their character from immigrant groups, such as Spitalfields (where the French silk weavers settled with their caged song birds and mathematical societies) and whole districts of the East End (settled by Jews, many fleeing pogroms in Russia and Eastern Europe). But there was not, until quite recently, a sense that London as a whole was composed of such myriad ethnic groups as can be found today. Anyone travelling around the capital today on its enclosed and privatized buses cannot fail to be aware that the continuous chatter on mobile phones is a veritable Babel of languages.

Things were very different in June 1948 when hundreds of Jamaicans first arrived in London. They were invited to a civic tea with the Mayor of Brixton and were afterwards introduced to local dignitaries. They had sailed to Britain on the SS *Empire Windrush* and the account of their arrival in the capital was headlined by the *Evening Standard*: 'WELCOME HOME'. These were the first black immigrants to come to London from the new Commonwealth in the post-war years. Many were ex-servicemen and they came decked out in their 'Sunday best' suits and jaunty hats. Like most immigrants they were poor and had had to save hard to buy a one-way ticket but they had high hopes for the future and were determined to begin by making a good impression. London to them was the promised land, a land of opportunity. The very friendly welcome they received was, in part, recognition of the great contribution made by the Commonwealth and Empire to the Allied victory in the Second World War. In the next fifteen years the pioneer Jamaicans from the *Empire Windrush* were followed by almost a quarter of a million more immigrants from former colonies and dependencies in the Caribbean, Asia and the Mediterranean.

The British Nationality Act passed by the Labour government in 1948 awarded British citizenship to everyone living in Commonwealth and Empire countries. Their status changed from being imperial subjects to citizens of the Commonwealth with full rights of entry and settlement in Britain. The legislation was inspired partly by idealism about Britain's role as the mother country and partly by a practical desire to hold the crumbling Commonwealth together by offering an incentive for membership. And there were good economic reasons to encourage immigration in that period.

The war had inflicted serious damage on factories, offices, roads, railways, public buildings and housing in the capital. Things had been patched up at the time, but there was much work to be done in the grand reconstruction plan to build a new and better London after the war. At the same time, war shortages meant that there was a huge pent-up demand for British goods at home and abroad, and manufacturing industry was geared up to fulfil a massive export drive, which in turn created a big demand for labour. The blitz alone had killed 30,000 London citizens, and many women who had taken waged labour during the war returned home when it finished, so workers were in short supply.

For large numbers of new Commonwealth citizens the war had created new and exciting opportunities. Many were prepared to fight the Nazis and joined up to serve in parts of the world that were far from their homes: a strong Caribbean contingent volunteered for war service in Britain (10,000 were recruited into the RAF to work as ground crews) and India provided 2 million men for the Allied forces, some of whom served in Europe. London seemed to offer great opportunities to these people. Most had been brought up in towns and villages where poverty and high unemployment were endemic. A few set their sights on returning to London to live, while others felt confident and worldly enough to go wherever there was well-paid work after the war.

But very few people from the new Commonwealth would make the passage to London until the early 1950s. For despite awarding British citizenship to everyone in the new Commonwealth, the post-war Labour government actually preferred to recruit European rather than colonial workers to ease the labour shortage at home, for they were considered more skilled and better suited to the British way of life. There were generous resettlement programmes for East European refugees who did not want to return home to their countries, now controlled by the Soviet Union. For example, around 30,000 Poles who had been in the armed services or who were prisoners of war settled in London with their families after the war. Even the enemies of Britain during the war – thousands of Italians and German ex-prisoners of war – were offered work permits and allowed to stay under the European Voluntary Worker Schemes. All these extra hands were supplemented by large numbers of Irish immigrants to London.

There was no direct recruitment of new Commonwealth workers in the immediate post-war years and those who did come paid for the voyage themselves and had no guarantee of work. These disincentives kept colonial immigration to London to a minimum. Just a few hundred West Indians were arriving in the capital each year in the late 1940s, and as late as 1952 the annual figure was still just 1,500. The vast majority of those leaving the West Indies to find employment abroad went to the United States instead, which was much closer to home and paid higher wages. The number of Indian and Pakistani immigrants arriving in London was also tiny at this time, at less than a quarter of the Caribbean newcomers. About one thousand people a year arrived from the island of Cyprus.

Most of these first immigrants who made the journey to London were skilled manual workers, or professionally qualified in some way, and they had high expectations of what could be achieved. Many believed that if they found a good job and worked hard for several years, they would be able to save up enough money to return home to their village or town, set up in business and lead a comfortable life. And for the pioneers, life in London in the early days could be sweet. Within three weeks all of the 492 Jamaicans who had arrived on the *Empire Windrush* had jobs, most typically as electricians, plumbers, coachbuilders, labourers and clerical workers. Hundreds of professionally qualified immigrants, particularly Asians, found employment in London as doctors and teachers. Although many had to be content with unskilled and unpleasant work that Londoners themselves did not want, they were at least able to find a job of some sort. Even in menial jobs, West Indian road sweepers, Asian factory shift workers and Cypriot kitchen hands were earning almost double the wage they would have received in a similar job at home.

Finding a place to live was not too hard. Naturally the newcomers wanted to be as close as possible to their work: for them a time-consuming and expensive commuter journey was generally out of the question. This was one reason immigrants tended to settle in particular districts. For Jamaicans it was to be south-west London, especially Brixton, where the first immigrants had been housed in old air-raid shelters in Clapham before they were directed to employment agencies in their search for work and a place to stay. The Asian settlement in Southall from the early 1950s onwards began because the personnel manager of Woolfe's rubber factory in that area had been a police officer in the Punjab in India, and he gave many Punjabi immigrants jobs there.

Cheap rented accommodation was all that immigrants could hope to get at first as they were in no position to buy homes and had no call on council housing. Brixton was especially favourable because it had long been a place where theatre and music-hall stars stayed and where there was less likely to be prejudice against black lodgers. The settlements, which soon began to grow into small ethnic colonies, were to have an enormous impact on the post-war social geography of the capital. Friends and relatives tried to live as close to each other as possible. They provided help in times of need, and their shared ties and culture gave them emotional strength in an unfamiliar world. But no vibrant West Indian or Asian communities took root until at least the mid-1950s. The majority of the pioneers were young men who worked all hours and saved most of their money, leading a spartan existence, usually in all-male households. Most looked forward to going back to their own countries when they had saved enough money.

THE CYPRIOT COMMUNITY

There was, however, a family-based Cypriot community. During the 1930s several thousand Cypriots had arrived in London, many of them settling in the Camden Town area. Most of them worked in the kitchens of Italian restaurants or in the sweatshops of the Jewish-run garment industry. Some Italians, interned during the war as potential enemies, sold their restaurants to their Cypriot employees for rock-bottom prices. The new Cypriot restaurants did surprisingly well: moussaka – a dish made of mince and aubergines – was enjoyed as a cheap and nutritious meal during the war. In the post-war years these new owners recruited friends and relatives from Cyprus to live and work with them in Camden. One Cypriot immigrant was John Nicolas, who came to London in 1947. He recalled:

> I was sent the invitation to come here by my father's cousin. And my profession was a hairdresser. So he said to me, 'What you like to do?' I say, 'I don't mind, I just want a job'. So we went to a hairdresser and

he said to me, 'You're better off not coming to me – go to a restaurant'. So I say, 'I don't mind, I want a job that's all'. So I got a job as a kitchen boy. It was better for me because whatever I got would be clear – I ate there and didn't have to spend my money.

The Cypriot community was then still very small, as were those of the other immigrant groups. In 1952 the total number of new Commonwealth citizens in London was little more than 10,000 and their tiny colonies had made little impact on life in the capital. Over the next decade, however, there was a spectacular increase in new Commonwealth immigration to London as the post-war boom in industry continued and there was pent-up demand for services in the capital.

The Cypriots were particularly well placed to take advantage of the increasing prosperity as Londoners began to benefit from the revived pleasure of eating out. The Cypriots in the restaurants had to work very long hours for low pay, but the wages were much better than they could hope to earn back home. On the rare occasions when they returned to their villages in Cyprus, their new wealth was immensely impressive to those they had left behind and this encouraged many more to emigrate to London. Panayiotis Stavrou Nicolas remembered being amazed at the affluence of his cousin John Nicolas, who returned to Cyprus in 1952 for a holiday after working as a kitchen hand in the capital for five years:

Every night John and his friends would go to clubs, bars, spending money, and we thought my God, in five years they became millionaires – these boys – so why not us! You know, we had to get to England, but to do that you had to be rich. I asked my father to give me some money to buy a ticket and he didn't have any money obviously. He says to me, 'The only way to do it is to buy a young pig. We feed it for six months, we sell it and then we buy the ticket.' So we did that. Well, it didn't fetch a lot of money and I had to borrow £8 from a cousin of my father as well. Eventually I got to London.

As well as restaurant work there was the rag trade, which had sustained the Jewish community since the early 1900s. By the 1950s their success was leading them into other businesses and professions where there was more status and less work. Educated Jewish sons were moving into professions and away from the clothing business to become doctors, lawyers or journalists. This created a great opportunity for the Cypriots, as tailoring and dressmaking were important traditional industries in Cyprus and many of the immigrants, both men and women, had the skills to ply their trade in London. Not much capital was needed as the sweatshops still used the Victorian technology of the sewing machine and steam press, and with long hours and hard work they could be made profitable.

From the mid-1950s onwards Cypriots had begun to take over London's clothing industry from the Jews. Most of the workers in the Cypriot-owned sweatshops and factories were recruited from among friends and relatives back home, and as the businesses prospered more people came over until several thousand were arriving in London every year. Tony Nicolas, who ran a clothing factory with his brother, recalled:

> After John had started work in the kitchens, the family had come over
> bit by bit and by 1953 more or less all of us were in London. Our
> sister, Nitsa, was working for a firm in Great Titchfield Street and
> when she was expecting her first child she had to stop work and her
> boss gave her a machine to work at home. And that's how our firm
> started. My other sisters stayed at home to help, then I stayed to help
> them. John gave up his work as a waiter and we brought another
> couple of machinists into the basement. We used to sleep there in the
> evening; we used to sort of push the machines aside and sleep in the
> same room. In those days we used to work nearly twenty-four hours a
> day – we put double the time in of anybody else because we were
> hungry for work. That's why we succeeded – through hard work. And
> I think within two years we bought a small factory in Chalk Farm
> Road, we stayed there three years then bought a bigger place off the
> Caledonian Road, then we bought a factory which was 15,000 square
> feet off the Holloway Road.

While the Cypriot community was becoming established in the clothing and restaurant businesses, the number of arrivals from the West Indies began to increase. Between 1955 and 1960 the numbers settling in London were about 20,000 each year. There were still plenty of low-paid, arduous jobs to be filled in the capital and more staff were needed in the hospitals, in public transport and in some other essential services which offered West Indian immigrants a way in. This was the time when Londoners were leaving the capital at the rate of 100,000 a year. However, employers did not simply wait for new recruits to arrive from the West Indies: they went out to recruit them.

ON THE BUSES

In April 1956 London Transport began taking on staff from Barbados, and later from Trinidad and Jamaica. The thousands of recruits had their fares to London paid for under a long-term loan system and places were found for them to live; then they were given training as bus drivers and conductors and on the Underground as guards and drivers. Enoch Powell, who later made the notorious 'rivers of blood' speech in which he warned of the dangers of immigration, was the Conservative Minister for Health when that department was involved in recruiting thousands of West Indian women as nurses. Some other organizations, like the British Hotels and Restaurants Association, were also active in recruiting labour in the Caribbean.

However, the great majority of settlers from the new Commonwealth arrived without any help or invitation. After 1952 their most popular destination, the United States, was closed off with new laws on immigration, and although London was much further away they at least had a right to go there. Colonial schooling had taught West Indians that Britain was the mother country where equal opportunity and freedom were enjoyed, whatever a person's creed or colour – a rosy picture endorsed by the letters the first arrivals had written home, naturally wanting to report that they had been successful and therefore, perhaps, exaggerating just a little. The favourable accounts of life in England encouraged many more West Indians to cross the Atlantic, and their rising numbers began to change the tone in the capital.

There was always a danger that ingrained views about the racial superiority of the English over their subject peoples would encourage prejudice. There was little or no sensitivity in films to the dangers of racial stereotyping, and it was in the cinema that the majority of Londoners had been given an impression of what 'blacks' were like. Most Londoners had never met a black man or woman face to face. Now, by the mid-1950s their numbers were increasing and there was talk of them 'taking over' certain areas. Not unnaturally there was a fear that the immigrants would accept poor pay and drive down wages. And, if they were skilled, they might throw Londoners out of work.

The consequence of all this was increasing job discrimination against non-whites. The blow of racial prejudice was to some extent softened by the fact that a greater proportion of this new wave of immigrants were unskilled and semi-skilled workers from poorer islands like Jamaica and, although they had hoped for something better, many did not complain when they were directed into dirty, low-status jobs as street sweepers and factory hands. However, more than a third of the newcomers were skilled or qualified in some way, and it was these that discrimination hit hardest. The first taste of this prejudice often came at the employment exchange. Whatever skills West Indians possessed, they would usually be encouraged to enter unskilled jobs. Myrtle Campbell was a qualified teacher who came to London from Jamaica in 1956. She remembered:

> I went to the Labour Exchange at Balham. And naturally I went to
> the professional section because I was a professional person and I
> wanted a good job. That caused a real fuss; they were very
> embarrassed there. I was told I would be unsuitable, and they sent me
> to the unqualified, unskilled section. And the jobs they offered me
> there were cleaning and washing jobs that I really didn't want to do.

Applying for jobs direct could be equally frustrating, since some employers and trade unions were reluctant to recruit new Commonwealth immigrants into skilled or white-collar jobs. A survey of West Indians in London undertaken in 1958–9 showed that more than half of them had had to accept jobs far below their level of qualification, as Myrtle Campbell recalled:

> I applied for a job in the South London Press, it was a clerical job for
> Palmolive and I wrote a letter applying for it. And they wrote back
> from their head office and actually offered me the job in writing. I had
> to go to the branch where I was to work and the man from head office
> would introduce me to the section I was working in. I remember
> when I arrived at the gate the gate-man said more or less, 'What are
> you doing here?' I produced the letter offering me the job and he
> eventually let me in muttering under his breath. I sat down but when
> the section leader came in he took one look at me and ordered
> somebody to take me straight away from the office entrance where I
> was sitting, down into the storeroom.

There was discrimination too when immigrants looked for a place to live. Notices announcing boldly, 'NO COLOUREDS' and 'EUROPEANS ONLY' appeared in boarding-house and newsagents' windows all over the capital. The same message was spelt out in many 'accommodation-to-let' advertisements in London newspapers. Whether or not landlords were themselves prejudiced, they were concerned that housing 'coloureds' might lower the tone of their property in the eyes of other residents. In order to obtain lodgings from a white landlord, immigrants often had to pay high rents and accept squalid conditions.

RACHMAN AND THE RACK RENTERS

One landlord who dominated this market in North Kensington and made a fortune out of it was Peter Rachman. He bought around 150 decaying houses in Notting Hill and Paddington, evicted white 'sitting tenants', using his henchmen to threaten them with dogs and smashing down their front doors. Once he had possession, Rachman packed in as many West Indian immigrants as possible, making huge profits. He favoured immigrants from the island of Trinidad and this, in time, gave a flavour to the district (see also Chapter Twenty-four).

As immigration continued, the first settlers were able to do something to protect the new arrivals from the effects of discrimination, helping them to find places to rent and jobs. West Indians, Cypriots and Indians all benefited from these 'migration chains' which, in time, inevitably led to the colonization of particular areas by particular ethnic groups. Many of the first wave of settlers had saved up to buy houses in their original areas of settlement in London where there was a large stock of old or substandard housing which could be bought very cheaply. These houses – built originally to attract the wealthy, servant-owning Victorian families – were often very large and although they enjoyed few basic facilities they could accommodate twenty or more newcomers desperate for a temporary home. The availability of cheap and friendly lodgings in West Indian-owned houses quickly turned Brixton into a reception area for Jamaicans coming to London, and its Caribbean population doubled from 5,000 to 10,000 between 1955 and 1960.

In time, West Indians settled in many different districts in London, but their concentration in places like Brixton and Notting Hill was, by the late 1950s, arousing increasing racial prejudice among local whites. Wherever they lived they were blamed for lowering the tone of neighbourhoods, bad housing conditions and increased rents. And they met with a frosty reception when they tried to join churches, drink in pubs and clubs or go to dance halls. Sometimes there was a firm colour bar and they were turned away at the door. Racist attacks in pubs and streets became almost daily events and West Indians began to arm themselves when they went out at night. Lionel Jeffrey recalled:

> To begin with when I came over from Guyana in 1949 things weren't too bad – people were friendlier. But when the masses came over to London there was a lot of bad feeling. You got everything – insults at work, in the street, 'Fucking niggers go home, we'll get you', that sort of thing. There was a fear that something violent was about to happen. Sometimes your friends would be beaten up or chased so I started walking around with a hammer in my pocket to defend myself. I always took a hammer with me, I didn't want to use it, but I didn't feel safe without it. And when I rode around on my bike I had an iron bar with me. I'd Sellotape it on to the crossbar so that it looked like part of the bike if the police stopped me for carrying an offensive weapon. You would always be asking your friends 'How is it in your area?' to see if there was any trouble. There was always something brewing in Brixton or Stockwell or Ladbroke Grove – the whites were getting very hostile there – and we got very little protection from the police. If things looked bad we'd be phoned up to go over and help out, because if there were a lot of us they'd leave us alone.

This racial tension exploded into London's first post-war race riot in Notting Hill in late August 1958. For several days and nights the homes of black tenants in the area were besieged by large crowds of whites, some of them several hundred strong, who smashed windows, shouted racial abuse and threw petrol bombs. At the same time gangs of white teenagers armed with iron bars, sticks and knives went 'nigger hunting', beating up any blacks they could find. This violence almost triggered a similar riot in Brixton, but police cordons managed to seal off the area and prevent white mobs from attacking their targets. In the next two weeks an escalation of attacks on black people was reported in Harlesden, Hackney, Stepney, Hornsey and Islington.

In response to these riots a Conservative Party campaign was launched for the introduction of immigration controls and there was much popular support for it. The issue of race relations became headline news, the favoured solution being to reduce or halt the flow of new Commonwealth citizens into Britain. To begin with, the attempt to control immigration had precisely the opposite effect to that intended, for while the new legislation was being debated and framed between 1960 and 1962 there was a last great surge of immigration to beat the expected ban. Indian and Pakistani arrivals in Britain swelled from 3,000 in 1959 to 48,000 in 1961; West Indian immigration increased from 16,000 in 1959 to almost 50,000 in 1960, then 66,000 in 1961; Cypriot immigration more than quadrupled in 1960 and 1961 when over 25,000 left for Britain; and from all corners of the new Commonwealth, like Hong Kong, immigration reached its highest ever level. Although many South Asians found work in the north of England, the great majority of other immigrants settled in London.

Despite reports of discrimination, London still offered the opportunity of a much better standard of living for the immigrants than they would have found at home. The houses of early settlers in Brixton, Southall and Camden Town became reception centres that were soon bursting at the seams. Though the first immigrants had never been sure how long they would stay in London, the impending ban on newcomers from their country panicked them into bringing over friends, relatives and kinsmen from villages so that they would not be stranded and separated from them should they decide to live in London long term.

When the Commonwealth Immigration Act came into operation in 1962 this final wave of immigration into London was abruptly halted, bringing to an end a brief flowering of liberal, 'open-door' policies towards Commonwealth immigration in the post-war years. From now on only Commonwealth settlers with guaranteed jobs would be allowed entry. The numbers and rights of new Commonwealth immigrants were then further reduced by legislation passed by both Labour and Conservative governments in 1968, 1971 and 1981. This was clearly racist in intent, for it was geared to restricting non-white immigration, while Irish and European immigration continued with no controls: a distinction was made between old Commonwealth citizens (from the white colonies such as Australia) and new Commonwealth who were the former subject peoples, overwhelmingly from India, Pakistan, the West Indies or Africa. An exception was made to the rules when first Kenya, in 1967, and then Idi Amin in Uganda expelled the Asian population, many of whom came to London.

Otherwise, the door was closed on new Commonwealth immigration when London's industries were beginning to go into decline. The affluent years were over, and news of the reduction in opportunities and jobs available in London discouraged new immigrants from attempting to come to the capital. And so the early 1960s marked a watershed in the story of their settlement of the capital. The main influx of first-generation immigrants, born and bred in the colonies, was now over.

A new era was beginning in which these immigrants would raise their own families, who would emerge as a generation of British-born Cypriots, West Indians and Asians. The hope had been that in time the various groups would be assimilated into the British way of life and would live in harmony alongside white Londoners in the same communities. And although this did happen, there was a natural tendency for people with the same language and culture and from the same regions of the new Commonwealth to stay together, so that distinct Mediterranean, Caribbean and South Asian settlements appeared. In some cases colonial villages were more or less transplanted on to the streets of the capital.

LONDON'S ETHNIC COMMUNITIES

Two quite distinct groups of immigrants came to London from Cyprus. The former British colony was divided between those of Greek origin and affiliation in the South and those of Turkish origin and affiliation in the North. There is a long history of conflict between these two communities and the island remains divided to this day. In London, a large number of Greek Cypriots who worked in the clothing and restaurant trade settled in Camden Town (dubbed 'Little Cyprus'), while the Turkish Cypriots tended to settle in different areas, notably in Islington and Hackney. Whereas the Greek Cypriots worship in the Greek Orthodox Church, the Turkish Cypriots are Muslim. Both communities developed their own clubs and community associations and have retained strong family ties while living in relative harmony in London.

Many of the West Indian settlements that emerged in London became outposts of the different Caribbean islands, each with its own identity. Jamaicans were concentrated south of the Thames in Brixton and Stockwell; Trinidadians and Barbadians settled to the west in Notting Hill; the Guyanese colonized north-eastern suburbs like Wood Green and

Tottenham; the Montserratians became established in Finsbury Park in north London; and Anguillans based themselves outside London in Slough. The geography of these settlements was often dictated by the chance factor of where immigrants from particular islands first found work and housing.

The West Indies span 2,000 miles of ocean and until 1960 the only way to fly from Jamaica to Trinidad was via London. The Jamaicans, who spoke an English-based patois, could barely understand the Franco-Spanish dialect of the Grenadians. Many of the islands had different religions. For example, most St Lucians were Catholics, Barbadians were Anglicans and many Guyanese were Hindu or Muslim. And there were important social divisions: Trinidad had a high proportion of white-collar professionals, while Jamaica consisted overwhelmingly of manual labourers. All the unique features of these cultures and the strong rivalries between them were transported into colony life in London. So strong was the separate identity of each island that each had its own clubs and associations, and there were very few mixed pan-Caribbean organizations in London.

The Notting Hill Carnival originated with the Trinidadians. It began as an August Bank Holiday event in the early 1960s, with steel bands parading the streets playing the latest calypsos; this was the traditional music of the East Caribbean and when mothers from those islands heard it in the streets many spontaneously stopped their chores and joined the revellers. They were re-enacting the old carnival celebrations that they had enjoyed back home in Trinidad. By 1965 there were dozens of bands and hundreds of dancers, kitted out in home-made ceremonial costumes. From these beginnings the Notting Hill Carnival went on to embrace the growing black pride of West Indians as a whole and become the biggest street festival in Britain.

The South Asian communities that became established in London during the 1960s were, like their Caribbean counterparts, quite separate from each other in culture and identity. One of the largest colonies was established in Southall, an immigrant boom town of the early 1960s. More than 50,000 Sikhs and Hindus came here from the Punjab area of India. The dividing line between India and the new state of West Pakistan drawn up by the British government after the Second World War ran right through the Punjab, creating social and political turmoil. Many Sikhs and Hindus who had lived in what was now Muslim West Pakistan fled back to the part of the Punjab remaining in India, but they lost their land and businesses in the process. The poverty and overpopulation in the Punjab encouraged migration to London.

This Indian colonization of Southall grew out of an earlier settlement of the area in the 1950s by Punjabis. Just as the Jamaicans of Brixton saved up to buy their own homes, so the new Indian settlers clubbed together to take out mortgages on properties in Southall. This was to form the foundation on which the later migration of friends, relatives and kinsmen was based. Southall was also very attractive to the Indians because it was conveniently close to Heathrow airport, which was not only often their first point of arrival but was also a big employer of cheap immigrant labour.

During the 1960s the Sikhs and Hindus began recreating many Punjabi institutions in Southall, the most important of which was family life. The pioneer Indian settlers had usually lived in all-male households in order to save as much money as possible before returning home. But when the decision was made to bring over wives and children in the early 1960s, the overcrowded and often squalid male homes practically disappeared. Families bought their own homes and money that had been saved was spent on furnishing and improving them.

The strict, male-dominated family traditions of the Punjab – one of which was the arranged marriage of children – were now resumed, much to the horror of some liberal Western observers. Similarly, the religious rituals of the Indian subcontinent were reasserted. In the pioneer period few immigrants had observed religious taboos on alcohol and tobacco and some Sikhs had stopped wearing their turbans, partly because it made it easier for them to get jobs. However, the 1960s saw a religious revival. Traditional customs were again practised, temples arose everywhere, often in abandoned Christian churches, and male Sikhs proudly began to wear their turbans and grow their hair and beards again, as a statement of their religious identity.

What emerged was a tightly knit culture with few points of contact with the white community. Many of the immigrants spoke little or no English, and they were disinclined to go to the local clubs, pubs and cinemas. This self-contained lifestyle actually protected the Indians from much of the everyday white discrimination that West Indians, for example – who shared the language and interests of many Londoners – experienced.

The most exclusive ethnic community to become established in London during the 1960s, however, was Soho's Chinatown. There had been an original Chinatown in Limehouse in the East End – a small settlement of grocery shops, lodging houses and eating places which had, since the mid-nineteenth century, provided a base for Chinese merchant seamen and dockers in London, many of whom were originally recruited by the East India Company. The running of Chinese laundries enabled hundreds to move out and set up independently, but the advent of the automatic washing machine and the launderette in the 1950s put them out of business. Fortunately a new taste for foreign cuisine (especially Chinese) and the growing popularity of eating out gave the Chinese in London an attractive alternative – the restaurant trade. Many sold their laundries and moved into catering. As a Pathé cinema documentary put it at the time: 'For Chinatown it's Wash to Nosh'. The Chinese community moved from east London to Soho in the West End, where they could open restaurants in an area long associated with dining out.

Such was the demand for Chinese food that thousands of villagers from Hong Kong were recruited each year to work as chefs, waiters and kitchen hands in the capital. Many were formerly rice farmers who came to London to better themselves and provide security for their families. The immigrants rarely spoke more than a few words of English and had no desire to mix with Londoners, whose way of life they found completely alien. By the mid-1960s part of Soho had become an island of Chinese culture, referred to by the newcomers as the Imperial City. But the strongest ties of all remained with the home villages back in Hong Kong. Savings were sent back every month; land or homes were bought with a view to going back eventually; and trips home were made every few years. For most young single men like Mr Mann, the motive behind visiting the home village was the quest for a bride. He recalled:

> I came over in 1959 to work in restaurant in London. There was much
> poverty in Hong Kong and I wanted better life. I write to my
> girlfriend there, she lives close to my village, and we talk about
> marriage when I come home. I save up to come back in 1962; that was
> when we get married. Then I come back to London, leave her there,
> because I didn't have a proper home for her to come to. I was very
> homesick and lonely leaving her. But in two years I had more money
> and a home and she come over to join me.

The rapidly growing ethnic communities in London during the 1960s developed their own economies to serve their needs. Restaurants serving authentic Cantonese and Indian food opened in the streets of Soho and Southall. The English who plucked up the courage to eat 'Chinese' or

'Indian' in the early days often just had egg and chips and a cup of tea which the proprietors provided. Many of the first Indian restaurants, nearly all of which were opened by people from Syhlett in Bangladesh (formerly East Pakistan), only made a profit by staying open late and enduring the unedifying spectacle of inebriated Londoners staggering in for a 'curry fight' after the pubs shut. A favourite Rugby club joke was to eat the flowers on the table. It took a while for a real appreciation of the food to become the norm. Similarly, ethnic shops selling traditional foods and costumes, at first almost exclusively for the immigrant community, in time attracted Londoners from many different backgrounds.

Some aspects of immigrant life remained, however, within the community. Run-down cinemas were given new life when, under Asian management, they began showing Indian films to packed audiences. And gambling clubs, ever popular with Chinese workers, sprang up all over Soho. Gerrard Street in Soho came to be called 'the Chinese People's Street', because it provided a great array of Cantonese eating places, grocers, book shops, travel agencies and so on, making it a regular place of pilgrimage for the Chinese from all over Britain.

The establishment of ethnic communities was not always welcomed by Londoners. There were dozens of unofficial strikes and walkouts staged by white people who refused to work alongside blacks. Street violence against non-whites also became a regular occurrence in the capital. The most turbulent area was Spitalfields, where a large Bengali community, recently arrived from East Pakistan, was eking out a living from long hours of toil in sweatshops. The local whites objected to their presence and took it upon themselves to intimidate the newcomers. They would go out 'Paki-bashing', attacking anyone they thought was Pakistani, sometimes with bottles, boots and knives.

When Enoch Powell rose to prominence with his rabble-rousing speeches advocating the end of immigration and a policy of repatriation, the London dockers and Smithfield porters downed tools and marched to the House of Commons in his support. In 1968, the year when Powell was making his most rabid speeches, the Labour government passed a new Race Relations Act offering protection to non-whites against discrimination in employment, housing and services.

MAKING A LIVING

From the mid-1960s thousands of Indian, Chinese and Greek family restaurant businesses followed the earlier example of Italian spaghetti houses, cashing in on the increasingly cosmopolitan tastes of Londoners. The opportunity that these restaurants offered to sample the food, music and atmosphere of different cultures was warmly welcomed by many Londoners. And in the process, conservative British eating habits were revolutionized. Mr Mann:

> I work as cook in Chinese restaurants for about ten years. Lots of people wanted Chinese food so I save up (it didn't cost a lot to open a takeaway). I borrow from a friend and a bank, then I start my business. I open it 1969. I had an advertisement in a local newspaper and I put up very big posters on my shop front saying when it would open. I also print a lot of menus with my name and address on them, then I take these menus round house by house so that people would know about the takeaway. It went well the business, the people were very friendly, they liked the food and often they come back for more.

During the 1960s some of the more successful and prosperous new Commonwealth families were moving away from their original colonies to more suburban homes, following a similar path to that trodden by the Jews in previous decades. Many were more devoted to traditional suburban values like pride in homeownership, church attendance and family respectability, than were the Londoners who were established there.

Cypriot families who ran successful clothing or catering businesses often moved north, first to Haringey, then to Enfield, Barnet, Brent and Waltham Forest. The symbols of success – detached homes and expensive cars – were very important to them and, as early as 1966, almost half the Cypriot householders in London were owner-occupiers. Another attraction of suburban life for Greek Cypriots like the Nicolas family was the open spaces, reminding them of the villages that they had migrated from. John Nicolas:

> To start with I lived with my sisters and brother in a house we bought near Regents Park. Then by the early 60s all the family started to move out to Finchley and the feeling was always to get out, as you did better in life. You wanted to be out in the open, because we came from a village and we liked the open; we missed all the countryside.

444

There was also a strong outward migration of West Indian families from the central areas to the London suburbs. One particularly popular area was Croydon, where around three-quarters of the several thousand-strong West Indian population were homeowners – a higher rate of home-ownership than was the norm among British-born London families. Most of the West Indian householders in places like Croydon were skilled or semi-skilled manual workers who saved hard to pay their mortgages. Many brought with them a passion for churchgoing and cricket that harked back to the days of the Empire. Myrtle Campbell remembered:

> It was the ambition of everyone coming over from Jamaica to have their own home. So for years we'd save every penny we could: no holidays, my husband gave up his drink and cigarettes, and he took every minute of overtime he could get, sometimes the children didn't see him from one week to the next. Well, we'd been living in rooms in Clapham and it was difficult with four children because there was no space and we didn't want them playing in the streets with all the traffic. We decided to move to Croydon and when we saw this home we just fell in love with it. It was about £8,000 at the time – it was a dream come true. The most important thing for us was that we had a back garden which gave the children so much more freedom to play. We were one of the first West Indian families in our end of the street and people were very friendly. The old woman next door was like a mother to the children and they used to play in her garden. And there was a lovely Roman Catholic church near here. We had the boys baptized there, then they became altar boys and we'd go to mass every Sunday morning. We were church people and we felt that our children should follow us. I suppose because I was a teacher I wanted the children to do well at school so I gave them a lot of tuition at home, reading them books, answering their questions, and it paid off because they all did well and my eldest son won a scholarship to the local grammar school. My husband was very keen on cricket – he played with the boys out in the back garden with a real cricket ball. It was a regular thing to have all the windows smashed. But they did well and Michael and Louis are both good cricketers now.

The corner shop, rapidly abandoned by Londoners in the face of competition from supermarkets, would certainly have become a rare sight in the suburbs had it not been for the entry of Asians into the retail trade. Newsagents, grocers, and off-licences could be bought at rock-bottom prices and the new owners made them profitable by opening all hours, seven days a week, and by using cheap family labour. They were to become a permanent and highly valued feature of London life, especially important to those who did not have a car to drive to a supermarket.

A GENERATION GAP

At the same time as many new Commonwealth immigrants were achieving respectability in the eyes of their suburban neighbours, so their children were also becoming more integrated into the mainstream 'white' culture of London. This mixing was greatest among children of families who were dispersed in the suburbs, but it also occurred in ethnic communities. For this generation of British-born non-whites went to schools where English was the first language, where 'Western' ideas formed the basis of the curriculum and where they mixed and made friends with the white London children. This education made them more receptive to the influence of Western books, magazines, radio and television than their parents, some of whom spoke little or no English.

The adoption of some Western and individualistic values by young Asians, Cypriots and West Indians created a generation gap between themselves and their parents. This conflict between the first and second generations of newcomers was heightened by the impact of Western 'pop' culture, which was embraced to some degree by many young people. Disputes with parents over dress, late-night discos and young love affairs often concerned teenage girls, who in some cases had marriages arranged for them and were expected to be virgins on betrothal. The patriarchal domination of women in these traditional ethnic cultures contrasted sharply with the freedom and sexuality encouraged in the new commercialized world of youth.

In fact, the 'youth culture' that bloomed in London during the 1960s was itself heavily influenced by non-whites, some of whom took advantage of the new careers it offered, especially in the music business. The Afro-Caribbean culture had influenced popular music for many decades and it was particularly important in the 'pop' explosion of the 1960s. Black rhythm and blues and modern jazz became cults among the London Mods; the

Ramjam Club in Brixton, featuring Gino Washington's band, became a seedbed for soul music; Georgie Fame and a number of other trend-setting singers increasingly employed black musicians in their line-ups; and ska and bluebeat were adopted as the music of the skinheads.

In all this new music there was a very heavy borrowing of traditional Afro-Caribbean dances which were much more informal and sexual than their British counterparts. Some of the most exciting young dancers featured on the television programme *Ready Steady Go*, for example, were West Indians. They helped to develop a modern style of dancing now taken for granted as part of our culture.

By the beginning of the 1970s, then, there were a number of different dimensions to the new Commonwealth experience in London. Important ethnic communities had been established; racial hostility and discrimination were on the increase and were directed particularly at these colonies; yet the more successful non-whites were becoming integrated into suburban life and a generation of London-born black children had grown up with white youngsters in the capital.

The recession which undermined London's economy from the early 1970s onwards had a profound impact on this emerging relationship between new Commonwealth minority groups and the mainstream culture. For it was precisely those areas of the capital's economy in which new Commonwealth workers were most heavily concentrated that bore the brunt of job losses. The rapid decline of the manufacturing industry, the sweated trades and public services in London hit the new Commonwealth groups hardest: their unemployment rate was twice that of whites and some of the inner-city areas like Brixton began to turn into ghettos where high unemployment, bad housing and social deprivation were concentrated. The position was worst for young blacks, many of whom were brought up in poverty and who benefited little from an education system that was geared to the needs and interests of white children. Most left school with few qualifications and were then confronted with racial discrimination by employers: the unemployment rate among West Indian youth in London rose to 40 per cent by the early 1980s. Almost daily experience of disadvantage and discrimination had a big influence on the attitudes of the new generation of London-born blacks, who by the mid-1970s represented about two in every five black people living in the capital.

The greatest impact was on West Indian youth, who formed the most deprived section of London's society. Out of their shared sense of resentment and injustice a new, defiant pride in being black was born. A collective Afro-Caribbean identity began to emerge among the younger generation, transcending the old island loyalties and rivalries. Whereas the older blacks had tried to fit into white society, some sections of black youth now turned away from it to form a distinct culture of their own. Some adopted Rastafarianism, a religious movement that grew up in the West Indies in the 1930s and looked to Africa as the spiritual homeland. It condemned white society as greedy and corrupt (referring to it as 'Babylon'), rejected the work ethic and celebrated the smoking of ganja (cannabis) as a way of achieving communion with God. And it was fuelled even more by reggae music, notably that of Bob Marley, who quickly became the high priest of Rastafarianism.

Street-wise 'hustling', usually involving illicit drink, drugs, petty crime and prostitution, became part of the disaffected culture of some young West Indians. One crime to emerge out of this twilight world in the 1970s and particularly favoured by black teenagers was robbing people as they walked home along dark city streets in places like Brixton. The disturbing image of young blacks flouting the law and attacking innocent whites was to unleash another wave of racism upon them in the capital. The resurrection of the Victorian term 'mugging' by the newspapers did nothing to allay anxieties which, in turn, grew into what sociologists have called 'a moral panic' – a widespread fear that is out of proportion to the scale of the problem. At the same time the Metropolitan Police swamped black areas with a new style of tough policing, resulting in many wrongful arrests which generated mounting resentment in the black community.

Such was the level of tension that insensitive policing was blamed (unjustifiably in some instances) for a series of incidents in which young black men were hurt. It came to a head in April 1981 in a weekend of full-scale rioting in Brixton, where relations between the police and much of the black community had almost totally broken down. Police officers were injured and there was looting and widespread damage to property. Scenes shown on television were the most frightening of the post-war era in the capital.

Fortunately, riots on the scale of Brixton were not repeated, but there were many other conflicts involving the police and young West Indians. In 1985, petrol bombs were thrown at Brixton police station after officers had accidentally shot a West Indian woman while carrying out a raid on a house. A week later, the death of a woman following a heart attack on the

Broadwater Farm estate in Tottenham, north London, was blamed on the police. The estate was set ablaze and when firemen arrived to try to get the inferno under control they were attacked. Police were sent in to protect them, among them PC Blakelock, a local bobby who was well known and respected. When he and others turned to run from a burning building he tripped and fell and, in a most horrible and tragic incident, a gang of young men wielding knives and machetes instantly pounced on him. When his lifeless body was examined he had forty stab and slash wounds and his head had been almost hacked off.

This shocking murder led to a good deal of soul searching about who was responsible for such a serious deterioration in relations between the forces of law and order and the first generation of London-born black youths. Broadwater Farm became a byword for a breakdown in community relations and trust. Eight years later, in April 1993, another shocking killing in the London suburbs brought the issue of racial hatred and the role of the police to the forefront of the capital's politics. Stephen Lawrence, the studious eighteen-year-old son of Jamaican parents living in south London, was on his way home with a friend when he was set upon while waiting for a bus and stabbed to death by a gang of white youths. The gang ran off but there were witnesses, including the friend who had been with Stephen.

Shortly after the teenager's death it became apparent that very little was being done by the local police to seek out the murderers, and Stephen's parents were shocked by the way they were treated by senior policemen. There was such public concern at the failure to track down the gang despite a huge number of tip-offs immediately after the killing that eventually an inquiry was held. A retired judge, Sir William Macpherson, with three others (a black bishop, a retired policeman and a doctor descended from Russian immigrants) went over the evidence and concluded in their report published in 1999:

> Stephen Lawrence's murder was simply, solely and unequivocally motivated by racism. It was the deepest tragedy for his family. It was an affront to society, and especially to the local black community in Greenwich. Nobody has been convicted of this crime. That is also an affront both to the Lawrence family and the community at large.

The report concluded that the police were 'institutionally racist' but drew back from concluding that such prejudice had prevented the conviction of any of the gang who killed Stephen Lawrence. There was a trial in the end but no convictions. For whatever reason, the collection of evidence that might have led to a successful prosecution was bungled.

The deeply worrying case of Stephen Lawrence was not the last of its kind to shock the public. In November 2000 a ten-year-old Nigerian boy, Damilola Taylor, was found bleeding to death on a stairwell in a block of flats near a library in Peckham, south London. He had a single cut just above his knee which appeared to have been made with the jagged edge of a broken beer bottle. Damilola did not say to those who came to his aid that he had been attacked; but he fell unconscious, the blood draining from his body. After the Stephen Lawrence inquiry the police were desperate to get a conviction. But again, a great deal went wrong. Four youths who went for trial were either dismissed or acquitted for lack of evidence and apparently irrefutable alibis. Finally, two black brothers, one of whom had a history of criminal offences, were convicted not of murder but of manslaughter, though they denied any involvement. There were no witnesses to Damilola's death other than his killers.

THE LONDON BOMBINGS

While racism has been and remains a critical issue in London, by far the greatest threats to public safety and order in the post-war years have come not from tension between whites and new Commonwealth immigrants, but from terrorists who have made the capital the principal target of their attacks. And these have not in any way discriminated between the social and racial groups in London's increasingly multiracial society. Anyone unlucky enough to be in the vicinity of a bomb will be a victim, regardless of religious belief or political affiliation.

The most sustained series of terrorist attacks on London came from the Irish Republican Army (IRA) which began a long, if intermittent, bombing campaign in October 1971 with an explosive that blew a hole in one of the most prominent landmarks at the time, the Post Office Tower. The Tower had had a revolving restaurant at the top but this was closed down after the attack as diners would have been too vulnerable. In 1975 there was a running gun battle between the so-called Provisional IRA and the police after four men launched an attack on a Mayfair restaurant. Taking two hostages, the men holed up in an apartment in Balcombe Street in Marylebone and the police laid siege. After six days the men released the hostages, a middle-aged couple, and surrendered. They were sentenced to life imprisonment, which lasted until 1999 when they were released in what became known as the Good Friday Agreement.

IRA bombing campaigns in the 1980s included a Christmastime attack on the Harrods store, Knightsbridge, in 1983 in which six people, including three policemen, were killed. Then, in the 1990s the bombing campaigns intensified. Attacks on railway stations meant that litter bins, ideal for planting bombs, were removed and notices appeared on Underground trains and buses warning of unattended packages. As a rule, the IRA gave some warning of attacks through coded messages, but in many explosions passers-by or police officers were killed. The City became a favoured target in the Irish Republican campaign to persuade the British Parliament to relinquish Northern Ireland.

In April 1992 a bomb exploded at St Mary Axe, injuring ninety-one people and killing three. The Baltic Exchange, where London agents arranged for goods to be put on to ships all around the world, was so badly damaged it had to be demolished; the Gherkin (see Chapter Nineteen) emerged from the ruins. A year later, a massive bomb caused an estimated £350 million worth of damage in Bishopsgate. City police set up road checks on all the routes into the Square Mile and it was surrounded by a low wall of what looked like giant Lego pieces. Police with automatic weapons became a common sight for lunchtime shoppers. One of the last attempted attacks was in 1996 in which a double-decker bus was blown apart when a bomber's explosive went off prematurely, killing him. After that Londoners felt the threat eased when they travelled around the city.

Although the Irish terrorists had targeted mainline railway stations they stopped short of blowing up crowded tube trains. After the attack on the Twin Towers in New York in September 2001, however, there was an awareness that if Islamic terrorists targeted London there would be no such scruples and no warnings. Public address systems still urged passengers to report suspect packages and not to leave anything suspicious lying around. But suicide bombers did not leave bombs in litter bins – they carried them on their backs. The horrific attack on commuter trains in Madrid in March 2004 raised the sense of unease in London. In that case, the bombers did not blow themselves up but left their explosives in rucksacks and set them off from a safe distance. More than 2,000 people were injured and 91 killed in that attack which proved to be, after some uncertainty, the work of an

Islamic group. Britain, and especially London with its large Muslim population, were bound to be attacked in the end, though the manner of the assault when it came on 7 July 2005 almost defied belief.

Four young men, all of whom had lived, for a time, perfectly conventional lives in the North of England, created home-made bombs, packed them in knapsacks and took a mainline train to London. They planned to synchronize the detonation of their bombs on four different Underground lines creating, as they saw it, a symbolic destruction on the four points of the compass. Three succeeded while one bomber, unable to get to the Underground, boarded a bus, blowing up some passengers who had felt pleased they had been able to get on it when the tube station had been shut.

When the explosions were first reported it was not clear what had happened. Then as the realization dawned that these were terrorist attacks there was speculation as to how the bombs had been detonated. Forensic investigation showed that the bombers had killed themselves and in time their route to the capital was pieced together by running CCTV footage taken at the time they travelled.

There was something uniquely disturbing for Londoners about these attacks for the bombers looked no different from thousands of other young men going about their business quite innocently. The rucksacks in which the bombers carried their explosives looked like those of any student. And the motivation of the bombers was at best obscure and at worst completely incomprehensible. The young men who took their own lives, leaving behind grieving families and friends, apparently believed that by blowing up themselves and a random sample of London's richly multicultural population (inevitably including some Muslims) they would go to 'paradise'.

London waited for the next attack and, sure enough, it was attempted later the same month on 21 July. But this time there was a failure in the manufacture of the home-made explosives and though the detonators went off, the bombs did not. The would-be suicide bombers found themselves unharmed in a carriage of terrified commuters and made a run for it. Six men, all of African origin, were eventually arrested and were on trial at the time of writing.

These bombings in the name of Islam have created a new problem in London. Those Muslims who do not condone the acts of the terrorists fear reprisals and a reaction against the whole Muslim community. On the other hand, the resurgence of Islam worldwide has led to more and more demands by Muslim leaders for the right to practise their own laws and follow the tenets of their own beliefs within the communities which have played host to them as immigrants. The wearing of the burka or face mask by Muslim women has caused a great deal of tension in London and in other European cities. This has raised the issue of 'multiculturalism' in the capital: to what degree should incomers adopt the rules and values of the host culture? Is there too much emphasis on encouraging ethnic and religious groups to live in isolation from 'mainstream' culture?

While that is debated, London carries on. In the year before the 7 July bombings the London Underground lines had carried the highest number of passengers in a year since the opening of the steam-driven Metropolitan line in 1862: 976 million. In the immediate aftermath of the bombings it was noticeable how many more Londoners were walking or cycling to work out of fear of further attacks. The bombs had put 15 per cent of the system out of action, anyway. Underground passenger figures fell by 20 per cent from that historic high point. In the second week after the attack they were already rising again and were only 15 per cent down. Then came the abortive 21 July attacks and numbers fell again, but not as much as after 7 July. Numbers were down at the end of July, but began to rise again the following month, and by the last week in September were almost back to the historic high again with a figure for 2006 of 971 million. On 8 December 2006, as Christmas shopping got under way, the Underground carried 4 million passengers in a single day, a record.

These buoyant figures are symptomatic of a great metropolis as vibrant as ever despite the bombings and attempts to disrupt it. In particular, the core of the great conurbation, that region referred to roughly and often misleadingly as the 'inner city', has experienced a revival that the post-war planners did not anticipate. And this has occurred at a time when London has been given back by central government some authority to plan for its own fate. A very familiar figure, a kind of scurrilous Dick Whittington and, in his day, almost certainly the best-known 'Londoner', resurfaced after years in obscurity as a mere Member of Parliament for Brent and left-wing *bon viveur* who made a tidy sum as a restaurant reviewer. The remarkable resurfacing of 'Red Ken' Livingstone concludes this people's history of London.

CHAPTER TWENTY-FOUR

Inner-city Dream

I F, BACK IN the 1950s, anyone had suggested that one day the great metropolis of London would have an American-style Mayor, like those celebrated potentates of New York or Chicago, the whole idea would have been dismissed as 'barmy'. In fact, that was the very word used in 1997 by Ken Livingstone, former leader of the long-gone Greater London Council, when Prime Minister Blair's government proposed that Londoners might in future *elect* a Mayor. In an article in the *Evening Standard* on 23 October 1997 Livingstone argued that only a handful of Labour MPs supported mayoral elections and precious few members of the public. However, the government went ahead in 1998 with a referendum held on 7 May, the same day as the local elections, asking: 'Are you in favour of the Government's proposals for a Greater London Authority, made up of an elected Mayor and a separately elected assembly?'

Only a third of the electorate bothered to vote but, of those that did, the 'Yes' votes were clearly in the majority in every London borough. In the run-up to the referendum the government had listed the capital's ills: a transport system 'creaking at the seams', fear of crime, poor air quality, run-down, dirty streets and a lack of jobs. 'London needs its own voice in shaping the City's future,' was the bold proposition. But who would be the people's elected Mayor? It dawned on the Blair government too late that the favourite candidate was none other than 'Red Ken' Livingstone, who emerged from obscurity to stake his claim as the leader London needed for this new dawn.

Reviled by New Labour as one of those radicals who had made the party 'unelectable' in the past, Livingstone at first tried to get back in as the official party nominee for the mayoral race. When he was turned down in favour of the no-hoper Frank Dobson and rivals from the Tories fell by the wayside (the pulp fiction writer Jeffrey Archer had to withdraw over a scandal), Livingstone announced he would run as an independent. When Livingstone was expelled from the Labour Party, Conservative leader

William Hague quipped in the Commons (where everyone knew how Blair hated Livingstone): 'Why not split the job in two, with Frank Dobson as your day Mayor and Ken Livingstone as your nightmare?'

When opinion polls revealed that the nightmare of Red Ken's return to London government was likely to become a reality there was just time for the government, in the framing of the Bill which would set out the powers and responsibility of the new Assembly and the Mayor, to allow as little leeway as possible. And when the elections were held in May 2000 many innovations were put in place to encourage, the government hoped, a higher turnout than was usual: it allowed voting over a whole week, put ballot boxes in Tesco supermarkets and set up an electronic system for counting the votes for Mayor. All very high-tech and largely a waste of time, as the turnout was the customary one-third of the electorate. Voters were asked to give a first and second preference for mayoral candidates. Ken came top but had just under 39 per cent of first-preference votes. On a second count, against Steven Norris the Conservative candidate, Ken won with nearly 58 per cent against his rival's 42 per cent. And so it came to pass that Ken Livingstone, who thought an elected Mayor for London was a 'barmy' idea, became the first person to enjoy that office. He did so with a total of 776,427 first- and second-preference votes from a total London electorate of just over 5 million.

Although as Mayor, Ken Livingstone had limited formal powers, he had been given an opportunity to make his presence felt and could claim to have been elected by a larger constituency than anyone before him. Further, to the immense relief of the government, it was clear that 'Red Ken' had mellowed a good deal, and before long he would be welcomed back into the ranks of the Labour Party, just before his re-election as Mayor of London for a second four-year term in 2004, with a slightly narrower margin than before. By 2006 moves were afoot to grant Mayor Livingstone and the Greater London Authority's elected members much wider powers than they had initially been granted, which has led some political commentators to speculate that London government is heading back to the days of the old London County Council and the GLC. This might well be the case, but London, now chosen to host the 2012 Olympics, is hardly the metropolis it was just after the war. In those days a modest festival on the bomb-ravaged south bank of the Thames was about all it could manage.

THE FESTIVAL OF BRITAIN

There is something about the Festival of Britain, the centrepiece of which was staged in London between May and September 1951, which lends itself to the idea that in its conception and design it was a watershed in both the country's and the capital's history.

First proposed during the war as a modern counterpart to the 1851 Great Exhibition in Hyde Park, the idea was pursued by Gerald Barry, editor of the left-wing newspaper the *New Chronicle*. Britain was effectively broke just after the war and holding a celebratory festival was, at that point, a very low priority. However, as the Labour government which had triumphed in 1945 approached the end of its five-year tenure in office, the money was found to stage the exhibition on the South Bank, much of which was derelict. The old Lion Brewery was demolished to make way for the festival grounds and its famous Coade stone lion eventually found a home on Westminster Bridge, rebuilt before the war (and opened officially in 1945) despite the protests of conservationists who wanted the old crossing preserved.

Although the government gave its backing, the prime mover for the Festival was the London County Council and the man most associated with it was Herbert Morrison, a cabinet minister in the Labour government. Morrison, inevitably dubbed 'Mr Festival' by the newspapers, said that the celebration was the nation 'giving itself a pat on the back'. It was, as it turned out, a huge success, attracting 8 million visitors in the few months it was open. There was a funfair in Battersea Park, and a wonderful collection of modernist structures such as the Skylon (which wags were quick to say was just like Britain herself as it had no visible means of support), and the Dome of Discovery with exhibits illustrating British contributions to science and exploration.

Most of the people involved in the Festival saw it as an expression of hope that out of the ashes of war an entirely new London could be built which would turn its back on the Victorian past. In particular, the rotten core of the metropolis – still pitted with bombsites now becoming treacherous playgrounds for a generation of London children – could be transformed with a new kind of architecture. On offer at the Festival was a chance to take a bus trip to view the brand-new Lansbury Estate created in burned-out Poplar – an example of the comprehensive redevelopment that planners regarded as the future. No more grim Georgian or Victorian terraces but brand-new homes on carefully designed inner-city estates with schools, shops and community centres all close by. Some of the Lansbury Estate show-houses had television sets on view.

Hugh Casson, who had overall responsibility for the architecture at the Festival, recalled for a BBC Television series:

> We all had, I suppose, in a way, rather naive views that England could
> be better and was going to be better – that the arts and architecture
> and music and healthy air and Jaeger underwear and all these things,
> which the garden city movement stood for, were in fact the keys to
> some sort of Utopia.

Playwright and humorist Michael Frayn had a similar view of the Festival, recalling it as:

> ... the last and virtually posthumous work of the Herbivore Britain of
> the BBC News, the Crown Film Unit, the sweet ration, the Ealing
> comedies, Uncle Mac, Sylvia Peters ... all the great fixed stars by
> which my childhood was navigated.

Frayn's 'Herbivores' were idealists with a social conscience, in contrast to the realists like the novelist Evelyn Waugh who hated the Festival, and Winston Churchill who thought it was a waste of time and money. In fact, it made a profit and left one lasting edifice – the very popular Festival Hall designed by LCC architects which has now been refurbished. The Labour government, on the other hand, did *not* last; it was voted out and the venerable Churchill returned to power in October 1951. Regardless of who was in power, however, the task of rebuilding London was inescapable, and the architects and planners of the London County Council were determined that it should be modernized with the Festival's Lansbury Estate as a model. A start had been made before the Festival but shortages of materials and capital had handicapped redevelopment and rehousing schemes, and the condition of homes in the worst parts of the inner city were terrible.

FROM WASTELAND TO HIGH-RISE

In 1945 huge tracts of inner London had been turned into a bomb-shattered and weed-covered wasteland. The blitz, followed by the doodlebug and rocket attacks on the capital, had devastated inner London's housing stock. In Islington, then one of the most poverty-stricken boroughs, 3,000 houses had been totally destroyed by Hitler's bombs. Many thousands more had suffered serious bomb damage to roofs, walls and windows, all of which had been hastily patched up. Islington's plight was not quite as desperate as that of the East End; a third of the housing in Stepney, for example, had been demolished and made uninhabitable by the blitz. However, the long neglect by the landlords who controlled its tenement slums, combined with lack of repairs and destruction during the war, meant that Islington had some of the worst housing in the capital. Three-quarters of its households had neither running water, an inside lavatory nor a bath.

It seemed to many Londoners that the promises of a better world, which had helped to sustain them through the sacrifices and sufferings of the war, had been pie in the sky. In Islington 12,500 families were on the council waiting list, among them the Cassallis. Ron Cassalli remembered:

> The housing conditions we lived in then [before the war] were atrocious. We had sixteen people using one toilet, three families queuing up and there were eight of us, my wife and six children, in two rooms. Then along came the war and the ceiling was damaged and water started seeping in through the cracks in it. We had eight people sleeping in this one bedroom with water seeping through the ceiling, buckets everywhere, and every now and then your bed got wet. And if one of the kids was ill, had a cough or something, it woke the others up. Terrible conditions to live in and to think we'd spent six years of our lives fighting a war, and we had to come back to this kind of thing. I was very annoyed; I felt really let down.

A mood of anger and desperation was in the air and in the summer of 1946 thousands of poor and homeless families took the law into their own hands by squatting in empty buildings and military camps. And in September of that year the Communist Party organized a well-publicized squat by about 1,500 East Enders in luxury West End flats under renovation. Hundreds of families carrying bedding and pots and pans converged on High Street Kensington and seized Duchess of Bedford House, a seventeen-storey block of flats. They also invaded other Kensington mansion blocks in Upper Phillimore Gardens and Holland Park, and captured the 630-room Ivanhoe Hotel in Bloomsbury. The squats ended after about two weeks when eviction notices were served, but the angry mood continued and was reflected in many individual acts of defiance. In the exceptionally cold winter of 1947, for example, the impoverished Cassallis used desperate measures to get free fuel for their fire, as Ron Cassalli recalled:

> Those were very hard days – so hard that when it got cold in the winter and you couldn't get coal we used to go next door (it was an empty house that had been bombed). And, first of all, we took the coal that was there in the coal cellar, then we took up the floorboards, then we used the banisters – anything that was burnable we would burn. And many a time I remember lying in bed thinking, 'How the hell am I going to pay these bills?' and even contemplating doing burglaries and things like that which I'd never done in my life. Things got so desperate, that's the way you felt.

But by 1948 things were looking up a little, although the first improvement felt by many was not in housing but in health care, when the National Health Service came into being at midnight on 4 July. With the coming of the welfare state, inspired by the Labour Party, people enjoyed new welfare rights. There was an enormous take-up of benefits in poor areas like Islington. Especially welcome was the free medical treatment and free spectacles and false teeth which the poorest had been forced to do without in the past. The creation of a comprehensive system providing health care for all, from cradle to grave, was one of the great social achievements of the post-war years.

And by the late 1940s things were also beginning to improve on the housing front. Production of the first prefabricated houses (quickly dubbed 'prefabs') was stepped up and many thousands of these rabbit hutch-like bungalows appeared on bombsites all over London. Although they were intended by the government to be a stop-gap measure with a short life they turned out to be a rare housing triumph of the post-war years. Inside they had all modern conveniences and they all had gardens, which was a dream for the likes of Betty Vodden who remembered being shown her new prefab in Islington:

> In 1947 my husband came out of the Navy and lodgings and houses were so hard to get, we couldn't live together. I went to live with my mother and we were well overcrowded there, and my husband lived

twenty minutes' walk away. This lasted for about two years and by then I had a son of eight years and a baby of eighteen months. So one day the woman who took my mother's rent came round and asked me if I'd go with her up the road. When I got to the top of the road she turned the corner and I knew there were eight prefabs there and I said to her, 'You're not taking me to a prefab?' She said, 'I am'. Oh, when I got there I was so thrilled with the lovely big gardens all waiting to be dug up. We went in through the side door and it opened on to the kitchen. It was beautiful: there was a fridge which was something I'd never had before, an electric cooker, electric kettle, lovely tops, wooden tops to everything. Everything was grand and I was really thrilled when she gave me the key, especially as we could live together then.

By 1948 the LCC rehousing programme in central London was beginning to bear fruit. At this period, the architecture was still on the modest scale of the interwar developments: it looked a little old-fashioned but it was what Londoners were happy with. The LCC insisted on a maximum height of six storeys for the flats it built. These made ideal homes for families like the Cassallis who were moved out from the tenement slums. Ron Cassalli remembered:

We were given a four-bedroomed LCC flat on the second floor which was absolutely heaven. The four main things we liked, in order of priority, were, firstly, to be able to sit in the toilet on your own, undisturbed, nobody knocking on the door, and to contemplate, and really enjoy yourself. Secondly to have a bathroom; thirdly, to have hot water and fourthly, to have the privacy of your own front door. Nobody could appreciate how marvellous it was unless they'd gone through the drama of having one toilet for sixteen people for all those years.

Even in its grandest project, the Lansbury Estate, the LCC insisted on a rich variety of housing design. Lansbury was begun in 1948 as part of the Comprehensive Development Scheme for Stepney and Poplar, which aimed to rehouse 100,000 people in the East End in a mixture of modern flats and houses. Community facilities like schools, churches, shops, civic centres and play areas were to be provided in abundance. As it turned out, however, the Lansbury model was not the beginning but the end of low- to medium-rise communities envisaged by the first generation of Labour politicians and planners. Their rather old-fashioned dream was to be replaced by a much more aggressive and modern approach to housing in the city.

The Conservative Party returned to power in 1951 and pledged to increase house building to end the continuing housing crisis, alleviated but not solved by Labour. Party politics was turning housing into a numbers game and the easiest way to register large numbers of new dwelling units quickly was to put up prefabricated high-rise blocks of flats. So wholesale slum clearance began as the decaying Victorian streets were demolished. These programmes of comprehensive redevelopment suited the London County Council architects and planners, just as it did the Conservative government in pursuit of election-winning claims for their efforts to solve the inner-city housing crisis.

A young generation of LCC architects was strongly committed to the modern movement in architecture and the futuristic dream of a city in the sky. Soon, daringly modern projects began to change the skyline of London's Victorian suburbs. Blocks of flats were built higher than ever before, often reaching up between eight and twelve storeys. This was the decade of great concrete-slab blocks, both long and tall. The grandest project in this style in inner London was the Loughborough Road Estate in Brixton, built between 1954 and 1957; most of its 1,031 dwellings were maisonettes contained in eleven-storey slab blocks and these prototypes later became the standard model for the LCC's housing programme.

The two-level apartments were designed with coal fires (central heating had not yet become a standard feature of council housing), but this made life complicated both for the designers and for the tenants. Coal had to be delivered in the lifts, the smoke from the fires was released through a system of flues and the ash was disposed of through chutes or through the lift. However, most tenants were, to begin with, very happy with their new flat life. The most popular feature of the flats was their generous room size, and the fact that each one contained a modern kitchen, bathroom and toilet.

In addition, there was a positive response to high-rise living. In the only serious survey of this in London, undertaken by sociologist Margaret Willis, the remarkable fact was documented that, after an initial period of anxiety, 90 per cent of families preferred to live on a high floor. Tenants preferred flats on higher levels because they were quieter. They often enjoyed spectacular views, too, and the air was more bracing. One of the first tenants to move on to the Loughborough Estate in 1956 was Pat Bloxham, who remembered:

When I moved up here it seemed strange to me – a great big place like this – and I really got scared. When I went outside I was terrified. I used to think that the walls were going to come away from me. When I was on the balcony, my legs just turned to jelly and I used to crawl to get inside again; it was terrifying. I wanted to run away. But after a while I got used to it and started to like it. My doctor told me if I lived up high it was better for your health – that's why I always used to be glad to be up high, to go out on the balcony and get all the fresh air. It was really lovely; you didn't want to go out anywhere, all you wanted to do was to stay up here in the sun and enjoy yourself. Oh, the views were beautiful! You look out and get Crystal Palace, the West End, you can see everywhere and everything; especially at night time when all the lights are on.

A DOOR CLOSES ON NEW HOMES

By the late 1950s the building of new flats had almost ground to a halt. The grand plan had proved to be hugely expensive, chiefly because the cost of land in the central areas was rising rapidly. Then a series of cuts in housing grants by the new Conservative government meant that councils in poorer London areas had virtually no money to spend on their housing programmes and could offer little hope to local families looking for a council flat. In Islington the housing waiting list was longer than almost anywhere else in London, and the council was forced to close it in 1957 when 16,000 families were waiting for new homes.

The best chance of being rehoused was through the LCC but it too had an endless queue of poor families needing accommodation. The upshot of all this was that many people were living in slum conditions, confronted by a faceless bureaucracy which kept them waiting interminably for new homes. The anger and frustration that this generated exploded into many daily dramas in the LCC housing offices. Jim Cattle, who worked as a porter at Smithfield Market, had been on the council waiting list for seven years. He remembered:

Their attitude was bombastic, dictatorial; it became a system of them and us. They had it, you wanted it, and they weren't going to give it to you. I used to be working from twelve o'clock at night and I'd come home about two in the afternoon, and instead of going to bed I'd go down to the LCC housing office with Doll, the kids and all. It got to the point where we'd been down there about three or four times that week. We were talking to a geezer behind the ramp and it just clicked, wallop, like that. I just did my nut. I said, 'I want to see the Housing Manager and I want to see him now.' (You had more chance of visiting God than one of the Housing Managers.) I shall never forget it to this day – I jumped over the counter, I pushed the geezer out of the way, went up the corridor, kicked the door open, and there was the old Housing Manager sitting there. And I just blew my top.

Although the housing drive in inner London was slowing down, the Abercrombie plan to remove people and jobs to the new towns (see Chapter Twenty-two) was now taking off and government money was going to Stevenage in Hertfordshire and Harlow in Essex rather than to the inner city. But because the whole system of dispersal of Londoners to new and overspill towns was heavily weighted in favour of the skilled working-class families, others, like the Cattles, soon discovered that there was no hope of them ever getting a council home in a new town. Jim Cattle recalled:

When they started to build these new towns like Stevenage, they said, 'Well, would you like to go?' 'Yeh, cor, I'd love to go.' 'What do you do for a living?' Well, when I turned around and said to them I work at Smithfield Market they looked at me and said, 'Well, you'd better go back there.' We weren't qualified for anything like that. I'd have given my soul for a house, but you were just banging your head against a brick wall. I put my name down and all that and they took your particulars, and that's as far as you ever got. Most people that went to these new towns were skilled people – mechanics, tool setters, and so on. After all, it was a new town being built out of the rubble and they wanted the craftsmen to go with it; they wanted the industries, they didn't want Tom, Dick and Harry going down there to take up the properties. So with me not being skilled we had no chance, no chance at all.

So in Central London it was the semi-skilled, unskilled, the old and the sick who were being left behind. But they were not to remain entirely abandoned; there were people who actually wanted to live in the inner city. Some incomers were new Commonwealth immigrants attracted by cheap rented housing, others were better off and were destined to transform the social composition of many areas: the pioneer middle classes who began buying up and restoring some of the old houses that were being sold off cheaply. They were given the mildly facetious nickname of 'gentrifiers', a term first coined by sociologist Ruth Glass in 1964.

The bug-infested Victorian terraces into which many working-class families had been crammed were regarded as potentially desirable by modestly well-off Londoners with a liking for traditional architecture and just enough money to turn them into attractive homes. Most of these houses had been put up by Victorian speculative builders to attract middle-class families with servants so the gentrifiers were, in effect, returning them to something approaching their original use.

THE GENTRIFIERS MOVE IN

Canonbury in Islington was one of the first parts of London to be gentrified and many of those who moved into its elegant Georgian town houses were young architects, among them Harley Sherlock who remembered:

> We wanted to be in the centre of things, we wanted to be where
> everybody was, we wanted a change from suburbia which wasn't where
> life was going on, we wanted to be part of London; we wanted to be
> where working people of all sorts were, and all this we found in
> Canonbury. In those days properties in Central London were cheap,
> nobody wanted to live in the centre. We bought two very nice
> buildings and each house I think cost us £2,650 which, by today's
> standards, is just ridiculous. Most people wanted to live in the leafy
> suburbs; indeed, my parents thought I was mad to come and live in
> dirty, grubby old London. But for those of us who were young and
> wanted to do something different, this was an absolutely marvellous
> opportunity. We were a sort of co-operative of young idealistic
> architects and we wanted to join the two houses we'd bought together.
> So we held a sort of house-warming party, we gave the guests pickaxes
> and crowbars and we showed them where to make a hole from one
> house into the other, one at first floor level and one in the basement.

And we offered a prize of a bottle of Schnapps for the first person to get through. This turned out to be very hard work in the basement because it was an eighteen-inch-thick brick wall, which was rather thicker than we'd expected, but it certainly was a good party. I think Canonbury started to become fashionable because it had a lot of very beautiful grand houses and people were getting tired of commuting into London every day. And, of course, there were articles being published at the time drawing attention to the fact that more and more people (I suppose they'd be called trendy people now) were hitting on the idea of moving into Central London. 'Good Housekeeping' magazine did a sort of article with fashion models standing on the steps of various pretty houses in Canonbury. It mentioned that five young architects and furniture designers had moved into the area. That was us.

When they were first built, many of the houses in places like Islington and Camden Town – always regarded as classic gentrifying boroughs – had been upmarket. They had gone downhill for a number of reasons but perhaps the most significant was the foul air of the inner city. (An exception was the really upper crust West End, which still housed the aristocracy and the very well-to-do in the Season.) It was the middle-class suburbs that were always liable to go downhill. The cutting of the railway lines ruined the attraction of many inner-city areas, not least because the trains were all steam-driven and belched soot over wide areas. The whole of London was heated and fuelled by coal and the soot and smoke from hundreds of thousands of chimneys blackened everything. In the satire *Diary of a Nobody* by the brothers Grossmith, the hapless Mr Pooter finds a house to rent in Holloway. As the garden backs on to the railway there is a slight reduction in rent.

Without cleaner air the Islingtons and Camdens would not have been colonized by the new middle classes. The passing of the Clean Air Act in 1956, progressively outlawing the burning of fossil fuels in the home and in factories and offering grants to replace the old hearth with an electric or gas fire, was crucial. It took a few years to produce a notable change in winter and the last really severe smog came in 1962–3 during bitterly cold weather, but from then on London air, the trees and the buildings were cleaner. At the same time steam trains were replaced by diesel engines and later electrified lines.

Another reason why middle-class families were looking for places to live in inner London was the realization that the delightful days of easy motoring and stress-free commuting by car from some far-flung rural idyll were well and truly over. Far better to live near enough work to walk or cycle or take the bus or Underground. By the early 1960s the movement of architects and media professionals back into places like Islington was increasing rapidly. As Canonbury filled up, so the newcomers discovered Barnsbury, and set about transforming what had deteriorated into one of the worst slums in London into a splendid period suburb. House-hunting young couples became experts at spotting the up-and-coming areas. They looked for sand and cement mixers in the road – tell-tale signs of renovation. And, most important, they noted how many houses in a street possessed brass door knockers and were newly painted. This was the badge of the pioneer and to outsiders it announced that there was a gentrifier within, determined to restore the house to its original glory.

This colonization of areas like Barnsbury by middle-class pioneers brought a new atmosphere and culture to wedges of inner London. In Islington, a Barnsbury Society was set up for the gentrifiers to press for schemes such as tree-planting, traffic control and pleasanter streets, all of which began to lend a special charm to the refurbished early nineteenth-century squares and terraces. A popular style with the gentrifiers was wittily called 'conspicuous thrift' – deliberately austere as opposed to the showy, conspicuous consumption of the really rich. Gentrifiers had often been rebellious students who disliked the brash materialism of the affluent society and preferred a natural and unpretentious look. Their furniture was stripped pine, their walls were painted white rather than papered, and their floorboards were sanded to remove the varnish, then left uncovered.

An indication of the changing character of Barnsbury can be seen in the census figures; the proportion of men employed in managerial and professional jobs rose from 3 per cent in 1961 to over 15 per cent ten years later. The social character of Islington in the early 1960s was fairly typical of London's inner boroughs. They contained three main kinds of housing and lifestyle. First, there were the up-and-coming areas, where a few thousand pioneer gentrifiers were busy restoring the surviving Georgian and early Victorian houses and squares. Second, there were dozens of council estates on which families enjoyed the comforts and convenience of living in modern flats. Third came the majority of people who could not buy a home and who lived in privately rented accommodation. In 1961 local authorities in inner London housed only about 20 per cent of the population. Slum clearance had only scratched the surface of London's housing problems. And among those left in the inner city a growing proportion were the poorer immigrants, the old, the sick and the families of unskilled workers.

By chance, a great scandal of the early 1960s which became known as the Profumo Affair led newspapers into the poverty-stricken streets of the once upmarket area of Notting Hill in west London, where huge stucco houses built for the well-to-do had long been in decay and were in dreadful condition, not untypical of London's huge unmodernized stock of rented flats and rooms. The district had provided a haven for West Indians, especially those from Trinidad (see Chapter Twenty-three), who had been taken in by Peter Rachman, the slum landlord notorious for winkling out legal tenants and cramming cheap properties with poor tenants.

THE PROFUMO AFFAIR

When the Profumo Affair hit the headlines in 1963 John Profumo was the Secretary of State for War in Harold Macmillan's government. He was accused in the House of Commons of having a sexual relationship with a high-class prostitute, Christine Keeler, who had also slept with the Russian Naval Attaché to London. At first Profumo admitted he knew Keeler but denied any affair. Later he had to admit that he had lied to Parliament and he was forced to resign. Investigation of the world in which Keeler lived led to Notting Hill and to Rachman and some seedy clubs. Although Rachman had died in 1962, stories of the violence he inflicted on innocent tenants in order to secure his fortune drew attention to the housing conditions in that part of London.

The Rachman scandal led to a government inquiry; published in 1964, the Milner-Holland report painted a grim picture of much of London's housing stock. Islington was one of the worst areas, for it had fewer basic facilities than anywhere else in the capital. Most of its households still did not have exclusive use of running water, a bath or a toilet. It also had the largest number of overcrowded households in London. The horrors of living in the 'inner city' became the subject of much concern in the newspapers and on television. Not only did hundreds of thousands of Londoners live in appalling conditions, a new and acute problem of homelessness was beginning to attract media attention. The most powerful indictment of the failure to tackle this social issue was the 1966 BBC drama documentary *Cathy Come Home* about a homeless woman and her children, much of it filmed in Islington.

It was clear that the policy of relocating families in the new towns had gone only so far to alleviate the post-war housing crisis in London, and that the building of council properties, though impressive, fell far short of what was needed. The Labour-controlled London County Council had been very active but was now a hopeless anachronism, as the built-up area of the metropolis went far beyond its old nineteenth-century boundaries. For many years there had been proposals to create a new authority to cover the whole of London, with a new configuration of local councils within it. This finally came about in 1965 when the first members of a new Greater London Council were elected and thirty-two new London boroughs created. Because the new authority encompassed the mostly Conservative-minded outer boroughs it was assumed that the Tories would dominate the GLC. But at the first election this did not happen. Labour won nineteen of the thirty-two boroughs and held sixty-four seats at County Hall compared with the Tories' thirty-four.

The new GLC continued the slum-clearance programme begun by the LCC. A new fashion for high-rise blocks of flats inspired by the French-Swiss architect Le Corbusier had captured the imagination of the LCC architects intent on giving London a contemporary appearance. Already in the 1950s there were blocks rising to eighteen floors in Southwark, twenty storeys in Paddington and twenty-four in Deptford. The Conservative government, anxious to keep the housing programme going for political reasons, encouraged high-rise building by offering from 1956 increased subsidy money for each extra floor built on a block. As new construction techniques evolved, tower blocks of flats could be built more and more speedily, their component parts or slabs prefabricated and hoisted into position by crane. Very soon the skyline of the old slums of London changed radically.

TOWER-BLOCK TRAP

The GLC put up no fewer than 384 high-rise blocks of flats in ten years and the boroughs were just as keen in their local building programmes. By 1971, more than a third of inner London homes were council-owned, a figure which rose to just under half in 1981. By that time in Islington, the classic 'gentrified' borough, 60 per cent of homes were council-owned. The private rented sector had shrunk and there was a kind of housing apartheid between the renovated Victorian terrace and the towering council block.

It soon became clear that the great advantages of high-rise building, the light and airiness of the apartments themselves and the modern conveniences they brought, were often outweighed by the drawbacks. Lifts would break down leaving tenants on the top floor stranded, or faced with a mountainous climb home. Poorly secured against intruders, the stairwells and lifts became horribly polluted and dangerous on many estates. Doreen Reid lived on one of the top floors of a high-rise block in Plaistow with her husband and baby Tracy in the late 1960s. She recalled:

> The first problem I discovered was the lifts; that was the first nasty experience. I had a rather large pram for Tracy when she was a baby. I went out one day and I came back and my lift wasn't working. Well, I had twenty-four flights of stairs to get up to my flat. It was very, very hard work and took me ages. I had visions of Tracy coming out of the pram, my shopping going everywhere, and I didn't attempt it again after that. So if the lift wasn't working then I just couldn't go out at all. I was virtually in the flat all the time until the lift was going. Sometimes it would take a day, sometimes two days, and I just couldn't get out at all because to take baby out in the pram was impossible.

Families with young children found they were trapped on upper floors with no outside area for the toddlers to play safely, as Doreen Reid remembered:

> There was virtually nowhere for Tracy, or any other child, to play. Our block was on a main road, so you had the traffic down there. The only place she could play basically was in her bedroom or the lounge area. The only time I could open the balcony door was if I was in the room with her continually because with young children, when they're growing up, they're into everything. I couldn't let her out – but I got neighbours complaining if she made too much noise indoors, like the tenant underneath or the tenant upstairs. I remember one day I was out in the kitchen doing some hand washing, and I thought to myself, 'Tracy's quiet, what's she up to?' And I called out to her and I got no answer. I thought, 'That's not like her.' I wandered into the lounge

and it was then I realized that the balcony door was open, and I thought 'Oh no!' I just went cold, literally cold; I stepped out on to the balcony, and I instinctively looked over the top because I fully expected to find Tracy at the bottom. When I looked down and found she wasn't there I came in and I looked in my bedroom first; she wasn't there, and then I went into her bedroom and there she was playing with her toys. But at the time it gave me a very bad fright.

When the Labour government was elected in 1964 it scrapped the high-rise subsidy and encouraged a return to low-level building. Architectural fashion was beginning to shift in that direction and the social problems of high-rise could no longer be ignored.

But the end of the high-rise era came dramatically and quite unexpectedly. On the morning of 16 May 1968 there was a loud bang in one of a number of 1960s tower blocks built in Newham. Tenants still in bed awoke to see a whole exterior wall of their flats fall away. An explosion had blown out one of the panels on an upper floor and those below had fallen like a pack of cards. The collapsing building left four dead and eleven injured – an astonishingly low casualty rate for such a densely populated block.

Long after the explosion, local rumour insisted that it had been caused by either an accident with a store of 'gelly' kept by a bank robber and safe blower, or an IRA bomb exploding prematurely. In fact, careful forensic examination of the apartment where it had occurred found no trace of explosives, nor any other evidence to support these local beliefs. The blast had, it was discovered, an entirely innocent explanation. Ivy Hodge, a fifty-six-year-old cake decorator, had put the kettle on her gas stove and lit a match to make herself a cup of tea. Somehow there had a been a build-up of gas which, when ignited, exploded with enough force to blow out a wall of her home and collapse one entire side of the block. Thus Ivy Hodge unwittingly brought to an end the programme of building high-rise blocks in London. (She lived to tell the tale, moving on to new accommodation, and, reportedly, taking her old gas stove with her.)

As soon as the cause of the explosion was known, all gas supplies were removed from existing slab-built blocks and the joins in them were strengthened at great expense. No new high-rise blocks were planned. Ronan Point was refurbished and reoccupied a few years later, but in 1986 it was knocked down along with other Newham tower blocks as the fashion for high-rise flats came to an abrupt end, giving way to an orgy of demolition. New techniques were devised for blowing them up so that they collapsed vertically in built-up areas, seemingly disappearing into the ground, leaving behind a skyline more like that of Victorian London.

A new concept replaced tower block building: the 're-hab'. Instead of knocking down Georgian and Victorian buildings in the inner city, they were to be renovated and given a new lease of life. The Labour Party's 1969 Housing Bill offered generous home-improvement grants to whoever owned these properties, especially in areas like Islington where there was a lot of old housing in poor condition. Only a few years earlier many old areas worthy of restoration were condemned and bulldozed in the clean-sweep planning phase of the mid-1960s. The most notorious piece of what was called 'planning vandalism' was the razing of the Packington Estate in Islington, a picturesque neighbourhood of Georgian terraces and squares close to the Angel tube station. A fierce local battle was fought to save it and strong arguments were put forward that refurbishment would cost less than rebuilding, but the planners won the day and another piece of Islington's prized Georgiana was returned to dust.

'Re-hab' and home-improvement grants were originally intended to improve the housing standards of the poorer people living in inner-city areas. Instead, most of the grants were taken up by middle-class gentrifiers and local property developers pushing more and more of the poorer families out of the Victorian suburbs. By the early 1970s there was a huge demand among professional people for old houses in central London suitable for renovation with the help of a home-improvement grant. In places like Camden the less well off who had bought their own homes found they were sitting on a goldmine and sold their run-down houses to young middle-class couples for what they thought were huge sums. In 1970 an early Victorian terraced house with three storeys would fetch around £5,000 – easily enough capital to buy a more modern home in places like Romford and Ilford in Essex.

Landlords, estate agents and property developers were, however, far more important than homeowners in exploiting this market for gentrification. They were ruthless in winkling out sitting tenants who had a legal right to stay. It was extremely difficult to sell a house unless it was fully vacant, and the profit to be made by means of a little unethical practice with a view to getting rid of tenants was too tempting. Some landlords locked tenants out of their lavatories, switched off the gas and electricity, smashed their windows and hired thugs to threaten them.

Another sharp practice was for a landlord to buy a property then report it to the local council as being unfit for human habitation so that the tenants had to be rehoused at public expense. Others offered tenants cash bribes to leave, usually £200, which some, ignorant of their rights, accepted. But, while homeowners were often eager to sell their houses, many private tenants wanted to stay as they had nowhere else to go, and the stage was set for many hundreds of bitter feuds between tenants and landlords.

In Stonefield Street in Barnsbury, Islington, with its attractive but run-down Georgian terraced houses, conflicts between tenants and 'winkling' landlords developed into a bitterly fought battle. From the late 1960s onwards there was pressure to get existing tenants out so that the homes could be renovated and sold at good profits. Landlords stopped doing basic repairs to homes to encourage tenants to give up and leave. Most went, but a few decided to stay and brave it out. Stonefield Street was one of the few streets where the old working-class community remained very much intact. Ray Spreadbury, a baker, had lived in the street since just after the war. He remembered:

> The actual words of the estate agents were 'Barnsbury is a chicken fit
> for plucking', meaning that they could wheedle and winkle tenants out
> and sell the houses to the gentry who wanted to move in. You see, the
> area's close to the City of London and it's also close to the West End –
> an ideal spot what with houses going cheap. Of course, we thought
> we'd got to do something about it, because we were a community in
> this street. There were all kinds of tradesmen living here; there were
> market tradesmen, bricklayers, carpenters, bakers; you name it, we had
> it in this street, and everybody knew everybody else. And if you wanted
> a job done you just sent to a particular chap. Anything you wanted you
> could get done, even our car repairs. Of course we were a bit reluctant
> to lose a community like that. So we decided that it was time to have a
> meeting and we met in a house round the square. I thought to myself,
> 'Well, the only way we can beat these people is to form ourselves into
> some kind of community group to really get down to it; so this is what
> we did. I was the one who was to be the chairman.

The tenants' association held meetings each week to campaign against bribery and harassment, but the battle reached its climax one day in September 1973, as Ray Spreadbury recalled:

People were being harassed by these winklers and especially people like Mrs Murphy who lived in number sixteen. I came along one day from work and there were workmen actually knocking her front wall down and her house was open. I knew that Mrs Murphy and her husband were both at work and I knew she wouldn't have given them permission to knock her house down just like that. They looked like cowboys. So I thought the best thing to do was to get in touch with James Pitt at the Housing Centre and get a solicitor on the job, to get an injunction and stop the work. That was what we did.

When Eileen Murphy came home from work she had a terrible shock:

There was scaffolding up and they'd pulled all the wall down. There were these great big men standing there with pickaxes, and things like that; well, I just didn't know what to do. There were bricks and mortar all over the place, and no cover to stop it getting through to the rest of the house. I went upstairs and there was this big scaffolding thing stuck on the bed with a note, a nasty note stuck to the ceiling, saying 'you dirty B'. I was really frightened because the house was all open at the front and anyone could get in. I didn't want to be pushed out, you see. I'd been there twenty-one years, and I didn't think I was of an age to be moved around. I didn't know what to do, I was scared. Then Mr Spreadbury came along and the neighbourhood lawyer James Pitt and Mr Cunningham, who was the MP for Islington.

In the ensuing legal battle the development company Preebles, responsible for demolishing Mrs Murphy's walls, lost their case. Islington Council were able to purchase and renovate much of Stonefield Street for the original tenants. But victories such as this were rare. Most of Islington's surviving desirable streets were gradually emptied of their original tenants to make way for gentrifiers.

Battles like that of Stonefield Street broke out across much of inner London in the 1970s as a new generation of pioneers moved into Georgian and Victorian streets and squares in places like Battersea, Brixton, Camden, Camberwell and Clapham. By then the enterprise of gentrification was changing in character – it was becoming highly fashionable.

To service the needs of gentrifiers, a new inner-city economy of upmarket small businesses and craftsmen's shops mushroomed. Shops selling antiques, furniture and old books, delicatessens, health food stores, wine bars and bistros, all became familiar monuments to the new affluent lifestyle. Old, semi-derelict shopping arcades like Camden Passage in Islington were transformed into busy and pricey emporiums for the gentrifiers. The money that fuelled this refurbishing of the inner city came from London's booming office economy and from expansion in media and the arts in the capital. And, as it became more and more fashionable to live in this stripped-pine belt in central London, so house and flat prices soared to astronomical heights. The average cost of a house in Islington, for example, rose from around £6,000 in the mid-1960s, to £30,000 in the mid-1970s, to £150,000 by the mid-1980s. In 2001 the average price of a terraced house in the borough was £467,000 and six years later would be more like £7–800,000. What had begun as a rather bohemian movement, often pioneered by men and women who were rejecting the suburban comforts and class snobbery of their parents' generation, had turned full circle. Increasingly, it was only those with an inheritance or on very high incomes who could afford to buy a house in a well-established, fashionable area like Barnsbury or Canonbury.

In the 1970s many commentators observed a deterioration in the quality of working-class life in inner London, as old communities were torn apart by comprehensive redevelopment of their areas. Crime, especially in the streets, grew alarmingly. In the old terraces of Islington and Bethnal Green people had struck up friendships with neighbours by talking in the garden, in the street or in the corner shop. Doreen Reid recalled:

> Where I used to live, everybody knew everybody in the street. You'd
> see your neighbour each day out in the garden; you'd have the odd cup
> of tea; either I'd make it or my neighbour would make it, and there'd
> always be something going on. We'd either be talking about the
> gardens or the children, or the dogs or whatever, but it was totally
> different when I moved into a tower block. There were about sixty
> families in it, but you might just as well have lived on your own
> because once you shut your street door you were on your own, you had
> no one to talk to. You felt like a prisoner.

Parents and grandparents had informally kept an eye on children and young people. This helped to contain and control the kind of serious crime and violence that flared up in the 1970s. But the new estates, where flats were much more isolated and surrounded by dark corridors, in a sense invited delinquency with their basement car parks, pedestrian tunnels and landscaped gardens, which were out of sight of adults and which quickly became night-time no-go areas of vandalism and violence. There were often few facilities like the traditional street-corner shop, pub or club, which in the past had been the meeting points of the local community.

In their classic sociological study, *Family and Kinship in East London,* Michael Young and Peter Wilmott documented an incredibly close and caring community which used to exist in the terraced rows of Bethnal Green in the 1950s. Practically all married daughters lived within a stone's throw of their mothers and some grandmothers might have sixty or so relatives living in their neighbourhood. But by the 1970s migration to new towns, to out-country estates and to high-rise developments scattered all over London had seriously undermined this kind of inner-city community. In the days of private rented accommodation it was at least possible for mothers to get flats in the neighbourhood for their married daughters as there were no 'regulations' governing who could get accommodation where. Local councils, on the other hand, did not see keeping families near to each other as a priority. Favouritism was frowned on and the 'point' rules applied to the allocation of flats. Older people got left behind as their families moved away, many living lonely and sometimes fearful lives, dependent on the state for basic services that might once have been provided by their families. The experience of the Cattle family in Islington vividly illustrates how the older generation were becoming stranded in the inner city. Jim Cattle recalled:

> We desperately wanted our two daughters to live close to us here in a
> council home in Islington and they desperately wanted to as well. We
> had a big battle with the council over this and they said there was no
> chance. I remember when my daughter had been on the housing list
> for four years and I went down and asked, 'Why is she being pushed
> aside like this?' He said, 'How long have you lived in the borough?' So
> I said, 'My family goes back six generations in this borough.' He said,
> 'Well, it's about time you moved over then and gave somebody else a
> chance.' Both my daughters have been forced to move out, one to
> Brighton and the other to South London. It was heartbreaking and
> we don't see each other or the grandchildren as often as we want. The
> reason it happened was because of the huge waiting list, and

gentrification as well has made it more difficult to find homes for our children. What has happened is that the old Islington community has been broken up. We've lived here for six generations and so have a lot of people like us but we're the last in the line now, we're the last generation. Islington's been taken over; we say it's been raped. When we look at the old people we see ourselves in a few years' time: isolated and dependent on authority and beholden to local government.

Most demoralizing to those forced to live on the new estates was their rapid physical decay in the 1970s. The transformation from showcase to sink estate in many cases took only several years, when appalling structural problems began to emerge. Walls and roofs leaked, drains became easily blocked and heating systems broke down. Often weeks or months passed before they were repaired. Some estates were infested with tiny, meat-eating Pharaoh's ants (so-called because they were unjustly accused of being responsible for one of the great plagues of Egypt). Shipped in accidentally from a much warmer climate, the ants first thrived in greenhouses before they moved into the warm air ducts of tower blocks and hospitals.

From the mid-nineteenth century, through the interwar years to the post-war world, there had been competing concepts of how best to improve the living conditions of the average Londoner. One was to build new suburbs so that they could move out of the centre and the other was to replace the slums in inner London with new housing. The Victorians had cheap workmen's fares on the trains and trams to encourage move-ment out to places like Hackney or Plumstead, and philanthropic housing to replace the rookeries with 'industrial dwellings'. From the end of the nineteenth century, the London County Council built some large estates beyond the borders of inner London at places like Becontree or Downham, moving Londoners out of the inner slums. When this proved problematic the LCC architects began to develop new estates of 'walk-up' flats in town. While London still had many local industries there were great advantages to having a workforce in town. After the war, the plan was once again to move Londoners out to new towns and accept that the population of Greater London would remain stable and much lower than it had been in 1939, at perhaps 6–7 million. But as London industries began to move out of the capital or to close down altogether in the face of competition from abroad there was a real anxiety that the capital would go into terminal decline.

THE BIG COUNCIL SELL-OFF

The coming to power of Margaret Thatcher in 1979 brought a wholesale change in the approach to all the economic and social problems of Britain and of London. Ostensibly there was to be a return to 'Victorian values', although it was not clear quite what that meant. In Margaret Thatcher's mind it certainly involved loosening the grip of what she regarded as the 'nanny state'. Local-authority housing, having suffered from such a bad reputation, was an obvious target, and legislation was quickly put in place to allow tenants to buy their properties at very favourable prices. This would, in theory, begin the creation of a 'property-owning democracy'. At the same time, council house building would be severely curtailed and what afterwards became known more generally as 'social housing' would be put in the hands of the unelected housing associations, some of them, like the Peabody Trust, survivors from the Victorian era of philanthropy.

Until 1982, local authorities in London were still building more new houses each year than private developers, but thereafter the building programmes were starved of government funds and fell from 14,000 completions in 1980 to the staggering figure of zero in 1994. Every year since the mid-1980s, the private sector has built more new homes than housing associations and local councils together.

Mrs Thatcher's disdain for the Greater London Council, with its offices in County Hall just across the Thames from the Houses of Parliament, was legendary. Under the leadership of Ken Livingstone, the self-styled militant Labour campaigner, County Hall cocked a snook at the Thatcherite government. Much of what was done in the way of subsidies for local fringe groups, satirized as 'Gay Whales Against Racism', was what became know as 'gesture politics': statements or policies which were no more than empty rhetoric. But there were attempts to tackle major issues in London such as the loss of manufacturing employment. Livingstone's GLC set up a Greater London Enterprise Board in an effort to attract new jobs to the capital. There was, too, a brief attempt to do something about the traffic congestion that was threatening to make London hopelessly unattractive to foreign businesses. A 'Fares Fair' policy reduced by a third the cost of travelling on public transport and was widely popular when it was introduced in 1981. Traffic congestion appeared to ease a little and travel on public transport increased. But there was a cost – an addition to the rates levied by the GLC on borough councils. This gave the

Conservative borough of Bromley a chance to challenge the Fares Fair scheme in the courts on the grounds that it had no Underground line and therefore should not be liable to subsidize it. After a long and expensive legal wrangle, ending in the Lords, Bromley and the Thatcherites won: the hugely popular Fares Fair policy had to be scrapped after just one year.

One of the central aims of Mrs Thatcher's plan for economic revival was 'deregulation'. All kinds of planning and other rules redolent of the 'nanny state' were to be removed to allow vigorous enterprise to flourish. This policy was behind the Enterprise Zone in London's docklands, the transfer of much planning control to the Docklands Development Corporation and the freeing-up of public transport services – both trains and buses – from statutory controls. When Mrs Thatcher was elected, virtually all bus and coach services in Britain, including those run by London Transport, were publicly owned and run, and fares were regulated by transport authorities. The deregulation of buses (the process for railways was a little different) brought in competition between private companies for the right to run services.

In London the process was more carefully regulated than elsewhere because of the enormous scale of the enterprise, but in time the old London Transport bus began to disappear as private companies came to negotiate contracts to work particular routes. It was not quite a return to the free-for-all of the 1920s and the racing between private buses and the 'Generals' – licensed vehicles of the General Omnibus Company – but startling none the less for Londoners who were used to the idea that a bus was a bus.

Mrs Thatcher regarded the metropolitan local authorities like the GLC (there were others for the big conurbations such as Birmingham and Manchester) as an 'unnecessary' tier of government and she planned their abolition. There was a great outcry, much of the opposition coming from members of her own party, but there was no relenting. A huge firework display on 31 March 1986 marked the demise of the Greater London Council, the toppling from power of 'Red Ken' Livingstone, and a return to the London of the days before 1889 when it had no overall authority at all.

The functions of the Greater London Council were divided between a number of local-authority organizations and ad hoc groups. There was a Minister for London, though nobody ever knew the name of the incumbent, a Minister for London Transport, a Traffic Director for London, a cabinet subcommittee on London, but no easily identifiable body or people concerned with the well-being and survival of the capital. In this respect Margaret Thatcher probably got closest to her ambition to revive Victorian values, for a constant complaint about London in the nineteenth century had been that it did not have an overall authority. And the capital had to wait until the ousting of Mrs Thatcher and her successors before there was a realistic proposal to return to it some semblance of self-government.

THE RETURN OF RED KEN

There is no more extraordinary story than the return of Ken Livingstone as the most prominent politician in London – a position made possible by his own political party which had for long regarded him as a liability. Enjoying a second term as Mayor, Livingstone has relished the new post he has made his own. His boldest scheme was to bring in a form of road pricing which had long been discussed as a way of alleviating congestion on the roads in the centre of town. The Congestion Charge has probably had less effect than it would have done had not Transport for London (part of the Greater London Authority which oversees Livingstone's office) received huge subsidies to increase bus services. Back in 1988–9, no subsidies at all were paid to London bus companies and they struggled to keep services running with insufficient funds to recruit drivers. By 2006, the transport budget was a generous £700 million or so a year.

Mayor Livingstone has nothing like the powers of his equivalent in New York or Chicago, but he has tremendous presence and influence and, as a politician, he never seems bothered about changing his mind about what is important. Whereas bus and Underground fares were frozen when he first came in, they have since risen sharply to raise revenue. He said he would never get rid of the much loved Routemaster buses with their back platform you could jump on and off of, then promptly oversaw the disappearance of nearly every one of them.

The changes that have taken place in London life between the abolition of the GLC and Livingstone's second term as Mayor have been huge. After years of decline, the capital has grown again since 1988. Its total employment has risen and, though in 2007 it still has an unacceptable level of unemployment, its buoyancy is tangible. There is no prospect of a return to the inner-city dreams of the post-war utopian planners who wanted London scaled down and less densely populated. It has even been argued by a planning think-tank, the Urban Task Force chaired by the architect Richard Rogers, that inner London would be more vibrant if the density of population were *increased*. Derelict or 'brownfield' sites left by abandoned manufacturing industries could be turned into new housing developments – a complete reversal of the policies for London evolved by Patrick Abercrombie and others during and just after the Second World War. In these early years of the twenty-first century London is not the ailing former capital of a lost Empire as many feared it might become, nor is it remotely like the metropolis envisaged by utopian planners: it is a vibrant, global city rejuvenated once again by its ability to adjust and adapt to new challenges.

BIBLIOGRAPHY

Sir Leslie Abercrombie, *Greater London Plan 1944* (London, 1945)

Alison Adburgham, *Shops and Shopping 1800–1914* (Allen & Unwin, 1981)

Jonathan Aitken, *The Young Meteors* (Secker and Warburg, 1967)

D. Atwell, *Cathedrals of the Movies: History of the British Cinema and their Audience* (Architectural Press, 1981)

Paul Addison

The Road To 1945: British Politics and the Second World War (Cape, 1975)

Now The War Is Over: A Social History Of Britain 1945–51 (BBC, 1985)

Christian Barman, *The Man who Built London Transport: A Biography of Frank Pick* (David & Charles, 1979)

T. Barker and M. Robbins

A History of London Transport Vol. 1: The Nineteenth Century (Allen & Unwin, 1975)

A History of London Transport Vol. 1: The Twentieth Century (Allen & Unwin, 1974)

Felix Barker and Ralph Hyde, *London as it Might Have Been* (John Murray, 1982)

Richard Barnes, *Mods!* (Eel Pie Publishing, 1979)

Tim Benton, 'The Biologist's Lens – The Pioneer Health Centre' in *Architectural Design, Britain in the Thirties* (1979)

Christopher Bigsby (ed.), *American Popular Culture and Europe* (Elek, 1975)

Charles Booth, *Life and Labour of the People in London*, 17 vols (Macmillan, 1902)

Brian Bowers, A History of Electric Light and Power (Peter Peregrinus, 1982)

Noreen Branson

Britain in the Nineteen Twenties (Weidenfeld & Nicolson, 1975)

Poplarism 1919–1925: George Lansbury and the Councillors' Revolt (Lawrence & Wishart, 1979)

Noreen Branson and Margot Heinemann, *Britain in the Nineteen Thirties* (Weidenfeld & Nicolson, 1971)

Christopher Breward, *Fashioning London, Clothing and the modern Metropolis* (Oxford: Berg, 2004)

Christopher Breward, Edwina Ehrman, Caroline Evans, *The London Look, fashion from street to catwalk* (Yale University Press in association with the Museum of London, 2004)

Chistopher Breward and David Gilbert (eds) *Fashion's world cities* (Oxford: Berg, 2006)

Peter Brimblecombe, *The Big Smoke: A history of Air Pollution in London since Medieval Times* (Methuen, 1987)

Fenner Brockway, *Bermondsey Story* (Bermondsey Independent Labour Party, 1949)

R. Douglas Brown, *The Port of London* (Lavenham Press, 1978)

Colin Buchanan, *Mixed Blessings: The Motor in Britain* (Leonard Hill, 1958)

John Burnett, *A Social History of Housing 1815–1970* (David & Charles, 1978)

Angus Calder, *The People's War: Britain 1939–1945* (Granada, 1982)

Angus Calder and Dorothy Sheridan, *Speak for Yourself: A Mass Observation Anthology 1937–49* (Jonathan Cape, 1984)

Ritchie Calder
  Carry on London (English Universities, 1941)
  Lesson of London (Secker and Warburg, 1941)

Iain Chambers, *Urban Rhythms: Pop Music and Popular Culture* (Macmillan, 1985)

John Connell, *The End of Tradition: Country Life in Central Surrey* (Routledge and Kegan Paul, 1978)

Peter Cowan, *The Office: A Facet of Urban Growth* (Heinemann, 1969)

Rosemary Crompton and Gareth Jones, *White Collar Proletariat: Deskilling and Gender in Clerical Work* (Macmillan, 1984)

Leonore Davidoff, *The Best Circles: Society, Etiquette and The Season* (Croom Helm, 1973)

Anna Davin, *Growing Up Poor: Home, School and Street in London 1870–1914* (Rivers Oram Press, 1996)

Nicholas Deakin and Clare Ungerson, *Leaving London: Planned Mobility and the Inner City* (Heinemann, 1977)

Alan Delgado, *The Enormous File: A Social History of the Office* (John Murray, 1979)

Bernard Donoughue and G.W. Jones, *Herbert Morrison: Portrait of a Politician* (Weidenfeld & Nicholson, 1973)

Ruth Durant, Watling: *A Survey of Social Life on a New Housing Estate* (P.S. King, 1939)

H.J. Dyos, *Victorian Suburb: A Study of the Growth of Camberwell* (1961)

H.J. Dyos and M. Wolff (eds), *The Victorian City*, 2 vols, (Routledge & Kegan Paul, 1973)

Lionel Esher, *A Broken Wave: The Rebuilding of England 1940–1980* (Allen Lane, 1981)

Bill Fishman, *The Streets of East London* (Duckworth, 1979)

Constance Fitzgibbon, *The Blitz* (Windgate, 1957)

Adrian Forty, 'The Electric Home: A Case Study of the Domestic Revolution of the inter-war years' in Open University, *History of Architecture and Design Course, British Design* (Units 19.20, 1980)

H.G. de Fraine, *Servant of This House: Life in the Old Bank of England* (Constable, 1960)

Peter Fryer, *Staying Power: The History of Black People in Britain* (Pluto, 1984)

Peter and Leni Gillman, *Collar the Lot! How Britain Interned and Expelled Its Wartime Refugees* (Quartet, 1980)

Di Gittins, *The Fair Sex: Family Size and Structure 1900–39* (Hutchinson, 1982)

Ruth Glass, *Newcomers* (Allen and Unwin, 1960)

David Goodway, *London Chartism 1838–1848* (Cambridge University Press, 1982)

Oliver Green and John Reed, *The London Transport Golden Jubilee Book* (Daily Telegraph, 1983).

Peter Hall
  The Industries of London since 1861 (Hutchinson, 1962)
  London 2000 (Faber and Faber, 1971)
  London 2001 (Routledge, 1989)
  The Containment of Urban England (2 Vols.) (Allen and Unwin, 1973)
  The Polycentric Metropolis: Learning from the Mega-city Regions in Europe (Earthscan Publications Ltd, 2006)

Leslie Hannah
  The Rise of the Corporate Economy (Methuen, 1983)
  Electricity Before Nationalisation (Macmillan, 1979)

Dennis Hardey and Colin Ward, *Arcadia For All: The Legacy of a Makeshift Landscape* (Mansell, 1984)

Paul Harrison, *Inside The Inner City* (Penguin, 1983)

Tom Harrisson, *Living Through The Blitz* (Penguin, 1978)

Guy Hartcup, *Code Name Mulberry: The Planning, Building and Operation of the Normandy Harbours* (David and Charles, 1977)

Geoffrey Hewlett (ed.), *A History of Wembley* (London Borough of Brent, 1979)

Dilip Hiro, *Black British, White British* (Pelican, 1973)

Hermione Hobhouse, *A History of Regent Street* (Macdonald & Janes, 1975)

Kenneth Hudson and Julian Pettifer, *Diamonds in the Sky: A Social History of Air Travel* (Bodley Head, 1979)

Antony Hugill, *Sugar And All That: A History of Tate and Lyle* (Gentry Books, 1978)

M. Hunter, *The Victorian Villas of Hackney* (Hackney Society, 1981)

Alan Jackson
   Rails Through the Clay: A History of London's Tube Railways (Allen & Unwin, 1962)
   Semi-Detached London: Suburban Development, Life and Transport 1900–39 (Allen & Unwin, 1973)

Henry Jephson, *The Sanitary Evolution of London* (1907)

David Johnson
   V for Vengeance: The Second Battle of London (William Kimber, 1981)
   The City Ablaze (William Kimber, 1980)

R.V. Jones, *Most Secret War: British Scientific Intelligence 1939–1945* (Hamish Hamilton, 1978)

Gareth Stedman Jones, *Outcast London* (Clarendon, 1971)

John Kellett, *The Impact of Railways in Victorian Cities* (Routledge & Kegan Paul, 1969)

David Kynaston, *The City of London four vols* (Chatto and Windus, 1994–2000)

Trevor Lee, *Race and Residence: The Concentration and Dispersal of Immigrants in London* (Clarendon Press, 1977)

Jane Lewis, 'Women Between the Wars' in Frank Gleversmith (ed.) *Class, Culture and Social Change: A New View of the 1930s* (Harvester Press, 1983)

Llewellyn Smith, *The New Survey of London Life and Labour* – 9 vols (P.S. King)

Norman Longmate
   How We Lived Then: A History of Everyday Life During the Second World War (Hutchinson, 1971)

The Doodlebugs: The Story of the Flying Bombs (Hutchinson, 1981)

Hitler's Rockets: The Story of the V2's (Hutchinson, 1985)

The GIs: The Americans in Britain 1942–45 (Hutchinson, 1975)

When We Won The War: The Story of Victory in Europe (Hutchinson, 1977)

If Britain Had Fallen (BBC and Hutchinson, 1972)

The Real Dad's Army: The Story of The Home Guard (Hutchinson, 1974)

Patricia Malcolmson, 'Getting a Living in the Slums of Victorian Kensington' in *The London Journal*, 1977

Oliver Marriott, *The Property Boom* (Hamish Hamilton, 1967)

Arthur Marwick

The Deluge: British Society and The First World War (Macmillan, 1965)

The Home Front (Thames and Hudson, 1976)

British Society Since 1945 (Penguin, 1982)

Henry Mayhew, *London Labour and the London Poor* (1861)

Mass Observation

War Begins At Home (Chatto and Windus, 1940)

People in Production: An Enquiry into British War Production (John Murray, 1942)

Ian McLaine, *The Ministry of Morale* (George Allen and Unwin, 1979)

George Melly, *Revolt into Style: The Pop Arts in Britain* (Penguin, 1970)

Les Miller and Howard Bloch, *Black Saturday, The First Day of the Blitz: East London*

Raynes Minns, *Bombers and Mash: The Domestic Front 1939–45* (Virago, 1980)

Leonard Mosley, *London Under Fire* (Pan, 1974)

National Federation of Women's Institutes, *Town Children Through Country Eyes* (1940)

Howard Newby, *Green and Pleasant Land? Social Change in Rural England* (Hutchinson, 1979)

Paul Oliver et al, *Dunroamin: The Suburban Semi and Its Enemies* (Barrie & Jenkins, 1981)

D. Olsen

Town planning in London in the Eighteenth and Nineteenth Centuries (New Haven, 1964)

The Growth of Victorian London (Peregrine Books, 1979)

Harold Orlans, Stevenage: *A Sociological Study of A New Town* (Routledge and Kegan Paul, 1952)

H.M.D. Parker, Manpower: *A Study of War-time Policy and Administration* (London H.M.S.O., 1957)

Sheila Patterson, *Dark Strangers* (Tavistock Publications, 1963)

Henry Pelling, *Britain and the Second World War* (Collins, 1970)

John Platt, *London: Rock Routes* (Fourth Estate, 1985)

William Plowden, *The Motor Car and Politics, 1896–1970* (Bodley Head, 1971)

Roy Porter, *London: A social history* (Hamish Hamilton, 1994)

David Reeder, 'A Theatre of Suburbs: Some patterns of Development in West London, 1801–1911' in H.J. Dyos (ed.), *The Study of Urban History* (Edward Arnold, 1968)

J. Richards, *Castles on the Ground* (Architectural Press, 1946)

Jack Rose, *The Dynamics of Urban Property Development* (E. and F. Spon, 1985)

Stanley Rothwell, *Lambeth At War* (S.E.1 People's History Project, 1981)

W. Rubinstein, *Men of Property* (Croom Helm, 1981)

Andrew Saint (ed.) *Politics and the People of London: The London County Council 1889–1965* (Hambledon Continuum, 1989)

Dennis Sharp, *The Picture Palace* (Hugh Evelyn, 1969)

Francis Sheppard
   London 1808–1870 The Infernal Wen (Secker & Warburg, 1971)
   London, A History (Oxford University Press, 1998)

Neil Stammers, *Civil Liberties in Britain during the Second World War* (Croom Helm, 1984)

Ronald Stent, *A Bespattered Page? The Internment of His Majesty's 'Most Loyal Enemy Aliens'* (André Deutsch, 1980)

Penny Summerfield, *Women Workers in the Second World War* (Croom Helm, 1984)

Penny Summerfield and Edward Smithies, *Crime in Wartime: A Social History of Crime in World War 2* (George Allen and Unwin, 1982)

Mark Swenarton, 'Having a Bath. English Domestic Bathrooms, 1890–1940' in *Leisure in the Twentieth Century* (Design Council, 1976)

David Thomas, *London's Green Belt* (Faber and Faber, 1970)

Ray Thomas, *London's New Towns: A Study of Self Contained and Balanced Communities* (PEP, 1969)

F.M.L. Thompson
   The Rise of Suburbia (Leicester University Press, 1982)
   Hampstead, Building a Borough 1650–1964 (Routledge & Kegan Paul, 1974)

Nineteenth-Century Horse Sense (The Economic History Review, New Series, Vol. 29, No. 1 Feb 1976)

Victorian England: the horse-drawn society (Bedford College, University of London, 1970)

The Second World War: A Guide to Documents in the P.R.O. (H.M.S.O., 1972)

Richard Titmuss, *Problems of Social Policy* (Longmans, 1950)

Tony Travers, *The Politics of London, Governing an Ungovernable City* (Palgrave Mamillan, 2004)

E.S. Turner, *The Phoney War on the Home Front* (Michael Joseph, 1961)

Neil Wallington, *Firemen at War: The Work of London's Fire Fighters in the Second World War* (David and Charles, 1981)

James Walvin, *Passage to Britain: Immigration in British History and Politics* (Penguin, 1984)

James Watson, *Between Two Cultures* (Blackwell, 1977)

Gavin Weightman
   London River, The Thames Story (Collins & Brown, 1990)
   Bright Lights, Big City, London Entertained 1830–1950 (Collins & Brown 1992)

Ben Weinreb and Christopher Hibbert (eds) *The London Encyclodpaedia* (Papermac, 1993)

Francis Wheen, *The Sixties* (Century Publishing, 1982)

Jerry White
   Rothschild Buildings: Life in an East End Tenement Block 1887–1920 (Pimlico, 2003)
   London in the Twentieth Century, A City and its People (Viking, 2001)
   London in the Nineteenth Century, A Human Awful Wonder of God (Jonathan Cape, 2007)

A. Wohl, *The Eternal Slum: Housing and Social Policy in Victorian London* (Edward Arnold, 1977)

Marion Yass, *This Is Your War: Home Front Propaganda in the Second World War* (H.M.S.O., 1983)

Ken Young and Patricia Garside, *Metropolitan London: Politics and Urban Change 1837–1981* (Edward Arnold, 1982)

Ken Young and John Kramer, *Strategy and Conflict in Metropolitan Housing* (Heinemann, 1978)

Michael Young and Peter Willmott, *Family and Kinship in East London* (Penguin, 1979)

Terence Young, *Becontree and Dagenham* (Samuel Siddars, 1934)

LIST OF ILLUSTRATIONS

Bottom © Gunnersby Park Museum
p14–15:   Gunnersby Park Museum
p16:   London Transport Museum

Picture Section Three
p1:   Top © Corbis
          Bottom © Corbis
p2:   Top © Associated Press
          Bottom © Corbis
p3:   Corbis
p4:   Top © Corbis
          Bottom © Corbis
p5:   Corbis
p6:   London Transport Museum
p7:   Corbis
p8–9:   Corbis
p10:   Top © Corbis
          Bottom © Corbis
p11:   Top © Popperfoto
          Bottom © Elsie Huntley
p12:   Top © Vestry House
          Bottom © Imperial War Museum (D 14784)
p13:   Top Foto
p14–15:   Corbis
p16:   Top © Popperfoto
          Bottom © Margaret Dent

Picture Section Four
p1:   Top © Alan Townsin
          Bottom © Alan Townsin
p2–3:   Mary Evans Picture Library
p4:   Top ©   Stevenage Museum
          Bottom © Corbis
p5:   Stevenage Museum
p6:   Corbis
p7:   Top © Rose & Ron Linford
          Bottom © Terence Conran
p8:   Unknown
p9:   Corbis
p10–11:   Corbis
p12:   Getty
p13:   Top © Corbis
          Bottom © Harley Sherlock
p14:   Top © Charles Milligan
          Bottom © Corbis
p15:   Jack Ailsby
p16:   Corbis

INDEX

Abbey National 176
Abercrombie, Sir Patrick 331, 406, 409, 413, 418, 420, 463, 480
Acton 14, 15, 69, 80, 81
Adburgham, Alison 30
Addison Act 169–70
advertising, in the interwar years 122–3, 142–3, 202
AEC (Associated Equipment Company) 288, 344–5, 347, 350–1, 353
Afro-Caribbean culture 446–7, 447–50
Agar Town 74–5
age profile, of present-day London xii, 426
Agers, Stanley 116–17
Ailsby, Jack 344–5, 347, 353
aircraft industry
  post-war 343–4, 350
  wartime 288–9, 289–90
air travel 397–9
Albert, Prince 94
Allnatt, Major 133–4
American influences 102, 108
  on British industry 118–20
  businessmen and industrialists 124–5, 126, 144
  and electricity 131
  on transport 145, 151–3
  West End 109–14
'Anderson' shelters 250, 264, 277
Archer, Jeffrey 454
aristocracy
  and American influences 113–14
  and the City 15, 17
  in the interwar years 114–18, 122–4
  and the London Season 18–19
  in the West End 33–4, 112, 114–18
art schools 359, 369–70
Ascot 27, 28
Ashfield, Lord 158, 159–60, 162, 164
Asian immigrants 341, 438, 440–1, 446
  from East Africa 438
asylum seekers 426
Attfield, Judy 410
Attlee, Clement 334, 406

Bailey, David 372, 376
Balcombe Street siege 450–1
Baldwin, Stanley 211
Baltic Exchange 451
Banfield, Jack 48–9
Bank of England 7, 8, 9, 12, 89
banking system 9–10
Barkers' Store 111
Barnato, Barney 114
Barnsbury, Islington 466–7, 472–3, 474
Barratt, Phil 265
Barry, Gerald 456
Basildon New Town 182
bathrooms, in the interwar years 195–6
Battersea Power Station 132
Bayswater 18, 25, 33, 34

Bazalgette, Sir Joseph 92
BBC (British Broadcasting Corporation) 119, 132, 201, 202
The Beatles 374
Becontree Estate 147, 169, 170, 174, 182, 197
Bedding, Edie 139–40
Bedford estate 20, 73–4, 95
Bedford Park, Chiswick 166
Bedford Square 20, 74
Belgravia 18, 24–5, 34, 50
Belsize estate 79–80
Belsize Park 14, 26
Bermondsey 36, 58, 183, 205, 217
  Jacob's Island 90–1
  in the Second World War 273, 285, 296
Bethnal Green 36, 39, 43, 44, 47, 97, 475
Betjeman, John 399
Bevin, Ernest 291
birth rate 192
The Bitter Cry of Outcast London 96
Blackwall 36, 38, 44
Blair, Tony 454, 455
Bloomsbury 20, 25
Bloxham, Pat 461–2
Bolster, Annie 106
Bonham Carter, Lady Charlotte ixfx, 27, 28, 52, 114
Bonnett, Lydia 181–2
Booth, Charles 31, 66, 76, 213
Bow Street Runners 87
Bradburn, Ron 398–9
Branfield, Jack 48–9
Brentford 80, 135, 136
British Empire xi, 124–5, 339–41
  and the City 4–5
  and Commonwealth trade 341–5, 348–9, 350
  Exhibition (1924) 124–6, 133, 134
British Leyland 351, 353
British Museum 356, 357
British Nationality Act (1948) 429
British Union of Fascists 221
Brixton 14, 66, 76
  black settlement in 326, 430–1
  Loughborough Road Estate 461–2
  riots (1980s) 84, 448
Broadwater Farm estate, Tottenham 449
Brown, Lal 196–7
Brunel, Isambard Kingdom 45
Brunwin, Mike and Rita 423, 424
Buchanan, Colin 135
Buchanan, June 258
Buckingham Palace 24, 263
building societies 171–3, 176–80
Burke, Thomas, *London in My Time* 108
Burns, John 85
Burr, Ernest 50–1
Burton, Montague 47
buses
  deregulation 478
  horse omnibuses 13, 14, 25, 56–7, 65

office workers 394
 walking suburbs 53–5
computers in offices 388–9, 401
Congestion Charge 479
Conran, Terence 377
conservation movement, and office development
  399–401
Conservative Municipal Reform Party 183
consumerism
 in the interwar years 126, 127, 130, 137, 140–2, 144
 post-war 347
 and wartime rationing 296–5
 and the youth market 369–72
Conway, Baron (later Marquess of Hertford) 21
Cook, Tom 395
Coronation (1953) xi, 339–41
corporatism, post-war 350–1
COS (Charity Organization Society) 96–7
Cotter, Michael 412
County Hall 120
County of London Plan 331–2
Covent Garden 12, 20, 331, 400
Crawley 351, 408, 411
crime
 and disorder in Victorian London 87–90, 93
 and new housing estates 474–5
 and the Second World War 313
crossing sweepers 52
Croydon 445
Cubitt, Thomas 24, 25, 72
cycling in London 147–8
Cypriot community 430, 431–3, 438, 439, 444

Dad's Army 243
Dagenham, Ford Motor company 144
Danbury, Essex 415
dancing 298–9, 361, 391
Dankworth, John 362
Davis, Mickey 261
Deacey, Willy 367–8, 372, 375
debutantes 27–8
Delon, Alain 367
Dent, Margaret 383, 397
department stores 28–30, 76, 109–10
Diary of a Nobody (Grossmith) 13, 30, 81
Dickens, Charles 13, 36
 Household Words 74
 Oliver Twist 206
 Our Mutual Friend 27
 Sketches by Boz 54, 93
Dingwall, T.E. 379
discothèques 375
Disraeli, Benjamin 92
divorce 329
Dobson, Frank 454, 455
Docklands 401–4, 478
docks and dockers
 and the City 6–8
 and Commonwealth trade 342, 348
 dockers and the 1886 riots 85
 East End 24–5, 36–43, 44–5, 48–9
 and the General Strike 211
 and the Port of London Authority 215–16, 401
 post-war job losses 352–3
 and the Second World War 302
 and shipbuilding 44–5, 303–4

dolly-bird secretaries 391–2, 400–1
domestic servants
 and clerks 12, 71–2
 and the First World War 108
 in the interwar years 172, 185, 187–9
 post-war cleaners in commuter villages 421–2
 and the Second World War 327
 West End 31–2, 116–17
Donovan, Terence 372, 376
door-to-door salesmen 140–1
Dorchester Hotel 113
Downham Tavern 199–200
Downham Wall 175–6
Draper, Charlie 273, 284, 292–3, 309–10, 317, 320, 321,
  322, 324–5, 335
Dresden, Allied bombing of 323
dressmakers 32–3
Duffy, Brian 372
Duke, James Buchanan 118
Dulwich 66, 71
Dunkirk evacuation 236–7
Dunton 181–2
Dyer, Dora 122, 180

Ealing 14, 61, 80
Eary, Emily 250, 255, 262, 276, 286
Eary, Rene 283–4
East End 35–51
 Cockneys 35
 docks 6, 24–5, 36–43, 44–5, 48–9
 housing 38
 in the interwar years 144
 Jews 47–8, 428
 population 47
 Port of London 36–7
 poverty 36, 42, 46–7, 49–51
 and the Second World War
  bombed-out families 252–4, 269–76
  bombing raids 246–9, 251
  class resentment 262–3
  homeless crisis 259–61, 269–70, 272–6
  V-2 rocket attacks 320
 suburban development 75, 83
 sweated labour 36, 43–51
 Zeppelin raids 103–5
Eastern European refugees 429–30
East India Company 7, 36–7, 40
economic depression, (1930s) 128–9, 173
education, in the interwar years 174
Edward VII, King 117
EEC (European Economic Community) 352
electricity
 in the interwar years 130–3, 185, 187, 193–5
 power stations 130, 131, 132
 vacuum cleaners 140–2
Elizabeth II, Queen 405
 Coronation of xi, 339–41
Elvin, Arthur 126
employment
 in the building trade 177–8
 in the City 17
 Commonwealth immigrants 429, 430, 434–6
 Eastern European refugees 429–30
 in the interwar years 127–8, 146–8
 new towns 409
 service sector 355